# A Richer Harvest

## By Sudhir Sen

Will the "miracle seeds" effect a real miracle and lift the world's needy nations from their dismal existence, or must millions of people starve and die with hundreds of millions forced to live a grim life of perpetual hunger? Can the planet sustain its galloping numbers with a fateful race between food and population already on hand, or must there be famines of staggering dimensions that would claim perhaps more victims than even a nuclear holocaust?

Dr. Sudhir Sen, a distinguished economist and agricultural expert, is convinced that the future need not be all that bleak, nor need it be scarred by an endless struggle against hunger and starvation

- if the world makes adequate and intelligent use of the amazing scientific and technological knowledge to speed up development;
- if the poor countries fully exploit the unique potential of dwarf wheat, miracle rice, and other high-yielding varieties;
- if all nations—rich, poor, and newly-rich—work together and adopt the right strategy to boost food production to the utmost possible extent and to ensure its equitable distribution within each and every developing country; and
- if such a collective effort—with seeds, fertilizers, credit, and other prerequisites—is mounted on a global scale without delay.

Written for the concerned citizen as well as for the specialist, *A Richer Harvest* is one of the most important books of the decade because it presents comprehensively, but also realistically and lucidly, what must be done here and now to safeguard the future of mankind in an increasingly interdependent world. Must reading for a time of hard decisions.

Dr. Sudhir Sen, a graduate of Calcutta University, obtained his B.Sc. (E... degree ... Econom... versity ... guished ... the firs... Damoda... first Ec... ... the Indian Embassy in Moscow). Subsequently, he served the United Nations in several responsible positions—as Director, UN Technical Assistance Board, New York; Resident Representative of TAB and Director of Special Fund in Ghana, and UNDP Representative in Yugoslavia. During 1967-68 Dr. Sen was Visiting Professor of Sociology at Brown University (Providence, Rhode Island), as a Senior Foreign Scientist Fellow of the National Science Foundation, Washington, D.C.

*a richer harvest*

NEW HORIZONS FOR DEVELOPING COUNTRIES

# A
# RICHER
# HARVEST

*New Horizons for Developing Countries*

SUDHIR SEN

*Orbis Books* — MARYKNOLL, NEW YORK

*Tata McGraw-Hill Publishing Co* — NEW DELHI

TO

*The scientists of India*
*who, by their vision, skill and dedication,*
*and in collaboration with scientific*
*and benevolent institutions from abroad,*
*are ushering in the long-delayed*
*revolution in India's agriculture*

Library of Congress Catalogue #73-89988
ISBN #0-88344-436-4

© Sudhir Sen, 1974
Published by Orbis Books, New York, USA, and Tata McGraw-
Hill Publishing Company Limited, New Delhi, and set in types
by P. K. Ghosh at Eastend Printers, 3 Dr. Suresh Sarkar Road,
Calcutta 700 014

DAVID E LILIENTHAL June 12/74

Dear friend Sen:

If only more people — whether Indian or American — grasped the concept and the spirit of your work and your writing the gloom I hear on all sides would be dispelled by an affirmative task to do.

I'm working hard, full of faith, and rejoice in the knowledge that there are men like yourself — not enough of them, true

Best
David Lilienthal

# Preface

My work on this study actually began about six years ago—at Brown University in Providence, Rhode Island. But in a broader sense I feel as if I have been at it for decades, groping—at first instinctively, then through conventional book-learning, followed by years of extensive travel and intensive home-work—for some effective clues to the solution of what has long been, and remains more than ever before, the world's number one problem—the problem of poverty.

The study was planned as a trilogy—to deal respectively with the roles of the three parties involved in development: the donors, the receivers, and the administrators of aid. And having just spent over a decade with the United Nations development programmers, I could not help but turn to them in the first place—to give a critical analysis of the kind of job the UN family, placed between the aid-givers and the aid-receivers, was doing as an aid-administering agency, and how and where its performance could be improved. That there was, and still is, wide scope—and a desperate need—for such improvement not even the most zealous devotees of the UN cause will deny, at least in moments of sober reflection. The besetting weaknesses of its programmes are three: they are not production-oriented; they are indifferent to, if not callous about, priorities; they show no understanding of the principle of complementarities.

The result is, to plagiarize one of my own chapter titles: "Low yield from high ideals." The losers are not only the developing countries, but also the UN itself.

For the developing countries have been denied the enlightened leadership which they have a right to expect from the UN to guide them—by the shortest and quickest route—to a better life. As a result, their progress has suffered cruelly.

As for the UN, its failure to grasp this leadership firmly and imaginatively has deprived it of what could have been a powerful instrument to strengthen its own foundations, to build up its moral prestige, and thereby to improve its prospects of tackling some of the more intractable political problems, despite the rifts of ideologies and the chill of a cold war. The UN, in that case, might not have been as impotent as it is today.

The first study was completed while I was still at Brown University.[1]

The second part of the trilogy looks at the problems from the field, that is, from the angle of the recipient countries. It examines, above all, the question of how to plan and implement high-quality country-programmes to secure the best possible use of both domestic and external resources, and thereby to make the maximum possible contribution to raise the living standards of the masses of people. This leads right to the heart of the question of priorities.

A well-conceived country-programme, I had long been persuaded, must have agriculture as its hard core. This conviction has been greatly re-inforced by two more recent phenomena—an accelerating demographic revolution and the advent of a green revolution. One poses a grave threat to man's future, the other gives him the best tool to counteract it. The population explosion multiplies the demand for food; the yield explosion in tropical agriculture offers the best—the only—hope to produce enough food in time to cope with it.

Not only that; an accelerating green revolution—provided its benefits are not confined to a few, but are diffused widely and wisely among the people—can help dampen population growth far beyond what even the best family planning programme can, by itself, achieve in a developing country.

How to make the green revolution a success—this is the question the second study is concerned with and examines in all its ramifications. This is also the foremost question all development planning must be concerned with today. For, if the green revolution succeeds, a great many other things will automatically fall into their proper places and will lift a whole economy to a far higher level of development. If it fails, it will not only drag down everything else, but will put a nation's very existence into jeopardy. The reward for success is extraordinarily high; so is also the penalty for failure.

Much of the study has been devoted to India—the country I belong to and know best, also a country which contains one-sixth of humanity, where problems are vast, complex and acute, where in fact the awesome drama of food-and-population race has entered the climactic phase. If the poverty problem can be solved in India, as I believe it still can, it can certainly be solved in most other countries within a reasonable time. These countries can greatly benefit from India's experience and learn what must be done as well as what not to do.

After Independence, India was faced with quite unique problems—both

---

[1] It was published under the title: *United Nations in Economic Development—Need for a New Strategy* (Dobbs Ferry, N.Y.: Oceana Publications, 1969), pp. 351-xiv.

in dimensions and in complexity. And these have been complicated by two other factors: demographic pressures and democratic antics. To crown it all, history gave India no time for experimenting, no elbow-room even for normal error.

Yet errors have been made, plenty of them, and some grave ones too. They sprang largely from dogmas and misconceptions—whether inherited from history, or hastily borrowed from abroad, or cultivated in India's lush emotional climate. The result has been a dangerously slow rate of progress at a time of exploding population, which now threatens to perpetuate poverty of the worst kind for all time to come.

The work has unavoidably grown in size. For, in order to develop its main thesis it became necessary also to examine the validity, or otherwise, of policies and ideas, often in historical perspective—not only to take a hard look at the trees and the forest, but also to clear a fair amount of jungle into the bargain. It has, therefore, been divided into two separate but related studies titled respectively:

*A Richer Harvest—New Horizons for Developing Countries*; and

*Reaping the Green Revolution—Food and Jobs for All.*

Dwarf wheat, miracle rice, and other high-yielding varieties of crops have opened up revolutionary possibilities; yet, by themselves, they can do very little. They must be cultivated with meticulous care according to prescribed practices with the needed inputs, and they must be backed by a broad spectrum of services and facilities. Only then can they produce a richer harvest. The problems and opportunities associated with them comprise the main field the first of the two studies is focused on.

But even a *richer harvest* will not be enough; it has to be the *richest possible*, especially in a country like India. Her arable land is now virtually static, around 350 million acres. Every acre of this land will have to work much harder to produce all the food and fibre needed to support her soaring population—350 million in 1951, 550 million in 1971, and 700 million in 1981, probably more. Her agriculture, it follows, will need to be restructured to achieve this goal, and, in addition, to absorb her exploding rural workforce to the maximum possible extent on jobs that will provide at least a subsistence income. These and related questions are discussed in the second study to indicate how one could gather a *full* harvest.

The third part of the trilogy, titled *Obligations of Affluence*, will consider certain aspects of the relations between rich and poor nations, also between the rich and the poor within a developing country.

If the fate of India and a great many other developing countries hinges today on the success of the green revolution, there is, also, an inescapable *sine qua non*: the highyielding varieties of crops must be matched by a highyielding variety of economics. It follows that the "traditional" brand of economics, as hitherto applied to these countries, will just not do. It must be impregnated by yield-boosting "genes," and for these one must often go far beyond the long-trodden ground.

To be more specific, development economics must centre primarily on the development of physical resources, especially land and water. In doing so, it must, with discerning judgment, choose the right kind of technology to suit each specific situation. In most cases—the main exceptions are oil-rich desert lands—it must concentrate most heavily on the production of food. It must give the highest priority to spatial development, especially with suitably-located market-towns to serve as nuclei for urbanization, and with networks of all-weather rural roads linking farms to the markets. It must provide for a massive expansion of production credit—or better call it "green revolution credit"—to finance the production and marketing of the new varieties, along with the supporting services and facilities. It must come to firm grips with the long-slighted problems of real land reform to free agriculture from the stranglehold of feudalism which, in most developing countries, has outlived colonialism. And it must lay far greater stress than hitherto on development-oriented education and on health-cum-family planning as indispensable tools of both economic progress and social welfare. These and other critical genes needed to evolve highyielding economics by "wide crosses," to borrow a phrase from modern biological engineering, with other disciplines have been scrutinized in these two studies.

So far the poor nations' progress has been heartbreakingly slow. For this the blame, only too often and too readily, is placed on them. Yet others, too, have contributed to it mightily, even if unwittingly, and they include planners and economists, aid-givers and aid-administrators.

"Do the best you can with what you have where you are"—a businessman's maxim—makes a lot of economic sense as well. One might even say that it contains the right mandate for those who are engaged in the challenging task of lifting two-thirds of humanity above the poverty line.

The development of the poor nations can be—it must be—greatly speeded up. And this can be done here and now, with the resources they have at their disposal. The biggest push in that direction will come when agriculture based on highyielding varieties of crops is combined with highyielding economics based, above all, on resource development with intelligent use of the miracles of science our age has been saturated with.

Development will begin to make real sense only when a marriage of the two is consummated. When this occurs, the world's poor nations will emerge out of a lingering twilight; and equipped with a winning strategy, they will finally begin to stride—by the shortest and the swiftest route—from age-old penury to the age of plenty.

New York                                                              SUDHIR SEN
February, 1973

# Acknowledgements

In preparing this study I have received help and encouragement from numerous sources but for which it would have been impossible to carry it through. Many of them have been mentioned in the text and footnotes with due acknowledgements. They need to be heavily supplemented, although no list can be complete and no expression of thanks fully adequate.

## International Sources

It is particularly hard to put in words all that I owe to Mr. Leonard K. Elmhirst, *inter alia* Founder-President of the International Conference of Agricultural Economists and of Political and Economic Planning (PEP), London. My interest in agriculture and rural development stemmed largely from the inspiration and opportunities he generously provided, beginning with 1939, and it was reinforced through active association with him on numerous occasions.

Mr. Elmhirst was kind enough to take the trouble of reading the book in manuscript and to help with critical and constructive suggestions.

*Ford Foundation.* My gratitude to Professor Forest F. Hill is deep and long-standing. Since 1948, first as Provost at Cornell University, then as Vice-President and more recently as Consultant of the Ford Foundation, he has helped me liberally with ideas, documents including his own writings, and valuable introductions. The numerous discussions with him served to clarify many basic concepts.

I have also received much help from Dr. Douglas Ensminger, the Foundation's Representative in India, and Dr. A. A. Johnson, Program Adviser, Agricultural Research and Development, who arranged two most useful rounds of discussions (in December 1969 and August 1972, respectively) with:

Dr. Harold A. Miles, IADP Team Leader (1962-65) and later a visiting Consultant, on agricultural credit;

> Dr. C. Stewart Holton and Dr. Philip Schroeder on plant protection;
>
> Dr. T. H. Quackerbush and Dr. Kampen on water problems;
>
> Dr. Joseph Ackerman on agricultural institutions; and
>
> Dr. B. A. Krantz, Agronomist, on the newly-established ICRISAT.

A few weeks' work, in summer 1970, at the Foundation's Library in New York was a great help.

*The Rockefeller Foundation.* A discussion at the Foundation's headquarters in New York with the late Dr. Will M. Myers, then Vice-President, and his colleagues Dr. Sterling Wortman and Dr. Clarence C. Gray, gave me some valuable insights.

Dr. Wayne H. Freeman, Rice Specialist, All-India Coordinated Rice Improvement Project, and Dr. S. V. S. Shastry, Coordinator, AICRIP, provided a comprehensive review of the rice improvement programme in India.

*USAID, New Delhi.* I am particularly obliged to Dr. Russel G. Olson for the information supplied on agricultural education, research and extension in India, and to both Dr. Olson and Dr. Clarence Gray, Chief, Inputs Division (now with the Rockefeller Foundation at headquarters) for arranging a series of discussions with experts of the Inputs Division (in December 1969), viz.:

> Mr. John T. Phelan, Chief, Soil and Water Management Division;
>
> Mr. W. D. Burgess, and Mr. D. L. Rucker, Advisers, Fertilizer Branch;
>
> Mr. C. J. Fredrickson, Plant Protection Adviser;
>
> Mr. J. S. Balis, Chief, Farm Machinery Division (with a second visit in August 1972);
>
> Mr. Darrel A. Dunn, Adviser, Credit and Cooperation;
>
> Mr. B. R. Gregg, and Mr. A. G. Law, Advisers, Seed Section;
>
> Dr. M. Gist Welling, Deputy Chief, University of Tennessee Team assigned to Mysore under USAID's India Agricultural Programs, who explained their approach and activities, and arranged some interesting field trips

Mr. Jerome T. French, now at USAID headquarters (Office of Development Administration, Bureau of Technical Assistance), supplied some mimeographed material giving a first-hand view of the green revolution in the Philippines.

*Agricultural Development Council.* I have benefited much from personal discussions with Dr. Arthur T. Mosher, Executive Director of the Council, and thanks to his courtesy I was able to use the library at the Council's headquarters in New York for several weeks.

*College of Agriculture, Cornell.* Dr. Kenneth L. Turk, Director, International Agricultural Development Programme, was good enough to supply a mimeographed set of papers prepared for a Symposium on Some Issues Emerging from Recent Breakthroughs in Food Production, held at Cornell, March 30 – April 3, 1970, which have meanwhile been published as a book edited by Dr. Turk.

*Food and Agriculture Organization.* I am grateful to Dr. A. H. Boerma, Director-General of FAO, for the generous facilities I enjoyed at the Agency's Headquarters in Rome during January-March 1970 for conducting my study. And my special thanks are due to Dr. Moni Moulik, then Director of FAO's Documentation, Library and Legislation Department, for his readiness to help with supply of documents at all times.

I must also thank Mr. Charles Weitz, currently Director, FAO Liaison Office with the UN, and Mrs. Lila Goldin of the Information Liaison Office, for supplying material from time to time.

*UNDP/UN.* The help received from Mr. John McDiarmid, Resident Representative, and Mr. Gvido Grisogono, Deputy Resident Representative, in India has facilitated my work on several occasions.

I have also received much valuable help, both professionally and otherwise, from UNDP/IAEA Project Manager Dr. Lars Fredriksson in Belgrade as well as in New Delhi.

Mr. Rafael Salas, now Executive Director, UN Fund for Population Activities (UNFPA), who had played a significant role in promoting the green revolution in his homeland, the Philippines, shed some interesting light on the ups and downs it has passed through.

Dr. Milos Macura, formerly Director of Population Division, has been a generous source of information and documents, so also Mr. Subhas Dhar, senior officer in the Department of Economic and Social Affairs.

*UN Library.* I am indebted to Mrs. Natalia Tyulina, Director, Dag Hammarskjold Library, its officers, and staff members. The facilities I have been enjoying in the Library have greatly helped me in completing this study.

## Indian Sources

*Indian Agricultural Research Institute.* My warmest thanks are due to Dr. M. S. Swaminathan, Director of IARI, now Director General, Indian Council of Agricultural Research (ICAR). The materials he was kind enough to supply, including copies of his own writings, have been a major source of information and ideas.

Both Dr. Swaminathan and Dr. N. P. Dutt, Deputy Director of IARI, arranged visits with IARI scientists, in December 1969 and again in August 1972, which have proved most helpful. In particular, mention must be made of:

Dr. H. K. Jain, Head, Genetics Division;

Dr. S. S. Bains, Head, Agronomy Division;

Dr. C. Dakshinamurthy, Head, Division of Agricultural Physics, also Head, Farm Operations Department in 1969;

Dr. S. P. Raychoudhuri, Head, Entomology Division;

Dr. S. Ramamoorty, Head, Soil Science and Agricultural Chemistry Division.

*Government of India*. Over the years I have received much help—in discussions and through supply of documents—from:

Dr. Samar Sen, formerly Additional Secretary, Planning Commission, and now Executive Director to the World Bank;

Mr. J. S. Sharma, Joint Secretary, Ministry of Agriculture, now Member-Secretary, National Commission on Agriculture;

Dr. Jyoti Bhattacharya, former Director, Programme Evaluation Organization (PEO), Planning Commission, now stationed in the FAO/IBRD Unit in Rome;

Dr. P. K. Mukherjee, also Director, PEO, Planning Commission, now serving in the ESA Department of the UN;

Mr. Tarlok Singh, ICS, formerly Member of the Planning Commission, now Deputy Executive Director, UNICEF, New York;

And more recently, in August 1972, from:

Dr. A. S. Cheema, Agricultural Commissioner; Mr. B. B. Vohra, Joint Secretary and Chairman, Central Ground Water Board, and Mr. J. K. Jain, Joint Commissioner (also in December 1969).

*Andhra Pradesh Agricultural University* (APAU at Rajendranagar, Hyderabad). Discussions were held (December 1969) with Dr. B. Appala Naidu, Director of Extension, and Dr. M. K. Adeni, Joint Director of Extension (Department of Agriculture), and others.

*All-India Coordinated Rice Improvement Project* (AICRIP at APAU headquarters). Most useful from my angle were the extended visits with Dr. S. V. S. Shastry, Project Coordinator, and Dr. Wayne Freeman, Rice Specialist. Together, they provided a full picture of the history, present status, and future prospects of rice-breeding in India.

*Mysore University of Agricultural Science*. A three-day visit (December 1969) gave me a first-hand idea about its activities. The discussions with the Vice-Chancellor, Dr. K. C. Naik, his colleagues, and Dr. M. Gist Welling (see above under USAID) were exceedingly helpful.

*West Bengal*. A personal visit with Governor A. L. Dias (11 August 1972) provided, among other things, an excellent opportunity to update my information about the State and its agriculture, also to check on some of my own conclusions.

Field visits arranged by the dynamic Director of Agriculture, Dr. A. K. Dutt, reacquainted me with old problems.

A visit to Kalyani University and discussions with its Vice-Chancellor, Mr. K. K. Sen, gave a first-hand idea about its problems, and in particular why, even in the twelfth year of its existence, it was unable to take off the ground as an agricultural university.

*Punjab Agricultural University.* My special thanks are due to Dr. Sukhdev Singh, Director of Research, for reviewing, during my visit to PAU on 22 August 1972, its many-sided research activities, also to Dr. S. S. Johl, Director of Research in Agricultural Economics, and Dr. R. N. Kaul, Acting Director, Agricultural Engineering Department, for giving the highlights of the work in their respective fields.

*Haryana Agricultural University.* During a short visit to HAU I could see and learn much, thanks to the kindness of Vice-Chancellor Mr. A. L. Fletcher and several faculty members who readily gave their time to explain the activities I was interested in.

A special debt of gratitude is due to the Governor of Haryana, Mr. B. N. Chakravarty, for the generous facilities which made it possible for me to see so much of Punjab-Haryana, including visits not only to PAU and HAU, but also to a number of farms with on-the-spot discussions with farmers.

### The Publishers

These acknowledgements will be incomplete without a word about my publishers. I am profoundly grateful to Mr. Philip J. Scharper, Editor-in-Chief, ORBIS BOOKS, whose understanding has sustained me through a difficult period. And he has spared me the horrors of deadlines which he has all along kept virtually open-ended, allowing my borings and musings to take their own time.

I have been fortunate also in my copublishers, Tata McGraw-Hill Publishing Company in New Delhi, whose generous understanding has relieved me of the pressure and has facilitated the work. For this I am thankful in particular to Mr. N. R. Subramanian, Executive Director, and Mr. Dipen Mitra, Editor-in-Chief of the Company.

### Manuscript Preparation

On a more mundane, but nonetheless vital plane I wish to record my thanks to Mrs. Susanne Zagorski and Mrs. Virginia Aquino for the care they have taken to produce an impeccably clean manuscript.

## Writer's Responsibility

As should be clear from the foregoing, I have drawn facts and ideas from a multiplicity of sources. However, for the contents of the book, including comments, views and analysis, the writer alone remains solely responsible.

# List of Abbreviations

| | |
|---|---|
| AEO | Assistant Extension Officer |
| AICMBS | All-India Coordinated Maize Breeding Scheme |
| AICRIP | All-India Coordinated Rice Improvement Programme |
| AIRCRC | All-India Rural Credit Review Committee |
| AIRCSC | All-India Rural Credit Survey Committee |
| APAU | Andhra Pradesh Agricultural University |
| APC | Agricultural Price Commission |
| ARC | Agricultural Refinance Corporation |
| BDO | Block Development Officer |
| CDP | Community Development Programme |
| CEO | Cooperative Extension Officer |
| CIAT | Centro Internacional de Agricultura Tropical (Cali, Colombia) |
| CIMMYT | Centro Internacional de Mejoramiento de Maiz y Trigo (Mexico) |
| CRRI | Central Rice Research Institute (Cuttack, India) |
| CWC | Central Warehousing Corporation |
| DAC | Development Assistance Committee of OECD |
| DVC | Damodar Valley Corporation |
| ETO | Exploratory Tubewell Organization |
| FAO | Food and Agriculture Organization |
| FCI | Fertilizer Corporation of India |
| FPC | Fertilizer Promotion Council |
| GNP | Gross National Product |
| HAU | Haryana Agricultural University, Hissar |
| HYV | High-yielding Variety |
| HYVP | High-yielding Varieties Programme |

| | |
|---|---|
| IAAP | Intensive Agricultural Areas Programme |
| IADP | Intensive Agricultural District Programme |
| IAMP | Intensive Agricultural Modernization Programme |
| IARI | Indian Agricultural Research Institute (New Delhi) |
| IAS | Indian Administrative Service |
| IBRD | International Bank for Reconstruction and Development (World Bank) |
| ICAR | Indian Council of Agricultural Research |
| ICGIAR | International Consultative Group on International Agricultural Research |
| ICRISAT | International Crop Research Institute for Semi-Arid Tropics (Hyderabad, India) |
| ICS | Indian Civil Service |
| IPC | International Potato Center (Peru) |
| IRRI | International Rice Research Institute, Philippines (Los Baños, Philippines) |
| IITA | International Institute of Tropical Agriculture (Ibadan, Nigeria) |
| IWP | Indicative World Plan (of FAO) |
| NCAER | National Council of Applied Economic Research |
| NDC | National Development Council |
| NES | National Extension Service |
| NPC | National Planning Committee |
| ODA | Official Development Assistance |
| OECD | Organization for Economic Cooperation and Development |
| PAU | Punjab Agricultural University |
| PCI | Pesticides Association of India |
| REC | Rural Electrification Corporation |
| SUNFED | Special United Nations Fund for Economic Development |
| TVA | Tennessee Valley Authority |
| UN | United Nations |
| UNDP | United Nations Development Programme |
| UPAU | Uttar Pradesh Agricultural University |
| USAID | United States International Development Agency |
| USDA | United States Department of Agriculture |
| VLW | Village Level Worker (of CDP) |
| WHO | World Health Organization |

# Contents

PREFACE      vii

ACKNOWLEDGEMENTS      xi

LIST OF ABBREVIATIONS      xvii


## PART ONE. THE SEEDS OF HOPE

1. *Neglected Assets of the Tropics*      3
   TWO WORLDS—CAUSES OF NEGLECT—IDEOLOGICAL CONFUSION—
   IMPACT OF HISTORY

2. *Axioms of Development*      17
   A. TRADITIONAL AGRICULTURE: POOR BUT EFFICIENT—PROFIT-MAXIMIZER
   OR RISK-MINIMIZER—NOT ALWAYS EFFICIENT

   B. AXIOMS OF DEVELOPMENT: CAPITAL ERROR—THE AXIOMS—PRE-
   REQUISITES OF AGRICULTURAL DEVELOPMENT

3. *High Hopes from Dwarf Seeds*      30
   A MIRACULOUS ESCAPE—THE GENESIS—BIRTH OF DWARF WHEAT—
   THE MIRACLE OF DWARF RICE—BIOLOGICAL ENGINEERING—PROMISE
   OF PLENTY

4. *The Stirrings of a Revolution*      44
   RAPID SPREAD OF DWARF WHEAT—RICE – A LAGGING MIRACLE—
   ADOPTION AND ADAPTATION—JAYA, PADMA AND AFTER—STIRRINGS
   OF A REVOLUTION—THE NEW VISTA—SOCIO-ECONOMIC ENGINEERING

# PART TWO.   NOT BY MIRACLE SEEDS
# ALONE—INDIA AS AN EXAMPLE

### I. Introduction

5. *A Fateful Race*                                                                69

    FATE AND FOLLY—AN IMPRESSIVE RECORD—UNIQUE PROBLEMS OF
    INDIA—A NEO-KEYNESIAN APPROACH—ONE MORE CHANCE

### II. Towards a New Agricultural Strategy—The Background

6. *Agriculture in National Plans—A Critique*                                      78

    QUESTION OF PRIORITY—AGRICULTURE VERSUS INDUSTRY DEBATE—
    THE TVA ERA—TRAVESTY OF TVA—A RECIPE FOR SLOW
    GROWTH

7. *Low Yield from High Ideals*                                                    93

    I. *Gandhian Economics*

    A UNIQUE PARADOX—A BLINDING VISION—THE CULT OF KHADI—
    CHARKA VERSUS MACHINE—OTHER ECONOMIC OBITER DICTA—A
    BAFFLING LEGACY

8. *Low Yield from High Ideals*                                                   107

    II. *Community Development and Panchayati Raj*

    WRONG ROADS—ETAWAH PILOT PROJECT—SUCCESS MISUNDERSTOOD
    —COMMUNITY DEVELOPMENT—MASS-PRODUCED PROTOTYPES—SHELL
    WITHOUT SUBSTANCE—AMENITIES BEFORE NECESSITIES. PANCHAYATI
    RAJ : COMPOUNDING THE ERROR—NEW SHACKLES FOR DEVELOPMENT

9. *Wrong Roads to Cooperation*                                                   125

    THE BACKGROUND—INTEGRATED RURAL CREDIT SCHEME—TOWARDS
    A COOPERATIVE MONOPOLY—ON THE INDIAN FARMER—AN UN-
    INSPIRING RECORD—BACK TO THE AXIOMS

### III. Towards a New Agricultural Strategy—Recent Developments

10. *The Food Crisis*                                                             139

    SOME BACKGROUND FACTS—SELF-SUFFICIENCY IN FOOD—A TURNING
    POINT—THE DROUGHT AND AFTER

11. *Intensive Agricultural District Programme (IADP)*
    *—The Background*                                                        151

    NEGLECTED BREAD BASKETS—THE COMPLEMENTARITY PRINCIPLE—
    THE 10-POINT PROGRAMME

12. *Package Programme (IADP) at Work*                                            159

    SIGNIFICANCE OF GUIDELINES : *a.* FARM PLANNING  *b.* CROP LOANS
    *c.* INTEGRATED APPROACH  *d.* INSTITUTIONAL SUPPORT—SELECTION

OF DISTRICTS—IMPERFECT SELECTION—INTER-DISTRICT VARIABLES—
FINANCIAL ARRANGEMENTS—A SLOW START—INHIBITING FACTORS

13. *A Decade of IADP*    176

THE ORCHARD BEARS FRUIT—RETARDING FACTORS

14. *IADP—An Appraisal*    186

CRITICISMS OF IADP—AN ADOPTION BREAKTHROUGH

15. *The New Agricultural Strategy*    195

NOT SO NEW—STILL A FLEDGLING—"FOOD ENOUGH" IS NOT ENOUGH
—NEED FOR NEW DIMENSIONS—FROM IADP TO IAMP—A MULTI-
TIER APPROACH—ECONOMICS OF SPEED—THE REAL CHALLENGE

## IV. Technological Needs of Intensive Agriculture

16. *Harnessing the Monsoon*    208

A BLESSING DESPITE PROBLEMS—IRRIGATION POTENTIAL AND PRESENT
STATUS—QUALITY OF IRRIGATION—MINOR IRRIGATION—NEW AP-
PROACH—GROUNDWATER DEVELOPMENT—RAINFED AREAS—MULTI-
PRONGED APPROACH—CHANGES IN AGRONOMY—ALIBI FOR PROCRASTI-
NATION—TASKS AHEAD—A GRAND VISION—A POSTSCRIPT

17. *Multiplication and Distribution of Improved Seeds*    235

LAGGING SEED-CONSCIOUSNESS—RECENT PROGRESS—TASKS AHEAD

18. *Chemical Fertilizers*    248

A LONG-DELAYED START—CONSUMPTION AND OUTPUT—LONGER-TERM
NEEDS—FERTILIZER PRICE—DISTRIBUTION OF FERTILIZERS—FERTILIZER
PROMOTION COUNCIL—SOIL CHEMISTRY

19. *Plant Protection*    265

FOOD FOR MEN OR PESTS—CONTROL THROUGH BREEDING—CULTURAL
PRACTICES—BIOLOGICAL METHODS—CONTROL THROUGH PLANT QUAR-
ANTINE—CHEMICAL CONTROL—WHY PESTICIDES—DDT CONTRO-
VERSY—USE OF PESTICIDES IN INDIA—AGRICULTURAL AVIATION—
WEED CONTROL—NEED FOR REALISM

20. *Farm Mechanization—Need for Selectivity*    284

A PROBLEM OF CHOICE—NEED FOR BETTER FARM IMPLEMENTS—
SPECIFIC NEEDS FOR HEAVY MACHINES—FARM MACHINERY FOR
GREEN REVOLUTION—DANGERS OF BLIND MECHANIZATION—TASKS
AHEAD

21. *Rural Electrification*    302

THE POWER GAP—POWER FOR GREEN REVOLUTION—A TIMID

Target—The Loaded Question—Electrification of Villages—
Tasks Ahead—The Financial Constraint—Let There Be Light
—Postscript on Power Famine

22. *Education, Research, Extension*      320

   I. Towards Agricultural Universities : A Mindless System—The
Seeds of Reform—A Monumental Struggle—The First Harvest

  II. Reorganization of Research : Rockefeller Foundation's India
Programme—Restructuring ICAR—Crop Research – Then and
Now—Research Takes Off—Some New Tasks

 III. Extension Service : The Weakest Link—From Amateurism to
Science—Rebuilding the Service

 IV. The Imperatives : Stay the Course—Build Science-based Extension—Give Scientists a Better Deal—Nourish the Golden
Goose—Expand Indo-US Collaboration—USA's Historic Contribution—A Footnote to History

### V. Other Prerequisites of Intensive Agriculture

23. *On Price Support*      355

    A Delayed Realization—"Bon Prix" or "Bon Marche"—Con-
sumer-oriented Prices—The Turnaround—Farmer Response—
Implementing the New Policy—A Fatal Hesitancy

24. *Marketing, Transportation, Storage*      376

    Post-harvest Underpinnings—Scarcity of Markets—Regulated
Markets—A Roadblock to Progress—The Roadblock in India—
Storage and Warehousing—The Missing Layer—How to Accel-
erate Progress

25. *Agricultural Credit*      398

   I. *From Cooperative Monopoly to Multi-Agency Approach*

    Needless Gyrations—"Credit Agricole"—Integrated Rural
Credit in Retrospect—Multi-agency Credit—A Dubious Step

26. *Agricultural Credit*      412

  II. *From Multi-Agency Approach to a Unified System*

    Two Fundamentals—Inadequacies of Multi-Agency Approach
—Evasive Palliatives—The Imperatives—An All-India Agricultural Credit Corporation—The Stake

27. *The Credit Shackles and Deficit Financing*      432

    A Gold-mine—Credit-Financing—PL 480 Funds—Deficit Finance
—The Grand Fallacies—Create Green-Revolution Credits

28. *On Administrative Reform*    452

    THE BACKGROUND—AN ANACHRONISM—DIAGNOSIS BY EXPERTS—
    APPLEBY REPORT AND AFTER—AGRICULTURAL ADMINISTRATION—
    DANGER OF WRONG REFORM

### VI. Conclusion : Road to Survival

29. *Road to Survival*    475

    A FITFUL WAR—SOME GLITTERING FALLACIES—PLANNING FOR HIGH
    GROWTH—GROWTH FOR WELFARE—GARIBI HATAO : A REALIZABLE
    DREAM

## PART THREE. NEW HORIZONS FOR DEVELOPING COUNTRIES

30. *Challenges and Opportunities*    495

    A DE GAULLE HOMILY—NOT FOOD AID, BUT FOOD PRODUCTION AID
    —RESOURCE-BASED DEVELOPMENT—PACKAGE APPROACH, THE ONLY
    WAY—NATIONAL COMPLEMENTARITIES—ROAD TO ABUNDANCE—
    BREAKING POVERTY-POPULATION SPIRAL

31. *International Aid to Agriculture*    514

    "LATE IN ALL THINGS"—DISENCHANTMENT WITH AID—UNDP :
    PREINVESTMENT FAD—FAO : KEYS TO NON-SUCCESS—A MOMEN-
    TOUS STEP—IBRD AID TO AGRICULTURE—US AID: AN ANGUISHED
    QUERY

32. *Towards New Horizons*    529

    THE MASTER-KEY : SELF-HELP—QUICKENING THE PACE

APPENDICES    535

SELECT BIBLIOGRAPHY    558

INDEX    565

*a richer harvest*

NEW HORIZONS FOR DEVELOPING COUNTRIES

# PART ONE

# THE SEEDS OF HOPE

# CHAPTER 1

# Neglected Assets
# of the Tropics

## TWO WORLDS

The most challenging task in today's world can be simply defined: how to rescue two-thirds of mankind from the age-old grip of dehumanizing poverty compounded by a population upsurge; and how, with that end in view, to harness modern science and technology in the underdeveloped countries to produce enough food, to curb the runaway population growth, and to produce other essential goods and services to meet the minimal needs of civilized life.

Today, luckily, it is possible to work for and realize these objectives. Modern science has made, and is still making, amazing progress in all directions; it has provided the *technical* means to tackle the problems involved. The industrially advanced nations are enjoying record-breaking prosperity; the vast reservoir of wealth they have created can readily produce the *financial* means, the capital, needed to build a better and brighter world to the lasting benefit of all.

The tools are there. What the world now needs are, first, a will to come to grips with the backlog of problems, and, second, a strategy, at once imaginative and practical, to realize the goals. Both are indispensable. Without the requisite will nothing much can be achieved; and without a well-conceived strategy goodwill and noble impulses will be of little avail. Compassion must be matched by understanding, and *vice versa*. An effective combination of the two has been largely lacking in the contemporary world. And this explains why so much misery is so readily tolerated, why it continues to coexist side by side with fabulous affluence.

The rich nations, with barely one-third of the world's population estimated at 3.5 billion in 1970, accounted for 87.5 per cent of its total gross national product, or G.N.P. The poor nations, numbering over one hundred, contained more than two-thirds of the world's population, but their share of the G.N.P. amounted to only 12.5 per cent. The combined G.N.P. of the rich nations grew, during 1960's, at an average rate of 6 per cent or more per year. The corresponding average for the poor nations was about 4 per cent; it kept only marginally ahead of the 3 per cent annual growth of their population, while their future continues to be shrouded in uncertainty.

The degree of affluence varies among the developed countries, and so does the extent of poverty among the underdeveloped nations.[1] At one end of the spectrum are countries like the USA, the UK, Germany, Japan and Soviet Russia with per capita incomes ranging from $3,500 to $2,000 a year. At the other extreme are countries like India, Burma, Pakistan, Ethiopia and Nigeria with an annual income of less than $100 per head.

This economic dichotomy of the planet, it is well to remember, is of quite recent origin and goes back to the industrial revolution which began just about two hundred years ago. This is a brief span even in man's recorded history, not to speak of the long stretch of his biological evolution extending over hundreds of millions of years.

How did this discrepancy arise? The simplest answer is that the march of history has unevenly spread science and technology over the world, that it has virtually bypassed what are now the underdeveloped countries.[2] The industrial revolution which began in England spilled over on both sides of the Atlantic and later, for special historical reasons, spread to a few remote countries—Australia, New Zealand, Japan and South Africa, but otherwise it hardly penetrated the rest of the world. As a result, the industrialized nations have been able to amass enormous wealth. Even a 3 per cent rate of annual growth would, over such a long period, add up to a massive figure; in actual fact, the growth rate has often been much higher, particularly in the period after the Second World War. Meanwhile, the rest of the world virtually languished in an environment of economic stagnation. And as the Pearson Commission reminds us, after World War II

---

[1] The definition of "poor" or "developing" countries is not free from ambiguities and some element of arbitrariness. The United Nations practice is to include in this category countries with a per capita income of less than $500 per year, which is good enough for our purpose. Most of these countries are concentrated in Asia, Africa and Latin America.

[2] The words "poor," "backward," "low-income" and "underdeveloped" are used more or less interchangeably with "developing" which is nowadays commonly favoured, especially in UN circles. Needless to say that they are used in a purely objective sense without any derogatory implications.

over sixty countries entered political independence "with a backlog of deep poverty."[3]

There is, of course, the handy one-word explanation offered by a great many people for the present backwardness of the developing countries, namely, *exploitation*. Few will deny that there has been, and still is, a lot of exploitation in one form or another; that the pattern of international trade has borne, and still bears, the stamp of onesidedness to the disadvantage of the poor nations; that this has been, and still remains, a formidable obstacle to their economic progress. Nevertheless, the theory of exploitation oversimplifies matters and distorts the historical perspective.

For one thing, it is only fair to remember that exploitation of the poor by the rich was by no means confined to the international field. Until very recent times there was plenty of it within a rich industrialized country where masses of people lived in shocking poverty. The concept of building and underpinning prosperity by sharing it on a nation-wide basis is surprisingly new. In general, the rich nations have discovered and accepted this truth only in the last generation. And even now its actual application is often marked by doubts and hesitancy, at times even positive resistance, conscious or subconscious.

The developing nations themselves, it must be added at least in parenthesis, have yet to grasp this truth. There has been, and still continues to be, a great deal of exploitation—of the poor and the weak by the rich and the powerful—within their own boundaries. Nor is there the slightest doubt that this, in most cases, seriously impedes their economic development and helps perpetuate their poverty.

Besides, strange as it may sound, the retarded economic growth of the poor nations may, with a good deal of reason, be attributed not to exploitation, but to a *failure to exploit*, that is, to develop and productively utilize their rich natural resources for mutual benefit. Historically, this has been the most critical omission. By and large, however, it has been the result not of an evil design deliberately created and perpetrated, but of a patent failure to understand the problems of well-phased resource development to achieve sustained economic growth.

This failure has been most serious in the field of agriculture. Yet it is here that the developing countries have their most pressing needs and also their best opportunities. The population must be fed; it provides them with a sizable potential market at their doorsteps; and, in general, they have—with some exceptions like the oil-rich desert countries of Kuwait, Saudi Arabia and Lybia—enough natural resources to grow not only the food needed for domestic consumption, but also to step up agricultural production as a whole with a much-needed surplus to help speed their overall economic growth.

[3] *Partners in Development*, Report of the Commission on International Development, Praeger Publishers, New York, 1969, p. 25.

In fact, the potential comparative advantages for producing food and a wide range of farm products lie, if anything, mostly in their favour. Many of them are inherently capable of turning out surpluses from their farms —food, fibre and other crops—not only for domestic consumption, but also for foreign markets, provided however the right kinds of science and technology needed for tropical agriculture[4] are developed with skill and care, and are applied systematically as an integral part of a comprehensive strategy that embraces and satisfies all the prerequisites for modernizing their agriculture. This vital condition has hitherto remained unfulfilled. Science and technology have made impressive strides in the developed countries and have boosted their farm productivity to unprecedented levels. The needs of tropical agriculture have, by and large, been ignored.

The result has been tragic. The population of the developing countries has surged ahead at an accelerated tempo. Their fragile economies have been saddled with the crippling burden of mounting numbers, of which 40 per cent or more are below 14 years in age and therefore fall in the non-earning categories. Their primitive subsistence-type agriculture is unable to produce enough food to cope with the fast-rising demand. Many of them are faced with increasing food deficits, so that they must either expend their scarce foreign exchange resources for importing foodgrains or helplessly drift into a deepening food crisis with all its grim implications.

These disastrous trends must be arrested, and reversed. Until this happens there will be no economic future for the developing countries. But it can happen only when tropical agriculture comes into its own. For, potentially, this is the most powerful generator of economic growth they possess. And it is from here that they must derive the big impulses for forward movement, especially in the initial stages of their economic development. It follows that their foremost concern today must be to capitalize on the high potential of their agriculture, to work out an effective strategy for the purpose, and to put it relentlessly into operation.

Luckily, the omens today look far more favourable than ever before, thanks to the remarkable scientific breakthroughs of recent years. Before turning to them, however, it would be worth taking a closer look at the reasons which have been responsible for keeping tropical agriculture in its present backward state. Such a look is necessary not simply to satisfy academic interest, but also to shed light on the remedial measures which will be needed as parts of the future strategy.

## CAUSES OF NEGLECT

Several factors have, in varying degrees, contributed to the long neglect

[4] Almost all the developing countries lie in the tropics and subtropics. For the sake of convenience the word "tropics" has been used frequently in a broader sense to cover the subtropics as well.

the natural resources of the tropics have suffered from despite their high productive potential: lopsided economic thinking, a dense ideological confusion, the blind operation of historical forces, and inadequate understanding, and misconceptions, about the prerequisites for developing a modern agriculture.

It is not possible, nor is it necessary in the present context, to delve deep into the history of economic thought. Yet it is worthwhile to recall, even if briefly, those doctrines which, from the days of the classical economists to our own times, have exercised a powerful influence on the attitudes and policies towards agriculture.

The classical system of economics[5] built around the three factors of production—land, labour and capital—with a few basic concepts had a simplicity of its own. To note its immediately relevant postulates, land was subject to the law of diminishing returns and gave rise to "rent" in the Ricardian sense of the term. By contrast, the manufacturing industry was governed by the law of increasing returns since costs came down as units grew in size. Supply of labour was supposed to be determined by the size of the population, and since population grew at a relatively fast rate, it constantly threatened to outrun the production of food, and to depress wages to the subsistence level. As for capital (goods), its quantum depended on savings as represented by the difference between production and consumption.

This system did not, even at its birth, fit the changing scenario of the Western world. The wheels of industrial revolution continued to move uninterruptedly, though the degree of its acceleration varied from time to time. Population grew steadily, but food production kept pace with it, while transcontinental communications opened up vast new sources of supply. Output of goods, volume of employment, overall income, living standards—all trended upwards. What began as an industrial revolution broadened into an all-embracing social and economic revolution. The Malthusian nightmare about population receded into the limbo of history as the evil dream of a fertile brain.

Technology continued to change and mould the Western world with repercussions which more and more penetrated into the remote regions of the earth. But economic theory continued to move mainly along its classical grooves. The genius of Marshall, Pigou and other neoclassicists was devoted primarily to the fashioning and refining of analytical tools; they managed to stay, even if at times with visible discomfort, within the classical framework. The dynamics of the modern world were, with impressive intellectual gymnastics, fitted into a static pattern. As Keynes put it in

---

[5] That is, economic theories developed in England by Malthus, Ricardo and others in the late eighteenth and the earlier part of the nineteenth century *prior* to John Stuart Mill.

another context, they were, in effect, applying Euclidean geometry to a non-Euclidean world.

Latter-day economists sensed this contradiction and sought to bring their theory in line with the phenomenon of economic growth. Yet in practice most of them fell back upon the device of an easy, but misleading shortcut. They recognized "technological change" as a separate factor of production and added it, mostly as an appendage, to the old system. Having made this perfunctory nod to the claims of dynamism, they hastily put it out of sight, well behind the classical trio of land, labour and capital, and then lapsed, with a more relaxed conscience, into the conventional static type of analysis. Most studies on economic growth have tended to lead, through a maze of elaborate analysis, to a point where there is in effect little change and growth.

No one doubts today that science-intensive agriculture can be tremendously productive; that land given by nature can be remade by man with capital, which need not always be large, and modern chemistry; that, as a result, the old distinction between good land and poor land has been largely blurred, and with it the Ricardian concept of rent; that, in fact, it is more pertinent today to distinguish between good farmers and bad farmers, and between science-starved subsistence agriculture and input-intensive commercial agriculture.

Similarly, science and technology have added new dimensions to the productivity of labour. Nor need they always be capital-intensive. The so-called "lumpiness" of capital holds good for certain industries, such as iron and steel, machine tools, automobiles, petrochemicals, fertilizers and pesticides, in general also for power generation. But a great many other industries, especially those producing consumer goods, are free from this constraint. Given the right technologies, they can be small, thinly capitalized, highly productive, and fully competitive. This has vastly altered the economies of scale, and therefore the validity of the old concepts of increasing or diminishing returns.

As for capital, radical rethinking is no less urgent. The greatest generator of capital is science and technology applied to idle resources, especially land and water (see Chapter 2).

The tools of economic analysis are now more numerous, more complex, and far more sophisticated. Computers can do instant data-processing on a massive scale; econometrics ensures a high degree of precision in the analysis; model-building, in its "micro" and "macro" incarnation, has gained fast in popularity. But sophistication has not been matched by insight or wisdom, and models are more apt to impress and dazzle than to inform and enlighten.

For example, economic growth or progress, it is now customary to emphasize, depends on the rate of capital formation, which in turn is conditioned by the rate of savings, that is, current production less current

NEGLECTED ASSETS OF THE TROPICS 9

consumption. This, according to some, constitutes the "iron law" of economic development.

The implications of this law are singularly uninspiring for the developing countries. Their per capita production is extremely low, and so is their rate of savings, especially when consumption is pushed up by rising population; and, this, in turn, keeps their production low. Thus, developing countries seem doomed to move in a vicious circle. They are poor because they are poor, and for the same reason they must remain so. Poverty, in short, is self-perpetuating. This conclusion is supposed to be in line with the law of economic growth, which holds the poor nations in an iron grip and denies them any means of escape.

If this reasoning were correct, the prospects for the developing countries would indeed be bleak. Luckily, it is not so. For, as will be seen later, especially in Chapter 2, this theoretical edifice, however skilfully erected, rests on palpably erroneous premises.


## IDEOLOGICAL CONFUSION

Classical economics served as the mainspring for the emergence of a militant theory which, thanks to its wide emotional appeal, has generated a great deal more heat than light and has further confounded the issues.

Karl Marx, it may be recalled, seized with alacrity the Ricardian theory of rent, rejected outright the Malthusian doctrine of population with its lugubrious predictions, enunciated his own theory of value which he attributed solely to labour, and prophesied the overthrow of capitalism and the ultimate victory of the proletariat through the dialectics of history.

An oft-forgotten facet of Marxian thought,[6] which is specially relevant here, is its rejection of the law of diminishing returns from land. As farms grew bigger, their costs of production, so it was argued, would fall, thereby giving rise to larger profits or "rent." Agriculture was thus placed on a par with industry. And both were supposed to be governed equally by the law of increasing returns.

That, by a rare dialectic twist of history, the rule *of* the proletariat would turn out to be a rule *over* the proletariat, is something which even Marx could not foresee. As Soviet Russia, with its awesome centralization under a one-party system, grew in science and technology, and built its political, industrial and military might, it became a powerful influence in spreading its own gospel of development far and wide, and in the process aroused excited hopes of speedy progress through ideological shortcuts. The package of dogmas it offered has tended to produce opposite effects. It has both stimulated and retarded progress.

[6] Theodore W. Schultz took special care to draw attention to this point in *Transforming Traditional Agriculture*, Yale University Press, 1964, p. 9.

2

On the positive side is its strong and unequivocal emphasis on education, on science and technology, on health services, on mobilization of manpower with productive employment for the entire working population. Illiteracy was recognized as an unmitigated evil, something like, say, malaria which had to be eradicated. There could be no compromise with it, and so in Stalin's Russia it was stamped out within record time.

The educational system was deliberately slanted towards science and technology. That economic and social progress would depend on the ability to acquire and promote scientific knowledge and modern technology was treated as axiomatic. It was set up as one of the foremost objectives and was pursued aggressively.

A no less remarkable feature of the Soviet system was its sharp accent on socialized medicine. Every citizen, it was assumed without any hesitation, was entitled to a minimum of medicare. Every effort has therefore been made from the start to expand the medical facilities and to make them available to the whole nation either free or at nominal cost.

A few other items must be entered on the credit side of the ledger. Geological prospecting of the country was carried out as a matter of high priority. The mineral base of the economy, it was rightly stressed, must be thoroughly explored as an essential first step for its development.

Unemployment was regarded as a social and economic waste for the simple reason that the jobless, apart from their own hardship, would function as consumers without being producers. Productive employment of the employable adult population, men and women, was therefore looked upon as one of the most important desiderata. Where necessary, large-scale public works programmes were initiated to achieve this end. Wages were admittedly low; on the other hand, every adult was entitled to, and provided with, a job with a minimum income.

Another significant feature of the Soviet approach was the concept of a multipurpose army—its utilization in peace time for public works and other nation-building activities. The net burden of maintaining a large standing army was thus substantially reduced.

Finally, mention must be made of certain aspects of Soviet finance. Unrestrained deficit finance, spiralling inflation, forced savings on massive scales, artificial exchange rates, frequent currency manipulations—these no doubt characterized it for several decades until, say, the mid-fifties. This, however, is not the whole story. In dealing with the nation-building functions listed above—education, health services, geological surveys, scientific research and experiments, substantial public works programmes—the Soviet authorities have shown much greater imagination than their Western counterparts with their rigid and negatively-slanted budget-balancing. They have treated expenditures on such items as social investments, have made generous allocations for them, and have reaped handsome dividends in return.

The Soviet shield has another side which is less attractive.[7] The negative factors stand out with such unmistakable clarity against the background of the last fifty years that it would be hard to miss or ignore them today. Soviet Russia, as is well known, has gone through revolutions covering all aspects of life. Its stormy upheavals were marked by two outstanding events, or rather an event and a non-event: it underwent a wrong revolution—the agricultural, and it missed a crucial revolution—the managerial. But for these two historical facts, Khrushchev would have had a better chance of catching up with the USA in production and in G.N.P., and life, too, would have been richer and fuller for Soviet citizens.

No one can help but admire the spectacular record of achievements Soviet Russia has to its credit. But many will find it hard to show the same admiration for its political and economic system. In fact, there is every reason to doubt, as many thoughtful Russians must be doubting today, if the system suits even Russia, especially in this age of super-technology and hyper-specialization. By all tokens, it is overcentralized, over-bureaucratized, and over-dominated by a single political party claiming omniscience which never existed and is even less likely to exist in future. No, the great achievements of Soviet Russia are not due to the excellence of its system, but primarily to the genius of its people, and its fabulous natural resources, though ingenious attempts are frequently made to sell it to others as something intrinsically superior.

Meanwhile, there are compelling reasons why the Soviet model will not suit India, Pakistan and other developing countries. Marxism and communism may connive at the population problem, and Soviet Russia, as one of the world's most sparsely populated countries, can do so with impunity. China's ideological fervour in this field has been less enthusiastic, no doubt because of her radically different demographic syndrome. This is well reflected in her stop-go policy about population control. Perhaps it is safe to predict today that realism will get the upper hand of ideology in China, and that it will soon opt, less equivocally, for a more stringent population control policy.[8]

For developing countries in general, population has become a problem of desperate urgency, and it must be tackled as such.

The Soviet system has been dominated, for reasons indicated earlier, by some overpowering biases: in favour of industries as against agriculture which has suffered from chronic neglect;[9] in favour of large-scale

[7] The comments contained in this section about the Soviet system were first made by the writer in a three-part article called "Socialism Today" which was published in the *Indian Express* on 3, 5 and 6 January, 1970. They have been used here with minor changes because of their obvious relevance in the present context.

[8] In fact, the "go-signal" in this stop-go policy has, for some time, been quite steady and prominent, and will probably be more so in the coming years.

[9] On 3 June, 1970, the Central Committee of the Communist Party approved a report condemning mismanagement in Soviet agriculture, admitting food supplies

mechanized farming as against considerations of productivity—"the bigger, the better" has apparently been the guiding motto in order to capture what were supposed to be the increasing returns resulting from the economies of scale; and in favour of state ownership and state management which turned farmers from entrepreneurs into paid workers and weakened the incentive to raise yield and income.

Such an approach does not fit in with the needs of the developing world, far less with those of India, Pakistan and other heavily-populated countries of Asia. Soviet Russia can poorly manage its large-scale collectivized, mechanized farms, and yet harvest enough grains to feed its 235 million people.[10] For the developing countries, especially of Asia, to grow enough food for the soaring population is literally a matter of life and death. For sheer survival a country like India must build up the Japanese type of small-scale, high-input farming with the utmost possible speed, treating it as the very heart of its programme for national development.

Meanwhile, Soviet agriculture has one aspect which, though mostly overlooked, is far more relevant to the developing countries. It is not the *kolkhoz* and the *sobkhoz*—the collective and the state farm—which naturally claim the limelight, but the countless small private plots which are still allowed to the Soviet farm workers and from which, through relatively intensive farming, they turn out large quantities of vegetable, poultry and other products. This private-lot farming, or Soviet-style "kitchen gardening," provides an eloquent hint of how much more Soviet farmers could, and would, produce were they not starved of incentives and were reasonably assured of the fruits of their own labour.

For developing countries it is of paramount importance today to take a leaf from Soviet experience. Indeed, it is vital for them to adopt the positive factors listed above and to incorporate them boldly into their own national development plans, just as it would be fatal for them to imitate the rest of the Soviet dogmas and to drift, whether deliberately or unwittingly, into an ideological neglect of their agriculture and of their pressing population problem.

## IMPACT OF HISTORY

Every philosophy, it has been said, is an apology. This cynical remark

---

were inadequate, and promising increased production. "The situation in grain production still does not satisfy us," said Mr. Brezhnev at the Committee's meeting. "The amount of vegetables and fruits being grown is inadequate ... the demand of the population for livestock produce, especially meat, is not being satisfied by far." Report in the *New York Times* on July 4, 1970.

[10] Not that it always happened that way. As the wit put it a few years ago, "Khrushchev sowed wheat in Kazakstan and reaped it in Canada!"

does contain an element of profound truth. We all rationalize—as individuals, groups, tribes, and as nations. No wonder that history should have its own quota of rationalizations.

This is well illustrated by the radical shifts which trade between rich and poor nations have undergone at different times and the somersaults in the theories and ideas that accompanied them. In the early eighteenth century fine cotton textiles of Indian origin found a ready market in England. The popularity they enjoyed and the competition they offered upset the woollen industry, the oldest industry of England and the "spoilt child of Parliament," and gave rise to protests which led to the imposition of heavy duties on imported cotton textiles. It is a commonplace of economic history how the continued keen demand for them gave a decisive impetus to the series of remarkable inventions for developing a domestic cotton textile industry, which ushered in the modern industrial revolution. By 1798, the import of textile goods from India was completely banned. The need for such a step to protect the domestic industry was in those days days taken for granted.

Only a few decades later, after a modern factory-based industry had emerged in England, came the great free trade era heralded by the Manchester School. Cobden, Bright and others conjured up the vision of world prosperity and peace through expanding commerce based on unrestricted exchange of goods. India's vast market was thrown completely open to the influx of imported manufactures. Her once prosperous textile and other handicrafts increasingly lost ground and fell victims at the altar of free trade.

The infant industry argument, the axiom on which continental Europe, America, Japan and others built up their modern industries, never touched the shores of India. And Friedrich List's name was barely known to Indian economists.

Yet even in this bleak milieu of blind free trade Indian entrepreneurship began to sprout, painfully but irrepressibly. Starting from 1854, a number of cotton textile factories sprang up, mainly in Bombay and Ahmedabad. There was no suggestion of giving any protection to them at any stage. On the contrary, when the exigencies of revenue led the government to impose moderate duties on imported cotton textiles, a countervailing excise duty was levied, in 1894, on cotton yarn above 20 counts, and it was converted, two years later, into an excise duty on mill cloth.[11] This was done under pressure from Lancashire to protect the principle of free trade—and thereby to protect for itself the Indian market against competition from Indian mills!

[11] Bitterly opposed by Indians, the cotton excise duty was looked upon as a symbol of their economic subjugation, somewhat like the Navigation Laws in early American history, and its abolition became a rallying cry for the national movement. After thirty years of agitation it was repealed, in 1926.

The free trade era ended with World War I, and after the War a new chapter began in India's economic history with the introduction of a policy of so-called "discriminating protection." Though a timid version of the infant industry argument as historically applied by many industrialized nations, it was nonetheless welcomed as a tardy recognition of a vital principle.

Another phase began with the Great Depression of the 1930's when markets shrank and a new wave of protectionism swept through the Western world. Great Britain initiated the principle of Imperial Preference which was embodied in the Ottawa Agreement of 1932 (and later also in the Indo-British Trade Agreement of 1939). It accorded preferential treatment to imports from Empire countries and thereby helped protect the Empire markets for British manufactures. Though a glaring departure from the hallowed principles of free trade, it was readily sanctioned in the name of expediency.

Since World War II several forces have been at work, sometimes at cross purposes. World trade has expanded steadily, but the rich nations have not hesitated to levy arbitrary tariffs on imports from the developing countries. They have made massive investments to develop synthetics which directly compete with primary commodities, the staple exports of the tropics. The Kennedy round of tariff-cutting has been confined to the developed nations; no corresponding benefit through tariff reduction has been extended to the underdeveloped world.

The developing countries, in their turn, have merrily gone ahead with the launching of new industries, often as a means of import substitution to save foreign exchange. This, in many instances, has proved to be a costly policy. Industries have been hastily conceived and poorly managed, requiring only too often heavy subsidies for their survival. They have thus become a drain on the limited national resources; and rather than promote growth, they have frequently hindered it.

Meanwhile, the days of Commonwealth Preference (as Imperial Preference came to be called after the dissolution of the Empire) have, it seems, been finally numbered. More stringent restrictions were recently imposed by Britain on imports of textile goods, including those from India and other Commonwealth countries. Even more important is the fact that Britain is now about to join the European Common Market* which has been busy building a common protectionist front against most developing countries.

All in all, the world seems to have drifted towards what one may call *big-power blocism* in international trade. One seldom talks or hears nowadays about international division of labour and the theory of comparative advantages. It seems they have been quietly cast to the four winds.

One of the most eloquent pieces of rationalizations that marked the

* Meanwhile, an accomplished fact.

colonial era was that the tropical countries were inherently cut out for agriculture and not industries, that they could best prosper as producers of primary commodities and trading them for imported manufactures, that such a global division of labour, reflecting as it did the comparative advantages embedded in nature's own scheme of things, best served the interests of all nations. The underdeveloped countries are struggling today with the crippling legacy left behind by this unabashed one-sidedness.

But the saddest feature of the economic pattern that dominated the colonial era is that even its much-advertised bias for agriculture was more apparent than real. It helped prevent, or retard, the growth of industries rather than promote agriculture. Barring a few exceptions, agriculture in India, and elsewhere, suffered from chronic neglect.

Some valuable research was done in tropical crops, but it was mostly confined to a few commodities of industrial and commercial importance, such as jute, rubber, palm oil, tea, coffee, cocoa, sugarcane. Research hardly touched the vastly more important category—the food crops which account for the bulk, about 85 per cent, of the agricultural output in the developing countries.[12]

Much progress was made in evolving improved and higher-yielding varieties of foodgrains in the temperate zones, but they had little relevance to tropical conditions. That the radically different ecology of the tropics would call for new crop varieties and production technology tailored to suit its own soils and climates is something that was not realized for a long time. Surprising as it may seem, it is only in the last decade or so that the world, both developed and underdeveloped, began to grasp this elemental fact with its far-reaching implications.

Pests and insects, too, pose an analogous ecological problem. Not only are they different, they are also more numerous; and they flourish and multiply far more easily in the hospitable climate of the tropics. They have to be subjected to intensive scientific study on a continuous basis as a precondition for evolving effective plant protection measures.

In India, to take this once again as a specific case, the vital importance of irrigation was at best partially recognized. Large-scale irrigation was developed only in a very few areas; and even in these cases it happened to be mostly seasonal, without storage reservoirs, without drainage, and without field-level controls. By far the most important, and successful, system of irrigation was built in the Punjab where the rainfall was too low, about 8 inches, to support crops, but where the snow-fed Indus carried a perennial flow.[13]

Yet irrigation was needed not only in the dry, but also in the wet regions—to free India's agriculture from the bondage of the monsoon that brings most of the rainfall concentrated practically in three months of

[12] See Chapters 3, 4 and 22.
[13] See Chapters 11 and 15.

the year. The intensity of cropping can be raised only if the rainwater is stored and spread over a longer period. This explains why, from ancient times, irrigation had become a major preoccupation of India's rulers. Elaborate systems of irrigation had been constructed in many parts of the country. But once the rights and responsibilities about land were confused following shifts in the political panorama, they fell into neglect and succumbed to the ravages of time.

As for land tenure, the changes introduced helped neither agriculture nor the actual tillers of land. In particular, the so-called "permanent settlements" made in the eastern provinces starting from 1793 created a class of callous intermediaries who, in effect, came to exercise full control over land, dominated the peasantry, pocketed a large slice of the income from agriculture, and rendered little or no service in return.[14]

Conservation of water and soil has a vital importance, especially in tropical agriculture; there never was, nor even now is, adequate realization of this fact. Poultry and fishery, despite their enormous possibilities, seldom received any attention. The moribund departments of agriculture, run mostly under civil service control, had little direct contact with farmers. There was no suggestion of anything resembling an agricultural extension service. And so whatever promising results were achieved through research and experiments tended to remain confined to laboratories and government farms.[15]

Another conspicuous omission was the absence of domestic facilities for producing chemical fertilizers, a key industry that supplies the lifeblood of modern agriculture. Or, here again perhaps the underlying presumption was that it was unsuitable for the tropics because it was an industry! In any case, the first steps for setting up the first fertilizer factory in India were taken in the last years of the pre-independence regime. The factory, established at Sindri in Bihar, went into production in October 1951.

These, then, are some facts from the past, a cross-section of history's track record. They have been recalled here only to set the perspective right. It is futile to quarrel with history; but it is fatal, in any analysis, to ignore it.[16]

---

[14] Problems relating to land reform are dealt with in *Reaping the Green Revolution.*
[15] There have been some striking exceptions, however. See Chapters 4 and 22.
[16] The remark made many years ago by a British friend, then a senior executive of a British-owned commercial firm in Calcutta, comes to mind. "You see, we have followed an ostrich-like policy in India," he told the writer with some feeling on the eve of India's independence. "It has always been a case of jute, tea, and coal—coal, tea, and jute, and we have refused to look further beyond." A good many Britishers would, at least implicitly, share this view today.

# CHAPTER 2

# Axioms of Development

## A. TRADITIONAL AGRICULTURE

**POOR BUT EFFICIENT**

Misconceptions about traditional agriculture have been both profound and widespread, and they have by no means been confined to the developed countries.[1] Theodore Schultz tried to demolish at least some of them. In a penetrating analysis he showed that the traditional farmer, contrary to the view almost universally held, was not an irrational being after all, and that he did display a lot of skill in using the meagre resources he had at his disposal.

Traditional farmers, Schultz argued, were hardworking, thrifty, shrewd, and empirically wise. However, the rate at which they "can accept a new factor of production depends upon its profit, with the allowance for risk and uncertainty," and in this respect their response was "similar to that observed by farmers in modern agriculture."[2] This view would suggest that there are "comparatively few significant inefficiencies" in the allocation of the factors of production in traditional agriculture."[3]

In support of this hypothesis Dr. Schultz cited two specific studies. One of them had been carried out by Sol Tax on a rural community in Panajachel in Guatemala, which he found "very poor but efficient," and

[1] For Indian misconceptions about the Indian farmer, see Chapter 9.
[2] Theodore W. Schultz, op. cit.
[3] Ibid., p. 37.

3

which he called "a society which is 'capitalist' on a microscopic scale."[4]

The second study was on a village called Senapur located in the Gangetic plain of India, which was made by W. David Hopper in the mid-fifties.[5] An observer "cannot but be impressed with the way the village uses its physical resources," said Dr. Hopper in summing up some of his main findings. "The age-old techniques have been refined and sharpened by countless years of experience.... Rotations, tillage and cultivation practices, seed rates, irrigation techniques, and the ability of the blacksmith and the potter to work under handicaps of little power and inferior materials, all attest to a cultural heritage that is richly endowed with empirical wisdom."

But were the people of Senapur "realizing the full economic potential of their physical resources?" Dr. Hopper left no doubt on the question. From the point of view of the villagers the answer, he said, must be "Yes." In general, each man came "close to doing the best he can with his knowledge and cultural background."

This conclusion is not surprising; in fact, this is what one should have suspected even on *a priori* reasoning. Living in a small world of very few opportunities and engaged in a pitiless struggle for existence, farmers in a traditional agriculture had to adapt themselves from generation to generation to an environment over which they had little control, and had to develop their innate skills to wring out of it whatever benefit they could to eke out a living. This is how they had to respond to the challenges they faced for sheer survival.

And this is true not only of farmers, but also of a great many other people in the backward economies—craftsmen, traders, workers in general. Their methods of work, though mostly crude and primitive, have their own rationale. By and large, they do the best they can with the tools and knowledge they possess in the conditions they live and work under; and in that sense they, too, are "poor but efficient." A little understanding with a touch of compassion would in most cases reveal that, contrary to the superficial verdict readily given by supercilious observers, they are not irrational in their general behaviour, that their backwardness essentially reflects a lack of opportunities, that it is wrong, if not cruel, to reverse this cause-and-effect relationship and to hold them responsible for their misfortune. It is to the credit of Schultz, Tax, Hopper and other similarly-minded social scientists that they have eschewed the beaten path, probed below the surface, and have employed scientific tools to explode some cherished myths.

[4] In *Penny Capitalism*, first published by Smithsonian Institution, Washington, D.C., in 1953, and reprinted by the University of Chicago Press in 1963. Quoted by Dr. Schultz, ibid.
[5] *The Economic Organization of a Village in North Central India*, Ph.D. thesis presented at Cornell University in 1957 (unpublished). Quoted by Dr. Schultz, ibid.

## PROFIT-MAXIMIZER OR RISK-MINIMIZER

While the thesis propounded by Dr. Schultz did have some valid points, he nonetheless overstated the case. For one thing, traditional agriculture can hardly be treated as something homogeneous. This omnibus label, when applied to the whole spectrum of underdeveloped countries, is liable to conceal notable differences despite the characteristics common to them all. There are degrees of "traditionalism," as of "modernism," in agriculture which one should be careful not to ignore.

Michael Lipton is reluctant to accept the Schultz-Hopper view that the Indian farmer is a "profit-maximizer." Based on his own experience in India, he argues that what the Indian farmer seeks above all is a "survival algorithm," a set of rules for farming that would ensure a tolerable minimum output.[6] He functions, in other words, more as a risk-minimizer. He would propitiate evil spirits or irascible gods even at some real economic sacrifice, for example, with grains or food. From his own angle this, too, is a part of his risk-minimizing effort.

The kind of farmer Michael Lipton depicts is a familiar prototype in rural India. Nor is this surprising since, with a great many people in India, agriculture has long been, to quote an old but nonetheless apt phrase, "a way of life" rather than a business in true sense.

However, there have been other prototypes as well. In several areas, especially in Punjab, Tamil Nadu, Mysore, and generally in areas close to large urban centres, farmers have been progressive and commercially-oriented, sometimes remarkably so. There is not the slightest doubt that a great many others could, and would, greatly improve their performance, even within the framework of the so-called traditional agriculture, if they were just provided with village-to-market roads. And if to these were added a reasonable price incentive, they would almost certainly give a far better account of themselves. Many of them have been psychologically ready for a more modern commercial type of agriculture, but have been held back by one or two adverse factors that could be remedied with comparative ease.

These facts contradict the generalized view one sometimes encounters in the Schultz school of thinking: that there can be no gradual transition from traditional to modern agriculture, that it has to be effected in one big leap with higher-yielding varieties, fertilizers and other inputs. In fact, the strongest feature of agriculture, from the angle of a developing country, lies in the fact that progress here is divisible and can be achieved on an instalment basis; that though it will ultimately call for large investments, it is much less subject to lumpiness of capital than industry so that small investments, if intelligently made, and if they are backed by the

[6] Paul Streeten and Michael Lipton, *The Crisis of Indian Planning—Economic Policy in the 1960's*, Oxford University Press, 1968, p. 116.

essential services, can produce significant results within a short time.

This, as is well known, is the strategy Japan followed for modernizing her agriculture in the early stages and used it, with conspicuous success, as the spearhead of her economic development. In more recent times Taiwan has demonstrated the effectiveness of the same strategy.

## NOT ALWAYS EFFICIENT

The view that traditional agriculture shows "comparatively few significant inefficiencies" does not always hold good. While on closer examination it does reveal a great deal more skill and practical wisdom than is commonly suspected, it also provides examples of much inefficiency, whether due to inertia or other factors.

As indicated earlier, it would not be correct to say that Indian farmers, even within the limits of their knowledge, generally make the best possible allocation of the factors of production. That the contrary can very well be true the writer discovered from his own experience during 1939-42 while engaged in rural development work covering a group of 15 villages in the Birbhum district of West Bengal.[7] Agriculture in this area was then virtually synonymous with the cultivation of a monsoon-fed rice crop. The methods used revealed much skill crystallized from long experience, but the yield was deplorably low—984 pounds of clean rice per acre— and there was considerable room for improvement. If the silted-up irrigation tanks, which had at one time dotted the undulating terrain, were reexcavated and put back to use, this alone could, by ironing out the effects of the rainfall, have raised the average annual output by as much as 50 per cent, apart from making it possible to grow a second crop on a sizable acreage and to raise some fish into the bargain.

Moreover, soil fertility was a sadly neglected subject. It could have been built up to a significantly higher level through such measures as using cowdung for manure rather than for fuel, composting, green-manuring, utilizing the available bonemeal, not to speak of the "human" manure which however was, and still is, mostly anathema to Indian farmers in contrast with their Chinese or Japanese counterparts.

Another negative factor was the monkey pest which posed a serious threat to the crops and, in particular, inhibited the cultivation of a winter crop even where enough water was available.

The farming community was desperately poor *and inefficient*, though

---

[7] Sudhir Sen, *Land and its Problems*, Visva-Bharati Economic Research Publication No. 3, Santiniketan, West Bengal, 1943. This publication contained the results of a study of the economic conditions in the fifteen villages which constituted the "Intensive Area" of the Institute of Rural Reconstruction at Sriniketan, a sister institution of Tagore's University at Santiniketan. See in particular Chapters 15 and 16 on "Low Yield and its Causes."

by no means unintelligent. Working in its midst the writer could not help wonder how a Japanese or a Chinese farmer would have handled the same resources. He had no doubt in his own mind that the latter, even under the conditions then prevailing, would have doubled the output of rice per acre and would have derived substantial extra incomes from ancillary activities, such as a second crop, poultry, fishery, cultivation of some fruits and vegetables. And he would have done so even without chemical fertilizers, and without waiting for a green revolution.

Why, then, was such obvious and readily realizable productive potential allowed to lie idle or to run to waste, above all in a country where the rural people had a considerable tradition of selfhelp? The answer was overwhelmingly psychological. The people had been *demoralized by history*—they had turned callous and had, apparently, lost much of the zest for living.

The area, at one time, had a number of flourishing industries and handicrafts. The most notable among them were cotton and silk textiles, lac and various lac products, indigo cultivation for dye manufacture, iron and iron products manufactured on a cottage-industry scale, apart from the more conventional types of village crafts—leather industry, pottery, oilpressing, and paddy-husking. But all of them had vanished, barring a handful of impoverished handloom weavers, potters and cobblers as if to help recall a nostalgic past. Trade and commerce were at a very low ebb, so also were the rivers—the Mor and the Ajay—which used to serve as arteries of communication and were now largely sand-filled. The incidence of malaria and other diseases had gone up sharply. The population had grown over the years despite the high mortality rates, and with it also the pressure on land and the size of the labour force.

Meanwhile, a class of absentee landlords had sprung into existence, who lived *off* land but *in* cities, who drained wealth from the countryside and offered little in return, who even neglected their long-established obligations for village welfare including excavation and maintenance of irrigation tanks. The silted-up tanks bore dreary testimony to this changed and one-sided landlord-tenant relationship.

In short, the clock of progress had moved backwards, and then seemed to stand still. The people had their eyes set on the past, and not on the future. The memories of a departed prosperity were still too vivid, also too bitter, in their minds. The prospects of a brighter future to be built with greater exertion on a shrunken foundation failed to enthuse them.[8]

What has been said about the Sriniketan villages holds good for many

[8] Leonard K. Elmhirst, Founder-President of the International Conference of Agricultural Economics, who had served as the first Director of the Sriniketan Institute during 1919-22, diagnosed the ills of the area as "malaria, monkeys, and mutual mistrust." While correct up to a point, the three M's were really symptoms of a malaise that ran much deeper.

other parts of India. As the old division of labour—between cottage industries, handicrafts, trade and commerce on the one hand, and agriculture on the other—disappeared and the extent of the market shrank, agriculture was increasingly forced to operate within much narrower limits, and, as a result, it became even more defensive and subsistence-oriented. The pressure of population, diminishing job opportunities, the apathy of landlords, oppressive rents, insecurity of tenure, almost certain post-harvest slumps in agricultural prices—these would have been enough, in any part of the world, to kill the incentives of a farming community to work more and to produce more.

There have, however, been exceptions, especially where history had a more benign influence, such as in the Indus Valley where large irrigation projects made the desert bloom or in areas close to expanding urban centres which provided growing markets for farm produce. In such cases farmer response has been both prompt and positive. In most areas, however, India's traditional agriculture moved a few steps backwards and, if anything, became a little more "traditional."

Before leaving this topic a more general word of caution seems necessary. Even where farmers are "poor but efficient," there should be no reason to glorify the low-level equilibrium reached in a traditional agriculture. There is the other side of the shield which must not be overlooked. The traditional *farmer* may be efficient, but traditional *agriculture* is not, and can never be. He may use the potential to the limit of his own capability; but even then a vast potential for production lies dormant and waits to be tapped with the combined input of science and technology, a wide range of manufactured items, and a multiplicity of skills. The allocation of his own resources and his own methods of farming may leave little room for improvement; yet government policies and actions may, and invariably do, fall far short of what is immediately practicable to improve agriculture and to set it on a rising curve of productivity per unit of land.

The distinction made above is vital; yet it has been blurred, and often ignored, in theoretical economics for reasons explained earlier. Theodore Schultz deftly skirted the trap laid by classical and neo-classical analysis. The so-called "technological change" economists are now apt to recognize as a new factor of production needs a deeper x'ray, Schultz argued, than is usually conceded. This general rubric, he pointed out, is "merely a bit of a shorthand for an array of (new) factors of production," a technology is always "embodied" in particular factors, to capitalize on it a *new* factor combination becomes essential. The old classification of factors into land, labour and capital is therefore not enough. One must, he insisted, treat each technological change as a new factor and carefully analyze its impact.[9]

[9] Theodore W. Schultz, op. cit., pp. 132-34.

This approach has an obvious virtue inasmuch as it recognizes, with refreshing clarity, technological change as the main lever of progress, and seeks to accommodate it, without equivocation, within the classical framework. Despite this, however, it remains essentially a halfway compromise. The approach can be, indeed it must be, broadened further to do justice to the concept of economic development in countries which are struggling to enter the modern age in the late-twentieth century. To this we now turn in the following section.

## B. AXIOMS OF DEVELOPMENT

### CAPITAL ERROR

Theoretical economics, it cannot be stressed too strongly or too often, has never been able to free itself from its classical shackles. Even in its modern version it has been hobbled by old abstractions. For explaining the problems of economic growth in the developing countries, it has been singularly unhelpful, and often a positive impediment.

This, in the final analysis, must be attributed to what can be rightly called *a capital error*. The standard definition of capital one nowadays encounters in most textbooks on economics is much too narrow and misleading. It is usually conceived in terms of plant and equipment, that is, producer's goods, or in purely monetary terms, that is, as savings which can be used for capital formation.[10] Such a concept has very limited relevance to a developing country.

### THE AXIOMS

To comprehend more fully the actual process of development and to chalk out, without too many costly deviations, the path a developing country must follow to achieve an optimum rate of progress it is absolutely essential to grasp more firmly a set of axioms which, at best, are implicit and, at worst, are ignored in the most prevalent economic thinking:

[10] A good example is what Ragnar Nurske said in his *Problems of Capital Formation in Underdeveloped Countries* (Oxford University Press, 1953), which, incidentally, gave the cue to a good many other economists: "There is the small capacity to save, resulting from the low level of real income. The low real income is a reflection of low productivity, which in its turn is due largely to the lack of capital. The lack of capital is the result of the small capacity to save" (p. 5). Or again, "The country's incremental savings ratio...is the crucial determinant of growth" (p. 142).

For an excellent review of the capital-formation approach and how it has grown into a major obstacle to economic progress in the developing countries, see Lauchlin Currie's *Accelerating Development*, McGraw-Hill Book Company, New York, 1966, Chapter 9 (pp. 121-39).

*One*, the assets of a developing country consist of its natural resources —its soils, waters, minerals and forests—along with the two universal and inexhaustible ones—sunlight and air. The profuse supply of sunshine and the growth-stimulating warm temperatures which usually characterize it must, on balance, be regarded as highly valuable assets which often confer on it comparative advantages for a wide range of products.

These natural resources constitute the *real* capital of a developing country. On them depends its ultimate economic destiny. How to develop, utilize, and conserve them on a sustained-yield basis—this is the crux of the whole question. This is what must be treated as the heart of development economics.

*Two*, if resource development is the only source of wealth, it can be achieved only in one way, namely, by harnessing science and technology to the task. This is how economic development has been achieved by the Western nations over the last two hundred years. This is how it must be achieved by the poor nations in today's world.

*Three*, science and technology have made tremendous strides in recent times and have opened up revolutionary possibilities, much of which could not be dreamt of even a generation ago. As a result, economic progress can be greatly speeded up. What took decades can now be telescoped into years.

*Four*, modern technology has not only an amazing range; it is also frequently divisible into tiny parts. Machinery can not only be massive, complex, and high-priced; it can also be small, simple, relatively inexpensive, and yet highly productive. The options are many; the risks of wrong and uneconomic choice are ever-present; the penalty it entails can be high. For the same reason the need for a sharp and vigilant eye for low-cost, yet speedy and high-payoff technology is all the more urgent.

*Five*, because one-third of the world is so rich today and has, over two hundred years, accumulated such vast wealth, the development of the remaining two-thirds should, at least in principle, be a much simpler task. If a fraction of this wealth can be channelled, or attracted, to the lagging economies to meet part of the pressing capital investment and foreign exchange requirements, their development would be greatly speeded up.

Charity, especially between nations, remains a rare phenomenon, and may have to be ruled out as a primary motive force; but the dictates of enlightened self-interest need not. This, coupled with a more equitable pattern of trade between the "have" and "have-not" nations, could greatly augment the financial resources of the latter to acquire the needed science and technology along with the essential plant and equipment in order to extract optimum wealth from their natural resources.

*Six*, it is customary to speak of land, labour and capital in one breath in cold-blooded classical style. But, surely, labour deserves to be given a more elevated status even if it must be called a "factor" of production.

The so-called labour force, in any economy, represents the vast majority of living human beings. And since the be-all and end-all of economic development is human welfare—"Maximum happiness of the maximum number" still remains a reasonably good motto for any society despite all the philosophical quibbling and the intangibles involved in working out the calculus of human happiness—the welfare of the working-class people must be a foremost concern in any development programme worth its name.[11]

*Seven*, the last point is reinforced by the fact that productivity depends overwhelmingly on the efficiency of the labour force. To build up this efficiency it is indispensable to give topmost priority to education and health services with adequate allocation of resources.[12]

And *finally*, involuntary unemployment of the employable people is not only morally wrong, it is also economically wasteful. The penalty for ignoring this plain fact is bound to be exceedingly high in the developing countries. Their fragile economies are groaning under the mounting child-dependency burden—some 45 per cent of their population fall in categories below 14 years, and is therefore too young to qualify for productive jobs. Clearly, they cannot, in addition, support a large unemployed population of adults without gravely endangering their future economic prospects.

Nor should there be any lack of productive employment in such economies which have barely touched the fringe of their development potential. Idle man-hours of the adult population put to work on idle, or semi-idle, natural resources can unquestionably accelerate the rate of their "capital formation" and production of wealth. The idle manpower can be turned into a valuable asset. No developing country can afford to let it run to waste without aggravating its problems of development and without further deepening the misery of its people.

These, then, are the axioms of economic development in the modern world. Despite their incontestable validity, it is surprising how often they are found missing in contemporary economic debates. For an explanation of this paradox perhaps one could best turn to a remark Keynes made many years ago: "The difficulty lies not in the new ideas, but in escaping from the old ones which ramify, for those brought up as most of us have been, into every corner of our minds."

It is no exaggeration to say that frequently scientists, engineers, and practitioners in applied economics, such as agronomists, power and indus-

[11] What about pampering labour, one might ask. Certainly it can, as it sometimes does, hurt an economy. The task is to steer clear of both pampering and exploitation.

[12] Not all education promotes development, as experience has abundantly shown. This, however, is an argument not against education, but against wrong education. As in the case of technology, wise discrimination is essential to ensure that the choice made is of the right kind to meet most effectively the specific needs in a given situation.

4

trial economists, also businessmen, industrialists, progressive farmers, even educated laymen with strong common sense, have shown better, even if instinctive, understanding of these axioms than "pure economists." Because of the very nature of their discipline and their upbringing they have to deal mostly with hard facts; this built-in safeguard in their case leaves little room for unrealistic theorizing and, in general, forces on them a more down-to-earth approach. On the whole, they have helped create, at least partially, a healthy countervailing force to what often threatened to be a misleading pull of theoretical economics as applied to the developing countries.

This, needless to say, is not a happy situation. To modernize the backward economies of the world's poor nations it is essential to modernize economic thinking as well, to discipline wayward theories based on archaic assumptions, and to align them firmly with the realities of actual life.


## PREREQUISITES OF AGRICULTURAL  DEVELOPMENT

Traditional agriculture is so largely based on subsistence farming that the two are usually treated as more or less synonymous. There has been a strong tendency, particularly in India, to take a romantic view of it and to uphold it as an ideal of simple life (Chapters 7-9). But its economic disadvantages are too patent to need recounting. It implies virtually nil division of labour, and therefore involves long hours of drudgery, poor resource utilization, meagre output, low income, and all-round misery.

It follows that the task of those genuinely concerned with economic development is not to provide a few improvised props to support it and to make it just a little more bearable, as has been attempted so frequently, but to rescue it from its age-old stagnation, to transform it into a productive apparatus with many times greater productivity, and therefore to end its isolation, to import into it the solid advantages of a wide division of labour, and to integrate it firmly with the entire national economy. The task, in short, is to effect the transition from an overwhelmingly subsistence to a predominantly commercial type of agriculture.

So transformed, a farm becomes a kind of a factory, and agriculture essentially an industry. In fact, modernization of agriculture is nothing but its *industrialization*. The requirements of the two—a modern factory-industry and a modern farm-industry—are surprisingly similar, though this has been overlooked surprisingly often.

It would be inconceivable to plan a modern factory without paying due heed to transportation facilities—to bring in equipment and raw materials, and to take out the factory output. When located inland, it would in most cases need adequate rail and road transportation.

Modern agriculture, too, needs exactly the same kind of transportation service—to bring inputs and machinery to the farm, and to carry the produce to the market, even though the scale of its operations and the nature of its products are quite different.

Nevertheless, there is also a fundamental difference between the two. In establishing a factory one has a choice of locations, usually a wide one; and it is possible to choose a site which is either already, or may easily be, provided with the requisite transportation facilities. This, of course, is the primary reason why factories crowd in large cities which are themselves the progenies of arteries of communication, and are sustained and continuously invigorated by the same lifelines.

How different it is with agriculture! The locational option here is—zero. Its operations must be carried out on farms whose locations are predetermined by nature. Agriculture is—to use a pedantic but nonetheless appropriate expression now very much in vogue—"location-specific."[13] Since farms are thus *pre-located*, they must be linked to markets mostly by roads which rarely exist and therefore have to be built mostly from scratch.

That farms must have outlets to markets is the most obvious fact about agriculture; and it is also the most neglected one. The presence or absence of these outlets is enough to spell the difference between modern and subsistence agriculture. To produce a marketable surplus is meaningless if it cannot be marketed. A farmer, knowing this fully well, will decide to produce only or mainly what is needed for subsistence, somewhat like a Robinson Crusoe in his insular isolation. Thus, the strategy for rescuing agriculture from its traditional strait-jacket must begin with the creation of market outlets.

Dr. A. T. Mosher tells us that the eminent British agricultural economist, Professor A. W. Ashby, was fond of saying, "If I could do only one thing in a region to spur agricultural development, I would build roads. If to this I could add a second, I would build more roads. And if to these I could add a third, I would build still more roads."[14]

No less important is the question of agricultural price. A manufacturing industry, as everybody knows, cannot survive long if its products are sold at prices below cost. This holds good also for the farm-industry; and if a farmer is unable to sell his produce at remunerative prices, all he can do is to confine himself to subsistence farming.

---

[13] To put the same point somewhat differently, industries other than those based on minerals, forests and bulky agricultural produce, are mostly "foot-loose," and enjoy wide locational options. By contrast, agriculture is "foot-bound," and its locational options are nil.

[14] Arthur T. Mosher in *Getting Agriculture Moving : Essentials for Development and Modernization*, Frederick A. Praeger, New York, 1965, p. 119. This is the most perceptive handbook the writer knows on the problems of modernizing agriculture. It sets forth, in lucid and persuasive terms, the interrelationships, the proper sequence for tackling them, and the common pitfalls to be avoided.

Also see Chapter 24 on "Marketing, Storage, Transportation."

The needs of the two are the same, but their comparative strengths are quite different. A manufacturing industry, even in an underdeveloped country, is better organized, commands greater resources, can within fairly wide limits adjust production to market conditions, and it can, in various ways, influence both the public and the government. The farmers, on the other hand, are disorganized, mostly poor and weak, tied by the very nature of their business to seasonal production, and exposed almost always to a brutal post-harvest slump in prices. This slump acts as a powerful deterrent; it is enough to compel the vast majority of farmers to cling grimly to the safe moorings of subsistence agriculture. Their risk-bearing capacity is close to nil. The operating formula they instinctively adopt in such a situation is: No risk, no loss.

Market prices directly affect farmers' incomes. Yet they are as helpless here as *vis-à-vis* the weather that determines their crop output. Only the government can help, and the government must step in and institute an agricultural price policy that would guarantee remunerative prices to the farmers, if it really wants to turn agriculture into a vehicle of economic progress. This is the second most essential prerequisite for modernization.[15]

To this should be added at least one more—research and extension. Like manufacturing industry, agriculture, too, is dependent on modern technology for its progress. Once again, the requirements, in a broad sense, are identical in both cases, but once again they call for entirely different policies and actions because the two industries are so different in nature. A manufacturing industry can buy the required technology, at home or abroad, with the resources it commands or can raise from the public and the governmental support it usually enjoys; it can hire the services of competent consulting firms to prepare blueprints for projects and to help implement them covering all phases from initial planning to the marketing of final products; if big enough, it can organize its own research to develop new and more profitable products or technologies. In short, it can usually fend for itself, and it very largely does so.

Farmers, on the other hand, must depend on the government both for supplying improved technologies and for communicating to them the skills needed to apply them. They must do so not only because they are mostly poor and ignorant, but for another overriding reason: Agriculture is a *biological* industry; there is no ready-made, transferable technology that would suit all farmers in all environments; it must be carefully tailored and continuously adjusted to suit the varying conditions in each case—soil chemicals, moisture supply, temperatures, solar energy, pests and insects. It follows that technology has to be locally tested and verified, and frequently readapted to local conditions.

And finally, its output and income potential must be demonstrated, convincingly, in local fields and under local conditions before farmers can be

[15] Discussed more fully in Chapter 23 on "Price Support."

expected, or even asked, to adopt it. Research and extension are the prime movers of modern agriculture. Without them subsistence agriculture can only remain permanently grounded.[16]

In all developing countries there are ready markets for agricultural produce, particularly for food which, on an average, accounts for as much as 85 per cent of their total agricultural output. And with the upsurge in population the markets are expanding rapidly. In fact, the demand is building up so fast that the problem—barring temporary and isolated exceptions—is not to find markets for larger production, but how to increase the production of food fast enough to support the soaring population. This is the biggest challenge in all developing countries.

But it is also their greatest opportunity. With the three prerequisites mentioned above—transportation, especially village-to-market roads, incentive prices, adaptive research with effective extension work—they can break away from stagnant subsistence agriculture, confidently launch on the modernization process, and give the first decisive impetus to production and income. The process can be greatly speeded up if adequate attention is paid to a good many other agri-supporting activities—in particular, supply and distribution of improved seeds, fertilizers and other inputs, production credit, storage and marketing facilities, farmer cooperatives, land improvement, processing industries, and, of course, education for development, and health services for rural communities.[17]

The three prerequisites, if supplemented by the other measures just listed, will greatly accelerate agricultural growth. And this, in turn, will spill over into other sectors and generate an overall economic growth rate far surpassing what is currently aimed at or considered feasible in most economic planning.

[16] For detailed discussion, see Chapter 22 on "Education, Research, Extension."
[17] Many of these items fall under the "five accelerators" of Dr. Mosher, ibid., pp. 123-69.

CHAPTER 3

# High Hopes from
# Dwarf Seeds

## A MIRACULOUS ESCAPE

Only a few short years ago, in the mid-sixties, the world's impoverished nations seemed precariously poised on the brink of an abyss. A famine of unimaginable dimensions stared them in the face. Its dark shadow lengthened visibly from year to year.

It was at this time that the Paddock Brothers,[1] in vivid and sensational terms, predicted that, by 1975, a world-wide famine would engulf the hungry nations. The grim projections they made contained no hint of a silver lining. On the contrary, they betokened an inexorable Greek tragedy from which there was no escape.

"Something will turn up, or will it?" This was the terse, rhetoric question they posed; and then with persuasive, almost contagious, pessimism they proceeded to answer it with a nerve-shattering negative. The hungry nations could not possibly improve their agriculture soon enough to avert the famine; the amount of food per person would continue to decline in the coming years, as it had done since the late fifties; the zero hour would strike some time around 1975. After serving this hair-raising notice on the world's food-surplus nations, they proceeded to give the USA—as if to flaunt their courage of conviction—an eerie assignment: to decide, well ahead of time, which nations to write off!

Hardly was the ink dry on these lugubrious words when something

[1] W. and P. Paddock, *Famine 1975? America's Decision : Who will Survive*, Boston, Mass., Little Brown. 1967, a sequel to the authors' *Hungry Nations*, Little Brown, 1964.

did turn up—the dwarf wheat and rice with record-shattering yields. Since then, fortified by an army of "dwarfs," the hungry nations have launched on a valiant fight to beat back the spectre of famine; and, to judge from the results to date, they have unquestionably booked a first round of resounding success. Their per capita supply of food has, almost overnight, ceased to decline; in most cases it is definitely on the increase; some have managed to wipe off their deficits and have begun to export food. It is no longer necessary to worry about writing off any nations, not even those which only the other day seemed saddled with staggering shortages. Instead, one can, at least for the foreseeable future, write off the apocalyptic pronouncements of the Paddock Brothers and of other prophets of the same genre.

This turnaround has few parallels in human history. The dwarf varieties of wheat and rice have completely altered the scenario in the developing countries. With dramatic suddenness, they have dispelled the thickening gloom, and have won the promise of plenty from the jaws of famine.

## THE GENESIS

Yet what appeared sudden and dramatic on the surface was far from so in reality. The dwarfs did not appear on the scene like some *deus ex machina* to carry out a last-moment rescue operation. They were, on the contrary, the work of a remarkable band of pioneers, the outcome of two decades of clear-sighted, painstaking research and experiments conducted by dedicated scientists.

The stage for the drama was set in Mexico, more than three decades ago, with the launching of a joint Rockefeller-Mexican programme for corn and wheat improvement. The fascinating story of this great scientific adventure need not detain us here; it has been told, authoritatively and colourfully, on a good many occasions.[2] However, some of its facets, in particular those that are specially relevant to the developing countries today, are worth recalling even if very briefly.

When, in 1941, the Government of Mexico turned to the Rockefeller Foundation for technical and scientific assistance to improve its agriculture, especially food production, it had, indeed, very good reasons to feel concerned about the situation. This was well exemplified by the status of wheat cultivation. The crop suffered heavily from rust diseases year after year; the yield was distressingly low—only 770 kilos per hectare

[2] In *Campaigns Against Hunger* by E. C. Stakman, Richard Bradfield, Paul C. Mangelsdorf, Cambridge, Mass., The Belknap Press of Harvard University Press, 1967. Also in numerous articles and reports by the Rockefeller Foundation scientists: J. George Harrar, Norman E. Borlaug, Robert F. Chandler, Sterling Wortman, and others.

(or 11 bushels per acre); the nation's wheat budget was in a chronic deficit; the gap had to be met with imports; and so, much of the nation's meagre foreign exchange resources had to be diverted away from urgent nation-building activities.

The request to the Foundation was an imaginative move; it signified an awareness of the need to inject modern science and technology into old and stagnating agriculture. Fortunately, the Foundation's response, too, was prompt and equally imaginative. It started off on the premise that "the greatest practical contributions to agriculture come through the fields of genetics and plant breeding, plant protection, soil science, live-stock management, and general farm management." It was, above all, this premise, firmly laid down by the Foundation's clairvoyant scientists, that was destined to give birth, some twenty-five years later, to a green revolution in tropical agriculture.

The first step, the Foundation felt, must be a quick reconnaissance of the field by a high-powered scientific team to diagnose the main problems and to lay down, in sufficiently concrete terms, the essentials of an action-oriented programme. Accordingly, a three-member Survey Commission[3] was appointed, which promptly carried out an intensive, on-the-spot study. Of the conclusions it arrived at, three are worth noting in particular:[4]

1. There was hunger in Mexico in 1941. The country had "many of the aspects of an overpopulated land." The level of subsistence was low; the dietary standards were bad.

2. The label "lazy loafers," often applied to the working people, especially in the countryside, was unjust. "The tragedy was not that they did not work hard enough but that they had to work so hard for what they got."

3. "The simple truth was that agricultural research and education were inadequate to the needs of Mexico."

The points are simple, yet how often they have been—and still are— missed even by erudite observers! What was true of Mexico, in 1941, is still true of most developing countries.

The Commission's recommendations were both forthright and farsighted. First, "the most acute and immediate problems, in approximate order of importance, seem to be the improvement of soil management and till-age practices; the introduction, selecting, or breeding of better-adapted, higher-yielding and higher-quality crop varieties; more rational and effective control of plant diseases and insect pests; and the introduction or

[3] The members were the three authors of *Campaigns Against Hunger* (immortalized by their admirers with the title, "The Three Musketeers of Agriculture") The mission worked in the field for two months in summer, 1941.

[4] Ibid., pp. 31, 26 and 30.

development of better breeds of domestic animals and poultry, as well as better feeding methods and disease control."[5]

The Foundation was therefore advised to assign four experts—respectively in agronomy and soil management, plant breeding, plant protection, and animal husbandry—as a "working commission" to cooperate with the Mexican Ministry in its agricultural improvement programme.

Second, the "basic philosophy" underlying the plan was that "most rapid progress can be made by starting at the top and expanding downward," and not by the alternative method of starting at the bottom and working towards the top.

One could, for example, start with a programme for improving the vocational schools of agriculture and for extension work directed towards the farmers. But then the schools could hardly be improved until the teachers were improved; extension work could not be improved until extension men were improved; and investigational work could not be made more productive until investigators acquired greater competence.

Third, the accepted goal was to help Mexico towards independence in agricultural production, in agricultural science, and in agricultural education. This called for two things: joint participation, that is, actually working with Mexicans to do the things that needed to be done, and not just telling them how they should be done; and a special type of fellowship for outstanding investigators and teachers in order to develop and utilize their potential as teachers and researchers to the fullest possible extent.

Fourth, the Commission's hopes "soared high and roamed wide," but it was realistic enough not to conjure up the vision of any "easy agricultural miracles on the Mexican horizon." And so it urged that the programme be continued for at least a decade.

To these should be added several other factors which were as good as axioms, both to the Commission and the Rockefeller Foundation. Research, education, and extension suffer from serious limitations when pursued in a separate and uncoordinated fashion, but when well-coordinated, they have a tremendous potential.

Then, there is the great urgency for research in a developing country. Extension alone, and other forms of education, observed the Commission, could make great improvement only when there was "a great reservoir of potentially useful but unused information." But in the Mexico of 1941 there was no such reservoir. Moreover, reservoirs had to be "constantly replenished with the results of research"; otherwise they would "run dry within a short time." This had been the case with many technical assistance programmes in agriculture and public health since they had to deal with living organisms and changing conditions.

Research alone would not improve conditions unless its results were

[5] Ibid., p. 33.

5

made "practically effective" through education and extension. The improvement could come only through "a combination of research, education, and extension—with research providing opportunities and furnishing materials for education and extension."

That the working commission of the experts would have to work as a team was taken for granted. Problems were interrelated; they could therefore be resolved only through a coordinated—or package—approach.

Last but not least, there was the question of the calibre of the experts. "The success of any undertaking depends upon the men who undertake it and the environment in which they work."[6] The Foundation has operated with a small number of experts, "handpicked" them with great care, and refused to compromise with quality. It not only decided to start at the top and work downward; it also insisted on starting only with top-calibre men of established professional competence.

The Commission's approach was "neither novel nor profound, but it did have the merit of being sound and sensible," modestly observed its members in retrospective judgment. "And it is equally sound and sensible today for other poorly developed areas," it added.[7]

So it certainly is. The approach, despite its simple appearance, was indeed profound. The developing world is strewn with wreckages of programmes, both national and international, because of the failure to grasp and apply its underlying principles.

## BIRTH OF DWARF WHEAT[8]

"On a job like this our science has to be good, but it has to be good for something; it has to help put bread into the bellies of hungry Mexicans" —this is how Norman Borlaug, the genetical architect of the dwarf wheat, defined his task as he took over control of the wheat programme.[9]

A down-to-earth visionary, he insisted that the programme had to be "a package deal" and must not be split up into "a lot of splinter programmes," that there was no room for "scientific sideshows" nor for chasing "academic butterflies." First things, he insisted, must be done first, and that meant producing a great deal more grain from the low-yielding wheat fields.

The groundwork had been laid by Dr. Harrar who had, in November 1943, "fired the first big gun of the wheat revolution," aiming it at stem rust. For rust control, he observed in unveiling his strategy, "resistant

[6] Ibid., p. 5.
[7] Ibid., p. 35.
[8] See, in particular, Stakman *et al.*, ibid., Chapter 5; and Dr. Borlaug's paper "Wheat, Rust, and People," *Phytopathology*, Vol. 55, No. 10, pp. 1088-98, October 1965. Printed in USA.
[9] Stakman *et al.*, ibid., p. 80.

varieties are the only answer." This climaxed in one of the most relentless breeding programmes the world had ever seen. Countless varieties, both native and exotic, were planted, studied, crossed and backcrossed, re-planted and re-analyzed. The world was ransacked for genes. "The plants of the world have a lot of wonderful genes in them if you can just find them and combine them," said Borlaug wistfully.

For him, breeding better wheats was not only a matter of genes, but also of—time. True, he seemed cut out for work which he apparently treated as synonymous with life. But there was something else to spur and inspire him, and, by example, to inspire others. Few people, at that time, could read the temper of the times with such uncanny foresight as Borlaug did, and few could detect so unerringly the early symptoms of an emerging food-population crisis. No wonder that he should have developed what his colleagues called the "wheat fever," which he successfully transmitted to his Mexican associates.

And so Borlaug was in a hurry; he worked almost round-the-clock, as if to beat the clock. In his anxiety to do so he pioneered the techniques of growing two generations of breeding materials each year, instead of only one as had hitherto been customary with plant-breeders. To save time, he had to beat the season; and so he initiated the ingenious device of hauling the breeding material 10° further in latitude and from low areas near sea level to an elevation of 8,500 ft. With this change in habitat he could find for his breeding materials the right season in what had been regarded as "off season." And with two generations a year, he could halve the time needed to develop new, improved varieties—from 6-8 years to 3-4 years.

Heresy, once again, paid off handsomely. Meanwhile, summer nurseries to speed plant-breeding work has become a common practice in many countries, including India and Pakistan.

By 1948, after numerous trials, four varieties were distributed—Supremo, Frontera, Kenya Rojo, Kenya Blanco. All four were foreign, and they were intended to serve as a stopgap arrangement while better ones were being evolved through hybridization.

By 1951, four new Mexico-bred varieties were released; Yaqui, Nazas, Chapingo and Kentana. All four were given high ratings—they were early-ripening, with stiffer straw they showed greater resistance to lodging and shattering, they had considerable rust resistance built into them, and they were high-yielding with grains of good quality. By then, the number of lines crossed totalled 2,000, and the breeding nurseries accommodated 50,000 varieties and hybrid lines.

In 1951, the battle, it seemed, had been virtually won. Mexico had several improved varieties of wheat; farmer acceptance, too, was rapid—70 per cent of the wheat acreage had been sown with them; acre-yield was sharply on the increase—thanks to the seed-fertilizer revolution many farmers reaped 45 to 60 bushels per acre from lands that had previously yielded only 6 to 10 bushels; Mexico was clearly on the way to self-sufficiency in wheat, a goal which it actually reached in 1956.

But for Borlaug, called a "perfectionist" by his colleagues, there could be no resting on the oars. The new varieties, significantly better as they were, still fell far short of his dream wheat. And this he continued to pursue with all his genius for gene-hunting.

Behind this, however, there was another compelling reason as well. The average commercial lifetime of an improved variety, he knew only too well, was limited, and much more so in the tropics than, say, in the USA or Canada.[10] And so breeding had to be pursued almost on a continuous basis to produce new varieties at fairly short intervals to replace old ones and thereby to forestall surprise attacks by pests and diseases.

For a while the rusts lay low. Then, during 1951-54, reincarnated as new races, they struck hard at the varieties just released. Dr. Borlaug had to look frantically for new genes to make his wheats more resistant. At the same time there was another critical question he had to resolve: should one stay substantially with the same varieties and simply make them more rust-resistant? Or, should one aim at quite different varieties that were not only more resistant, but also significantly higher-yielding? Borlaug decided to raise his sights once again.

It was clear by then that the main barrier to higher yields was the morphology of the wheat plant. Even the newly-bred varieties, despite their stiffer straw, tended to lodge, or fall over, on soils enriched with chemical fertilizers. And unless this lodging problem were overcome, production showed signs of levelling off at 3,000 to 4,000 kg per hectare. Moreover, machine-harvesting was coming into vogue replacing the old hand-sickle method; and this, too, pointed to the need for non-lodging non-shattering varieties.

Could the wheat plant be stiffened and shortened, so that it could stand erect with long heads containing plenty of kernels and holding them tight until they ripen for harvest? This was the dream wheat Dr. Borlaug and his colleagues now set out to build. The immediate objective was to dwarf the plant, and this called for some recessive genes. The search for them was aided by a combination of circumstances that was both fortuitous and fortunate.

Soon after World War II, Dr. S. C. Salmon, a representative of the U.S. Department of Agriculture, came across the now-famous "Norin" dwarfs in Japan; and some of them he shipped to the States as part of his routine duty. These were used as breeding material by Dr. Orville A. Vogel at the Agricultural Experiment Station of Washington State University, where he developed several interesting lines of wheat with dwarfishness

[10] In "Wheat, Rust, and People," loc. cit., he put the average lifetime at only four years, with only one exception, Lerma Rojo, that lasted nine years.

derived from the Japanese parent, Norin 10. Among them was a variety called Gaines which was cultivated in the Pacific Northwest to establish a world record in yields—up to 216 bushels per acre.

Dr. Borlaug obtained some of this Norin 10-based material and began crossing them with his improved Mexican varieties. The first time he made the cross, at Chapingo, Mexico, he reportedly lost the whole crop to rust, except a few kernels he managed to salvage. These he planted in his test plots at Ciudad Obregon where they sprouted and matured. Next time he took no chance; "we crossed them with everything we had," he said.

Out of these crosses with the Norin recessive gene there emerged a whole set of new varieties which, with some local adaptations, have established spectacular yield records in the developing world.

The first breakthrough came in 1961—Pitic 62 and Penjamo 62 were released in that year. With these varieties better farmers of Mexico were able to obtain yields as high as 7000 kg per hectare (105 bushels per acre). This was 2½ times the peak yields previously established in the country! They demanded much higher rates of fertilizer application and irrigation, but they stood them very well. This non-lodging quality contributed to the yield increase, but so did other factors—heavier tillering, better grain-filling qualities, and nonsensitivity to photoperiod (that is, they were not affected by changes in day length and date of planting). Because of this last characteristic and high resistance to rust and other diseases, they were endowed with a wide adaptability and could be cultivated almost in all wheat-growing countries.

Observed Dr. Borlaug in 1965: "The importance of these new varieties have been so great that in four years they have taken over 95 per cent of the area cultivated to wheat in Mexico." The quantities they yielded would previously have been considered "purely hyperbolic."

The wheat revolution in Mexico was now a reality. As the foregoing account shows, it was not a case of happenstance, nor was there anything serendipitous about it, even though there was a touch of good luck in hitting on Norin 10 at an opportune moment. It was, from the start, planned and executed as a man-made revolution through purposeful research by dedicated scientists.

## THE MIRACLE OF DWARF RICE

The story of the miracle rice is much shorter. It did not start until 1962, and the start was "a running one," to quote the words of Dr. Robert Chandler, Director of IRRI.[11]

The fast take-off with rice was possible largely because its path had

[11] The International Rice Research Institute was established in 1960 at Los Baños, Philippines, by the Ford and Rockefeller Foundations in cooperation with the Government of the Philippines. It was headed by Dr. Robert F. Chandler Jr., as Director.

been charted by wheat. Borlaug and his associates had to spend many years chasing the vision of an ideal wheat plant before it took firm shape. Chandler and his colleagues could save those years in shaping an ideal rice plant. What they needed to do was mainly to copy the plant-type of dwarf wheat, and to apply the same methods and principles to engineer it into existence.

The establishment of IRRI was another landmark in the history of tropical agriculture. Three-fifths of mankind depend on rice as the basic food crop; it is, far and out, the most important crop grown in Asia. Yet its average yield in South and South-East Asia was only 1500 kg/ha. This contrasted with an average yield of 5000 kg/ha in Japan; in Australia, Italy, Spain and the USA, the yield levels were more or less of the same order (Table 1).

What, then, could be more important for tropical agriculture than to raise its rice yields to the temperate-zone levels? This is the task IRRI set out to accomplish with a single-minded concentration of effort. It assembled 20 agricultural scientists from eight nationalities, and started, in 1962, experiments at its own station to raise yields, using the best-known tropical varieties and applying to them heavy doses of fertilizers, but only to discover that the yields, instead of going up, actually went down.[12]

The old varieties[13] were tall and leafy; under heavy application of fertilizers, they became even taller and leafier; this increased the shaded area where plantings were dense, cut down on the rate of photosynthesis and therefore also of grain formation; worse still was the lodging problem—when nourished with heavy doses of fertilizers, they responded by falling over long before the harvest time, and this drastically cut down on their yields. To crown it all, they were subject to virulent attacks by pests and insects which thrive merrily in the humid tropics.

This litany of woes dictated the tasks for the scientists. What they needed to do, above all, was to restructure the rice plant—it had to be short, sturdy, erect-leafed, non-lodging, disease-resistant, and fertilizer-responsive with a high grain-building capacity. In other words, what had just been accomplished with wheat in Mexico would have to be repeated with rice, and substantially for the same reasons.

By 1963, Dr. Chandler was able to sum up the conclusions in the following words: "Modern experience in Japan and elsewhere supports the thesis that increases in yield will result primarily from the development and use of early-maturing, short-stemmed, stiff-strawed, and non-lodging varieties

[12] For an authoritative account of this story, see Dr. Chandler's statement: "The Case for Research," in *Strategy for the Conquest of Hunger, Proceedings of a Symposium*, 1968. The Rockefeller Foundation, New York.

[13] Commonly known by the generic term "Indica" which are grown in the tropics, as distinguished from the "Japonica" varieties, which are short-strawed, fertilizer-responsive, and high-yielding, and have long been grown in temperate climates like Japan's.

that respond to nitrogen under field conditions and are insensitive to length of day. Naturally, they should have resistance also to blast disease and to as many other diseases (and insects) as possible."[14]

Some 8000 strains of rice were assembled and screened to detect the desirable genes for use in the breeding programme. In one important respect the search was simplified. Several short varieties of rice were already in cultivation and doing well in Taiwan. These were brought over to IRRI and systematically crossed with the tall tropical varieties. One cross turned out to be a remarkable success—between Dee-geo-woo-gen, a short variety from Taiwan, and Peta, an Indica variety developed in Indonesia but widely cultivated also in the Philippines.[15] The Dgwg dwarf gene did the trick—it imparted dwarfness to the hybrid plant.

But a good many other characteristics had to be built into it—in particular, it had to be made resistant to the stem borer, to the blast, leaf blight and other diseases, and also insensitive to day-length. And so the breeding work continued with innumerable crossings and recrossings; three experimental crops were grown every year, thus outdoing the Borlaug record established in Mexico. This hastened the breakthrough, which came in 1965, just three years after the first Dgwg-Peta cross.

In that year a selection, carrying the label IR 8-288-3 in the experimental plot, gave an outstanding performance in the yield trials. This was the famous IR8 soon hailed in Asia as the miracle rice.

As for its principal characteristics, one can do no better than quote Dr. Chandler: the plant was short, hard, dark green with upright leaves; it tillered heavily and gave medium-long grain of dry cooking quality; it showed moderate resistance to tungro virus disease, and, in many localities, seemed highly resistant to the rice blast disease; it was insensitive to photoperiod, and could therefore be planted at any latitude within the tropics.

As for yield, it gave excellent results under heavy doses of fertilizers and topped almost everything tested at IRRI; what was particularly significant, it proved an equally good yielder outside the Philippines, as was revealed by cooperative tests all over Asia. The yield potential was over 9,000 kg per hectare, or about six times the average yield from the tall traditional, or Indica, varieties. Response to nitrogen was excellent; in the dry season it gave 28 kg of grain for every kg of N added; in the wet and cloudy monsoon season, the yield was lower—15 kg of grain per kg of N. Without fertilizer, it yielded as much as local varieties, and so farmers had nothing to lose. (See Figs. 3 and 4.)

Though IR8 ranks as a historic breakthrough, there is still much room

[14] Robert F. Chandler, Jr., "An Analysis of Factors Affecting Rice Yield." *International Rice Commission Newsletter*, XII, No. 4, 1963.
[15] Peta had been developed by Dutch plant-breeders some thirty years earlier. Its parentage was partly derived from a West Bengal variety called Latisail.

for its improvement—in grain shape and size, in eating and cooking qualities so as to suit consumer preferences, in making it more resistant to
major diseases, in growth durations so as to meet the specific needs of
particular situations. Accordingly, IRRI is pressing on with its crossing
and breeding programmes. Its objective is to produce, within a decade
or so, 15 to 20 varieties "so versatile and varied" as to be able to satisfy
all requirements in the tropics.

But the IR8 plant-type, Dr. Chandler and his colleagues believe, has
come to stay. It is, indeed, the ideal rice plant for the tropics—short,
upright, heavy-tillering, an avid consumer of fertilizers, giving yields
hitherto undreamt of. It is rightly looked upon as IRRI's great contribution to tropical agriculture.

## BIOLOGICAL ENGINEERING

The dwarf wheat and rice, as seen above, are creations of modern plant-
breeder-geneticists. They are products of what has been aptly called
"biological engineering," which, in itself, represents a remarkable breakthrough in scientific techniques, and has profound implications for tropical agriculture. A little reflection will show why.

Crop improvement through selection of better-yielding plants is no
new phenomenon; it dates back to neolithic times. Breeding of new and
better varieties through systematic attempts to combine the desirable
genetic traits of different lines is a much more recent development; however, this, too, has a history of more than a century.

But until recently, most of this plant-breeding work took place in the
temperate-zone countries, which benefited from its results. And since
agriculture is a biological industry—it has to do with living things
like plants, insects, pests—those results were not applicable to tropical
countries.

True, some breeding work did take place also in the tropics, but they
were almost invariably confined to industrial or export crops, such as jute,
rubber, cotton, oil palms, tea, coffee and cocoa, while little or no effort
was made to improve food crops through breeding. This was a great void
in the economies of the underdeveloped countries. For, food crops account
for four-fifths or more of their total agricultural production.

Even in those exceptional cases where some breeding work was undertaken on major food crops like wheat and rice, as for example in India
from around 1900, the breeder's sights were kept consistently low; the
primary goal it aimed at was to protect a meagre yield, not to boost it.
This indifference to yield had its own logic—for even the "improved"
varieties had to fit traditional agriculture which, almost by definition,
operated without fertilizers, without pesticides, and almost always on
soils drained of plant nutrients.

This also explains the negative characteristics of the traditional varieties of wheat and rice which Borlaug, Chandler and their colleagues discovered and wrestled with after the first round of experiments with them. These varieties had to be fast-growing; for they had to outgrow, and outwit, the weeds in their competition for the limited plant nutrients of the unfertilized soils. They were slow-maturing, also tillered slowly in instalments; this enabled them to "weather" the spells of drought which frequently hit them even during the wet season. Insects and pests were common, but in unfertilized lands their attacks were less severe—they took their own share of the crop at different stages between sowing and harvesting, yet left a residue for human use although, in the circumstances, it could only be small.

Thus, an equilibrium had been established among plants, soils, insects, and humans. And even when plants were touched up by breeders, it was only to stabilize a low-level equilibrium with low-yielding plants deliberately, even skilfully, adjusted to low-fertility conditions. These plants were not intended for chemical fertilizer—they had been bred away from it. And so when heavy doses of fertilizers were applied to them, they responded, predictably enough, not with more grain, but with rank growth. Quick-growing and weak-strawed, they drooped and lodged, and evaded the strain of extra photosynthetic work.

Meanwhile, the scientific world marched on. Modern genetics opened up a new chapter with exciting possibilities for making rapid advances in many fields, including agriculture. New techniques were developed for plant-breeding, such as alteration of germplasm by irradiation, genetic mutations including "alteration of single genes or breakage of chromosomes and rearrangement of the segments," screening and crossing on massive scales, including "wide crosses," that is, between different species or genera.[16]

Irradiation—by x-rays and ultraviolet rays—to alter the germplasm had already been in vogue; but its scope was now widened by nuclear energy, gamma rays and neutrons. Nevertheless, the most important tool relied upon by plant-breeders is still an old one, modernized and made vastly more effective, namely, screening on a massive scale to pinpoint the needed genes.

What the world has been witnessing, since the 1940's, is a germplasm revolution, brought about by a combination of factors—rapid communication, new techniques, a truly international attitude among plant-breeders ready for quick exchange of ideas and breeding materials. Germplasms can now be collected, literally by the thousand, from all over the world and screened quickly and efficiently; once promising characters have been

[16] President's Report on *The World Food Problem* gives a brief summary of recent advances made in this field with some examples, esp. Vol. II, pp. 202-3, The White House, Washington, D.C., 1967.

isolated, crossings are made, again by thousands; and two or more generations are grown on experimental plots per year, often at different elevations, to hasten the breeding process. As a result, new varieties with much
higher yields can now be turned out at a much faster rate than would
have been conceivable only a decade or two ago.

Once again, these developments took place in industrial countries of
the temperate zones; and coupled with new advances in fertilizers and
pesticides, they boosted their agricultural productivity to unprecedented
levels. The underdeveloped countries were unable to participate in this
genetic-cum-chemical revolution in agriculture. Their acre-yields stagnated at primitive levels, while those of the developed countries swung
sharply upwards.

## PROMISE OF PLENTY

Against this background it is easy to see why the emergence of the dwarf
wheat and rice should be hailed as an event of momentous significance.

They have shattered the long-held myth about tropical agriculture—
that it was not only backward, but had no future because it could not
pay its way; they have shown that, on the contrary, it is a vast treasure-
house of potential wealth, which bids fair, some day, even to outperform
the temperate-zone agriculture.

They have revealed, more vividly than ever before, the root cause of
the world food crisis which, until recently, used to scare mankind: That
crisis arose from the fact that modern science and technology were not
only developed, but were also dammed up, in the Western world and
could not flow into the tropics to "fertilize" its arable lands; that, as a
result, the poor nations were condemned to live with poor plants and
poor soils that were incapable of turning out enough food to support
their burgeoning populations.

They have also demonstrated how, in practice, science and technology
can be effectively harnessed through sustained production-oriented research backed by education and extension.

They have, through this demonstration, brought a new message of hope
to the developing countries where the majority of their one-and-a-half
billion inhabitants not only live in chronic hunger and malnutrition, but
have long accepted them in a mood of helpless resignation.

That mood is visibly changing today. For the realization is spreading—
still slowly, but inexorably—that what has been achieved with wheat and
rice in a few countries can be repeated, time and time over again, with
other crops and in other countries.

The dwarfs have kindled high hopes, and with perfect reason. They
have clinchingly proved that hunger, in today's world, is an anachronism.
Indeed, it can be eliminated surprisingly fast despite the surging popula-

tion, faster than a great many experts are still apt to believe, provided the storehouse of man's knowledge is drawn upon resourcefully, the right techniques are selected and applied systematically, and wastages—of resource, talent, and time—are avoided scrupulously.[17]

[17] Fortunately, the family of high-powered international institutes for improvement of crops grown in tropics and subtropics is expanding fast. See Chapter 31 under "A Momentous Step."

# CHAPTER 4

# The Stirrings of
# A Revolution

## RAPID SPREAD OF DWARF WHEAT

National production programmes, argued Dr. Borlaug some time ago, should be organized not for a "slow, steady increase of yields," but for a "revolution in production." When yields are changed from 500 to 5,000 kilos per hectare, "a cataclysmic reaction occurs across the whole spectrum of human activity."[1]

This is, no doubt, the objective he had all along in mind; and this is what he has helped accomplish with a remarkable measure of success. The dwarf wheat and rice have set in motion a chain of events which may well be called cataclysmic. In many developing countries a revolution in production is already under way. The most convincing proof of this can be found today in three countries—Mexico, India, and Pakistan—and in the production of the two major food crops—wheat and rice—and, to some extent, also of corn (maize), sorghum, and millets.

*Mexico.* Since the wheat revolution began in Mexico, it has also made the maximum impact here. During 1941-45, her wheat imports averaged at 253,600 tons a year. The yield, on an average, amounted to 600 kg per hectare.

By 1956, the domestic production of wheat had almost trebled—to 1.2 million metric tons; yield had doubled—to 1,200 kg per hectare; and the nation had become self-sufficient in wheat for the first time since 1900.

[1] Norman E. Borlaug, "National Production Campaigns" in *Strategy for the Conquest of Hunger, Proceedings of a Symposium,* 1968. The Rockefeller Foundation, New York.

Thereafter the trend not only continued, but accelerated, so that Mexico became a net exporter of wheat. During 1962-66, the wheat exports, on an average, amounted to 276,000 tons a year, with a peak of 684,500 tons recorded in 1964. By then, the average yield had surpassed 3 tons per hectare, or 45 bushels per acre (see Fig. 1).

In the best wheat-producing areas, the yield exceeded 5.25 tons per hectare (80 bushels per acre) on large farms and 6.6 tons per hectare (100 bushels per acre) on smaller farms. These are the yield levels realized by farmers in Denmark and Belgium, which are recognized as world leaders in wheat yield per unit area.

*India.*[2]  The dwarf wheats first arrived in India in 1963, and in Pakistan a year later. By then, both countries had been sufficiently intrigued by the possibility of growing the new Mexican wheats locally *as direct transplant.* Who could advise them better on this matter than Dr. Borlaug, the father of the dwarf wheat? Accordingly, the Rockefeller Foundation was requested to assign him for a short period to assess the situation on the spot. The verdict Dr. Borlaug gave after a rapid reconnaissance was positive—he saw no reason not to proceed with the direct-transplant idea. And so, on his return, he promptly despatched dwarf seeds to both countries to be tried out—on an experimental basis.

India received seeds of four dwarf and semi-dwarf varieties in bulk— 100 kg of each—and small samples of 613 promising selections. The material was grown and studied in all the main wheat-growing areas. At Delhi, Ludhiana, Pusa and Kanpur, two varieties—Lerma Rojo and Sonora 64— yielded over 4,000 kg per hectare, as compared with an average per-hectare yield of 800 kg over the previous three decades. A fivefold increase in wheat yield! The impact was immediate—and sensational.

There was no time to lose. The country was already in the grip of a desperate shortage of food. So the following year, in 1964, at the height of summer the seeds were multiplied in the heights of the Nilgiri hills in South India. And almost immediately thereafter, in the *rabi* (winter) season, the new wheats were field-tested all over the country at no less than 155 locations under the All-India Coordinated Wheat Trials Programme which had meanwhile been organized by the ICAR.[3]

The results were subjected to a detailed evaluation—pathological, physiological, agronomic, qualitative, which led to the release of the two varieties for general cultivation. At the same time cultural practices needed to optimize their yields were established through extensive trials. Again, seeds were multiplied in Nilgiris in summer 1965. At the same time a programme was launched for national demonstrations, which were car-

[2] Documents put out by IARI (Indian Agricultural Research Institute, New Delhi), have been used as source material, esp. *Five Years of Research on Dwarf Wheats,* 1968.

[3] See Chapter 22 on "Education, Research, Extension."

ried out by competent scientists at some 100 different locations within irrigated areas, all on farmers' fields.

To speed up cultivation of the dwarf wheats, 250 tons of Lerma Rojo and Sonora 64 seeds were imported from Mexico, and these were distributed by IARI to the state seed farms and some 5,000 farmers. The following year, in 1966, the seed imports soared to 16,000 tons, which were sown on 400,000 hectares (1 million acres).

Meanwhile, India's plant breeders, in collaboration with the Rockefeller Foundation, had been busy not only adapting the dwarf strains to local conditions, but also making them more disease-resistant and adjusting the grain quality to suit the consumer's taste. One major drawback of the Mexican wheats, from India's angle, was its colour—it happened to be red whereas wheat-eating Indians have a definite preference for golden or amber seeds. Besides, the Mexican type was too soft and not so well suited for making *chapati* (unleavened bread), the most popular form in which wheat is consumed in India.

The intensive breeding work culminated, in 1967, in the release of six Indian variants of dwarf wheat: Kalyan Sona, Sonalika, Safed Lerma, Chhoti Lerma, Sharbati Sonora, and PV 18. All were amber-seeded and highly rust-resistant.[4]

Kalyan Sona (the "Golden Bliss") combines with medium maturity and heavy-tillering other attractive qualities—very high yield, amber grains, and good *chapati*- and bread-making properties. It has rapidly gained in popularity, but has a close competitor in Sonalika (the "Gold-hued") which is also amber-coloured and, in addition, has bolder grains which fetch a price premium, and matures more quickly and therefore fits better into multiple-cropping cycles.

Safed Lerma (or "White Lerma") closely resembles Lerma Rojo 64A, its Mexican parent, in all respects except that its grain is white and semi-hard as against the red and soft grain of the original. Chhoti Lerma( or "Small Lerma"), unlike the above variants, is a two-gene dwarf, white-seeded, with more pronounced non-lodging and rust-resistance properties.

Of all the Indian-bred wheats the one most prized is Sharbati Sonora (which may be somewhat freely translated as "Model Sonora"). It has been bred at IARI by Dr. M. S. Swaminathan and Dr. George Varghuese from the original, two-gene Mexican strain Sonora 64; the method used was irradiation with gamma rays, which altered the grain colour from red to amber—after this cosmetic change it could fetch about Rs. 20 more per quintal, the price premium allowed by purchasers for amber over red wheats. Its other qualities, such as disease-resistance and yield-capability, remained unaffected; when grown according to specifications,

[4] For their parentage and detailed characteristics, see *Five Years of Research on Dwarf Wheats*, ibid. pp. 5-8. For their nitrogen-responsiveness, yield, and profitability, see Table 2.

the yield could be as much as 6000 kg per hectare. Its bread-making qualities, too, are rated exceptionally high.

The mutation breeding by gamma rays yielded another significant bonus. It raised the protein content of the Mexican strain—from 14.0 to 16.5 per cent; it also upgraded the quality of the protein—per 100 grams the lysine content rose from 2.4 to 3 grams. Sharbati Sonora provides a clue to the extent to which high yield might be combined with high quality in breeding new varieties of food crops.[5]

What has been the impact of dwarf wheats on production? By any measure it has been truly spectacular. India's wheat production in 1960-61 amounted to barely 11 million metric tons; four years later, in 1964-65, thanks to very good rainfall, it reached what was then a record level—of 12.3 million tons. But since then, it has established year-to-year peaks with 16.5, 18.7, 20.0 and 23.2 million tons respectively in the four years ending with the 1971 harvest.

Part of this increase was no doubt due to an extension of the acreage under wheat, which rose from 12.9 million hectares in 1966-67 to 15 million in 1967-68, and has since then slowly climbed to reach about 18 million hectares in 1971-72. Thus, the total area sown to wheat rose barely by 50 per cent since the early 1960's.

Within this total, however, the acreage under dwarf wheat grew by leaps and bounds—from a largely experimental start with 400,000 hectares in 1966 to (in million hectares): 2.4 in 1967, 4.9 in 1968, 5.7 in 1969. This uptrend still continues, though somewhat more gently. Thus, in five years dwarf wheat came to be grown on 15 million acres. The spread has been phenomenally rapid, for which history has hardly any parallel. And it is this fact that mainly explains the doubling of India's wheat crop within five years.

In 1968, when production spurted by almost 4.5 million tons over the previous year's level, the government issued a "Wheat Revolution" stamp to commemorate the occasion. There was enough cause for this thanksgiving celebration. In less than a decade the wheat output had doubled; the biggest jump came just after the two disastrous droughts; and it signalled the beginning of a new era, an era of rapid transition from dismally low to astonishingly high yield per hectare.

In 1972, India harvested as much as 26 million tons of wheat, or more than three times the level she used to accept as normal in the late fifties.

In 1963, Dr. Borlaug, then on his first visit to New Delhi, expressed the view that India could double her wheat crop within a decade. This evoked cynical smiles from many, both in India and abroad. In 1971, while in New Delhi on one of his periodic visits, he recalled his earlier prediction, and felt gratified that it had come true within a shorter period than

[5] Problems relating to protein gap and protein quality are discussed in *Reaping the Green Revolution*, Chapter 7.

he had deemed feasible. Then he added confidently that India could, once again, double her wheat harvest within a similar period. There are still skeptics who would reject this rosy prognosis, but their ranks have considerably thinned meanwhile.

*Pakistan.* The story of the diffusion of dwarf wheats in West Pakistan closely parallels that of India, and can therefore be told briefly. A handful of breeding material was brought over, in 1961, by a Pakistani worker who had gone to Mexico to participate in a short practical training course on wheat breeding. This material helped establish, in the next two years, the superior yield-capability of the Mexican dwarfs which outyielded the local varieties at least in a 2:1 ratio.

After this nodding acquaintance with the new varieties, Pakistani and Mexican scientists, aided by the Rockefeller Foundation and FAO, started a breeding programme, which resulted in the release of the main hybrid dwarfs—Mexipak 65 and Indus 66.

Meanwhile, following a visit by Dr. Borlaug in 1964, Pakistan, like India, decided to import dwarf wheat seed from Mexico on a large scale for direct transplantation. Accordingly, 250 tons of seed were imported in 1965, which was multiplied both on government and private farms. Yields of Mexican dwarf varieties were 3,226 to 3,411 kg per hectare— some farmers raised as much as 4,000 kg/ha—against an average yield of 922 to 1,106 kg/ha from local varieties.

In 1966, Pakistan made a very large import of Mexican seeds, amounting to as much as 42,000 tons, which were again multiplied for distribution. By then, the locally-bred hybrid dwarfs, too, came on stream, and Pakistan was able to produce all the dwarf wheat seeds it needed for commercial planting.

Thanks to these steps, wheat production in Pakistan recorded a steep rise—from a base level of 4.6 million tons in 1965 to 6.7, 7.2 and 8.4 million tons in 1968, 1969 and 1970 respectively.

In 1965, Pakistan had introduced an accelerated wheat improvement programme, modelled on the Mexican programme which had proved so successful. The goal was to achieve self-sufficiency by 1970. It was actually reached in 1968, two years ahead of schedule. In that year Pakistan had nearly 3 million acres under dwarf wheat; it reaped a huge crop of 6.7 million tons, or 50 per cent more than in the previous year, against a national target of 5.4 million tons, and thus became a surplus producer of wheat.

*Other Countries.* So far wheat revolution has made the most striking progress in India and Pakistan; and in both countries it is making further headway with expanded plantings of dwarf wheat and a well-organized programme to breed improved strains of high-yielding varieties. However, the Mexican-type wheats are now spreading to other countries of Asia, the Middle East and Africa, such as Turkey, Egypt, Afghanistan,

Iran, Kenya, Nigeria, Syria and Ethiopia. Some of them have breeding programmes to develop dwarf varieties of their own.[6]

*A Gamble?* As seen above, during 1964-66 India and Pakistan had resorted to imports of dwarf wheat seed on a daring scale. History had seen nothing remotely approaching this venture in direct transplantation. Was it a "gigantic gamble," a "wild irresponsible risk," as it was characterized by many at that time, including some well-known experts? They viewed it with trepidation, decried the impetuous switch almost overnight to exotic varieties on a commercial scale, and waited suspensefully to see the crop perhaps decimated by unsuspected races of pathogens. The apprehension proved misplaced; both countries harvested enormous crops, thanks to the fantastic yields of the dwarf strains. The critics heaved a sigh of relief over such rare good luck.

Dr. Borlaug heartily dissented. He had full confidence in the varieties he had evolved, because of the unusual breadth of adaptability and the high degree of disease-resistance they had been impregnated with. In addition, they had been field-tested and subjected to careful scientific evaluation during 1963-64, before a massive switch to them was finally agreed upon.

The importations of seed, Dr. Borlaug estimates, resulted in a saving of three to five years. Pakistan, he cheerfully observes, has done in three years what it took 13 years to accomplish in Mexico.[7] And India's record, as seen above, is not much different.

By his scientific skill, robust faith, and an all-consuming sense of urgency, Dr. Borlaug has rendered to India-Pakistan a service which is unique and unforgettable.


## RICE—A LAGGING MIRACLE[8]

The first high-yielding variety of rice to be introduced in India was Taichung (Native) 1, or TN-1 for short, which was released in Taiwan in 1952. A cross between Dee-geo-woo-gen (literally "brown-tipped, short-legged") and a tall drought-resistant indica variety, it was short-statured, fertilizer-responsive, and exceptionally high-yielding. Though grown quite

[6] See *Proceedings of the Third FAO/Rockefeller Foundation Wheat Seminar*, mimeo., FAO, Rome, 1970. This document gives a detailed account of the diffusion of dwarf wheats, the problems encountered, and the future outlook, country by country.

[7] "National Production Campaigns" in *Strategy for the Conquest of Hunger*, loc. cit.

[8] The writer is grateful for much valuable information he received, in December 1969, from Dr. S. V. S. Shastry, Coordinator, and Dr. Wayne H. Freeman, Joint Coordinator, All-India Coordinated Rice Improvement Project, in personal discussions with them at the AICRIP Centre in Hyderabad, which Dr. Shastry was good enough to supplement with detailed, specially prepared, background material.

7

widely within Taiwan, it did not spread to other Asian countries for quite a while.

However, TN-1 found its way to IRRI soon after the Institute was established, and immediately became the centre of attraction because of its promising characteristics. From there it was brought over to India in 1963, by the late Dr. G. V. Chalam, who was then the General Manager of the newly-established National Seeds Corporation of India. In that year, he visited IRRI in search of seeds of improved varieties of rice, felt deeply impressed by what he heard about TN-1, returned to India with two kilograms of its seed, and distributed it for cultivation at different places in the 1964-65 *rabi* (winter) season. The results created a shock wave—8000 pounds of paddy-in-the-husk were produced per acre, as against 1,000 to 1,200 pounds per acre normally obtained by farmers from local varieties.

The following summer saw a poignant contrast. A drought raged in the country and played havoc with *kharif* rice; but here and there, in small pockets, TN-1 thrived with staggeringly high yield, almost mocking at the shortage. Then raged something else—an intense debate on the wisdom of adopting it for cultivation on a nation-wide scale, for which large imports of dwarf wheat seeds could serve as a precedent. Some scientists shrank back in fear and advised against such a headlong plunge.

And indeed, they had good reasons to counsel caution. TN-1 had hardly been tested in India and contained many imponderables—unlike dwarf wheat, it had not been fortified by a seasoned hand like Borlaug's; its prophylactic attributes were therefore largely unknown—what was known was its marked proneness to bacterial leaf blight. And suppose a sudden outbreak of disease in epidemic proportion destroyed the crop—memories of the Irish potato famine apparently floated before their eyes—it would be a national calamity, a man-made one and, therefore, also a national scandal. In that case, the High-Yielding Varieties Programme which had just been launched would receive a mortal blow right at its start.

But the go-ahead school which included—apart from indomitable Dr. Chalam—some eminent scientists and the then Minister of Food and Agriculture, Mr. Subramanian, had an even more powerful case. What was certain was that TN-1 would yield a far bigger crop, notwithstanding the threat of disease which might not occur after all; and even if it did, the damage could be kept well within tolerable limits with pesticides and other protective measures, so that the country could, even then, count on a bigger harvest. Finally, what was the alternative? Only the ghastly certainty of acute shortage and near-famine conditions. This was the clincher; to play safe in times of a national crisis was—unsafe. TN-1 held out the promise of an early escape from a dreadful bind. If it still looked like a gamble, it was a good one, warranted on rational calculation.

So IRRI was approached with an emergency request for one ton of TN-1 seed which was airfreighted to India in June, 1965. A few months later five more tons arrived by ship from Taiwan; and the following year, Taiwan made a handsome donation of 80 tons of the same seeds to India. These were promptly multiplied and distributed, mainly by NSC. In 1965-66, TN-1 was sown on 1,500,000 acres, representing a 10,000-fold jump from 150 acres in one single season!

About the same time came the heartening news of a breakthrough at IRRI with IR8. Seeds of the new dwarf rice arrived in India in 1966, and were planted, on an experimental basis, in many areas. The results were uniformly reassuring. Steps were therefore taken to multiply IR8 seed which, it was assumed, would soon elbow out TN-1 from the HYV Programme.

The area under IR8 rose from a token level of 30 acres in 1966 to 250,000 acres in kharif 1967 and to 4.0 million acres in kharif 1968. By then, over 5.0 million acres were planted to dwarf rice, doubling the previous year's acreage and trebling it since 1966.

The new varieties spread with a rapidity that took the nation, and many outside observers, by surprise. Farmers in many places were dazed by the size of the crops they harvested. This helped improve the country's food supply position, and provided a much-needed insurance against the vagaries of the monsoon. The decision to gamble on TN-1 and later on IR8 stands fully vindicated, even in terms of immediate gain. The longer-range benefits, there is no more doubt today, will be incomparably greater and will sweep through the whole economy.

### ADOPTION AND ADAPTATION

The acreage under dwarf rice, after the initial spurt, has hit a plateau. Some disillusioned farmers, after a quick try with them, even reverted to the traditional varieties. The output of rice in the country, after recovering from the drought-induced slump, has revealed no noticeable upward thrust, despite a sizable increase in the area under the dwarf varieties (Table 3A-B). A good many people have been baffled by these facts. Others find in them enough reason to question the very significance of dwarf rice.

Such an attitude, however, reflects only a superficial view of things. It ignores the fact that a new variety, no matter how promising, does not spread automatically. It always encounters a host of practical problems; these must be overcome before it can be adopted by farmers on a significant scale. Moreover, even the best varieties have to be adapted to local conditions. This involves more work for plant-breeders who must turn out new and more custom-made variants to fit different ecologies.

In both respects dwarf wheat was more fortunate than dwarf rice.[9] The Mexican wheat had a high degree of resistance to rust and other diseases. This was not the case with TN-1, its vulnerability to bacterial leaf blight was well known even in its homeland—Taiwan.

Besides, wheat in India is grown as a winter crop in a dry and sunny climate of moderate temperature when the risks of attacks by pests and insects are relatively low. By contrast, rice is grown overwhelmingly as a summer crop during the wet monsoon months when pests and pathogens flourish most in the hot and humid climate. In Taiwan, where water is not a serious problem, TN-1 is cultivated in the dry season to escape leaf blight. In India, on the other hand, rice culture is so largely dependent on the monsoon rainfall that TN-1 could not be shifted to the dry months, except on a limited scale where good irrigation was available.

Both TN-1 and IR8 revealed other problems, once they were tried out in farmers' fields. They are highly susceptible to gall-midge, an insect that thrives in some areas of India and South-East Asia, but is not present in Taiwan or the Philippines. Besides, both varieties are temperature-sensitive; when grown in north India or at high elevations, low night temperatures, it has been noticed, tend to delay their maturity.

Summer cultivation of dwarf rice entails two other major problems. To exploit its high potential, strict regulation of water supply is absolutely essential; but this is also the most difficult condition to satisfy in India today. Only one-fifth of the cropped area is under irrigation; most of the irrigation consists of erratic flushing, with no field control and with little or no heed for its timing and dosage;[10] and all this is compounded by a notoriously erratic monsoon.

Both TN-1 and IR8, being insensitive to photoperiod or day-length, can grow under cloudy skies of the monsoon, unlike the tall indica varieties which enter into the flowering and grain-building phase only as the monsoon tapers off, and thereafter they need several weeks of sunny skies for their grains to ripen and be ready for harvest.[11] As a result, the dwarf rices have a much shorter duration and ripen just when the monsoon is at its peak, which often hampers their harvesting. Worse still, in the high humidity their grains tend to germinate.

The remedy, it has been suggested, is to instal electric driers so that the grains may be dried up promptly after harvest to conserve their dormancy. This certainly would be the most logical step. But it also means

[9] The problems about dwarf rice have been cogently stated by W. David Hopper, and Wayne H. Freeman, in "From Unsteady Infancy to Vigorous Adolescence—Rice Development," *Economic and Political Weekly*, Review of Agriculture, 29 March, 1969.

[10] Discussed in Chapter 16.

[11] Some indica varieties of coarse rice, such as *aus* and *boro*, are insensitive to day-length and are therefore early-maturing. They are grown to a limited extent in the north-eastern areas of the subcontinent.

that the adoption of dwarf rice is contingent upon the availability of driers and electric power.

Finally, there is the question of grain quality. The dwarf rice produced a miracle in terms of yield, but its grain—coarse to medium coarse with a "white belly"—lacked consumer appeal. Initially, in view of the acute food shortage, it was accepted *faute de mieux*; but once the worst was over, its acceptability markedly sagged.

The official price policy for rice did not help either. Coarse-grained rice was procured by government at relatively low controlled prices, while finer varieties could be sold in the free market at substantial premiums. This discouraged the adoption of dwarf rice by farmers, and even induced them to divert acreages back from the new to the old and finer varieties, thus keeping down the tonnage of production.

Here, then, is the ironical situation: The tall indica rejects fertilizers and gives a pathetically low yield of fine-quality rice which is eagerly accepted by consumers. The dwarf avidly absorbs fertilizers and gives a fantastically high yield of coarse rice which consumers are unwilling to accept. Can the quality of the tall indica be combined with the yield of the exotic dwarf? This is one of the major tasks scientists have been grappling with.

As seen earlier, a somewhat similar problem arose also with dwarf wheat when it was first introduced. And although efforts for further improvement of its grain quality still continue, the primary task was resolved rather quickly—as soon as the colour of the Mexican wheat was changed from red to amber.

The problem with rice is much more difficult for two reasons. Unlike other grains, rice is eaten "whole"; and India's consumers, especially her rice-eating elite, is fastidious about quality—they want the kernels to be fine, long and white. Besides, rice is grown on a much larger scale and under widely varying conditions; a good many varieties will therefore be needed to suit different ecologies.

Moreover, not only the varieties, but also the cultural practices have to be adapted to local conditions, and this calls for extensive trials both in experimental plots and farmers' fields. For example, the dwarf wheats, on first plantings, gave yields which fell far below expectation. There followed a series of coordinated agronomic trials. It was soon established that, for best results, the dwarfs needed shallower planting—the optimum is 4 cm deep against 8 cm for native strains, also late planting—a few weeks' delay beyond the customary sowing time proved essential because of their short duration.[12]

Proper land-shaping is, of course, essential; an uneven surface would mean uneven distribution of moisture and plant growth, and therefore

[12] See, in particular, the papers by Dr. R. G. Anderson and Dr. Bill C. Wright in *FAO/Rockefeller Foundation Third Wheat Seminar Proceedings*, 1970, cited earlier.

lower yield. Precision in fertilizer application and uniform planting at proper depth can make a difference of 10 to 15 per cent in yield; this underlines the need for some kind of fertilizer-seed drill to ensure uniform plant stands and plant growth.[13]

The regimen for irrigation, as may be presumed, is exacting: first irrigation at the time of crown root formation, that is, about three to four weeks after sowing, three more irrigations at late tillering, flowering, and dough stages respectively, and two or three more extra irrigations on sandy soils.

Determination of fertilizer requirements is another vital part of the exercise. It includes, first and foremost, the quantity of nitrogen to be applied, in what doses, at which stages, and how; rates, timing, and the method of application are all essential. Other chemicals and trace elements are sure to be needed, depending on the results of soil analysis. To mention one obvious instance, most Indian soils are critically deficient in phosphorus. All food crops—rice, wheat, maize and others—will give far better results when nitrogen is applied in proper combination with phosphorus in adequately irrigated fields.[14]

A similar package of sophisticated cultural practices is needed also for dwarf rice. Not only that; every high-yielding variety of every crop must be accompanied by a package of tailor-made practices evolved out of extensive field trials. If it takes time to determine them, farmers take time to learn and apply them, more so where the needed services and facilities are still in an embryonic stage.

Yet when the dwarf wheat and rice first arrived in India, farmers rushed in, scrambled for seeds and inputs, and did the best they could to capitalize on what looked like a rare opportunity. Many booked large profits; others discovered that there were more things involved in the high-yielding varieties than they had suspected; some withdrew in disappointment. Dwarf rice caused more casualties because it entailed more problems, also more intractable ones, than dwarf wheat.

Even with wheat, things were not all that rosy. This can be best illustrated with an example from West Pakistan. The wheat revolution was hailed as a resounding success when, in 1968, the country overfulfilled the target and became a surplus producer in one big leap. But the euphoria gave place, almost with equal suddenness, to misgivings the following year. The yield of Mexipak 65, the most highly prized dwarf wheat of Pakistan, sagged to an unexpectedly low level; farmers began to express serious doubts about its value; so an official Committee was appointed to unravel the facts.

The Committee's findings showed that the deterioration in yield was due to a combination of factors. Weather had played a part—there was

[13] See Chapter 20 on "Farm Mechanization."
[14] See Chapter 18 on "Chemical Fertilizers."

an abrupt rise in temperature in the first fortnight of March, and a dry spell at most of the places just at the critical time of growth and development. Besides, the area under Mexipak had doubled from the preceding year; farmers had cultivated it on all types of soils without considering their suitability for raising a good crop of wheat. Another shortcoming was that most farmers, for whatever reason, had failed to apply fertilizer in the recommended doses. To crown it all, the Mexipak seed the majority of farmers had used was not pure; they had grown their own seed but without roguing it properly (that is, without weeding out the foreign plants).

Nevertheless, too much should not be read into facts of this kind. Essentially, they conform to the normal pattern of development, especially in an agriculture that has just begun to modernize. Progress, in such cases, follows a zigzag course, frequently with two steps forward, one step back. This need not cause concern as long as the trendline points distinctly upward with continuous effort to improve it.[15]

## JAYA, PADMA AND AFTER

The dwarf wheats developed in Mexico have a rare breadth of varietal adaptation; in fact, they were bred with this as one of the primary objectives in view. Some of them have proved equally high-yielding in locations between 0° to 50° latitude and over a wide range of longitudes, and they have a high degree of disease-resistance. According to Dr. Borlaug's own estimate, they were 75 per cent "pre-adapted" so that the changes needed to fit them to local conditions amounted, at best, to 25 per cent.

It was not so with TN-1, not even with IR8, though this was regarded as definitely superior. Indian scientists were aware, at least partially, of their limitations. Nevertheless, when TN-1 first arrived in India via IRRI, in 1964, they were deeply impressed by its plant architecture—sturdy straw, dwarf stature, good tillering, erect leaves, its high fertilizer-responsiveness, and its amazing yield. As Dr. Shastry puts it, TN-1 has been "more a concept than a variety."

The concept, however, was invaluable—it pointed to India's rice-breeders what to aim at and how to get there by the shortest route. Accordingly, an intensive programme of hybridization centering on TN-1 was launched in November, 1965. Barely three years later, in 1968, India was able to release her own home-bred dwarf rice: Jaya and Padma.

This was a remarkable achievement. After wandering aimlessly in scientific wilderness for over half-a-century, India's plant geneticists were, at last, able to dazzle the nation with a spectacular performance. They

---

[15] Dr. M. A. Bajwa's paper on "Wheat Research in Pakistan," in *FAO/Rockefeller Foundation Third Wheat Seminar Proceedings*, ibid., describes how Pakistan is trying to overcome the current problems.

produced varieties of uniquely high yield potential and were able to compress the entire breeding work within an incredibly short time-span.

How could they suddenly stage this near-miracle? Two things helped: the dwarf indica TN-1 which provided an excellent basic design to work on, and a radical reorganization of agricultural research in India, which occurred around the same time and was itself tantamount almost to a revolution.[16]

An All-India Coordinated Rice Improvement Programme (AICRIP) was established in 1965, and immediately it became the pivot of a country-wide hybridization programme. During 1965-68, over 300 primary crosses were made, mainly between the dwarf indicas from Taiwan and the tall commercial varieties of India, and 150,000 progenies were studied by plant breeders in different states. Out of this elaborate process emerged Jaya and Padma; on careful scrutiny they were found to stand up well, in yield as in other essential attributes, against both TN-1 and IR8.[17]

A cross between TN-1 and a tall indica from India known as T 141, Jaya outyields IR8 by 10 to 12 per cent, responds better to fertilizers, shows greater stability for yield, also scores over it in "earliness" by 7 to 10 days. It was named Jaya, or "victory," to symbolize a successful break-through, more so as it outperformed IR8, till then universally regarded as *the* miracle rice.

In all other respects Jaya is almost a replica of IR8—in plant type, grain type, and adaptability. Like the latter, it is sensitive to low temperature and does not therefore suit the cool climates of extreme north or of high elevations; like IR8 and TN-1, it is highly susceptible to gall-midge and should not be grown where, or when, the pest is serious; like these and other dwarf rices, it cannot be grown in deep water and flood-affected areas. Finally, the Jaya grain is average in quality, and "white-bellied," like that of IR8.

Like Jaya, Padma, too, is a cross between the tall indica T 141 and TN-1, except that it is the "reciprocal of the cross for Jaya." In plant type and nitrogen-responsiveness it is similar to TN-1. However, in earli-ness it has an edge over the latter by seven days; its yield is lower than that of TN-1 by 8 per cent, but this is more than compensated by its better grain type, whence the name Padma which implies "good-looking."

The main strengths of Padma are its earliness which makes it a better fit in multiple cropping, and its slender grain which makes it more accept-able to consumers.

Several other varieties have been developed from crosses with TN-1. A promising one is Hamsa, made by Andhra Pradesh Agricultural Uni-

[16] See Chapter 22 on "Education, Research, Extension."
[17] For a detailed account, see "New High-yielding Varieties of Rice—Jaya and Padma" by Dr. S. V. S. Shastry, Project Coordinator (Rice), AICRIP, in *Indian Farming*, February, 1969.

versity (APAU), from the cross HR 12 × TN-1. Its main virtues are its superior grain quality and tolerance to low temperature. Its yield is somewhat lower than those of the other main dwarf varieties, but its slender, translucent grain makes it a winner in the market-place, while its low-temperature tolerance makes it more suitable for multiple-cropping cycles in many areas with cool climates or seasons.

Another dwarf variety developed by the Department of Agriculture, Kerala, is Nellu, a cross between a local indica and TN-1. Because of its earliness it suits Kerala's cropping patterns; but because of its red kernel it is unlikely to have much appeal outside the state.

Jaya and Padma were both released on 23 December, 1968. The National Seeds Corporation (NSC) undertook to multiply their seeds. It may be assumed that before long they will spread over wide areas, especially the plains of India, displacing TN-1 and IR8, until the time comes for them to be replaced by even better varieties.

Jaya and Padma are only the first fruits of the recently established AICRIP breeding programme; and many more are expected to emerge out of its crowded pipeline. One of the varieties people are expectantly waiting for is dwarf Basmati, a slender-grained, aromatic, élite rice highly prized in most rice-eating countries. Apparently, it is now approaching the release stage.[18]

All in all, India has become, within the brief space of a few years, a vast laboratory for rice-breeding. Well might the IRRI Director, Dr. Chandler, say: "So far as rice is concerned, India is the most exciting place in the world today."

Meanwhile, at IRRI, too, exciting things are happening on an extended scale under Dr. Chandler's inspiring leadership. The release of IR8 in 1966 was followed by IR5 in 1967, and IR20 and IR22 in 1969. The institute is engaged in an intensive breeding programme with the main emphasis laid on three factors: improvement of grain quality, greater disease and insect resistance, and development of a broad spectrum of new varieties to meet all conceivable needs.[19]

The strong points of IR8 and IR5 are their high yield and fairly wide adaptability to tropical conditions, but they are poor in grain quality (that is, appearance and milling quality) and are also vulnerable to bacterial blight disease. IR22 largely rectified these deficiencies, combining high quality of grain with high resistance to the bacterial blight, but it is susceptible to the green leafhopper and, through it, to the tungro virus,

[18] Rice in India is grown under widely varying conditions—from sea level to 3000 metres altitude. To meet the varied needs an intensive programme of "minikit demonstrations-cum-trials" (to use IARI's phrase) has been in progress. In summer 1972, it covered 17 varieties, including Basmati dwarfs.

[19] For a review of IRRI's research programme and current priorities, see Dr. Chandler's keynote address delivered at Rice Research and Development Meeting of West Africa Rice Development Association, held in Rome, 22-26 March, 1971.

8

and it lacks enough resistance to certain rice blast disease. IR20 is far more resistant to all of them; its grain quality is good, though apparently inferior to that of IR22. Nevertheless, because of its greater resistance to a wider range of diseases, it is, as Dr. Chandler reports, spreading rapidly among farmers, especially in the Philippines, East Pakistan (now Bangladesh), South Vietnam and Indonesia.

The task of the breeder is not an easy one. His aim is nothing less than to combine the right plant type for high yield, generalized disease resistance, and superior grain quality. As he sets out to tackle this complex task, he is constantly faced with the problem of gene compatibility. The gene he introduces to further improve his handiwork may, and frequently does, knock out some desirable attributes as well. And so he may make headway on one front only to slip on another, which makes the going both arduous and long-drawn-out.

Among other things, IRRI has embarked on an intensive crossing programme using materials of different genetic origin; and it hopes to produce a series of new varieties which would be sufficiently resistant to all the main diseases and insects that commonly attack rice crops. This, it estimates, will take at least another 10 years.

In addition, IRRI's breeding programme aims at several other objectives. New varieties will be developed with varying growth durations—from 100 days or less to 150 days—and not photoperiod sensitive; variable duration is particularly important from the angle of multiple-cropping cycles. Some photosensitive varieties, however, are deemed necessary for cultivation in certain areas during the monsoon.

A second category will consist of cold-resistant varieties to be grown in cooler temperatures—either at high elevations or in winter in the northern plains of the tropics. IR8, as seen earlier, is not suitable for these

Some deep-water varieties are needed for cultivation in monsoon-areas, nor are its existing derivatives.

submerged lowlands, as in West Bengal, Bangladesh, and other deltaic areas of the tropics. Work on this group recently got under way.

Finally, there is a special urgency to breed drought-resistant varieties suitable for growing in uplands and other areas under rainfed conditions, since the major part of the rice acreage in the tropics falls in these categories.

Even this bald listing of the requirements[20] is enough to indicate the magnitude of the tasks involved. But IRRI is busily at work, and so are rice-breeders in other countries, especially India, with continuous exchange of varieties, breeding materials, and information, and with far-flung cooperative arrangements for field-testing. There is no longer any doubt

[20] IRRI's work naturally includes intensive experiments to determine the specific cultural practices that must accompany every new variety. Another top-priority item it is working on is multiple cropping systems.

that the problems, despite all their intricacies, will be resolved, that new dwarf varieties of rice—more resistant, better adapted to varying physical conditions, high-yielding, and finer-grained—will begin to flow out before long.

"India's wheat and rice programmes," says Carroll P. Streeter, "have been like two powerful jet planes at the airport. Wheat rolled down the runway first and is now well aloft. Rice has only barely lifted off the ground, but it is beginning its climb."[21] This is no exaggeration, certainly not so far as breeding is concerned.

But as Mr. Streeter rightly points out, rice will not gain height as fast as wheat. For, unlike wheat, it has to negotiate cloudy skies and serious operational problems. Yet this is not a reason to lose, but to take heart. For, what is at stake here is far more than rice. In India, for example, agriculture accounts for one-half of the national income, and rice alone accounts for 40 per cent of the total agricultural production. Rice culture is the biggest building block of the national economy. When, after initial hesitancy, the dwarf rice finally gets airbrone, it will also lift the whole economy with it.

## STIRRINGS OF A REVOLUTION

As indicated earlier, dwarf wheat and rice initially spread with blitz-like rapidity. In the four years ending 1968-69, their plantings in developing countries rose from 23 and 13 acres to 18.3 and 11.5 *million* acres respectively, or for the two crops taken together, from 36 acres to 29.8 million acres. "It is probably safe to say," to quote the remark of two well-known agriculturists, "that never before have so many farmers made so important and dramatic a shift in cropping practices in so short a period of time."[22]

In 1968-69, of India's 39.4 million acres sown to wheat, 10 million acres —or over a quarter—were already under high-yielding varieties. In Pakistan, the proportion was even higher—the new wheats were planted on 6 million acres or 40 per cent of the total wheat acreage of 15 million.

The impact of dwarf wheats in the Middle Eastern countries has so far been much less striking. In 1969, the share of these varieties ranged from almost nil to a maximum of 6 per cent in Afghanistan and 10 per cent in Turkey. However, in Egypt, a locally developed high-yielding variety of wheat, Giza 155, accounted for 15 per cent of the wheat area

[21] F. Streeter Carroll, *A Partnership to Improve Food Production in India*, A Report from the Rockefeller Foundation, New York, 1969, p. 26.

[22] F. F. Hill, and S. Lowell Hardin, "Crop Production Successes and Emerging Problems in Developing Countries," in Kenneth L. Turk, ed., *Some Issues Emerging from Recent Breakthroughs in Food Production*, Cornell University, Ithaca, New York, 1971, p. 5.

in 1968-69, and was expected to rise to 75 per cent the following year.

The miracle rice spread quite fast in South and East Asian countries. Released on a large scale in the wet season of 1967, it was immediately planted on 13 per cent of the Philippines' 7.9 million acres of rice lands. By 1969, the percentage rose to 31.6, when the country had 2.5 million acres under IRRI rice.

In the same year, dwarf rice plantings in India and Pakistan accounted for 6.50 and 1.14 million acres, or 7.1 and 4.2 per cent of their rice lands, totalling 91.3 and 27.2 million acres respectively.

In 1969, Indonesia and Burma had 416,000 and 470,000 acres, or 2.0 and 3.8 per cent of their respective rice acreages, under IRRI-type rice. Other countries, taken together, had 460,000 acres planted to the new varieties.

The impact of the high-yielding varieties on national food budgets has been most significant in Pakistan, India, and the Philippines. As seen earlier, Pakistan became an exporter of wheat in 1969; in the same year it also had a small exportable surplus in rice.

India, too, has been approaching self-sufficiency in foodgrains. In 1972, she became, for the first time in decades, a surplus producer of wheat, though her overall food budget still remains precarious with rising population and still-lagging diffusion of dwarf rice.

In the Philippines, the country that pioneered the miracle rice, the turnaround was even more remarkable. A substantial importer of rice— during 1963-66, the imports exceeded 300,000 tons a year—it became a rice-surplus country in 1968 when it was able to export 60,000 tons, mostly to Indonesia.[23]

The contribution high-yielding varieties have made to additional food production is difficult to calculate. The very rapidity with which they have spread tends to defy all follow-up efforts; besides, there are other factors—weather and acreage expansion—which should be taken into account, in addition to fertilizers and other inputs, more and better irrigation which must go hand in hand with the high-yielding varieties.

However, for south and south-east Asia, FAO provisionally estimates an increase of 9 per cent in rice and 20 per cent in wheat production in 1968-69, equivalent to about 20 million tons of foodgrains.[24]

Another FAO study covering 14 food-deficit countries in Latin America, the Far East, the Near East, and Africa, showed that their aggregate cereal production in 1969 had gone up by 24 per cent as compared with

[23] N. B. Cabanilla, in *Technological Innovation in the Philippines: High-yielding Rice Varieties* (University of the Philippines, mimeo. Thesis, 1969) gives a detailed account of the development. The country's rice picture has recently been confused, mainly because of domestic politics and a sudden weakening of the key administrative agency. In addition, the miracle rice varieties were badly damaged in 1971 by a Tungro virus outbreak.

[24] *The State of Food and Agriculture*, 1970, FAO, Rome.

the 1964-66 average. They still have to import grain to support their expanding populations; but their net aggregate imports have already been reduced by 25 per cent.

These are heartening facts, even after due allowance has been made for increases in wheat and rice acreages, partly at the expense of other crops. To talk of surplus foodgrains for export, it has been argued, is meaningless for developing countries where the masses of people still suffer from chronic undernourishment. This certainly is true; yet, surely, it is a tremendous relief, and a big step forward, to have a surplus, and not a deficit, at the present low level of consumption. Moreover, what has made possible today's surplus should raise tomorrow's level of consumption—and with it the general living standard—to a more satisfactory level, once its potential is more fully exploited.

What has been the effect of rising food production on agricultural income? Dr. Anderson estimates that in India the gross additional income from wheat for the three years ending in 1968-69 amounted, on a conservative basis, to $1.85 billion.[25] According to Dr. Borlaug, additional wheat harvested in four years—1967 through 1970—added as much as $3 billion in India and $1.1 billion in Pakistan to the gross value of their agricultural production. And he further estimates that farmers cultivating Mexican-type wheats in these two countries have increased their income more than fourfold, to $162 per hectare as compared with $37 they previously obtained from growing local wheats.[26]

Rising food production and agricultural income by no means exhaust the benefits derived from the high-yielding varieties; they are only the end-results coming out of a long pipeline. No less significant are the vast changes the HYV's are forcing into the whole production process and the enormous job and income opportunities they are creating all along the way: A seed industry, rapid development of tubewells, spurt in fertilizer consumption, increasing use of pesticides for plant protection, a surge in the demand for farm machinery (tractors, threshers, seed-fertilizer drills, driers), growing emphasis on multiple cropping, rural electrification, expansion of fertilizer and pesticide industries and agro-business of various types, rapid growth of agricultural credit—these are the direct results of the adoption of dwarf wheat and rice.

In addition, they have made a decisive impact on official policy. Agricultural research has been reorganized; the extension service is being revamped; there is deeper realization of the need for an incentive price system for farm products, for genuine land reform to give the farmer an abiding stake in good farming, and for better marketing facilities.

[25] R. G. Anderson, in *Proceedings of the Third FAO/Rockefeller Foundation Wheat Seminar*, loc. cit.
[26] Norman E. Borlaug, *Mankind and Civilization at Another Crossroad*, 1971, McDougal Memorial Lecture (mimeo.), FAO, Rome.

These changes, so far as India is concerned, are discussed later item by item, along with the progress made, the difficulties encountered, and the tasks that lie ahead to meet adequately the specific requirements of an HYV-based agriculture.[27]

What is abundantly clear already is that the dwarf wheat and rice have thrown India's traditional agriculture into a melting-pot. The farmers are clamouring for the new seeds, and are ready to pay almost any price for them—it is reported that there are constant pilferages from experimental plots of unripe seeds of an unreleased variety of triple-gene dwarf wheat; and they are yearning for the latest knowhow, better services, and greater facilities.

A revolution is clearly under way. Its stirrings are visible on a broad front.[28] How fast it will spread and how far it will go, how much prosperity and welfare it will generate and for how many people, will, from now on, depend overwhelmingly on one thing: how wisely and deftly its forces are stimulated—and regulated—by official policies and various administrative agencies.

## THE NEW VISTA

When the joint Rockefeller-Mexican programme was initiated, there was widespread skepticism about the future of wheat. Officials and farmers were almost unanimous in their view that Mexico lacked the climate and soil for good wheat production; the country, they assumed, would always remain dependent on wheat import; all that the government could do was to reduce the degree of this dependence.

This was not surprising. What Mexico overlooked, and what most people—in both developed and underdeveloped countries—continued to overlook until very recently are: first, varieties can be evolved, thanks to the modern techniques of biological engineering, to fit almost all climates (except deserts); and, second, soil, too, can be largely amended with modern chemicals to fit the new varieties. Agriculture, in short, need not be a helpless prisoner of soil and climate. Science has given it some remarkable escapes.

How completely Mexico's scepticism about wheat was exploded in just about a decade has already been seen. But wheat was only the starting-point; the revolution that began with it fanned out in all directions until it blossomed into an all-round agricultural revolution. It had to be so; the powerful forces of transformation it unleashed were soon at work all over the country, and before long they revolutionized the old system.

To put it more concretely, the dwarf wheat had to be nourished with

[27] Mainly in Chapters 16 through 29.
[28] Carroll Streeter describes them in vivid terms in his information-packed write-up: *A Partnership to Improve Food Production in India*, op. cit.

well-measured and well-timed doses of water and fertilizers; it had to be protected against pests and insects with effective measures including the use of pesticides in right doses at the right time; farmers had to be taught these sophisticated cultural practices and, therefore, field demonstrations had to be organized; they had to be supplied with genetically pure seeds, chemical inputs, and essential farm machinery; all this called for a competent extension service staffed with scientifically trained personnel; and behind it all there had to be a vigorous programme of research and education.

In addition, farmers needed sizable credit to take care of their increased outlays, expanded facilities to market their swollen crops, and adequate price support to earn an adequate profit.

But what was good for wheat was good for many other things as well; and once a new framework was created on the above lines to accommodate the dwarf wheat, it could be used, with the same effectiveness, for other high-yielding crops and, to a large extent, also for livestock development. Thus, the wheat revolution spilled over into other areas and stimulated many-sided progress in her agriculture.

It is not simply the yield surge of dwarf wheat, but this broader, rapidly unfolding scenario of Mexico's agriculture that should serve as an inspiration, and as a model, to the developing countries. The facts are readily available,[29] and all we need do is to touch upon only a few salient points of this success story.

The record-breaking progress Mexico has made in wheat production has already been noted. With minor increases in acreage, the output was boosted from 400,000 tons in 1941 to 2,200,000 tons in 1969 (Fig. 1); as a result, 253,600 tons of net annual *imports* of wheat were replaced by net *exports* of 276,000 tons, or more, a year.

Corn, the most important cereal in Mexican diet, has been a good second to wheat. Because of wide variations in physical conditions—altitude, slope, temperature, moisture supply—corn cultivation in Mexico is more difficult than, say, in the USA's corn-belt. Nevertheless, the breeders have developed several categories of hybrid corn custom-made for different conditions: early-maturing, late-maturing, "tropical" hybrids suitable for altitudes below 1000 metres, "temperate" hybrids for altitudes of 1800 to 2400 metres; some for irrigated lands, others for areas with sparse rainfall; some frost-resistant varieties, others to withstand drought.

It took time to breed such widely diversified varieties. But once they were put to work, production rose sharply, aided by improved cultural practices, especially greater use of machinery and fertilizers (Fig. 2). Between 1941 and 1958, the area planted to corn increased by 75 per cent to 7.5 million hectares, yield per hectare doubled to 1200 kg, and total

[29] Roberto Osaye, "Mexico: From Deficits to Sufficiency" in *Strategy for the Conquest of Hunger*, loc. cit., gives the highlights of this historic transition.

output more than trebled to 9 million tons a year. A net importer of corn in the early 1940's—the import reached a record level of 162,800 tons in 1944—Mexico became a substantial exporter—the corn export peaked in 1965 with 1,347,000 tons.

The goals of self-sufficiency have been fulfilled, or exceeded, with other crops: rice, potatoes, barley, sorghum, sesame, sugarcane, coffee, a number of horticultural crops, and several fruits. Great progress has been made also with poultry and poultry products, cattle and dairy produce, and other livestock. In 1967, Mexico's total exports amounted to $1.2 billion; two-thirds of this, or 65.4 per cent, consisted of agricultural products.

To complete the picture, mention must be made of one more factor: the growth in population, which rose from 20.5 million in 1942 to 45.5 million in 1967. The annual growth rate is 3.2 per cent, one of the highest in the world; 1.5 million new-borns are added to the nation every year; and one-half of the population is now below 20 years in age. Self-sufficiency in food was attained despite the soaring numbers. It would be more secure, however, and living standards would rise much faster in the future, if the growth rate of population could be sharply curtailed.

How far has the proximity to the USA helped Mexico? Can other developing countries emulate her example? Presumably she has derived some benefit—psychological and, to some extent, perhaps also material —from being a next-door neighbour of a modern giant. But her real benefit came not from any special relationship with the USA, but overwhelmingly from the agricultural science and technology she imported from this source, and adapted and applied systematically to her own conditions. And since the USA has no patent right on them, other countries, too, can do the same and stage repeat performances as often as they like.

## SOCIO-ECONOMIC ENGINEERING

The agricultural revolution of Mexico can be repeated in other tropical countries.[30] To do so, however, they must bear in mind two fundamentals. First, miracle seeds are really not a miracle; they very much represent a man-made phenomenon. Nor are they a "once-and-for-all innovation"; they are only "an invention of a new method of innovating."[31] The so-called miracle must be constantly watched, and frequently re-made and re-adapted to changing conditions, particularly to forestall pests and pathogens.

And second, miracle seeds alone will not do. They will yield up their

[30] Apart from Mexico, there is another country which has much to teach in tropical agriculture, namely, Taiwan, and to some extent also Israel.

[31] As Zvi Griliches aptly observed about hybrid corn, quoted by Hill and Hardin in the paper cited earlier in this Chapter. The remark, of course, holds good for other crops as well.

stored wealth only when they are cultured with the requisite skill and care, and they will be so cultured only when the skills are properly taught, the needed ingredients are adequately supplied, and facilities are provided to garner the wealth and to turn it into cash.

To put it differently, with the tools of modern genetics, scientists can now build plants to fit practically every physical environment; and where moisture is not a limiting factor, they can make them astonishingly high-yielding with heavy doses of applied nutrients. But the environment itself, in the broadest sense of the term, must in turn be fitted to the progenies of biological engineering. Scientists have drastically restructured the wheat and rice plants for the tropical milieu. What is now needed is to restructure the milieu—in all its major socio-economic components—so that it may worthily accommodate the prodigious dwarfs.

In short, biological engineering must be accompanied by socio-economic engineering. It is the "wide cross" between these two different types of engineering that can produce a new hybrid type of economy which will be truly high-yielding.

How long should it take to reconstruct the traditional environment in order to effectuate a marriage of the two brands of engineering? The prevalent view still is that it will be a slow, laborious process. And the example frequently cited in its support is that, even in the dynamic environment of the USA, hybrid corn took thirty years to saturate the entire corn-belt. This is largely explained by the fact that the so-called corn-belt is not physically homogeneous. For example, what was good for Iowa and northern Illinois, the first states to benefit from hybrid corn, was not suitable for Alabama and Georgia, which obtained tailor-made hybrids much later—only in the late forties. A time-span of 10 to 12 years between the first appearance of an improved variety and the saturation of the area it is designed for is accepted as normal even in the Western countries.

Such a view suffers from its very virtue—the patience and understanding it breathes dilutes the sense of urgency. The point at issue is not how to explain delays, but how to save time. The first is the easiest thing to do in view of the multitude of obstacles that stand in the way in a developing country. But it is the second that matters—how, despite these obstacles, the diffusion rate can be greatly speeded up so as to make spectacular progress within a short time.

Plant-breeders are now able to produce improved varieties for the tropics at a much faster rate; by adopting new techniques including summer nurseries, they have slashed the time into one-half of what, until recently, was accepted as normal in the USA and other countries. The varieties they are breeding lap up fertilizers, and work day and night, in season and out of season, to turn them into grain, and so they produce mature grain in about half the time to give four to five times more yield.

9

Surely, it is time also to accelerate their adoption and to compress it into a much shorter time-period.

These, then, are the larger issues which are pressing for solution today: how to enlarge the corps of trained scientists and to help them expand their research work to breed high-yielding varieties of crops on a larger scale; how to ensure that the new varieties will be grown according to their cultural specifications so that they will really give high yields; how to speed their diffusion among farmers so as to reach full area saturation expeditiously; how to make sure that the benefits of the high yield are diffused widely in the rural communities, and beyond; and how, through these and other measures, to win decisively the race between food and population.

Much of this study is concerned with a thorough analysis of these questions with specific reference to one country, namely, India. The problems involved here are numerous and complex; they are also critically interlinked so that failure to tackle one will jeopardize the success of the whole. They have, therefore, been examined, one by one, with an assessment of the past progress and the future needs.

For a case study India, admittedly, is untypical. Her problems are intimidating in their complexities because of the vastness of the country and its diversity, which have been compounded by the misdoings of history, hoary dogmas, misplaced ideologies, false starts, and hasty commitments.

All these make the task of socio-economic engineering in India incomparably more difficult, but they also make it more, not less urgent. The stakes here are exceedingly high, involving as they do the future of one-sixth of mankind. In a larger sense, they are indeed even higher. For, what happens in India, the giant underdeveloped country, has a tremendous significance for the entire Third World.

The stakes can be won. They can be won even with the cards as fate has dealt her, if they are played boldly and skilfully. Success in India's protean struggle against hunger and poverty will have an electrifying effect on other developing countries. Her very example will help set them on the right road and redouble the pace of their development.

# PART TWO

# NOT BY MIRACLE
# SEEDS ALONE
# —INDIA AS AN EXAMPLE

CHAPTER 5

# A Fateful Race

## FATE AND FOLLY

In the early fifties India received plenty of plaudits for the vision she had shown in launching her national development plans. But as time went on, as the plans failed to make more than a dent in the low living standards of her people, and as she visibly drifted towards a deepening food crisis, disenchantment grew, and criticisms of her plans, both at home and abroad, became louder until, by the mid-sixties, her stock sank to a disconcertingly low point.

Here as elsewhere, the proof of the pudding, it was implied, had to be in the eating; the slow growth rate, it was therefore inferred, could only reflect faulty planning. Without doubt mistakes had been made, some grave ones too. But if the planners had erred, so also did most of the critics most of the time.

Criticism, to be of real value, must be based on correct diagnosis; only then there would be hope for remedy. Unfortunately, this was not always the case. Much of the criticism, even when well-intentioned, was not sufficiently well-informed and therefore easily missed the mark. Indeed, at times its very vulnerability produced a hardening of attitude on the other side.

For example, it is customary to compare the economic performance of India, as reflected in her growth rate, with that of other countries, such as Pakistan, Korea, Taiwan, Mexico, Yugoslavia, at times also mainland China if and when facts were available. Comparisons can no doubt be useful, but they have to be made with due circumspection. For they usually involve a good many variables which can easily vitiate comparisons of this nature, such as historical background, natural resources, population pressure, climatic factors, geographical location, quantum of foreign aid, both military and non-military. Indeed, it would be more meaningful to compare a country like India not with others. but with herself; and to enquire where and how her own performance could, and should, have been better.

Even here one should be careful to distinguish between two things: What is due to a legacy from history or to some *force majeure* such as a natural calamity, and what can be legitimately attributed to the decisions of the policy-makers. In short, between fate and folly.

## AN IMPRESSIVE RECORD

This is not the place to attempt an overall appraisal of India's achievements since she became independent, on 15 August, 1947, after a surgical operation that split the subcontinent three-way and created two separate countries. However, some brief comments are necessary in order to set the perspective right.

The progress made by India since independence, despite nagging doubts to the contrary, is most impressive judged by any standards, past or present. In the seventeen years between 1950-51 and 1967-68, industrial production rose by over 7 per cent per year—from 73.40 to 192.60 (1956= 100). The gains recorded in the major industries during this period are shown in Table 6. As will be noticed, the installed capacity of power rose almost sixfold—from 1.83 million to 10.19 million kw; power generation multiplied more than seven times—from 5.30 to 39.40 billion kwh; production of steel ingots increased from 1,690,000 to 6,310,000 tons; of railway wagons from 2,900 to 11,900; of cement from 2,730,000 to 11,500,000 tons; of caustic soda from 12,000 to 275,000 tons.

Even the older industries substantially raised their production over the same period. The output of jute textiles went up from 837,000 to 1,156,000 tons, of cotton cloth from 4,215 to 7,509 billion metres, of paper and paper boards from 134,000 to 537,000 tons. Significant progress was made by chemicals, rubber goods, light engineering, and a broad spectrum of consumer goods industries which mushroomed during this period.

In agriculture, as will be seen later (in Chapter 6), the progress, in absolute terms, has been no less remarkable. All told, more has been achieved since independence than in the preceding half-century or more.

The gross national product, at current prices, rose from 95,300 to 231,200 million rupees between fiscal 1951 and 1967. Expressed in real terms, i.e., in 1948-49 prices, the rise was much less but still quite appreciable—from 95,300 to 149,500 million rupees. But in per capita terms the increase in *real* income was very small—from 266.5 to 298.0 rupees, or only 31.5 rupees over a period of sixteen years. In other words, real income per head rose barely 1.5 per cent a year.

This brings us to what is by far the most disturbing fact about the Indian situation—the explosive growth of population. At the time of independence, the total population of India was estimated at 350 million. By 1970, it went up by 200 million to 550 million—that is almost like adding the entire population of Africa or of Latin America or of the USA and pyramiding it on a constant resource-base. This is not all, for the projections are even more alarming. Some 15 million people are being added to the country every year. By the end of the current decade the total, even on a conservative estimate, will reach or surpass 700 million. The figure staggers imagination, so does the crushing burden it will impose on a still struggling economy. As things now stand, it threatens to nullify all future development effort.

The effort will indeed be nullified unless ways and means are found to greatly speed up economic growth in a way that will make the quickest impact on living standards and will help dampen the runaway population growth.

## UNIQUE PROBLEMS OF INDIA

India's achievements have been "dramatic and important," observed the Pearson Commission. However, "the problems rather than the achievements have usually been highlighted."[1] This is undoubtedly true. Nor are the reasons for it hard to find. Most people, particularly the critics abroad, are apt to judge India's performance by what they see on the surface—a surging population, a dishearteningly low rate of growth in per capita income, little visible prospect of raising her people well above the subsistence line, and, until recently, uncertainty about her ability even to feed them.

Such judgment, however natural, fails to make allowance for the unique constellation of circumstances in India.

First, no other nation in world history has ever set out to develop its country with so many formidable obstacles as India. *She has started late, with little inherited capital, but with a vast population, living mostly at an appallingly low level, and multiplying fast.*

Second, India is attempting economic development under a *democratic system* of government. This often impairs, if not cripples, the decision-making capacity, particularly in a country of great regional diversity due to race, language and cultural tradition. It also sets stringent limits to capital formation through belt-tightening. For, the vast majority of people have no savings to offer, but they have votes to cast at election times.

[1] *Partners in Development*, loc. cit., p. 286.

Unlike Stalinist Russia and Maoist China, she cannot squeeze capital out of the people through draconic methods.

And third, there is the overwhelmingly important *time factor*. India's economy has long been riddled with scarcities—of food, capital, foreign exchange, and a good many other things. But her worst scarcity lies somewhere else—in the TIME she has at her disposal to tackle the enormous tasks she has been saddled with. Time, in India, is in desperately short supply. She has been caught in a fateful race between population growth and economic development. The race began in a low gear, but it accelerated surprisingly fast and has already entered the climactic phase.

This last point is worth pondering because of its disquieting implications. It means, first of all, that India must achieve development not only at low cost, but also at high speed; she must avoid not only the waste of resources, but also the waste of time; her economic policies and programmes must be geared firmly to these dual objectives.

It means that India cannot afford to follow the trial-and-error method in a relaxed fashion and to learn the hard way from her own experience, as has been the case in the last two decades, with a callous squandering of her precious time. It means that she must, instead, learn from the experience of others, both past and present, to the utmost possible extent to minimize the risks of failures or of lost motions.

It means that, at times, India must forego what might normally be regarded as quite legitimate experimentation, and take calculated risks. This is precisely what she did when she decided to adopt, so wisely and so successfully, the miracle rice and wheat on a massive scale, dispensed with the much longer process of initial trials and experiments under local conditions, ran the risks of diseases to which the new varieties might have been susceptible, and took whatever precautionary measures she could to cope with whatever diseases might break out.[2] This trade-off—of traditional safety for the time she could salvage—was perfectly sensible and deserves to be repeated in a great many other programmes and activities.

For the same reason it is most unfortunate that the government should have decided to postpone more or less indefinitely the space satellite project[3] which was so wisely conceived to introduce satellite broadcasts on birth control, hygiene, farming, national integration, elementary school subjects. India simply cannot afford not to give the foremost priority to a project like this.

Scarcity of time means that India must more quickly shed some of her long-cherished dogmas, harness her wasted idealism to constructive goals, and shape and mould her institutions to meet the needs of faster growth.

It means that she must show greater discrimination and better judgment

[2] See Chapter 4, especially the subsection : *A Gamble?*
[3] In July 1970, the government took the decision to postpone the project "at least by a year." At this point its future still looks uncertain.

in adopting borrowed ideas, ideologies and institutions from abroad, many of which will never fit the unique mixture of her problems and opportunities, which can easily become, as they have been in the past, imported impediments to progress. It also means that, in this age of big-power rivalry and bloc-building, she must not hesitate to straddle ideologies, and to accept unreservedly concepts, ideas and institutions irrespective of their source when, with necessary adaptation, they can help her overriding objective of rapid development.

It means that friendly governments, international institutions, and foreign experts in general, while giving aid or advice, should approach their tasks with more caution and a greater sense of responsibility, bearing in mind the grave implications of the advice they render, how it can, even when well motivated, cut both ways and may result in actually hindering development either because it is technically inappropriate for local conditions or because it overlooks the emergency character of the situation, and is consequently too costly in terms of time.

And it means that the government and its economic planners must promptly jettison a fundamental concept they have routinely followed so far—the fetish of a predetermined rate of economic growth derived from a preconceived rate of savings based on a rough-and-ready estimate of national income calculated in monetary terms. Planning has too long been engrossed in a hollow debate about the annual growth rate the national plan should aim at—whether, to be more specific, it should be four, five or six per cent per year.[4]

Such a planning concept is totally misplaced in the context of India. It springs from false notions, it displays limited vision, it breathes defeatism even before the first well-aimed shots are fired in the war against overpowering poverty. The foremost task before the planners is to tap the unused and under-used productive potential of the economy, the "slacks" it is littered with today, which are directly responsible for the deplorably poor rate of economic growth and the intolerably low annual increment in per capita income.

Where, then, are these slacks? They lie, first of all, hidden in the soils which could be coaxed to yield many times more crops—food, fibre, and a wide variety of raw materials—than they do now. They lie in the wasted waters which can be harvested more carefully and put to use far more skilfully. They lie in the public-sector industries which can work far more efficiently to turn out handsome profits instead of piling up disgusting losses; in the idle plant capacity in the private sector, most of which can work to fuller capacity, sometimes on two or three shift basis, to raise production by a wide margin; in the exceedingly low man-hour productivity which can be substantially raised under a well-conceived incentive system and without resorting to more capital-intensive equip-

[4] See Chapter 29, the subsection on "Some Glittering Fallacies."

10

ment. They lie in the vast reservoir of unemployed and under-employed (including what may be called "pseudo-employed") manpower, both in rural and urban areas, which can be used on countless productive jobs —to provide crucial underpinnings to agriculture, to build essential public works, especially roads, schools and hospitals, to promote housing projects, to create a vast network of small or cottage industries, viable and vibrant, in place of the present moribund, subsidy-fed units. They lie in the under-used scientists starved of incentives and of funds to carry out vital production-oriented research work, and in the wasted talents of thousands of young professionals struggling for jobs or for creative opportunities, and, in sheer frustration or despair, deciding in increasing numbers to migrate abroad in quest of what they are unable to find at home. The list could be lengthened.

As John Lewis in his perceptive analysis of the Indian situation rightly pointed out, an excessively "savings-centred" approach to the problems of development finance has led to "a disappointingly timid" policy in employing the idle manpower.[5] The Third Plan he called "bold" in overall endeavour and "tough-minded" about priorities, but with a conspicuous exception, namely, "in the matter of activation of idle manpower."[6] The Indian planners, he charged parenthetically but no less pertinently, were "encumbered no little by inappropriate economic theories learned mostly from the West." The upshot is that "Indian planning has tended to be too cautious, too afraid of making mistakes, too little animated with an uncompromising determination to activate idle resources." This, he correctly diagnosed, is due to the fact that, despite independence, it still looks too much like "the progeny of an administrative system dedicated to the prevention of wrong-doing rather than to the marshalling and energizing of 'right-doing.' "[7]

## A NEO-KEYNESIAN APPROACH

Lewis's reference to the "inappropriate economic theories" learnt by Indian planners mainly from the West deserves a little elucidation. The inappropriateness he had in mind stems from implicitly equating the conditions and problems of the *developed* West with those of an *underdeveloped* country like India. The equation is patently wrong because of the very fact of underdevelopment in the latter case. Yet, interestingly enough, it does hold good in essentials if the perspective is slightly altered to envision the realities as they are, unblurred by theories.

For example, the crux of the thesis Keynes developed in his later years

[5] John P. Lewis, *Quiet Crisis in India*, The Brookings Institution, Washington, D.C., 1962, pp. 68-69.
[6] Ibid., p. 112.
[7] Ibid., p. 135-36.

was to achieve full employment—of idled plant capacity and of jobless workers—in a Western economy. The mechanics he advocated to attain this goal was a judicious mixture of fiscal and monetary measures in order to expand aggregate demand with a deliberate unbalancing of the national budget, that is, a substantial dose of deficit finance, in times of an economic slump. The expanding demand in its turn would, he argued, lead to fuller use of the plant capacity and reemployment of the idled workers.

Full employment must also be the broad objective in India, as in any other developing country. Clearly, it cannot be achieved by concentrating attention on a few modern factories; it would be absurd to think it can. Underdevelopment is a kind of perpetual slump; for an economy languishing in this backward state there is one and only one way out—by activating its idle natural resources which, so to say, constitute its "plant capacity."

Similarly, to cope with the massive problems of unemployment aggravated from year to year by the swelling population, there is one and only one effective means—rapid development of these resources tied in with comprehensive public works programmes to build essential supra- and infrastructures for the economy. For this purpose deficit finance on a substantial scale is indispensable, and it would be perfectly justified as long as it is directed to create employment and to extract maximum possible wealth out of the resources.

Under such a policy the aggregate demand, it may be assumed, will grow fast; in a country like India it is not likely to hit any ceiling for decades to come. Nor should the inflationary situation worsen under such an approach. Production is bound to rise *pari passu* with the growth in demand—in an economy like India's one can confidently count on what may be called *demand-push production*. And this would be the only way to counteract the *population-push inflation* which is already acute and threatens to become increasingly more serious.[8]

Thus, the basic concepts of resource development, public works programmes, manpower mobilization and deficit finance can be embalmed in Keynesian theory and terminology without undue violence to them. That this would involve a radical policy shift for India goes without saying. Yet this is precisely what she needs most urgently today for two inescapable reasons.

What Lewis, about a decade ago, called the "quiet crisis" in India, giving a clear warning in the guise of a euphemism, has already become

---

[8] This section partly echoes the writer's views on resource development and deficit finance expressed in his book *United Nations in Economic Development*, op. cit., esp. pp. 289-91. They are briefly repeated here because of their importance in the present context, and to avoid a break in the chain of reasoning. Also see Chapter 27 of this study on "Credit Shackles."

turbulent and now threatens to get out of control. Can it be contained? This is the fateful question that faces India today. The hour is late; the trend is ominous; the crisis, fed by the demographic upheaval, has gained powerful momentum. Nevertheless, the writer does believe that the trend can still be halted and reversed, the crisis momentum can still be braked, provided the policy shift is effected forthwith, and the "old economics" is unreservedly replaced by the kind of "new economics" indicated above.

The second reason is no less compelling. The "inappropriate theories" which have so long been treated as sacrosanct, have demonstrably failed to deliver the goods. As a result, they now stand discredited in the eyes of a great many people, particularly of the fast-growing generation of educated young men and women who have learnt their economic theories mainly from the "East." The pendulum shows every sign of swinging to the other extreme. The implications of such a swing are too serious to contemplate. For, should this happen, one set of costly dogmas will be replaced by another, the objective of rapid economic growth will continue to be a casualty, and in the process India's future will be irretrievably mortgaged.

Such a tragedy must not be allowed to happen because of thoughtless, and heartless, adherence to obsolete dogmas in a mood of complacent passivity. To forestall it, India must build her own *eclectic economic model*, culling the needed ingredients, boldly and imaginatively, from all ideological camps. And she must do so before the sands of time run out.

## ONE MORE CHANCE

When India became independent very few people realized the full gravity of the situation, the himalayan tasks that lay in front of her, and how few chances history had given her to tackle them. The excitement of independence blurred the vision, and a mood of exultation distracted attention away from the frightening realities.

Even Prime Minister Nehru could not read the signs of the time (any more than he could read the inscrutable writings on the Chinese wall). He talked about the future, but hewed closely to a rigid past; he planned to build a new India, but mechanically relied on the old system; he preached dynamism, and practised a desultory approach. And so the few priceless chances history had vouchsafed India were unwittingly thrown away.

By 1965, only eighteen years after independence, the smouldering crisis gathered to a climax; the nemesis, it seemed, would overtake the nation. For a while a great many people came to believe as if the population-food race would soon be lost for ever. In this moment of spiralling despair came the dwarfs—the seeds of hope that dispelled the gloom and sprouted into a promise of plenty. The miracle wheat and rice have enacted a second miracle—they have given India one more chance to mobilize her forces, to overhaul her strategy, and to launch a concerted attack on the terrifying enemy—the goliath of poverty—until victory is finally won.

This is the message of the dwarfs. Will India heed it? And do so before it is too late? She must, unless she is willing to write off her future as a nation. The next decade—the nineteen-seventies—will for her be the most decisive period in her four-thousand-year old history. In these ten years the issue will, in all probability, be clinched either way.

The signs are hopeful today, more so than at any time since her independence. She has learnt enough costly lessons; she has had an awesome glimpse of the dark abyss, and has shuddered back from its brink. Above all, she has caught the message of the dwarfs, has drawn new hope and inspiration from it, and is now far better equipped, both materially and psychologically, to forge ahead with her tasks.

CHAPTER 6

# Agriculture in National Plans—A Critique

## QUESTION OF PRIORITY

Has India neglected her agriculture? Many Westerners, at least until a few years ago, felt convinced that she had done so. And criticisms were frequently levelled on this ground, particularly against her first three Five-Year Plans.[1] Yet this was always a simplistic view which failed to do justice to the Government's thinking and policies.

Progress in India's agriculture was, for a good many years, undeniably slow. This, however, was due not to any lack of concern on the government's part, nor to any reluctance to allocate sufficient resources. It reflected a genuine inability to understand the complexities of agriculture, its inherent growth potential, and the concrete measures needed to raise its productivity. This deficiency, it should be noted, was by no means confined to the Indian administration. Foreign experts who, from time to time, came to give advice to the government often did no better, while some of them inadvertently helped deflect India's agriculture along unrealistic channels.

After independence the Government of India turned to economic development with a bias not against, but in favour of agriculture. The bias was genuine; it could not be otherwise for some solid reasons. The

[1] For example, *The Wall Street Journal*, while commenting editorially, in its issue of 30 March, 1967, on Pope Paul's encyclical on *Development of Peoples* did not hesitate to pass the obiter dictum that "the Indian government neglected agriculture for fashionable industrialization." This is typical of a widely held view, though it has been toned down as a result of the green revolution.

Congress Party was committed to the philosophy of Gandhi, which had its focus on rural welfare. Political expediency, too, pointed in the same direction since the villager had now acquired the right to vote. And finally, free India was born in the shadow of a food crisis, a crisis that has given the government little respite ever since.

All the Plans gave high priority to agriculture in unequivocal terms. This can be best illustrated with a few extracts from the different Plans.

"For the immediate five-year period, agriculture, including irrigation, and power have topmost priority. Without a substantial increase in the production of food and of raw materials needed for industry, a higher tempo of development in the latter cannot be sustained. The economy has first to be strengthened at the base, and a sizable surplus created in the agricultural sector and mobilised for sustaining increased employment in other sectors." This is how the First Five-Year Plan explained its pattern of priorities.[2]

The Second Five-Year Plan emphasized the principle of balanced development and the "inter-dependence" of agriculture and industry. Accordingly, agricultural programmes were intended to provide "adequate food to support the increased population" and the raw materials needed for a growing industrial economy, in addition to producing "larger exportable surpluses of agricultural commodities."[3]

The Third Plan was, if anything, even more categorical about the role of agriculture. In the scheme of development it envisaged for its five-year span, "the first priority necessarily belongs to agriculture. Experience in the first two Plans, and especially in the Second, has shown that the rate of growth in agricultural production is one of the main limiting factors in the progress of the Indian economy." Agricultural production, it went on to say, had to be increased "to the largest extent feasible," and "adequate resources" had to be provided for realizing the agricultural targets.[4]

A year later the Planning Commission reiterated the same theme in even stronger words: "Agriculture has the highest priority of all India's plans for development, today and over the future... the reasons for a sharp step-up in farm production are urgent and compelling."[5]

That the priority for agriculture was real and not lip-deep should be clear from the actual allocations made for it under the different Plans. In crores of rupees they were:[6]

[2] *The First Five Year Plan—A Summary*, Planning Commission, Government of India, 1952, p. 13.

[3] *Second Five Year Plan*, ibid., 1956, p. 259.

[4] *Third Five Year Plan*, ibid., 1961, p. 49.

[5] *Towards a Self-reliant Economy—India's Third Plan, 1961-66*, Planning Commission, Government of India, 1961, p. 169.

[6] Compiled from official reports. The figures show minor discrepancies owing to adjustments made from time to time in different publications.

| | Agriculture and community development | Irrigation and flood control | Total | Percentage share |
|---|---|---|---|---|
| First Plan | 372 | 365 | 737 | 33.0 |
| Second Plan | 510 | 820 | 1,330 | 29.3 |
| Third Plan | 1,377 | 664 | 2,041 | 23.0 |
| 1966-69 | 1,266 | 457 | 1,723 | 24.0 |
| Fourth Plan | 2,333 | 964 | 3,297 | 22.6 |

True, the Second and the Third Plan laid greater stress on industrial development. This, however, was not done at the expense of agriculture, the provisions for which were steeply raised at the same time. Nor should too much be made of the fact that over the years agriculture had a falling share of the national Plans; for, in absolute terms, they not only remained large, but showed quite a sharp rise from Plan to Plan.

What about implementation? There was a shortfall of a few percentage points for each Plan, and the margin of under-fulfilment was somewhat wider than for other sectors, mainly because of the relatively slow progress with the large river valley projects. Yet judged by the normal standards of performance on government-sponsored development plans, there was nothing unusual about the shortfalls. They are, it seems, both regrettable and unavoidable. One need not, however, exaggerate their effects. For, the fact remains that the declared objective of the government has been to achieve a more balanced growth between agriculture and industry; and that it has consistently pursued this goal according to its own light, as is clearly borne out by the structure of the Plans.

And it is borne out also by the results achieved. The area under irrigation was rapidly extended—from 55.8 to 85 million acres; by 1971, it was expected to reach 111 million acres or about one-third of India's total cultivated land. Between 1950-51 and 1964-65, the total grain production rose from 54 to 88 million tons; the output of jute and cotton was doubled to support the mills; production of sugarcane and sugar, too, was almost doubled to cope with the rising demand; other crops like oilseeds, coffee and tea showed sizable increases.

The progress, measured by an absolute yardstick, was indeed remarkable. In normal times, or even one generation earlier, it would have been hailed as a tremendous, record-breaking achievement. But, alas, the times were not normal because of one overwhelming factor—a record-breaking upsurge in population. It neutralized most of the production gains; and as per capita consumption rose, a deficit yawned. The wolf was never quite out of the economy. Meanwhile, agriculture continued, and still continues to be largely a gamble in monsoon. Even a partial failure, apart from affecting the rainfed crops, could neutralize much of the irrigation gains. And the monsoon failed, dismally, in two consecutive years—in 1965 and 1966. For this cruel turn of events it would be unfair to blame the government or its planners.

## AGRICULTURE VERSUS INDUSTRY DEBATE

No, there has been no *deliberate* neglect of agriculture on India's part. She was much too harassed by an intractable food deficit and the consequent foreign exchange drain to be so myopic. Yet agriculture *was* neglected in the sense that she could have greatly improved her performance even within the short period of two decades, within the existing framework of her so-called traditional agriculture, and with the limited resources she had at her disposal, and she *should* have done so in view of the pervasive crisis that dominated her economic scene ever since independence. India did err; and human though it was, the penalty she was required to pay was heavy, particularly in terms of the valuable time she lost in the process.

But if India has erred, so also have her critics, and sometimes quite conspicuously. It has, for example, been suggested that good weather and better crops in the early fifties played havoc with the Second Five-Year Plan. As the food gap narrowed, so it is suggested, worries diminished, the worst seemed to be over, a kind of euphoria gripped the nation, attention was diverted to industries, and though substantial resources were allocated to agriculture under the Second Plan, its practical problems were not subjected to analysis and debate.

Others have expressed similar views about India's planning in general. The charge quoted earlier—that India had indulged in "fashionable industrialization" to the neglect of her agriculture—became at one time a fashionable refrain with her critics. Yet such views do scant justice to the actual denouement of events, nor to the real needs of a vast country like India.

Even before independence India had been anxious to go ahead with industrial development.[7] In fact, lack of adequate opportunities to promote modern industries had long been a major national grievance. But the years immediately following independence were not propitious to launch an industrial programme. The scars of partition had yet to be healed; the violent civil disturbances which erupted in many places had to be quelled; the millions of refugees pouring in from across the frontiers had to be integrated, and a new national unity had to be forged; the food situation, which sharply deteriorated as a direct result of the partition (see Chapter 9), had to be given urgent attention with large allocations of foreign exchange. In such conditions a broadbased programme of

[7] This should be clear from the various reports prepared, during 1939-42, by the National Planning Committee with Pandit Jawaharlal Nehru as the Chairman.

11

industrial development had to wait for better times. India turned to it just as soon as the pressures seemed to ease.

Was this an irrational policy? The "agriculture-firsters" have been wrong on several counts. They have ignored the large industrial potential of the country, its comparative advantages in many fields, its need for exports, or import substitution, to earn or to conserve foreign exchange, the contribution that industries must make to build up national income and to create employment. Their worst error has been to overlook the fact that a vigorous non-farm sector is an essential concomitant of modern agriculture. Rigid adherence to an agriculture-first philosophy can only spell agricultural stagnation. The two must be synchronized, and rationally integrated.[8]

The sharpest criticism of this school has been reserved for India's steel industry which has been a favourite target of attack. Here again, it has been warranted neither by facts nor by logic. At the time of independence, India had two steel mills with a total capacity of 1.3 million tons a year. Domestic demand far exceeded domestic production, the trend was sharply upward, and steel imports were already consuming a good deal of foreign exchange.

Also from a long-run angle, it was essential to develop the fuel-metal base of the economy, the more so since in this case the comparative advantages were unmistakably in India's favour. In the eastern region alone she has some two billion tons of rich, easy-to-mine iron ores with 50 to 60 per cent iron content. And close by are abundant deposits of coal; though much of it is not of ideal quality, especially because of its high ash content, it can be washed and beneficiated at a fairly low cost.

Steps for a new steel mill would have been most appropriate soon after India became independent. Yet nothing was done for several years to increase steel production; even the First Five-Year Plan, drawn up in 1951, made no provision for it. Why? Because, as mentioned earlier, the emphasis was still largely on agriculture and irrigation, particularly on massive high-dam projects. Some Indians, though relatively few,[9] deplored this as a most unfortunate omission; on any objective criteria, they held, expansion of the steel-producing capacity should have been given a very high priority.

A few years later Mr. George Woods[10] came to India as head of a World Bank Mission and urged immediate steps to increase steel production. To drive the point home, he used a striking equation: for India

---

[8] See Chapter 30 for comments on the complementarity of farm and non-farm sectors.

[9] The writer happened to be one of them.

[10] This was several years before George D. Woods became President of the World Bank. He was still President of the First Boston Corporation when he first came to India as head of the World Bank Mission.

"steel is food," he insisted. Following his recommendation steps were taken to increase the capacity of the two main steel mills by about half a million tons. The World Bank gave a special loan for the purpose.

In 1953, the government negotiated with the Krupp-Demag consortium of West Germany an agreement to set up a new steel factory; the location selected after much debate was Rourkela in Orissa. The Second Plan provided for two more mills in collaboration, respectively, with Soviet Russia and Great Britain; the former was located at Bhilai in Madhya Pradesh, and the latter at Durgapur in West Bengal. The fourth steel mill, which at one time became the subject of a hot political debate between the U.S. and India, is being erected at Bokharo in Bihar with the help of Soviet Russia; progress has been slow, and it is already behindhand by several years. The capacity of the two old mills in the private sector has been further increased in successive stages.

The annual steel production in India currently amounts to about nine million tons of ingots. By the end of the Fourth Plan, or March 1974, the capacity is expected to reach 16 million tons. Given the highly favourable raw material base for the industry, abundance of labour, the experience acquired over the years, the size of the country, its soaring population, and the rising domestic demand, the capacity is still much too modest. What she needs is to expand it further and more rapidly over the coming years.

India did not err in giving priority to the steel industry. Her real error lay somewhere else—in not planning and managing the new steel mills far more competently than she has done so far. The first mill was needlessly delayed by six to seven years; attempts to make belated amends for them led to an undue concentration on heavy industries in the Second Plan; the combination of slow-maturing, capital-intensive steel and high-dam projects (see below) put heavy strain on the economy and fed the forces of inflation.

The location of the steel mills was determined less by economic than by political factors, more particularly by regional pulls and pressures. The so-called "dispersal of industries," then officially advocated as a guiding principle, proved handy for the purpose. The principle was intrinsically sound, though far more for light industries than for steel factories which allow very limited locational flexibility. If, for example, the first, and not the third, steel mill had been located at Durgapur, there would have been a minimum saving of some 200 million dollars in capital costs on related civil works, and of at least 18 months of time in completing the project, with a corresponding benefit to the economy and saving in foreign exchange. The estimated savings alone would have been enough to finance, say, 100 new medium-sized light industries in the country.

By far the most serious weakness of the public-sector steel mills lay in their management, mostly by civil servants not only lacking in technical competence, but inclined, like most civil servants, to run them on bureaucratic lines rather than as cost-conscious business concerns.

The cumulative effect of all these and other factors should not be hard to imagine: continual production troubles, lagging output, high-cost steel, and substantial annual loss. It had been hoped and assumed that India, with her comparative advantages and most up-to-date plants, would produce steel at a competitive price and would build up an export trade to earn foreign exchange, in addition to meeting her rising home demand. These hopes were dashed; with mismanagement her comparative advantages were squandered away.

What has been said above about the steel mills applies, by and large, to public-sector industries in general. The zeal to expand government-owned undertakings has not been matched by a concern to run them well. As a result, they are yielding woefully poor return on the large investments while many of them are piling up sizable losses.

The private sector has suffered from a different brand of mismanagement. There was no attempt to master the sophisticated art of regulating a complex modern economy in the interest of public good. The approach, inspired by nationalistic-cum-socialistic motives, turned out to be maladroit, doctrinaire, often counterproductive. The private sector was allowed monopoly rights where it badly needed competition; it was pampered and sheltered when it should have been thrown open to market forces; and it got off with malpractices which deserved to be severely penalized. At the same time it was "regulated" by bureaucratic fiats to protect public interests when market forces could have done a better job; it was castigated and overtaxed when it needed encouragement and incentive; it was subjected to hidebound rules where initiative and freedom were essential. It was, in fact, not so much regulated as strangulated.

Yet in this confused environment of anomalies India's private sector has built up a record of remarkable achievements. How much more it could have achieved had policies been more enlightened and less dogma-ridden!

All in all, the private sector remains one of the most precious and most hopeful assets of India. Properly utilized, it could, as it still can, give a tremendous boost to her economic growth in all sectors, including agriculture. Its contribution to agriculture could be enormous if industrial planning and policies were deliberately slanted towards that end.

There were solid grounds indeed to criticize India's industrial policy, but they were mostly missed by most of her critics. Those who indulged in a blanket disparagement of her industrialization programme came perilously close to betraying a hidden bias. In any case, they were in error because they ignored the plain fact that industry must grow hand in hand with agriculture to create markets for farm products, to produce and distribute a wide range of manufactured inputs, to provide a great many other industrial props needed to support modern agriculture. The one-sided criticism did not help India; it only served to create resentment and to perpetuate her errors.

## THE TVA ERA

India's planning in general, and for the agricultural sector in particular, was skewed, almost incorrigibly, by massive long-term commitments which had been made in the pre-planning years, mainly in late 1940's. This was what may be called the TVA phase of economic development, to which several factors had given a powerful impetus. The saga of the TVA, which had spread far and wide, touched the shores of India during the war and immediately kindled great enthusiasm. This was all but natural since TVA seemed to provide the key to the solution of the two problems which loomed largest in a monsoon-ridden country like India: flood control and irrigation. And it also showed how with these could be combined not only power generation and navigation, but quite a few other ancillary benefits.

The TVA idea received its first big impulse in 1943 when West Bengal was hit by a triple disaster: the war which, at one point, touched Calcutta; the Damodar flood which disrupted major arteries of rail and road communications, and isolated Calcutta for several critical months; a famine, one of the worst in India's history, which took an estimated toll of three million lives. In this emergency situation it was decided to apply the TVA-type of multipurpose treatment to the Damodar river system, long notorious for its monsoon turbulence and the destructive floods it periodically inflicted on the low-lying areas.

The services of some TVA engineers were hired, by the then British Government of India, to investigate the problems and to prepare the preliminary blueprints. By 1945, there emerged a fascinating eight-dam multipurpose project for flood control, irrigation, power generation, and navigation. The cost, after the first revision, was estimated at about $200 million; the payoff was high because of its location in an exceptionally resource-rich region with 1,040,000 acres of fertile irrigable land, large deposits of coal, iron ores and other minerals, a ready market for power, proximity to the port of Calcutta, and its large urban market. The dams were medium-sized, and so the waiting period between investments and realization of the benefits was kept relatively short. The Damodar Valley Corporation or DVC, for years known as "India's TVA," was officially launched on 8 June 1948.[11]

[11] As a Government of India employee, the writer was required, during 1946-47, to help secure an agreement among Bengal, Bihar, and the Centre, the three parties involved in the project, and later, from 1948 through June 1954, to serve the DVC as its chief executive officer.

While the DVC was still on the anvil, some Indian engineers got busy to forge their own TVA's. And some of them proved adept not only in irrigation, but also in political engineering. Nor did they have too much difficulty in obtaining the needed blessings from the highest quarters.

One example will illustrate the point. During this TVA phase of India's economic development, a well-known Indian engineer used to proclaim off and on that he was going to build the highest dam in the world, suggesting implicitly a new yardstick for measuring national greatness—the height of a dam and the millions of cubic yards of concrete poured. Yet such flamboyance used to flatter many egos and invited surprisingly few frowns. That many engineers, in India as in other countries, would, if left to themselves, like to build monuments to themselves regardless of the time and cost involved is a commonplace of history. But India had yet to discover this.

Thus, at the dawn of her independence India relied, wistfully, on her highdam-builders. State after state clamoured for its own multipurpose project; even the top political leaders, understandably enough, joined in the chorus and followed the lead of their technical experts. This kind of development is by no means an exclusively Indian phenomenon, but it was a luxury India could least afford.

The commitments made were heavy, and once made, they ran into many years—from a minimum of four or five to ten or more. In fact, one of the primary motives for launching on five-year planning was to introduce, though belatedly, some "family planning" in this field and to put a brake on the commitments which were piling up on account of long-term, high-cost, high-dam projects. The First Plan mainly bunched together those which were already under construction and put a virtual ban on new ones. It was more significant for what it kept out than for what it brought in.

This fact was admitted, though in oblique official idioms, in the Plan document. In the First Five-Year period, it observed, "the development of irrigation, power and transport will take up the bulk of the resources available to the public sector"; progress in the industrial field would therefore depend "to a great extent on the effort in the private sector."[12] This was the real genesis of the First Plan. Its underlying principles were discovered *ex post facto*, presented in well-articulated terms, and were duly solemnified.

The table on the opposite page will show at a glance the investment made in major and medium irrigation projects under the different Plans.

By 31 March 1971, India had taken up 557 irrigation projects under the first three Five-Year and the three subsequent Annual Plans. Of these, 73 were classified as major and the balance of 484 as medium projects; and 345 of the total had been actually completed by that date. In addition.

[12] *The First Five Year Plan—A Summary*, p. 13.

OUTLAYS ON MAJOR AND MEDIUM IRRIGATION PROJECTS

*(In Crores of Rupees)*

| Plans | Total for Plan[13] | Total for Irrigation |
|---|---|---|
| First Plan | 1,960 | 300 |
| Second Plan | 4,600 | 380 |
| Third Plan | 8,577 | 580 |
| Annual Plans : | | |
| 1966-69 | 6,757 | 414 |
| Fourth Plan | 14,398 | 857 |

about Rs. 600 crores were spent on *minor* irrigation projects under the first three Five-Year Plans; thereafter outlays on them were substantially stepped up (see Chapter 16).

Included in the 73 major irrigation projects are parts of the giant multi-purpose projects, such as the DVC, Bakhra-Nangal, Hirakud, Kosi and Nagarjunasagar. To complete the picture it should be remembered that large sums of money had been invested in some of them during 1945-51, which are not included in the various Plan figures.

These large projects in any case would have entailed long periods of gestation. The periods were further lengthened because of the adherence to the traditional method of slow departmental, or force account, construction. Delayed completion meant higher project costs as overheads were piled up; and it also meant a longer waiting period with a corresponding loss of benefits.

There were other deficiencies which were overlooked in the excitement of highdam construction. Ancillary works like village channels were not constructed in time. As a result, a large part of the irrigation potential, even after it had been created at high cost, remained idle for several more seasons. Actual utilization has consistently lagged behind by a needlessly wide margin because of this faulty coordination.

A grave weakness of India's irrigation works, both old and new, is that they are designed only for unregulated flow irrigation through the command area. The river valley projects, unlike the older works, provided for large reservoirs behind high dams, and tens of crores of rupees were spent to impound millions of acre-feet of water; yet they ignored the vital need to control and regulate the irrigation water where it mattered most—at the field level.[14]

Coupled with this there was another strange omission, by both British and Indian engineers, namely, of drainage, even though it is as vital for agriculture as irrigation, and must go hand in hand with it. The penalty

[13] Excludes private-sector outlays.
[14] See Chapter 16 for further comments.

for this disregard is writ large over many areas—in terms of excessive salinity and other soil afflictions.

The general practice is not to line the irrigation canals, though Punjab is a notable exception. Their banks tend to crumble, especially in the wet season; they are often choked with weeds, as is the case with the DVC and the Chambal projects; the evaporation rate in the dry-weather period is too high; and their maintenance costs are pushed up, though, as a rule, they are not maintained properly and the costs are "saved."

Finally, no effort was made, until the early sixties and the initiation of the IADP (see Chapters 11-14), to develop intensive agriculture with modern inputs in the areas irrigated from the river valley projects.

The result was not only long delays in reaping the benefits from the projects and exceedingly low return from the heavy outlays, but also a tragic waste in terms of resource-use.

## TRAVESTY OF TVA

It was the TVA concept—of extracting maximum wealth out of the natural resources through an integrated approach—which had triggered the explosion of river valley projects in India. Yet they ended in what is a travesty of the TVA idea.

This was highlighted by another unforgettable event—the dismemberment of the DVC. This is not the place to tell the exciting story of this great experiment packed with revealing episodes—how it began as a pacesetter in post-independence India and, backed by three World Bank loans, established a remarkable record of achievements on many fronts; how, before long, it was involved in a long series of wearisome battles to defend its autonomy embodied in a charter unanimously passed by India's democratic Parliament, in order to pursue the cause for which it had been established with tremendous enthusiasm; how Central and State ministers, innocent of the fundamentals of the corporate device and of the essentials of resource development, increasingly frowned upon the very idea of an autonomous body and made steady inroads upon it despite the clear-cut provisions of the law; how engineers, inspired by an all-too-familiar professional rivalry, ceaselessly manoeuvred to grab the project and to bring it securely under their own control; how senior civil servants, more concerned with their own future than with the fate of the project, retreated along the line of least resistance into the alibi-ridden stronghold of divided responsibilities; and how, under the impact of these converging forces, the integrated multipurpose project began to disintegrate until, by the mid-sixties, it was converted almost completely into a single-purpose project for power generation. The effects of this amazing short-sightedness were far-reaching. They are worth noting, at least briefly, because of the indelible mark they have left on India's recent history.

A senseless fiat from the Centre divested the DVC of the responsibility for headwaters control, soil conservation, and reforestation in the Upper Valley and transferred it to the State Government of Bihar, although this ran directly counter both to the letter and the spirit of the DVC Act. It virtually brought to a halt the excellent progress the DVC was making in carrying out these key functions. The result is not only continued neglect of land in the Upper Valley, which has long been badly eroded and gullied, but also accelerated erosion which, year after year, dumps heavy loads of silt into the reservoirs down below, thereby drastically cutting into their useful life.

This shocking lack of resource-sense still characterizes India's river valley projects. She has yet to show a much deeper realization, not simply in official literature but in actual action, of the great urgency to conserve the life-giving fluid on the sloping land, to promote conservation farming, to rebuild forests, to minimize erosion, to protect and lengthen the life of the reservoirs, and to put them more fully to productive use for fisheries and recreation.

Some time ago, on a visit to Durgapur, the site of a new industrial complex including a steel mill, a gas plant, a chemical factory, two power stations, and a bunch of other factories which have mushroomed there, the writer, to his horror, found that the main river Damodar, above the DVC-built irrigation barrage, was for a long stretch covered with a dense carpet of water hyacinth. There could hardly be a more eloquent testimony to the mismanagement of public-sector enterprises.

A primary responsibility of the DVC under its charter was to develop the agricultural potential of the Lower Valley. And as noted earlier, over one million acres of fertile alluvial soil was to be serviced with irrigation. The whole area was ideally suited for perennial cropping, once water supply was assured.

Yet within a few years the question of jurisdiction was reopened; an unholy wrangle started as to who should be responsible for this function; the sterile debate lasted for years; and in the end it was decided to transfer it to the State Government of West Bengal, though its record in agricultural development, both before and after independence, had been one of the least inspiring in the country.

It is sad to reflect what might have happened. If its unique potential were properly developed, the Lower Valley would have become a granary for feeding the entire region, including the sprawling city of Calcutta plagued by chronic food shortages. It would certainly have reduced India's food deficits of the fifties and the sixties by one million tons of grain, or more, a year with a corresponding saving of foreign exchange.

12

And it could have averted the tragic famine that raged, in 1967, in the adjoining districts of Bihar.

Finally, the turmoil in Calcutta and in West Bengal, which is increasingly attracting world-wide attention, might have been prevented, and their history differently written, but for the mutilation of the DVC. The fate of the two was interlocked, though very few realized it then and do so even today.

Had the DVC project been executed as originally planned, the Lower Valley would have developed a prosperous agriculture and provided a base for a host of new industries. Like a powerful magnet, it would have attracted masses of people away from the already overcrowded city of Calcutta. This was the only way the city could have been saved from the crushing pressure of population, with the assurance of maintaining a reasonable level of amenities for civilized living. This golden chance was thoughtlessly thrown away.

The magnet has been working powerfully, but in the wrong direction. The large hinterland of Calcutta remained virtually undeveloped, barring Durgapur; millions of refugees poured into the city after the partition of Bengal; others streamed in from rural areas not only from within West Bengal but also from the upcountry States of Bihar, Uttar Pradesh and beyond, in search of work which frequently did not exist; and there was, of course, the natural increase of population within the city. Since independence the population of Calcutta metropolitan area has almost trebled; its utilities, old to start with and overworked during the war, were totally inadequate to cope with this staggering burden; transportation was battered, services decayed, and most of the city increasingly put on the appearance of a vast slum.

The State Government has long been tinkering with the problems of Calcutta, while town-planners, Indian and foreign, have been engaged in preparing ambitious blueprints for urban renewal. Yet this is doomed to remain a futile exercise. The problems can never be solved as long as so many millions remain bottled up within the city precincts. Its renewal cannot be generated from within; it can come only from outside, with a rapid development of its neglected hinterland, the potentially rich rural slums, which alone can halt the present influx and turn it into a massive outmigration. This presupposes precisely the type of regional development which was envisioned in the DVC a quarter of a century ago.

The din of controversy has died down. The facts now stand out with unmistakable clarity. The establishment of the Damodar Valley Corporation was an act of rare foresight and statesmanship; its subsequent mutilation remains an act of monumental folly.

It has been argued that, in India's economic planning, there has been no deliberate neglect of agriculture. Yet West Bengal, one can say with very good reason, is an exception. Here agriculture has suffered from gross neglect which cannot be dismissed as accidental. One of the most urgent needs of the state was land reform; the government enacted a law, but made a mockery of it in practice.[15] It allowed jurisdictional issues to get the upper hand of developing the rare food potential of the Damodar Valley; instead of urging and encouraging the DVC to speed up progress, it began to compete with it. It proceeded to set up power stations within the DVC area on its own account, in violation of the DVC Act and with tacit disapproval of the Centre, when the same money and effort could have been devoted to more pressing and much more rewarding tasks. Even the industrial complex it has built at Durgapur with large investments of capital would have made much greater sense within the framework of a comprehensive programme of regional development with the initial emphasis sharply laid on two sectors: promotion of intensive agriculture along modern lines, and building up a more adequate and more up-to-date transportation and communication system to open up the countryside.

The greatest tragedy of West Bengal is that it has for years been saddled with large food deficits, although with its extraordinary natural endowments it could easily be a major food-surplus state as well as an important source of jute and other industrial raw materials. This, by itself, testifies to the chronic neglect its agriculture has suffered from, which in turn has been the most important single factor for turning it into a problem state.

The crisis which is now brewing here, and which constantly threatens to spill over into several other states, can still be overcome, an era of prosperity can still be ushered in, provided however eyes are, at long last, turned in the right direction, and the disastrous omissions of the past are speedily made good.


## A RECIPE FOR SLOW GROWTH

India's planning was far from perfect; indeed, it bore distinct imprints of far-reaching compromises, much of which is inevitable in a democracy. Nevertheless, it did accord high-priority treatment to agriculture, and it did back it up with substantial allocations. The "agriculture-firsters," to borrow a handy label from John Lewis, did not, at least *prima facie*, fare too badly.

It was not the inadequacy of allocations which was the real villain, but the *quality* of agricultural planning, which was never of a high order. This must be attributed very largely to the fact that planning in this sector was dominated by the "irrigation-firsters," who in turn were dominated by the "highdam-firsters." In fact, what passed for planning was,

[15] Discussed in *Reaping the Green Revolution*, Chapter 11.

as seen earlier, mainly a fortuitous mix of projects, most of which were already under way.

There is little doubt that India's agricultural economy, and therefore the country as a whole, would have been incomparably better off if the number of high-cost river-valley projects had been initially kept down to one or two, and the funds so released were devoted to a great many more small and quick-maturing irrigation projects. There was not only vast scope, but also great need for such projects, although they began to attract anything like adequate attention only in the final phase of the Third Five-Year Plan. And if this type of planning were accompanied by other essential inputs, it would have given the most attractive capital-output ratio with a very low foreign-exchange cost. As it happened, India virtually settled for what could give her only the lowest output for very high capital input—with high dams, large investments, slow completion, slipshod irrigation, and indifference to inputs.

The causes of India's economic woes are not hard to determine. In a large measure they are due to historical and demographic factors. But they have also been compounded by her own follies. Her veteran engineers have run away with the river valley projects; her senior civil servants have run away with the public-sector undertakings; and, meanwhile, her politicians, aided and abetted by the bureaucracy, have shackled the private sector. All this would in any case have added up to an excellent recipe for a snailpaced economic growth.

And as if to reinsure this, her rural planning has been inspired by high ideals which, like her high dams, were mostly premature. They were noble but impractical, and more elevating for the soul than for the economy.

# CHAPTER 7

# Low Yield from
# High Ideals

## I. GANDHIAN ECONOMICS

### A UNIQUE PARADOX

Few subjects have been so charged with emotions, and so packed with fallacies, as rural development. And ironically enough, the most prolific source of both in India has been her greatest national leader. As Mahatma Gandhi[1] created, inspired, and guided a country-wide movement for political freedom based on his twofold principles of truth and nonviolence, he also extended his "applied religion" to rural India to lift it from its misery and degradation, defined the goals it should aim at, and laid down an action programme it should follow to realize them. And all along he preached and pursued them with a relentless tenacity and a burning concern for people's welfare which were at once the foundation and the measure of his greatness. But the goals he laid down and the programme he prescribed were diametrically opposite to what rural India desperately needed for its modernization. They added up to a passionate advocacy of the past and a resounding negation of science and technology without which it could never be regenerated.

---

[1] Mohandas Karamchand Gandhi, it may be added specially for the benefit of non-Indians, was called *Mahatma*, literally The Great-souled, by the people. Gandhi protested, but the title stuck. More commonly, he is referred to as Gandhiji—the north Indian suffix *ji* indicates both respect and endearment.

## A BLINDING VISION

Take, for example, the most important asset of rural India—land. For almost three decades Gandhiji pleaded that in India it could, in general, provide employment for three to six months, that the cultivator needed alternative employment for his idle time, that the only practicable alternative was hand-spinning and hand-weaving. And all through those years he travelled all over India with his *charkha*, or spinning-wheel, which had become almost a bible to him—an extension of his soul, preached the gospel of spinning and day after day, without fail, he did his own spinning—in the privacy of his cottage, in public gatherings, even in trains when on travel. Spinning, like prayer, became a part of his daily ritual.

Perhaps never in history have so much altruism and energy been expended to achieve so little, such nobility of soul has been matched by such futility of purpose, saintliness has been a substitute for science on such a scale. The greatness of Gandhiji was directed not *towards* building up agriculture but *away* from it, not to rescue it from the deplorable neglect it had suffered from, but taking the neglect for granted, to look for palliatives elsewhere.

What Gandhiji failed to see was that the cultivator was under-employed because his land was under-utilized, that he was impoverished because his land was starved of production-ingredients, that the only rational course, also the most rewarding one, was for him to move, by the shortest possible route, to better farming. Instead, he put up the passionate plea that low-payoff farming should be supplemented, on a nation-wide scale, with a lower-payoff hand-spinning.

The blind eye Gandhiji turned to agriculture had a pervasive effect. It coloured the attitude of the national leaders, influenced the policies of the Congress Party and, after independence, of the national government, and directly contributed to a gross undervaluation of the role of agriculture in economic development.

How different things would have been if Gandhiji had the vision to realize that what India, with its large population (in 1919 when he launched the national movement, the total for undivided India was already 320 million), needed most was the Japanese type of agriculture—with small holdings, mostly under peasant proprietorship, and highly intensive.[2] He as well as other Indian leaders might very well have arrived at this conclusion had they been sufficiently in touch with the outside world. This, however, was not the case. Perhaps the worst feature of the colonial rule in India was that she had been completely cut off from the rest of the world—from continental Europe, from America, from

[2] The writer felt convinced, in the 1930's, that Japan provided an almost perfect model for India. This was later emphasized in his study on *Land and Its Problems*, published in 1943 by Visvabharati Economic Research, Santiniketan, (West) Bengal.

Japan and China. All communications ran to and from England; most ideas and values, particularly in the economic field, flowed from there; and they were mechanically applied to India, by Britishers and Indians, though quite often they had little or no relevance to Indian conditions.

## THE CULT OF KHADI

The classic misdirection was not confined to agriculture, but was extended to rural industries as well, with results that were no less damaging. With Gandhiji the last word in industries was hand-spinning and hand-weaving. Till the last day of his life he sang the glory of *khadi*[3] which, to him, was not only a thing of beauty and a joy forever, but also a source of spiritual uplift. And he nonviolently imposed it on the whole nation.

In a speech delivered around 1926 in Chittagong, now in East Pakistan,[4] Gandhiji pleaded for khadi in a public gathering in words which are well worth quoting: "You say khadi is coarse, khadi is expensive. If it is coarse, remember the slavery of India is coarser than the coarsest khadi. If it is expensive, tear into two, and it will no longer remain so."[5]

The plea, one must admit, made a lot of political sense. Cotton textiles were the largest single item of import from Britain, on which India expended vast sums of money every year. Khadi was the most important part of the movement to boycott British goods, which was conceived as the most effective means of putting economic pressure on Britain. But with Gandhiji the distinction between ends and means was always thin, if not non-existent. He employed the means he chose with an all-consuming passion, and so the ends he envisaged tended to get lost in its blaze. While in the eyes of his countrymen khadi made political sense in the fight for freedom, he invested it with economic, and after some time even with spiritual, sense as well. Thus, khadi became a goal in itself, the ideal industry for rural India, and soon it grew into a cult.

In the early thirties he broadened his industrial programme, mainly under pressure from some of his closest followers, and so to hand-spinning and hand-weaving he added a few others, such as paddy-husking, oil-pressing, hand-made paper, and pottery. But in all these cases he extolled manual labour and primitive tools, and rejected the use of modern equipment and power, not to speak of factory industry. He glorified pure manual labour uncontaminated by modern machinery. It became, in his case, almost a kind of spiritual penchant.

---

[3] That is, handwoven cloth made out of handspun yarn; also called *khaddar*.
[4] In "Bangladesh" since December, 1971.
[5] Quoted from memory.

## CHARKA VERSUS MACHINE

Soon there arose a vigorous controversy between the advocates of the spinning wheel and those who voted for modern industries, between the *charkhaites* and the *machinites*. The writer recalls the experience he had in 1939 at the meeting of the National Planning Committee headed by Pandit Jawaharlal Nehru as Chairman. The discussions bogged down in dreary rounds of debate on the relative merits of Gandhian philosophy and modern industrialization, on *charka* versus machinery. Each school tirelessly reiterated its point of view and held its own ground with equal fervour. Ideals were pitted against ideals; the clash, as usual, generated a good deal of heat, but showed no sign of producing any light to penetrate the dense ideological confusion.

Or, to change the metaphor, the debates proceeded along two parallel lines which promised to extend into eternity without showing the slightest inclination that they would ever meet at any point.

The experience was discomforting to the writer who had freshly returned to India after a long stay in Europe.[6] It impelled him to examine this tough dilemma which had so clearly become a roadblock not only to economic progress, but even to rational thinking. The attempt to clarify the fundamentals resulted in an essay-type study which was published in 1941.[7]

The central thesis of the study is worth noting since time has not detracted from its relevance. The fundamental task in rural India was to achieve greater production, higher incomes, and more employment for more people. The thrust of India's industrial development, owing to historical forces, had hitherto been not towards "wealth-producing" and "job-creating," but towards "wealth-redistributing" and "work-robbing" industries, such as rice mills, oil mills, textile mills, tanneries and shoe factories. The economy was hardly enriched by such industries, considerable sums of money were spent on imported machinery, and large numbers of people were thrown out of employment. To that extent Gandhiji and the anti-machine school had both facts and logic on their side. Joblessness had been mounting in the villages. No rational policy could blink at such an elementary fact.

But outright rejection of machinery, it was argued, would be an equally tragic error. The population was already vast, tens of millions were living at or below the subsistence level, millions were jobless and incomeless. The only way to rescue them from poverty was to work towards a careful mix of labour and machinery to increase production as

[6] He had spent over ten years (1928-39) in continuous study and work, mainly in England, Germany and Italy.

[7] *Conflict of Economic Ideologies in India—An Attempt at Reconciliation*, Visvabharati Economic Research, Santiniketan, (West) Bengal, 1941.

well as new jobs. Such a policy would not militate against Gandhiji's primary objective of promoting rural welfare. It was, indeed, the only way to realize it.

India's iron and steel industry, for example, had created both wealth and jobs, and had supported a host of subsidiary industries. Its job-creating potential could be greatly increased if the processing work were decentralized and, as far as possible, carried out in a large number of small workshops equipped with relatively simple and low-cost tools and equipment.

A modern, well-equipped tannery would be warranted on several grounds. It could assemble and treat hides and skins in quantity, much of which was either exported as low-priced raw materials, or was simply wasted. It could produce leather of far better quality than a village tanner by his primitive methods. And it would salvage not only raw materials, but also human beings—the *chamars* or tanners and the *muchis* or the cobblers who belonged to the lowest of the low castes because of the filthy occupation they were engaged in, and were treated as untouchables. A modern tannery, by taking over the dirty work, would directly help Gandhiji's fight against untouchability.

But once better grade leather was produced, the processing business—for making shoes and other leather goods—could and should be decentralized and carried out in small inexpensively-equipped, and usually family-type, workshops. Such a policy would give the best combination of production, quality of goods, and the number of economically sustainable jobs.

A modern bonemeal factory would be highly desirable to process a valuable raw material which was either wasted or exported at a nominal price, and to produce locally a valuable soil nutrient to build up soil fertility.

It is not necessary here to multiply these examples. However, a brief comment should be in order about cotton textiles, the classic handicraft of India and the main plank in Gandhiji's economic programme.

Some intensive studies carried out by the writer during 1939-40 in rural areas and urban markets led him to three main conclusions. First, hand-spinning was not an economically viable industry—hours of intensive work at the spinning-wheel would give an output worth only a few annas or cents. Its opportunity cost was hopelessly high. Second, hand-weaving was far more remunerative and produced enough income to support a weaver family on a modest level. The income would be sub-stantially higher but for the high cost of millspun yarn, the high margin of middlemen's profits for marketing the finished goods, and the high interest paid on loans advanced by moneylenders.

And third, the economics of the handloom industry could be greatly strengthened if steps were taken to supply low-cost yarn, to organize

13

marketing in order to eliminate the middleman, to provide credit at lower interest, to introduce improved *power-driven* looms, and to supply better, consumer-oriented designs and patterns from, say, a central design school.

Such measures, it was clear, could be taken only by the government. The proposals the writer worked out included the establishment of a government-owned spinning mill which would supply yarn, both dyed and undyed, to weavers at cost, and a design school since good designs would fetch a high price premium and would also help create an export demand.[8]

A weaving industry, organized and supported on these lines, could not only hold its own, but could throw the organized mills on the defensive because of its lower wage-cost, lower overheads, flexibility of operations including design changes. It could provide decent employment to millions of people in rural and semi-rural surroundings, and could thereby help alleviate senseless urban concentrations.

The plea made in the reconciliation study was not to reject machinery which would be fatal, nor to introduce it blindly which, too, was bound to produce tragic consequences, but to adopt it with great discrimination and after a case-by-case analysis, always with one primary objective in view—to hit the optimum combination of output, incomes, and jobs. In a great many instances this could be best achieved when a modern factory was established as a kind of mother industry to support a large number of small but efficient workshop-type industrial units for fabrication or manufacture of either parts or finished goods. This had long been the pattern of industrial development in Japan[9] where the assembly line frequently ran through countless workshops in semi-rural setting. Here again, the writer felt India would be wise to take her cue not from the Western countries, but from Japan.

The "reconciliation study" was published in 1941. By then the leaders of the national movement had been put into jail. A copy was all the same sent to Pandit Jawaharlal Nehru. In a letter written from District Jail, Dehra Dun on November 24, 1941, Mr. Nehru said *inter alia*:

> I want to congratulate you on your essay on the "Conflict of Economic Ideologies in India." I think it is a concise and very able present-

[8] The proposals were publicly made by the writer at a meeting held in Calcutta in 1940. It was presided over by late Dr. B. C. Roy who was Chief Minister of West Bengal from 1950 until his death in 1962. The proposals were warmly commended by Dr. Roy, but nothing came out of them.

[9] In recent years, with the burgeoning industrial progress in Japan, greater sophistication and bigger establishments, the old pattern has been changing. Nevertheless, Japan still remains a striking example of decentralized industrial operations. She has achieved conspicuous success in bringing industries to rural areas rather than shifting rural people continuously to expanding industrial centres, and has thus achieved a healthier rural-urban balance.

ment of the case and, for my part, I agree with the approach and the general conclusions. I can understand, although I may not wholly agree with, the special emphasis that each group puts on its own viewpoint. But what distresses me is the way in which it refused to consider calmly and dispassionately the other's viewpoint. How we become slaves of our own words and slogans!

He was sorry, he added, that the National Planning Committee was "in cold storage." He wanted it to continue to function in spite of his absence but "the others" were not agreeable to this.

The controversy was not resolved. Even after all these years there has been no real reconciliation between the two schools. In actual practice the machinites have carried the day with the backing of the government, and hundreds of modern factories—from steel mills, machine tools, ship-building, aircraft, automobiles and trucks to all kinds of consumer goods and processing industries—have sprung up in the country. At the same time the economic philosophy of Gandhiji has been accommodated to a considerable extent, and a number of uneconomic cottage industries have been kept alive with substantial government subsidies, even though the ranks of devout Gandhians have been decimated by time. In general, it is the politics of his economics which has prevailed. The most extravagant expression of this politics is the levy imposed on power-looms which, with effective organization, could compete with, even undercut, the tex-tile mills, to support hand-looms which have much less viability and are a drag on the economy.[10]

Thus, the problem persists. The biggest single task before India has been how to optimize production *and* employment, and, with that object in view, how to work out the right combination of men *and* machine. But because the problem has been wrongly posed—as men *or* machine—it has hitherto evaded a rational solution. As a result, there is, in a great many cases, either too much of machinery or too little of it, with adverse effects on both production and employment.

Today the same problem looms in another vital area and is pressing for an imaginative policy. As the green revolution spreads, the question of farm mechanization gains in urgency. Blind advocacy of mechaniza-tion or blind opposition to it is bound to produce disastrous results (see Chapter 20).

## OTHER ECONOMIC OBITER DICTA

Gandhiji had definite views on a number of other economic issues. They

---

[10] It is odd to reflect that the Congress Party which had fought so hard for the removal of the cotton excise duty because it penalized the Indian mills for the benefit of Manchester, now tolerates this invidious tax on power looms which can

are worth noting because of the influence they have exercised in shaping development policies.

1. *Population.* Gandhiji was uncompromisingly against birth control, except through abstinence. Any other method was, in his view, immoral and totally incompatible with the tenets of nonviolence. His position was, if anything, somewhat more rigid than that of the orthodox catholic church.

India's population was growing at an annual rate of some four million a year in the 1940's. This is what was assumed at that time. Would Gandhiji have changed his mind had he been faced with today's more explosive growth? It is safe to assume 'no', though he might, and probably would, have pleaded for abstinence more strongly than before. The fact is that in his *Weltanschauung* population was not, indeed it could not be, a really serious problem. A human being is born not only with a mouth, but also with two hands. A plot of land to grow food and a spinning-wheel to produce some cloth were all that he needed, in a climate like India's, to live the kind of life Gandhiji had in mind.

Would the people embrace the philosophy of such pristine simplicity in sufficient numbers? Could they really afford to do so when the very fact of living together as a nation created so many other indispensable needs—for health, education and communication, to mention only the most obvious? Gandhiji never worried about such questions. He donned his spiritual blinkers, walked along the path he had chalked out for himself, and tirelessly preached his own views.

Within a few years after independence India adopted a family planning programme. The initial allocations were small; progress in the first decade was almost negligible. Those who criticize India on this account will do well to remember that she was the first among the developing countries to accept family planning as a national policy, that such realism in Gandhi's India called for real courage, that it took time for the government and the people to be psychologically attuned to such a radical change in traditional values, that in the fifties the gravity of the problem was universally underestimated. The ground India has covered in this field is commendable. That it is still far from adequate is another matter.[11]

2. *The Cow.* Gandhiji shared the old Indian attitude to the cow, the "holy" animal—this "holiness," in its origin, was nothing but an extension of the pervading Indian view that *all* life is sacred, mingled with a feeling of special gratitude for an animal that contributed so much to

only benefit textile mills in Bombay, Ahmedabad and other places at the expense of many enterprising weavers.

[11] The subject has been discussed at length in *Reaping the Green Revolution*, Chapter 15: Lagging Progress in Family Planning.

sustain human life. Gandhiji was shocked to find how often Hindus, while professing to worship the cow, starved and ill-treated and mercilessly exploited her. Once again, as defender of the oppressed, he registered his protest. He gave up using cow's milk in any form, and drank goat's milk instead for the rest of his life.

This act of "noncooperation" did not help the cause of animal husbandry. That man, cattle and land formed an economic nexus with relations of interdependence did not concern him, nor did the problem of surplus cattle population which weighs heavily on India's limited resources. Many Indians were content to draw two superficial conclusions from this act of protest: Gandhiji had fads about food, so he drank goat's milk; and he shared the orthodox Hindu sensitivity towards the cow, and was therefore so keen on cow protection.[12]

3. *Diet.* As regards fads about food, for years Gandhiji's meals consisted of a glass of goat's milk and about a dozen dates. This was perhaps the most original, also the most meagre, menu ever adopted by a national leader. It reflected Gandhiji's supreme unconcern about both calories and the science of nutrition.

The main beneficiary of this self-prescribed dietetics was—the goat. It basked in the vicarious glory of nonviolence and came to enjoy a more elevated status than was justified by its economic value. The goat is a poor converter of protein, a poor producer of milk, and the worst enemy of afforestation. In India, as in so many other countries, goat-induced erosion is a common phenomenon.

4. *Medicine.* Gandhiji did not believe in modern medicine, and, barring very few exceptions, stayed away from it. He advocated and personally relied upon "nature cure," occasionally supplemented by the old indigenous system of medicine. It was futile to expect that he would personally see any urgency in developing an up-to-date national health service in India.

5. *Prohibition.* A major plank in his programme of social reform was prohibition. One of his main objectives was to protect the health and the meagre incomes of the depressed class of people who were often addicted to indigenous liquors made in villages, mainly out of palmyra juice or rice, under unhygienic conditions.

After independence, prohibition continued as a national policy, and almost all state governments enacted legislations to carry it out. But the law was honoured mainly in its breaches, even health permits officially issued on medical grounds became a major loophole, bootlegging and blackmarketing flourished, illicit and unhygienic liquor-making became

[12] India's cattle problem has been examined in *Reaping*, etc., Chapter 3: The Holy Cow Enters the Scientific Age.

a prosperous cottage industry. The country lost an estimated total of Rs. 200 crores (or $400 million at pre-devaluation rate) in revenue, and spent perhaps another Rs. 50 crores (or $100 million) for the administration of prohibition laws.

The policy was reversed a few years ago when a severe financial stringency forced the government to end this costly exercise in futility. State after state ceased to be dry. A liquor industry, on factory scale, is now growing in the country. Grape cultivation was recently introduced as a new crop in areas which few had suspected would be suitable for it. It has already struck firm root, vineyards are spreading surprisingly fast, and a beginning has been made, especially in Hyderabad region, to turn the surplus grapes into wine. With this the prohibition movement has, one may say, died its official death.

6. *Education.* Boycott of all educational institutions—schools, colleges, universities—was an important part of Gandhiji's noncooperation movement. Countless students responded to his call all over the country, including the cream of the academic community; in fact, talented students were often the most willing to respond. Even after the movement subsided, many of them never returned to academic life—noncooperation remained very much in the air. Instead, they withered in a political wilderness with their idealism.

Gandhiji was not kindly disposed to the type of Western education Indians were receiving. The system certainly needed reform as many thoughtful people agreed. But the spirit of rejection overshadowed the need for reform, and the net result was not better, but less education.[13]

7. *Class Struggle.* Progress, Gandhiji always insisted, must be achieved through peaceful and nonviolent means—whether the goal was political freedom or economic development or social reform. As the Congress Party moved more and more towards radical programmes and policies, he warned it about the risks of violence. Asked about his views on class struggle which some believed to be "inevitable," Gandhiji explained his stand as follows:[14]

Class struggle there had been always. It could be ended if the capitalists voluntarily renounce their role and become all labourers. The other was to realize that labour was real capital, in fact, the maker of capital. What the two hands of the labourer would achieve, the capitalist would never get with his gold and silver. Could any one live on gold! But labour had to be made conscious of its strength. It had to

[13] For more detailed comments on the poor quality of education in India, see Chapter 22 of this study.

[14] While addressing 500 workers in Midnapore district, (West) Bengal, on 2 January 1946, and recorded by his associate and secretary, Shri Pyarelal.

have in one hand truth and in the other nonviolence, and it would be invincible.

The pronouncement was wholly consistent with Gandhiji's philosophy, and wholly inadequate as a practical guideline for national policy to bring about genuine reconciliation between capital and labour. It was noble and poetic, but also unreal and futile.

8. *Land Reform.* Property, in Gandhiji's eyes, was a public trust; therefore, it had to be used for public good. The principle ignored the fact that, within limits, private property too has its *raison d'être*. In any case, it left unanswered the practical question as to how to persuade the property-owners to serve the public good in practice. The only definite guideline he laid down, here as elsewhere, was that the change must be accomplished nonviolently.

For a great many people it was but a short step from nonviolence to passive preservation of a status quo even with glaring injustices. After independence, the principle of nonviolence, quite understandably, acquired an added appeal when the leaders discovered that the vested interests were the best vote-getters. This explains, among other things, why true land reform, despite voluminous legislation, has hitherto proved so elusive.[15]

9. *Back to the Village.* India has been rent with this cry ever since Gandhiji launched his noncooperation movement. It has been a cry in the wilderness. The flow of people, all these years, has been persistently in the reverse direction—from the villages to the urban centres; and in more recent years, with the population upsurge, it has swelled into tidal proportions.

Once again, Gandhiji thought through his heart and viewed the past with romantic eyes. British rule had disrupted the old equilibrium of village life blessed with idyllic happiness; the damage had to be repaired. The cities were symbols of Western culture, artificially planted on the Indian soil, which thrived on exploitation of the village people; this had to be ended. The lure of the cities was drawing away the rural elite, depriving the villages of both wealth and leadership; the drain had to be stopped. Once again, Gandhiji fought, almost superhumanly, against a rising tide, but to no avail. He failed because he was fighting for what was foredoomed to be a lost cause.

What Gandhiji could not realize was that, while the British ruled, time did not stand still—not even in India. Her population had gone up sharply, the village economy was already overcrowded, it was too small a unit to contain the exploding population, far less to support it with food, jobs and income even on the modest level of the pre-British days.

---

[15] Problems relating to India's land reform are discussed in *Reaping the Green Revolution*, Chapter 11.

The old system, rendered obsolete by the march of time, had to give way to something new and vastly different in dimensions, with villages merged or linked together by networks of roads to create more modern and much larger semi-urbanized communities. This was the only route India could take to reach the goals Gandhiji had upheld before the country with so much passion and compassion—the liberation of the masses of people from political, economic and social bondage, and a life of dignity and self-respect for them. It was pointless, indeed self-defeating, to attempt to put the clock back with a nostalgic hand.

The back-to-the-village ideology has been ingrained in the Indian mind too long and too deeply, thanks to Gandhiji's teachings and preachings. It has fatally faulted India's planning from the start. To this day, her rural planning has remained *too rural*. With eyes rivetted on a by-gone past, she is still backing into the future, with results as awkward as they are tragic.[16]

## A BAFFLING LEGACY

The period of national movement—from 1919 to Gandhiji's death in 1948—is looked upon as a glorious epoch in India's history. So indeed it was, culminating as it did in national independence. But in another sense, it was a period of wanton waste. After historians, British and Indian, have sung to their hearts' content the glories respectively of the British rule and the Gandhian movement, some stubborn facts will still stand out against a turbulent background, like the peaks of the Himalayas, rugged and clear, appealing to high heavens.

It is fascinating to speculate how radically different could have been the course of events if, for example, India had been granted Dominion Status around the same time as Canada, or if, even half-a-century later, the Montagu-Chelmsford reforms were put to work without fatal equivocation. What a difference it would have made to India and to the world! But that was not to be. Reason prevailed, but only after irrationalism had run its full, sterile course. In that sense, history has cheated India and mankind including, the writer believes, also Britain.

In two World Wars Britain was bled white—in defence of the Empire and of liberty. They imposed a heavy drain also on India as she was automatically dragged into them. In addition, she had to pay a fantastically heavy price to win her own liberty. For one whole generation her best talents—at all levels from the top national leaders to the student community—were invested in agitation, platform speeches, prison-going. Much of the flower of British manhood fell on the battlefield. India's

[16] The pattern of spatial development India needs today to replace the obsolete village units is examined in the companion study (*Reaping*, etc.)—see especially Chapters 18-20.

sacrifice took a different form. She had to cripple herself—nonviolently.

Gandhiji achieved almost the impossible. In a large subcontinent disarmed, impoverished and demoralized, riven with differences, and inhabited by masses of ignorant and illiterate people, he conjured up a vast national movement, yet guided it, on the whole with amazing success, into nonviolent channels. His courage, patriotism, personal charm, examples of sacrifice to the point of self-immolation—all combined to produce an electrifying effect. Millions of people were swept off their feet, and thousands of educated Indians off their minds as well.

Without the support of the masses the political movement would get nowhere—it would have no teeth, not enough propelling force. But a mass movement needed mass appeal. So with his unfailing instinct, Gandhiji set about the task, ostentatiously upheld traditional values, and, like a master artist, aroused, mobilized and guided emotions on a gigantic scale. Nationalism, in such conditions, could not but lead to a revival of traditionalism along with obsolete dogmas and ideas. Reason had dictated the need for an emotional upheaval; reason thus became the first casualty in that upheaval. This is the other side of the glorious epoch of Gandhiji's leadership. It was an age of tumultuous retreat from reason.

However inevitable, this was for India a frightful price to pay. And as fate would have it, the price has been compounded by two other phenomena.

The value-system Gandhiji used for one whole generation to win national freedom was, in many respects, just the opposite of what free India needed for her development. It called for a radical change in values and ideas, a change that could come only with a new generation of leaders. But history has denied India this psychological breathing-space. Barely did she emerge out of her long political upheaval when she was thrown right into a spiralling demographic upheaval.

Moreover, the long national movement had awakened the masses and kindled their expectations. This was the gift of Gandhiji. But so far mass expectations have found their most important fulfilment not in the economic, but in the political field—in mass enfranchisement. India became a full-fledged democracy in one big leap, the largest democracy in the world, but also the poorest and the most illiterate.

In Western countries economic and social development was spread over a long period; and during this period they were pretty well shielded from demographic and democratic pressures. By contrast, India has been singularly unlucky. At the very threshold of her development, she has been confronted with both kinds of pressures on an unprecedented scale.

And the ultimate tragedy is this: Even the people of rural India, who were so dear to Gandhiji, derived little lasting benefit from his superhuman effort and sacrifice. For years he suffered with them and for them; his compassion knew no bounds; yet it yielded hardly any tangible

14

mitigation of their actual suffering. He acted like a fond mother, innocent of swimming but plunging after a drowning child, to perish together, clasping it to the bosom. This was soul-stirring, but not life-saving.

It is a baffling legacy that Gandhiji has left behind with his self-
effacing commitment to the people, coupled with his anti-machine, anti-
medicine, anti-science stand. India's problems have been immeasurably
complicated because he inextricably mixed ethics with dogmas, struggled
to make poverty more bearable rather than to cure it, upheld obsolete
ideas with a spiritual fervour few could resist, disarmed reason with
charm, and fought with values which, even if relevant for winning political freedom, were definite impediments to winning freedom from want.

Yet the legacy contains, though implicitly, an inescapable imperative:
to be at least sane, even if not saints; to see truth and nonviolence not
through Gandhiji's eyes, but through our own; to accept firmly his first
principle, but to reject, with equal firmness, most of the specific applications he advocated, as *non sequiturs*; to share his concern for the people
fully and deeply, but to evolve and apply better and more effective
measures to promote their welfare; in short, to marry his ethics with
modern science.

This is precisely what poet Tagore had in mind when, sadly reflecting
on contemporary trends, he observed: "If I had Gandhiji's courage and
strength of character, I would have used them differently." The words
echoed the inner feelings of other thoughtful Indians.

The poet held Gandhiji in high esteem and deep affection, but with
characteristic vision he deplored the rapid drift of the nation towards an
age of unreason.

Many Indians vividly recall how the poet castigated Gandhiji's pronouncement that the earthquake which had devastated much of Bihar
in 1934, was nothing but a divine dispensation, a punishment to the
people for practising untouchability. This was pandering to superstition,
Tagore charged furiously, wholly unwarranted even in a worthy cause
because, in the long run, it could only hurt the nation.

India has not yet been able to effect the marriage of Gandhian ethics
and modern science. Prime Minister Nehru gallantly tried, but failed. He
bowed reverentially to Gandhiji's teachings, proclaimed allegiance to
science and technology, juxtaposed them, and deluded himself into believ-
ing that he had struck the right synthesis between the two. In reality, he
fell between two stools, and with him India suffered the same fate.[17]

[17] A personal note may be in order here. The writer did not "non-cooperate" with
school and college—such non-cooperation, he felt, was a tragic error. He did not
spin—he was unimpressed by the economics of khadi. In 1922, when the first wave
of enthusiastic adoption of khadi was very much on the wane, he took to it as a
mark of respect for Gandhiji and as a symbol of economic nationalism, maintained a
wardrobe of four pieces of khadi, followed his "wash-and-wear" principle until September 1928 when he left for London for higher education.

CHAPTER 8

# Low Yield from
# High Ideals

## II. COMMUNITY DEVELOPMENT AND
## PANCHAYATI RAJ

### WRONG ROADS

Rural India has long been a victim of high ideals. This is no doubt what happened *before* independence when the fundamentals were lost in the emotional confusion that accompanied the national movement. This is what was repeated *after* independence when, in the early fifties, two far-reaching commitments were made—for community development and co-operative credit—which sidetracked the essentials and set the country on the march—along wrong roads.

Both ideals were boldly conceived—they were to build their respective institutional network covering the whole country. Both were nobly motivated—their declared objective was to inspire and assist the rural people to achieve quicker economic and social progress. Both bypassed the first-things-first principle—they showed little understanding for the fact that community development and cooperation are "later-generation" institutions, that they are the arch and the coping-stone, not the foundation, of rural development. There was little awareness of this difference. The result was a design for development turned upside down.

### ETAWAH PILOT PROJECT

The immmediate precursor of the community development programme in

India was a pilot project which had been launched, late in 1948, in the Etawah district of U.P. (Uttar Pradesh).[1]

The story of the Etawah project need not detain us here. Considerable literature has grown around it. In addition, it has been described fully and authoritatively by Mr. Albert Mayer who was its architect-in-chief and the driving force behind it.[2] Only a few brief comments are made here in so far as they appear specially relevant in the present context.

In spring 1948, the writer had an interesting talk with Mr. Mayer in New York.[3] Mr. Mayer was about to start, somewhere in North India, an experimental project on rural development covering a group of villages; he had already had considerable discussions and correspondence about it with Prime Minister Nehru and other Indian leaders; he was most eager to go ahead with it, but was still largely feeling his way and was wondering how best to shape and design it. Its location was apparently still open, though a decision seemed impending.

At this point the writer put up a strong plea to locate the project in the Damodar Valley[4]—with flood control, year-round irrigation for a large acreage, fertile soil, power supply, good communications and other facilities, it would provide an ideal framework for such a project. The DVC, too, needed a comprehensive project for rural development to put to the maximum possible use the facilities it was going to create with large capital outlays. The two projects were essentially complementary. Together, they could give a powerful demonstration for regional development and thus set up a model for others to emulate.

Mr. Mayer was swayed by the logic. "What you are saying is whether

---

[1] There had been several other experiments in the same broad field, notably at Tagore's Institute of Rural Reconstruction at Sriniketan referred to earlier (in Chapter 2, p. 20, footnote). This could, with very good reason, be called India's first "community development" project, though the phrase itself is of more recent vintage.

As for the background and basic philosophy of Sriniketan, reference may be made to the writer's book: *Tagore on Rural Reconstruction*, Visvabharati Economic Research, Santiniketan, 1942.

[2] In *Pilot Project, India* (The story of rural development at Etawah, Uttar Pradesh), University of California Press, 1958.

[3] The writer had first met Albert Mayer in 1944 when Mr. Mayer was stationed in Calcutta as an officer in the United States Army Engineers. A professional architect and town and rural planner, he was keenly interested in Indian villages. This led to his informal association for a while with a Bengal Government project which later grew into the Haringhata Milk Supply Centre for Calcutta. Mr. L. K. Elmhirst, then Agricultural Adviser to Bengal Government, three New Zealand dairy and poultry experts, and the writer actively worked for this project in its early stages.

[4] He had an axe to grind! He was then returning to India—after serving a tour of duty as Economic Adviser to the newly established Indian Embassy in Moscow and a four-month on-the-spot study of the TVA based in Knoxville, Tennessee, and was due to join the DVC as its chief executive officer. He was very well aware that the DVC, for its own success, would definitely need such a project.

there should be one success or two failures," he remarked thoughtfully, though somewhat too pointedly.

As a follow-up, he took up the proposal with Prime Minister Nehru through a personal letter. Mr. Nehru agreed that the proposal had merit, but preferred not to put all eggs in one basket, and favoured Uttar Pradesh for the new project. In fact, a decision to that effect had been virtually made, and only the formal stamp of approval was awaited. Was there at least a subconscious preference to have the new project located in the Prime Minister's own state? This may well have been the case.

The writer always regretted that the two projects could not be combined. The analogy of "eggs and baskets" had little validity; it ignored their crucial complementarity, the need for a better-rounded project, which, once successfully incubated, would have produced spectacular results—one lasting and resounding success serving as a model and as a pace-setter for the whole country, rather than two partial successes, each enjoying a brief summer of glory, only to be swept aside by the confused march of subsequent events.

Not only that; a combination of the DVC and Albert Mayer's pilot project would, by strengthening themselves mutually, have greatly improved their chances to withstand the predictable onslaught by the forces of confusion. It would have helped avoid some of the worst blunders committed later, especially in the costly river valley projects;[5] and it would have ushered in something very similar to the Intensive Agricultural District Programme, or IADP,[6] at least a decade earlier.

As for the Etawah project itself, Mr. Mayer—after his searchings into the Indian "highways and byways and no-ways," to use his own phrase—arrived at conclusions which showed remarkable perceptiveness, especially for one with an entirely different professional and cultural background.[7] Regular government work on rural development was "accomplishing very, very little." The system and the attitudes it entailed were "really deadly."

The old Civil Service remained stubbornly aloof. The Gandhian constructive workers went to the other extreme. They not only believed in full involvement, but tended to "over identify with the people's hardships." They were unable to provide the leadership needed for material improvement. Agriculture, for example, did not receive much attention from them. Their approach "assumed the existence of more saintly people than the world contains." There would "not be enough of them to go round," Mr. Mayer suspected.

Missionaries were doing a lot of useful work. But as a rule, it did not reflect sufficient involvement of the people, nor enough "sense of urgency." And in a country where "government is pervasive" and handled

[5] See Chapter 6, especially the last two sections.
[6] Discussed in Chapters 11-14.
[7] Ibid., pp. 16-22.

even matters like supply and credit, its aloofness from government was a handicap.

"Single-lobe" development attempted from time to time, such as brick roads here and there or public sanitary facilities, was not doing much good. Such works, almost always, suffered for lack of maintenance and quickly fell into disuse.

To build "model villages," though occasionally attempted by some idealists or enthusiasts, would, Mr. Mayer felt, be "simply a *tour de force.*" They would have "no real roots," and the country could not afford too many such examples. He doubted if the concept of a self-contained village was at all realistic.

These were all sound conclusions which more or less coincided with those of many thoughtful observers. This was generally true also of the approach Mr. Mayer finally worked out: initially to emphasize economic matters—agriculture, animal husbandry, fish culture, local industry, and related activities—to secure more and better products and higher incomes; such a programme, if effectively carried out, would create enough good will and confidence for close cooperation between the project representatives and the village people; and this, in turn, would pave the way for the final step—to improve the quality of village life in all its aspects, including sanitation, housing, community facilities. Once that stage was reached, villagers, one might safely assume, would not only accept, but demand such good things for better living.

Essentially, this is nothing but the classic approach of community development which sprang into prominence particularly after World War II. Why, then, was Etawah considered so novel, and was greeted with so much fanfare?

In the Indian context the most novel feature of Etawah was that it steered clear both of the ingrained apathy of officialdom and of the glowing emotionalism of Gandhian workers. It treated rural development as what it always should have been—an immensely *practical* affair to advance *material* welfare among rural people. It supplied enough idealism, or empathy, combined it with a down-to-earth approach, and impregnated it with professional competence. Once the goals were defined and the paths clearly chalked out, it pursued them tenaciously, systematically, and in business-like fashion.

All this was possible because Etawah was blessed with a rare asset—the personality of Albert Mayer, who mobilized the personal support of Prime Minister Nehru,[8] and of Pandit Govind Ballabh Pant, then Premier of

---

[8] On 17 June 1946, i.e. more than a year before independence, Mr. Nehru in a letter to Albert Mayer said *inter alia*: "Just at the beginning some people, used to the old type of authoritarian British expert, who neither understood nor cared to understand Indian conditions, might view any foreign intrusion with some suspicion.... But we can get over them given the chance." Ibid., p. 8.

Uttar Pradesh, and had also secured, at least in principle, the blessings of Gandhiji before his death. Such high level political support ensured adequate funding for the project. Last but not least, Mr. Mayer handpicked high-grade experts, Americans and Indians, to serve as a team on the project.

By 1951, the Etawah project became a major success story which, aided by American genius, was dramatized and publicized in a world hungry for such examples. It was hailed as a model for rural development, in India and abroad; soon it was indiscriminately grabbed as a panacea for all rural afflictions. An orgy of imitation followed, and, within a few years, rural India was thrust into a custom-made strait-jacket which has proved more suffocating than conducive to growth and progress.

## SUCCESS MISUNDERSTOOD

The Etawah pilot project was unquestionably a success. What escaped its admirers, however, was the fact that it was far more a success for the pilot than for the experiment as such; that its achievements were due to a very rare combination of circumstances which made it unique rather than typical; that, for the same reason, its repeatability was strictly limited.

Mr. Mayer himself had argued that India could not afford too many model villages which were "simply a *tour de force*." The same remark could be applied, with almost equal force, to the model project he had himself piloted. In leadership, political support, extent of funding, and the number and quality of experts, Etawah was exceptionally lucky. One could not realistically expect to multiply such a model.

The need to generate self-propelling force within the pilot project was recognized from the start; therefore, the initial emphasis, as seen above, was laid on economic matters. Striking results were achieved in several directions—for example, in increasing both output and income from agriculture, especially from the cultivation of wheat, potatoes and peas,[9] also with the cooperative brick-kiln industry which spread rapidly and became, in its own right, a success story.[10] Several other industries were pursued —flaying, bone crushing, fruit and vegetable canning, sericulture, but evidently the results were meagre.

This brings us to what was the real weakness of the Etawah approach. It recognized that economic development was vital, and that it must perforce precede other activities however desirable in themselves, yet it did not concentrate sufficient efforts on what is the heart of the rural economy—agriculture. It realized, at best only vaguely, that by far the biggest and most rewarding task in rural India was to modernize its agri-

[9] Ibid., esp. pp. 283-87.
[10] Ibid., pp. 272-78.

culture. And it showed little real understanding as to how best to go about it.

The cost of the Etawah project was high in terms of leadership, political support, expertise, and money. It was even more costly in another respect—in terms of *time*. Several valuable years were spent for learning, and for not learning, what should have been obvious, both on *a priori* reasoning and on the strength of the experience already accumulated both within India and in other countries.

A dozen pilot projects planted immediately after independence in different parts of India, especially where river valley projects were under way—this is what was done more than a decade later in launching the IADP—would have made a great deal of sense. But it made none at all to put all eggs in one single Etawah basket, and to wait patiently over a long incubation period, while rural India, stimulated by decades of national movement and continuously starved of real development, was getting more restive and less nonviolent. The very restraint of the earlier years was destined to explode later into uncontrollable impatience.

## COMMUNITY DEVELOPMENT

*a. Mass-produced Prototypes.* The Etawah project was no doubt a major improvement over the previous exercises in rural development. Nevertheless, it is no exaggeration to say that despite more coherent planning and practical-minded approach, it too largely missed the main "highway" of rural development, namely, agriculture, and got lost in numerous "byways and no-ways." And as a pilot project, it soon became instrumental in leading India in the same direction—towards a maze of no-ways—in the name of community development.

What happened next is a familiar story. Suffice it to recall here the more important facts and to reflect briefly on their consequences.[11]

Before launching the Etawah project Albert Mayer had felt convinced of the "desperate importance in India" of making some specific things work well as "radiating demonstrations" rather than to give high-level advice that was not planted anywhere.[12] The project he planted late in 1948 with 64 villages grew in three years to embrace over 300 villages in the same district; in addition, it was reproduced at four other centres

---

[11] The literature on community development in India, both official and unofficial, is vast. The most authoritative account of its growth and philosophy will be found in *Community Development—A Chronicle, 1954-61* (Ministry of Community Development, etc., Government of India, 1962), and *Community Development—A Bird's-Eye View* (Asia Publishing House, London, 1964), both by Mr. S. K. Dey who served first as Community Projects Administrator and later as Union Minister for Community Development and Cooperation.

[12] *Pilot Project, India*, ibid., p. 6.

within UP State. The demonstration, it seemed, had reached the stage of "radiation."

Late in 1951, a proposal was developed, in consultation between the Ford Foundation and Planning Commission, to set up 15 new projects in 15 states, each covering 100 villages with five training centres for village extension workers.[13] The new projects were due to start in April 1952.

Even before this happened, however, the Planning Commission urged the creation of a Community Projects Administration which was to organize initially 55 projects, each embracing 300 villages.[14] The proposal was embodied in the First Five-Year Plan, and an allocation of Rs. 90 crores was made for the purpose. Steps were promptly taken to create a far-flung administrative apparatus which was to consist of: a Department at the Centre (later turned into a Ministry), a Development Committee and Commissioner in each state, a Development Committee and Officer in each district, a Project Executive Officer in charge of each project and with a staff of some 125 supervisors and Village Level Workers to serve under him.

The die was now cast for the next and much bolder step. Barely a year passed when a decision was taken to create a permanent National Extension Service (NES) for the entire country, and a plan was drawn up for operating the combined CD-NES programme. The main unit was now going to be the so-called "development block," each would consist of 100 villages and cover an area between 150 and 170 square miles with a population between 60,000 and 70,000 as then estimated. Each block was to be provided with a "schematic budget."

As for the execution of the programme, three phases were envisaged in a rising order of intensity: a "pre-intensive," or NES, phase thinly covering a wide area, followed by an "intensive," or CD Programme, phase with the full complement of a CD block staff and stepped-up intensity in the activities, paving the way for the final or "post-intensive" phase when the people themselves would take over from the official workers and become their own pilots. By then the villages in a block, it was assumed, would have reached the take-off or self-propelling stage.

The pattern was well-stylized. Then followed years of block-building and laborious creation of a vast network of NES-CD services. It took about ten years to "saturate" the country. In January 1969, rural India stood delimited into 5,265 blocks. The total expenditures incurred on the CD-NES programme by then amounted to Rs. 571 crores.[15]

[13] It was blessed by Paul G. Hoffman, then President of the Ford Foundation, during a visit to India.

[14] The Indo-U.S. Technical Cooperation Agreement was signed early in 1952. There were clear indications that U.S. assistance would be available for community development. The prospect of aid was no doubt the main reason for the decision to embark upon a much broader-based programme.

[15] Or more than a billion U.S. dollars at the pre-devaluation exchange rate. Plan

15

The Community Development Programme (CDP) was officially launched with 55 projects on 2 October 1952. The date was no accident—it was Gandhi's birthday. The Programme was Gandhian only in the broad sense that its objective was to serve the cause of the rural people, though in both concept and methods it was quite different. Linking the CDP with his name had of course its value. It lent an aura of sanctity which the programme would otherwise have lacked.

*b. Shell Without Substance.* What about the quality of the projects? It is amazing to reflect how little heed was paid to it. The workers, particularly at the village level (the VLW's), were mostly too young and too inexperienced to further the cause the CDP had in view; poorly trained and poorly paid, they looked less like development workers than like an army of minor officials in any other government department. The last task they were qualified for was to provide guidance to improve agriculture. The fact that they were saddled with a multiplicity of activities—for health, sanitation, education, construction of roads, schools, village halls, and so on—made matters, if anything, even worse.

In the heyday of the noncooperation movement when an army of Congress workers were let loose on rural areas, the cynical villagers in some parts used to say tauntingly: "Look, the three-anna baboos are coming!"[16] The CDP was of course in a much stronger position. For one thing, the Congress Party was now in the saddle; the village workers were no longer volunteers, but officials backed by governmental authority. What is even more important, the government in its benevolence had loosened the purse-strings, and money was flowing to the villages through *their* hands.

That this generosity would be enough to create an irresistible demand for more and more CD projects it should have been easy to foresee—for anyone with the least insight into human psychology. For, nowhere in the world are people averse to staking a claim to a pork-barrel should luck favour them with the opportunity. Yet, oddly enough, this demand was adduced as the most convincing argument for a dizzy expansion of the CDP.[17]

---

allocations were substantially larger. Details about CD blocks—growth from Plan to Plan, state-wise distribution, financial allocations, actual expenditures, and stages of development (viz. NES, CD and post-CD)—will be found in the official publications of the CD Ministry and the Planning Commission, esp. the Five-Year Plans. The reference year-book called *INDIA* (Information and Broadcasting Ministry) reproduces the basic statistics. See *INDIA—1969*, pp. 256-63.

[16] The term "baboo," used mainly in Bengal, implies cleanly dressed in Indian style, wedded to desk work as junior official, and prone to sneer at all dirty work. Three annas, about four British pence, were needed to be a Congress member and therefore to acquire the title of a rural worker.

[17] "Soon after the programme began, demands came for its wide multiplication.

Albert Mayer was perturbed by the developments. "It is relatively easy to multiply the mechanics of the early prototypes, but not so easy to multiply and reproduce their inner content," he wrote on one occasion. And it is easy to be unaware in the rush that "one is doing the former at wonderful speeds at the expense of the latter." The anguished words, alas, came too late. Firm commitments had already been made. The CDP rolled on crushing, like a steamroller, the sensitivities which were regarded as the hallmark of a true community development project.

A combination of material and moral elements, as tested at Etawah, was considered far superior to "any more spectacular hot-housing methods."[18] Or, as D. P. Singh put it, community development, in the long run, should become "a people's programme with Government participation and not *vice versa*." The NES-CD programme never measured up to these high expectations. Almost from its birth, it began to wither in a bureaucratic hothouse. And it has all along remained a government programme with very little people's participation, though it has been milked as far as possible by the rural elite.

*c. Amenities before Necessities.* The true character of the CDP was not immediately revealed. The flow of public funds was large enough to produce some results. It was easy to bunch them together—miles of roads constructed or improved, village lanes paved, wells dug, schools built, adult literacy centres opened, leaders trained, and so on—to produce a glowing account of the achievements. And with judicious window-dressing, one could easily impress the visiting dignitaries, more so when they usually arrived with a friendly predisposition. Faith in the CDP initially ran strong. It left little room for objective judgment. Rural India, it was readily assumed, was at last coming out of its economic doldrums.

The bloom soon began to wear off. The congeries of projects, it was gradually realized, were not planned and executed properly, nor were they well-maintained; they did not make much of an impact on the rural economy; and they yielded anything but a satisfactory return on the use of public funds.

In fact, the CDP workers, though stationed in the field, were oriented more towards their headquarters than towards the villages, more inclined to impress their remote masters than to serve the near-by farmers, and predisposed to measure progress by the amount of money spent rather than by the results achieved. The appropriations under the Plans were liberal, more than the CDP was able to spend. As a result, how to spur expenditures and narrow the gap between the two became a primary

---

The demand grew so heavy that it was impossible to resist." S. K. Dey, in *Community Development—A Chronicle, 1954-61*, p. v.

[18] *Pilot Project, India*, ibid., p. 312.

concern; and this led to a lot of hastily conceived projects trumped up through eleventh-hour efforts towards the close of fiscal periods.

Moreover, the benefits were mostly confined to the upper layers of the rural community—landlords, moneylenders, big farmers; and only to a very small extent they filtered down to the under-privileged—small farmers, artisans, and landless workers. Thus, in the main the CDP enriched the few; contrary to initial expectations, it did little to advance the cause of social justice.

Finally, the programme was at its weakest where the stake was the highest—in agriculture. A good many activities were routinely reported, such as quantities of improved seed distributed, fertilizers introduced, compost pits dug, area green-manured, new acreage brought under irrigation. But the approach was haphazard, the quality of work was poor (for example, improved seeds were seldom improved), the results were far from commensurate with the efforts, the overall impact was negligible.

On the positive side, perhaps the best contribution the CDP made to agriculture was initiating farmers in the use of chemical fertilizers. It gave them a foretaste of what fertilizers could do. While this positive entry augured well for the future, it was not enough to alter the overall balance-sheet of the CDP's performance in agriculture, which remained decidedly unsatisfactory.

This last point is confirmed by Mr. S. K. Dey whose voice ought to carry special weight since, as Union Minister, he was in direct charge of the entire community development programme in India. The "amenities programme," he recorded on 28 September 1956, was "rather out of proportion to the less spectacular efforts on the economic side." Four years later, on December 4, 1960, he made an even more forthright admission: "The second mistake was not to give adequate emphasis at the very start of the programme to production, particularly of food."[19]

These were also the views of a UN Mission which, in 1959, critically examined the working of India's community development programme. It confirmed what many Indians had known and deplored: the programme had given precedence to amenities over necessities. "In view of the over-shadowing danger of starvation," it urged, "the community development programme must put priority on increasing agricultural production."[20]

It is sad to reflect that so high a Mission should have been necessary to arrive at such a self-evident conclusion. The core of the community development philosophy is to discover the "felt needs" of the people and to concentrate efforts to meet them; for, once these needs are met, they would be "motivated" for voluntary cooperation. How much research

[19] In *Community Development—A Chronicle, 1954-61*, p. 62 and p. 121.
[20] *Report of a Community Development Evaluation Mission in India*, United Nations, New York, 1959 (unpublished). The Mission consisted of Professor René Dumont, Dr. Margaret Mead and M. J. Coldwell.

should have been necessary to discover that the most acutely felt need of a starving people was—food? The failure to see such a plain fact shows how far the human mind can at times wander away from realities in pursuit of sophistry. This failure, more than anything else, made a mockery of India's community development programme.

*d. On U.S. Support.* There remains one intriguing question: Why did Americans give such a priority to the community development programme? Though there is no simple answer, there are some factors which help explain why things happened the way they did.

A good many people—Americans, Indians, and others—had persuaded themselves, especially after the Etawah experiment, that community development was going to be the wave of the future in the developing countries. The Etawah team, inspired by its own pioneering work, was understandably anxious to see it spread fast; the glowing accounts that followed captured headlines at home and abroad, especially in the USA; and soon there developed the usual selling pressure.

"Community development was certainly not Gandhian in inspiration, although it has been so interpreted," says Doreen Warriner; "Americans wished it on to the Indians, though they were willing victims."[21] This is quite true; however, in fairness, it is well to remember that in those days selling a new idea to India was often a surprisingly simple job. All that was necessary was for one or two high-placed Indians to mobilize the support of one or two big names from abroad in order to secure the personal blessings of Prime Minister Nehru. By no means were all Indians sold on the community development projects. Many harboured grave misgivings about them, particularly when they entered the mass-production stage.

These facts, while relevant, still do not add up to an adequate answer to the question posed above. For, *prima facie*, it is unbelievable that of all countries the USA, left to itself, should give priority to community development rather than to agriculture *per se*. It was too well aware of the role of agriculture in a developing economy, in general also too hard-headed in its thinking, to opt so readily for something so nebulous, even if idealistic. For this there was probably a deeper reason—the prevailing political climate—and the chill already perceptible in Indo-American relations.

As John Kenneth Galbraith wrote later in his *Journal*, in those days the Indian Government "regarded technical assistance activities—agriculture, public health, education and so forth—with considerable suspicion ... an invasion of sovereignty, a possible cover for cold war penetration ... Whenever India Government asked for help, a great effort was made to

[21] *Land Reform in Principle and Practice* by Doreen Warriner, Clarendon Press, Oxford, 1969, p. 197.

respond. 'At least they were asking us.' " As a result, technical assistance became "a hit-and-miss affair, helping here and missing there, and maybe doing occasional damage by diverting attention from first essentials."[22]

Just about a month earlier he had noted down in the same vein: A few years ago all American activities were "regarded with much suspicion. Accordingly, when we were asked for help—in remedial reading, occupation therapy, flower arrangement—we were delighted and responded enthusiastically. The resultant pattern of technical assistance activities was wholly haphazard."[23]

The community development programme was not the best nor the most important the administrators of the U.S. aid programme could visualize for India. Such a suggestion would be unfair. It was perhaps the best that was *available to them* at that time, and it was supported by them *faute de mieux*. Here is an excellent example to show how priorities could be distorted by the cold war, how development could be hurt by the political fallout of big-power rivalry in an atomic world.

Another instance of the same kind of fallout may be noted in passing. When the first press report about U.S. military aid to Pakistan came out in 1953, a senior civil servant in the DVC, with the instinct of a bird flying ahead of a coming storm, argued that in the future it would be politically inexpedient to recruit experts or order equipment from the U.S.A. This was the beginning of the end of several years of highly productive Indo-U.S. collaboration on what was then proudly called "India's TVA." The label itself was quietly dropped, especially after TVA's image was successfully tarnished in its own homeland.

## PANCHAYATI RAJ

Before long the weaknesses of the NES-CD venture began to surface. Even the official evaluation reports sounded a discordant note—discreetly, yet unmistakably. Nor could they be readily brushed aside as the inevitable growing pains of an infant organization. For they continued to be repeated in successive reports backed by a wealth of data collected straight from the field which were hard to ignore.[24]

Search, or rather talks, began for a remedy. And the same romantic impulse which had already landed rural India in two mammoth misadventures—NES-CD programme and cooperative credit scheme (see next Chapter)—almost irresistibly led her into a third, the so-called *Panchayati Raj*.

[22] *Ambassador's Journal*, Houghton Mifflin Company, Boston, 1969. In letter dated May 10, 1961 to President John F. Kennedy, p. 110.

[23] Ibid., on April 12, 1961, p. 67.

[24] *Evaluation Reports on Working of CD and NES Blocks*, Programme Evaluation Organization (PEO Series), Planning Commission. The first instalment of critical comments came out with the Third Evaluation Report, April 1956.

The aura village life had come to be surrounded with in the minds of most Congress leaders was not confined to the village economy, but was extended to village democracy based on *panchayats*.[25] It was never warranted by historical facts, for only in exceptional cases did the village council function effectively. Indian villages were always caste-ridden with rather rigid social stratification despite the occasional veneer of democracy.

Yet the faith in a largely mythical past dies hard. How indomitably, and incurably, it has survived to this day is evidenced by the amazing ease with which it has managed to ride roughshod over the stark realities of today's village life—its shrunken economic base, its seething population, its appalling misery, its revolting inequalities and injustices, its intriguing factions, its ceaseless feuds. To think of building rural democracy on such a foundation calls for a degree of surrealism seldom matched in history. Yet this is the venture India suddenly decided to embark upon!

Voices harking back to the past and pleading for a return to the village panchayat had never been completely stilled, and, after independence, they became distinctly more audible. When the community development programme began to falter, the idealists lost no time in pressing for their pet panacea. The anaemia of the CDP, they confidently diagnosed, was due to the lack of people's participation; it was lacking because they were denied the opportunity to exercise responsibility; the remedy, promptly derived from these premises, was to decentralize responsibility to be exercised by the people through their democratically-elected organs.[26] That this neatly-structured logic was less than perfect, both in its inductive and deductive aspects, did cause discomfort to some sceptics and to quite a few seasoned administrators. But it did not trouble the policy-makers; with them it was a matter of faith, a faith that conquers all criticisms, including reason.

The First Five-Year Plan had indicated in broad terms the "important role" the village panchayat could play.[27] The Second Five-Year Plan was both more explicit and more emphatic. The subject, it stressed, "requires careful and objective study"; it therefore recommended "a special investigation under the auspices of the National Development Council"; and pending this investigation, the existing non-official agencies, i.e. district

[25] Derived from *pancha* or five, a panchayat originally meant rule by a village council consisting of five *elected* members. *Panchayati raj*, or rule based on panchayats, is now treated as synonymous with rural democracy.

[26] The ebullient Union Minister Mr. S. K. Dey registered a characteristic confession later. Writing on 29 December 1960, he admitted, with profound hindsight, that the CDP had made two mistakes: not to have entrusted the development programme, as far as it lay within village confines, to the panchayats from the start, and not to have given priority to production, particularly food. *Community Development—A Chronicle*, op. cit., p. 121.

[27] *The First Five-Year Plan—A Summary*, December 1952, p. 53.

councils and development committees, should be strengthened and reorganized so as to be more widely representative in their composition. Their functions, too, were delineated in some detail, though they were still restricted to an advisory and supervisory role.[28]

In accordance with this recommendation, the NDC set up a "Team for the Study of Community Projects and National Extension Service" under the Committee on Plan Projects (COPP). The Team, under the Chairmanship of Balvantray Mehta, took barely three months to produce a three-volume report in which it blessed the philosophy of community development, deplored the lack of representative and democratic institutions to supply the "local interest, supervision and care necessary to ensure that expenditure of money upon local projects conforms with the needs and wishes of the locality," and plumped for immediate planting of panchayati raj all over the country.[29] The swiftness of the performance aroused widespread suspicion that the Team, set up to carry out a "careful and objective study," had trimmed its sails to the prevailing ideological wind.

The Study Team urged that "there should be a devolution of power and a decentralization of machinery, and that such power be exercised and such machinery controlled and directed by popular representatives of the local area." To give effect to this principle it recommended a three-tier system:

*a.* An elected panchayat at village level with provisions to coopt members to represent women, scheduled castes, and scheduled tribes. The list of its obligatory duties should include water supply for domestic use; sanitation; maintenance of public streets, drains, tanks, also of panchayat roads, culverts, bridges, drains, etc.; keeping records about cattle; collection and maintenance of statistics; supervision of primary schools; distress relief; welfare of backward classes. It should, in addition, serve as the *panchayat samiti's* (see *b.* below) agent for executing schemes of development.

*b.* A *panchayat samiti*[30] at the block level, consisting mainly of members elected by the *panches* of the village panchayats, and some members coopted to represent disadvantaged sections, such as women, scheduled castes and scheduled tribes.

Of great significance in the present context are the functions of the *samiti*, including as they do the development of agriculture in all its aspects—selection, procurement and distribution of seeds, improvement

[28] *Second Five-Year Plan*, 1956, pp. 160-63.

[29] Team for the Study of Community Projects & NES, *Report*, Committee on Plan Projects, New Delhi, November-December 1957.

[30] A *Samiti*, in this case, is best rendered as a "council," though it can also mean "assembly" or "association."

of agronomic practices, provision of local agricultural finance with assistance from the government and the cooperative banks, minor irrigation works, improvement of livestock. In addition, the list includes promotion of local industries, drinking-water supply, public health and sanitation, medical relief, relief work in emergencies, construction and maintenance of roads (other than those of village panchayats), management and administrative control of primary schools, fixing minimum wages for non-industrial labour under the Minimum Wages Act, welfare of backward classes, maintenance of statistics. Finally, the *samiti* would have to safeguard the growth and efficiency of the village panchayats in its area.

The list hardly errs on the side of modesty!

*c.* A *zila parishad*[31] at the district level. Once the block-level *samitis* and the village-level panchayats are brought into existence, they will become the pivots of local executive work; the importance of district level activities will therefore diminish, and various bodies like district boards and district school boards will become redundant. Nevertheless, the parishad will have other important, though non-executive, functions to perform. It will coordinate the activities of the *samitis* within the district, examine and approve their budgets, recruit and post officials like the VLW and the primary school teacher, coordinate and consolidate block plans, distribute government funds among the blocks, and assume a general supervisory role.

The *parishad* was conceived as a heterogeneous body comprising the presidents of the panchayat samitis, members of the State Legislature and the Parliament representing the district partly or wholly, all district level officers of development departments—medical, public health, agriculture, veterinary, public health engineering, public works, education, backward classes welfare—and the District Collector as the Chairman. Thus, officials and elected representatives were to sit together, deliberate on issues within their jurisdiction, and exercise equal voting rights.

As for finances, there would of course be the usual Central and State funds. It was specifically provided, however, that these funds should, with very minor exceptions, be "assigned to the panchayat samiti to be spent by it directly or indirectly." In addition, the samiti was empowered to raise supplementary revenues from a dozen other sources, even though their yield, as was foreseeable, could make no more than a marginal difference to their total budget.

A village panchayat would receive grants from the *samiti* just as the latter would receive grants from the government. The panchayat would also be authorized to collect supplementary tax revenues from a variety of sources.

[31] *Zila* = district, and *parishad* = council or assembly.

16

These, in broad outline, were the main proposals of the Study Team, which were endorsed, on 12 January 1958, by the NDC. They became the blueprint for what was hailed as "democratic decentralization." Those with a penchant for slogan-making acclaimed it with an appealing rhyme: "After *swaraj—panchayati raj!*" Translated freely, it means, "self-government or independence culminates in decentralized democracy."

Soon came a spate of legislation passed by state after state. The blueprint remained substantially the same, but within its broad framework there were considerable variations. Rajasthan was the first state to pass, in October 1959, *panchayati raj* legislation, Andhra Pradesh was a close second, and with short time lags they were followed by most of the other states.

The country has been well "saturated" with *panchayati raj* institutions. Village panchayats have been established in all states and almost in all Union territories. The two higher tier bodies—the block *samiti* and the district *parishad*—have been set up in all states except Jammu and Kashmir, Kerala, Nagaland, Madhya Pradesh, and parts of Bihar.[32] These gaps, it may be presumed, will be gradually reduced.

Thus, India has been through another hectic round of institution-building which took almost a whole decade. And the end is still not in sight. Emphasis is now laid on "consolidation" of these institutions. The states are reviewing their own legislative provisions from time to time and making whatever adjustments are considered necessary in the organizational setup and administrative procedures.

*New Shackles for Development.* The community development programme, as started in India, was itself an act of faith. When it began to develop the predictable symptoms of a multiple malaise, *panchayati raj* was promptly prescribed as a sure remedy, a faith-cure. This is the most question-begging enterprise India has undertaken so far. The questions it provokes are many, obvious, and disquieting.

It is no secret how New Delhi has re-made Westminster democracy after its own image, and how this performance has been repeated, even more vividly, in the various state capitals. How, then, will democracy function in caste-dominated, faction-ridden rural India?

Given the feudalism, and the interminable feuds, which still dominate the rural life, will democracy planted from above cement unity? Or, will it freeze, and possibly aggravate, the existing disunities?

How will the interests of the great majority—the poor, the weak, and the ignorant—fare under the new system? To put it differently, will rural democracy mould rural plutocracy, or will it be the other way round? If the latter, would it not come perilously close to an abdication of responsibility by the higher authorities, leaving the many at the mercy of the few?

[32] Position as of early 1970.

What guarantee is there that the public funds entrusted to a *samiti* and by it to the village panchayats would be actually used for public, and not for private, benefit? Vigilance, it has been argued, is the antidote to corruption. But will enough vigilance be forthcoming in an effective form? From where?

Can the *panchayat samiti* do anything like justice to the impressive array of functions it has been loaded with? Will it have the required technical competence and adequate administrative ability?

The *samiti* officers, as envisaged by the Study Team, will consist of a chief officer and various technical officers in charge of agriculture, roads and buildings, irrigation, public health, veterinary, cooperation, social education, primary education, etc. They will be "lent" or seconded by the state government which will continue to be responsible for their salaries and conditions of service; but they will all be responsible to the *samiti*. The technical officers will be accountable to the chief officer for "administrative and operational matters," but for technical matters they will report to the "corresponding district level officers."

How is such a system, bravely founded on the dubious principles of dual allegiance and divided responsibility, going to affect performance by individual officers? Will democratic decentralization lead, under such circumstances, to administrative demoralization?

And will the state government be able to recruit, in conditions as they exist today, enough qualified technical people of the requisite calibre to staff the large number of blocks? Is there not a real danger that, as in the past, quality will be sacrificed in this numbers game?

The last questions provoke yet another: Can the village, handed down from a hoary past, and the block, recently created by an administrative fiat, be accepted as the most rational operational units in today's India from the angle of economic development and efficient administration? Would it not be more practical and much wiser to build further on the existing structure of district administration, which has been consolidated over a long period of British rule, to radiate from there into the villages to speed up their development with roads and markets, agricultural research and extension, secondary schools, hospitals, and other essential services, and to respond progressively to the needs of villages or groups of villages, in light of actual experience, to provide for a more intensified development? Is it not the only way one could make the best use of the still-limited supply of really competent technical and administrative leaders, the only way also to demarcate what would be the most logical units of operation in different agro-climatic regions since these, except by a miracle, are unlikely to be conterminous with today's villages or even blocks?

Why, in any case, throw the existing system into the melting-pot and the country into the throes of another upheaval with all the attendant stresses and strains, and do so in the name of development which is visibly hindered by such an avoidable exercise?

Time, it has been held, will demonstrate the superiority of the *Panchayati raj* system in the long run, even if development suffers meanwhile, Will it? Is it not the uncontrolled voice of faith once again luring the country away on a suicidal course of vast distractions? And can India afford this waste of time when population explodes, violence mounts, and chaos impends? Have we not squandered enough precious years, thoughtlessly and recklessly?

To put these questions is, in most cases, also to answer them.

The community development programme was launched in India as a cure-all for rural ills. Its true potential, even to start with, was vastly exaggerated. Planted from above, it built no communities, and produced little development. Then, at a breakneck speed, it was centralized, bureaucratized, and amateurized. To cure these avidly cultivated ills and to restore it to its pristine purity, a new panacea was prescribed—in the form of *panchayati raj*. With this *coup de grâce*, the programme is being more and more politicized! The new institutions, created to serve as the vehicle of grass roots democracy, threaten to grow into formidable new shackles for development in general.[33]

---

[33] The literature on *panchayati* raj is vast, confused, and still growing, with considerable state-to-state variations in legislative content and actual operations, and with no uniformity in the terminology used. Most of it is dull "officialese" and, perhaps unavoidably, tendentious in character. However, a good review of the developments with critical comments will be found in *The Process of Planning—A Study of India's Five-Year Plans, 1950-1964*, by A. H. Hanson, Oxford University Press, 1966, esp. pp. 427-43.

CHAPTER 9

# Wrong Roads to
# Cooperation

## THE BACKGROUND

To community development and *panchayati raj* has to be added another high-ideal low-yield programme—the programme for credit cooperatives. Together, they constitute the trinity of rural development in India. And together, they have paved the path for her economic stagnation.

Cooperation in India has a fairly long history behind it. It started with the passage of the Cooperative Credit Societies Act of 1904.[1] As the title of the Act implies, it was confined mainly to credit; in fact, its declared objective was to combat rural indebtedness. The initiatives for the cooperative movement came from the government; and to this day, the government has retained full direction and control over the "movement."

The Act of 1904 was amended and broadened in 1912; its actual workings were reviewed from time to time; and, with surprising consistency, whole-hearted commitment to the principle has been matched by candid confessions about the paucity of results. The record did contain occasional bright spots, thanks to the sporadic achievements of some dedicated individuals. Besides, in a few areas the government showed commendable initiative, and by a vigorous pursuit of the goal, set up isolated examples of success. However, they could not make much difference to the overall record. It remained one of apathy among members

[1] Even earlier Fredrick Nicholson, in a Report in 1895-97, had made the suggestion to use cooperation as a remedy for rural indebtedness. The only result, however, was some sporadic individual efforts. The Famine Commission of 1901 stressed the need for starting cooperative credit societies, which led to the Act of 1904.

of primary societies, uninspired leadership, poor management, meagre results.

This was recognized by the Royal Commission on Agriculture in 1929. It emphasized, however, that "if cooperation fails, there will fail the best hope of rural India." The same sentiment was echoed, in 1952, by the Rural Credit Survey Committee. "Cooperation has failed, but it must succeed," the Committee asserted. But success continued to prove elusive. As Sir Malcolm Darling, a veteran of the cooperative movement in India, wrote in 1957: "The path of cooperation is strewn with wreckage."[2] Little has happened in the intervening years to alter this verdict.

*Integrated Rural Credit Scheme.* The stage for today's disillusionment was set, back in 1951-52, by the All-India Rural Credit Survey Committee (AIRCSC) referred to in the preceding paragraph. The Committee carried out an extensive survey and collected a wealth of data which confirmed, in more precise quantitative terms, what had long been suspected by knowledgeable people: the bulk of the credit, or 84 per cent of a total of Rs. 750 crores, came from moneylenders and the borrowers' relatives; the government's share was 3.3 per cent; the commercial banks, which had steered clear of agricultural credit as something that fell outside their ambit, accounted for only 0.9 per cent. But the most shocking revelation was the share of the cooperative societies—a mere 3.1 per cent!

Why did the cooperatives make such a dismally poor show after five decades of effort to spread the gospel of cooperation accompanied by benevolent official pampering? The Committee traced their woes to what it called a fundamental defect in the structure of rural credit and defined it rather pedantically as follows: In rural areas the landlord may also be the moneylender, the moneylender may also be the trader, while the educated person may be a subordinate official. And all of them, linked as they are directly with the outside world of finance and power, wield their influence not to promote the good of the village, but to serve their own interests. The cooperative movement failed because of the "total incompatibility to combine the very weak in competition with the very strong." To expect that the weak could, by their own efforts, emancipate themselves from the grip of the vested interests was an illusion.

The dice were loaded against the weak; the conditions had to be changed; but they would not be changed if left to the forces that were at work in rural areas. The forces of transformation, the Committee insisted, could be generated "not by cooperation alone but by cooperation in conjunction with the State."

Its recommendations centred on what was called the Integrated Scheme of Rural Credit. Briefly, it urged the creation of a three-tier structure—

[2] *Report on Certain Aspects of the Cooperative Movement in India*, Planning Commision, 1957.

an apex bank at the State level, central cooperative banks at the district level, and large-sized societies at the primary level; separation of short and medium term from long term loans; introduction of a crop loan system to help farm production, with a close link between credit societies and marketing organizations; coordination of all cooperative agencies to ensure utilization of loans and their prompt recovery; and, perhaps most important of all, substantial state participation in the share capital of the cooperative credit institutions at all three levels, to enable them to withstand the pressure of vested interests.

The Committee's recommendations were accepted in toto by the Central and the State Governments. Soon they became a major plank in official policy and an integral part of the Five-Year Plans which made generous allocations to implement it. This policy, with marginal adjustments, continued to dominate the rural scene through the mid-sixties until its patently inadequate approach was highlighted by the march of events.

*Establishing a Cooperative Monopoly.* Neither the Survey Committee's diagnosis nor the remedy it prescribed contained anything startlingly new, except that it should, with so much exuberance, prescribe a remedy which had already been tried out and found sadly wanting. Cooperation in India was born as a government enterprise; it did not sprout from below but was, like community development, planted from above; it failed to strike root and, in most cases, wilted in a bureaucratic hothouse. These were established facts which could not escape even a superficial observer. Yet the Committee failed to take note of them and fervently pleaded for a much larger measure of government support. The recipe, in other words, was substantially the same as before. The only difference was that, henceforward, it was to be administered in heavier doses.

The Committee, in short, excelled in the degree of faith it evinced in an already exploded dogma. And this exaggerated faith paved the path to another fatal pitfall. According to its findings, agriculture got "less than four rupees out of every hundred financed by commercial banks." Or, looked at from the cultivators' angle, the credit they obtained from these banks "was less than one per cent" of their total borrowings, and even this was confined only to a few districts. From this the Committee concluded that although cooperation was inadequate, in the prevailing conditions "*there was no alternative to the cooperative form of association in the village for the promotion of agricultural credit and development.*"[3]

The logic was indeed curious. In essence, it was like arguing that since the villages had no highways and were almost entirely dependent on mud roads, the ideal mode of transportation for them would be bullock-carts! But the designers of the Integrated Scheme were not baffled by this palpable *non sequitur*. How to open up the rural areas and plant modern

[3] Italics supplied.

dynamic institutions for their development—this had all along been by far the most important question in this context. The Committee did not discuss it. Instead, it decided to treat agricultural credit and development as a closed preserve of the cooperatives!

Modern joint-stock banks, if agriculture-oriented and equipped with trained staff, could help modernize agriculture and revitalize the co-operative societies. This was the obvious and most logical approach. Yet it was summarily ruled out by the Survey Committee which proceeded to establish a monopoly of rural credit for the cooperatives. As it happened, even the State Bank of India, which was created on the Committee's own recommendation by nationalizing the old Imperial Bank, was kept at an arm's length.

The cooperatives, ensconced as monopolies for supply of rural credit, had neither the incentive nor the opportunity to grow into efficient units. Instead, they began to develop their political muscles, aided by the antics of an infant democracy; and soon they themselves grew into powerful vested interests. As a rule, they resented suggestions of competition and often did their best to forestall it to safeguard their privileged position. Meanwhile, rural areas continued to be starved of credit, though the situation has somewhat improved after the recent policy changes.[4]

That the cooperative movement has, in general, been less than a stunning success is now admitted on all hands. In fact, there has, so far, been a lot of "movement," but little real cooperation. Spoon-fed more liberally than before, it has, in recent years, expanded impressively in size, but it displays more flabbiness than robust health.

To take a few key figures, the number of primary agricultural credit societies stood at 171,804 on 30 June, 1968, after declining by 6,931 in the previous twelve months, evidently because of the elimination of "dormant societies." However, even the reduced number contained 22,714 dormant societies covering 41,504 villages. And 30 per cent of the total, significantly enough, were working either at a loss or without profit. The advances rose from Rs. 24 crores in 1951-52 to Rs. 535 crores by 30 June, 1968; but overdues on that date amounted to Rs. 171.0 crores, or 32 per cent of the total loans.

The All-India Rural Credit Review Committee (AIRCRC), reporting in summer 1969, ruefully admitted that the rosy forecast made about the potentialities of cooperative development under the Integrated Credit Scheme of 1951-52 "substantially failed to materialize," and that there had been "serious and avoidable failures on the part of those who implemented the policy." It was bitter over the intrusion of politics, both state and local, into the working of cooperatives.

Even according to official reports, cooperatives have, by and large, failed to deliver the goods, and only in three States—Gujarat, Maharashtra

[4] See Chapter 25, especially the section on multi-agency credit.

and Punjab—they have, owing no doubt to a combination of favourable factors, been able to show satisfactory progress. The reasons for this failure are no longer open to question. The cooperatives have long been in credit—and, to a limited extent, in other—business; yet, from the start they have been weak in business experience and managerial talent. Most of them are too small in size to be efficient operating units. In addition, they have been afflicted with the same triple malaise as community development projects: they have been centralized, bureaucratized, and, in recent years, increasingly politicized.

Today the problem of rural credit poses a major, if not the most serious, threat to India's future development. True, some steps have been taken to improve matters, but they are still very much in the nature of palliatives. The problem calls for urgent and radical rethinking, with far-reaching changes both in policies and in credit institutions. Otherwise it can nullify the benefits of the package approach based on modern inputs,[5] brake the current momentum of development, and even bring the new-born green revolution to an abrupt halt.[6]

## ON THE INDIAN FARMER

The pre-independence regime in India was reputed for its chronic inaction. Her post-independence years have been characterized by wrong actions. These, in turn, have stemmed from two deep-rooted misconceptions—about the farmer and about agriculture. Before concluding these reflections on her past it would be worth looking into both a little more closely.

Take, for example, the Rural Credit Survey Committee which has been the sheet-anchor of agricultural credit policy all these years. It proclaimed a renewed commitment to the ideal of cooperation; it earnestly sought ways and means to rescue it from its nagging woes, also showed wisdom in proposing an integrated credit system with crop loans and stable agricultural prices. But on the most crucial issues—the problems of the farmer —it did most of its thinking not through the head, but through the heart. This vitiated much of the diagnosis it made and the remedies it proposed.

The cultivators of India, the Committee stressed with considerable feeling, were victims of vested interests—landlords, moneylenders, traders, even officials. The remedy, it argued, was to bring the state into the picture in order to create a strong countervailing force and to give vigorous government support to the *cooperatives* at all levels. The premise was at best a half-truth, while the conclusion was a clear *non sequitur*.

The farmers were victims not only of the vested interests listed above,

[5] See Chapters 11-14.
[6] Problems relating to credit are discussed further in Chapters 25-26 on Agricultural Credit and in Chapter 27 on "The Credit Shackles."

17

but also of something else—of governmental inaction in a number of vital fields. They could be so easily exploited because the government was doing so little for their education to liberate them from ignorance, for their health to free them from malaria and other debilitating diseases, for land reform to give them their rightful security of tenure as tillers of land, and for agriculture to introduce the rudiments of modern farming. Had the government addressed itself properly to these areas, which, after all, represented the elementary duties of a modern state, the farmers would have grown in knowledge, skill and self-reliance, and the counter-vailing force, one could confidently assume, would have gradually emerged from within the village itself, without requiring artificial credit, and non-credit, crutches from outside.

The emphasis on cooperatives, however laudable, was decidedly pre-mature. For, of all institutions genuine cooperatives are the most difficult to build and to operate, especially because they postulate a relatively high degree of development and of social justice, in terms of education, health, jobs-and-income, which was noneexistent in rural India.[7]

The weak and the strong could not combine, the Committee had rightly argued, and therefore the weak had to be strengthened with the backing of the state. But how? Surely, the status quo in the village could not be changed just by projecting into it a larger measure of governmental authority. For, the authority itself could be pre-empted by those who throve on the status quo. To be more specific, the government-backed cooperatives, it had been assumed, would protect the weak and deal out even-handed justice. This could not but be wishful thinking as long as the old pattern of economic, political and social power continued un-changed. The cooperatives, with few exceptions, came to be dominated by the strong—that is, by the rural elite plus the officialdom, while the weak were left in the lurch more or less as before. No prophetic quality should have been necessary to foresee such an eventuality.

The failure to evolve sound policies for rural development reflects, in the final analysis, a failure to understand the farmer and his needs. Sym-pathy for him has been over-abundant—in speeches and writings, even in legislation; but it was seldom translated into hardheaded analysis and sound practical action. The Indian farmer in most cases "lacks one square meal a day"—this well-known cliché was repeated ceaselessly, but he was never given what he most sorely needed—a fair deal.

The Indian farmer was not only much misunderstood, but was also much maligned; he was both undercared and underrated. He was prodded and goaded on the plea that he needed to be "awakened," even when he was awake and perhaps kicking; he was to be rescued from his ingrained

---

[7] Cooperation in India, because of some accidents of history, concerned itself mostly with credit societies where success is most difficult to achieve, compared with marketing and supply cooperatives. See Chapter 25.

inertia and was therefore entrusted to the care of amateurs; he was subjected to inspirational talks long after he had been made cynical by gar-
rulous inaction and frustrated hopes; he was served overdoses of stimulants
and denied the most elementary inputs.

This was a very good case where one could apply Occam's Law of
Parsimony, or "Occam's Razor,"[8]—that one must not evoke more complex reasons to explain behavioural phenomena when simpler ones are
adequate. The traditional view of the Indian farmer, at least until very
recently, was that he was unprogressive—unreceptive of new ideas and
unresponsive to incentives; that he was "timeless," "changeless," and
"tradition-bound," as if these were his congenital traits. Yet in reality,
he was wedded to subsistence farming because he knew that was the
only way he could subsist. He was denied—by fate and by government—
any valid alternative. The timeless, changeless farmer fretted only too
often in roadless, helpless isolation.

What is surprising is that the traditional view should have persisted so
long even in the face of impressive evidence to the contrary. For example,
long ago when the cultivation of jute was first introduced in Eastern
India, cultivators promptly adopted it on a wide scale; the market for raw
jute was well organized, and as a cash crop jute, they found, was more
remunerative. The cultivators were usually quick in adopting new and
improved varieties of jute introduced from time to time by the All-India
Jute Research Institute.

Some rich and hardy varieties of sugarcane evolved at Coimbatore,
South India, in the early thirties spread over the country with amazing
rapidity. Spurred by protection, sugar factories sprang up in several
provinces and, in barely a decade, India became self-sufficient in sugar.

Where access to large urban markets was fairly easy, farmers took to
the cultivation of vegetables and fruits on an intensive scale, based on
whatever knowledge and resources they had at their disposal. Many of
them readily adopted new and improved varieties; their production was
fully market-oriented; they were sensitive to price fluctuations, and, in
general, quite shrewd in calculating their own profit margins and incomes,
though a long chain of middlemen mercilessly cut into both.

No less significant is the case of chemical fertilizers cited earlier. It was
a revelation to see how the "unchanging" farmers, hitherto unaware of the
existence of artificial fertilizers, began to take active interest in them as
knowledge spread and food prices soared, and how, within a few years,
their demand exceeded the available supply, giving rise to something
incredible and profoundly meaningful—a sizable black market in fertilizers.

[8] William of Occam, fourteenth-century English philosopher, framed the Law to
counter the tendency, then widely prevalent among scholastic theologians, to explain
nature in complex, metaphysical terms. Like a razor, the Law "shaved away" these
explanations and substituted simpler ones in their place.

These are striking evidences to show that the Indian farmer is far from unresponsive. He is cautious, but not callous; he plays safe, as he must, because he cannot afford to take chances. Yet like farmers elsewhere in the world, he, too, can be persuaded when someone has something really worthwhile to offer and when its benefit is convincingly demonstrated to him.

The fact is that, until recently, the Indian farmer had been offered very little indeed—in terms of improved seeds, fertilizers, assured water supply, better agronomic practices, price incentives, crop loans, marketing facilities. This was particularly true of foodgrains production which dominates India's agriculture and accounts for 85 per cent of the total acreage under crops. Thus, the boot is on the other leg. It is the government that has been unresponsive in the sense that it failed to assess and meet the farmer's needs.

The evaluation reports on the Intensive Agricultural District Programme[9] are full of praise, even enthusiastic, about the Indian farmer and his eagerness to adopt better technology. But they are far less so about the quality of the manifold facilities and services which he is entitled to, and which, in a modern state, must be supplied by the government.

The two main programmes launched by the government—community development and cooperative credit—were unable to provide these specific services. Not only that; they were faulted by a major miscalculation. Contrary to the ideals they professed, they were inadequately selfhelp-oriented; instead, they soon grew into vast spoonfeeding agencies.

What the programmes failed to see is that, under application of massive state aid, the traditional society would "droop and lodge," like the traditional varieties of wheat and rice under application of heavy doses of fertilizers. The task of *biological engineering* today, as was seen earlier (Chapter 3), is to build a new *plant type*—strong-strawed, erect-leafed, able to absorb a maximum of fertilizers and of solar energy. *Social engineering* faces a similar task today—to build a new *peasant type*—robust, self-reliant, energetic, able to absorb fresh ideas, and quick to exploit new opportunities.

The two engineering tasks are complementary, and equally vital for the green revolution. Only when both tasks are tackled adequately, and co-ordinatedly, the revolution will roll on with assured momentum.

## AN UNINSPIRING RECORD

"We stretched traditional agriculture almost to the very limit during the first three plans," observed Mr. Subramanian, former Union Minister of Food and Agriculture, some time ago. India could not depart earlier from the traditional path, he argued, because "the new varieties of seed were

[9] See Chapters 11-14.

just not available." She created new irrigation facilities, increased extension services, instituted the package programme. Only thereafter "qualitative change" was feasible.[10]

Such a view would be soothing to the soul, if it did not do violence to the actual facts. That a great many things had been done under the national plans for—or in the name of—agriculture, no one can deny. Nor can it be denied that a great deal more could, and should, have been done years before the arrival of the high-yielding varieties. The overall record is anything but inspiring. It is packed with errors—of omission and commission, with wrong policies and missed opportunities. Let us illustrate.

To leave the farmers at the mercy of seasonal price slumps was deplorable. It was also inexcusable, especially when one recalls how consistently the pre-independence regime used to be criticized for its failure to eliminate such slumps which were treated as an evidence of exploitation. Such powerful price deterrents were enough to kill all farmer initiative. The remedy need not have waited for the arrival of the new seeds.

In fact, much better results could have been achieved even with the old seeds if enough attention had been paid to their quality. As Mr. Dick Leeuwrick pointed out in April 1969, India's wheat yields had been so low, "despite the excellent breeding work" that had been conducted for many years, at least partially because of the failure to maintain "varietal identity." For, new varieties, in the absence of proper care to safeguard their purity, "soon retrogress to an 'average' type."[11]

The black market in fertilizers, which sprang up in the mid-fifties, was sufficient testimony to the fact that there was no need to wait for the high-yielding varieties to promote fertilizer use on a much wider scale.

True, the fertilizer-responsiveness of HYV has reached levels beyond all dreams. But the failure of pre-HYV varieties to respond to fertilizer application has, in recent writings, been frequently exaggerated. Their response, though not spectacular, was quite significant, as was borne out by early IADP experiments. Besides, fertilizer experiments in India were usually carried out in a slipshod fashion, mostly without soil tests. But for this, they would, in all probability, have given a better response.[12] In any case, FAO studies on fertilizer experiments carried out in many developing countries have confirmed that fertilizers used in moderate doses give appreciable increases in yield even without varietal improvement.

The intensity of cropping was abnormally low in India, even in irrigated areas. It should have been raised long ago with more determined

[10] "India's Program for Agricultural Progress," by C. Subramanian in Rockfeller Symposium on *Strategy for the Conquest of Hunger*, Rockefeller Foundation, New York, 1968.

[11] "Reaction to New Wheat Varieties," *Seed Specialists' Seminar Proceedings*, New Delhi, April 8-11, 1969. Mr. Leeuwrick was then a Ford Foundation expert with IADP.

[12] See Chapter 18.

effort. There was no shortage of demand for food crops. The main deterrents were a price structure which inhibited production, and lack of transportation, especially village-to-market roads.

The worst errors in the pre-HYV days, however, were made in India's river valley projects. Here the writer can do no better than quote himself from an article published in December 1949:[13]

\*               \*               \*

### Three Crops a Year Programme

In his remarkable lectures on the "Ancient Systems of Irrigation in Bengal," delivered at the Calcutta University some twenty years ago, Sir William Wilcocks eloquently recalled "the days when travellers considered Central Bengal as rich as Egypt and the Burdwan Raj as claiming first rank in productive agricultural value in the whole of India." There is no inherent reason why a three-crops-a-year programme, after the pattern of the Egyptian agriculture, should not ultimately be feasible in the lower Damodar Valley. The view is no doubt held by some that the cultivator will not make more than a partial use of the irrigation facilities to grow a second crop because, according to them, the fatalist in him is stronger than the "economic man." Such pessimism is, however, hardly warranted by facts. For even now the cultivator does show a good deal of skill in doing his job, although he is not only shackled by the monsoon and frequently crippled by malaria but has, in addition, only primitive tools to work with. It is significant that, as a rule, he grows a second crop wherever feasible in the lower Valley, often laboriously lifting the water from tanks and ponds. The steep rise in agricultural prices during and after the war has impelled him to exploit such opportunities even more fully, which shows that he is, after all, not so oblivious of his self-interest nor wholly impervious to normal economic incentives.

It should not be overlooked that in one important respect DVC's approach to the irrigation problem will differ from the past practice followed in India. Though irrigation should include not only planned provision of water, but also its planned use, the latter has only too often gone by default, perhaps because of the tendency to treat irrigation as the exclusive jurisdiction of the irrigation engineer without any direct association with the agriculturist as well. No wonder that the irrigation task should be considered to be over as soon as water has been made available to the cultivator, no matter whether the latter actually avails himself of the facilities or not. Translated into business terminology, this means that

---

[13] "Damodar Project's Food Potential Strengthens Priority Claim" by Sudhir Sen, Secretary, DVC, *CAPITAL Annual Supplement*, Calcutta, December 22, 1949. This bit of self-plagiarizing has been indulged in to help straighten a distorted view of the past, to avoid a possible suspicion of "wisdom by hindsight," and because the ideas contained in the extract are still largely valid.

attention has been concentrated on the *production* aspect to the neglect of the equally vital function of *marketing*.

The DVC cannot afford to rest content merely with the passive function of supplying water, but will have to promote its use actively in every possible way for the double reason that, as a business undertaking, it must look after its own profit and loss account, and, as a public corporation, it has a specific statutory responsibility for promoting social and economic welfare in the area. If, for example, the DVC finds that the cultivator is not making adequate use of the water for growing a second, or even a third, crop even when such a crop is definitely an economic proposition, it will have to examine the causes closely and devise suitable remedies. Given the large latent demand for water in the lower Damodar Valley, there is no reason why the Corporation should not be able "to sell" all the water, especially if it develops and exploits the "market potentialities" with the enterprise characteristic of a modern commercial undertaking by adopting such measures as low promotional rates for water in the early stages, test demonstration through selected farmers, coupled with such inducements as the provision of free or subsidised seeds, manures, fish fry, even water.

As a result of such measures the intensity of cropping in the area should rise steadily. In, say, ten years' time from the introduction of perennial irrigation, it should be possible to convert the entire irrigable area into a twice-cropped area, the proportion of which at present amounts to only 6 per cent of the total land under cultivation. Besides, DVC's agricultural programme must include proper drainage, soil improvement and conservation, better manuring, better seeds and strains, scientific crop rotation and better agronomic practices. Irrigation accompanied by such measures ought to bring about a big rise in the acre output of rice and other crops. A 100 per cent increase in production per acre, both for kharif and rabi crops, is by no means an absurd proposition. It is well known that China grows twice, and Japan three times as much rice per unit of land as India. Given the unusually favourable climatic factors and the high fertility of the soil, there is no reason why the lower Valley should not be able to produce more rice per acre of irrigated land than China. Similarly, it should be possible to double the average output of rabi crops per acre with a considerable improvement in the quality of the produce. Lastly, a third crop in the Damodar delta is a distinct possibility in the not too remote future, and, as in the lower Nile Valley, it should gradually become a permanent feature of agriculture in this area.

From the angle of marketing the agricultural produce, hardly any other area in this country is more favourably situated than the lower Damodar Valley. The large and expanding market of Calcutta and industrial areas lies almost next door, while the coal-fields of Bengal and Bihar as well as other urban areas in and around the Valley, including Jamshedpur, should draw their supplies largely from the lower Damodar area. Feeding these areas, especially the ever-increasing mass of people in Calcutta, is becoming a more and more difficult problem, and is imposing a considerable strain on the transport system of the country. Nothing could be more logical in the circumstances than to develop the agriculture of the perennially irrigated lower Damodar region primarily to meet the food requirements of these urban areas. This will call for a diversified pattern of agriculture in place of the present monoculture of rice, in order to meet the urban demand for milk, eggs, fish, meat, potatoes and other vegetables, and fruits, which will yield a much higher income than from the cultivation of foodgrains. If properly replanned increased yields of rice per acre should go hand in hand with a diminishing rice acreage and an increase in the area devoted to vegetables, fruits, fodder, sugarcane and other miscellaneous crops. The rabi cultivation should make substantial provision for potatoes, sweet potatoes, and other heavy-yielding vegetables.

### Use of Fertilisers

However fertile the soil in the lower Valley may be, perennial cropping cannot go on indefinitely without impoverishing the soil, unless steps are taken to build up and maintain its fertility. A proper crop rotation with leguminous crops whenever feasible can in large measure take care of the need for nitrogen. Better utilisation of farm-yard manure, with proper composting of all vegetable matter, can go a long way to maintain fertility. This can be supplemented by dressings of "green manure," especially before the cultivation of kharif crops. It is well known that the strength of agriculture in Japan and China is largely due to the care with which the farmers utilise every possible source of plant food including cattle and human refuse as well as dry leaves, weeds, straw and farm-yard waste which are all put into a compost pit and turned into valuable manure. The Indian farmer cannot continue for long to starve his land of the vital organic matter without starving himself in the end. Above all, he cannot afford the continued waste of night-soil, which is one of his cheapest and richest sources of organic manure.

Our villages today are mere "dung heaps," said Gandhiji, emphasizing the need for cleansing village lanes and streets of all rubbish, much of which, he urged, could be turned into manure and thus become a source of wealth. "Excreta picked up are golden manure for the village fields," he said in a striking passage, though at present "this rich manure, valued at lakhs of rupees, runs to waste day by day, fouls the air and brings disease into the bargain." The Royal Commission on Agriculture, more than twenty years ago, laid special stress on the need for utilizing night-soil as manure and strongly recommended that all municipal authorities should be induced to convert it into poudrette through scientific methods.

It is curious that the so-called grow-more-food campaign should have been conspicuously silent about this vast and untapped source of national wealth.

The use of fertilisers should no doubt expand, but it would be obviously more economic if they are used to supplement, and not to supplant, the inexpensive manures mentioned above. Under perennial cropping special care will have to be taken not to upset the delicate mineral balance of the soil. As in other countries, phosphates and potash, and even lime, are almost sure to become the critical minerals so that, sooner or later, they will have to be applied to the soil in judicious doses in order to maintain the proper mineral balance.

*       *       *

Let there be no illusion about it. The record of India's performance in agriculture is far from gratifying. Many mistakes have been made, and some tragic blunders too. But for them, she could have attained self-sufficiency in foodgrains long ago, and could have maintained it despite population growth. And but for them, her problems now would have been far less overwhelming. What India needs today are not alibis for the past, but greater objectivity and stricter scrutiny of her track-record with its achievements and failures, to draw the right lessons from them, and to use them as valuable ingredients for perfecting the strategy for the future. There is no need for breast-beating, but a good deal of soul-searching is definitely called for.

## BACK TO THE AXIOMS

India has strayed too far from the axioms of development set forth earlier (in Chapter 2). She has been tricked by her own idealism which has led her on to wrong and devious paths.

At the root of her trouble lies an ingrained habit, which is largely the result of a generation-long emotion-packed national movement: to substitute sentiment for reason, idealistic impulses for scientific analysis, to apply heart-solutions to what are preeminently head-problems. As a result, her biggest problems have proved more intractable and have eluded solution, while a disaster continues to loom on the horizon.

To conquer poverty and hunger, India must, first of all, conquer these fatal proclivities. She must shake off her lingering nostalgia for a by-gone past, temper her idealism with science, and gear her policies to the axioms of development. More specifically, she must realize:

That it is senseless to pursue the chimerical goal of a village-centred economy when the world itself has been thrown into a melting-pot in this fast-changing scientific age; that one must re-pattern and re-structure the entire economic life to meet not yesterday's dreams, but today's realities and tomorrow's needs;

18

That the vote is not a valid substitute for bread; that however valuable as a tool of progress, it is meaningless in the hands of starving, illiterate masses; that it will acquire real meaning only to the extent they are provided with tangible economic opportunities to improve their lot;

That, in her four-thousand-year-old history, she has never been confronted with a crisis of such gravity and magnitude as stares her in the face today; that the sheer weight of numbers threatens to submerge her, and that her very survival is at stake today; that in the next ten years or so, the die will be cast, either way, for all time to come;

That if the population explosion is a gift of modern science and technology, suddenly thrust upon an unsuspecting world, so is also the green revolution which has burst upon the underdeveloped world with the same suddenness; that the green revolution, if fully exploited, can not only soften the impact of the population problem, but can help solve it once and for all;

That, to exploit the full potential of the green revolution, however, it is imperative for her to embrace science and technology wholeheartedly, to mobilize all her resources on a nation-wide scale, and, above all, to put to the fullest possible use the talents of her own people, particularly of the scientists, since these talents represent her proudest, most valuable, but also her most underused asset; and

That, in order to do so, India must disengage herself from hasty and erroneous commitments of the past, eschew the romantic paths, substitute science and technology for emotional amateurism; that, in short, she must go back to the axioms.

But it is not necessary for her to surrender her ideals; indeed, she must not do so, for as long-range goals, they are still valid. All she needs to do is to change the means she has been relying on so long, and to use science and technology, fully and systematically, because these are the only tools that will deliver the goods. The plea here is not for giving up, but only for *reculer pour mieux sauter*. It does not spell the end of her dream; it is a call for a fresh start with solid assurance of its ultimate realization.

CHAPTER 10

# The Food Crisis

## SOME BACKGROUND FACTS

Nothing is causeless,[1] as Orwell reminded us; certainly not the food crisis of India. The stage for it was set long ago, longer than people are usually aware. A lagging economy with few industries, a rising population, growing pressure on land, neglect of agriculture which languished in the subsistence type of farming of the pre-scientific age clearly bore the seeds of a future crisis. The situation steadily worsened over many decades. The outside world took little notice of it, except on occasions of such dramatic development as the Bengal famine of 1943.

An analysis of foodgrain production in India shows that, despite sharp fluctuations, the long-term-trend was distinctly downward. For the twenty-five years ended in 1924-25, the annual production averaged at 70.16 million tons; in the twenty-three years ended in 1947-48, that is, the last year of undivided India, the annual average was 67.39 million tons. In the first period, there were thirteen years when the production was 70 million tons or more, and in four of them the level reached or exceeded 80 million tons. In the second period, only six years saw production levels of, or more than, 70 million tons, and there was not a single 80-million ton year.

The figures are even more telling when expressed in kilograms per caput. The population of undivided India rose from 284 million in 1900-1 to 410 million in 1947-48. Annual production of foodgrains dropped from 236.32 kg to 186.95 kg per caput over the same period.

After partition, India's population stood at 354 million in 1948-49, and

[1] In this section the writer has used part of his article entitled "Damodar Project's Food Potential Strengthens Priority Claims,"—published in *CAPITAL—Annual Supplement*, Calcutta, 22 December, 1949, and cited in the preceding Chapter.

production in that year amounted to 57 million tons, giving only 164 kg per head. In the two years 1950-51 and 1951-52, this per capita figure dropped to 151 kg owing to poor harvests.

It may be added that the long-term decline in food production was, in all probability, sharper than is reflected in the figures cited above; for, in the earlier decades, production tended to be underestimated, particularly in the permanently-settled areas of North-East India.

This secular trend in food supply was accelerated by several factors since the early forties. India emerged out of the war years with her traditional year-to-year carryover completely depleted. Immediately thereafter she was faced with a number of poor crop years. On top of this came the heavy influx of refugees—some ten million people—from both East and West as an aftermath of partition. West Punjab, long regarded as the granary of India, was converted overnight, like Burma in 1937, from an internal into an external source of supply; it exported men to feed in lieu of food to feed them with.

Nor was this all. After the partition India had to make frantic efforts to produce enough jute and cotton for her textile mills which had been cut off from the sources of their raw material supply. This entailed transfer of a substantial acreage from grain to fibre.

Meanwhile, per capita consumption began to rise perceptibly. Soaring prices of foodgrains enabled the cultivator to retain a larger proportion of the output for his normally underfed family; this led to a fall in the marketable surplus. There began, at the same time, a noticeable shift of purchasing power to people in the lower-income brackets, particularly the working-class, the bulk of whose income is spent mainly on foodstuffs. Even rationing in urban areas, paradoxically enough, seemed to have contributed to the same result. For a country of chronic under-nourishment offers little scope for general belt-tightening in emergency conditions, so that rationing ends by pooling not excesses over a given minimum nutritional standard, but deficits by which the average consumption falls short of it. The cumulative effect of all these factors was to widen the gulf between demand and supply.

And overshadowing them all was the continuous growth of population. Around 1949, it was assumed that the average rate of increase was something like one per cent per annum!

In the pre-planning period grain imports rose alarmingly from year to year, as should be evident from the table on the next page. India had an adverse balance of payments amounting to about Rs. 200 crores in 1948-49. Foodgrain imports alone accounted for no less than 65 per cent of this total.

In the three years preceding the First Five-Year Plan the imports averaged at about 3 million tons a year, and some Rs. 750 crores worth of

IMPORTS OF FOODGRAINS INTO INDIA

|  | Quantity<br>in 1,000 tons | Value<br>in crores of Rs. |
|---|---|---|
| 1943-44 | 326 | 8.4 |
| 1944-45 | 327 | 15.8 |
| 1945-46 | 931 | 26.0 |
| 1946-47 | 2,569 | 88.9 |
| 1947-48 | 2,656 | 108.7 |
| 1948-49 | 2,840 | 130.0 |

foreign exchange had to be expended on them. Long renowned as a "sink for precious metals," India was fast becoming a sink for foodgrains.

## SELF-SUFFICIENCY IN FOOD

"India must be self-sufficient in food within three years—this is what the government has decided." So was the writer told by a senior administrator in Delhi in 1952, soon after the initiation of the First Plan. This was the reply he received in response to his plea to take urgent steps to tap the Lower Damodar Valley for food production.

Self-sufficiency in food by 1955! How was this going to be achieved? By an official declaration? It was not fashionable to raise such awkward questions in those days. Not that the leaders and policymakers were not worried about the food situation. Indeed, they were; for they knew only too well how the grain imports were bleeding the economy of foreign exchange. They were anxious to stop this drain, and to save and devote the resources to other development work, especially to industries. They hoped, and believed, that the drain could be stopped before too long.

The general mood, both inside and outside the government, was a mixture of concern, hope, and complacency; but it was the last element that was most evident. And at least *prima facie*, there were some good reasons to support a relatively optimistic view. The river valley projects were under construction; they would extend the irrigated area which would lead to larger production. The Community Development Programme had been launched; the multiplicity of activities it embraced did include minor irrigation projects and other items to help agriculture, and they, too, would sooner or later make an impact on farm output.

What about the weather? After all, India had lived with the monsoon for ages, and, though unpredictable, it was in general bountiful; the odds should not vary tremendously in the future; good years and bad should, as hitherto, pretty well balance themselves out. Meanwhile, the extension of irrigation should provide at the least some extra insurance.

All this sounded quite plausible, but only on the surface. To anyone probing deeper below, the balance between supply and demand looked dangerously precarious. Domestic production fluctuated upwards, but the demand rose steadily and at a faster rate. Even in years of good rainfall, the gap persisted. It continued to be closed with imports coupled with that never-failing element—wishful thinking.

The last element was for a while bolstered by what looked like reassuring facts. The First Plan had assumed a base production level of 54.87 million tons of foodgrains a year and had targeted for 62.59 million tons to be reached in 1955-56. That year the actual production amounted to 65.85 million tons, thus overshooting the target by a comfortable margin. With the rising production grain imports fell substantially—in 1954 and 1955 they amounted only to 840,000 and 755,00 tons valued at Rs. 49 and Rs. 35 crores respectively (Table 7). The day of self-sufficiency almost seemed to have arrived.

The rosier outlook was due to a combination of factors: past efforts to extend irrigation, to introduce fertilizers, and—good luck. The monsoon, still the main determinant of the volume of production, had behaved surprisingly well for a string of years, through 1955.

This fact was not overlooked in preparing the Second Five-Year Plan. It was recognized that with increasing population and rising incomes, the consumption of foodgrains was bound to go up. The production target was set at 75 million tons to be reached in 1960-61,[2] which was 10 million tons above the assumed base level of 65 million tons in 1955-56. In addition, the Plan provided for imports aggregating six million tons; a substantial part of the total was to be imported in the first half of the Plan period. This was considered essential to meet the rising demand, also to replenish the stocks with the government, which were running low. The Plan breathed no euphoria; it was still haunted by a sense of unsolved crisis though somewhat muted by the knowledge of good harvests.

The good luck did not last long. Production faltered—in 1957-58 it barely touched the previous high of 68.9 million tons reached in 1953-54; then in the following year it slumped to 62 million tons. It did pick up thereafter—for the following six years it averaged at 78 million tons, and then, in 1964-65, it shot up to a record figure of 88 million tons. But the year-to-year gyrations continued within wide margins with an ever-present threat that a poor harvest might suddenly upset all calculations and unhinge the national plan.

Meanwhile, the population curve, which could move only in one direction, began to rise more steeply, though still somewhat stealthily; the full measure of the uptrend was not suspected by the government, not even

[2] *Second Five-Year Plan*, p. 262. The target was considered inadequate and was raised, in November 1956, from 75 million to 80.5 million tons (*Third Five-Year Plan*, p. 302).

by demographers, at home or abroad. The divergent movement of the two curves—of food and population—carried an awesome omen. The gap between the two could, at any time, yawn into a disaster.

## A TURNING POINT

This, then, was the situation in the late fifties: For over a decade India had wistfully chased self-sufficiency in food, and had at one point come tantalizingly close to it, but only to find it receding fast into a dim horizon.

Heavy investments had been made in agriculture, especially in high-dam projects for flood control and irrigation, but they were still yielding a meagre return. Far-flung organizations had been built up for community development, but the slow-moving machinery was used mostly for amateurish tinkering with an obsolete pattern of agriculture. The farmer was ready for a big leap forward, but the government was not yet ready with a well-thought-out forward policy. Some elements of such a policy had been developed, but incoherently through isolated action while several key factors were still missing, and all of them were yet to be integrated to form an effective strategy. India was already caught in a fierce race between population and food, but the government was still unaware of its full gravity.

Things have changed since then almost in every respect, and changed radically. The critical gaps and weaknesses have been, or are being frantically filled or remedied. India's agriculture has, at long last, been consciously placed on the uphill path of modernization. A new revolution has been sparked in the countryside and, despite inevitable ups and downs, it is clearly moving ahead. As a result, the food-and-population race has lost some of its terror, and, at least for the immediate future, victory seems within reasonable reach.

How did all this happen within the brief span of a decade? Three main factors converged to bring about this spectacular reversal of trends: a Ford Foundation study, two disastrous droughts in two consecutive years, and the advent of the high-yielding varieties of wheat and rice.

The study made by a team of twelve consultants, in 1959, marks a watershed in the history of India's agriculture. Sponsored by the Ford Foundation on the joint request of two Central Government ministries, namely, Food and Agriculture, and Community Development and Co-operation, it included specialists in all the interrelated fields: soil and water, plant breeding, seed improvement, agricultural extension, animal husbandry, public administration, rural sociology, credit, cooperation and home economics. Its primary task was to investigate the problems, and to make practical recommendations to achieve more rapid increases in food production. It was headed by Sherman E. Johnson who served both as

Chairman and as Agricultural Economist. And it worked closely with an equal number of Indian associates designated by the Central Government.

The Team arrived in India in January 1959, toured extensively in the country, held numerous discussions at different places, and about three months later, in April 1959, submitted its report on "India's Food Crisis and Steps to Meet It." This was, in many ways, a remarkable document. It combined a rare breadth of vision with a depth of understanding which had been lacking so long; it mingled sympathy with realism and candour; it made farsighted, highly practical, and most timely recommendations; it was incisive, at some points almost blunt.

"India is facing a crisis in food production," declared the Team in a forthright fashion. "More specifically it is a crisis in foodgrains production. . . " The entire nation, it urged, "must be made aware of the impending food crisis, and steps must be taken to meet it." And then as a more direct warning it added: "Adequate supplies of food may indeed be essential to survival of democracy, because freedom from hunger is prerequisite to enjoyment of other freedoms. *If elementary wants, such as food and clothing, are not satisfied, the other freedoms may be sacrificed for food enough.*"[3]

According to the Team's estimates, *five* million persons per year had been added to India's population during the First Five-Year Plan; *seven* million per year would be added during the Second Plan period; and this would go up probably to *ten* million per year during the Third Plan period ending in 1966. Although there was considerable emphasis on family planning, no slowing down of population growth could be expected by that time.

The conclusion reached by the Team was startling: "Food will have to be provided for 80 million more people by the end of the Third Plan." And this explosive growth in population would raise the total from 360 million in 1951 to an estimated 480 million by 1966.

With these demographic projections in view, the Team recommended an annual target of 110 million tons of foodgrain production for the Third Plan, to be reached by 31 March, 1966, which represented a steep rise of 36 per cent over the revised official target of 80.5 million tons. The consumption requirements of cereals and pulses were estimated at 88.0 million tons; to these were added 12.6 million tons or 12.5 per cent of total production, for "seed, feed and wastage," and 9.4 million tons for "stock requirements and safety margin."

The suggested target allowed a small increase in per capita consumption

[3] *Report on India's Food Crisis and Steps to Meet It.* By the Agricultural Production Team sponsored by the Ford Foundation, and issued by the Government of India, Ministry of Food and Agriculture and Ministry of Community Development and Cooperation, April 1959. See esp. pp. 11-12. It is often referred to as the Ford Foundation's "Crisis Report."

—from 13.3 ounces of cereals and 2.4 ounces of pulses per day in 1956-57 to 15 ounces of cereals and 3 ounces of pulses for the projected population.

Foodgrain production in the previous five years had averaged at less than 68 million tons a year. This left a gap of 42 million tons to be bridged in seven years! Even if the sights were lowered and the target set at 100 million tons, the additional requirement would still be 32 million tons!

To meet this impending crisis the Team sketched out a comprehensive programme. It pinned its highest hopes on chemical fertilizers to which it gave topmost priority. Next in importance were hybrid maize, multiplication and distribution of improved seeds, and plant protection. Among its other major recommendations were measures for soil-and-water conservation, agricultural extension work, livestock development with practical steps to deal with the urgent but sensitive problem of surplus cattle. The Team laid great stress also on the need to strengthen agricultural administration, and to give it a more pronounced scientific orientation; to reinforce research and experiments; to expand and improve the facilities for credit, supplies and marketing; to press ahead with land reform to provide security of tenure; and to take appropriate steps to change the food habits in order to lower grain consumption and to redress imbalances in diet to secure better nutrition.

Food enough, the Team urged, must be made "a central objective in the crusade for the new India." But the problem could be solved only if the work were organized "on a war footing."[4] Agriculture, it therefore insisted, must be given the highest priority in the coming years, adequate resources must be allocated for the purpose, and an all-out emergency programme must be immediately undertaken on a national scale.

Finally, to meet both immediate and long-term objectives, the Team made another most significant plea: Given the shortage of trained manpower and of essential supplies like fertilizers and pesticides, efforts must be heavily concentrated in areas with the greatest potential for producing the most important crops—rice and wheat, and tailor-made production programmes must be worked out and introduced in each of these areas.

The publication of the report fell like a bombshell on a smug official world. The furore it caused was mixed with visible resentment. The initial reaction, even in otherwise sober and knowledgeable circles, was one of shock and disbelief. The population forecasts were considered exaggerated, if not alarmist, so also the estimates of food requirement in the Third Plan period and the extent of the food gap. The overall picture drawn by the Team was viewed as much too gloomy. Exception was taken to some of its comments which were considered less than objective and, in some instances, not altogether relevant.

Worst of all, there were whispers that the Team had revealed a sub-

4 Ibid., p. 14.

19

conscious bias in favour of agriculture at the expense of industrial development to which the government and its planners had so wholeheartedly committed themselves. These reactions served to show how little India was psychologically ready to grasp the full implications of her surging population and her lagging food production, and how little she understood the interdependence of agriculture and industries.

Despite these initial reactions, however, the Team's Report marked a decisive turning point. It shattered the lingering mood of complacency, drove home the fact that India's population growth was definitely outpacing her food production, and compelled a steeply upward revision of both.

Nor did the Team stop with a mere Cassandra-like prediction. With a keen sense of realism, it worked out a bold strategy indicating how India could in fact arrest this trend and win the food-population race. The hard core of that strategy consisted of concentration of effort, with a combination of modern inputs and improved practices, in the most productive areas to maximize impact within the shortest time. The government was wise enough to accept, in June 1960, this recommendation without demur and to embark upon a programme of intensive agriculture in selected districts. This was a historic decision which, as will be seen in the next four Chapters, was destined to yield solid results within a short time and to facilitate the transition to a modernized agriculture.

## THE DROUGHT AND AFTER

Thus, a major proposal of the Ford Foundation Team was accepted, and steps were taken to initiate the new programme, though at a rather unhurried pace. Otherwise there was, as yet, little visible change in the general attitude to the Team's other expostulations—its estimates of population growth, the extent of the food gap, the gravity of the looming crisis, its plea for giving the foremost priority to food production, for making much larger allocation of resources, and for launching an all-out emergency programme to arrest and reverse the disastrous trend. And suspicion still lingered in some minds that the food situation was painted too dark, perhaps to divert attention away from the programme of industrialization the country had launched in its Second Five-Year Plan with renewed hope and enthusiasm, though no one cared to explain who would benefit, and how, from the pursuit of such a neo-Machiavellian economic policy.

Yet after the Crisis Report things could no longer remain the same. The seeds of doubt and self-questioning it had planted soon began to work imperceptibly below the surface. Thoughtful minds gradually turned to a re-examination of the realities of the situation and the wisdom of the basic policy mix embodied in the Five-Year Plans. Then came a thumping vindication of the Team's projections and conclusions, not via logic and foresight, but in a most freakish way—through a grim display of the whims of Rain God.

In 1965 even the long notorious monsoon outdid its previous records. Vast tracts of the country were denied its capricious showers. In many areas crops could not be sown; if sown, they failed to mature and withered under a merciless sun. Even where they struggled and survived, they lost much of the grain-bearing capacity, and could give only a very poor yield, poor even by the pathetically low standards of India. The result was a bitter harvest—of extensive crop failures, a steep decline in the output per acre, and dark prospects for the future. Millions of people stood aghast staring at the sunbaked earth, with no sign of vegetation in sight, and with no water within easy reach even to meet the minimum human needs. It seemed as if Nature had suddenly carried out a well-planned scorched-earth policy on a gigantic scale.

Soon the country was in the grip of widespread starvation and near-famine condition. The government's preoccupation now was to procure foodgrains—in millions of tons—from all over the world, haul them across the high seas, unload them frantically at the congested ports, and rush them to the stricken areas. For several years India had lived on a hand-to-mouth basis. Now it became very much of a "ship-to-mouth" affair.

For months much of the country was turned into a vast relief establishment. It was dotted with feeding centres hurriedly set up on an *ad hoc* basis, operated by the government at all levels and by philanthropic institutions, both domestic and international. In all this, time was the essence of the matter. Cost was no concern. It had become, literally, a matter of life and death.

And lives were saved in millions thanks to the timely assistance—grain and other food, ocean freight, finance—generously extended by governments and benevolent institutions from abroad, particularly from the USA, to help India tide over this calamity. The worst was averted, though countless people perished as direct and indirect victims of starvation.

Then came something even more unexpected. This grim tragedy, with some minor variations, was enacted for a second time, in 1966. Two widespread droughts of unprecedented severity in two successive years—few had believed this could happen in India. Yet it did, and it shook the nation to the core. Once again the government launched on massive procurement operations all over the world; once again it had to haul millions of tons of grain across thousands of miles, unload them and rush them inland over hundreds of miles, distribute them through countless relief centres to tens of millions of people simply to enable them to keep body and soul together.

And once again it had to do all this regardless of cost, and at the expense of the planned activities on the development front. Grain imports soared to 10.6 million tons in 1965-66 and 8.7 million tons in 1966-67. The cost, in foreign exchange, amounted to Rs. 505 and Rs. 433 crores respectively leaving out generous grants and donations. The economy had come almost to a standstill. It was time to struggle and survive, also to pause and ponder. No complacency could outlive such a traumatic experience. It died finally in the drought.

A dazed nation now set out to review its past policies with the blinkers finally cast off. It could no longer be denied that the high priority hitherto given to agriculture had not been high enough in India's uniquely perilous situation; that the past programme, based largely on an incoherent assortment of projects, had not been adequately production-oriented; that these omissions had to be made good as fast as possible to forestall future disasters; that food production had, indeed, to be organized "on a war footing." The pharse had been repeated from time to time as a hollow slogan; but now it became a deadly reality. Out of this dearly-bought realization was born a new national policy.

Once the frantic pressure of relief work was lifted, the government launched a series of bold measures to achieve a rapid increase of food production. It took steps to expand the fertilizer industry and to establish several new factories; made liberal allocations to import fertilizers and pesticides to meet the immediate needs; enlarged the provisions for small irrigation projects and tube-wells; gave new price incentives to the farmers; liberalized agricultural credit; reorganized and reinvigorated the research and extension programmes; and set out to strengthen the agricultural infrastructure, along with a series of agro-industries and other corporate bodies. Many long-standing gaps were filled through belated official action.

This post-drought surge in government initiative was powerfully aided by a miraculous coincidence—the arrival of the high-yielding varieties of dwarf wheat from Mexico and of dwarf rice from the Philippines, described in Chapters 3-4. Seldom did a nation need a scientific windfall so desperately, and seldom did history oblige more mercifully.

The combination of normal weather, government measures, and high-yielding varieties has enabled India not only to stage an amazing recovery, but also to feel the first sensations of a yield-breaking revolution. The total foodgrain production, after reaching a peak of 88 million tons in 1965-66 had plummeted to 72 million tons in 1966-67, to rise moderately in the following year to 79 million tons. But in 1967-68 it spurted to 96 million tons, a record harvest, followed by another record in 1968-69 with a total of 98 million tons.

New year-to-year growth is now projected for the early seventies. And barring unexpected mishaps, the trendline should continue upward in the coming years.

## NEW PROJECTIONS

India has travelled a long way in the brief span of a decade or, more correctly, in the late sixties. The distance covered can be gauged from a few simple facts.

India's population, according to official estimates, crossed the 500-million mark some time in mid-1967. A Reserve Bank of India study made in January, 1967 projected that, by 1976, the total would rise to 630 million. Her foodgrain requirement would then reach 152 million tons a year—130 million for consumption, 18 milion for seed, feed and wastage, and four million for additional stocks.

The Registrar General of India projects that the population would increase by 2.5 per cent, or about 15 million, a year during the Fourth Plan period; and that the rate would fall thereafter, reaching 1.7 per cent a year by 1980-81, assuming that, by then, the birth-rate would drop from 39 per thousand in 1968 to 26 per thousand while, over the same period, the death rate would further decline from 14 to 9 per thousand. In other words, the population which stood at 527 million in 1968 would shoot up at least to 600 million by the end of the Fourth-Plan period, that is, by March, 1974. These estimates, which are in line with those of the Reserve Bank cited above, have been adopted by the Planning Commission for the Fourth Plan. By and large, they also conform to the projections made by the United Nations.[5]

The target for foodgrain production set by the Commission for the current Plan period is a 31.6 per cent increase—from 98 million tons in 1969 to 129 million tons in 1974.

The following statement made on the eve of formulating the Fourth Plan is illuminating: "The pace of development in the agricultural sector sets a limit to the growth of industry, of exports, and of the economy as a whole and constitutes a major condition for achieving economic and social stability and improving the levels of living for the mass of the people. *The success of the Fourth Plan will be judged, above all, by performance in agriculture.*"[6]

Such a forthright declaration about agriculture would have been unthinkable only a few years earlier. It is a measure of the profound policy shift that has occurred in India.

In 1967, when India was still in the grip of an acute food shortage with

[5] Since the above was written, the results of the latest decennial census have been published, according to which India's population stood at 547.37 million on 31 March, 1971; this represented an increase of 108.30 million over the preceding 10 years. During the same period her birth rate declined from 41.7 to 39 per 1000, and her mortality rate from 22.8 to about 16 per 1000. India's population growth, family planning programme, and related issues are analyzed in *Reaping the Green Revolution*, esp. in Chapter 15.

[6] *Fourth Five Year Plan, 1969-74 (Draft)*, p. 112. Italics supplied.

famine raging in several areas, especially Bihar, an eminent US agriculturist with a life-long experience behind him told the writer that he felt more reasssured than before about the future of India's agriculture. The basis for his confidence was rather unusual. He recalled how, in his own country, agriculture had for decades suffered from neglect, how even the most pressing reforms were continually put off owing to governmental indifference and public apathy, but how fast things changed once the country was plunged into the great depression, and how truly the foundations for its future agricultural prosperity were laid in those early days of the New Deal era when a series of far-reaching measures were rushed through the Congress to meet a national emergency. This he clearly expected to happen also in India.

And this is precisely what has happened after the drought and the famine. The blows of fate opened the eyes. This, in turn, led to a package of policies and reforms which had long been overdue.

CHAPTER 11

# Intensive Agricultural District Programme (IADP) —The Background

## NEGLECTED BREAD BASKETS

The low population projections and the food production target of the late fifties needed steep corrections. But this was not enough; there remained the formidable question: how to meet an almost 40 per cent higher target within the brief space of six years.

Of all the steps recommended by the Agricultural Production Team to meet this challenge, by far the most significant was its forceful plea for concentrating efforts and resources in a few selected areas possessing the highest potential to make the quickest impact in terms of increased output. India had to build up the granaries for her present and future population. Some areas richly endowed by nature and further developed with large public investments were clearly carved out to serve this purpose. They deserved priority treatment, and it was most urgent to accord it to them.

"Probably the greatest opportunity for immediate increase in food production," observed the Team in the Crisis Report, "lies in the improvement of water management, fertility and cultural practices on lands now irrigated, where opportunities for 2 to 3 crops a year exist." Immediate steps should be taken in these areas to provide adequate systems of water conveyance and distribution to the farmers with necessary technical and financial assistance, and with special attention to land levelling and land preparation to ensure more uniform distribution of water.[1]

Then, stressing what had long been obvious to some Indians whose protestations were greeted with solemn indifference, the Team went on to say: "India can make greater and more immediate gains in food production by intensifying expenditure of time and effort on water management than by constructing large-scale irrigation projects which take years to develop." A primary concern of the Third Plan should therefore be to allocate substantial funds "to aid cultivators in making better use of available water."

The Team drew pointed attention to the wasted potential of the river valley projects, long noticed and lamented by quite a few knowledgeable people.[2] In many of the irrigated areas water was available to grow two, even three, crops a year. Yet only 12 per cent of these areas were actually growing more than one crop. And even for this single irrigated crop use of fertilizer and good seed was rare. The result was an exceedingly low yield. Most farmers, for example, harvested only one-half ton of wheat per acre in irrigated areas where a few were already getting 1.1/2 tons per acre.[3]

For India as a whole, the irrigated fields, according to official estimates, produced only one-fifth to one-fourth ton more foodgrains than unirrigated fields. This was "an extremely low return on investment in irrigation." Yet this is the estimate the government used in appraising the benefits from new irrigation projects. Thus, good agricultural practices were not even expected on newly irrigated lands!

All this points to what has been a congenital weakness in India's irrigation engineering carried over from the British days. The engineers specialized in planning for just enough return—about 4 per cent—to service the capital in perpetuity. There was no suggestion of amortizing the capital, of earning a profit, certainly not of optimizing production for the benefit of the farmers and the economy. The objective was to provide *some* irrigation, and to provide it as a service by the government and therefore at the lowest possible cost. This was the rationale behind the piecemeal planning of irrigation projects. Its inevitable result was a deplorably low yield and a highly wasteful resource-use.

In an attempt to remedy this grave weakness the Team made some specific recommendations. Among other things, it urged that for each new major irrigation project an adequate percentage of the total cost should be earmarked and made available to start educational and other necessary technical work on irrigated land; that this work should begin

[1] Loc. cit., pp. 146-47.

[2] See Chapter 6.

[3] This point, once again, explodes the thesis that India could do nothing to increase acre-yields before the arrival of the HYV's.

*at the same time* as the engineering construction phase of the project; and that it should include research and demonstration, using water from wells or tanks, *as long in advance* as possible.

Ironically enough, this is precisely what the DVC had set out to do soon after it was established. Demonstrations, particularly for improved methods of rice cultivation, were laid out at selected places in the Valley. They included better seeds, careful land preparation, and what was particularly significant, moderate application of chemical fertilizers. This was, in essence, the so-called Japanese method of rice-culture adapted to the local situation. The yield per acre was 100 to 150 per cent higher than what was considered normal for the area. Local farmers frequented the DVC plots. Their interest was visibly kindled; they even began to put questions and ask for some of the inputs. The demonstrations were demonstrably catching on.[4]

Once again all this proved premature in the Indian context. The DVC, as a business undertaking, was anxious to prepare the ground, well in advance, for an optimum utilization of the irrigation water, to maximize production and other benefits, and of course to strengthen its own balance-sheet. But such an approach was too much of a break all too suddenly with an apathetic past. The hostility it aroused among the status-quo-minded veterans successfully made a fiasco of the DVC's irrigation enterprise. But for this melancholy turn of events much of India's subsequent history might have been differently written. The millions of tons of foodgrains which were imported from overseas sources could and should have been produced at home, in her own irrigated areas.

In January 1958, when the country was faced with a widening food gap, the National Development Council gave the "clarion call" to increase food production. At the same meeting, the NDC highlighted the fact that four million acres of land were under potential coverage of irrigation, that the marginal food deficit could be wiped off if India utilized the water which had been harnessed at enormous cost but was running to waste for lack of field distributaries and ancillary facilities.

While commenting on these facts, the then Minister of Community Development and Cooperation drew attention to another anomaly. His own Ministry had spent hardly 40 per cent of the allocation made for minor irrigation works. This, to quote his own words, came to him "as a shock."[5]

---

[4] This promotional work was pioneered by a young Cornell-trained Indian agronomist, Dr. A. K. Dutt, who combined high technical competence, hard work including actual field operations, and an infectious enthusiasm to an extent still rare in India. At present he is Director of Agriculture in West Bengal.

[5] S. K. Dey, *Community Development—A Chronicle: 1954-61*, Government of India (Publications Division), 1962, p. 90.

20

## THE COMPLEMENTARITY PRINCIPLE

India's irrigation policy had to be rescued from its long-standing follies. This is what the Agricultural Production Team sought to achieve with the recommendations cited above. Its authoritative views forcefully expressed in a unanimous voice had a telling effect. They heralded the end of a long era of blind domination of India's agriculture by her irrigation engineers. This rescue operation was, in itself, an event of tremendous significance.

The irrigated areas are what one may call India's potential bread baskets. This, in effect, was the first major point the Team sought to drive home. The second point it made was no less significant. To develop these baskets irrigation was not enough. Water is an indispensable input, but by itself it can raise yield only to a limited extent. Truly remarkable results can be obtained only when water is combined with other essential inputs—improved seeds, fertilizers, pesticides, etc.—and better agronomic practices. All these elements complement and reinforce one another; it is their interaction which boosts yield. Modern agriculture must be intensive, and it must be built on the principle of complementarity of inputs.

Today this may sound almost like a platitude. Yet not so long ago Dr. Kellogg could, without overstating things, remark: "Failure to grasp this vital principle of interactions is the greatest present technical handicap to agricultural development in the newly developing countries."[6]

Balanced supply of plant nutrients, adequate moisture in the rooting zone of the soil, well-adapted crop varieties of high genetic potential, and plant (and animal) protection—"all these four essentials must be changed simultaneously," he emphasized. "Rarely can economic progress be made only with one change."

The principle was certainly not familiar in India. The search for self-sufficiency in food led to a series of *ad hoc* measures, such as grow more food campaign, Japanese method of rice cultivation, introduction of so-called improved seeds, a compost and green manure drive, and of course extension of irrigation. They came like waves in successive stages, created artificial excitement for a while, and then vanished leaving very few traces behind. The poor management of water even in irrigated areas was in itself a measure of how little the complementarity principle was understood. Where it is at work, water supply could not but be strictly regulated and efficiently managed.

The Community Development Programme violated the principle no less glaringly, though in a different sense. It brought together *all* aspects of

[6] Charles E. Kellogg, "Interactions in Agricultural Development." In *Science, Technology and Development*, paper presented at UN Conference on the Application of Science and Technology to Development (Oct. 1962), and World Food Congress, Washington D.C. (4-18 June 1963).

rural development into one comprehensive programme—health, education, public works, housing, social welfare along with agriculture, fishery, poultry and animal husbandry. It preached and practised an omnibus complementarity of all aspects of rural life. The more limited and specific complementarity we are concerned with, namely, of agricultural inputs to raise crop yields per acre, was swallowed up in the process.

The earlier policy was to spread the development efforts on a fairly uniform basis throughout the country. The treatment of all areas on an equal footing ensured a kind of geographical equity. But it also failed to produce striking results in any particular area. Moreover, since the potentialities of the areas varied enormously, it inevitably involved a sacrifice of much larger production from the favourably-endowed areas. Thus, its drawbacks far outweighed considerations of equity. It was jeopardizing overall national interests and was not helping, but hindering development. A radical change of policy was clearly overdue.

The change came through the twin principles of concentration and complementarity. This, as the Team rightly implied, was the only rational approach India could adopt, not only to meet her emergency situation, but also to rebuild her agriculture on a modern foundation.[7] The underlying reasons are so important and are still missed so often that they deserve to be restated.

First, in the fifties India's production of foodgrains had increased at an average rate of 3 per cent per annum; of this, 1.6 per cent was due to yield improvement and the balance to extension of the cultivated area. The rise in acre-yield was only marginal, and even this small increment could not be guaranteed for the future. The most urgent, also the most obvious, need for her was to achieve a very substantial rise in her proverbially low yield per acre. Such a rise was technically feasible, but it could be brought about only in one way—by introducing yield-boosting technologies on an intensive scale.

Second, the surest way to achieve significant yield-breakthroughs with rapid increases in overall production was to concentrate efforts in the "most responsive areas" where the infusion of science and technology

---

[7] "We agree that concentration is essential beginning with water, plant and plant production (sic) and fertilizer—the things that get good grains," observed John Kenneth Galbraith, former U.S. Ambassador to India. "Nothing else is so important; everything else may consume scarce energy." *Ambassador's Journal—A Personal Account of the Kennedy Years*, Houghton-Mifflin Company, Boston, 1969, p. 67. This entry in the Journal is dated April 12, 1961. By that time IADP had already been launched.

He pressed for "concentration of energies on a few subjects concerned with bread-grain production," and helped bring about the necessary reform in the U.S. aid operations in India (under what was still called TCM). He also successfully pleaded to have the Peace Corps programme in India identified "pretty closely with agriculture." (Ibid., p. 209 and p. 95).

would yield the maximum benefits. These, clearly, had to be irrigated areas.

Third, yield breakthroughs, as indicated earlier, would be possible only when improved technologies and practices are adopted in combination, not in isolation.

And fourth, this combined approach is the only way to improve the payoff from capital investments in irrigation.

What about the other areas and the question of equity? The Team was by no means oblivious of this sensitive issue. The normal activities in other areas, it explicitly urged, should not be curtailed but should continue as before. In other words, the most responsive areas must be made to produce a great deal more; the higher production would redound to the benefit of the country as a whole, but this need not, and should not, occur at the expense of other areas.

### THE 10-POINT PROGRAMME

The logic behind the proposal was unexceptionable, and so it prevailed. In June, 1959 it was accepted, in principle, at a high-level Inter-Ministerial Committee of the Government of India. However, to work it out in more precise and practical terms, a second Team was sponsored by the Ford Foundation. Composed of three agricultural experts, this Team arrived in October, 1959, made a rapid survey of the selected areas in the various States and, in consultation with the Central and State Government experts, outlined what it called "Suggestions for a 10-Point Programme to Increase Food Production."

This pilot programme, as the Team underlined, had a fourfold objective, viz. to determine how rapid increases in food production could be best brought about, providing at the same time practical experience which could be used in other areas; to increase the farmer's income; to improve the economic resources of the village; and to create an adequate agricultural base for more rapid economic and social development.

The 10-Point Programme once again stressed the fundamentals involved and spelled out their practical implications in considerable detail. Farmers should be given *adequate price incentives* to increase production; they must also be provided with necessary *aids and services* to do so; a *farm plan* must be developed for each holding in direct consultation with the farmer; and on the basis of this plan, he must be given *enough credit* to purchase the additional inputs. In addition, village plans should be prepared for increased production, and village leadership strengthened along with village organizations such as cooperatives and panchayats.

Clearly, such an intensive approach could not, at least to start with, be applied to a large area. The limited resources alone—manpower, inputs, and finance—dictated the need to restrict it in scope. Besides, it was only common sense, the Team argued, to try it out first as an experimental programme, in order to draw appropriate lessons from experience, and then only to decide on its further extension.

The criteria for selecting the experimental areas had been laid down by the first Ford Foundation Team in broad terms, and they were now reiterated by the second one: Only those areas should qualify in the first instance, which had a specially favourable combination of physical and other factors and, consequently, would respond most favourably to an intensive treatment, leading to rapid gains in production. Quite obviously, such areas must, among other things, be already equipped with maximum irrigation facilities and be exposed to a minimum of natural hazards like floods.

Even such high-potential areas were then starved of essential inputs like fertilizers, and were thus prevented from making the big contribution they otherwise could to the country's depleted granary, and from earning a handsome return on the large capital sunk in the irrigation-cum-flood control projects. What could be more sensible than to choose these areas for an intensive effort directed to step up acre-yield to help meet a galloping grain shortage and place the finances of these projects on a sounder basis?

This was the immediate goal. But there was a longer-term one which was no less urgent. It was clear to both Ford Foundation Teams, as it had been for years to thoughtful Indians, that the economic salvation of India depended overwhelmingly on one thing: a quantum jump in her acre-yield based on scientific farming and multiple cropping. Such an objective could be reached only in stages. Yet the first decisive step in that direction was to apply, in selected areas enjoying optimum conditions, an integrated approach based on whatever improved technologies were already known and could be immediately applied, and to build further on this foundation by incorporating new results of research and experiments as soon as they became available. This is precisely what the pilot programme set out to accomplish.

It was widely believed that even the then known improvements, if intensively and systematically applied to the most responsive areas, would lead to large increases in output. Meanwhile, the Rockefeller Foundation through its plant-breeding programme—on wheat and maize in Mexico and on rice in the Philippines—was opening up new horizons for tropical agriculture; and it was also actively assisting India in crop research.[8] The Ford Foundation Team attached great significance to this work. While advocating that the integrated programme it recommended be launched forthwith based on the improved technologies then available, it urged that the progress of the Rockefeller Foundation-assisted crop breeding work be watched carefully in order to adopt its results as soon as they emerged out of the experimental stage and were ready for wider application.[8]

The methods and practices embodied in the "10-Point Pilot Programme" were, for the most part, not new in India. What *was* new, however, was the simultaneous application of all these elements in an optimum combination to achieve maximum increases in production. The main elements involved in this programme were:

1. Adequate and timely supply of *credit* on the basis of *production plans*. The credit was to be supplied by cooperative societies, and these were to be strengthened for the purpose.
2. Adequate and timely supply of *production requisites*, such as fertilizers, pesticides, implements. Again, all these inputs were to be channelled mainly through cooperatives.
3. Arrangements for *marketing* and other services. Once again, reliance was placed on cooperatives on the ground that they alone would enable the producers to secure full market price for their surpluses.
4. Adequate *storage* facilities for supplies, such as seeds, fertilizers, pesticides and implements, and for the farm produce. It was important to ensure that the cultivators would not have to travel long distances to procure supplies and to market their produce.
5. Intensive educational efforts, particularly through scientific *demonstrations* to disseminate improved agronomic practices. The existing and additional trained staff would be used for the purpose. The same staff would also supervise the operation and "follow-up" of production plans.
6. *Transport* arrangements to ensure mobility of supplies and staff. The existing facilities had to be strengthened.
7. *Village planning* for increased production. The primary emphasis would be on the production of rice, wheat and other major food crops. A strengthening of village organizations like cooperatives and panchayats was considered essential.
8. Establishment of agricultural implements *workshops,* and of seed and soil-testing *laboratories.*
9. Formulation and execution of local *works programmes* having a direct bearing on production increase.
10. Analysis and *evaluation* of the programme—from its initiation to its completion.

This, then, is the genesis of the Intensive Agricultural District Programme, the celebrated IADP. It was a far-sighted innovation, and through it were planted the seeds of a revolution in India's static agriculture—even before the arrival of the high-yielding varieties.

[8] See Chapter 22 under "Rockefeller Foundation's Programme," also the relevant sections in Chapters 3-4.

# CHAPTER 12

# Package Programme (IADP)
# at Work

## SIGNIFICANCE OF THE GUIDELINES

The initiation, expansion, working and impact of the IADP, or the "Package Programme" as it is commonly called, will be discussed in this and the next Chapter. Before proceeding further some reflection on its main guiding principles should be in order.

The 10-Point Programme, as just seen, sought to bring to a single focus all the essential elements needed to realize one overriding objective, namely, a rapid increase in production. This was in striking contrast with the earlier policies which had prevailed so long and were characterized by a piecemeal approach and haphazard infrastructure-building without much concern for results in terms of production and payoff.

The new programme, in effect, consisted of two related packages—of inputs and services respectively—both converging on one single objective, namely, to raise farm productivity. Farm planning was therefore rightly made its cornerstone.

### a. Farm Planning

The goal was no less than to effect, by the shortest route and at the quickest pace, a multiple transition from traditional to scientific farming, from mainly subsistence-oriented to mainly market-oriented production, from low-intensity to high-intensity cropping; in general, from a static, low-input, low-yield, low-income to a dynamic, science-based, high-input agriculture with sharply rising yields and incomes. These points, repeatedly stressed in IADP literature, were not new. What is new about the IADP is that it did not stop simply with the enunciation of these objectives, but as an action programme set systematically to bring about this transformation, relying on farm planning as its chief instrument.

Such planning, to be really fruitful, had to satisfy a number of basic conditions. A farm plan must be prepared by competent men with the requisite scientific and practical experience. It must be assured of the essential production inputs—quality seeds, fertilizers, plant protection materials, improved elements; without them it will remain a pointless exercise. In addition, there must be assurance that, based on the farm plan, enough production credit, or crop loan, would be available in time to enable the farmer to buy the needed inputs. The plan must be simple enough to be understood by the farmer, and inexpensive enough to be within his financial reach. It must be properly phased so as to move, in suitable stages, from a relatively simple start towards greater sophistication.

Accordingly, farm planning was divided into three broad phases. The first-stage task was to draw up and implement a simple plan with the emphasis laid on the use of a "package of improved and tested agricultural practices," but restricted only to *key crops*. This, it was recognized, must be the first logical step for the vast majority of farmers in their long journey towards scientific farming.

The second phase aimed at a twofold objective—to introduce further refinements into the package of improved practices and to apply them to *all crops* and *all other activities* on the farm. For the third phase sights were raised still higher: to make the best possible use of all available resources and all latent opportunities to maximize farm income. The *whole-farm* management on modern lines, embracing all its varied components, was the ultimate goal.

The farm planning exercise, as a little reflection will show, has wide-ranging implications. Its purpose, simply put, is to work out "the optimum combination of enterprises, practices and methods." To achieve this, however, every enterprise must be examined, and every practice, technique or method, old and new, scrutinized and evaluated on the basis of input-output and cost-return analysis; the demand and supply in the market and the behaviour of prices must be constantly studied.

Nor is this all. The variables involved in the calculus of cost, output, price and profit are numerous. There may be new scientific knowledge, fresh technological advances, more productive strains or varieties, major shifts in supply or demand or both, unexpected movements, up or down, in market prices. This means that the picture of comparative advantages and opportunity cost may be, and under present-day conditions mostly is, in a constant state of flux. Efficient farm management presupposes that a farm plan must be frequently reviewed and adjusted to the changing conditions in order to take advantage of new and more promising opportunities as they appear on the scene.

Farm planning in the third phase will clearly require exceptionally qualified extension agents with an appropriate scientific background and well conversant with the multi-faceted problems of farm management. There must also be adequate facilities for research and studies on management problems and on market conditions.

The journey of a thousand miles, as the saying goes, must begin with the first step. The uphill task of modernizing subsistence-type inputless moribund agriculture must start with a modest plan, simple enough to be understood by the simple-minded farmer and by the newly-trained extension worker, and modest enough to be financed from the existing credit organizations, which in practice meant cooperative societies. But even in this early stage a farm plan, it was specifically laid down, must result, first, *in substantial increases in agricultural production even on very small holdings*, and, second, *in increased sale of crops providing more net cash income*.

This emphasis is particularly significant. The simple farm plan was to serve as an eye-opener to give the farmer the first glimpse of a new vista of possibilities that lay in front of him, to whet his appetite for progress with the first sizable instalment of extra production and extra income, and to set him securely on the path of scientific farming with the promise of a better life for himself and his family.

Even a simple farm plan is, however, not all that simple; it has severely practical implications which need to be objectively faced and adequately tackled. In order to minimize risks on this score, the IADP made the following stipulation: First, the farm plan, or crop plan, must emphasize the *added cost* and the *added return* for each crop due to improved practices. In both cases, the stress should be on the *cash* costs and the *cash* income. Second, production inputs—improved seeds, chemical fertilizers, plant protection materials, and others—must be made available on the basis of the estimates as worked out in the farm plan. Third, the cooperative societies must provide the required short-term production loan based on the production plan. In addition, a farm plan proforma was developed to suit the needs of each area characterized by similar conditions. It comprised all the basic elements, such as: an inventory of the available resources, the existing land-use and cropping system, improved production practices to be adopted, production supplies to be purchased for cash, production credit which was to be tied to the additional production resulting from improved practices and not to tangible security, expected net return from all enterprises, and a repayment plan. And finally, to facilitate the procurement of credit, the proforma included a credit application, which linked credit requirements to production needs.

21

Thus, the actions needed were carefully thought through. Yet the success even of the simple farm plan hinged on factors which lay outside the IADP's competence: quality of extension workers, capacity of the cooperatives, availability of inputs and credit. They involved vital policy matters which the IADP could at best partially influence, but was in no position to mould to its satisfaction.

### b. Crop Loans

The idea of crop loans against well-conceived farm plans was no less significant. Vast numbers of Indian cultivators are steeped in debt, often from generation to generation, mostly to moneylenders who lend money at extortionate rates of interest. Because of this heavy indebtedness, they are uncreditworthy. And because they are unable to obtain loans even for productive purposes, they are deprived of what is often the best means to improve their economic situation and, consequently, their credit rating. For them it is a case of: once in debt, always in debt.

Crop loans can provide a way out of this cruel dilemma. The underlying idea is quite simple: loans should be given based on a credit rating not of the farmer, but of the farm plan. If the plan is prepared by competent technicians, embodies improved production technologies, and promises a big increase in output, the farmer should be left with a substantial surplus even after retiring the loan from the proceeds realized from the sale of his produce after harvest. Clearly, this will work only if the credit is scrupulously used for implementing the farm plan for which it is specifically granted. This means that there must be the machinery with trained staff to supervise the utilization of the credit at different stages—from the time it is granted to the time of its repayment. Assuming that these conditions are satisfied, improved farm technology can be relied upon to free the farmer from the clutches of the moneylender and from his chronic impoverished state.

The concept of the crop loan was by no means new in India. For example, its importance was recognized by the Rural Marketing and Finance Subcommittee of the National Planning Committee, and much of the Subcommittee's Report was concerned with the mechanics of an effective crop loan system.[1] The Rural Credit Survey Committee, in its Report published in 1953, devoted considerable attention to the subject. In fact, crop loans were central to its plea for adopting what it called an integrated system of rural credit covering all requirements from production to marketing.[2]

[1] The writer served on the Subcommittee as its Member-Secretary. The NPC did its planning work during 1939-41 with Pandit Jawaharlal Nehru as its Chairman.
[2] Report of the Rural Credit Survey Committee, Reserve Bank of India, 1953, Vol. I.

Nevertheless, there was a crucial difference between the earlier proposals and the IADP approach. Crop loans are production loans; to be effective they must be geared to a production-boosting programme based on improved methods and technologies. This was the case with IADP farm planning, but not with the earlier proposals which came to naught because of this critical omission.

### c. Integrated Approach

The fate of the package programme hinged on another major assumption which had to be constantly borne in mind. This was made clear in the original 10-Point Programme which unequivocally stated that "the full food production potential can be realized only when *all the essential elements are combined into an integrated impact programme.*" If any one component were deficient in quantity or in quality, it would affect the anticipated results; and if a major input or service were missing, it would jeopardize the entire programme. If, for example, no pesticides were available, the entire crop might be damaged or lost as a result of pests or diseases. In short, the principle of interaction worked both ways. And the weakest link would determine the strength of the chain.

### d. Institutional Support

The programme, it will be noticed, relied heavily on cooperatives—for credit, supply of inputs, and marketing of farm produce. This was perhaps inevitable, given the commitments repeatedly made by the government to the ideals of cooperation and community development, later also of panchayati raj. Nevertheless, the tie-up was unfortunate; for, these ideals, attractive as they are, are also among the hardest to realize. True cooperatives can blossom and flourish only after their prospective members have already tasted progress and have learnt to take initiative to promote some common interest. But in the early stages of development they are seldom effective as a vehicle of economic and social progress. And where the masses of people are weak and live in appalling poverty, as is overwhelmingly the case in rural India, the cooperative is likely to prove a non-starter.[3]

The excessive reliance on cooperatives was due not to any inherent logic, but to idealistic predilections. It vastly complicated what was already a highly complex task: effecting a marriage of India's agriculture with modern science and technology.

**SELECTION OF DISTRICTS**

From the formulation of the 10-Point Programme it took just about

[3] See Chapters 9 and 25.

a year to initiate the IADP officially. An outline scheme was drawn up, which provided that the pilot project should be introduced in seven states; that in each state it should cover a whole district; and that, of the seven districts, four would be predominantly rice-growing, two wheat-growing, and one millet-growing.

The states selected were: Andhra Pradesh, Bihar, Madhya Pradesh and Tamil Nadu (Madras) for rice, Punjab and Uttar Pradesh for wheat, and Rajasthan for millet.

The next step was to select suitable districts within these states. The state governments concurred in the fourfold criteria laid down by the Ford Foundation Teams for selecting the districts to ensure best possible response. Briefly, each district was required to have:

a. Assured supply of water, as far as possible;
b. A minimum of natural hazards—that is to say, the area should be free from flood, drainage or acute soil conservation problems requiring long-term attention;
c. Relatively well-developed village institutions like cooperatives and panchayats; and
d. Maximum potential for increasing output within a comparatively short time.

The districts selected by the state governments on the basis of these criteria were:

1. Thanjavur in Madras, i.e. Tamil Nadu.
2. West Godavari in Andhra Pradesh.
3. Shahabad in Bihar.
4. Raipur in Madhya Pradesh.
5. Aligarh in Uttar Pradesh.
6. Ludhiana in Punjab.
7. Pali in Rajasthan.

As noted earlier, the first four districts are devoted mainly to rice, the fifth and the sixth to wheat, and the seventh to millets.

The Government of India, on 11 June 1960, approved the selection and gave the green signal to go ahead with the programme. While doing so, however, it wanted the programme to be extended to all the fifteen states of the country, and decided that all of them would be treated on equal terms as regards help from the Centre. It emphasized further that the programme be so developed as to make it possible to apply its essentials, in due course, to other areas as well. The extended IADP coverage and the stress laid on the repeatability principle breathed an optimism for the future. The desire to see the package programme cover the whole country some day was in itself a welcome sign. But it also betokened a lack of appreciation of the complexities involved—of the organization, the supply line, the trained scientific personnel needed for the purpose. Coverage, once again, threatened to overwhelm quality. Little thought was given as to how to reconcile the two.

The second group of districts selected in accordance with the Government of India decision consisted of:

1. Alleppey and Palghat in Kerala.
2. Bhandara in Maharashtra.
3. Burdwan in West Bengal.
4. Cachar in Assam.
5. Mandya in Mysore.
6. Sambalpur in Orissa.
7. Surat in Gujarat.
8. Jammu and Anantnag districts—six blocks in all—in Jammu and Kashmir.

In all these eight districts the principal crop is rice. However, ragi and sugarcane occupy a sizable area in Mandya district, while Surat has a considerable area under jowar and cotton.

The basic data regarding the fifteen districts are given below:[4]

### BASIC DATA ABOUT IADP DISTRICTS

| | No. of blocks | No. of villages | Gross cropped area in 1000 hect. | Gross irrigated area in 1000 hect. | Population in million |
|---|---|---|---|---|---|
| Group I: 7 districts | 141 | 14,120 | 4,509 | 1,879 | 12.29 |
| Group II: 8 districts | 173 | 13,707 | 3,571 | 785 | 13.83 |
| Total | 314 | 27,827 | 8,080 | 2,664 | 26.12 |

It is worth noting how these IADP data compare with the corresponding all-India figures (See Table on p. 166).

Thus, the 15 IADP districts, taken together, covered about 5 per cent of India's villages, and about 6 per cent of the C.D. blocks, gross cropped area, and population.

## IMPERFECT SELECTION

The districts were supposed to be selected by applying the four criteria laid down for the purpose. How far were they actually satisfied?

[4] *IADP—Second Evaluation Report* (1960-65), Expert Committee on Assessment and Evaluation, p. 4.

EXTENT OF IADP COVERAGE[5]

| | All-India | In IADP districts | % |
|---|---|---|---|
| No. of C.D. blocks | 5,240 | 314 | 6.0 |
| No. of villages | 566,878 | 27,827 | 4.9 |
| Gross cropped area in million hectares | 137.90 | 8.08 | 5.9 |
| Gross irrigated area in million hectares | 26.30 | 2.66 | 10.1 |
| Population in million | 439.07 | 26.12 | 5.9 |
| No. of districts | 320 | 15 | 4.7 |

The 15 IADP districts, taken together, accounted for just over 10 per cent of the total irrigated area. This was a higher proportion than their share of the gross cropped area, also of the villages, C.D. blocks and population. Yet in absolute terms it was surprisingly low, especially in view of all the emphasis that had been laid on introducing intensive agriculture in irrigated areas. The first group of districts, it is true, had a larger acreage in the irrigated category, but even there it amounted to only 42.7 per cent of the cropped area. In the second group it was only 22 per cent.

Besides, there was considerable variation among the districts. For example, the ratio of irrigated to gross cropped area was 52 per cent in Burdwan, in the other districts it was much lower and varied from 3 to 35, although in some cases high rainfall to some extent compensated for the deficiency.

Moreover, the very definition of "irrigated areas" poses a big problem. At one extreme is assured year-round irrigation capable of supporting multiple cropping, an ideal condition which prevailed in comparatively few cases. At the other extreme "are areas which would receive just one or two flushings" during the rainy season, especially when the monsoon begins to taper off. This is mostly the case with the older irrigation projects (see Chapter 16).

Even this very limited irrigation is by no means assured; much depends on the adequacy, or otherwise, of the monsoon rains. For example, in Raipur district 120,000 hectares are classified as irrigated; but irrigation was designed mainly to supplement the rainfall, especially in September-October, and thereafter the canals would run dry.

The IADP criteria laid stress on "assured rainfall." This, in the context of India's agriculture, is not a very meaningful phrase either, because of the erratic monsoon and the very wide seasonal as well as year-to-year

[5] *India 1969*, Government of India. The figures for gross cropped and irrigated area are for 1964-65. The population figure relates to 1961. The all-India total of districts shows some variations as new districts are created from time to time. The official total for 1970 was 339, some of which are hardly agricultural.

variations. Once again, Raipur district well illustrates the point. With an average rainfall of 55 inches (140 cm), it is classified as an "assured rainfall area." Yet in four out of the first seven years of the IADP, it suffered from droughts.

In fact, even the best irrigated district is only half-irrigated and half-rainfed. In West Godavari, for example, only the delta region enjoys irrigation from the Godavari canal network, while the upland area continues to depend on the monsoon.

Finally, even where irrigation is provided for the greater part of the year from large projects, two difficulties are frequently encountered: the area covered is too large and the dosages of water are too small; and no control is provided to regulate the supply of water at field level. These weaknesses, as seen in the previous Chapter, are built-in features of almost all major flow-irrigation projects so far developed in India. They are no less a part of irrigation in Burdwan, Thanjavur, West Godavari and several other IADP districts.[6]

As noted above, Raipur is subject to frequent droughts; so also are three other districts—Sambalpur, Pali, Bhandara. On the other hand, five districts—Cachar, Burdwan, Aligarh, West Godavari and Thanjavur—have considerable parts exposed to periodic floods.

As for village institutions, the cooperatives were far from well developed in the IADP districts; in most cases they lacked the capabilities needed to support a new dynamic programme like the IADP. The panchayati raj institutions fell short of the requirements by an even wider margin.

Thus, the fifteen districts, though selected by applying fairly well-defined criteria—assured water supply, minimum exposure to natural hazards, well-developed village institutions, all intended to ensure maximum potential for a rapid increase in production—were, contrary to initial expectations, not distinguished by anything like ideal conditions. They contained sizable pockets which, in comparison with the country as a whole, had better than average facilities for irrigation; but they had also large areas which were no better. In the other two respects they were not markedly superior to the all-India average.

This leads up to some important conclusions: The results achieved in the IADP areas have, by and large, been due not so much to any exceptionally favourable conditions they enjoyed as to the exceptionally intensive treatment that was applied to them. But for their inherent limitations, even better results could have been legitimately expected. Also, the district averages did not correctly reflect the gains in production made in irrigated areas. Although substantial, they were diluted by the presence of large dry pockets.

[6] Irrigation problems of India are analyzed more fully in Chapter 16, also the recent attempts to develop assured irrigation especially with minor projects.

## INTER-DISTRICT VARIABLES

The districts selected for the package programme were far from uniform as regards the level of development they had reached, both in agriculture and in agro-institutions. In that sense, they were themselves very much of a mixed package. The main points of difference are worth noting since inter-district differences affect inter-district comparisons.

The districts are located in different "agro-climatic zones"; this is reflected in their main cropping patterns. In 12 out of the 15 districts, the principal crop is rice; in two it is wheat, and in one, millets.

The average *size of farms* is the largest in Ludhiana, about 7.5 hectares; in the other districts it is mostly around 2.5 hectares. Labour supply is more than plentiful in some, such as West Godavari, Thanjavur, Palghat, Alleppey. This helps intensive cropping at low cost, but also creates a more pronounced social problem of equitable wealth-sharing.

The *irrigation* facilities in general leave much to be desired has already been indicated. This, of course, directly affects the production of cereals. At the start of the programme, only 6 per cent of the acreage under major cereals was irrigated in Surat, about 30 per cent in Raipur and Sambalpur, 43 per cent in Mandya, and 53 per cent in Aligarh. In Thanjavur and Godavari, most of the rice is irrigated; in Cachar and Alleppey nearly all of it depends on rainfall, which is usually adequate; Bhandara, Raipur, Sambalpur also depend largely on rainfall, which is mostly erratic. In the fifteen districts taken together, just over half of the rice acreage is irrigated; for wheat the proportion is much higher—80 per cent; for other cereals it is only 20 per cent.

Fertilizer or *plant food use* per hectare of important crops can be taken as a broad indication of the stage already reached in agricultural development. The relative position in fertilizer use at IADP's start was as follows: Mandya, Thanjavur, Alleppey and West Godavari came at the top—Mandya, for example, used 19.7 kilos of $N + P_2O_5$ per hectare of major crops and West Godavari 7.3 kilos. Next came Burdwan, Ludhiana, Palghat, Surat, Shahabad and Raipur in that order, with average plant food use varying from 4.4 to 1.9 kilos per hectare. In the lowest category were the remaining five districts—Bhandara, Aligarh, Pali, Sambalpur and Cachar; the fertilizer use here was negligible, about one kilo per hectare on an average.

The *crop yield* data showed wide differences among the districts. For the base period, that is, the three years preceding IADP's initiation, they revealed the following position:

> The yield, in terms of *hulled* rice, in the twelve rice districts averaged 14.4 quintals per hectare—16.1 on irrigated and 12.3 on rainfed land; the national average for the same years was 12.1 quintals per hectare.

Wheat yield averaged 9.4 quintals per hectare in IADP districts—10.3 on irrigated and 5.4 on rainfed farms, as against an all-India average of 8.3 quintals.

Maize, jowar and bajra yields in IADP districts were 11.0, 4.6 and 4.4 quintals per hectare respectively. The national average for jowar was practically the same, for the other two it was slightly lower.

In *infrastructure*, none of the districts were up to the mark, and almost all of them had undeveloped parts. However, the deficiencies were particularly serious in Bhandara, Raipur, Sambalpur, Shahabad and Cachar. Communication facilities, so essential for agricultural development, showed wide differences. They were relatively good in Ludhiana and very poor in Raipur. In this respect the IADP districts, taken together, were presumably more or less representative of conditions obtaining in the country as a whole.

Finally, if the districts were uneven in development and disparate in their physical as well as socio-economic characteristics, even a single IADP district was far from homogeneous. The potentialities for development varied, often quite significantly, within the district boundaries. The West Godavari district, for example, consists of almost two distinct parts, the upland and the delta region, with sharp differences both in configuration and other conditions. Substantial differences exist within other districts, such as Raipur, Aligarh and Thanjavur. In short, while the district is a convenient administrative unit, it is seldom a rational unit for agricultural planning. Given the wide intra-district differences, it needs to be demarcated into more meaningful agro-climatic zones. After the first few years' experience, the IADP administration increasingly took cognizance of this fact and its practical implications.

Thus, some main aspects of the original 10-Point Programme have been gradually, though perhaps subconsciously, de-emphasized. The IADP set out to apply the ten-point approach to a few hand-picked districts possessing unusually favourable conditions for bringing about a rapid increase in food production. The district has proved much less useful as an operational unit than had been initially assumed. As seen above, the selected districts were not exceptionally, but only marginally more favourable than the rest of the country. This makes one wonder what would have happened if they had been chosen on a random sampling basis, instead of going through the elaborate motions of selecting them by applying a prescribed set of criteria. The end-result might not have been significantly different.[7]

---

[7] Attempts have been made to justify this on the ground that the selected districts were truly representative of the country as a whole. This, however, is precisely what the IADP had decided *not* to do. It wanted the districts to be not just average but exceptionally promising.

22

These points are stressed here only to set the perspective right, to separate what constitutes the crux of the IADP from its less relevant trappings. By far the most important part of the package programme is the package itself, both in concept and in content, comprising as it does all the essential ingredients needed to modernize subsistence agriculture and their systematic application in an integrated fashion to a sufficiently large and fairly representative cross-section of the country covering about 5 per cent of its total cultivated area. It is this planned attempt to make full-blooded transfusion of modern science, technology and management that has generated a new dynamism in India's long-languishing agriculture, and has opened up fascinating prospects for the future.

## FINANCIAL ARRANGEMENTS

The financing of the IADP involved a tripartite arrangement—among the Ford Foundation, the Central Government, and the state governments. The formula adopted for cost-sharing has some interesting features.

The Memorandum of Agreement, signed on 18 June, 1960, between the Government of India and the Ford Foundation, stipulated that the financial assistance from the latter would be confined to the first group of IADP districts; that, furthermore, it would be limited to 100 Community Development blocks out of the 140 blocks which comprised this group. For the remaining 40 blocks as well as for all the 173 blocks covered by the second group of districts, the required finance would be found from domestic sources.

The Government of India, on the other hand, decided that there should be no discrimination among the states; that, accordingly, the programme should be carried out on the same pattern and with the same intensity in all the states. This meant, first, that the financial burden accepted by the initial group of seven states set the level for the remaining eight; and second, that the commitments made by the Ford Foundation for the first group of districts had to be taken over by the Central Government in respect of the second group.

The obligations assumed by the three parties may be briefly mentioned. The Ford Foundation agreed to bear, in respect of 100 blocks in the first group of states, 50 per cent of the cost of the additional staff plus the full cost for half-a-dozen other items: transport (capital and recurring), survey and evaluation, implement workshop, scientific demonstrations, staff training, and soil-testing laboratory, and quality seed programme.

The state governments would meet 25 per cent of the additional staff costs starting from the second year, plus the full cost of equipment for demonstration and of local works. They were also required to build storage godowns under the normal Plan schemes of the departments of cooperation in the states.

The Government of India would bear all other costs for the Programme, including 50 per cent of the additional staff costs in the first year and 25 per cent thereafter.

To strengthen the cooperatives, it was decided to make an outright grant to them as "a special bad debt reserve." This grant was shared on a 50:50 basis between the Centre and the state governments.

The Memorandum of Agreement was to remain in force for an initial period of five years. It was subsequently extended through 1970.[8] The Board of Trustees of the Ford Foundation appropriated $10.5 million in March, 1960; of this the major part, $6.9 million, was committed on 18 July, 1960. While the financial assistance has been confined to 100 blocks in the first-group districts, the technical assistance, i.e. the services of Ford Foundation experts, has, from the beginning, been extended to all the fifteen districts on equal terms.[9]

## A SLOW START

A new programme like the IADP could not be transplanted overnight from the blueprint to the field. That the ground would need to be prepared in advance was recognized by its designers, who laid down in some detail the steps which were considered necessary for the purpose.

Accordingly, each district was first required to go through a "preparatory stage," with attention concentrated on several important items, namely: selection of areas within the district for implementing the programme; creating a general awareness among the farmers and non-official agencies like panchayats and cooperatives and securing their participation; strengthening the cooperatives in the areas selected for coverage; selection, appointment and posting of additional staff; training of staff; organization of a resource and production "bench-mark survey"; assessment of the supplies needed; construction and/or hiring of storage godowns in order to bring the supplies within easy reach of the farmers; and strengthening of transport arrangements.

Once this essential preparatory work was completed, the programme entered the second phase, that is, of actual operation and execution. And with this the centre of gravity shifted to the activities indicated earlier, namely, preparation and follow-up of production plans for farms and

[8] It has been extended through the Fourth Plan period, i.e. through 31 March, 1974.

[9] For details, see India's "Package Programme" by Neil A. Patrick, Ford Foundation, New Delhi, mimeo., Sept. 1972, which gives a comprehensive review of the IADP. It reached the writer after his manuscript had been completed and delivered.

villages; adequate and timely supply of credit based on such plans, and of production requisites, such as seeds, fertilizers, pesticides, and implements, all mainly through cooperatives; intensification of extension education work through field demonstrations and use of information media; arrangements for marketing and other services through cooperatives; and programme analysis and evaluation.

The extent of the required preparatory work and, therefore, of the time needed to complete it varied considerably since the districts were at varying levels of development, both in agriculture and cooperation. The first to enter the operational phase was Thanjavur (Tamil Nadu), in April 1960; it was followed, six months later, by West Godavari (Andhra Pradesh) and Sahabad (Bihar); and by April 1961, they were joined by the remaining four districts of the first group of states.

It was inevitable, however, that the coverage of the programme, even after its initiation, would grow slowly, particularly in the early stages. In fact, the state governments were advised to proceed cautiously in the first year or two, and a broad guideline was laid down for the purpose. It suggested a target of about 20 per cent of the cultivated area for the first year, and a gradual rise up to 65 per cent or more in the next three years, leaving the balance, that is, the longest lap, to be covered in the fifth year.

In implementing the programme, preference was given to those C.D. blocks which were relatively well established and therefore had the normal complement of staff. The year-to-year progress in coverage in all the fifteen districts is described in the IADP Evaluation Reports, especially the first one (for 1961-62), and need not detain us here.

The next step was to recruit and post the additional staff. The process proved more arduous and time-consuming than had been assumed. The general recommendation made to the states was to reinforce the normal complement of C.D. staff with the following additions:

a. *At District level*: one Project Officer, four to five subject-matter specialists (for agronomy or soils, plant protection, farm management, agricultural engineer, information), and one Assistant or Deputy Registrar of Cooperative Societies.

b. *At Block level*: ten Village Level Workers (V.L.Ws. for short), up to four Extension Officers (Agriculture), one Extension Officer (Cooperation), and four to five Cooperative Supervisors.

The block-level staff, computed at the above rate, reached a sizable figure. On an average, a district would require 200 V.L.Ws., up to 80 Extension Officers for agriculture, 20 Extension Officers for cooperation, and at least 80 Cooperative Supervisors. To these were to be added six to seven relatively senior professionals at the district level. To arrive at the overall total for all the states, these figures had to be multiplied by fifteen.[10]

To recruit and place this additional staff was in itself a difficult task. The procedures for financial clearances and recruitment did not help matters. Formal approval of the Government of India specifying the staff in different categories, issue of detailed sanctions by the state governments after the customary period of gestation in their finance departments, setting in motion the recruitment machinery, screening of candidates, formalizing the appointments, and their actual placement in the field—all these are standard rituals, and they consumed considerable amount of time.

It took twelve to eighteen months to set up the field organization, and even then practically none of the seven Group-1 districts had the full complement of the block-level staff like A.E.Os. and V.L.Ws. An acute shortage of V.L.Ws. was felt in several districts; the gaps were gradually filled mostly by drawing upon more seasoned V.L.Ws. from other areas.

## INHIBITING FACTORS

That a major innovation like the IADP would encounter numerous hurdles was a foregone conclusion. No one even with a superficial familiarity with conditions in rural India could have any illusion on that score. The authors of the package programme set about their tasks with open eyes, ready to face whatever obstacles came in the way, and willing to negotiate them, with patience and fortitude, as best they could.

Not only was the setting up of the administration a slow process, its performance continued to be adversely affected by unfilled vacancies, frequent staff transfers, shortages of trained personnel, inadequacy of training to meet this deficiency. Not infrequently fertilizers and other essential supplies failed to reach the farmers in time. Cooperative credit did not measure up to the expectations, and was often unavailable at the right time or in the right amount.

The administration needed time to acquire an understanding of the new programme and had to learn from experience, often relying on a trial-and-error method. Farm planning, the cornerstone of the programme, well illustrates this point. The Extension Service lacked knowledge, equipment and adequately trained staff to do justice to its tasks; not enough hard data were available on which it could confidently build its recommendations to the farmers; the concept of crop loans against production plans was much too novel to the credit institutions to gain ready acceptance.

[10] The total Block level requirements were estimated at: 3000 VLW's, 770 AEO's, 350 CEO's, and 600 cooperative supervisors.

Even the production plan proforma was not easy to work out and was evolved only after much fumbling and futile experimenting with unpractical approaches. The form first introduced in some districts was much too elaborate, overloaded with input-output calculations, and consequently "it never got off the ground." This dictated the need for something simple, workmanlike, sound and yet easily intelligible to the masses of cultivators. The result was the adoption of the simple-plan formula for the first stage. The plan was now restricted to only *one* important crop. It included "a package" of improved practices, but based strictly on research, soil analysis, results actually obtained on experimental and demonstration farms, and tested methods successfully adopted by progressive farmers in the same locality. This was the only practical way to initiate the farm planning approach, to prove its usefulness to the farmers, also to train the extension workers in what was for them, too, an admittedly new task. The first essential step was to see that the farm planning concept was understood and accepted by the farmers. Refinements of its techniques could logically follow only thereafter, as extension workers gained experience in its intricacies, as farmers felt more convinced about its benefits, and as the supply lines for both credit and essential farm inputs were better organized.

Progress was particularly slow in setting up the key supporting activities, such as the establishment of soil-testing laboratories, a quality seed programme, implement workshops, an information service.

A very severe handicap, all along, has been the untrained quality of the great majority of the V.L.Ws. To make matters worse, they were often required to do all kinds of jobs unrelated to the tasks to which they were expected to give undivided attention, that is, stimulation of agricultural production.

Another major weakness of the IADP, as of India's public sector undertakings in general, has been a defective administrative set-up, painfully evident in a lack of unified responsibility at the district level with full control over all inter-related disciplines (see Chapter 28).

And to compound these weaknesses there has been a rapid turnover of personnel at all key levels. For a programme like the IADP, staff continuity is absolutely essential in order that the workers may be imbued with its spirit, get acquainted with the tools of operation, gain insight into the practical problems, acquire on-the-job experience, establish personal contacts with farmers, win their confidence, and learn the art of persuasion. A rotating staff can never acquire these qualities, and without these qualities no agricultural extension service can be effective.

"Failure on the part of the State Governments to maintain a reasonable continuity of staff in spite of repeated requests to do so," to quote from the Second Report, "must be identified as an important operational weakness of the IADP. Frequent staff transfers, particularly when ... there was need for more and more specialised and intensive technical guidance to the cultivators, greatly retarded the progress."[11] This has been a sadly recurring theme in all the IADP Evaluation Reports.

To this long list of difficulties should be added another—the droughts of 1965-67 which could not but adversely affect the IADP's work, although its main activities, including the off-take of fertilizers and other inputs, were maintained at a fairly satisfactory level even during this critical period. Notwithstanding the teething troubles, the freaks of nature, and the inevitable shortfalls, the IADP did manage to establish for itself an impressive record of achievements. This is one of the most heartening facts about India's agricultural development today.

[11] *IADP—Second Evaluation Report (1960-65)*, p 11.

# CHAPTER 13

# A Decade of IADP

## THE ORCHARD BEARS FRUIT

It takes time to get a new programme under way, especially when it involves wide departures from previous approaches, reminded Sherman E. Johnson in reviewing a decade of development in India's agriculture. To give more emphasis to the remark he then added: "When a farmer plants an orchard, he does not expect much fruit in the first four years. Similarly, rapid production increase should not have been expected from the intensive district programme in the first four years. Nevertheless, some districts were reaching the first fruit bearing stage when the severe drought struck in 1964-65."[1]

Since then all the IADP districts have been bearing fruit. A rich harvest has already been gathered—in terms of immediate results and of lessons for the future. A review of both would be interesting in itself, especially since even now not enough is known about this fascinating story not only to the outside world, but also to large sections of the Indian public. Accordingly, an attempt is made to give, in this and the following chapter, a fairly full appraisal of the IADP experiment—its achievements as well as its problems and future prospects.[2]

[1] Sherman E. Johnson, *Observations on a Decade of Indian Agricultural Development*, The Ford Foundation, New Delhi, March 1969.

[2] The basic information and data have been drawn mainly from the Reports of the Expert Committee on Assessment and Evaluation on the Intensive Agricultural District Programme, Ministry of Food, Agriculture, Community Development and Cooperation (Department of Agriculture), Government of India. New Delhi. The Fourth Report called *Modernising Indian Agriculture*, published in 1969, gives a review of IADP for the period 1960-68. In the text and the footnotes these reports have sometimes been referred to simply as Evaluation Report(s) on IADP.

*First,* the IADP has finally exploded the lingering myth about the Indian farmer and has set the perspective right. It has given the farmers over a large cross-section of the country the sensations of rapid progress, created a new dynamism in the stagnating countryside, generated demand pressures for more and better facilities and inputs, which, often working backwards, are making their impact on the official policy. This, in itself, is a major achievement, since the modernization process must begin in the minds of farmers and policymakers.

This was acknowledged as early as 1964-65 by the then Central Minister of Food and Agriculture, Mr. C. Subramaniam, at the time of working out the programme for the Fourth Plan. After stressing that the fundamental departure involved in the new strategy was the emphasis laid on science and technology, he went on to say: "... it is one of the miracle stories of modern development that the allegedly backward, tradition-bound Indian farmer has been so responsive to the new technology. This has been in a large measure due to the pioneering efforts of the intensive agriculture programme through which the package approach to agriculture was introduced."[3]

The administration could be so impressed by the "miracle" because it had so completely misjudged the potentialities of Indian agriculture and ignored the "economic man" in the Indian farmer, and had so long denied to both the benefits of modern science and technology. The miracle, in the main, revealed its previous miscalculations and policy deficiencies, as seen earlier.[4]

*Second,* the IADP played an active role in developing the new strategy for the Fourth Plan, in formulating the High-Yielding Varieties Programme (HYVP), and in implementing both.

A negative result emerging out of the early IADP experiments set in motion an important chain of events. The traditional varieties, it was found, did not respond adequately to the new technology; under heavy doses of fertilizers they tended to lodge.[5] This highlighted the need to experiment with exotic varieties, which, in conjunction with other factors, helped usher in the HYVP.

In the IADP districts the two programmes immediately began to reinforce each other. Higher production targets were set for these districts, which effected the switch to the new varieties at a faster rate than the rest of the country. For example, in 1966-67 and 1967-68 the ratio of HYV area to the total cropped area was 100 per cent higher in the IADP

[3] "India's Program for Agricultural Progress," in *Strategy for the Conquest of Hunger,* loc. cit., p. 19.

[4] Especially in Chapter 9.

[5] Sometimes it is assumed that there was no room for fertilizers in pre-HYV days, that the fertilizer-responsiveness of traditional varieties was nil. This is an exaggeration (see Chapter 9).

23

districts than in the country as a whole. By that time these districts had most of the cropped area already "saturated" with the new varieties.

*Third,* the IADP has sought to improve staff operations; and, despite the inherent weaknesses of the old system, it has achieved a fair measure of success. In particular, its general approach to provide, at the district level, unified leadership for agricultural development through a team of competent specialists headed by a Project Officer has stood the test of time. It therefore deserves to be adopted in other areas more fully and systematically, and with fewer loopholes and lapses.[6]

The teams' efforts to improve farm planning and to upgrade farmers' skills and practices did not, in the first few years, result in much production gain. But the spadework they did so patiently was destined to pay off later. The high-yielding seeds could do so well almost from the start because they fell on a ground which had been so well-tended in advance.

*Fourth,* the IADP has, from the beginning, laid great stress on staff training, and soon developed three distinct, though inter-related facets: A period of orientation training to acquaint the staff with its objectives, methods and procedures; training in technical subjects on a scientific-cum-practical basis to qualify the staff to give technically sound guidance to the farmers; and training to improve skills as farmers move on to new or improved methods and techniques. The training programme was therefore conceived in flexible terms so that it could be redesigned and upgraded in keeping with the rising levels of technology adopted by the farmers.

To enrich the quality of training, the IADP seeks to make increasing use of the technical knowledge emanating from various sources, such as the agricultural universities, Indian Agricultural Research Institute (IARI), the Central Rice Research Institute (CRRI), the International Rice Research Institute (IRRI) in the Philippines, and others. More recently, it began to concern itself with the training of extension officers in farm management, which has been organized with the help of the U.P. Agricultural University (UPAU).

The staff training programme is vitally important to the IADP for two obvious reasons. Since it has to rely largely on the untrained and undertrained staff of the C. D. blocks—even the new recruits are seldom adequately qualified—it is absolutely essential to upgrade their knowledge and skills. Besides, to introduce progressively higher technology in farming, the extension workers must be given training at correspondingly higher levels.[7]

---

[6] See comments made in Chapter 28 under "Agricultural Administration."

[7] Even such in-service training will, in many cases, be only a stopgap arrangement. The quality of extension agents must be vastly improved, and this will require well-trained scientists to be drafted into the service in large numbers. See Chapter 22, Part III on "Extension Service."

*Fifth,* the IADP concept won early recognition as evidenced by the fact that, in 1964-65, it was extended to 114 districts under what was called Intensive Agricultural Areas Programme (IAAP). The basic approach of the two programmes is identical; the difference between them is only one of intensity. Given the shortage of resources, and trained men, IAAP has to manage with a simpler staffing pattern and also without some of the supporting facilities like soil-testing laboratories and implement workshops, which form an integral part of the package in the IADP districts.

What is significant, however, is that only after four years of IADP's experience, it was deemed desirable to extend the package approach, even if in a somewhat diluted form, over a much wider area.

Moreover, the IADP districts have considerable "spill-over" effects. Neighbouring areas have benefited from their activities, while other districts are using them as training-ground for their own people.

*Sixth,* an IADP-type of undertaking tends to benefit primarily the large, commercially-minded farmers, particularly in its early stages, since they are the first to take quick advantage of the new opportunities to augment their output and income. But IADP has not been oblivious of the medium and small farmers. On the contrary, it realized quite early that the programme, in the final analysis, would stand or fall largely by its ability to involve the smaller farmers, to lead them by stages to intensive scientific farming, and thereby to make their farms economically viable.

Clearly, small farmers have a large contribution to make in solving the country's overall food problem. True, 62 per cent of them, with less than 5 acres each, farmed less than one-fifth of the area as owned or rented land. But what they lack in size they can often make up in intensity. Indeed, they have to; otherwise in most cases they will be unable to reach and cross the subsistence level of income. Through intensive farming they can, and must, help solve the nation's food problem and also assure for themselves a better future. Otherwise plans for rural welfare, as for the nation's economic progress, will remain largely meaningless.

Keenly aware of these considerations, IADP has actively sought to involve small farmers in the modernization process. This concern also explains its anxiety to maintain able and stable field staff in full strength with the requisite mobility so that each farmer may be approached and served individually.

Its confidence in the small farmers' ability has already been vindicated. In many places they have booked handsome gains in productivity. Indeed, according to the last evaluation report, the small farmers in some IADP districts, such as West Godavari, Raipur, and Thanjavur, are "in the forefront of production and often ahead of the medium and large farmers."

And this, the report points out, is the direct result of a programme deliberately designed to involve all farmers.[8]

*Seventh,* in most cases, the IADP activities are still in the first stage of transition. A Stage II programme was introduced selectively in villages which had attained a certain level of development. Results have so far been uneven. However, it is significant that some of these villages are engaged in an endeavour to bring about all-round improvements in agriculture. Their aim is not only to cover the entire cultivated area, but also to involve all farmers, big and small, to implement a group of diversified projects, such as small irrigation, animal husbandry, poultry farming, pasture development. In Raipur district, the Stage II village concept has apparently been further amplified and is applied to larger areas, each comprising a cluster of four to six contiguous villages.

A Stage III programme is also envisaged by IADP. Its objective is to develop "growth centres" in rural areas with emphasis on agro-industries so as to integrate agriculture and industry more effectively. So far only one district, Ludhiana in Punjab, is sufficiently advanced to enter this stage, though one or two others seem fairly close to it.

The second and third stage programmes are still confined to limited areas, and progress so far has been small. Their main value lies in the fact that they indicate the directions which future development must take, though the underlying ideas are still somewhat too general.[9]

*Eighth,* in input-use technologies IADP has made substantial contributions, both by introducing improved practices and methods and by pinpointing the deficiencies based on actual field experience.

That *water-use and management,* so vital for agriculture, had been sadly neglected was recognized by IADP. In some IADP districts, demonstrations were laid out, but, according to the latest evaluation report, the problems involved proved beyond IADP's capacity to cope with. More specifically, the work suffered for lack of trained staff, research information on water management, and data regarding water requirements of particular crops in given conditions.[10]

*Fertilizer use* in the IADP districts has increased about tenfold in the seven years since 1961-62. In this respect, as also in using farmyard manure and green manure, they have been far ahead of the non-IADP districts.

The same remark applies to *improved seeds,* the use of which increased about five times in the IADP districts during 1961-68. There was, however, no corresponding impact in terms of actual production. This, as mentioned earlier, is ascribed to the fact that the improved seeds of tradi-

[8] Fourth Evaluation Report, loc. cit., para. 2.15.
[9] The writer has discussed the issues involved in *Reaping the Green Revolution,* op. cit.
[10] Water management problems have been analyzed in Chapter 16.

tional varieties responded poorly to chemical fertilizers; on an average, they gave only about 10 per cent higher yield over the seeds normally used by the farmers, which was not enough to justify the extra price margin for the improved seeds.

These views, though frequently encountered, are not quite convincing. There are good reasons to believe that the so-called improved seeds were not sufficiently pure, that fertilizer application was perfunctory, that irrigation and drainage left much to be desired.

In any case, the situation changed completely once the exotic high-yielding varieties were introduced. The farmers were quick to grasp their value. Since then they have been ready to pay a substantial premium for seeds of these varieties, when their quality is assured.

*Plant protection* measures have increased significantly, about sixfold, in the IADP districts during 1961-68. The protection work is also much better organized in these districts compared with other areas. For example, a widespread yellowing of TN-1 crop was reported in 1966-67 from several states including Madhya Pradesh, Orissa, and Maharashtra. There was much panic in the country. The non-IADP districts waited helplessly for the plant protection experts from outside to visit the stricken areas. In IADP districts, the disease was quickly identified—it was caused by an attack of fulgerids and jassids, and effective measures were promptly taken to counteract it.

The problem of pests and diseases has multiplied manifold with the introduction of high-yielding varieties (see Chapter 19). Farmers are pretty well aware of the new risks, and so they are increasingly asking for a more effective plant protection service. In some places they have made it clear that, despite the risks of pests and diseases, they will continue to cultivate the high-yielding IR-8; that all they want are adequate supplies of chemicals and equipment along with the necessary technical guidance; and that they are ready to foot the bill.

*Ninth,* in marketing and storage IADP could not break much new ground; and so its performance in this field has not been noticeably better than in non-IADP areas. Nevertheless, it has been able to make two noteworthy contributions. First, it has stressed the importance of modernizing the rice processing industry, helped establish the first four modern rice mills in the country, and organized training courses for paddy-processing technicians. And, second, it has demonstrated the importance of paddy-drying units and storage silos. The need became particularly urgent when sizable tracts of samba-lands in Thanjavur district began to grow two rice crops with the short-duration ADT-27. The IADP helped set up 30 drying and storage centres in the district.

*Tenth,* in developing the essential *supporting services* IADP's contribution has been substantial.

All IADP districts have been equipped with *soil-testing laboratories,* each with a capacity to handle 30,000 soil samples annually. It took time to install them, sometimes as much as four to five years, owing to usual administrative and procedural delays. Some of them, especially the late-starters, have not yet reached the stage of full capacity utilization. In general, there is room for improvement in their working. The time lag between the collection of soil samples and the transmission of the test results back to the farmers has, at least in some districts, been much too long. Besides, the tests are still conducted too much in an *ad hoc* fashion. There is need for more purposeful research on the correlation between soil tests and fertilizer response.[11]

Nevertheless, IADP has laid the foundation of what must be an integral part of modern, fertilizer-intensive farming. The soil-testing service, though new particularly at the district level, is steadily gaining ground, as farmers more and more realize the value of this tool to determine the fertility status of their farm lands. Here again, IADP districts are well ahead of other parts of the country.

*The agricultural implement workshops* in IADP districts have pio-neered in several directions. Among the implements IADP has developed and successfully promoted are paddy-threshing roller, seed-cum-fertilizer drills, and power threshers. In some districts it has also popularized "custom work" in tractor operations.

In one district, the simple paddy-threshing roller has replaced the traditional method of threshing paddy, slowly and laboriously, by a team of eight to ten bullocks, thus saving much time and economizing on bullock power.

The district of Ludhiana has reached an advanced stage in *farm mechanization*. Power-operated wheat-threshers are now widely in vogue; so also are seed drills and planters, both bullock-drawn and tractor-drawn. A more recent development is the tractor-drawn harvesting equipment, which has been introduced in the market. Since private industrialists have actively entered this field, IADP has rightly decided to leave to them the manufacture of such equipment and to use its own limited resources for demonstration, testing and training.

Once again, IADP has broken ground in an important field and has made encouraging progress. But a great deal still remains to be done. The evaluation report candidly observed that the performance of the work-shops "has not been up to expectation," and that they have been "loaded with repairs and maintenance jobs of vehicles and tractors," mostly at the expense of the more urgent tasks, particularly demonstration work and training activities.

There is one fundamental issue which has received little attention from IADP, namely, to what extent farm mechanization should be encouraged, and how the often conflicting claims of productivity and employment

[11] See Chapter 18, last section.

should be reconciled. This all-important question will be examined later, especially to exemplify the need for discriminating judgment.[12]

Effective extension work requires well-organized *agricultural information units* for prompt dissemination of useful information about locally-adapted district programmes, to encourage the adoption of new practices, often by publicizing major successes booked by individual farmers in the same region, to alert farmers about important demonstration work planned or under way, to broadcast significant results achieved from such work, to give timely warnings about threats of pests and diseases, and, in general, to bring to the farmers any useful knowledge—scientific, commercial, or otherwise—which may affect their operations.

From the start the IADP has treated such information units as an essential component of its extension work. These units, by disseminating the needed information both directly and through the local press, have reinforced the hands of the subject-matter specialists and the village-level workers in their extension activities. The All-India Radio, through its Farm and Home Unit, has also helped the IADP, especially in connection with its programme at the district level.

The purpose of the so-called *bench-mark survey and assessment* was to ascertain the extent to which new and improved practices were being adopted by farmers, and with what results, measured especially in terms of yield improvements. The field work embraces agronomic and agro-economic enquiry for sample cultivators' holdings within sample villages, and crop-cutting experiments on major food and cash crops in fields selected at random. To facilitate comparisons of production trends between IADP and non-IADP districts, "control areas" were set up in the latter. These were also expected to help assess the feasibility of extending the programme further at a later date.

Ideally, a resource and production bench-mark survey should be carried out prior to initiating the programme. This, however, did not prove feasible, and so the survey was started only after the programme had been launched. To a limited extent, the districts did compile data through agronomic and crop surveys. But the data could not be analyzed quickly enough since, for lack of facilities at the district level, they had to be referred to the Institute of Agricultural Research Statistics (IARS) in New Delhi.[13]

The IADP also envisaged special studies on major problems affecting the programme. The intention was to conduct them mainly as case studies; operational research units were therefore set up in the first group

---

[12] In Chapter 20 on "Farm Mechanization."

[13] In hindsight, this was perhaps no great loss. "Control areas" are less significant when, for example, yield surges dramatically, as indeed was the case after the arrival of the HYV's. This induced IARI to delete the control area technique altogether from its National Demonstrations programme (see Chapter 22).

of seven IADP districts. But, according to the latest evaluation report, they have not functioned well for lack of qualified staff, failure to follow the technical guidance, and inability of the project authorities to appreciate their usefulness. Concurrent evaluation through operational research studies was conceived as a valuable aid to progress. But, the report regretfully observes, little use has so far been made by it.[14]

*Eleventh,* despite a slow start and numerous obstacles, the foodgrains production has registered handsome gains in IADP districts. The gain has been spectacular in the case of wheat—about 260 per cent compared with the base period of 1958-61; it has been moderate for maize—about 100 per cent; and rather small for rice—only 38 per cent.

Not all these gains have been due to the high-yielding varieties. In the first four pre-drought years grain production, it has been estimated, went up by about 25 per cent in the first seven IADP districts. Even these earlier results were deemed sufficiently promising to induce the Government of India to extend the IADP approach to 114 additional districts under the IAAP, as seen under point five above.

To take a more striking example, wheat production in Ludhiana district nearly doubled in six years prior to 1966-67 when Mexican dwarf wheats made their first appearance. The new varieties gave a further boost to yield per acre with results which were truly remarkable for wheat, rather modest for maize, and, at least so far, unexciting for rice.

The overall increases in production are quite considerable even in absolute terms, but two factors greatly enhance their significance. First, tremendous effort is needed, in the initial stages, to overcome the accumulated forces of inertia and to generate the first forward motion. This wearisome phase is now over; the point of acceleration has been definitely reached.

And, second, the tempo of future progress can, indeed, be accelerated if the obstacles, now clearly identified, are squarely faced and overcome with appropriate action or strategy in each case.

## RETARDING FACTORS

This brings us to what must be regarded as another outstanding achievement of IADP. It has not only registered progress in many directions, but has brought, even forced, to the surface the factors that have been impeding it. It has shown no inhibitions about its own shortcomings or failures, and has publicized them with a refreshing candour. It has focussed the full glare of its searchlight on the obstacles, whether man-made or God-given, which are acting as drags on development. Even its negative results have thus come to acquire a high positive value. For progress, to indulge

[14] Fourth Evaluation Report IADP, p. 17. Studies of this kind can be best undertaken by the expanding network of agricultural universities (see Chapter 22).

in a platitude, is achieved only when problems are correctly diagnosed and adequately treated.

What, then, are these retarding factors? In pursuance of its dual role of path-finding and pace-setting,[15] IADP has probed into this question periodically in its evaluation reports. The Second Report, which covered the years 1960-65, regarded the present administrative system as a major handicap. And then it went on to state that "the Government's basic policy regarding credit, marketing, prices, industries, import, investment and land are not conducive to the full realization of the benefits of this impact programme."

To achieve a more rapid rate of progress at the district level, the Report emphasized, it was essential to tackle the following categories of problems: providing a better economic climate to encourage farmers; strengthening and stabilizing the staff situation; ensuring adequate supplies of technical inputs and production credit; improved distribution and management of irrigation water; and speeding up the development of high-yielding, disease-resistant varieties of all major crops.

The same diagnosis and the same prescription have been made virtually in all the evaluation reports on IADP. In the last report published in 1969, they have been made even more comprehensively and incisively.

The main problems listed above, along with their practical implications, will be examined, especially in Chapters 16 through 28, indicating as clearly as possible the lines along which action must be taken if, capitalizing on the IADP's experience, and on the vast new opportunities opened up by the high-yielding varieties, a full-fledged programme for modernization of India's agriculture is to be launched on a nation-wide scale.

[15] Subsequently, this role was assigned primarily to five out of the 15 IADP districts, viz. Ludhiana, West Godavari, Sambalpur, Raipur, and Thanjavur. Designated as "Innovative Districts," they constitute a kind of pilot areas within the IADP pilot programme.

24

CHAPTER 14

# IADP—An Appraisal

## CRITICISMS OF IADP

The IADP has not been above controversy. That a pioneering experiment of this nature would attract criticisms from different sources was inevitable. It would be worthwhile to review and evaluate the criticisms as far as possible to arrive at a balanced appraisal of IADP's performance and to help draw the right lessons from its experience. This would also be in the true spirit of the IADP which went out of its way to arrange for strict evaluation of its activities every two years.

In examining the criticisms, a point-by-point approach is adopted for both clarity and convenience, even though they might appear somewhat over-schematized.

1. Concentration of resources favoured a limited area and discriminated against the rest of the country.

By implication, this challenges the very concept of IADP. Yet its justification rests on solid reasons, which may be restated briefly:

a. Not all lands are equally endowed by nature; some are more productive than others. It is both common sense and sound economics to tap the full productivity of high-potential areas. Essentially, this is no different from sinking capital and other resources to extract coal, iron ores, and other minerals from areas where nature has deposited them.

b. In effect, IADP sought to develop India's "bread-basket areas" to increase food production rapidly. This is absolutely essential both from the short- and the long-term angle. It would be foolish, and economically ruinous, to import millions of tons of foodgrains from remote sources when they can be produced domestically at reasonable cost in these areas.

c. India must develop an intensive agriculture on modern lines and increase output per acre severalfold. This she can and must achieve to feed her population, to speed economic growth, and to raise living standards. A start in that direction has to be made somewhere, and the best areas for a start are those which would quickly yield the best return on the invested resources. While relieving the immediate pressure for food, they would also serve as national demonstration areas, broadly indicating the path the nation as a whole must travel.

d. IADP was *not* conceived at the expense of other areas; it was *additive*, not *subtractive*. Activities in other areas, it was insisted by all concerned, should continue at least at their pre-IADP levels. The new experiment, if anything, was expected, by its very example, to lead to an intensification of efforts in other areas as well. And this is what actually happened as evidenced by the launching, in 1964, of the Intensive Agricultural Areas Programme (IAAP) in 114 additional districts.

2. IADP made the rich farmers richer and the poor ones poorer.

The rich and resourceful farmers, it is true, were quick to grasp the new opportunities and were able to buy the inputs and machinery and to obtain liberal credit. This was only natural and there was nothing inherently wrong about it. It only means that an output-booster like IADP does not solve *all* problems, nor is it, in fact, supposed to do so. Increasing production is in itself a tremendous task. To derive full benefit from it, IADP's efforts must be supplemented by other appropriate measures.

The kind of measures needed in this case is quite clear. The wealth of the affluent farmers must be taxed properly and the proceeds used for general economic and social development. In addition, small farmers must be given the special attention they need—more specifically, inputs, credit, technical guidance, and services must be made available to them to place them on a par with their bigger and more powerful competitors. In short, small farmers must not be allowed to suffer just because they are small. Through farm planning and other measures, IADP has tried to serve them more intensively and, as noted earlier, with very encouraging results.[1]

3. IADP districts were overstaffed and scarce administrative resources were overconcentrated.

Intensive agriculture needs intensive staffing. This is specially true in a country like India where farms are tiny in size (about five acres on an average) and large in number (over 50 million); where farmers are mostly illiterate and are just taking the first faltering steps into the scientific age; and where the supply line of farm credit and inputs is yet to be organized and the responsibility for ensuring the supply devolves, at least in the present transitional stage, on the extension service workers. As agriculture is modernized, as technologies advance and grow complex, more and not less professional workers are needed in relation to the number of

[1] In *Reaping the Green Revolution* the writer has tried to show how small farmers can prosper, provided they are given equal treatment and opportunities.

farms served. This has been the experience in developed countries.

As Sherman Johnson points out, in the typical Corn Belt countries of the United States the average is one professional worker for 150 farms. In IADP districts the ratio is one worker to about 400 farms, with the added difference that in India the government personnel must give much of their time to questions relating to credit, fertilizers, and other inputs, which in the USA are handled by other agencies.[2]

Unless staffing is adequate, small farmers are the first to suffer, for it is they who need greater individual attention from professional workers if they are not to be left in the lurch in an age of rapidly advancing technologies. Already it seems their interests are less well protected in IAAP than in IADP areas because of the fact that the former operates only with a skeleton staff. Those who complain about rich farmers getting richer should be the last to object to the more intensive staffing pattern of the IADP districts.

Here, again, what India needs is to build other areas up, not IADP areas down. For this she has to mobilize the available scientific manpower more fully, use it more effectively, expand and improve the educational and training facilities, and build up, just as fast as feasible, the strength of her scientific manpower to the requisite level.[3]

4. The IADP district is not a logical unit. It is an administrative, not a farm district.

This is quite true, as has been noted earlier. Even then it does not necessarily invalidate the district as an operational unit. In fact, there are several points decidedly in its favour. A district has long been a well-established unit, for both administrative and developmental work; it has already been handling a good many agricultural and agri-related activities; its headquarters is located in a township possessing at least a minimum of physical and other facilities; it thus provides a good base on which to build further; finally, it is large enough, yet not too large, to support the additional professional staff required by IADP.

That a district cannot be treated as a single unit from the angle of farming technology goes without saying. Plans and programmes must be tailored to fit the different agro-climatic zones. IADP may not have given enough weight to this fact in the early stages of its path-finding venture, but today it is well aware of the problem and the kind of treatment it needs.

As intensive agriculture spreads, farm districts based on agro-climatic zones will emerge, and since they will, in many instances, not be conterminous with the present district boundaries, one can foresee the need to carve out new and more homogeneous units of what may be considered

---

[2] Sherman E. Johnson, op. cit.

[3] For an analysis of the problem and requirements, see Chapter 22, especially Part III on "Extension Service."

optimum sizes for maintaining a network of essential agri-support activities. This is still some way off in the future. The district-based IADP operations should not be an obstacle to such a transition. In fact, the better they are organized in terms of the quality of staff and the services, the easier should be the transition when the time comes.

5. Farm planning proved a flop and did not go much beyond a paper exercise.

The start, as already explained, was a fumbling one, too detailed and theoretical to be of much practical value. But things did improve with the adoption of a simple farm plan as the first stage. The direct contacts and consultations between extension workers and farmers aimed solely at increasing their farm output was something new in India; it had a tremendous educational and psychological value. Farm planning, it should be remembered, is the crux of the IADP philosophy, and it is also the toughest task in the whole programme. When it succeeds, everything else will. This calls for patient and persistent effort to improve its quality along with the supporting services.

6. Despite all the talks about the package programme, it virtually meant only supply of fertilizers; seeds were unimproved, and pesticides were unavailable.

The criticism is valid, but only in the sense that a half-full glass is also half-empty. IADP's success has been admittedly partial, and uneven. It has been particularly marked in pushing the consumption of fertilizers, which in itself was a major contribution. Building up a modern seed industry has proved difficult, its importance is now almost universally recognized, and much progress has also been made in that direction. Pesticide use is picking up; the need for plant protection measures is now much better appreciated, and progress is being steadily made. The practical problems involved in each case are discussed at some length in other Chapters.[4]

7. The IADP districts were already among the, if not the, most advanced and progressive in India. The results achieved here were due to this fact rather than to the approach or the effectiveness of the programme.

The original idea was to select districts which had exceptional potential for a rapid increase in food production. The selection was, however, very much diluted in practice. Besides, all the districts contained both wet and dry areas, sometimes quite large underdeveloped pockets of the "run-of-the-mill" type. In any case, the really valid comparison is between IADP districts as they were in 1960 and as they are today, and not between these districts and the rest of the country. As seen earlier, the progress made by them in one decade has been impressive. For this the credit must

[4] In Chapters 17, 18 and 19 respectively.

go, above all, to IADP which has served as the guiding as well as the driving force in these districts.

8. Water-use and management were neglected for several years, and in this respect IADP failed to implement the vitally important recommendations of the Crisis Report.

This, unfortunately, is true. Water is India's by far most important natural resource. Yet for reasons indicated earlier, it has suffered from chronic neglect. How much more IADP could have achieved within ten years in terms of scientific water management is a moot point. Perhaps progress could not but be slow since past trends and hardened habits could not be reversed overnight. Perhaps all concerned, including the policymaking authorities, could learn only from experience in this case, and, therefore, needed convincing field demonstrations to show the deficiencies of water management before they could realize the gravity of the problem and the urgency of immediate remedial measures. This, at least, IADP has achieved with undeniable success. As a result, there is today a far greater awareness of the problems and their importance—a new water-consciousness—and much stronger determination to tackle them.[5]

9. IADP efforts to increase production were a failure until the arrival of the high-yielding varieties.

This is an exaggerated view. As seen earlier, compared with pre-IADP levels, production of wheat did rise substantially and of maize significantly even in pre-HYV days, while rice, for special reasons, showed only a slight increase both before and after the HYV.[6] Besides, it should not be overlooked that Indian scientists had expected large gains in yield from traditional varieties if backed by the package of inputs and improved practices. This hypothesis needed to be tested in the field, and the field tests virtually disproved it. The actual results fell far short of early expectations.

10. IADP has neglected research, nor did it recognize the ingrained weaknesses of agricultural research in India.

This has been a serious, and recurring charge. Neglect of research in IADP has been called by some a major error. This also underlines the previous point (ninth item) which implies that IADP overlooked the significance of plant-breeding work.

The criticism itself overlooks several pertinent points, as Sherman Johnson has been at pains to explain:[7]

a. The Food Crisis Report, as he reminds us, did lay great stress on research both in natural sciences and in economics. It recognized the seminal importance of plant breeding and urged: "The rice and wheat

---

[5] See Chapter 16.
[6] See Chapter 4, especially under "Rice—A Lagging Miracle."
[7] Sherman E. Johnson, op. cit. pp. 5 and 7.

breeding research work should be intensified ... to supply the needed high yielding plant-disease and insect-resistant (*sic*), stiffer strawed varieties that will respond to higher levels of soil fertility."[8]

b. The overriding objective, in 1959, was to achieve rapid gains in food production. Researchers at that time felt confident that yield per acre could be greatly increased, even doubled, if only the improved techniques already known were actually applied by cultivators. The body of available technical knowledge, it was assumed, should be adequate for a good start. The real task was to make an organized effort to bring the existing knowledge to the doors of the farmers, to ensure adequate supply of inputs and remunerative prices for their produce, and to help them learn the required skills. This is what IADP set out to accomplish.

c. The Rockefeller Foundation, under a cooperative programme with the Government of India, had been carrying on crop research work. In addition, the Economic Cooperation Administration (present USAID) was helping in organizing agricultural universities in India on the pattern of Land Grant Colleges with facilities for practical research.

These facts dictated the strategy adopted by IADP. That it needed an adequate research base was abundantly clear. There was no point in duplicating the effort. But there was clear need to supplement it through a proper division of labour to produce maximum overall impact. The Rockefeller Foundation was helping India to achieve a *genetical breakthrough* in crops research. The IADP was conceived to prepare the ground for what Sherman Johnson aptly called an "adoption breakthrough." Research scientists might, for example, produce results which would double the crop yield. But what good would this be unless the results were actually adopted and applied by farmers? Now, there is no automatic adoption of research results. Farmers have to be taught, even tempted. They must be shown how to grow a new variety or use a new technology; they must be convinced that it would be sufficiently profitable for them to do so; they must be sure of obtaining the required inputs and credit; they must be assured of a remunerative price. This is the other side of the research coin, which had been practically ignored. The primary task IADP undertook for itself was to make good this major omission. It did not neglect, but supplemented research in a most vital respect.

Meanwhile, engineering research had received little attention in other programmes. The Ford Foundation, therefore, sponsored it at two IADP centres. Besides, research and studies in farm management problems at the district level were envisaged in the programme, though they remained one of its neglected facets.

11. The quality of extension workers has seldom been up to the mark. In general, it has been very poor.

This is very true. The reasons are also well known. IADP inherited

[8] The Food Crisis Report, loc. cit., p. 185.

the community development staff who were mostly untrained and un-qualified for giving assistance in scientific agriculture. It had to do the best it could with them, but the best it did, even after developing its training programme, was frequently not good enough. Much of IADP's problems stems from this source. This crippling deficiency, unless urgently rectified, will continue to impede the march of the green revolution.

12. The importance of a public works programme, especially road construction, has been overlooked.

The 10-Point Programme had specifically included this in the IADP package to serve a twofold objective—to provide employment to rural people and to build up the essential structural support for agriculture. But this provision has been virtually ignored in practice, as the IADP Evaluation Committee has dolefully observed time and again.

The absence of a comprehensive public works programme, especially in rural areas, reflects a major failure in India's development planning. This grave omission has continued for years and now threatens to spell disaster on a nation-wide scale. One of the foremost tasks today is to make belated amends for it with the utmost possible speed.[9]

13. There has been "administrative slippage" in implementing the pro-gramme.[10]

This is not only true, but was also inevitable, given the conditions in which IADP was launched and administered. The Ford Foundation ex-perts and consultants naturally served in an advisory capacity, and they would advise mainly the Government of India. From there the line of authority ran, in successive steps, to the state governments, the district officers, the block-level staff, and the village-level workers. Instructions and efforts were both diluted in the process. This explains much of the shortfalls in performance which have been noted above.

14. Agriculture cannot be "packaged."

The phrase "package programme" is useful, but it can be misleading as well. It vividly expresses the need to bring together a number of elements —inputs and improved practices—for a synchronized application to capi-talize on their high complementarities. This is the only strategy that could bring about a yield explosion and put India's subsistence agriculture definitely on the march. Without it her agriculture would at best continue to limp along.

The package itself must, however, be flexible, constantly adapted and re-adapted to changes in technology, to differences in soil, water, and climatic conditions, to movements of market prices. The basic *concept*

[9] Discussed further in *Reaping the Green Revolution*.

[10] The phrase was used by Dr. Arthur T. Mosher, President, Agricultural Develop-ment Council, during personal discussions in July 1970, which gave the writer some fresh insights as well as confirmations of his own views about India's agriculture in general and IADP in particular.

of the package holds good for all conditions; its actual *contents* must, however, be varied to fit the specific needs of specific situations in order to achieve the best possible results.

The package programme was not conceived as a straitjacket; the need for dynamism was all along fully recognized. It was rightly assumed, however, that, within the cosy confines of the package, agriculture would have an assured growth until it was ready, like a chrysalis, to emerge out of its protecting shell, to unpackage itself and to take to the wing to fend largely on its own.

### AN ADOPTION BREAKTHROUGH

A proper evaluation of IADP must go beyond the tangible production gains it has achieved. Its real significance has been overwhelmingly educational and, therefore, far transcends the immediate results. In essence, it has been a kind of super-demonstration project to discover what it takes to develop tropical agriculture, also to rediscover some of the old axioms, for the benefit not simply of India's cultivators, but also of the government and its economic planners, of businessmen and the public in general, and what is no less important, of the foreign experts and consultants working in India.

Free India did not inherit any worthwhile tradition of agricultural development, and so she lacked any definite sense of direction in this field. As she began to grope around for one, her idealistic impulses led her into one blind alley after another. Here was a rare opportunity for her advisers, particularly Americans with their unique record of achievements in agriculture, to help her chalk out the right course. But they, too, largely failed her and inadvertently fed her romantic weakness.

Had an IADP-type of programme been launched soon after India's independence, or even in 1952 when the Ford Foundation, followed by the U.S. aid programme, enthusiastically plumped for community development as the wave of the future, the subsequent course of history would have been entirely different. The food-population syndrome would not have assumed such a virulent form, agricultural and economic growth would have been immeasurably speeded up, there is every reason to believe that, by now, real community development enterprises would have spontaneously sprouted and dotted the countryside, that India's example would have inspired others. Alas, that was not to be. The cart was resolutely put before the horse; a state-financed welfare package was offered when the primary need was for a science-based production-stimulating package; the result was a special brand of bureaucratized amateurism that avidly laid the foundation for collective stagnation of rural India.

To note in passing another example of well-meaning misdirection, for

25

several years Calcutta Metropolitan Planning Organization (CMPO) has been at work with handsome financial support from the Ford Foundation. Its approach has been too academic, too town-centred, too much like Western-type highly capital-intensive urban renewal projects, too dependent on a massive inflow of funds which is nowhere in sight. It has kindled great expectations, caused deep disappointments, and has wasted years of valuable time.[11]

IADP provided a refreshing contrast to these undertakings. As a production-oriented action programme it allowed little leeway to stray from the realities. Its down-to-earth, or rather down-to-farm, approach compelled all concerned to grapple with them constantly, to learn by doing and by seeing, as new technologies and practices were introduced and actually tried out in the field.

In the initial years the IADP package yielded much narrower margins of extra production and income than had been expected, due to weak response of farmers to still-hesitant price incentives and weak response of traditional varieties to chemical fertilizers. These hard facts could be learnt only from actual field results assembled by a functioning IADP.

Among the other facts brought to a focus by IADP were ill-organized supply and distribution of inputs, inadequacies of production credit, poor water management, fitful research largely unrelated to production problems, low quality of extension service, weaknesses of the administrative system, lack of transportation and other facilities. These deficiencies had long been known or suspected, but very little was done about them. IADP, by vividly demonstrating their crippling effects on farm productivity, forced the government's hands to adopt remedial measures. Thereby it ushered in a second, but no less crucial adoption breakthrough.

Meanwhile, the Rockefeller Foundation, busily engaged in crop research and plant breeding in Mexico, the Philippines and also in India, engineered the epoch-making biological breakthrough.[12] It was the meeting of these two breakthroughs, around the mid-sixties, that gave birth to a green revolution in India.

---

[11] Problems relating to regional planning and town-building are dealt with in *Reaping the Green Revolution.*

[12] The research and breeding work pioneered by the Rockefeller Foundation has been broadened in successive stages with the help of the Ford Foundation, USAID, and, more recently, the World Bank.

# CHAPTER 15

# The New Agricultural Strategy

## NOT SO NEW

What passes for new agricultural strategy in India today is not all that new when seen in a historical perspective. It has been at work in the developed countries of the temperate zones for a century or so, though it has been refined and reinforced with new advances in science and technology. These advances which have been amazingly rapid in the last quarter century, have introduced greater sophistication into their farming. Modern agriculture has, in recent years, been further modernized.

Japan has, of course, long been the classic land of intensive agriculture. It takes the pride of place among the world's nations, both developed and underdeveloped, in two important respects. Her holdings are the smallest in size—the average is only 1.2 hectares, or 2.3 acres. Her yield per unit of land, however, is generally the highest—the average yield of rice in 1966-67 was 5,090 kilograms per hectare, or 4,534 pounds per acre.

The introduction of modern science and technology in India's agriculture on a significant scale had to wait for a more auspicious time. That time came only a few years ago, especially with the arrival of the dwarf varieties of wheat and rice, which, again, were evolved mainly from Japanese dwarf strains and adapted to the tropical climate. The high-yielding varieties have sparked a new dynamism in India's agriculture, as in that of several other countries. They have paved the way for modern science and technology. The strategy, which is about a century old in the modernized countries, is now being adopted and applied in the old world—in the tropics and subtropics—for the first time. This is what makes it new.

In recent years India has, without doubt, made rapid strides in placing her agriculture on a sounder basis. Accumulated omissions of the past have been, and are being, made good at long last. Some warmly held misconceptions have been hurriedly buried. The shackles of home-made dogmas have been increasingly shattered. All this is epitomized in the new strategy.

## STILL A FLEDGLING

Born in the midst of convulsions, the strategy is still in its infancy, a fledgling still struggling to take off. It needs to be nurtured with care and affection; it has to be strengthened and developed in many ways. Only then will India be in a position to boast a full-fledged strategy.

"The fundamental departure in the new strategy," as Mr. C. Subramanian, its most ardent spokesman, has stressed on several occasions, "was its emphasis on science and technology." It is a kind of three-dimensional approach consisting of a High-yielding Varieties Programme (HYVP), adoption of modern chemical technology, and incentive prices backed by a price support policy. All three meant a major break with a deeply entrenched tradition; all three gave rise to fierce controversies—scientific, economic, and political; in all three cases wisdom prevailed in the end, thanks to a combination of forces—the new vistas opened up by the dwarf varieties, the IADP exercise in intensive agriculture and the hard lessons already booked, the obstinate food gap, the new "short tether policy" adopted by the U.S. Government in supplying food from its surplus stocks in the mid-sixties, the drought, and the vigorous leadership provided by Mr. Subramanian as Minister of Food and Agriculture.

The immediate objective the new strategy aimed at was to secure a rapid spread of the high-yielding varieties. A five-year target was fixed for the purpose—over 32 million acres were to be brought under these varieties by 1970-71. An HYVP was inescapable to close, or even narrow, the food gap. But, by itself, it could not get off the ground. It needed other components.

"Genetic manipulation" and "chemicalization of agriculture," in Mr. Subramanian's words,[1] are the twin pillars of the new strategy. Both, however, call for strong scientific underpinnings. Research was therefore reorganized and revamped in order to press ahead with plant-breeding work, including further improvement, field-testing, and local adaptation of the high-yielding varieties, and to ensure a steady flow of improved practices and new technologies. Emphasis was laid on training workers for the extension services—the "transmission belts" to carry science and technology from laboratories and experimental plots to the farming community. And all this had to be accompanied by price incentives, that is, guaranteed remunerative prices, since otherwise no farmer would adopt

---

[1] "India's Program for Agricultural Progress" in Rockefeller Symposium, loc. cit.

new technologies, however productive and attractive they might be from a purely scientific angle.[2]

These policy changes, synchronizing with the IADP experiment, have made a major impact on India's agriculture. The outlook has incomparably brightened. Yet while there are good reasons to feel encouraged about the future, there is still none for jubilation. Since complacency flourishes so easily on the Indian soil, it is most important not to lose sight of the perspective, to paint the future rosier than it really is, and to confuse possibilities with realities.

The actual modernization of India's agriculture is a long way off. A beginning, albeit an encouraging one, has been made; nonetheless, it is only a beginning. The journey is bound to be long, arduous, full of pitfalls with inevitable slips though, hopefully, not too many.

Besides, the new strategy bears the distinct stamp of improvization. Its components were hastily assembled in a crisis atmosphere; they are still not firmly rooted in deep convictions, nor adequately backed by long-range policy commitments.

The fact is that India's agricultural policy has too long been obsessed with one single thought—how to produce enough food for the nation, eliminate the imports and save the foreign exchange, and this has led to a continuous quest for shortcuts based on short-term measures. That the nation's food budget must be balanced goes without saying. What has not yet been realized, however, is the insufficiency of self-sufficiency in food as a long-term national goal. A policy that sets its sight no higher is destined to come to grief.[3] It will never be able to realize this limited goal on a durable basis just because the goal is so limited. India's food problem is so vast and so complex that it can never be solved in isolation and by itself. It postulates an all-round modernization of her entire agriculture.

Whatever may have been the justification in the past for chasing such a narrow objective, there is none today, after all the sufferings the country has gone through, and after the great opportunities the high-yielding varieties have opened up. From the frantic efforts of the past to close the food gap through a confused mass of short-term decisions India must turn towards a *total* development of her agriculture in *all* its aspects. This is the only way she can ever expect to lay permanently the spectre of famine, the only way she can maximize production, employment and income, the only way she can significantly raise the living standards of the masses of her people.

[2] For reorganization of research and extension, see Chapter 22; for price support policy, see Chapter 23; for discussions on fertilizers and pesticides, see Chapters 18 and 19.

[3] Disillusionment came sooner than expected. A severe drought hit many areas in July-August 1972; the kharif crop suffered an estimated loss of 14 million tons; buffer stocks have been sharply drawn down; frantic efforts are being made to fill the gap with the next rabi crop. Much will depend on the 1973 monsoon.

The sight must be raised. The goals for agriculture must be broadened and redefined to replace the jungle of artificially fixed targets in the national plan. The new strategy will be really meaningful when it is correspondingly broadened to subserve the larger goal of achieving an all-round development of agriculture, fully supported by all essential agri-related services and facilities.

### "FOOD ENOUGH" IS NOT ENOUGH

The drought-spurred policy changes, as noted above, led, among other things, to the declaration of a new deadline for making India self-sufficient in food, a goal which, like a will-o'-the-wisp, had constantly receded beyond the reach of a wistfully chasing government. This time it was to be reached within five years, that is, by 1970-71.

The deadline was not exactly met. However, with foodgrains production now well above 100 million tons a year, the deficit has been sharply reduced (see Table 7). Despite continued population growth, India has moved closer to self-sufficiency than almost at any time since the early fifties.

By 1973, or thereabouts, the total output should reach, if not exceed, 110 million tons, barring any unusual setbacks due to bad monsoons. This would roughly correspond to the estimated annual requirements. Apparently, therefore, production and consumption should soon be more or less in balance, and this will obviate the need for imports.

It would be unwise, however, to feel elated over this development and to rely heavily on it. For the balance would still be both superficial and precarious. First, a total of 110 million tons does not make anything like adequate allowance for seed, feed, and wastage, nor for the stocks to be carried as a safety margin, especially against a "rainless" day. The minimum need for the first item would be, say, 12 million tons, and for the second another 10 million, making a total of 22 million tons.

Second, population growth will continue unabated through the Fourth Plan period, probably also for several years thereafter. On a conservative estimate, 75 million will be added to India's population by the mid-seventies, making a total of some 625 million.[4] This will be a rise of about 14 per cent. The demand for foodgrains should increase at least correspondingly.

Third, per capita consumption of grains has tended upwards for many years owing to several factors as seen earlier. The trend will almost cer-

---

[4] The latest census results published meanwhile show that the population, on 31 March 1971, was somewhat lower than projected—or 547 million. The current plan-period should therefore end with a lower figure—perhaps close to 600 million. This does not, however, affect the main argument.

tainly continue in the foreseeable future since most of these factors will still be at work.

Fourth, the nutritional standard in India is abnormally low and will have to be raised, and this is likely to give a further push to the demand for foodgrains, both directly and indirectly. For example, the emphasis on livestock and poultry development has been growing lately. The current Plan has made substantially larger provisions for both. This will add to the demand for grains to be used as animal feed.

And, finally, it is not enough to produce enough foodgrains. There is, in addition, the problem of producing, simultaneously and in sufficient quantities, fibre—especially cotton and jute—and a number of other essential commodities, such as sugarcane, oilseeds, tobacco. The demand for all these products has been going up, yet the output has in some instances been lagging. In particular, there has been a sizable transfer of acreage from cotton and jute to rice and wheat owing to the relatively high prices commanded by the latter. It will not help matters if the food crisis is resolved by creating a raw material crisis.

The Fourth Plan, as finally adopted, has set the target for foodgrains production at 129 million tons to be reached by 31 March 1974. This is about a 30 per cent increase over the actual level of production in 1969-70. Yet it is doubtful if even this steeply stepped-up target makes adequate provision for buffer stocks and for seed, feed and wastage.[5]

Can India reach this level of production by the appointed date and hold it firmly? Can she ensure that production thereafter will increase by a minimum of, say, five million tons a year to keep pace with the annual population growth and some rise in demand?

It would be foolhardy to answer these questions unconditionally in the affirmative. All one can say is that today it is *definitely possible* for her to create the indispensable preconditions which would warrant affirmative answers. This means, first, she must fully capitalize on the valuable experience of an eventful decade, especially with intensive agriculture in IADP districts, the high-yielding varieties programme, and the so-called new agricultural strategy which, in actual fact, is still on the anvil; and, second, she must no longer aim simply *at* self-sufficiency in food, an urgent but nonetheless restricted goal which has so long warped her vision, and fix her gaze *beyond* it on a far more ambitious goal: *an all-round development of agriculture with an all-out national effort.*

---

[5] With a steeply rising population and sharp periodic monsoon swings, India needs much larger buffer stocks than hitherto assumed, to cover the risks adequately. According to press reports, China faced the 1972 below-normal harvest with 39 million tons of foodgrains carried over as stocks.

## NEED FOR NEW DIMENSIONS

The staggering problem of feeding India's seething population has been made vastly more baffling because it has been persistently underestimated, resulting in an endless tinkering process with feverish short-term measures to achieve a patched-up hand-to-mouth self-sufficiency. This cultivated myopia has been her worst enemy. Her future hinges on how soon she can get rid of it and envision a much broader and worthier goal for the nation.

This should, in a sense, no longer prove difficult. For, recent history has simplified the task. It has dictated unmistakably what India needs most urgently today, namely: an aggressive long-range plan, say, for fifteen years, which will aim at a food production target of no less than 200 million tons to be reached by 1985; which will have built into it all the other sectoral programmes to fully modernize agriculture and to maximize benefits—in terms of production, income, and employment; which will be backed by a nation-wide mobilization of vast manpower and other resources. To achieve these objectives she must formulate and launch both short-term and longer-range policies and programmes.

In other words, India's agriculture must be rescued from its present rickety, *ad hoc* policy framework. It must be given vastly expanded dimensions to embrace a great many more nation-building objectives which have so far been either ignored or only partially recognized. An adequate national plan for agricultural development in India should aim at the following broad objectives: [6]

a. To double foodgrain production in fifteen years from the current level of about 100 million tons, or to reach a level of 200 million tons a year. This may look too ambitious. Yet only a target of this order will put India's food production comfortably ahead of her population growth, leave enough margin for buffer stocks to make her self-sufficiency fully *weather-proof*, and enable her to divert a sizable proportion for use as feed for her expanding livestock and poultry industries, to meet seed requirements adequately, and to put up with the inevitable loss due to wastage.

b. To improve the quality of diet and to increase its protein content for the masses of people in general, and for children in particular. This will, among other things, call for special emphasis on animal husbandry with an expanding dairy industry, on poultry and poultry products, fishery development—both inland and marine, on production of pulses,

---

[6] The eleven items listed here—from a. to k.—give in outline what may be regarded as an adequate national plan for agriculture. The immediate problems involved in intensive agriculture, along with the ground covered and the tasks ahead, are analyzed in Chapters 16 through 29. How to gather a full harvest—items b. through k. along with population problems—are discussed in the companion study: *Reaping the Green Revolution.*

also on measures to improve the protein content of foodgrains.

c. To evolve a more productive and less risky pattern of agriculture for the rainfed areas which constitute 80 per cent of India's 350 million acres of arable land. Overwhelming dependence on an undependable monsoon over such wide areas has been the weakest feature of her agriculture, and this is what has made her quest for self-sufficiency in food so largely a futile speculation. Her agriculture will never be fully proof against monsoon vagaries, but their impact on output and income can be effectively cushioned in a good many ways, such as better agronomic practices, changes in the cropping pattern, custom-made varieties, new and more appropriate technologies, and of course extension of irrigation wherever feasible. The task is complex, gigantic—and vital.

d. To boost farm incomes. Multiple cropping, mixed farming, improving the quality of products, substitution of more profitable items as cash crops or truck crops—these and similar measures are essential to make a real success of the farming business.

e. To produce a variety of industrial raw materials, in increasing quantity and of improving quality, such as cotton, jute, oilseeds, rubber, silk, wool, and leather. Production of tea, coffee and sugar will have to be increased considerably to meet the rising demand.

f. To build up export earnings. Many tropical products, both processed and unprocessed, are inherently suitable for developing a flourishing export trade. The potential is vast. Only a fringe of it has so far been touched.

g. To extend and better manage forests and to tap forest wealth on a sustained-yield basis to meet the growing demand for paper, timber, and cellulose.

h. To protect and improve land and build up soil fertility. Only too often land has been callously neglected or ruthlessly exploited, with the result that its productivity has been gravely impaired. Past damages must be repaired, and the wasting assets must be fully rehabilitated and put to productive use.

i. To build up an expanding non-farm sector to perform a triple function: to give support to agriculture through agri-business, to create larger markets for increasing farm products, and to draw away, at least partially, surplus labour from overcrowded farms. Meanwhile, the expanding farm sector will provide growing markets for many more industrial goods.

j. To build up an adequate supporting structure for agriculture, especially roads, markets, silos, godowns, warehouses, power supply, and refrigeration facilities. And, all this must go hand-in-hand with spatial planning and town-building, a vastly important but so far also a grossly neglected subject in India.

k. And, finally, to provide employment to the exploding rural population. Intensive agriculture, with its exceptionally high job-creating poten-

26

tial, both directly and indirectly, remains by far the best hope for India to find productive jobs for the tens of millions of people mushrooming in rural areas.

These objectives indicate the broad dimensions of an adequate national plan for agricultural development India so badly needs today. The tasks are stupendous, but so also are the opportunities. What fascinating prospects will such a plan open up, not simply for her agriculture, but for her entire economy! And what a powerful impetus it will give to her G.N.P., putting to shame the timid four or five per cent growth rate on which India's planning pundits have riveted their gaze so long!

## FROM IADP TO IAMP

The experimental programme carried out in IADP districts for ten years has set the stage for bolder action on the wider front just outlined. A great deal has been achieved and learnt, as both positive and negative results, to justify a giant step forward and to extend the programme in its essentials to all the 320 districts of India—to embark upon what in the last IADP Evaluation Report has been called an All-India Intensive Agricultural Modernization Programme, or IAMP.

The feasibility of the programme should no longer be in doubt. It will, of course, have to be adapted to local situations—to the agro-climatic and agro-economic conditions in each case. But such adaptation should be no hindrance. It is part and parcel of the IADP approach, and it must be so in any sensible programme of agricultural development.

The farmer has seen the light and has tasted progress; he is ready, often restive, for a forward leap. The government's basic policies are now more realistic; its price policy which, by design or accident, was long oriented towards urban consumption, has been recast, at least partially, to provide incentives for farm production. Deficiencies still persist in several fields of basic policy; but there is now much greater awareness, and willingness, to face them with open eyes and to rectify them with reasonable speed.

The long-neglected inputs of modern agriculture—seeds, fertilizers, pesticides, and the rest—are receiving more urgent attention; their supplies, from domestic sources and from imports, are expanding more rapidly. The high-yielding varieties have greatly improved the economics of input-intensive agriculture, and have brought it within the reach of masses of farmers. Research and experiment, with a more pronounced problem-solving slant, is broadening in scope as it gains in urgency. Greater emphasis is laid on the training of extension workers. Several agricultural universities have been in operation to serve as "knowledge centres."

The convergence of the genetic breakthrough, the adoption breakthrough, and the policy breakthrough has created a most auspicious occasion to build rapidly on the past experience gained, especially, from the intensive efforts made for intensive agriculture under the package programme, and to launch a *total* effort, a big push forward, to develop and modernize agriculture in its entirety and all over the country.

## A MULTI-TIER APPROACH

IADP can and should be expanded into a *national* programme for modernizing India's agriculture. Obviously, this will take some time— IADP cannot be blown overnight into a fullfledged IAMP. Given the constraints of resources, one must resort to a realistically phased approach.

Besides, quality must be safeguarded at all cost. Amateurism, as experience has shown, habitually threatens to invade programmes of this type, but it is totally incompatible with modernization of agriculture and must therefore be kept at an arm's length. The strength of IADP lay, above all, in its quality-consciousness. Not that it always succeeded in attaining the requisite quality; in fact, quite often it failed to do so. But it was, all along, painfully conscious of the deficiencies, persistently struggled to remedy them, and steadfastly refused to compromise with quality. This is what has distinguished IADP from other operative programmes and has enabled it to build for itself a record of solid achievements.

It is absolutely essential to maintain, and improve, the quality of performance in the IADP districts, and to strengthen their organization and facilities, where necessary. These districts have, by and large, come to serve as models for others. It is important to ensure that their value as models is enhanced, and not diminished.

Moreover, the five "innovative districts" have been entrusted with two other essential roles: to serve as the *field laboratory* where new ideas, approaches, and methods can be tried out to discover new opportunities and to set up new directions; and to act as the *engine* that can help determine the optimum attainable rate of progress and thus set the pace for others. It will not help the cause if their "laboratory functions" are neglected or scaled down in scope, or if the "engine" is dismantled and its horse-power scattered over a wide area. To reduce the intensity of activities here in order to speed up intensive agriculture in other areas would be ironical and counterproductive. The risks of such "scatteration" are real, especially in a democratic society. But they must be effectively guarded against.

The innovative districts, in short, must continue to innovate. Their capacity should not only be left unimpaired, but should be further reinforced as and when deemed necessary. In embarking upon an All-India IAMP, the first task, then, is how *to combine speed with quality* and to work out an optimum combination of the two. This underlines the need for adopting what has been called "a multi-tier approach" embracing four categories of areas, all operating simultaneously but at varying levels of intensity. Stated in the descending order of intensity they are:[7]

a. The five innovative districts of IADP, with the most intensive programme, comprise the first category. Based on research and experiments, they will continue to strike out new paths and set the pace for others. However, even these districts are at present mostly in the first stage of development. They will have to move on towards the second and the third stage much more rapidly to embrace *all* major agricultural activities and to involve all farmers irrespective of the size of their holdings.

b. Next in this stratification are the remaining ten IADP districts which resemble the first group in all respects, except that they will have no experimental and innovative role.

c. The 114 IAAP districts and a few other areas now operating at or near the IAAP level of intensity constitute the third category. The most proximate goal for them is to complete the first stage of the full package programme.

d. And, finally, there are the remaining districts, about 190 in all, covering about two-thirds of the country. The first task in this case is to initiate the IADP, to start with, in a somewhat thinner form as in the IAAP districts, and then to work as fast as possible towards the full IADP status in its first stage.

This, in broad outline, is the multi-tier all-India agricultural modernization programme which has been recommended in the last Evaluation Report on IADP. This is the most constructive proposal that has emerged in India since the IADP was launched in 1960. And it is the best vehicle one could design to carry the green revolution rapidly to all parts of the country. The technological needs of intensive agriculture on an all-India scale will, of course, be enormous. These needs, the prerequisites of a truly meaningful IAMP, will be discussed in the next two Parts (Chapters 16 through 28) along with the fascinating prospects it holds out for the future.

### ECONOMICS OF SPEED

A caveat must be entered here about what may be called the economics of speed.

In carrying out a comprehensive IAMP India must, as stressed earlier, combine *quality* and *speed*. On both counts she has hitherto been found sadly wanting. Things have improved in recent years, but not remotely enough. Almost everywhere, the pace is still far too slow; there is still a shocking lack of a real sense of urgency; the very sight of self-sufficiency in food has tended to give rise to premature elation, even in quarters which should know better and should have no excuse to over-

[7] *Modernising Indian Agriculture*, Report on IADP (1960-68), Vol. I, pp. vi-viii.

look its fragile character. Meanwhile, the country continues to drift towards a demographic abyss.

Not only does the administrative machinery grind slowly with its fragmented responsibilities and a prolific growth of rules and regulations, even experts and technicians are still used to a tempo more appropriate to the mid-Victorian era than to the late-twentieth century. How often experimental programmes and pilot projects are recommended and initiated with a complete disregard for the time factor to achieve what would at best be only marginal advantages!

This all too common tendency is by no means confined to Indian professionals. International experts and consultants—economists, sociologists, agriculturists, irrigation specialists, demographers, town-planners, administrators, and others—serving under both bilateral and multilateral programmes frequently end up their reports by routinely recommending pilot projects. They may be, and often are, good, even though not necessarily excellent, as specialists. But hailing as they do from Western countries whose development was spread over two long centuries, they are inured to a different pace and are often unable to combine a sense of urgency—a time-sense—with their professional competence.

Not infrequently they suffer from another inhibition. The underdeveloped world is so often so different from their own and its problems so unrelated to their own background of experience that they themselves must get acquainted with their tasks and acquire on-the-job experience. This largely explains their cautious approach and their love for pilot projects even where, given a little extra vision or imagination, these could be dispensed with.

And, finally, many experts, being subject to normal human failings, are more interested in themselves than in development, and quite successfully slip into development programmes, both bilateral and multilateral.[8]

The pilot projects in community development were more time-consuming than fruit-bearing, and they prepared the ground for a nationwide misadventure. There are constant talks of pilot projects in various fields—for water technology, growth centres, functional education, administrative reforms in districts, and what not. Even IADP districts have at times been inclined to overplay experiments at the expense of development.

How often does one hear the eloquent plea, especially from international experts, that it takes time to change, to develop, to modernize, without any attempt to measure the length of the time needed and with-

---

[8] Those who suspect these views are too critical should see what John Kenneth Galbraith has to say on the subject in his *Ambassador's Journal*, op. cit., pp. 110-11, where in a letter to President Kennedy he gave his own views about the very mixed quality of technical assistance experts in lively phrases sprinkled with biting sarcasm.

out any suggestion to shorten it.[9] And how rare, alas, is the counter-plea that time is precious in today's underdeveloped world and must be husbanded with the utmost care, that development can and must be speeded up, that the modernization process must be telescoped into the shortest possible time-period! Conventional cost-cutting is no longer enough; it must go hand-in-hand with unconventional *time-cutting*.

Luckily, there have been some outstanding exceptions. The most memorable of them is the Ford Foundation Team on India's Food Crisis and its classic plea to adopt a war-like strategy to avert an impending famine. There are other names which would be hard to forget, such as John Lewis who "quietly" turned on his searchlight on India's gathering crisis; Frank Parker, Ralph Cummings, and Marion Parker who did so much for education and research in agriculture.[10]

Then there are those stalwart-pioneers of the Rockefeller Foundation —E. Stakman, George Harrar, Norman Borlaug, Robert Chandler, and their colleagues—to whom India as well as the whole underdeveloped world owes a debt too deep for words.

To these names must be added at least one more, Forest F. Hill of the Ford Foundation, who made it a mission to help plant, jointly with the sister Foundation, international institutes for crop research to fill a critical void in tropical agriculture.

Norman Borlaug, the chief architect of dwarf wheat, stands out as an embodiment of that restless impatience which the developing countries so badly need today. He deliberately set out to build a seed packed with explosive force to meet the historic challenge of this explosive age. And this he did with a thumping success. The seed he created, after twenty years of uniquely dedicated work, has exploded in the underdeveloped world, shattering much of the old myths, cynicism, and sloth.

And Robert Chandler and his team, taking the cue from Borlaug's remarkable handiwork, staged a repeat performance—this time with rice —and produced the same explosive impact. Most significant of all, the repeat performance was compressed within three brief years.

Here is a classic example which illustrates how time can be saved when a programme is framed with imagination, geared to a definite goal, and inspired with a sense of overriding urgency. This is the kind of example which practitioners in international development must learn to emulate.

Let there be no misunderstanding. Research and experiments, along with adaptive research and local verification trials, constitute the very soul of modern scientific agriculture. They cannot and must not be

[9] *An Evolving Strategy for India's Agricultural Development* by Douglas Ensminger, The Ford Foundation, New Delhi, June 1968, gives an excellent account of India's struggles in this field, along with an able apologia for past misconceptions, omissions, and errors.

[10] For their historic contributions in this field, see Chapter 22.

dispensed with or bypassed. Without them, agriculture will be eternally condemned to a low-yield primitivity.

But we must be equally on our guard not to promote fancy research projects, spin out experiments in a leisurely fashion, make a fetish of pilot projects. Stringent "family planning" is absolutely essential here with strenuous efforts to cut down the *time-cost* to a minimum.

## THE REAL CHALLENGE

Can India immediately launch an Intensive Agricultural Modernization Programme, or IAMP, on an all-India scale? She certainly can, if the multi-tier approach is adopted with graded levels of intensity for different tiers, yet all moving up toward an optimum.

Can she afford such a programme and find the resources needed for it? She can, and she must. There will unquestionably be numerous bottlenecks owing to shortages of trained men, of materials and machinery, of research and a host of other needed facilities. They can and must be overcome with appropriate actions to make the best possible use of whatever resources are already available and to expand them with every feasible speed.

Meanwhile, the least troublesome of all bottlenecks should be what is commonly believed to be the most serious one—money. India must be ready to finance an IAMP largely with created money, or credit. She cannot afford not to afford it.[11]

And, finally, will the government be willing to launch an IAMP, to mobilize the necessary resources and to back it up with the requisite political leadership? Here lies the crux of the matter, the real challenge. Once again, the answer is crystal-clear. It can and it must. For what is at stake here is nothing short of national survival. A government that shirks this challenge can be sure to stand accused of the gravest default at the bar of history.

[11] See Chapter 28. The Credit Shackles and Deficit Financing.

CHAPTER 16

# Harnessing the Monsoon

## A BLESSING DESPITE PROBLEMS

Most people in India are apt to bemoan the problems the monsoon has piled on her agriculture. Droughts and floods are an all too common phenomenon; sometimes, as in the mid-sixties, they can assume catastrophic proportions. Even in a year of normal rainfall, its distribution is usually too uneven to meet crop requirements—too much or too little water almost always leaves behind a trail of woes and damages. And, in the post-monsoon months, most of the land runs out of moisture needed to support crops. How to ensure optimum supply of water in the fields has all along been the biggest problem in India. Her agriculture has been enslaved by the monsoon.

Yet it is sobering to reflect what *might* have happened. Given her latitudinal location, India could easily have been a vast desert land. She escaped from such a fate at a surprisingly low price—with only one single pocket of sandy or arid land—because of a gigantic freak of nature: the emergence of the towering mountain range in the north. The monsoon clouds rushing from the south and south-west in the hot summer season are trapped by the Himalayas and are turned back to the plains to drench them in merciful showers, or are turned into torrents and sent down the mighty rivers—the Indus, the Ganges and the Jumna, the Brahmaputra. The Himalayas also act as a protective wall in the winter months; they deflect the massive cold winds blowing from Central Asia away from the Indian plains which, as a result, enjoy a much milder, mostly frost-free, winter than would otherwise have been the case.

Abundant rainfall, a hospitable climate, a wide range of temperatures thanks to the high-altitude mountains in the north, also in the centre and in the south—all this explains the extraordinary diversity of flora and fauna, which has enriched India. For the same reason a great variety of crops—many crops of temperate climates in addition to those of the tropics and subtropics—can be grown here. And most important of all, year-round cropping is feasible wherever year-round water supply is assured.

Monsoon, without doubt, does create some problems, but in spite of them it remains a rare blessing. Mother Nature has not spoonfed India in well-measured doses. But she has been more than generous with the supply of her milk of kindness. So far India has handled this life-giving fluid indifferently or clumsily.

What India has yet to realize is that water is the most valuable asset she has been endowed with; that for her it is equivalent to both food and cash; that it provides, along with the land resources, the surest means to abundance; that she must husband it with a Spartan—or should we not say, a Japanese—sense of economy.

Like a prudent individual who finds his whole year's wages advanced to him in one single quarter, India must learn to live on her monsoon supply. But so far she has "woefully failed to budget this liquid cash which nature gives her in one bountiful season. Hence floods are followed by scarcity of water. Hence the land is starved of water and the people are starved of food. What we receive in three months, we must spread, as best we can, over twelve."[1]

In 1945, Sir William Stampe, then Agricultural Adviser to the Government of India, had expressed the paradox of scarcity amidst plenty in vivid words: "As one flies over these arid areas of India, one cannot but wonder why millions of tons of horse-power in the hills above should crash to waste yearly within sight of toiling peasants beneath whose feet millions of tons of water sweep silently through sands to the sea."[2]

The Ford Foundation Team of 1959 expressed a similar view in its Crisis Report: *"India is blessed with one of the largest water supplies of any country in the world, but only a small portion of its potential has been developed."*[3]

Time has compounded the penalty for the past neglect. A gigantic and well-coordinated effort is needed to make amends for it. Otherwise it would be meaningless to talk about "genetic manipulation" and "chemicalization of agriculture." Without water the seeds of green revolution will not germinate; $H_2O$ in right doses must have precedence over N, $P_2O_5$, $K_2O$ and other nutrients. The new agricultural strategy is thus a hostage to the $H_2O$ problems.

[1] From *Breaking the Bondage of the Monsoon* by Sudhir Sen, published on the DVC's Fourth Anniversary, 7 July, 1952, by its Staff Association..

[2] In an address delivered at the East India Association of London in September, 1945.

[3] The Crisis Report, op. cit., p. 142; italics in original.

## IRRIGATION POTENTIAL AND
## PRESENT STATUS

The annual rainfall in India over the years averages at about 42 inches. The figure, however, conceals sharp year-to-year swings. In a good year it can go as high as 50 inches, while in a bad one it can drop as low as 31 inches.

Even more striking are the regional variations in a given year. At one end of the spectrum is Cherapunji, the famous monsoon trap in Assam, with an average annual precipitation of 430 inches, the highest in the world. At the other end is the Rajasthan desert with an average of only 5 inches a year.

The State of Assam and the West Coast lying at the foot of the Western Ghats are classified as areas of very heavy rainfall. Next comes a broad belt of what is called "moderately high rainfall," comprising the Eastern States, most of north Indian plains and the east-coast plains extending from Orissa southwards. Finally, there is the narrower belt of relatively low rainfall, which runs from the Punjab plains across the Vindhya mountains into the western part of the Deccan where it broadens to embrace the Mysore plateau.

Thus, irrigation, or water management, in India has a threefold task: to stretch the monsoon supply into the dry-weather period; to transfer the excess supply, as far as possible, from the wet to the dry or deficient areas; and to iron out the intra-seasonal fluctuations in many areas with an adequate rainfall in absolute terms. In addition, there are cognate tasks of drainage, prevention of water-logging, and of what is the biggest of them all in dimension—flood control.

The average annual supply of surface water has been estimated at a total of 168 million hectare-metres (h.m.).[4] Of this total, 56 million, or just one-third, are considered usable for irrigation, given the physiographical limitations. Of this usable total, only 9.5 million had been actually used by 1951. This was almost doubled—to 18.5 million—under the three Five-Fear Plans; it rose further to 20.5 million by March, 1969, and is expected to reach 25.5 million by the end of the Fourth Plan (31 March, 1974).

The 56 million h.m., it has been assessed, could ultimately irrigate 60 million hectares, or about 150 million acres. This might, according to the Planning Commission, turn out to be "somewhat on the low side." In

[4] The estimates cited here were prepared by Dr. A. N. Khosla in 1949 in his "Appraisal of Water Resources: Analysis and Utilisation of Data," and have since then been used by the Planning Commission. *Fourth Five-Year Plan, 1969-74 (Draft)*, pp. 182-83.

The irrigation potential, as revised in 1972, stood at 71 mill. ha. from all sources. The entire increase fell under "major and minor works," which now account for 56 mill. ha. against the earlier estimate of 45 mill. ha.

fact, reasonably hard long-term hydrological data are still so rare for many areas of India that the entire exercise cannot but be regarded as highly conjectural. Nevertheless, these are the only estimates currently available of the annual volume of surface water and its usability; and, as such, they have received the official stamp of approval. In any case, they do give, even if on a rough-and-ready basis, some indications about the quantitative aspects of India's overall irrigation potentialities.

The growth of irrigation in recent years, as compared with the ultimate potential, is shown below:

*(in million hectares)*

|  | From major and medium works | From small works | Total |
|---|---|---|---|
| Total potential | 45.0 | 15.0 | 60.0 |
| Developed by March 1951 | 9.7 | 6.4 | 16.1 |
| „ by March 1961 | 14.4 | 6.6 | 21.0 |
| „ by March 1969 | 18.6 | 8.1 | 26.7 |
| Balance to be developed | 26.4 | 7.0 | 33.3 |

The new *potential* created for irrigation between 1951 and 1969 is substantial, and represents an increase of 60 per cent—from 16.1 to 26.7 million hectares. Its *actual utilization*, as was noted in Chapter 6, lagged behind by an appreciable margin which, even according to official figures, amounted to as much as two million hectares. By 1969, the gap apparently narrowed to half a million hectares, mainly no doubt because of the fact that, in the later sixties, the emphasis shifted away from large river valley projects to minor irrigation works.

The point to be noted in particular is that, in spite of the development of the last two decades, more than half of the total irrigation potential, equivalent to 33 million hectares (82.5 million acres), is yet to be realized.

As for *groundwater*, it has been estimated that about 22 million hectare-metres can be ultimately exploited through deep tube wells to irrigate the same number of hectares. However, these estimates are even less firm at this stage than the hydrological data for surface water.

The Exploratory Tubewells Organization (ETO), which was set up in October 1954, has investigated only about 18 million hectares in 16 different regions in its first fifteen years. It has yet to explore most of the country; in fact, some of the states are yet to take the first serious steps for initiating groundwater investigations. The Fourth Plan contemplates a sharply stepped-up programme for the ETO (see below).

The present position may be briefly summed up as follows: The total land area of India covers 326.8 million hectares (818 million acres). The reporting area in 1965-66 (the latest year for which figures are available) was 305.6 million hectares. The *net* area sown in the same year was 135.8 million, and the *net* area irrigated *from all sources* was 26.4 million hectares. This last figure had the following breakdown by source: 11 million irrigated from canals, 4.4 million from tanks, 8.4 million from wells, and 2.6 million from miscellaneous sources such as lift irrigation from rivers and streams.[5]

The drought and the high-yielding varieties have stimulated the extension of irrigation, particularly from minor works. As a result, by March 1969, facilities were created to irrigate 37.6 million hectares—26.7 million from surface water and 10.9 million from underground water.

This compares with an overall potential of 82 million hectares—60 million from surface and 22 million from groundwater resources. There is thus still a gap of over 44 million hectares, or 110 million acres, between the potentially irrigable area and the area actually irrigated at present.

This gap, the Planning Commission urges, should be closed "within the next few plans"—in about 15 years for groundwater and about 20 years for surface water. For the Fourth Plan the Commission has recommended a programme which will narrow it by about a quarter. The new potential, to be created by 31 March, 1974, should irrigate 10.5 million hectares —5.7 million from major and medium projects and the rest, 4.8 million, from minor works comprising both surface water schemes and deep tubewells. Even after the Fourth Plan there will, according to these figures, still be a balance of as much as 33.5 million hectares which will need to be serviced with irrigation.

**QUALITY OF IRRIGATION**

As seen above, less than one-half of the estimated water-use potential has been developed so far to irrigate just about one-fifth of the net area sown with crops. Mere acreage is, however, not a good enough yardstick to measure progress. Since the sole purpose of irrigation is to grow more and better crops, the questions of dosage and timing are all-important to meet deficiencies and to eliminate excesses of water supply. Judged by these criteria, the quality of India's irrigation, in general, has been simply deplorable.

[5] Source: *Indian Agriculture in Brief*, Ninth Edition, Directorate of Economics and Statistics, Ministry of Food, Agriculture, etc., Government of India, New Delhi. These figures, especially those about acreages irrigated from different sources, show some discrepancy as between different official publications, presumably due to such factors as lack of uniform definitions, different years of compilation, estimates used in some instances, and periodic revisions of some data.
The official estimates for 1968-69 were as follows (in mill. ha.): reporting area 305.7, net area sown 137.5, net area irrigated 28.77 from all sources—from govt. canals 10.86, private canals 1.00, tanks 3.85, tubewells 3.07, wells 7.67, and other sources 2.32.

The earlier irrigation projects, barring one or two exceptions in South India, did not provide much storage facilities, and relied more or less exclusively on the river flow.[6] In years of poor monsoon, when the rivers ran low, they could give only poor irrigation. Even in years of normal rainfall, they were often unable to provide, at the tail-end of the monsoon, the critical doses of irrigation needed by kharif (summer) crops. And they did not, or could not, support rabi (winter) cultivation. Some rabi crops were still grown here and there on a very limited scale; but they were due to the ingenuity of isolated farmers who managed to coax out of the drying land an extra crop as a kind of bonus.

With the multi-purpose storage projects started mainly after the war, the quality of irrigation improved in two respects.[7] Thanks to the storage reservoirs, kharif irrigation was fully assured, and in each case substantial facilities were created for a second, or rabi, crop. But like the earlier projects, they too continued to suffer from several grave defects. They have provided for old-style flow irrigation, but as a rule with no means to regulate the quantity of water on the fields; there was no change from the "wild flooding method" of irrigation,[8] no land-levelling to secure even distribution of water, and no attention was paid to the problem of drainage and to the damage excess water could inflict on crops and soils. Finally, irrigation, as seen in Chapter 11, was not accompanied by other measures—fertilizers, improved seeds, and better agronomic practices—to raise yield per acre. The extra yield from irrigation remained exceedingly low, only a small fraction of what it could have been under a system of efficient water-soil-input management.

The result has been a very poor return on the heavy investments of capital.[9] For the 18 years ended 31 March, 1969, they amounted to Rs. 1,747 crores, or over $3.5 billion at the pre-devaluation rate of exchange, and they had been preceded by sizable investments, amounting to several hundred crores. The Fourth Plan has made a provision of Rs. 857 crores for the five-year period through March, 1974.

An incredible feature of India's irrigation policy, a leftover from the colonial days, is that it is considered enough to earn 4 to 5 per cent return on the invested capital so as to meet the service charges. There is no suggestion of improving the output-input ratio, not to speak of maximizing the benefit, and of course none to amortize the investments. Financial sights have been kept astonishingly low. And so what, under good

---

[6] The Indus, India's main snow-fed river, has a substantial natural storage in the Himalayan heights, which gives it a large perennial flow.

[7] See Chapter 6.

[8] The Crisis Report, Ford Foundation, op. cit., p. 146.

[9] The return was further reduced by the utilization lag. According to Agriculture Ministry's estimate, in April 1970 only 83 per cent of the potential was utilized; the remaining 17 per cent, or 3.8 million acres, received no water and, as a result, some Rs. 350 crores of investments yielded no return.

management, should have been a major source of surplus, has turned out to be a veritable sink for development capital. This could not but badly hurt economic growth.

To complete this catalogue of woes, mention must be made of another lamentable fact: how the extension of canal irrigation without heed to drainage is creating havoc in many areas, particularly in the Indo-Gangetic plains. The subsoil water level has been rising, and millions of acres have been affected by or are threatened with water-logging.

An official study published in 1963[10] sought to focus attention on the problem. Large areas, it emphasized, "are getting water-logged, and are going out of cultivation." If attention were not paid to remedy the situation, it emphasized, "the result could be catastrophic."

The worst state to suffer is the Punjab, the cradle of the green revolution, where irrigation was considered to be at its best. The year-to-year data show that water-logging has been steadily increasing, and no less than 2.5 million acres have already been affected. Some improvement, it seems, has taken place in the meantime, following the introduction of surface drainage measures.

A large acreage in the Punjab—429,000 acres in the canal irrigated area and about 224,000 acres outside it—have been recorded as damaged by salt accumulation. The actual position seems much worse. Over 3 million acres, the study estimates, are either visibly affected by salts on the surface or contain enough salts to lower crop yields.

To cite another disturbing case, in Uttar Pradesh an estimated 3,100,000 acres are lying waste because of saline or alkali soils and the state has an equally large area suffering from soil salinity.[11]

What is the explanation for the absurd irrigation policy hitherto pursued in India, the planned waste on a colossal scale? The broad answer is of course the lack of resource-sense and the failure to understand the role of agriculture in economic development. There is, however, also a more specific answer as was briefly indicated in Chapter 11. Obviously, irrigation cannot be treated as an end itself; it must, under any rational scheme of things, serve as the handmaid of *agricultural* development. Yet in India the two functions were arbitrarily separated, which ensured virtual autonomy for the irrigation engineers. The explanation for this strange set-up lies perhaps in the fact that most government-sponsored irrigation projects were conceived in very narrow terms—either as "famine relief" or as "protective" works—to protect the kharif crops against spells of drought by diverting the river flow with wiers and canals into the fields, mostly planted with rice. Even after independence

[10] *Study on Wastelands including Saline, Alkali and Waterlogged Lands and their Reclamation Measures*, Committee on Natural Resources, Planning Commission, New Delhi, 1963, pp. 105-6.
[11] Ibid., p. 11.

India's irrigation engineers remained largely wedded to an outmoded past and managed to keep the agriculturists at an arm's length, if not to usurp their position.

Thus, the extension of irrigation, though impressive at first sight, is anything but inspiring when its quality is taken into account. The damage done by past omissions and commissions is enormous. Here is a costly legacy; and the nation must address itself to the task of repairing it as best, and as fast, as possible.

### MINOR IRRIGATION[12]

Wells, tanks, and other small irrigation works have traditionally played an important role in India's agriculture. Of the 56 million acres (gross) irrigated in 1951, small projects accounted for as much as 32 million acres (gross), as against 24 million acres irrigated from major-medium works. Though individually small, their overall impact is quite substantial.

Moreover, minor irrigation has a number of built-in advantages. An official publication stated that in many irrigated areas, "half of the water diverted from the rivers and streams is lost in conveyance and half of the water given to the fields is lost before it gets to the roots of the plants."[13] The seepage problem is particularly serious in large surface projects with unlined canals.

By contrast, water loss due to conveyance and evaporation is much less in well irrigation. Proximity to the source of supply, ease of delivery, greater flexibility about the timing and the quantity of supply are all positive factors in its favour. They also widen the options regarding the crops to be grown since the supply of water can be readily adjusted to meet the specific requirements in each case. And, finally, small projects are inexpensive, they are easy to build and maintain, also to operate, especially when power is available. All this results in a payoff which is both quick and attractive. When assured water supply is combined with improved seeds, essential inputs, and better agronomic practices, the pay-off can really soar.

Most wells in India used to be shallow masonry structures. A new phase in minor irrigation began in 1952 when, under an agreement between the Government of India and the U.S. Aid authorities, construction of 2000 tubewells was undertaken in Punjab, U.P. and Bihar.[14] The number was later increased to 2885. A study carried out in the late fifties showed that tubewell irrigation alone had raised crop yields by 45 to 100 per

[12] Irrigation works with a financial ceiling of Rs. 1,500,000 each were, until recently, classified as minor. From 1 April, 1970, this ceiling has been raised to Rs. 2,500,000 each; for hill areas it has been set slightly higher—at Rs. 3,000,000.

[13] *Better Use of Land*, Ministry of Community Development, Government of India, New Delhi.

[14] "Operational Agreement Number 6" between the Government of India and the Technical Cooperation Mission under the Indo-American Aid Programme.

cent, without the use of fertilizers, without multiple cropping, and without a switch-over to crops best suited for cultivation under irrigated conditions.[15]

Despite all the points in their favour, minor irrigation works were eclipsed under the first three Five-Year Plans when attention was concentrated on large-scale surface-irrigation projects. Then came the droughts—the unfilled reservoirs, the feebly flowing rivers, the dried-up irrigation canals revealed the weakness of the past policy and the dangers inherent in it. Small irrigation projects, it was suddenly realized, must be given a far bigger role to play. This conclusion was soon reinforced with the arrival of the dwarf wheat and rice. Intensive agriculture with the new seeds called for assured and intensive irrigation, a condition which large surface-irrigation projects were in most cases unable to satisfy. Minor irrigation thus scored a major victory; and along with the dwarf varieties, it moved to the forefront of the green revolution.

After the droughts high priority was given to minor irrigation, particularly to wells, tubewells and pumpsets, to achieve quick and assured irrigation.[16] In the three fiscal years ended 31 March, 1969, 161,000 new tubewells were installed, raising the total for the country to 286,000 (only 16,000 were state tubewells, the rest were all private); 596,000 wells were dug to reach a total of 5,700,000 dugwells; diesel pumpsets installed for irrigation, which had been steeply rising, increased by over 185,000 to a total of 650,000; the number of electric pumpsets jumped more than 100 per cent to 1,021,000. In three years 692,000 minor irrigation projects—mostly dugwells and tubewells, to some extent also for lifting water from rivers, streams and lakes—were energized, a remarkable development by previous Indian standards.

The progress of minor irrigation programmes can be best judged from the following figures:

|  | First Plan | Second Plan | Third Plan | 1966-69 |
|---|---|---|---|---|
| 1. Financial: | | | | |
| Rs. in crores | 65.62 | 171.28 | 427.85 | 513.32 |
| 2. Physical—in million gross acres: | | | | |
| (a) New irrigation: | | | | |
| Surface | 1.50 | 2.00 | 3.50 | 2.25 |
| Ground | 3.50 | 3.00 | 5.00 | 4.25 |
| (b) Other benefits: | | | | |
| Stabilization, suppl. irrigation, embankment, etc. | 4.50 | 4.00 | 4.30 | 3.70 |

[15] This is another example to show that substantial yield improvement was possible even before the arrival of the high-yielding varieties or of fertilizer-intensive agriculture. See Chapter 9.

[16] The data used in this section have been drawn mainly from: *Report of the*

The area irrigated from minor works of all types, after making allowance for their usual depreciation, reached an estimated total of 47,000,000 acres (gross) in 1968-69—20 million from surface and 27 million from groundwater schemes.

As for the future potential, it is estimated that *new* surface-water schemes could irrigate *additional* 35 million acres (gross); that the groundwater "recharged" by annual rainfall, if tapped properly, could bring another 55 million acres (gross) under irrigation; and that some 3 million acres would be restored to irrigation after repairing the works that were lying derelict in 1968-69. They add up to an impressive total of 93 million acres (gross). This is *twice as large* as the area at present irrigated from minor projects.

## NEW APPROACH

The recent spurt in minor irrigation has been accompanied by several wholesome policy changes. There is now a definite shift from extensive/protective irrigation of the past to intensive/assured irrigation. Such a shift is a *sine qua non* for cultivating the high-yielding varieties with heavy fertilizer application, also for creating confidence among the farmers that the new technology would really benefit them substantially.

To bring about the shift it is essential to introduce supplemental irrigation, especially in the command areas of large irrigation projects dependent on run-of-the-river supplies. With this object in view, farmers are being encouraged to set up private wells, tubewells, and pumpsets to supplement the canal water with supply from their own works as and when needed. Besides, the state governments are executing tubewell or river pumping projects to feed the canals with fresh supplies or to irrigate non-command areas when available in compact blocks at convenient locations.

It is now agreed that, in accordance with this policy change, all new irrigation projects—major, medium, and minor—should be planned and designed for higher irrigation intensities to meet the optimum requirements of the crops to be grown; that the command areas of state tubewells should be scaled down; and that the "conjunctive use" of surface and groundwater should be adopted to the utmost possible extent.

The principle of conjunctive use has been extended also to finance—*all* sources of funds should be simultaneously tapped to finance minor irrigation programmes of all types. Accordingly, to the Plan Sector and

---

*Working Group for formulation of Fourth Five-Year Plan Proposals on Minor Irrigation and Rural Electrification*, Dept. of Agriculture, Ministry of Food, Agriculture, etc., Government of India, New Delhi. It has been supplemented by *Fourth Five-Year Plan (Draft)*, and *India—1969*.

28

the Community Development Sector have now been added the so-called institutional sector which comprises agencies like the Land Development Banks, Agricultural Refinance Corporation, Central Cooperative Banks, and Agro-Industries Corporations.

The principle of pooling is applied, finally, also to the fields. What has been called the "selective compact area approach" should facilitate maximum development with irrigation from different sources, extension of power lines, electrification of pumpsets, field levelling and other construction work, supply of inputs, and improved agronomic practices.

Minor irrigation works, as was to be expected, have proved highly remunerative, so much so that the demand for them is rising steeply, outrunning what the administration is ready to cope with. Past subsidies have been scaled down, and are being eliminated in most cases. The policy, as now contemplated, is to restrict them to farmers with very small holdings, who may genuinely need such help.

As for loans, the more well-to-do farmers, it is felt, should be able to finance themselves from their own resources. They should be granted loans, if at all, sparingly and for short periods.

*Fourth Plan Targets.* Encouraged by the progress made in recent years, the Working Group referred to earlier pleaded for a bolder programme for the 1969-74 period. The main targets it recommended were: new irrigation for 14 million acres (gross)—4 million from surface and 10 million from underground water; and an additional area of 7.50 million acres to benefit from such measures as stabilization, supplemental irrigation, drainage, and embankment.

In physical terms, the proposals provided for digging 1,000,000 new wells, boring 510,000 wells, deepening 350,000 wells, erecting 375,000 private and 6,300 state tubewells, and installing a total of 1,850,000 pumpsets —two-thirds electric and one-third diesel—to energize 975,000 dugwells, and 375,000 tubewells while 500,000 were earmarked for surface schemes to pump water from rivers, streams, and lakes.

The cost was estimated at Rs. 1200 crores of which the bulk or Rs. 750 crores, it was suggested, should come from institutional sources, Rs. 325 crores from private investments, and the balance of Rs. 125 crores from the Plan Sector.

The targets were substantially scaled down in the Fourth Plan. The actual provision made was Rs. 476 crores to create new facilities for irrigating 8 million acres. The reason was, as usual, lack of financial resources; and, as usual, it betrayed a lack of real-resource sense.

## GROUNDWATER DEVELOPMENT

There remains one other major source of supply—much talked about and well-publicized, but virtually unused so far, namely groundwater.

The Exploratory Tubewell Organization (ETO), as mentioned earlier, was set up in October, 1954, but progress to date has been slow and spotty because of inadequate capacity, lack of highgrade expertise, sluggish and uncoordinated approach.[17]

Yet, as experience has clearly demonstrated, groundwater exploration can be highly rewarding. In the two drought years extensive investigations were carried out for drinking water in areas which had previously been ruled out as unsuitable for groundwater exploration, such as: areas south of the Ganges in Uttar Pradesh and Bihar—in the districts of Benaras, Mirzapur, Shahabad, and Gaya; in the hills of Banda and Jhansi; in the coastal belt of Andhra Pradesh, between the delta and the hills; in southern Tanjore, and in the coast of Orissa. In all these areas aquifers, including some artesian, have been struck, sometimes at great depths. The finds took many by surprise, including the official world. Started as a desperate gamble in an hour of national crisis, the venture has handsomely paid off. These aquifers can serve as a most valuable source of irrigation in what has hitherto been set aside as arid or semi-arid land unfit for cultivation. They are yet to be exploited to put the barren land to productive work.

In its first fifteen years the ETO has done exploratory work in 16 regions covering 70,000 sq. miles; it drilled 1,646 wells with a total footage of 900,000 running feet. About 24,000 sq. miles, or over a third of the area explored, proved "groundwater worthy"; this would create a potential for 12,000 deep tubewells to irrigate an estimated area of 2,400,000 acres (gross). During this period, a sum of Rs. 10.92 crores was spent on the exploration work.

For the Fourth Plan the ETO programme will be intensified. It is proposed to investigate 74,000 sq. miles, of which 29,000 sq. miles may prove groundwater worth enough for installing 14,500 additional tubewells to irrigate about 2,900,000 acres (gross). The five-year outlay is estimated to be Rs. 12 crores. Thus, the programme for 1969-74 is expected to exceed, both in physical and financial terms, the ETO activities of the previous fifteen years.

Much more significant, however, is the revised strategy which is now being adopted. First, emphasis is laid not only on exploration, but also on exploitation. It is not enough just to strike groundwater and to delineate the area of its occurrence; the ETO, it is now urged, must make quanti-

[17] The Report of the Working Group on Minor Irrigation, etc. referred to earlier contains a detailed account of the ETO's activities, its shortcomings, and recommendations for its future work.

The groundwater potential, acc. to revised estimates received from official sources in Dec. 1972, looks even brighter. The total is now placed at 26.5 million hectare-metres, enough to irrigate 35 mill. ha. This is the new target for ultimate development against the earlier one of 22 mill. ha. In 1968-69, 12.99 mill. ha. were irrigated from groundwater.

tative assessments and prepare feasibility studies for groundwater development to irrigate compact areas. As such studies are completed with design, pumpage and other particulars, it is intended to implement them with institutional finance, especially from the Agricultural Refinance Corporation.

Second, the ETO activities have so far been confined mainly to the alluvial and semi-consolidated areas, although 70 per cent of the total geographical area of the country consists of hard-rock formations. In these areas open wells and dug-cum-bore wells would be a most valuable source of irrigation. Encouraged by the successful strikes it has, in recent years, made in several rocky areas, the ETO plans to undertake hard rock exploration more systematically, with priority given to those parts which are chronically affected by drought.

Third, integrated studies of ground and surface water resources are essential, particularly in the drainage basins of the major river systems, to ensure balanced development of both, based on changes that may occur in the hydrological regime. The need for such studies was strongly emphasized by a team of two experts from the Water Resources Division of the United States Geological Survey, which visited India in September-November, 1966.[18] The ETO is building up its strength, with staff and equipment, to undertake such studies.

Even this brief account leads up to some important conclusions. The groundwater resources have a vital role to play for irrigation, especially in the dry areas. The task is vast, and the ETO has been unable to do anything like justice to it; nor is there any guarantee that it will fare appreciably better in the future, despite the attempt to expand its capacity with more staff, more equipment and more facilities for in-service training. For, the work, because of its very nature, does not lend itself to departmental, or force account, operations. Herein lies the real snag. It would be far more rational to farm it out to competent commercial concerns.

A policy of contracting out the work to private enterprises will have some solid advantages. It will greatly speed up progress—not just of exploration, but of what should be the real objective—of utilization, as measured in terms of the acreage actually brought under irrigation with groundwater and deep tubewells. It will be less, not more expensive—earlier exploitation of the resource will, it may be assumed, yield extra benefits to lower the net costs of commercial services. And, finally, it will spare the government a great many headaches, and will save much of its energies, which could be profitably deployed on other urgent work.

In fact, some indirect steps have already been taken towards enlisting private enterprise for this work. The ETO has several special projects on

[18] Messrs. Paul H. Jones and Walter Hofmann.

hand, such as groundwater assessment study in Rajasthan with assistance from the United Nations Development Programme (UNDP); groundwater investigation in the Gaya district of Bihar with assistance from the Netherlands Government; and Terai Seed Development, a World Bank-assisted project for developing a large-scale seed farm along modern lines. Though the ETO will continue to have overall responsibility for these projects, they will be executed with the help of foreign experts and private enterprise.

An even more straightforward example of the new trend comes from Andhra Pradesh where a programme, costing Rs. 60 crores, has been proposed to tap the aquifers in the delta region. The work is expected to be entirely in the private sector. This is an imaginative move. Andhra Pradesh has shown the way; other parts of India would be well advised to follow suit.

In the past years the government has spent substantial sums of money on oil exploration. Despite some sharp criticisms, this has been a wholly justifiable undertaking, for which the government deserves to be unreservedly complimented. Thorough geological prospecting, as emphasized in Chapter 2, is one of the first imperatives of economic development, especially in a vast, over-populated, and under-prospected country like India. For the same reason groundwater prospecting and development deserves to be pushed vigorously, with the same purposeful tenacity as has been evinced for oil exploration. The payoff from aquifers, when combined with HYV seeds and fertilizers in the tropical environment, will be exceptionally high, and should far exceed the payoff from oil.

## RAINFED AREAS

At present only 20 per cent of India's net cultivated area—340 million acres—is classified as irrigated from one source or another. And the remaining 80 per cent is dependent on the erratic rainfall for growing crops—a fact that is habitually lamented in India. Yet, as stated at the outset of this Chapter, the really lamentable fact is not the failure of Nature to give more, but the failure to turn to reasonably good account what she has already conferred. The problem, in general, is man-made, not God-given.

To set the perspective right, it is necessary to take a close look at the overall picture (see Table on p. 222).[19]

The assured rainfall areas (Category A) contain some pockets where the rainfall is very heavy, 100-150 inches or more, and the problem is one of excess water. Over most of the areas in this category, however, the

[19] The data relate to 1964-65, the latest year for which complete figures are available. The net irrigated area has somewhat increased since then, but the broad pattern still holds good.

| | A. Assured rainfall areas | B. Medium rainfall areas | C. Dry rainfall areas | Total |
|---|---|---|---|---|
| Range of rainfall | Above 45″ | bet. 30″ & 45″ | below 30″ | |
| Net area sown—million acres | 102.7 | 121.7 | 115.8 | 340.2 |
| Net irrig. area     „     „ | 17.0 | 26.6 | 21.0 | 64.6 |
| Net irrig. area as per cent | 16.5 | 21.8 | 18.1 | 18.9 |
| Crop-growing season in unirrig. areas | 110 to 135 days | 90 to 105 days | Less than 90 days | — |

rainfall is fairly well distributed in the kharif season, though there may be occasional dry spells of two to three weeks. With drainage and irrigation, almost the entire cultivated area could be conditioned for three crops a year, or continuous cropping, if adequate steps are taken: to tap systematically the available surface and sub-surface water with both major and medium works and ordinary wells, tubewells, and lift irrigation; to provide for drainage and reasonable flood control, along with reclamation of fertile, marshy lands; and to change the cropping pattern suitably, relying mainly on new short-duration, photoperiod-insensitive, high-yielding varieties.

Most of the areas in Category B need to be treated substantially on the same line as A-Category lands. Drainage is imperative, though the disposal of excess water will be much less of a problem in this case. If the available water—surface and subsurface—is properly used, and crop varieties are carefully chosen, most of the B-Category lands should grow at least two good crops a year. For post-monsoon irrigation main reliance will have to be placed on storage tanks, ordinary wells, and shallow tubewells. Moreover, groundwater exploration may radically alter the picture in many instances. Where rich, subterranean aquifers are struck, deep tubewells in combination with rainfall, surface works, ordinary wells and shallow tubewells, should make it possible to develop perennial irrigation with perennial cropping. In such cases B-Category lands will be elevated to Category A; in addition, they will enjoy greater immunity from drainage and flood control problems than the latter.

There remains Category C comprising some 116 million acres, where average rainfall is less than 30 inches. Even here the situation is not nearly as desperate as might appear at first sight. For one thing, some 21 million acres of C-Category lands are already under irrigation. The irrigated area can certainly be further extended even with the available monsoon and subsurface supply. In addition, there are the prospects of groundwater. If vigorously pushed through, the exploration should lead to new finds of aquifers. The rating of C-Category lands will then vastly improve. Once equipped with deep tubewell irrigation, they should rank among the best available in the country.

Besides, much of the areas included in this category has 20 inches of rainfall or more. This should be enough to grow a good short-term crop provided the available rainwater is saved and stored with meticulous care, the right kinds of crops are grown, and the right cultural practices are adopted for the purpose. In short, the potential of C-class lands is very much underrated. There is considerable room for upgrading these lands, especially through irrigation and/or water conservation, and for improving both production and income from them.

### MULTI-PRONGED APPROACH

Thus, the rainfed areas do have a number of problems, but they are by no means insoluble. What is needed to solve them is a multi-pronged attack.

The first obvious step is to extend the area under irrigation. Even according to the current official estimate, which is probably too conservative, there is enough potential to double the irrigated area—from about 20 to 40 per cent of the net acreage under cultivation. Once this potential is fully utilized, the size of the problem will be substantially reduced.

As is to be expected, irrigation is unevenly distributed over the country. As against an all-India total of 20 per cent, some states—Maharashtra, Gujarat, Madhya Pradesh, and Mysore in particular—have facilities for irrigating less than 10 per cent of the cultivated area. Moreover, they have an undulating topography with rocks at shallow depths. In these rather peculiar conditions, minor surface projects are essential to make the best possible use of the available precipitation. The practice, long in vogue in these areas, has been to construct irrigation tanks, sometimes as a chain at different levels so that, apart from irrigating the crops, they also recharge the underground water in their vicinity. Many of these tanks are now in a derelict condition. They need urgent attention for renovation; in many instances, they could be widened and deepened to increase the capacity and to cut down on the rate of evaporation; at times they may have to be relocated, if cost considerations so dictate; and where warranted, they should be supplemented with new tanks and or dugwells. In all cases they will need foolproof arrangements for their future maintenance.

What will happen in years of short rainfall? The benefits will, admittedly, be less, but they should still be substantial, unless there is a complete failure of the monsoon which, luckily, is rare and normally occurs once in several decades. Agriculture, nowhere in the world, is weather-proof. The business of good farming, everywhere, is to make the best one can, given the weather and other physical conditions.

This points to what is by far the most important requirement in unirrigated and unirrigable areas, namely, water-harvesting. Unfortunately, in most of these areas most of this water is still allowed to run to waste, often eroding and gullying the land. It is absolutely essential to stop this callous resource-waste, to ensure that the available water is scrupulously stored by every conceivable means—in dugwells, in tanks and ponds, along the contours through impermeable and properly-aligned bunding, and in the soil itself—to protect the land and to grow crops to the utmost possible extent.[20]

## CHANGES IN AGRONOMY

Once maximum effort has been made to salvage the available moisture supply, agronomy should come into play to take care of the remaining problems. The farming practices may, and in most cases will, need to be adjusted. More specifically, greater emphasis will have to be laid on soil-and-moisture-conserving methods of cultivation.

Intimately related to this is the choice of crops to be grown. Much of the trouble today arises from the old habit of growing traditional crops, especially rice and wheat, on lands lacking enough moisture to support them adequately. High-yielding varieties of shorter duration can go a long way towards solving the problem while greatly improving the yield. A number of such varieties are already available. They can be further improved, and more varieties can be evolved, tailor-made to suit the specific soil, water and climatic conditions of these areas.[21]

Even after such adjustments, there will still remain a sizable residue, running into many millions of acres. The most economic use for such land would be to put it under pastures for livestock development, under orchards to grow fruits, or under forests to produce fuel wood, timber, and other forest wealth.[22]

Most rainfed areas at present grow a precarious summer crop, which represents only a fraction of their inherent potential. With skilful water-harvesting—from both surface and underground sources—coupled with scientific agronomy, their economics can be vastly improved. Much of these areas can be made to grow two, sometimes even three, crops of the high-yielding types. The promise of a many times richer harvest is within reach. What is needed to realize it is to cease blaming fate unfairly, and to start systematic action on a broad front.

[20] A recently-created Water Development Cell in Agriculture Ministry has been trying hard to promote groundwater development. The various proposals it has formulated, apparently on Joint Secretary B. B. Vohra's initiative, deserve prompt and wholehearted support.

[21] See Chapters 3, 4 and 22.

[22] Discussed in *Reaping the Green Revolution*.

## ALIBI FOR PROCRASTINATION

Water and soil constitute the foundation of India's economy, as of most other developing countries. Both have hitherto been slighted and abused. The penalty for this has already been high, as reflected in eroded and parched-up lands with drained-away fertility, in one of the world's poorest acre-yields, in the pervasive misery and want. The penalty for continuing the past policy will be fantastically higher if only because of the sharp upswing in population. The only hope for the future lies in putting the water and soil to the maximum productive use with the utmost possible speed.

Today there is a growing water-consciousness in the country, as evidenced by the stepped-up effort to extend minor irrigation of all kinds. But as yet there is no sign of a burning sense of urgency.

The Planning Commission has set up a Panel on Water Resources to advise on: long-term planning of water resources, including their assessment, exploitation and conservation; integrated use of surface and underground water; important matters like "water-logging and salinity"; proper distribution and management through such measures as land-shaping, construction of field channels, and provision of adequate drainage, now considered essential for optimum utilization and conservation of water and for intensifying agricultural productivity.

The Planning Commission is also giving attention to special studies and investigations in order "to improve the efficiency of water management," both public and private, after taking into account all relevant factors, such as soil conditions, plant-water relationships, farm practices and farm management.[23]

The Indian Agricultural Research Institute (IARI) has established a Water Technology Centre with the help of the Ford Foundation and the University of California for intensifying research and training on all aspects of water-use.

Under an agreement reached in 1968, four Pilot Projects for Soil and Water Management have been established, with assistance from USAID, in four of the principal soil and water resource areas. The projects will adopt a team approach, bring together all related disciplines, study such problems as group-irrigation with drainage and water control, adjustment needed in land ownership, cropping patterns in the interest of better water-use, inter-relationships of crop, water and inputs, conservation measures with field design, layout, and construction. In addition, the projects will provide facilities for training technicians at different levels.

An Irrigation Commission has been appointed by the Centre with wide terms of reference. It will, among other things, review the development

[23] *Fourth Five-Year Plan, 1969-74 (Draft)*, p. 130.

29

of irrigation in India since 1903 when the last Irrigation Commission submitted its recommendations; report on the contribution made by irrigation to increasing the productivity of land and in providing insurance against the vagaries of rainfall; to examine the facilities available in chronically drought-affected and food-deficit areas and the minimum irrigation works they would require; to outline a programme of irrigation of all types to attain self-sufficiency in cereals and to maximize the production of other crops; to examine the administrative and organizational set-up for planning, execution and operation of irrigation works, for "speedy completion of projects and reduction of their gestation period."

An elaborate questionnaire was issued by the Commission late in 1969. It will take about three years to prepare and submit its recommendations.

All these steps apparently display a laudable, though much too belated, concern for this vital problem. What is most needed today is not more diagnosis, but determined application of remedies already known, not what may prove better on paper at a future date, but what is good and acceptable in practice right now. No elaborate investigations or sophisticated studies should be necessary to correct the glaring omissions and deficiencies. For example, the Ford Foundation Team, in 1959, gave an excellent analysis of India's water problems.[24] The recommendations it made should have served as a blueprint for action. Unfortunately, they did not do so, and, strangely enough, not even for the IADP.

It is time for a firm commitment, not for a new commission; time for action, not for procrastination; time to mobilize, not to grope for a strategy.


## TASKS AHEAD

The tasks that lie immediately ahead should no longer be in doubt. Assured water supply is an indispensable underpinning of the green revolution. The primary objective of scientific water management must therefore be to provide optimum irrigation, or moisture supply, for the maximum number of days over the largest possible acreage. This dictates the kind of action programme that can and should be undertaken immediately:

1. The area under irrigation should be extended at a much faster rate to exploit the full potential. A more definite timetable ought to be laid down to turn the potential—110 million acres of irrigable area—into actual. It should be possible to telescope the minor irrigation development, including deep tubewells for groundwater, into fewer years.

2. All existing irrigation works must be examined *de novo* to provide them, as far as technically and economically feasible, with supplementary works—minor canals, village channels, inlets, outlets, and

[24] The Crisis Report, ibid., pp. 140-52.

controls—to regulate the supply of water at the field level. The distribution system, in many instances, may very well need construction of terminals and sub-terminals. They will, in a sense, correspond to the substantiations of a power grid with a network of transmission lines for power distribution.

It is certainly not going to be easy to build such "irrigation grids" out of the existing systems of irrigation canals. There are likely to be physical or technical difficulties; large additional financial outlays will be needed in most cases; and, perhaps worst of all, strong opposition to remodelling of irrigation works is likely to be encountered from vested interests that might stand to lose the benefit of the present "thin" seasonal irrigation. The integration of groundwater and the augmentation of total supply, with or without adjustments in the cropping pattern, should provide the best means of overcoming such opposition and finding a way out of the political difficulty.

In any case, there is no escape from such remodelling of major and medium surface irrigation projects. Where persuasion fails despite effective demonstration of its benefits, some legal action may prove unavoidable.

3. India has taken ages to wake up to the great potential value of the vast quantities of water stored by the monsoon, year after year, just below the surface. The realization is still rather dim. That the water which flows on the ground and which is stored below it must be tapped to grow crops, supplementing one with the other, is now presented as a great discovery. This, itself, shows how neglectful has been the past attitude. The conjunctive use of both, which is now being emphasized, is the only sensible approach. It should be unequivocally adopted and applied all over the country.

Again, supply of power provides a good analogy. Just as seasonal hydro-power is firmed up, say, with thermal power from coal as in the Damodar Valley, so also seasonal water supply for crops, whether from surface irrigation canals or from direct rainfall, can on many occasions be profitably supplemented, or firmed up, with underground water.

4. The exploration of groundwater—that is, of aquifers—should be greatly speeded up. The ETO could best serve as an all-India coordinating body. But actual exploration, quantitative assessment of groundwater occurrences, feasibility studies, design, construction, and actual utilization could be far more effectively, speedily, and economically carried out as package operations by competent firms in the private sector.

5. In remodelling the existing irrigation systems, facilities must be created for proper drainage. Its importance should be brought home to all concerned, including farmers relying on minor irrigation.

6. Surface drainage schemes should be developed and speedily exe-

cuted to put back into use the millions of acres which have been thrown out of-cultivation by drainage congestion. The states of Punjab and U.P. alone contain about 3.4 million acres of such land. The Committtee on Natural Resources of the Planning Commission estimated that this acreage could be reclaimed and restored to full production at a cost of Rs. 36 crores. To bring an equivalent new, and probably less fertile, area under irrigation would cost Rs. 119 crores. A modest investment, it argued, "could play a significant part in helping to close the estimated gap of 28 million tons in our foodgrain requirements by 1965-66," as was projected at that time. The Committee pleaded that the attitude should be "drastically oriented" towards "holding what-we-have," and that surface drainage for removal of excess water "to safeguard and promote many interests should occupy an important place in the Plan for water resources development."[25]

There are millions of acres, especially in the lower portions of river deltas, which are waterlogged not because of faulty irrigation, but because of their low elevation and the large supply of water they receive in the wet months. As a rule, such deltaic land is highly fertile, much of it could be reclaimed at a moderate cost and could grow two to three crops a year. Such areas should be given a high priority in any programme for land and water development.

7. In future all large-scale flow-irrigation projects must avoid the tragic errors of the past. They must be planned more rationally to provide for optimum utilization of water. And facilities for regulating irrigation water—both in the canals and in the fields—and for adequate drainage must be built into them from the start.

8. In areas which will continue to depend on rainfall, systematic efforts must be made to capture and store it in wells and tanks, on the land through gully-plugging and contour-bunding, in the soil through moisture-conserving cultivation of crops. Skilful water-harvesting can greatly alleviate the situation in most of the "dry" areas.

9. Maintenance, servicing, and repair of irrigation works call for far greater attention than they are receiving at present. This is true of all works—major, medium or minor. Experience has shown how quickly tanks, wells, tubewells, pumpsets, and contour bunds can fall into disrepair.

As energized tubewells, both public and private, multiply, the need for efficient servicing outfits gains in urgency. This function can be best performed by private enterprise which, to judge from past experience, will readily step in if it receives due encouragement.

[25] Study on Wastelands, etc. loc. cit., pp. 112-13. This and the paragraph immediately following provide fresh examples to show that India's agriculture in the pre-HYV days need not have been all that helpless, and that the food crisis was not primarily due to an inexorable fate.

10. Finally, there is the question of better water-use. Some 40 to 50 per cent of the irrigation water, it is estimated, is lost in the conveyance and the distribution system, and 40 per cent of this in the field channels alone. Clearly, lining of conveyance and distribution systems and of field channels, which would eliminate most of these losses, deserves a high priority. Ayacut development, proper land-levelling, piped distribution in the fields—all would contribute further to the same end. The harvested water must be budgeted properly to maximize the benefit.

These, then, are the essential steps needed to harness India's water resources. Since the drought years they have found increasing recognition in principle; and in several instances, they have been reflected in action. The most promising policy change, as pointed out earlier, is the emphasis now being laid on minor irrigation projects, especially wells and tube-wells, and on the combined use of both canals and underground waters. Some surface drainage schemes have also been introduced, especially in Punjab, with good results.

Besides, a beginning has been made in remodelling the large surface irrigation projects. In particular, controls have been established in the Hirakud project in Orissa and in the Mayurakshi project in West Bengal, to minimize the wastage of water due to uncontrolled gravity flows in the canals. Much more is, however, necessary than such *ad hoc* measures to provide for what is most essential, namely, assured, intensive, yet controlled irrigation at the field level.

Of much greater promise is the so-called ayacut (or command area) development programme, which seeks to remedy the defects encountered in areas receiving surface irrigation from major and medium projects. It provides for large-scale land levelling and shaping, construction of field channels and field drains, better utilization of water in general to help maximize agricultural production. The programme is being executed in parts of Andhra Pradesh, Mysore, Maharashtra, Tamil Nadu, and Rajasthan. To start with, ten pilot projects have been taken up, all sponsored by the Centre and each containing about 4000 hectares in fairly compact blocks with a high percentage of unutilized potential, all due to be completed by early 1970's. This is the kind of development that is needed in the command areas of *all* large and medium surface irrigation projects as far as the physical conditions will permit.

Once the worst defects of the present system have been remedied, it will be possible, and necessary, to introduce further refinements. Scientific water management calls for crop-water correlation data on an extensive scale. To secure optimum utilization of water, such data will have to be compiled throughout the country, both for irrigated and unirrigated conditions. The variables here are numerous: configuration of land, soil conditions, nature of crops and their different varieties, agro-meteorological climate, seasons of the year—all these will affect the correlations.

Accordingly, adequate compilation of data will require experimental plots to be set up in different parts of the country so that the field data may cover at least the major combinations of these variables.

It will also be necessary to set up field demonstrations in different parts of the country and within easy reach of the farmers, in order to initiate them in more efficient management of water under conditions if not identical with, at least essentially similar to, their own. Such demonstrations will necessarily be a major function of the extension service.

As noted earlier, a beginning has been made to compile crop-water data, to improve water technology, and to carry out experiments and demonstrations in the field. The work envisaged at the four USAID-assisted pilot projects and at the Water Technology Centre at IARI will be particularly useful, once the structural weaknesses of the existing irrigation systems have been remedied and the worst examples of water wastage have been stopped.

At last progress is being made towards better water management. But the scale of operations is still too small, and it all looks very much like a slow-motion performance. Can it be speeded up, and can the total effort be multiplied several times? India has the knowledge, the scientific manpower, and the labour force to mount such an effort. All she needs to do is to mobilize them, to build the right organizations, and to put them to work.

But what about financial resources? Lack of funds, it is taken for granted, is the worst constraint India has to wrestle with; and this now is proclaimed with a tiresome frequency from both public and private forums. Yet it is the worst piece of fiction India has inherited from the past and has perpetrated so long. The constraint is mental, not real.

Can India allow her water resources to run to waste, and starve her land and people in the process? Surely, she must cash in this liquid wealth. And if she is immediately short of tangible cash to do so, she has to create the necessary credit. The water, the soil, the new seeds, and the tropical sun—together they provide the most generous collateral even the most conservative banker could ever ask for.[26] The spell cast by financial orthodoxy has done enough damage to the cause of development. It is high time to demolish this fetish.


A GRAND VISION

What about India's rivers whose monsoon turbulence dispenses flood and havoc in many areas as they struggle to carry the massive volumes of waters to empty them into the sea? The rivers will have to be tamed, trained, and put to productive work. Clearly, India will need high multi-purpose dams, plenty of them, to store water in order to control floods,

[26] See Chapter 27 on "The Credit Shackles."

to generate power, to provide irrigation, to create or to improve facilities for navigation where feasible, and to develop a host of valuable ancillary activities like industrial and domestic water supply, fish cultivation, recreation facilities. This was the dream that inspired India on the eve of her independence and led to the simultaneous launching of a number of large river valley projects.[27] That dream is still valid. All the remaining rivers should, in due course, be similarly, or even better, treated. It remains an exciting long-range goal.

On a still longer view, there is an even grander vision. Can the surplus waters of the mighty North Indian rivers be diverted southwards by canals to link up with the rivers of South India and to bring irrigation to the rainfall-deficient areas up to the Mysore plateau? This admittedly grandiose scheme has been actually suggested by some Indian engineers.[28] It need not be ridiculed as a figment of imagination. Such ambitious projects may very well prove indispensable to support the population as it soars to and beyond 700 million. Incidentally, such an engineering feat will be a fitting epilogue to the ancient story, immortalized in India's epics, of how the Aryans, some four thousand years ago, carried culture and agriculture from the Indo-Gangetic plains to the remote parts of the south.

Nothing is inherently wrong with these dreams. The decisive question is their timing. The day of their realization will be hastened if, in the immediate future, the water resources are developed and utilized on the lines indicated above. They will prepare the ground and create the capability to embark upon more ambitious schemes. It is the wrong timing—the urge to take up last things first—which has been the source of so much trouble in India. It must be resisted in the future.

## A POSTSCRIPT

It is over two years since this Chapter was written. Meanwhile, the Irrigation Commission has published its Report (June 1972); and, as expected, it confirms the conclusions set forth above. In fact, its findings had, to a large extent, been anticipated by some thoughtful executives in the Central Ministry of Agriculture.[29]

The Commission estimates that, of the accumulated irrigation potential of 8.9 million ha., 1.7 million ha. (4.2 million acres), or almost a fifth, remain unutilized. This is not a revelation. What the Report does is to

[27] See Chapter 6.

[28] By Dr. A. N. Khosla in particular. Of late, it seems, megalomania has once again gripped India's engineering and political leadership. Backed by "expert" counsel from abroad, it is reportedly ready to make commitment to such a grandiose scheme in wanton disregard of the grave implications of cost and time factors.

[29] For example, in *Balanced Development of Surface Water Resources* by B. B. Vohra, Ministry of Agriculture, April 1970.

give a more up-to-date measure of the colossal waste that has been known to exist for about two decades.

Even the so-called "100 per cent utilization" of the irrigation potential is largely meaningless. For it simply means that water has been made available to the whole area a project is intended to cover, but it ignores how this water is actually used beyond the outlets, in how many instalments it is made available, at what intervals, and in what doses. The Report urges that, in formulating irrigation schemes, the very important question of "correct intensity" should be given full attention. The strange thing is that there should have been such a default in the first place.

Since the absence of field channels is a major factor behind the serious lag in utilizing irrigation potentials, the Commission argues that the state governments should find ways and means to overcome the practical difficulties and to ensure their timely construction. It has taken a whole generation to realize that village channels are a vital component of an irrigation project, that their construction must be carefully synchronized with that of a storage reservoir!

Another familiar item stressed afresh in the Report is the need for proper land-shaping to achieve efficient irrigation. The state governments and their agencies, it is suggested, should be called upon to take appropriate steps.

The Commission also underscores the well-known fact that the water losses incurred in transmission are at present disproportionately high—amounting to almost 50 per cent—which can be drastically cut down if the channels are lined. And it gives the interesting estimate that "lining can save enough water to irrigate an additional 6 million hectares," that is, 15 million acres, apart from other benefits it will confer, such as: saving land, reducing land cost and earthwork, easier and less costly maintenance, higher velocities in transmitting water—nearly three times that of unlined channels—and prevention of percolation damage to adjoining agricultural land.

Foreseeably enough, neglect of drainage comes in for some of the severest criticisms. The effective answer to water-logging is a properly designed drainage system. "In fact the menace of water-logging would not have attained the present proportion if attention had been paid to drainage along with irrigation." The importance of drainage, it goes on to say, is so well recognized in advanced countries that "it is always considered an integral part of any irrigation scheme." And it wants "the greatest attention" to be paid to this item. The comments are unexceptionable. But they also provoke the question: Was it necessary for India to pay so little attention to so vital a matter for so long?

On sedimentation of reservoirs, the Commission's findings are most disturbing. Data collected for 22 storage reservoirs show that they are silting up at an alarming rate—far higher than what had been assumed by the planning engineers. The following figures show the position of six storage dams in terms of acre-feet of silt deposits per 100 sq. miles of catchment area as worked out in the studies of the Soil Conservation Directorate:

|  | Assumed siltation rate | Observed rate |
|---|---|---|
| For Bhakra | 105 | 154 |
| Maithon, DVC | 28 | 300 |
| Panchet, DVC | 47 | 251 |
| Ramganga, UP | 90 | 377 |
| Tungabhadra | 90 | 382 |
| Nizamsagar | 6.33 | 104 |

The picture revealed in the Report surpasses the apprehensions of even the most confirmed pessimists. Thus, the huge public investments made in India's well-publicized river valley projects are now being rapidly buried in sands.

To remedy the situation, the Commission recommends what it calls "a time bound programme of soil conservation." The work, it suggests, should be completed in 20 years, but on the worst-affected projects, it should be compressed into half the time.

The Commission is critical of the neglect from which areas supposed to be serviced by surface irrigation projects have suffered in the past. It therefore wants command area, or ayacut, development to go hand in hand with the engineering works, with the two fully integrated right from the planning stage. This is all very sound, also all too obvious, and one wonders how it could be ignored all these years.

Ayacut development, the Commission recognizes, is an "exceedingly complicated task" as it will include administration and coordination, extension services, surveys, consolidation operations, water courses and field channels, land-shaping, research, demonstration and farmers' training, credit needs, infrastructure in regard to communications, marketing centres, warehousing and storage, agro-industries, etc. These activities must be accompanied by construction of all-weather roads, transportation systems, better markets and provision of remunerative prices for farm produce.

All this will call for coordination of many government departments and agencies, at both Central and state levels. The Commission, therefore, believes that a special administrative agency has become a necessity for expeditious development of command area under major and minor projects.

What the Commission does not realize is that the task is too vast, and too complicated, to be handled by a single administrative agency. Nor

30

can it be done speedily and efficiently, if at all, through rigid, rule-ridden government departments.[30] The only sensible approach would be to set up new administrative agencies, one for each large river valley project. Each agency must be endowed with enough authority to tackle the problems on the spot on a decentralized basis. And it must be entrusted with the responsibility not only for ayacut development in the irrigated area, but also for soil conservation and related work in the upper catchment area. The two functions are integrally related, and best results can be achieved only with unified responsibility for both.

This is what the DVC was established to achieve a quarter of a century ago. The combined follies of administrators, engineers, and politicians have played havoc with it, and have successfully set back the clock of progress. Yet the approach embodied in the DVC Act is as valid today as it was in 1948 when the Act was passed amidst loud acclaim. Time has fully confirmed this, also greatly increased the urgency.

Will the government belatedly muster enough wisdom to undo the damage that has been wantonly inflicted on one of the nation's great pioneering undertakings? And, beyond that, will it show enough vision to apply systematically the same treatment to all the other dam-cum-irrigation projects? The reward for such a move will be dramatic. The penalty for continued dillydallying in this vital field will be staggering.

[30] As for the proper role of agriculture departments in a system based on a rational division of labour, see Chapter 28.

# CHAPTER 17

# Multiplication and Distribution
# of Improved Seeds

## LAGGING SEED-CONSCIOUSNESS

The genetic breakthrough does not automatically lead to a production breakthrough. There's many a slip between breeding a high-yielding variety and a bumper crop. The easiest slips relate to seeds.

From breeder to foundation to registered to certified seed, and from processing, storage to packaging, labelling and distribution to farmers is a long chain fraught with risks at each point. The genetic purity of the seeds and their viability must be fully safeguarded all along the line. Otherwise, the seeds of hope will turn into seeds of frustration.

The task is inherently difficult. It is incomparably more so in India where, until recently, there was no seed industry, no system of production and distribution of quality seeds, no seed laboratory for quality-testing, no seed law, no clear-cut standards, no mechanism for seed certification, no concern for genetic purity; in short, no real seed-consciousness. What a contrast does this present, for example, to Japan where varietal breeding, particularly of rice, and meticulously careful handling of seeds at all stages have, since the late-nineteenth century, spearheaded progress in agriculture with steadily rising productivity!

The so-called improved seed programme, which was initiated in India in the early fifties, did not prove equal to the task. The operation was entrusted to the State Departments of Agriculture; under their control the seeds of selected varieties of cereals, pulses, and cash crops, already known in the area and accepted as improved or superior, were multiplied; the distribution was left mostly to the C.D. Blocks and the Grain

Gola (or Storage) Societies; their principal aim was to saturate a target area within a given period with "improved" seeds. But there was no quality control; the breeder seed, of genetic purity and in the requisite quantity, was not always available; the foundation seed multiplication, in such conditions, was anything but satisfactory. The improved seed pro-gramme went through a lot of motions, but it could bring about little tangible improvement.

There were other anomalies no less striking. Improved seeds given to the Grain Golas in some areas were loaned by the latter to parties who would repay them the following year *in kind*, with an interest of 12.25 per cent, from the crop grown with these seeds. In practice, however, the repayment was made with nondescript seeds, and these were re-issued as improved seeds the following year.

The programme provided for a subsidy from the state governments, it being assumed that the farmer would not pay the full price even for good seeds. As a result, the size of the programme depended on the extent of the subsidy a state could afford. Worse still, sometimes the subsidy was collected for seeds supposed to have been distributed, even when this was actually not the case.

Then there was the wholly impractical emphasis on self-sufficiency in seed for each C.D. block, which led to the decision to set up, in each block, a small seed farm of 25 acres. This reflected a gross under-estima-tion of what it takes to build modern seed farms in terms of expert know-ledge, guidance and supervision, equipment and machinery, and storage facilities. A 25-acre farm is too small a unit to support these economically. Nor can it provide the degree of physical isolation needed for multiply-ing seeds of certain types, especially of cross-fertilized varieties. It was only in December, 1964 that this arbitrary limitation of size was sup-pressed in favour of larger seed farms of 300 acres or more.

In general, little distinction was made, in actual practice even if not in theory, between "seed" and "grain"; and what passed for seed was mostly nothing but untested, nondescript grain. Incidentally, this non-chalant attitude towards seed largely explains why so little benefit was derived from the earlier work of plant breeders in India, who did turn out several improved varieties of wheat and rice.

Yet the distinction between seed and grain is vital, of *seminal* impor-tance, to agriculture. As a geneticist or seed technologist would put it, a seed, strictly so called, is an "embryo," a living organism, embedded in the "supporting" or the "food storage" tissue. The business of seed technology is to protect this biological entity and look after its "welfare," while the focus of food technology is on the second component—the supporting tissue.[1]

[1] See, for example, the paper presented by Mr. N. S. Gill, Assistant General Manager (Quality Control), National Seed Corporation Ltd., at the *Seed Specialists'*

The indifference towards quality seed, which had prevailed until very recently, should, however, cause no surprise. It epitomized the more general indifference towards scientific agriculture. Since it is a biological industry, good agriculture depends on good seed, and vice versa. One cannot exist, or advance, without the other.

## RECENT PROGRESS

Against this depressing background the progress made in recent years stands out as truly remarkable. Once again, the Ford Foundation's Crisis Report marked the real turning-point. It diagnosed the then existing situation in depth; pointed up its manifold inadequacies; emphasized the overriding importance of improved seeds which, under conditions of high fertility and good crop management, "can make the greatest contribution to increased production"; reiterated that the seed of an improved variety "is a living organism" possessing genes which could assure "superior performance" only when high genetic purity was maintained and the seed was of good quality; urged the creation of an adequate organization with qualified seed specialists; and made a set of strong and detailed recommendations, all directed towards one primary objective: to help build up "a seed multiplication and distribution industry geared to modern plant-breeding concepts."[2]

In doing so the Team was clearly looking ahead. There was already unmistakable evidence, based on the breeding work done by the Rockefeller Foundation in Mexico and, to some extent, also in India, that new varieties of amazing potential would soon emerge which would double and treble acre-yields. Once officially released, the rate of their spread was going to be determined, above all, by the ability to multiply and distribute to cultivators quality seed of high genetic purity. There was no time to lose if a major bottleneck was to be averted, and if the new opportunities were to be quickly cashed in. This realization breathed an added sense of urgency into the Team's recommendations. Its intention was to take time by the forelock. Luckily, it has worked.

Most of the measures it recommended have, meanwhile, been acted upon. As a result, a more adequate framework has been created for a modern seed programme. The main developments since then may be briefly noted:[3]

---

*Seminar* held in New Delhi, 8-11 April, 1969; included in Mimeographed Proceedings.

[2] The Crisis Report, loc. cit., Chapter 10 on "The Multiplication and Distribution of Improved Seeds," pp. 194-214.

[3] The *Seed Specialists' Seminar Proceedings* referred to earlier gives a thorough review of developments to date, problems on hand, and the programme chalked out for the immediate future. This Seminar was convened under the joint auspices of the National Seeds Corporation and The Rockefeller Foundation.

1. *Variety Release.* No orderly seed programme is possible if new varieties are released in a pellmell fashion. Streamlining the release procedures is, therefore, one of the first desiderata. There is an even more important prior question: Varieties must be thoroughly tested and screened to identify the best ones—in terms of yield, disease resistance, and the extent of adaptation, with official release restricted to the topmost few for propagation and cultivation. Otherwise too many varieties would spoil the cause.

This is precisely what was happening in India at that time. This situation has, meanwhile, been rectified. Thanks to the initiative taken by the Ford and Rockefeller Foundations, an all-India coordinated variety-testing programme has been established for the important crops, along with a Central Variety Release Committee and an associated Committee in each state to attend to the tasks at the state level.[4] Together, they have laid the foundation for a modern seed programme. The seeds to be multiplied and distributed are now unequivocally identified. And their number, too, is kept within more manageable limits.

2. *Variety Release Procedure.* The old system was slow, passive, and not much concerned about impact or results. A few kilos of seeds of an improved variety would be "released" to interested farmers who would try them out; and, if the results proved satisfactory, it would gradually spread from there. After some time, if the spread proved appreciable, the variety would be given the seal of approval, and "released" officially.

This timid, *ex post facto* method of release would be completely out of place in today's conditions when the objective is to disseminate the high-yielding varieties at a fast rate. Nor is there any need for such exaggerated caution. The accelerated breeding programme, as recently established, provides for extensive variety trials, agronomic experiments, quality evaluation, and screening for proneness to diseases and insect attacks. Besides, the breeders themselves have been made fully responsible to maintain breeder seed from generation to generation, with guaranteed varietal purity and in conformity with the accepted standards of physical purity and germination (see below). Given these developments and the regular supply of pure breeder seed, the old time-consuming procedures can be safely circumvented. Thus, the ground has been cleared for launching an accelerated programme of seed multiplication as an essential first step to rapid dissemination of the high-yielding varieties.

3. *National Seed Corporation.* The 25-acre seed farm at the block level was an anachronism. It was too small to book the economies of scale and the benefits of advanced technology, and, therefore, unsuitable to serve as the base for a modern seed programme. The Food Crisis Report left no doubt on this score. It, therefore, urged the creation of a broadbased

[4] Food Crisis Report, op. cit., pp. 207-8; also see Chapter 22, the section on "Reorganization of Research."

organization to handle high quality stock (foundation) seed on a national scale, which led to the establishment, in 1963, of a National Seeds Corporation (NSC). This was a landmark in India's belated attempt to repair the long neglect on the seed front.[5]

The primary function of the NSC, as laid down in its charter, is to serve as the custodian of foundation stock; to multiply and distribute both breeder and foundation seed to serve as stock seed for further multiplication as registered and/or certified seed; to initiate a quality control programme and, for this purpose, to provide the much-needed professional leadership; to act as the clearing-house for the design of seed-processing facilities. At a time when each state tended to go its own way, when uniform standards were conspicuous by their absence, and when the purity of improved seeds was far from assured, the NSC was conceived as the vehicle for distributing high quality stock seed through the length and breadth of the country.

4. *Breeder Seed.* The pivotal role of breeder seed is now much better understood. The responsibility for maintaining regular supplies of genetically pure breeder seed has been thrown where it logically belongs—on the breeders themselves, that is, on the base laboratories or institutions. The plant breeder best knows the characteristics of the improved variety he has developed. He and his assistants are, therefore, best fitted to maintain the breeder seed by resowing it year after year. As long as their variety figures in a seed multiplication scheme, it should be their concern to produce and supply breeder seed of 100 per cent genetic purity.

Some laboratories, it is reported, had difficulty in fulfilling this function for lack of funds. The NSC came to their rescue with advances, partly also to enable them to increase their output of breeder seed which the Corporation will need for its foundation seed programme.

Be that as it may, it is absolutely essential that competent laboratories are provided with adequate funds, whatever may be their source, to enable them to produce and maintain pure breeder seed of high quality. Failure to do so will entail incomparably greater economic loss as it will undermine the very foundation of the national seed scheme and thereby of the green revolution.

5. *Foundation Seed.* As noted earlier, the NSC has been made responsible for maintaining the foundation stock of all important seeds. It has also been agreed by all concerned that the Corporation will make it available both to private growers and state governments, who, in turn, will multiply it into certified seeds for farmers. To ensure the purity of the foundation stock, it will have to be produced every year from

[5] It was fortunate that (late) Dr. Will M. Myers of the Rockefeller Foundation (Vice-President until 1969) and Dr. A. A. Johnson, a member of the Ford Foundation's Agricultural Production Team and now the IADP Director in New Delhi, actively helped in preparing the blueprint for the NSC during 1960-61.

breeders' stock directly obtained from laboratories. This underlines the urgency of ensuring an adequate supply of pure breeder seed once a year, which is at present not the case. Some of the newly-established agricultural universities are arranging, or have arranged, to produce both breeder and foundation seed for the NSC.

6. *Certified Seed.* The scope has been considerably widened, and seeds for this category can now be grown by a number of agencies—Central and State Government farms, selected growers, private-sector business, Seed Producers' Cooperatives. This has been possible because, under the recently-passed seed law (item 9 below), standard procedures on an all-India basis have been introduced for testing and certifying seeds. The NSC is normally not expected to enter into this particular seed business, though it may have to do so exceptionally—for example, to speed pre-release multiplication when a new variety is about to be introduced.

7. *Modern Seed Farms.* Rigid adherence to 25-acre block-based seed farms has been given up. Instead, the emphasis has been shifted towards large, well-managed, mechanized farms located in areas where irrigation is assured, so that only high-quality seeds of uniform standards would be produced under controlled conditions and under close supervision of competent specialists.

A number of large farms are already in existence. The Centre intends to set up ultimately one large farm of 10,000 acres or more in each state. The states in their turn will also run relatively large farms, up to 500 acres in size. Six large-sized farms, established by the Centre on freshly reclaimed land, are being turned into seed farms. Two more farms of this type are proposed to be set up in the Fourth Plan period.[6]

How far India has moved in the direction of modern, large-scale seed farms can be judged from the Terai Seed Development Project located in U.P. and scheduled to be completed in 1973. The project is sponsored by the Central Government and assisted by the World Bank. Estimated to cost Rs. 20 crores, it will cover 16,000 hectares, or app. 40,000 acres, with double cropping, and will produce quality seeds of high-yielding varieties of wheat and rice, and of hybrid maize, sorghum and pearl millets. On completion, it is expected to turn out 5,000 tons of seeds per year.[7]

8. *Seed Law.* The Seeds Act, which became law on 29 December, 1966, along with the Seed Rules framed under Section 25 of the Act and notified on 2 September, 1968. has filled another long-standing void. Modelled on the legislation in force in the developed countries, it provides the standard kit of legal tools so essential for developing a sound seed industry.

The responsibility for implementing the Act has been vested in a

[6] *Fourth Five-Year Plan, 1969-74*, Planning Commission, New Delhi, p. 129.
[7] Ibid., p. 130.

Central Seed Committee constituted by the Central Government with 28 members. In addition, there will be a sub-committee in each state to advise the state government on implementing the Seed Act, and four Central sub-committees dealing respectively with: cereals and pulses; vegetables and horticulture crops; all other crops not covered by these two groups; and what is of special interest in the present context, Seed Testing, Certification, and Seed Law Enforcement Procedures.

The Seed Act, the Seed Rules and the related bylaws have thoroughly covered the ground. India now has a modern seed law. The next important step is to enforce it fairly and efficiently.

9. *Seed-testing Laboratories.* High quality seeds must be genetically pure, of high germination, free from all foreign material like weeds and other crops, and free from seed-borne diseases and insects. Visual observation, however seasoned, is not enough to verify the qualities. In particular, genetic impurities, germination, and many seed-borne diseases can be detected only with specialized modern equipment. This is why well-equipped seed-testing laboratories manned by well-trained seed analysts constitute the backbone of a seed certification scheme. All the state governments are now setting up such laboratories. The Seeds Act requires the states to have at least one laboratory each for purposes of the Act. They may, if they so choose, have a second one to analyze routine samples received from ad hoc parties for testing and certification.

10. *Seed Processing.* The first seed processing plant was built in India in 1960. Great strides have been made since then; within the brief space of nine years, the number of plants set up rose to about 100. Many pieces of equipment needed for them are now manufactured within the country, such as driers, threshers, shellers, small and medium size cleaners, seed treaters and moisture meters. Some items are still imported, and it will be necessary to do so yet for some time.[8]

The Planning Commission estimates that, in all, about 350 processing plants would be needed by the end of the Fourth Plan period, each with a capacity of 1000 tons of seeds over two seasons. Attempts will be made to have the remaining plants installed in the public, private, and co-operative sectors.[9]

11. *Seed Storage.* Processing is not enough; it must go hand in hand with proper storage. The storage problem is particularly acute in India as high temperatures and high humidity can play havoc with seeds. It has been further aggravated with the introduction of short-duration varieties since their seeds tend to germinate prematurely during the wet season.

[8] For details about seed processing plants and equipment, see paper by Mr. B. R. Gregg, Seed Processing Specialist, USAID, and Mr. S. S. Virdi, Agricultural Engineer, NSC, in *Seed Specialists' Seminar Proceedings*, loc. cit.
[9] *Fourth Five-Year Plan, 1969-74*, p. 130.

31

However, IADP has already demonstrated how this problem can be best tackled. The two seed processing plants it has installed, respectively in Thanjavur and West Godavari district[10], have demonstrated that, despite unfavourable temperature and humidity, seed viability can be maintained satisfactorily from harvest to planting time, with the help of modern seed drying and processing equipment. As the seed processing storage specialist of the Ford Foundation has shown in West Godavari district, the key is to bring down the moisture content of the paddy to safe levels, prior to its storage. This type of drying-cum-processing plant with facilities for storage in controlled temperature and humidity should become an essential component of the improved seed programme.

11. *Marketing and Distribution.* By far the biggest challenge lies here —how to carry the improved seeds to the doorsteps of the millions of farmers living in over half a million villages scattered all over the country, often in inaccessible areas. Already the capacity of the seed-processing plants is outrunning the available storage capacity and the capability of the existing marketing organization to handle the processed seeds. Yet, unless the improved seeds reach the farmers in time and are actually used by them for production, the mountain in labour will produce proverbially poor result.

Here, too, progress is being made. The most reassuring sign is the increasing involvement of the private sector in seed production and distribution. The NSC broke new ground in this case. From the start it took the realistic view that the task was far too big to be handled by the state governments and the cooperatives. It supplied foundation stock to private growers and initially bought back from them the certified seeds for marketing. The move induced the state governments to extend help and encouragement to the private operators. Several private organizations are now producing good seeds, and some are marketing them under their own trade names.

The NSC and the Agricultural University at Pant Nagar have jointly organized a large seed programme involving many growers in Terai, U.P. (see above). Their plan is to undertake seed marketing to meet a substantial part of the requirements in U.P. and the neighbouring states. The I.C.I., which is setting up a fertilizer factory at Kanpur, has indicated its willingness to utilize its network of fertilizer agents to distribute part of the seeds produced in Terai. A similar practice of distributing seeds through fertilizer agents has been adopted by Parry and Company in the South.

The growing role played by the private sector is the most hopeful sign. In Indian conditions this is the quickest and the surest way of building up an effective system of seed distribution on an adequate scale.

[10] Referred to earlier in Chapter 13. See also Dr. A. A. Johnson's paper in *Seed Specialists' Seminar Proceedings*, loc. cit.

## TASKS AHEAD

"A modern seed program in India has not yet come of age. It is clearly moving forward, and it is headed in the right direction." These remarks made by Dr. A. A. Johnson in April, 1969 very well sum up the current situation.[11]

The present shortcomings are both quantitative and qualitative. To come of age, the programme will need a great deal more effort—scientific, organizational, and entrepreneurial—to expand the facilities and services, and to improve their quality. The main requirements are implied in what has been said before. It is, however, worth bringing them into sharper focus.

The Variety Release Committees, though established only recently, have been functioning well, so also the plant breeding work and the coordinated variety-testing on a national scale. As a result, new high-yielding varieties are emerging faster out of the pipeline.

From the angle of the seed industry, this raises some important questions. Should the older HYV's be replaced by the newer ones? Or, should they exist side by side with the latter? And if so, for how long? Unless reasonably hard answers are available to these questions, it will be well-nigh impossible for the NSC and the industry to undertake orderly multiplication and marketing of seeds. Advance quantitative assessments of requirement, by each variety and for each sowing season, is essential even if on a rough-and-ready basis. New varieties, coming in waves, can disrupt all calculations of the seed producers.

The clue to this vexing conundrum should not, however, be hard to detect. Clearly, the objective, at least for some years, must be to replace the old low-yielding *deshi* (indigenous) varieties by HYV's giving three to four times higher yield, and not to replace an older HYV swiftly by a newer one just because the latter is slightly more improved and gives a marginally higher yield of, say, 10 to 15 per cent. The second approach will produce chaos in the seed market, hold up the spread of the HYV's, and make it impossible to saturate with them the targeted acreage, viz. 25 million ha. to be reached in five years, or by 31 March, 1974, from the present base level of 9.2 million ha., which would call for a cumulative increase of about 25 per cent a year.

It takes time for a variety to spread among farmers. With planning, organization, and drive, the process can be accelerated. But even then each variety, once introduced, must stay around at least a few years. The spread of a new HYV, it may be assumed, will rise rather sharply to start with, the curve will then tend to flatten out, hit a plateau, and gradually slope downwards.[12] It would neither be feasible nor desirable

[11] In *Seed Specialists' Seminar Proceedings*, ibid., p. 114.

[12] For an excellent analysis of the problems, with comparative examples of the

to displace the older HYV's straightaway by newer ones. They will have to coexist for some time.

Once this basic question is settled, and the varieties to be accommodated within the seed multiplication programme are definitely known, it will be possible to tackle more systematically other important issues:

1. It is essential to undertake market studies in order to appraise farmer attitude and assess the requirement of each HYV seed. The seed-fertilizer distributing agencies, extension service, and cooperatives can be particularly useful for conducting such studies.

2. Matching supply and demand over a single season or year will be too much to expect, however good the market forecasts. Besides, a safety margin would in any case be desirable in order not to risk inhibiting the spread of the HYV's because of a possible seed shortage. This points to the urgency of building up adequate storage facilities for carrying over foundation and certified seeds, say, on a two to three year basis.

Storage, however, remains a major bottleneck, and at present constitutes a serious threat to the entire programme. Since preservation of viability depends on the level of moisture content, both in the processing stage and during storage, no seed programme can succeed, especially in the adverse climatic conditions of India, unless ample storage facilities are available with proper temperature and humidity control. These points as well as the present inadequacies of seed storage in India were underlined by a Seed Review Team in 1969. The recommendations it made need to be implemented as a matter of high priority.

3. The combined drying-processing-storage plants successfully introduced in two IADP districts with assistance from Ford Foundation experts have provided a model for other areas. They should be treated as an indispensable component of the improved seed programme, and multiplied all over the country. Incidentally, the drying and storage facilities are needed both for the seed industry and for cultivating short-duration crops, particularly rice, in the wet season since otherwise its grain loses dormancy and begins to sprout.

4. The seed processing plants, as mentioned before, have grown rapidly in number, but their performance still leaves much to be desired. The quality of locally manufactured equipment, particularly cleaners, needs improvement.

The Indian Seed Team recommended that, as a longer-range policy, steps should be taken to develop and produce domestically all types of equipment of the requisite quality so as to make the country self-sufficient

---

spread of hybrid maize in the USA and of improved rice varieties in Japan, see Dr. Wayne Freeman's paper on "Seed Problem and Seed Production of New Rice Varieties" in *Seed Specialists' Seminar Proceedings*, ibid. However, as stressed in Chapter 4, the old pattern can be improved, and every effort should be made to spread the HYV's more rapidly.

in this respect within a few years. However, it took the realistic view that, meanwhile, in order not to inhibit progress, essential equipment should, when necessary, be imported from abroad, while trying to keep it down to a minimum.

5. A Seeds Act has, at last, come into existence. But the process of its implementation has been slow. Almost two years elapsed between the passage of the Act and the formulation of the Seed Rules. There is an urgent need to speed up progress.

6. Seed certification is still in a rudimentary stage. So far little headway has been made for certification based on field inspection of crops for varietal purity, proper isolation distance, and supervision at harvesting.[13] This is a serious gap which will have to be filled as early as possible.

7. Progress is being made in establishing seed-testing laboratories, but there is a long way to go. Once again, the pace needs to be quickened. As explained earlier, there can be no effective quality control without properly equipped laboratories run by properly trained specialists.

8. The nascent seed industry has so far attempted to handle mainly dwarf wheat seeds, hybrid maize, some sorghum and millets, and some HYV's of rice, though so far to a very limited extent. The volume of improved seeds to be handled for these lines, particularly for dwarf rice, is bound to grow by leaps and bounds. And to these will have to be added other lines fairly soon—pulses, soya beans, oilseeds, various cash crops, vegetables, fruits, grass and fodder, flowers. The scope is enormous, so also is the need.

9. In addition, there is a large export potential. In fact, small amounts of seeds are already being exported. The Indian Seed Team, after going around many foreign countries, came back fully convinced that India could enter the seeds markets of Europe, Canada, and other countries in a big way because of the comparative advantages she enjoys in this field. Seed production in Europe and Japan, in general, is costly because of the high wages of labour; and they can grow only one crop in the temperate climate. India's labour costs are low; she is in a position to grow two to three crops a year of many varieties; and she has also developed the techniques of crossing and double-crossing for seeds.

India's export prospects are considered particularly good for cereals, millets, vegetable, and flower seeds, provided they are pure, of high quality, and properly certified. Large-scale production, with proper isolation conditions, would be essential. Large government farms, especially the one at Terai, are at present better placed to provide for the required isolation. Seed villages, it has been suggested, could also be organized in shaded valleys of Kashmir and in other mountainous areas.

10. The main responsibility for seed distribution still rests on depart-

[13] *Fourth Five-Year Plan, 1969-74*, p. 130. It also lists, though in general terms, the present deficiencies of the seed programme.

mental agencies. This is the result of the emergency programme which was launched to meet the food crisis. There was no other organization that could undertake to produce and distribute improved seeds. The government had to step in and do the job through its own departments.

But today, as the Indian Seed Team emphasizes in its Report, the situation has "vastly changed"; it calls for a "massive expansion" of seed producing, processing, and distributing units. It is "unconceivable" that the departmental agencies could cope with this task. Moreover, they have other, even more pressing responsibilities to attend to, especially farmer education through extension agencies. A dynamic marketing system can be created only if cooperatives and private enterprises are developed and harnessed to the tasks. It is essential to make greater effort in that direction, and to provide necessary encouragement and incentives for the purpose.

11. Initially, to promote the spread of improved seeds, subsidies were resorted to, and low seed prices acted as a deterrent to private enterprise. Later, when private growers entered the HYV seeds market, prices were often pushed too high. There is obvious need to keep seed prices at reasonable levels which would leave adequate margins for growers and distributors without, however, pushing up prices too high and thereby imposing an undue burden on farmers.

Given such a policy, there would no longer be any need for a seeds subsidy. The farmers, in the last few years, have become quite quality-conscious; significantly enough, they readily pay a premium for certified seeds bearing the NSC tag. "The real demand constraint," as the Seed Team underscores, "is quality rather than price."

12. Improved seeds have, according to reports, been adulterated by traders in some cases. This is not surprising in a country known for non-enforcement of its food and drug laws and of inaction even in cases of gross violations. Nothing can, however, so effectively destroy farmer confidence as adulteration of HYV seeds. It merits, and should be meted out, exemplary punishment. Administrative softness here would be fatal.

13. The National Seeds Corporation is the pillar of the improved seeds programme. There has, however, been a tendency to load it with extraneous functions, such as imports of foreign seeds, wheat, rice, and other crops. These must not be allowed to conflict with its primary duties: to procure pure breeder seeds on an adequate scale, to multiply them into foundation seeds, to store and distribute them on a nation-wide basis. Whether the NSC earns 4 or 6 per cent a year on its invested capital should be immaterial, compared with efficient and adequate discharge of these vital responsibilities.

14. As the seed programme grows and matures, it will call for research on various aspects of seed technology, such as seed maturation, embryo culture, isolation distances, seed protectants, germination and dormancy,

seed vigour, storage and moisture interrelationships, and a host of problems relating to drying, processing, and packing, all with one supreme end in view—that the seeds of the green revolution will not lose their propelling force.[14]

15. Good seeds alone will not do. The release of every new HYV must be accompanied by a tailor-made package of services for its cultivation, and the farmers will have to be initiated in them through field demonstrations. This is the biggest task for the extension workers. Such farmer education will have to continue for *each* HYV, irrespective of the time of its release, at least in the foreseeable future.

16. And, finally, there is the problem of organization and training. The task is vast, embracing as it does production, maturation, drying, processing, treating, bagging, storage, certification, enforcement of seed laws, transportation, and marketing. Quality control presupposes close cooperation among all the parties involved—the Central and State Departments of Agriculture, research stations, the NSC, the private sector and the cooperatives. An effective seed programme will need a large army of scientists, specialists, and technicians, and, therefore, an effective research and training programme to produce them.

Let there be no mistake about one thing, the HYV seeds, packed with rare genes, are unique creations of scientific genius. They must be preserved in their pristine purity; protected against weather, apathy, and profiteering; and handled with skill, care, even affection. Only then will the miracle seeds continue to produce miracles; otherwise not.

---

[14] Mr. N. S. Gill, in the paper cited earlier in this chapter, identifies the more important areas of research.

# CHAPTER 18

# Chemical Fertilizers

## A LONG-DELAYED START

Water, seed, fertilizer—this trio constitutes the core of yield-increasing technology. Traditional irrigation, traditional seeds, and no fertilizer—this was the pattern of India's agriculture until the sixties. The result was one of the lowest acre-yields in the world. The first real break came with the initiation of the IADP which carefully chalked out the path for transition from primitive to modern agriculture, from input-starved to input-intensive farming. But the break did not, and could not, immediately lead to a breakthrough. Modern fertilizers were applied in heavy doses, but the traditional seeds responded to them rather weakly. Yield improved, but not strikingly.

Then came the virile, dwarf varieties which produced sensational results —they shattered the age-old, low-yield equilibrium and flung the door wide open to modernism. Intensive irrigation, improved seeds, heavy doses of chemical fertilizers have set in motion an upward spiral in acre-yield. And, in combination, they have set India's languid agriculture finally on the march.

The fertilizer-hungry dwarfs must be spread rapidly, nurtured skilfully, and fed adequately if they are to fulfil the promise of a richer harvest. Can India satisfy these conditions? Can she, in particular, feed the dwarfs with enough chemical nutrients so that they may in turn produce enough food for her expanding family? Here again, the progress already made inspires confidence about the future prospects.

The birth of the chemical age in India's agriculture was far from pain-less. Prejudices ran deep, and, like stubborn tropical weeds, they were hard to eradicate. In the fifties the small domestic production from the

Sindri factory and the limited imports were mostly used up by large plantations. The Indian farmer, it continued to be argued, was not interested in chemical fertilizer; nor could he afford it—given the relative price of the input and of his produce, it would simply not pay for him to use it. This reasoning, or rather this unreasoned assumption, persisted even though it was frequently belied by glimpses of growing black markets in areas where farmers had chanced to witness the magic effect of the chemical powder.

On this confused and hesitant scene, the Crisis Report of the Ford Foundation Team burst like a flood of light. Chemical fertilizers, it stated in emphatic and authoritative terms, held out the best, if not the only, hope for India's future—to increase production rapidly enough to overcome the deepening food crisis.[1] It opened a lot of eyes, but a lot more, sometimes even of scientists, remained at best half-open.

In the early sixties, even the small supply—production at Sindri plus limited imports—could not be easily marketed. There were serious holdups despite the large potential demand, a fact that played into the hands of the anti-fertilizer school. In 1964, the Government of India, in the Ministry of Food and Agriculture, appointed a Committee to investigate the fertilizer problem in all its aspects. Fortunately, this Committee was headed by an able and rather unconventional civil servant with a sensitive and creative mind, Mr. B. Sivaraman, then Chief Secretary in Orissa, who later became the Secretary of Agriculture in New Delhi. It made short shrift of dogmas, preconceived notions and some pseudo-scientific theories which had so long acted as roadblocks.

The fertilizer response of crops in India was supposed to be poor.[2] Apparently, this conclusion was based on the results of a large number of fertilizer trials carried out in different parts of the country. The mass of data collected and analyzed in accordance with modern statistical methods could not but impress a lot of people. But what about the *quality* of the trials themselves? As it happened, they were all carried out without any pre-trial soil analysis! There was no knowledge of the basic fertility levels of the soils, of the missing plant nutrients, and of the specific doses needed by particular crops. The experiments were thus vitiated from the start.

Many of the experiments were carried out only with nitrogen, though most of India's soils suffer from an almost chronic phosphate deficiency because of continuous cultivation of grains through centuries. This critical deficiency had to be met and supplemented with a judicious dose of potash. Mere nitrogen application could not be of much avail.

The amateurish type of fertilizer trials held the ground for over a

[1] The Crisis Report, loc. cit., pp. 170-179
[2] The response *was* poor, especially when contrasted with dwarf wheat and rice; but was higher than what was assumed, and it varied from crop to crop.

32

decade. It ended with the reorganization of the ICAR in 1965 when a Soil and Water Division was created and placed in charge of a competent scientist.[3] From then on, determination of the basic fertility level became a precondition for all fertilizer experiments. Such experiments are no longer considered necessary to answer the general question if fertilizer response is sufficiently significant in India. The response, it is now accepted, is as fully adequate here as in other countries.

The earlier experiments had led to other dubious conclusions: that the available varieties were not fertilizer-responsive; that the grain response to fertilizers in terms of price was too low—10 times for nitrogen, six times for $P_2O_5$ and none for potash—to leave any safe profit margin to the cultivator; that, in a bad year, he might not recover even the costs. In any case, the arrival of the high-yielding varieties gave the quietus to this kind of controversy; they showed that the grain response could be as much as 26 times the nitrogen application. There is every reason to believe, however, that the earlier biases had discouraged the use of fertilizers and had helped keep down the level of consumption under the first three Plans.

Ammonium sulphate happened to be the first fertilizer introduced in India, both as import and as a domestic product. This gave rise to the belief that no other fertilizer would suit the Indian soils. A scientist went the length of establishing this thesis by carrying out elaborate field trials with ammonium sulphate, calcium ammonium nitrate and urea. The explanation for this startling result was a simple one. His field trials had been so laid out that they were more favourable to ammonium sulphate. Thus, what the trials really established was the bias of their initiator.

Only water-soluble phosphates, it was strongly held, would be suitable to India. The notion died hard. And even after a *tour d'horizon* of foreign countries had revealed that 30 per cent water-soluble phosphate was, by and large, good enough for most areas, a compromise was struck for a 50 per cent soluble compound.

The use of ammonium nitrate was generally banned in the country on the ground that because it was an explosive, its handling would be risky. The farmers' ability to learn, given proper instructions and demonstrations, was underrated. This is confirmed by the skill they are increasingly displaying in handling poisonous pesticides.

Another widely prevalent view was that fertilizer use would be too costly for food and other non-cash crops; that, in any case, only plantations and cash crops needed phosphate and potash. The only valid point in this reasoning was that, in the early sixties and before the arrival of the HYV strains, the fertilizer-grain relationship was such that it did tend to act as a deterrent, though probably even here its practical implication had been exaggerated. Doubts about the value of NPK were finally set

[3] For the details of reorganization, see Chapter 22.

at rest with the advent of the high-yielding varieties and the drought-induced spurt in cereal prices.

Another major obstacle to overcome was the one-sided advocacy of compost and green-manuring. It was widely believed that these were not only cheaper, but also indispensable, to maintain soils in a healthy condition; and it was implicitly assumed that they would be an adequate substitute for chemical fertilizers. The high fertilizer prices, especially after the rupee devaluation, provided the anti-chemical school with a handy argument to press their familiar thesis. But it was already late in the day. The farmers had "tasted" fertilizers and were pressing for more; the responsive dwarf strains had opened up new vistas with their spectacular yield potential; the drought had plunged the country into a grave food crisis. In the face of such formidable facts traditionalism had to beat a hasty retreat.

The value and the limitations of compost and green-manuring have tended to be both ignored and exaggerated. They are valuable particularly because they are cheap; a thrifty farmer should therefore make the best of both. The old practice of burning cowdung is a reckless waste and a drain on soil fertility. Yet, oddly enough, despite all the talks of compost-making and the emphasis laid on it all these years in community development work, perhaps 50 per cent of the cowdung supply continues to be burnt as fuel.

As for green manure, it is most useful if it can be grown and ploughed under before the onset of rains. A fertilized legume can serve the dual purpose of building up soil fertility while supplying green fodder for livestock. Obviously, green-manuring must rationally fit into the cropping system of a farmer so as to add to, and not detract from, his overall income.

The limitations of compost and green-manuring must not be overlooked. They can serve only as a *basal*, and not as a *top* dressing. A green-manure crop will need time to decompose before it can effectively serve as plant food. And, finally, there is the quantitative aspect. Intensive agriculture, if it is to maximize farm income, will need large quantities of plant nutrients, of which compost and green-manuring can supply only a small fraction. To rely mainly on the latter in cultivating, for example, the high-yielding varieties of wheat and rice would be an economic folly. It would mean throwing away most of their yield potential, and therefore many times more income than what could be saved through this self-imposed constraint.

An important conclusion emerges from what has been said in this section. The new strategy for agriculture rests on the foundation of science and agriculture. But not all scientists are sufficiently objective or scientific in their approach, analysis, or even in their attitudes. They may sometimes have their blind spots or biases, be wedded to pet dogmas, may even trim their sails to the prevailing political wind. The world of science contains pitfalls which must be guarded against. Sometimes science has to be rescued from scientists.

## CONSUMPTION AND OUTPUT

Details about consumption, domestic production, and imports of fertilizers are given in Appendix (Tables 11-14, Charts 12-13), which show that until very recently consumption was negligible, even in absolute figures. In 1951, it amounted to just over 40,000 tons of nitrogen (N), about 13,500 tons of phosphorus ($P_2O_5$), and 8,000 tons of potash ($K_2O$). It picked up in the following years; but even a decade later, for the year ended 31 March, 1962, it amounted to only 242,000 tons of N, 66,000 tons of $P_2O_5$, and 29,000 tons of $K_2O$.

The mild uptrend continued in the early sixties, reflecting, to a considerable extent, the activities initiated by IADP (Chapters 11-14). Then came a real spurt following the two droughts, and, within a few years, the consumption in all three categories shot up severalfold. Estimated annual consumption on the eve of the Fourth Plan and the targets tentatively set for the next five years are shown below:

| | Year ending 31 March, 1969 (in million tons) | Year ending 31 March, 1974 (in million tons) | % Increase |
|---|---|---|---|
| Nitrogen (N) | 1.40 | 3.70 | 164 |
| Phosphorus ($P_2O_5$) | 0.40 | 1.80 | 350 |
| Potash ($K_2O$) | 0.18 | 1.10 | 511 |
| Total | 1.98 | 6.60 | 231 |

Thus, the rise in fertilizer use is expected to be substantial in the Fourth Plan period. If all three categories are taken together, the annual rate of consumption will be more than trebled by 1974.

The domestic output of fertilizers has shown a fairly steady increase (Appendix A, Table 11). Between 1951-52 and 1968-69, the production of nitrogen (N) rose from a nominal level of 11,000 to 650,000 tons, and of phosphatic fertilizers in terms of $P_2O_5$ from 16,000 to 320,000 tons. There has so far been practically no production of potassic fertilizers in India—only 1,000 to 2,000 tons of "Muriate of potash" (about 60% $K_2O$) is produced annually in the country.

The Fourth Plan targets for domestic production, to be reached by 31 March, 1974, are 3 million tons of N and 1.5 million tons of $P_2O_5$ against an estimated requirement of 3.7 million and 1.8 million tons respectively. This will leave a gap of 2.10 million tons to be met by imports, including the entire $K_2O$ requirement estimated for 1974. Thus, despite the increase in domestic capacity and production provided for in the Fourth Plan, the deficit to be met from imports will increase more than 100 per cent. If only N and $P_2O_5$ are considered, the deficit will no doubt be much less, but even then it will go up from 830,000 to about one million tons.

These figures show that there is a strong case for an immediate upward revision of the targets for domestic production. The case will, of course, be stronger still if a faster rate of growth in fertilizer use is postulated as is eminently desirable, if not indispensable, in India's struggle for survival.

## LONGER-TERM NEEDS

Clearly, the use of chemical fertilizers is spreading in India. It is visibly picking up momentum and should continue to do so more rapidly after the Fourth Plan. What must not be overlooked, however, is the fact that, notwithstanding the progress made so far, India still stands on the threshold of the fertilizer age. Its consumption, judged on a per capita or per hectare basis, is among the lowest in the world as will be vividly clear from the following chart.

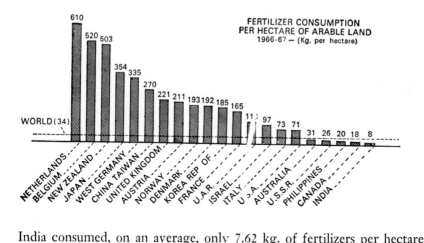

FERTILIZER CONSUMPTION
PER HECTARE OF ARABLE LAND
1966-67 — (Kg. per hectare)

India consumed, on an average, only 7.62 kg. of fertilizers per hectare in 1966-67; this was less than a quarter, or 23 per cent, of average world consumption amounting to 33.55 kg. per hectare of arable land. Since then, the figure for India has almost doubled in just about four years, but even then it is less than one-half of the world average. Moreover, it lags way behind the consumption in most other countries, including China (Taiwan), Republic of Korea, and UAR, not to mention the countries of fertilizer-intensive agriculture par excellence, such as Netherlands, Belgium, New Zealand, Japan and West Germany.

What, then, should be a desirable long-range target for fertilizer consumption in India to be reached, say, in the next twenty years? This question may appear somewhat speculative. Yet an approximate answer should not be too difficult if the relevant factors are taken into account.

*First,* the productivity of India's agriculture has been dismally low. As shown in Appendix (Table 10), in 1966-67 per-hectare yield of rice, maize and wheat in India was only about 20 to 30 per cent of the levels achieved in the high-yield countries. At last the Indian yield has begun to look up. Every effort must be made to speed this trend. Given the present yield data, the minimum objective before India should be to treble or quadruple the yield of cereals per hectare.

*Second,* so far as wheat is concerned, the genetic breakthrough has already brought this target within reach. Eleven varieties, treated with optimum doses of N, gave yields ranging from 3,154 to 4,415 kg. per hectare. Five of them responded positively to nitrogen doses of 120 kg. N per ha. and beyond; the best response came from Sharbati Sonora at all levels up to a dose of as much as 160 kg. N per ha.[4]

The economic optimum for nitrogen fertilization of dwarf wheats, it has been estimated, is around 120 kg. N per ha., assuming a cost of Nitrogen at Rs. 2 per kg. and of wheat at Rs. 0.80 per kg. At 120 kg. N per ha. the response is about 20 kg. of grain for every kg. of N. As for phosphorus, past experiments indicate that for dwarf wheats the economic optimum is about 60 kg. $P_2O_5$ per ha.; at this level each kg. of $P_2O_5$ yields 23 kg. of grain.

For dwarf rice, definitive data regarding optimum levels of fertilization are not yet available, mainly because cross-breeding to evolve better-adapted and more disease-resistant varieties is still in progress. That they will, like the dwarf wheats, be heavy consumers of fertilizers goes without saying. After all, the primary objective of the geneticists is to breed varieties which will absorb heavy doses of fertilizers to give a high return in terms of grain.

To judge from the experience with IR8 and its recently released variants—Jaya and Padma (see Chapter 4), the optimum levels of NPK for dwarf rice will at least equal, and probably exceed, those of a dwarf wheat like Sarbati Sonara. The same remark should substantially hold good for hybrid corn and millets.

*Third,* the High-Yielding Varieties Programme (HYVP) is being extended with a target to cover 25 million ha. by March, 1974, representing almost a threefold increase in five years. The irrigated area is expected to rise from 37.6 to over 48 million ha. by the same year. The multiple-cropping is on the increase—the Fourth Plan aims at extending it by 9 million to about 14 million ha. Even in rainfed areas the possibility of double-cropping has significantly increased in many instances, if the

[4] See Appendix, Table 2.

introduction of short-duration HYV's is accompanied by better moisture-conserving methods of farming. These developments will yield full benefit in terms of output, income and profits only when the intake of fertilizers is pushed to the optimum limits.

*Fourth*, intensive agriculture must be extended soon from cereals to pulses, cash crops, potatoes, vegetables, and fruits. The intensity of cropping will perforce be less in rainfed areas than under conditions of assured irrigation, but on an average it can and must be very much higher than the present level. And this, again, presupposes correspondingly higher levels of fertilizer consumption.

And, *finally*, in today's India *fertilizer is food* because of the need to feed her vast population, born and yet to be born. The only hope for her to sustain the huge population lies, first, in spreading fast the fertilizer-hungry dwarf varieties on the widest possible scale; and, second, in feeding them profusely with fertilizers so that they may turn out the mounting tonnage of foodgrains in time to forestall the gigantic food crisis that still lurks in the offing.

Against this background it is easy to see why fertilizer consumption in India must multiply rapidly in the coming years. Could India reach, latest by 1990, the level of fertilizer use now prevailing in Japan, that is, about 350 kg. per ha.? This will represent a steep, about 24 times, rise from the current level. Yet given the requisite will and the right strategy, even such a target should be quite feasible. And given the demand projections for food and other agricultural produce, a target of this order appears indispensable. No further disaster should be necessary to arrive at such a transparent conclusion.

As the data given above indicate, several countries—the Netherlands, Belgium and New Zealand in particular—consume much more fertilizers per hectare than Japan. This is probably due to the stringent use Japan has traditionally made of organic manure of all kinds—of plant, animal and *human* origin. In keeping with her strong sense of economy, she has, through this combination of organic and inorganic fertilizers, endeavoured to build up soil fertility at a relatively low cost.

Recently, official policy in India has been reoriented towards making greater use of organic manures; and with that object in view, a new programme has been proposed in the Fourth Plan. The intention is to set up ultimately a series of mechanical compost plants to manufacture organic manure of good quality out of urban waste. Initially, three to four pilot plants of different types will be set up to try out and evaluate their economics as well as suitability. Besides, it is also proposed to undertake chemical treatment of the sewage effluents by modern methods, and, to minimize the space needed, the possibility of "pre-drying" the effluents will be explored. Finally, emphasis is laid on the green-manure programme. The coverage under this programme, estimated at 10 million ha.

in 1968, is due to be increased considerably and will form part of the intensive system with crop rotations which is now emerging in the country.

An urban compost scheme is already in existence and, apparently, about 4.6 million tons were distributed in 1968. Rural compost production in the same year was estimated at 148 million tons. These figures are perhaps no more than informed guesses. However, they do show greater "manure-mindedness" even in official circles.

This new emphasis on organic manures—both compost and green-manure—is most welcome. It is to be hoped that the programme for both will be pursued vigorously. While, clearly, they cannot supplant chemicals, they can nevertheless supplement them significantly. And since they are cheaper than chemicals, they certainly should be used to the utmost possible extent.

There is an additional reason as well. Organic manures help maintain a proper ecological balance, whereas chemicals are liable to upset it and cause damage to the environment, especially if they are used in excessive doses. Thus, considerations of both economy and environmental protection underline the need for making the maximum possible use of organic manures as a source of plant nutrients.

### FERTILIZER PRICE

Only a few years ago it used to be assumed that, to promote fertilizer use, a subsidy was essential. Even in the mid-sixties some wanted a large sum to be earmarked for the purpose in the Fourth Plan. After the devaluation of the rupee, in June 1966, imports became much more costly; as a result, the emphasis was shifted towards expanding the domestic production on the ground that this would keep the rupee price low and would also save valuable foreign exchange. At the same time there were second thoughts about the wisdom of imposing a large subsidy on a visibly weakened economy. This, it was now argued, could be obviated if the guaranteed minimum prices were fixed at levels which would leave a fair margin of profit to the farmers. However, investigations to determine the appropriate levels of guaranteed prices led to an unsuspected conclusion: the farmer was found to be better off by using the fertilizers even at the prevailing prices because it actually lowered his unit cost of production and increased his overall profit. This knocked down the case for a subsidy, which was reduced in 1967 and was completely removed in 1968.

The black market in fertilizers reportedly continued even thereafter, thus further clinching the case against subsidy. In the face of these facts, it was hard to argue that high fertilizer prices were impeding production. The idea of a subsidy was therefore altogether discarded in the

Fourth Plan proposals, though exceptions were made in some special cases —for pilot projects, poor farmers, and backward areas.

What about the *level of fertilizer prices*? It is certainly pertinent to ask if they could be lowered *without* subsidies, and *without* weakening the farmer's incentive to use this input. For, other things remaining equal, this would lower the costs of agricultural production and would therefore benefit the consuming public and the economy in general.

Fertilizer prices, in a broad sense, will no doubt be determined by the play of supply and demand. More specifically, they will depend on the cost of imports, the cost of domestic production, the efficiency of distribution through wholesale and retail trade including transportation costs, the official price policy, and farmer demand. The government can do little about the cost of imported fertilizers, which will mainly depend on world prices, except planning, as a long-range policy, to replace imports by expanding domestic production. The potential farmer demand for fertilizers in India, at least for the foreseeable future, is unlimited. The main price determinants, apart from the volume of this demand, will therefore be the other three factors.

The present costs of domestic production are undoubtedly high, and the indications are that there is considerable room for reducing them through better management, higher efficiency, and fuller utilization of the existing plant capacity. In 1969, according to reports, only 50 per cent of their capacity was actually utilized by the domestic fertilizer factories. There could be no excuse for such wasteful operations which could not but push up the unit costs of production.

The need for cost-cutting cannot be stressed too strongly. For, fertilizer costs are the most important single item of direct costs in crop production, amounting as it does to as much as two-thirds of the total in intensive farming. As a result, they have a major impact on the cost levels of agricultural production and on the prices of primary commodities, which ultimately work themselves into the whole economy and the general cost of living.

Not that the government has been unaware of these facts. Given the strong demand within the country, producers were tempted to take advantage of the seller's market. Even public-sector factories were not immune from this temptation. However, in an attempt to keep in check the retail sale price, the government laid down that no public-sector factory should push the price beyond what is charged by the Fertilizer Pool. One such factory, however, gave its own interpretation to this rule and equated its price at the factory gate with the Pool's retail price charged to the farmer in the village!

In 1969, the government suddenly decided to impose a 10 per cent excise duty on fertilizers. This unexpected move was due to an unusual reason. Agricultural incomes were rapidly going up; the affluent farmers

33

were growing in number, yet they were making no contribution to the exchequer, even though such contribution was badly needed for capital expenditure to strengthen the rural economy itself; an agricultural income-tax, long talked about and fully warranted in principle, was time and again ruled out as unfeasible under democratic politics. An excise duty was therefore imposed on fertilizers as a *pis aller* to tap the growing rural wealth.

Whatever may be the explanation, it is a bad tax. It further pushes up the cost of fertilizers when, if anything, effort should be made to bring it down; it is inequitable in its incidence since the same flat rate is uniformly applied to all farmers, rich or poor. It is inopportune, coming as it does when the new agricultural strategy is still suffering from teething troubles. And finally, it is self-defeating since it keeps up the support prices for grains, looks like a disincentive in the farmer's eyes and may thus kill the golden goose.

From a subsidy for fertilizers to an excise duty on them within the brief space of three years—this is too much of an abrupt switch. It cannot help but undermine farmers' confidence in a sound and stable official policy at a time when this remains a *sine qua non* for future progress.

The growing rural wealth must be tapped for revenue. There can be no difference of opinion on this point. But the fertilizer excise is a poor device with a poor yield. The government must find other ways and means that are more rational and are also much more adequate.[5]

## DISTRIBUTION OF FERTILIZERS

The organizational pattern for distributing fertilizers initially had several unusual features. The Fertilizer Pool, an official body, was made responsible for handling most of the supply, indigenous or imported. Until 1964, the Pool operated almost exclusively through the State Cooperative Marketing Organizations which, as a result, practically enjoyed monopoly privileges. Phosphates, other than imports, were distributed by the factories themselves. As for potash, in the absence of domestic production an Indian Potash Supply Agency was formed, mainly by the plantations and distributors of fertilizers, to procure potash from abroad; the quantity imported was small, and its distribution was handled by the Agency. Thus, overwhelming reliance was placed on cooperatives while private enterprise was given no more than a peripheral role.

This system soon proved utterly inadequate for the task. The cooperatives, with a few exceptions, were too small, too weak in resources and management, too much dominated by the official bureaucracy and the rural elite to cope with this new responsibility (see Chapter 9). These

---

[5] Problems relating to agricultural income tax are considered in *Reaping the Green Revolution.*

weaknesses, long known and long connived at, soon proved intolerable. As the demand for fertilizers soared, they put the new strategy for agriculture in jeopardy.

No wonder, then, that the Fertilizer Committee, in 1964, should have taken a grim view of the situation. It drew pointed attention to the magnitude of the task, warned that attempts to maintain a cooperative monopoly would end in disaster, and urged an immediate shift to a multi-agency system of distribution. In effect, this meant that fertilizer distribution, instead of being a closed official business as hitherto, should be thrown open to manufacturers and private distributors. Most of the states gradually made the switch; but in some of them—Punjab, Hariyana and Gujarat—the vested interests proved too strong and successfully resisted the change. In 1969, after a critical holdup in fertilizer distribution in Punjab, the heart of India's wheat revolution, the government issued a new Fertilizer Control Order, amending the licensing authority for retail distribution, which finally ended the lingering cooperative monopoly in these three states.

Domestic manufacturers were given, in January 1969, the freedom to market their products in areas of their own choice, while the government retained the option to buy up to 30 per cent of their output at negotiated prices. As a result, they are now substantially free to promote and sell their products.

Recent experience has clearly demonstrated the vital role private entrepreneurs can and must play in distributing essential agricultural inputs. Many of them are building up their marketing organizations and are working aggressively to promote fertilizer sales. By doing so, they are also setting up an example which public-sector factories would do well to emulate. Instead, some of the latter, it seems, have sought to widen their profit margins by cutting too deeply into the distributors' margins and have thereby impaired their own competitive capacity. For orderly trade it is essential, as was emphasized by the Fertilizer Committee, to stabilize reasonable margins at different stages in the chain of distribution from the factory to the farmer.

## FERTILIZER PROMOTION COUNCIL

The agricultural targets set for the five-year period through March, 1974 assumed, among other things, a growth in fertilizer consumption at a compound rate of 30 per cent a year. As against this, the *actual* growth in the 1969 crop seasons was only 10 to 12 per cent. This unexpected setback was due to a combination of factors. Much of the earlier demand originated from the spontaneous adoption of the new technology by progressive and more resourceful farmers: some slowdown after this initial spurt was therefore quite natural. Weather, too, played a part; in

Tamil Nadu, for example, an unusually dry period was followed by excessive rains.

But there were other contributory factors as well. Fertilizer prices were going up, aided by the 10 per cent tax discussed earlier and the rising incidence of sales taxes levied by state governments. Meanwhile, agricultural prices tended downwards; the Agricultural Prices Commission hinted at the possibility of lowering the foodgrain prices, and this had an adverse effect because of the prospect of a cost-price squeeze (see Chapter 23). The phosphate offtake was low; in fact, the setback in fertilizer consumption was more marked in phosphate and potash. For bajra, jowar and maize, the fertilizer use showed an appreciable drop as some farmers reverted to the *deshi* (indigenous) varieties because of unattractive input-output price relationship.

And, finally, the green revolution in rice was still lingering unexpectedly long in the offing. Despite all its promise, IR8 proved too disease-prone and encountered too much consumer resistance to gain wide acceptance. Only 5 to 6 million acres were sown to this variety. A real breakthrough in rice is yet to come, though given the vigorous breeding work now in progress in India, it cannot be delayed much longer (see Chapter 3). Meanwhile, the flooding situation continues to be a discouraging factor; flooding must be cut back if fertilizer use for kharif crops is to be optimized.

Thus, in 1969 the green revolution showed signs of faltering as fertilizer consumption, the most important yardstick for measuring its progress, revealed a disappointing rate of growth. The concern it caused led, late in the year, to the proposal to establish a Fertilizer Promotion Council (FPC) as a statutory body with participation of the Centre, the state governments, and the Industry—in both public and private sectors. The move was prompted by a recognition of what was called the "mutuality of interest" among these parties in accelerating the use of chemical fertilizers and, consequently, of the need for jointly mounting an intensive promotional campaign.

To achieve its objective, the FPC will systematically deal with all factors which impinge on fertilizer consumption, such as input-output prices, fertilizer response of new seed varieties, irrigation and rainfall, acreage under the high-yielding varieties, credit availability, extension work, marketing and other related services. It will pay special attention to small farmers, dry cropping areas, regions with high but underutilized potential, command areas of some large projects, like Nagarjunasagar and Kosi, where stress is being laid on integrated development. It will engage in the full gamut of those activities which are indispensable to its promotional effort, such as extension, soil-testing, demonstration, publicity with full use of audio-visual and broadcast methods, and training of marketing perosnnel. It will not duplicate the work of existing institutions, nor will it serve merely as a passive coordinator, but will act as a spearhead, filling critical gaps, and strengthening and supplementing current activities as and where necessary.

The minimum programme will involve a coverage of 80 to 100 districts out of a total of 330 districts in the country. The FPC's budget, as envisaged in the proposal, will consist of a non-recurring expenditure of Rs. 1 crore and a recurring annual expenditure of Rs. 1 crore. The Industry will be involved not only in the management of the Council, but also in the actual field activities, and will contribute not only money to meet a part of the FPC's finances, but also its experience and expertise.

This last point is the most significant of all. The Industry, so long kept at an arm's length, is now given a worthy role. And private enterprise, hitherto frowned upon, is at last welcomed as a partner in a common cause, and is entrusted with tasks it is best fitted to fulfil.

This sorely-needed change in official policy has certainly not come too soon. It is now devoutly to be wished that this principle of joint enterprise will be pursued vigorously and extended rapidly to other fields of activities.


## SOIL CHEMISTRY

Fertilizer use, to be really effective and economical, must go hand in hand with scientific soil-testing and precise appraisal of the plant nutrients needed for different crops. This interrelationship, though earlier ignored in India, is now recognized as indispensable, particularly by agronomists. Even more significant is the fact that an awareness of its practical implications is spreading not only in the official world, but also among the farming communities. Much progress has also been made in creating soil-testing facilities, though a great deal more remains to be done.[6]

A beginning for soil-testing on modern lines was made in 1952 when the Government of India, with assistance from the U.S. Government, set up 24 Soil-Testing Laboratories through IARI, each with a capacity to analyze 10,000 samples per year. This was a good start, but far from enough to meet the requirements of intensive agriculture. Accordingly, while initiating the IADP, it was decided to set up 15 laboratories, including five from the old ones, and to equip them for handling 30,000 soil samples each per year. Assistance in this case came, as indicated earlier, from the Ford Foundation.

The 34 laboratories now in existence are, in general, expected to tackle all major tasks relating to soil analysis: to make fertilizer recommendations for nitrogen, phosphorus and potassium on the basis of test results;

---

[6] Much of the factual information used in this section is based on documents supplied by IARI, for which debt is acknowledged.

to examine soils for pH and the requirements, if any, for acid soils, to assess soluble salts and alkali conditions, and to advise on gypsum requirement for alkali soils; to supply information on soil texture; also to analyze irrigation water and advise farmers accordingly. All this work is conducted under the overall responsibility of IARI.

In addition, IARI introduced one mobile soil-testing van in 1957 to tour the country and to analyze samples on an ad hoc basis. By 1968, it had handled some 20,000 samples in different states. A second mobile van was started in 1967 by the Directorate of Extension, Ministry of Food and Agriculture, and this was followed by a third one, in 1968, by the State Government of Mysore. The Extension Directorate now plans to start 34 additional mobile vans, which will raise the total to 37 and will thus greatly increase the capacity for handling soil samples.

The mobile vans help to create among the farmers an awareness of the importance of soil-testing through talks, films, discussions and demonstrations; they also take samples, analyze them on the spot, and make manurial recommendations to the farmers. Apart from this prompt service, the mobile vans, through their propaganda, help stimulate the flow of samples to the stationary laboratories.

The maintenance of the soil-testing instruments has proved to be a major problem even in the stationary laboratories. It will be even more difficult in the case of the mobile vans, partly because of poor roads in rural areas, and partly because, in the case of a major breakdown, no repair services will be readily available.

To augment the capacity for soil-testing the state governments, on their own initiative, have set up 40 more Soil-Testing Laboratories. The Fertilizer Corporation and the private sector have added another 25 laboratories, thus bringing the total to 99. Besides, IARI plans to set up, through the Indian Council of Agricultural Research (ICAR), an Auto-analyzer in Delhi with a capacity to analyze 40 samples per hour.

Meanwhile, IARI has prepared soil-test summaries based on about 1.6 million samples analyzed in the existing laboratories by the end of 1969. As an interim measure, these summaries can serve as a rough-and-ready basis for making fertilizer recommendations.

Thus, as this brief review shows, much progress has been made in building up a soil-testing service. Yet compared with the magnitude of the tasks in India, it must still be rated as modest. For one thing, the coverage is still much too thin. The service has to be expanded so as to cover the entire cultivated area of some 140 million hectares, of which a sharply rising proportion should grow two, three or more crops a year. As the intensity of cropping grows with heavy fertilizer application, the need for soil-testing services will gain correspondingly in urgency. For only through careful soil-testing in relation to individual crops can one ensure balanced use of fertilizers and optimization of profits.

The *quality* of the service, too, needs to be improved in most cases. Many laboratories are still ill-equipped and ill-staffed. To overcome the deficiencies, it is essential to provide adequate in-service training to the existing staff and to recruit large additional staff with the requisite scientific background. To do justice to the tasks, hundreds of well-trained, well-qualified soil chemists will be needed for the service even in the near future.

The mobile soil-testing vans have no doubt their utility in the short run for making the service quickly available to a large number of farmers. But from a long-term angle this is not good enough. The objective should be to establish, at each district headquarters, a stable, well-staffed and well-equipped soil-testing laboratory to service the farms which should be easily accessible by all-weather roads.

The practical implications of plant nutrition and of the problem of maintaining soil fertility at the optimum level should be self-evident. Yet even today they are fully grasped only by relatively few people in India. The emphasis so far has been on nitrogenous fertilizers because of their quick impact on yields. That intensive cultivation will soon create or aggravate other deficiencies—especially of phosphate and potash—has not received enough attention. The use of phosphatic fertilizers has lately increased in some IADP districts, particularly in Ludhiana, Raipur, Madhya Pradesh and Thanjavur, but even in these cases it continues to lag behind the optimum. As for potassic fertilizers, their use, except in Kerala, has so far been very limited.

There is yet another aspect, somewhat more subtle but no less vital, which has so far been almost ignored in India, namely, the importance of *trace elements*. An example from Japan's experience will illustrate the point.[7] In the 1930's it was found that some rich lands were deteriorating in fertility with a decline in yield. The cause was later traced to the heavy use of ammonium sulphate fertilizer, or, more specifically, to the sulphate-radical contained in this compound, which exercised a deleterious effect on the rice crop grown on such soils and made it particularly susceptible to a disease called *akiochi*. It took several years to discover that the disease was really due to lack of certain minor elements in the soil, mainly to iron deficiency. The remedy followed from this—the addition of a small amount of iron filings was enough to neutralize the hydrogen sulphide. It was also necessary to add silicate, some manganese and other bases in order to make good the loss of trace elements due to leaching.

Increasing intensity of cropping, it should be clear from the above, calls for increasing sophistication in the application of science and tech-

---

[7] *Agricultural Development in Japan*, edited by Takekazu Ogura, published by Japan FAO Association, Tokyo, 1963, p. 648.

nology. This is true particularly of soils. For a flourishing agriculture the first and foremost requirement is to keep the soils in good health. This can be done only when up-to-date soil-testing laboratories are available within easy reach, to serve as health clinics, for periodic check-up of soil conditions.

# CHAPTER 19

# Plant Protection

## FOOD FOR MEN OR PESTS?

There can be no green revolution without adequate plant protection. This is a truism to scientists, but its full import is by no means clear to others. Let us therefore recall a few simple facts.

First, what is food for man is also food for pests and insects, often also for rodents and animals. Their attacks may come at any point in the long chain of production—against the seeds before they are sown, the plants when they are green and tender, the grains as they begin to form or to ripen, the harvested grains when they are in storage. The better the food, the greater are the temptations it offers, and the higher the risks of depredation it entails. Lush crops provide feasts for pests. And weeds flourish in well-fertilized fields.

Second, new varieties usually bring with them new races of pathogen, and therefore new hazards of diseases. They lie in a dormant state and bide their time, but only to explode when the moment is opportune. What is safe now may not be so later, and what is safe in one place is not always so in another. This changing scenario needs constant watching. It calls for effective measures to forestall pest attacks as they threaten to develop and spread, in any case long before they assume epidemic proportions.

Third, a different set of diseases may be caused, directly or indirectly, by "malnutrition," resulting from soil deficiencies or from unbalanced fertilization, including lack of essential trace elements. In such instances, the causes must be correctly identified, and the right chemistry worked out and applied for cure.

And, finally, there is the all-important economic aspect. Intensive agriculture raises productivity per acre, but only with a greater outlay of cash, which can be quite burdensome, particularly for poorer farmers. The prospects of a richer harvest inevitably entail risks of heavier losses. The risks must be guarded against, and this makes plant protection all the more imperative.

An adequate programme of protection and control involves intensive work on several fronts: breeding for resistance, cultural practices including weeding, seed treatment, biological methods, and application of chemicals.

## CONTROL THROUGH BREEDING

The ideal method of pest and disease control is through breeding resistant varieties, building into the seeds the genes that would neutralize or counteract the pathogens. It is ideal not simply because prevention is better than cure and because it is more economical than chemical control. Any developing country would find it hard to solve the practical problems of supply and distribution, of training and organization, more so a country like India with its size and complexity. To reach its 50 million farmers with enough pesticides and equipment, and to teach them to apply these at the right time, in the right doses, and in the right manner is, by any standard, a gigantic task. Plant breeders, to the extent they are successful in evolving more resistant varieties, can reduce its magnitude and thereby bring it within more manageable proportions.

Dr. Norman Borlaug, the architect-in-chief of rust-proof dwarf wheat in Mexico, had little doubt on this score. In traditional agriculture rusts are not "aggressive," and epidemics are seldom of any magnitude in fields where wheat plants are "scattered and undernourished." But the moment one starts to fertilize and plant a dense stand with adequate moisture supply from irrigation or rainwater, conditions change radically. "Unless new varieties have built-in genetic resistance to rust," warned Dr. Borlaug, "this disease will destroy the crop despite all of the other inputs and despite all the farmer's efforts."[1]

The present transition from the tall to the entirely new dwarf varieties has placed on plant breeders a new responsibility of great urgency. The old varieties, low-yielding and weak-strawed as they were, could claim one virtue—they were fairly well adapted to their respective environments and had acquired a high degree of resistance to major diseases. This equilibrium has now been upset. The dwarfs have brought with them the promise of high yield, but along with it also much greater hazards of new diseases. The breeders must, through continuous research and testing,

[1] Dr. Norman E. Borlaug: "National Production Campaign" in *Strategy for the Conquest of Hunger, Proceedings of a Symposium*, The Rockefeller Foundation, 1968, p. 100.

build into them the right kind of genes so that, in their recreated form, they may be much more disease-resistant.

Nevertheless, as scientists know only too well, no variety, however ingeniously bred, can attain full immunity; even to start with, it will remain vulnerable, though to a much smaller extent; and this vulnerability will, almost inevitably, increase with time. In short, no variety remains indefinitely dormant. "Generally, resistance of crop varieties to plant pathogens is lost within 5 to 15 years."[2] In the tropical climate the realistic period is probably pretty close to the lower limit.

Breeding for resistance has gained momentum in India, and much progress has already been made. The pathogenic problems encountered with dwarf wheat and rice are discussed elsewhere along with the status of research to overcome them.[3]

Two conclusions follow from what has been said above. First, breeding for resistance is an absolutely essential first line of defence. But this Maginot line can be breached. For plant breeders there can be no resting on the laurels. The search for desirable genes to breed high-yielding, high-resistant and better quality strains is an endless one in modern agrobiology; and so they must continuously breed, test, watch, appraise and breed again in order to adapt and re-adapt their strains. And, second, breeding alone cannot be relied upon to control diseases. It should go as far as possible to make varieties immune at least from all major known diseases. But it will still need to be supplemented, and often quite heavily, by other control measures.

## CULTURAL PRACTICES

Good cultural practices have long been recognized to be an essential method of pest control. Even in this chemical age it has by no means lost its importance because it has some definite advantages. It reduces the risks of pests at the very source; it can, within limits, be quite effective; and, being preventive, it is also cheap inasmuch as it helps cut down on pesticide costs.

To take a few examples, quick disposal of crop residues after harvest helps keep down pest population; proper cultivation of soil is important —it brings hidden pests to the surface where they are liable to die of exposure or be destroyed by their natural enemies.

The cropping pattern should provide for suitable rotation. Successive cultivation of the same crop in the same field creates a favourable environment for dormant races of plant pathogens, while rotation of crops works in the opposite direction. The corn blight which struck large areas of the

[2] *The World Food Problem, A Report of the President's Science Advisory Committee*, Washington, D.C., 1968, Vol. III, p. 137.
[3] In Chapter 22 on "Research, Extension, and Education"; also see Chapter 4.

USA in 1970 and inflicted heavy damages, has been attributed to "mono-biotic culture," that is, cultivation of corn year after year without any rotation because it is found more profitable to do so.

Timing, too, can be an important factor since pest activity often fluctuates with seasons. For example, Taichung/Native I, the first dwarf variety of rice to arrive in India, proved highly susceptible to pests when grown in the monsoon season, but much less so in winter. Even compara-tively resistant varieties should, as far as possible, be sown or planted at a time when they have the best chance to escape from a major pest attack.

Proper *seed treatment* can serve as a valuable prophylactic and prevent a good many diseases. This, for example, is true of the nematode diseases, to which all varieties of wheat now grown in India are susceptible. These diseases, it has been established, are perpetuated by nematode galls which are harvested with the seed crop and thus remain as a contaminant. They can be largely eliminated by a simple process—all that is necessary is to soak the seeds for one-half to one hour in a solution of 20 per cent brine (Sodium chloride plus Potassium chloride) and to strain off the floating nematode galls from the top. The seeds so treated must be thoroughly washed three to four times before they are dried and sown.[4]

The salt water treatment of seeds has been an old practice in Japan's rice cultivation. "One of the significant technological innovations of the early period was the device of placing rice in salt water to separate sound from immature seed which floated to the top." This technique was devised in 1882 by Dr. Tokitaka Yokoi who was then head of the Fukuoka Agricultural Experiment Station. In fact, it was developed by Dr. Yokoi from a similar practice followed by farmers, which came to his notice in the course of his field observations.[5] Incidentally, this is a characteristic feature of Japan's agriculture, especially in its early period, when research was largely oriented towards adopting and adapting the improved practices of the more progressive farmers and to spread them over the farming community at large.

The value of proper seed treatment to counteract seed and many soil-borne diseases and pests is now more or less universally recognized For example, in the USA 60 to 70 per cent of the area is sown with treated seeds while the proportion in the UK is even higher. But in India, even in the mid-sixties, it was only 1.3 per cent! The Fourth Plan proposes that, by 1974, the area sown with treated seeds should reach 26 million ha. (65 million acres) or almost 20 per cent of the total.[6]

---

[4] *Five Years of Research on Dwarf Wheats*, Indian Agricultural Research Institute (IARI), New Delhi, 1968, p. 36.

[5] *Agricultural Development in Modern Japan*, op cit., p. 644.

[6] *Plant Protection—Report of the Working Group for the Formulation of the Fourth Five Year Plan Proposals*, New Delhi, 1965, p. 9. Also, *Fourth Five Year Plan 1969-74*, p. 133.

## BIOLOGICAL METHODS

Apart from breeding resistant varieties, biological methods of control have other interesting possibilities, namely, through useful parasites and predators. In some instances quite significant results have been achieved through these methods. For example, the President's Science Advisory Committee cites the case of the "cottony cushion scale" which has been controlled in the USA since the 1890's by the "Vedalia beetle introduced from Australia," and of Klamath weed in the western United States and pricklypear in Australia, which were "virtually eliminated as major pests" following the introduction of insect parasites. Over 110 cases were reported by 60 countries where biological control of different insect pests had been wholly or partly successful.[7]

Attempts have been made to cultivate and commercially exploit certain parasitic organisms (e.g. Bacillus thurigiensis) as means of control. While some successes have been achieved, these methods have obvious limitations. Their effectiveness depends on such factors as host density, host behaviour, humidity, perennial crops, etc. which cannot be controlled. The bacilli cannot search out the host, and this necessitates repeated applications to provide thorough coverage. Even more serious is the fact that while they are at work, the crops must continue to be damaged by pests, for periods extending to 2-4 weeks.

It is true that parasites and predators introduced from outside have shown good results in several instances. But almost always they relate not to short seasonal crops, but to evergreens such as forest trees, coconuts, and certain fruit trees. In such cases the parasites or predators can establish themselves and gradually extend their work without requiring repeated releases.

This kind of what may be called eco-biological, or "bioenvironmental," method of pest and insect control, using nature to control nature, is fascinating to contemplate. It is certainly worth pursuing with patience and tenacity, both to extend the horizons of scientific knowledge about the behaviour of plants, pests and insects, and to book whatever successes may be achieved in the process for plant protection, always remembering that the end-results might at times turn out to be highly rewarding. Moreover, it has the added attraction that, unlike many chemicals, it causes no damage to the environment; on the contrary, it helps maintain a proper ecological balance.

But the practical limitations of this method must not be ignored. It calls for long-drawn-out research, often extending to many years; progress is uncertain; and even when positive results are achieved, their practical application is far from easy. To rear the useful parasites in

[7] Loc. cit., Vol. III, p. 137.

laboratories, to make sure about the host-parasite adaptation, to maintain the proper female : male ratio in the fields—these are all difficult and delicate tasks. There may be other slips as well—the parasites may not establish themselves after release, in which case fresh releases, usually in very large numbers, will be necessary. And, finally, different parasites may be needed at times to control a single pest or pest complex, which would further limit the practical usefulness of this method.

In India, attempts have been made on a limited scale to control insect pests through these techniques. At first, the aim was to control sugarcane borers, woolly asphis of apple, and cottony cushion scale of citrus. Later, under the Second and Third Plans, attempts were made to control the *nephantis* caterpillar of coconut and San Jose scale of apple. In the Second Plan period, 11 stations were established—in Madras, Kerala, Andhra Pradesh, Mysore, and Maharashtra—to combat the coconut pest and some 63.5 million parasites were released. The number of stations were later increased to 17 and targets for release of parasites were fixed for each state. Meanwhile, steps have been taken to breed and release the parasites of San Iose scale in Himachal Pradesh and in Jammu and Kashmir.

Plant protection scientists in India, as in other countries, are apt to stress the value of the biological techniques of control and the need to exploit their potential more fully. These techniques have no doubt their value and, as already noted, they ought to be pursued and applied wherever they hold out enough promise of reasonably good results. But too much should not be expected from them, nor too soon. The "ifs" and "buts" involved in these methods are numerous, and the scope of their effective applicability is inherently limited. The insect pests of sugarcane, coconut, and apple, on which biological methods are being tried in India, represent almost ideal cases where they are most likely to be successful. On the other hand, there are many areas where they can be ruled out almost on *a priori* grounds. In particular, this kind of biological technique can provide little or no protection for what we are primarily concerned with here—bumper crops from high-yielding varieties of wheat, rice, and other foodgrains.

## CONTROL THROUGH PLANT QUARANTINE

Plant (and animal) protection programmes have habitually included quarantine measures for enforcement at important check-points. As part of such measures, proper certification of seeds and nursery stocks is insisted upon. The objective is, of course, to forestall the spread of diseases or of pathogens from one country or region to another, or from one locality to another within the same country. This is particularly important in cases of serious outbreaks of diseases. Normally, governments forearm themselves with adequate legislative powers in order to deal with such situations and to localize, control and, wherever possible, to eradicate the pests and pathogens.

In India, a Central Act called Destructive Insects and Pests Act has been in existence since 1914. Its main purpose is to regulate the import of plant and plant materials and domestic quarantines. Since independence, the states, with the exception of West Bengal, have passed their own Agricultural Pests and Diseases Acts with jurisdiction within the state boundaries.

In recent years the plant quarantine work has made considerable headway. Control stations have been established at all the main seaports—Bombay, Madras, Calcutta, Cochin, Visakhapatnam, and later also at Kandla and Bhavnagar—and at the four international airports—Bombay, Calcutta, Madras, and Delhi. Some more have been, or are being, established, including a few along the land frontiers.

Incidentally, these stations serve an important commercial purpose as well. Most countries while importing plants and plant products require from the exporting countries official certificates that these are free from pests and diseases. State governments perform this function at present on behalf of the Centre. This means that adequate facilities for inspection and fumigation have to be provided at the seaports and airports. With the growing foreign trade the existing organization apparently finds it hard to cope with this work.

The domestic quarantine, at the inter-state level, has not been working too well, according to official reports. It is also admitted that some newly introduced pests and pathogens have spread quite rapidly. Here, again, one must realistically appraise the value of a quarantine system and remember what it can and cannot achieve. It is most useful as a tool for localizing and controlling pests and diseases in cases of serious outbreaks. It is also essential for export certification—given the current regulations, an exporting country must, in its own interest, make sure that the agricultural commodities it wants to export are of a high quality, of the desired grade, are free from disease, and are credibly certified as such on the basis of their disinfection or disinfestation, without which they will not fetch the desired price and may not be exported at all. Lastly, it can also, within limits, control the spread of pests and pathogens, whether of foreign or of domestic origin.

It is this last point which needs to be heavily qualified. No national frontiers can be hermetically sealed so as to keep out all pests and pathogens of foreign origin. Leakages are bound to occur. As Dr. Harrar pointedly reminds us, containment of pathogenic micro-organisms within prescribed areas is a well-nigh impossible task in this jet age. Many known and even more unknown virulent pathogens are "fellow travellers" through national and international trade channels and transportation systems, and "a goodly number ride the jet streams."[8]

For the same reason in a country like India, these microorganisms—and there are literally countless races of them—are bound to find their way from one area to another, despite the inter-state quarantines. And here is the most important fact to remember: many of these pathogenic races, once they escape through the quarantines, can multiply at an astonishing rate and assume menacing proportions within an incredibly short time.

## CHEMICAL CONTROL

The chemical methods of pest control have many advantages. Great progress has been made in the last two decades in developing and perfecting these methods based on the supply of an ever-widening range of pesticides. As synthesized materials, they can be produced according to different formulae to meet particular needs; they can be standardized with meticulous care, stored for indefinite periods and transported over long distances, without losing their efficacy; and they can be applied at short notice almost to any situation to produce quick results. Today they provide an effective tool to bring under control any sudden and serious outbreak of pests.

The equipment for quick and effective application of pesticides has been similarly improved through constant research. The improvement of technology has entailed higher costs. Nevertheless, the actual cost of plant protection by chemicals to a modern farmer remains quite low, thanks largely to his high per-acre productivity.

Unlike biological agents, chemicals are not affected by environmental factors in their effectiveness. They can be applied, with a reasonable guarantee of success, on numerous pests and diseases under widely varying conditions. Occasionally there may be a resurgence of pests calling for repeat applications of chemicals. But this need not present any serious practical problems.

Another noteworthy feature about chemicals is the number of ways in which they can act—as contact or fumigant poisons, as attractants or repellants, as sex-sterilants. They can, according to requirement, be used either singly or in combination with other chemicals, sometimes also in conjunction with biological agents, either in a synchronized form or in appropriate sequence.

Another spectacular breakthrough was the principle of selectivity (see below) under which chemicals would hit, almost like precision bombing,

[8] "An International Approach to the Study and Control of Plant Disease" by Dr. George Harrar, President, The Rockefeller Foundation, in *Strategy towards the Conquest of Hunger*, New York, 1967, p. 140.

the deadly targets without, however, affecting the beneficial plants or organisms, as is the case with selective weed-killers.

To this armoury of wonder chemicals are now being added even more fascinating variants to control pests not by killing them directly, but by creating physiological disorders. To this category belong "anti-feeding" compounds, attractants like food or sex lures, sex sterilizers which would make the males of an insect population infertile, prevent them from multiplying and thereby soon eliminate them altogether.[9] Many "chemosterilants" are now being investigated and evaluated, and some of them at least should reach the operational stage in the near future.

## WHY PESTICIDES

In general, chemicals provide the quickest, most effective, and also the most versatile means of pest and insect control; and given the yield potential of modern agriculture, they have a favourable cost-benefit ratio. But what about safety? In India, even before the use of pesticides had hardly begun, people began to express fears about the dangers they would involve to human life as well as to fish and animals. Some extremists conjured up the spectre of the extinction of wildlife and permanent damage to human beings.

More recently, as the campaign against DDT and other pesticides in the USA, mostly led by ardent conservationists and nature-lovers, became increasingly louder, it reinforced the hands of the traditional anti-pesticide school, to which, strangely enough, even some scientists, engaged in plant protection, gave quiet allegiance. It is most essential to correct the distorted views and to set the perspective right.

First of all, it must be noted that much of the problem arises from an almost ingrained misconception about poison in a layman's mind. As every scientist knows, poisoning is a function of two things—the dosage and the body weight of man or animal. Those who would ban the use of pesticides in India should, for the same reason, be ready to put a similar ban on all poisonous drugs and medicines. Yet few, if any, would be willing to do so.

Second, biological control, whether through breeding of resistant strains or through introduction of biological agents, should be attempted to the maximum possible extent. However, for reasons discussed earlier, by itself it will be far from adequate. In particular, crops of high-yielding varieties will have to be heavily protected with substantial use of pesticides, more so in the early stages pending successful breeding of much more resistant varieties.

[9] "A striking example of a new approach to insect control is the use of a male-sterility technique to control the screw-worm in the Southern United States." *The World Food Problem*, President's Report, loc. cit., Vol. III, p. 138.

Third, India's agriculture has just entered the chemical age. In fertilizer consumption per hectare of arable land, it still stands close to the bottom of the list of countries. The same is true of pesticides. Their use, in 1969, taking all kinds together, amounted to 10,790 grams per hectare in Japan, 1,870 grams in Europe, 1,490 grams in the USA. In India, it is only 149 grams. The figures speak for themselves. Is it the time for India to be scared away from the use of pesticides?

Fourth, intensive agriculture is expensive. To capitalize on the potential of the high-yielding varieties the farmer must liberally use modern inputs, especially fertilizers. The total outlay—on seeds, water, fertilizers, also labour, equipment, power, and other ancillaries—would add up to several hundred rupees per hectare. He must avoid risks of loss and must protect his crops as best he can. He has begun to realize that adequate protection is not possible without pesticides and is therefore increasingly demanding this input. Interestingly enough, the Indian farmer has also shown how quickly he can acquire the skill to handle and apply such toxic products as folidol and endrine, once the techniques are demonstrated to him.

It follows that a rational policy about pesticides should be not a ban on their use—this will be fatal for the future of agriculture—but to use them scientifically, with good judgement and with all due precaution. Pesticides must be accepted as an indispensable component of modernized agriculture, but adequate steps must be taken to ensure that they *are* used effectively, economically, and safely. Research and vigilance will be needed to satisfy these conditions. With increased use of pesticides, the pest populations may undergo alterations, both genetic and ecological; as a result, new pesticidal chemicals may be needed for their control. New and better or cheaper formulations are continually coming on the market; they will need to be followed and, where justified, should be introduced after whatever adaptation may be necessary.

As for safety, some pesticides are highly toxic to man, animals, and wildlife. It is essential to establish safe practices in handling them at all stages—from manufacturing through distribution to their application by the farmer in the field. Caution is also needed in applying certain pesticides that are toxic to fish and wildlife. That increased use of chemicals may, under certain conditions, become a health hazard cannot be denied. The Ford Foundation Team of 1959, while urging the use of pesticides for plant protection also sounded a warning: "As more pesticides are used, residues on food may become a problem, and fuller implementation of pure food and drug laws will be necessary."[10]

Substantially the same recommendation was made by the Thacker Committee, which was appointed by the Planning Commission in 1965, to investigate the problem of pesticides and the dangers associated with them. This action was prompted by the exaggerated fears entertained by

[10] Report, loc. cit., p. 191.

some people even before an effective plant protection programme was developed. The Committee's main recommendation was what one might well have anticipated, namely, proper rules and regulations should be laid down and enforced so as to forestall or "immunize" the dangers of misuse of pesticides and fungicides.

This is sound advice given by the government's own scientists. The debate on pesticides should be settled on this basis, once and for all. The sooner that happens, the better. Otherwise blind opposition to chemical control will only provoke its blind advocacy. And in the process its *regulated* use might well become a casualty.

## DDT CONTROVERSY

In recent years the campaign against DDT has gained considerable momentum, particularly in the USA. Arizona banned it early in 1969; other states led by Michigan and Wisconsin followed the example; and in Congress, Senator Gaylord Nelson of Wisconsin reintroduced his bill to outlaw DDT nationwide.

In an editorial on "Twilight for DDT,"[11] the *New York Times* pointed out that the revolt against this powerful pesticide was part of a wider awareness of "how fragile and endangered man's environment is." And then it went on to comment: "There is no doubt that DDT has been spectacularly effective. But it is known that it is highly persistent and that its residues have accumulated in fish and in the entire food chain at levels which are potentially dangerous." There were other safer substitutes which could be used in some cases in lieu of DDT; in others, nature too could "cope" if its own balance of forces were left undisturbed. The lead given by Arizona, Michigan, and Wisconsin, it concluded, should be followed by other states.[12]

This revolt against DDT is not hard to understand. Broadly speaking, it has been due to three factors: over-use of this pesticide largely under the high-pressure salesmanship of the manufacturing interests; under-exploitation of biological and other alternative methods of pest and insect control; and the over-emphasis of the conservationists on the evil effects of chemical control *per se*.

It cannot be denied that the U.S. attitude to DDT has scared a lot of people in India and elsewhere. Yet it would be little short of tragic if its abuse in the U.S.A. were to prevent its legitimate use in the developing countries. For, it is one of the most potent tools they now possess to control pests and insects, to protect their crops, and to raise the effective productivity of their lands.

[11] On 20 April, 1969.

[12] The USA, it seems, is now well on the way to put a complete ban on the use of DDT.

There is another vital aspect of this controversy which must not be overlooked. Chemicals, particularly DDT, have been instrumental in achieving complete or nearly complete eradication of many deadly pests and diseases such as malaria, typhus, yellow fever, plague. This, in turn, has greatly lengthened the average expectancy of life, and has thereby directly led to the present explosive growth of population. Thus, in a very real sense, nature's own balance of forces, or the ecological balance between the human and the insect or pest population, has been radically altered. Must we now blindly fight against DDT and other chemicals which alone can help establish a new and more tolerable equilibrium between man and his environment, without which the world will not be able to produce enough food to sustain its surging population? Such a policy would not only be tragic, but also ironical.

The two United Nations agencies directly concerned with the DDT issue are WHO and FAO. The verdict jointly given by their experts, in December 1969, after reviewing "all available animal data on all aspects of toxicology of DDT pertinent to man," should indeed command respect. Though there are still some unresolved questions about its effect on the environment and on human health, they agreed that DDT, along with some other organochlorine insecticides will continue to play "a vital role" in food production and crop protection in many countries.

More than half the total insecticides used by developing countries consists at present of DDT and some other organochlorine compounds because of their low cost, user safety, safety in their storage and transport, and of the lack of suitable substitutes. To replace them by more expensive and frequently more toxic chemicals would be beyond the financial resources of some countries; and this might entail new risks for which they are not prepared.

The experts therefore recommended the continued use of DDT, but wanted it to be restricted to those pest problems for which no other satisfactory solutions are now available, and urged that "all unnecessary or excessive use" of this chemical should be avoided. India and other developing countries can do no better than heed this sound and authoritative advice.

## USE OF PESTICIDES IN INDIA[13]

Luckily, the counsel of reason has prevailed despite misgivings and premature controversy. The use of pesticides has been spreading rapidly, as can be seen from Chart 14 which gives actual consumption, domestic

[13] Some of the information contained in this section was supplied by Dr. C. J. Fredrickson, Entomology Adviser, USAID in New Delhi, during a discussion on 10 December, 1969. Also see his article "It's Your Move" in *Looking Ahead*. Pesticides Association of India, 1969.

production, and imports since 1960 with projections through 1975. As is to be expected, the uptrend was particularly marked after the introduction of the high-yielding varieties. The total consumption is still small, even in absolute terms. On the other hand, plant protection by chemical means is a new activity which was virtually unknown only a few years ago. The only chemical used in quantity was DDT, and it was used almost exclusively as an insecticide to control the malarial mosquito. Against this background, the growth in the *agricultural* use of pesticides appears quite remarkable.

Another significant fact is the growth of the domestic pesticide industry which produces no less than 16 out of some 20 compounds currently used in the country. The official policy is to attain self-sufficiency in the major pesticides; accordingly, licences have been allocated to domestic manufacturers to expand their capacity. If fully utilized, they should meet most of the requirement through 1975. Both demand and domestic production are rising sharply, and will almost certainly continue to do so for many years. But there will almost certainly be a continuing need for some import as new pesticides come on the international market with promise of more effective or more economic control under Indian conditions.

Initially, pest control was treated as a function of the state governments or the panchayat organizations. All that the programme then aimed at was to distribute some hand or power sprayers to the Blocks—in some states to the panchayats—to be used either directly or on a loan basis for plant protection in their respective areas. The state governments stockpiled pesticides at their own cost and distributed them through the Block and panchayat organizations. Inevitably there were hold-ups, and the stocks did not move fast enough. The state-operated service was weak even to start with; and after the HYV programme was launched, its utter inadequacy became glaringly obvious to all concerned, and this led to a completely new approach to the problem.

Every state has now set up one or more organizations, equipped with sprayers and transport vehicles, so that each may tackle epidemic areas at the rate of 500 to 2000 acres per day. The Centre has established 14 similarly equipped stations of its own located in different places. An aerial wing has been added to the Central set-up for plant protection.

Even more significant is the reliance now placed on the private sector. Marketing of pesticides has been largely de-officialized; only buffer stocks for urgent action in case of epidemics are kept by state government organizations, while the main responsibility for distribution has been largely transferred to the manufacturers and private sector distributors. Private firms are urged to provide custom services in spraying, from both ground and air, and to persuade big farmers to buy their own power-spraying equipment to take care of plant protection on a do-it-yourself basis. They are also more and more relied upon to provide free demonstrations and trials on farmer's fields to stimulate pesticide use.

The private sector has readily responded to the call and is striving to fill the gaps in supply and distribution. A more forthright official policy and less ad hoc decisions could greatly facilitate this task. For example, in 1968 the subsidies on pesticides, which had been as high as 50 per cent in some states, were suddenly withdrawn without serving any advance notice to the industry. Taxes levied under the Central sales tax law on interstate sale of pesticides are too high, even higher than the state sales taxes on fertilizers. Such levies cannot but act as a deterrent to the chemical means of control, which is still in its infancy. They ought to be substantially reduced, if not altogether eliminated.

A progressive pesticide industry in India will require a steady inflow of technical knowhow, equipment, essential raw materials and, in a good many cases, also foreign collaboration, for which the flourishing pharmaceutical industry of India can serve as a good precedent. The government has recognized this need and has so far followed a fairly liberal import policy allowing preferential customs duties. The need for such a policy is likely to persist for some time to come.

Suggestions have also been made to abolish, or at least to reduce substantially, the excise duties on raw materials used by the industry; and for tax concessions for free demonstrations and trials held by the industry on farmers' fields. The idea of such tax rebates does indeed make sense in the early stages of pesticide development and promotion.

Finally, there is the important question of credit—for manufacturers, for dealers and distributors, and for farmers. The demand for credit, already strong, will rise rapidly as the use pesticides spreads. The symptoms of a credit famine are already there. Some progress has been made to meet it, but much more remains to be done.[14]

### AGRICULTURAL AVIATION

The march of modernization of India's agriculture is highlighted by another fact—the growth of agricultural aviation. An aerial wing has been established in the Plant Protection organization of the Central Department. At one stage the plan was to expand the initial fleet of seven by adding another 100 planes during the Fourth Plan period. However, wisdom prevailed, and it was decided to encourage the private sector increasingly to undertake the work of aerial spraying on a custom service basis, which is subsidized by the government. The present aim of official policy is to enlarge the private sector coverage in order to bring down the unit cost of spraying and with it the amount of subsidy.

A few figures will illustrate the present trend. The area covered by

[14] Discussed further in Chapters 25-27.

aerial spraying of pesticides and fertilizers rose from 408,000 acres in 1966-67 to 980,000 acres in 1967-68 and to 2,000,000 acres in 1968-69. Of this last total, the Central Government's share was 344,000 acres while the balance was accounted for by the private sector. In the same year it was not found feasible to spray about 325,000 acres in Punjab and Hariyana for lack of aircraft, and 300,000 acres in Uttar Pradesh for lack of the required insecticide (i.e. ULV). However, in UP half a million acres of sugarcane were covered with aerial spraying to protect the crop which was attacked by sugarcane leafhopper and black bug.

The fleet for agricultural aviation, which consisted of 32 aircraft—six owned by the Centre and the rest by the private sector—is being strengthened with the addition of 50 units financed with a $3 million loan from the Export-Import Bank of the USA. Under this expansion programme, it is significant to note, only four aircraft will be added to the government fleet and the balance will go to the private sector.

The pesticide industry is conducting demonstrations in aerial spraying. A beginning has been made to spray jute crops from the air with pesticides to control pests and with urea to boost their growth as seen in the preceding Chapter. USAID has assisted this project with both finance and technology. It is also cooperating in another project of a similar nature, namely, to spray 10,000 acres of rainfed wheat with urea, mixed with pesticides where needed. The target for aerial spraying of pesticides is 20,000,000 acres to be reached by 1973-74. This is about 10 per cent of the total area to be treated with pesticides in one form or another.[15]

The advantages of aerial spraying are clear. It obviates the problem of reaching a large number of small farmers, mostly in isolated villages with poor transportation facilities in general and often none in the wet monsoon months, to ensure adequate deliveries of pesticides to them in time, to provide them with the necessary spraying equipment, and to teach them, through demonstrations, how to do the job effectively and safely. The limitations of aerial spraying are also equally obvious. It can be applied only when large areas are sown with the same crop more or less at the same time and therefore require the same kind of chemical treatment, as is, for example, often the case with kharif rice. Where this homogeneity of crops is lacking over fairly extensive tracts, it will be of little avail.

Two facts stand out from what has been said above. First, the need for pesticides is no longer in doubt. In fact, the Indian farmer is increasingly convinced of its absolute urgency. The chemical method of pest control is spreading fast, though the ultimate needs will be many times larger. And, second, there has been a major turnaround in official policy, and

[15] The figures cited here are intended to illustrate a trend which bids fair to gain momentum in the coming years.

reliance is now increasingly placed on private enterprise, not only for the production of pesticides but also for their distribution, for demonstrating their usefulness, and, where appropriate, for the actual spraying operation, especially from the air—all, of course, within the general policy framework laid down by the government. This, indeed, is the right kind of division of labour between the government and private enterprise. As in the case of seed handling and fertilizer distribution, the logic of circumstances has forced the government to rely heavily on the private sector also for pesticide distribution and application. This is an important lesson learnt from the costly school of experience. No dogma should be allowed to weaken it.

## WEED CONTROL

In an adequate programme of plant protection in India weed control must be given vastly more attention. Like insects and pests, weeds will thrive on well-fertilized soils and will relentlessly compete with crop plants. Scientists sometimes like to dramatize the rate at which weeds can multiply. A barley plant, for example, may produce 50 seeds, but a poppy weed as many as 17,000. In any case, there is no doubt that weeds grow luxuriantly in the hot and humid tropics with its profuse sunshine.

Scientists also like to roll out other impressive statistics about the world of weeds. In all, the planet contains more than 30,000 species of weeds; of these about 1,800 cause economic losses every year, and 50 to 200 usually infest and damage the major food crops; of these, again, 10 species—perennial weeds and grasses—cause as much as 90 per cent of the crop losses in the world.[16] The most significant fact is that *all these ten species are present in India.*

Gardening, it has been said, is a controversy with weeds. In fact, this controversy extends much wider; for weeds are in eternal competition with food and other cultivated crops, and rob them of light, moisture, and plant nutrients. Many of the reservoirs and irrigation canals constructed in India with vast capital investments in the post-independence years have been invaded by weeds. The Chambal River Project, for example, was built to irrigate 1.4 million acres with a 240-mile long main canal, a system of distributaries totalling 1,000 miles in length, and a discharge of 6,000 cfs at the head. Within five years the growth of submerged aquatic weeds has, according to some reports, cut down the flow by 90 per cent. In the Damodar Valley area it is pathetic to see how vast areas above the Durgapur barrage have been covered by water hyacinth. In West Bengal, fish culture has badly suffered for decades because most

---

[16] These are nut grass, Bermuda grass, barnyard grass, jungle rice, guinea grass, goose grass, Johnson grass, water hyacinth, thatch and lantana.

of its cultivable waters are choked by this ubiquitous water pest.[17] Such examples can be easily multiplied.

There is no hard estimate of the losses caused by weeds in India. According to some, it should be as high as 24 to 50 per cent. Even if the loss is very conservatively assumed to be only 10 per cent of the crops grown, the total, on account of the major crops alone, would run into hundreds of crores of rupees a year. Failure to grow crops or to raise fish because of weed infestation results in large additional losses.[18] Of more immediate concern are the huge potential losses which will ensue from the cultivation of high-yielding varieties with intensive fertilization unless weeds are kept under effective control. Here again, modern chemicals hold out the best hope for success.

The discovery of selective weed-killers in 1944 marked a major victory in man's age-long struggle against weeds. One of them—2.4 dichloro-phenoxy acetic acid, or "2.4-D" in shorthand, rapidly gained in popularity. By 1950 it was, in the USA alone, used for weed control over 18 million acres of small grains and 4 million acres of corn. Since then the acreage has grown fivefold or more, aided by the stream of herbicides that flowed out of the chemical factories. By 1967, the sale of herbicides in the USA more than matched the total sales of all other pesticides taken together—insecticides, fungicides, nematocides and rodenticides, and accounted for $700 million out of a total turnover of $1.3 billion at the manufacturers' level.

The economic implications of herbicides or weedkillers can be best judged from a few examples. A gallon of a particular weedkiller, it has been estimated, can destroy more weeds in one single application than seven men working with hoes for seven hours. Or, one man working in cotton fields can, with one pound of chemical, do the weeding work previously done by 100 labourers. Besides, there are several hardy perennial weeds which cannot be controlled by any means other than these chemicals. Most dicot weeds can be controlled by 2.4-D; with pre-emergence application, it can prevent the annual germinating seeds of weed grasses, also of broadleaved weeds though for shorter durations of four to six months.

Used in combination with improved seeds, fertilizers, irrigation, and other pesticides, weedkillers have boosted productivity. In a Nebraska experiment with open permanent pastures, application of 2.4-D raised the forage yield from 1,100 to 2,800 pounds per acre. In Maryland, alfalfa production was pushed up from 3,000 to 4,600 pounds per acre with the help of the herbicide CIPC.

Chemical weed control has led to impressive gains in the yield of

---

[17] For rapid siltation of storage reservoirs, see Chapter 16, "A Postscript."

[18] Problems relating to fishery development are analyzed in *Reaping the Green Revolution*.

cotton, sugarcane, and other products. It has cut down on manual labour, raised production from mechanized farming, and pushed down unit costs. In strawberry cultivation, it has reduced the cost of weeding from $200 to $30 per acre. For most tilled crops, labour for hoeing and for pulling out weeds by hand has become not only old-fashioned, but also too expensive for farmers.

And, finally, herbicides can help control water weeds that invade irrigation and drainage canals, ponds, lakes and streams, and interfere with their economic uses, a phenomenon which is all too common in tropical countries.

The discovery of the chemical methods of weed control with the rapid flow of new herbicides has ushered in something like a green revolution in the developed countries, especially in the U.S.A. Agricultural productivity in the U.S.A. and in Japan has been among the highest. It is significant that in both countries application of pesticides of all kinds, including weedicides, on a per hectare basis, continues to be exceptionally heavy. Chemical plant protection and weed control have undoubtedly made a major contribution to this productivity in recent years, though no precise correlation can be established between the two, especially since pesticides and herbicides must be used in combination with other essential inputs.[19]

In the U.S.A. today herbicides alone, as mentioned previously, account for more than 50 per cent of the total annual outlay on pesticides. This ought to serve as an eye-opener. The use of pesticides, though on the uptrend in India, is still in its early stages. The total consumption, taking together all kinds of pesticides, amounted to 28,200 tons in 1968-69, or 178.4 grams per hectare, while the targeted total for 1973-74 is 68,400 tons. The share of herbicides in this total is about 2 per cent!

Yet the weed problem is much bigger and more intractable in India than in the U.S.A. Even now weed infestation is seriously impeding proper land and water use in many parts of India, the worst sufferers being the low deltaic areas like West Bengal. The problem will grow vastly more in dimension with the shift to the high-yielding varieties and multiple-cropping accompanied by fertilizer-intensive agronomy. Weeds, unless adequately controlled, will threaten to smother the green revolution.

But would it not be better, cheaper, also more humane to do the weeding by manual labour when wages are low, and the countryside is filled with countless landless and jobless adults? There is certainly a case for labour-intensive weeding where this does not unduly push up costs nor seriously affect productivity, especially by upsetting the time-table in a cycle of multiple cropping. Manual weeding is slow and arduous, but

[19] For more information on this point reference may be made to *World Food Problem*, President's Report, loc. cit., Vol. III, pp. 138-139.

even back-breaking work, one can legitimately argue, is better than no work. Nevertheless, even in such cases the objective must be to employ the land fully, to maximize output and income, and to open up better and more paying job opportunities for the rural unemployed. Besides, it may be safely assumed that even now in many places manual labour may prove too expensive, certainly too slow, to cope with the problem of weeding in short-duration crops. In such cases extensive use of modern weedkillers is likely to provide the only effective answer.

What about pollution? Weedicides can no doubt do damage to the environment. Once again, it is a question of balancing opposing factors and exercising the right judgment. That food production must be pushed up to keep pace with the surging population goes without saying. But compatible with this overriding requirement, every effort must be made to minimize the use of all chemicals—fertilizers, DDT and other pesticides, and weedicides—that are likely to pollute the environment.

**NEED FOR REALISM**

As the green revolution blossoms and spreads, it will have to be protected, carefully and scientifically, at every step. Eternal vigilance is the price of a richer harvest.

Clearly, every method of plant protection must be used to its optimum point. The breeders must continue to evolve varieties with built-in resistance. Cultural practices must be improved with emphasis on seed treatment, field preparation, crop rotation, and sowing schedules, so as to minimize pest and disease hazards. Research on ecobiological methods must continue to open up new possibilities; and full use must be made of them wherever they prove effective. Quarantines, too, have to be established to localize, as far as possible, pests and pathogens as well as epidemics. Finally, there is the wide range of pesticides which must be used, at the right time and in correct doses, to complete the protection. Modern agriculture needs an up-to-date armoury for plant protection. And the armoury must include all the amazing weapons modern science has invented for the purpose.

There is a widespread illusion, even among educated Indians, that one could cash in on the full potential of the high-yielding varieties without waging a relentless war against insects, pests, and weeds, or that this war could be successfully waged without the aid of modern high-potency chemicals. This is a dangerous illusion which must be resisted. Otherwise the green revolution may very well be nipped in the bud.

CHAPTER 20

# Farm Mechanization—
# Need for Selectivity

**A PROBLEM OF CHOICE**

Technology today confronts the developing countries with an *embarras de choix*. The options it offers are so numerous and bewildering that the risks of wrong choice are ever-present. And wrong choices are being constantly made, hindering development.

This is particularly true of machinery and equipment. The criteria needed for their selection should not be difficult to lay down, at least in principle: the machinery must, first of all, raise production, and the more it contributes towards that end, the better; it should not be too costly (capital-intensive), especially in terms of foreign exchange; it should not be difficult to operate or to maintain; and it should yield quick and tangible return.

To all these should be added yet another: it should not needlessly displace labour. For, the most pressing need in the developing countries is a rapid rise in opportunities for productive employment; as population swells, the urgency grows. The last thing they need, or can afford, is labour-saving machinery that "saves" labour, but does not significantly add to production.

How to maximize both production and employment—this must be the guiding principle and constant concern of policymakers. Yet, as explained in an earlier Chapter,[1] India has not been able to work out the optimum combination of man and machine in her industry, mainly because of the

---

[1] In Chapter 7.

polarized attitudes of the opposing schools and the consequent refusal to explore the middle ground.

The same danger now looms in India's agriculture. Once again, the issue is posed as "whether or not," as a choice between extremes: mechanization or no mechanization of farming. And, once again, the prevailing tendency is to ignore the truly relevant questions, namely: where, why, when, and how much. As will be seen below, some mechanization is absolutely essential in the interest of production; but there is another kind which would simply displace labour, which may even reduce acre-output, and would therefore be wholly unwarranted.

This is not an issue that can be disposed of offhand, or settled in the abstract. It calls for strictly objective analysis of every socio-economic situation to ensure wise discrimination and selectivity.

## NEED FOR BETTER FARM IMPLEMENTS

It has been estimated by the President's Science Advisory Committee that at least 0.5 horsepower per hectare is needed to achieve high yields. The available horsepower per hectare of arable land and land under permanent crops is: 1.02 in the USA, 0.93 in Europe, 0.27 in Latin America, 0.19 in Asia, and 0.05 in Africa. The Asian average of 0.19 consists of three elements: .05 human, .09 animal, and .05 tractor horsepower.[2]

Assuming that this rough-and-ready assessment is by and large valid, the per-hectare horsepower available in Asia is only one-third of the required minimum. Nor is this the whole story. The human and animal power, which together account for almost three-quarters of the total, is used very inefficiently, mainly because of the poor quality of the tools and implements.

For example, bullock power, wooden plough, hand sickle for grain-cutting, threshing under bullock feet have been the mainstay of India's agriculture almost down to this day; and, in general, the results have been wasteful all along the line. Improved implements, even if bullock-drawn, and better tools, even if manually operated, could bring significant gains in efficiency and output. For instance, a mouldboard steel plough gives much better results than the wooden plough. To achieve superior tillage, discing and harrowing have to be added. Improved ploughs can drastically reduce the number of ploughings—from 5-8 for some crops to a single ploughing plus two cross harrowings—and yet give a better seed bed in much less time and with much less labour.

[2] *The World Food Problem*, loc. cit., Vol. II, p. 397. This section of the Report (pp. 396-400) argues the case for better farm machinery in developing countries. The Ford Foundation's Food Crisis Report gives a brief but penetrating analysis of India's need for improved agricultural implements and partial mechanization, pp. 235-38, also pp. 154-55 and p. 189.

*Timeliness* in farming operations is an all-important factor, in India as elsewhere. But the ability to carry out the operations in time often depends on the quality of the implements used. For example, in Raipur district, which mostly grows monsoon-fed crops, particularly rice, the fields, baked in the pre-monsoon hot weather, cannot be ploughed until they are softened by enough rainfall. Then follows a race against time. For best results seeding must be completed in 10 to 15 days to take full advantage of the short rainy season. Experiments carried out have shown that each day's delay in seeding beyond the optimum period entails 1 per cent loss in output. Yet the available bullock power and ploughs cannot, even theoretically, complete the operations in less than 27 days; in practice, they take much longer.

What has been said of Raipur holds good for many other areas where the soils are clayey and crops are unirrigated.

Timeliness in seeding has another aspect. If enough time can be saved at the onset of the monsoon, and in harvesting the kharif crop, there may, in many instances, still be enough moisture left in the field *to grow a second crop*, with or without a little irrigation from tanks, surface wells, and the like. This kind of "fine-tuning" calls for more efficient, often power-driven, equipment. The use of the right equipment in such cases is an excellent investment. It is time-saving when to salvage time is to salvage a whole crop.

This shows that in many cases machines can help overcome what is the chief constraint on tropical agriculture, namely, supply of moisture. Where irrigation is assured, there is greater flexibility of operations and, to that extent, less need for power. This, it has been suggested, might be the reason why Egypt and Taiwan are able to maintain high yields with comparatively small horsepower—0.4 and 0.3 respectively per hectare, which are well above the Asian average, but are well below the estimated level of requirement. It is significant that Egypt has 100 per cent and Taiwan 60 per cent of their arable lands under irrigation, against 20 per cent in India. This points to the conclusion that India would need relatively more power and more machinery of suitable types to make efficient use of her seasonal rainfall.

Proper *placement of seed and fertilizer* can make a marked impact on yield. Tests conducted on maize cultivation have shown that yields rose by as much as 40 per cent if, unlike conventional methods, seeds were placed in right depth with improved implement. Grain drills helped raise average output by some 12.5 per cent. Line sowing, drilling, and dibbling are doubly useful—they add to the yield and cut down on the seed costs.

The hand-sickle method of *harvesting* and the traditional device of *threshing* under bullock feet are laborious, slow, and wasteful; the grain loss involved is considerable. Better sickles and bullock-drawn harvesters, though far from modern, would be a major improvement over the still-prevalent primitive methods. Threshing could be greatly improved with the Opland thresher, and, where appropriate, with small power threshers.

The role of *the wheel* has, in general, received scant attention in India, both in her rural and urban economy. The head-basket or similar methods of load-carrying, which are still all too common, gives the lowest performance per man-hour with a maximum of physical strain. Hand-operated carts and tools on wheels—wheel barrow for transporting, wheel hoe for weeding, and the like—can make a lot of difference. Bullock carts, with better-designed and rubber-lined tyres, could often significantly improve rural transportation. And there is, of course, an undeniable need for a host of tailor-made, power-driven equipment on wheels. Imaginative attention to the use of wheels can, at a small cost, lighten labour, save time, and greatly improve performance. One thing is certain: the green revolution will need millions of wheels of all kinds, well-designed and well-adapted, and driven by human, bullock, diesel, or electric power if it is to roll on more smoothly and speedily.

What about the *quality* of bullock power? At present there are 70 million draught bullocks in India, which vary enormously in size, breed, nutrition, strength and, therefore, in their usefulness as draught animals. The Fourth Plan recognizes the need to upgrade their quality with better feed and breed, and to improve the quality of the implements hauled by them.[3] This is no doubt a sound decision in the conditions now obtaining in India. For years to come bullocks will remain a major source of power in her agriculture. It will take time to reduce their number significantly even where mechanization is likely to prove more economic. In the short period, therefore, substantial gains can be booked in terms of productivity with better-bred and better-fed bullocks harnessed to improved farm implements.

Why has so little progress been made all these years in such an obviously important field? The explanation lies mainly in the fact that subsistence agriculture was long accepted as almost inevitable, both before and after independence, not only by Britishers but also by educated Indians; while it continued to be glorified, along with the village economy, by Gandhians who believed in poverty and suffered with the poor. The result was an official policy which pampered farmers with subsidies and denied them opportunities for self-help. And just as little attention was paid to roads, markets, inputs, and price incentives, little attempt was made to improve tools and implements.

In addition, there was a widespread tendency to assume that Indian farmers were not able to handle anything but the most primitive tools. Denied the opportunity to develop skills, they were blamed for lacking them.

Yet enough evidence had already accumulated to disprove this thesis.

[3] *Fourth Five Year Plan 1969-74*, p. 135.

It is not necessary to recall the deftness displayed by Indian artisans for centuries in numerous handicrafts, though the exquisite products they turned out should have dispelled misgivings about their ability to acquire what are inherently simpler skills needed to operate modern tools and equipment. In more recent times they have repeatedly demonstrated their adaptability. They are crowding hundreds of modern factories to work as skilled labourers; they are increasingly taking to bicycles, both in rural and urban areas;[4] they are already using irrigation pumps, tractors and other power-driven equipment; they are rushing to the cities in large numbers to serve as cab and truck drivers—in fact, they often display truly impressive skills in maintaining and operating old vehicles as taxi cabs which, in a Western country, would have been junked years ago.

In the last few years a number of new machinery have been introduced in the IADP districts, such as drills and planters, drawn by both bullocks and tractors, wheat-threshers and electric driers. The rapidity with which they are spreading, especially in Ludhiana district, has taken the sceptics by surprise.[5]

The real constraint is not the lack of farmer's ability, but the lack of the required facilities. What is badly needed today is to shed old misconceptions, to evolve or adapt better and more efficient tools and implements, to make them available in sufficient quantity, and to demonstrate their advantages. The primary initiative for these measures is taken by the government in all advanced countries, mainly through agricultural institutions and the extension service. Obviously it must be so also in India.


SPECIFIC NEEDS FOR HEAVY MACHINES

Better hand tools and improved bullock-drawn implements, as seen above, can make a major impact on performance and productivity in most cases. But there are exceptions where heavy tractor-drawn equipment is clearly needed to achieve good results.

Much of the soils in India consists of a heavy clay which cannot be adequately tilled with bullock-power. Because of this limitation, such soils, though otherwise productive, often lie idle. Yet with tractor-drawn tillage equipment, they can be easily brought under cultivation. Such machine ploughings, if provided occasionally, should be enough in some cases; once the soil is sufficiently loosened up, bullock-power can do the rest. Other areas may need thorough tillage by powerful tractors at least once a year.

---

[4] "The successful operation of bicycles is more complicated than many improved farm implements, yet cycles are found in many villages." The Food Crisis Report, loc. cit., p. 235.

[5] See Chapter 13.

The time factor, as seen in the case of Raipur district, is relevant also here. For rain-fed kharif crop, pre-monsoon tillage is most desirable. But before the rains the soil is too hard for bullock-power, and once the rain sets in, it is too slow to complete the seedbed preparation in time. Only tractor-driven equipment can provide a way out of this dilemma.

The same kind of problem arises quite often after the monsoon when at stake is nothing less than the fate of a second crop. The Narbada Valley and its adjoining regions provide a typical example. The monsoon tapers off around mid-September; about 10 days are needed for the black, clayey soil to run dry before the bullocks can physically move in; yet the deadline for completion of sowing is mid-October. Since bullock-power cannot work to such tight schedules, the inevitable result is poor seedbeds, delayed sowings, high rate of seeding, and poor yields. Tillage by tractor-drawn heavy machines can cut right across this tangle and thereby raise yield by 50 per cent or more, without aid from any other input.

All over India there are large areas of village commons which are potential croplands of good economic value, but which are now only a wasting asset. Overgrazed and overtrampled, they have solidified with a hard, impermeable surface. They yield, at best, a poor pasture in the wet season and are often liable to heavy erosion. Bullock-drawn ploughs can barely make a scratch on them. If properly tractor-ploughed and reconditioned with suitable organic matter, they could be converted into high-grade arable land. Millions of acres could, in this way, be resuscitated for fully productive agricultural use.

Once the process of reconversion is completed, the need for tractor tillage will be reduced. However, it will persist in those cases where the soil is very clayey and where time-saving in seedbed preparation, whether before or after the monsoon, is essential for maximum crop production.

For reclaiming waste-lands, tractor-drawn equipment is sometimes indispensable—for example, where they are infested with tough, deep-rooted grasses which cannot otherwise be eradicated. The Central Tractor Organization was set up, in 1948, to reclaim waste-lands of this type in Madhya Pradesh, and this was followed by a few other projects of the same type. There are still many areas which need similar treatment.

In the deltaic regions many large tracts of marshy lands can be reclaimed and turned into fertile croplands. Such reclamation work can be frequently combined with the development of fresh-water fisheries, for which there is an enormous potential. The tasks are in most cases too vast and too complex to be tackled exclusively through manual labour—with hand shovels and head-baskets. For speed and quality of work, it is essential to employ modern equipment for pumping, draining, dredging, for moving earth, building roads and levees, bridges and culverts. The payoff on this type of mechanized operations should be exceptionally high.

37

For soil-and-water conservation work, especially contour-bunding, tractors would be desirable in many places for speed of work, to ensure proper alignment of bunds, and, of course, where soils are too difficult to tackle otherwise.

In the examples cited above—and more could be added to them— modern power-operated machinery will help develop or upgrade land, extend cultivation, raise yields, increase cropping intensity, produce more income, and create new jobs. Mechanization, in such instances, is not only justified, it is a must. To turn it down, on ideological or any other ground, would be sheer folly.

## FARM MACHINERY FOR GREEN REVOLUTION

India has a super-abundance of man-power and animal-power. Why, then, should she need engine or electric power at all? The answer should be clear from what has been said above: the first two types are *not necessarily* interchangeable with the third. Yet it is very often assumed, implicitly or otherwise, that they are *always* so, or that they are *never* so. This false premise has been, and continues to be, the source of much confusion.

Clearly, man-power and bullock-power, just because they are already there, must be put to optimum use; land and water resources must be put to work so as to give optimum yields; and, for this purpose, full advantage must be taken of the advances made in science and technology. These criteria should help determine how, in practice, the three types of power can be best combined.

Since conditions vary widely within the country, the optimum mix, too, will vary from place to place. And it will vary also over time in the same place since with time conditions change—new and more productive techniques and technologies may be available, cropping plans may be changed in favour of higher intensity and larger overall output, population may grow, bullock-power may diminish, shortage of farm labour may develop in isolated pockets, and so on. The exercise, in short, is an unending one. Modernization means growth and change; with it farm economics enters a state of flux. To achieve the best results, management problems have to be continually examined and adjusted *de novo*. In such examination the economics of mechanization must figure as a major component.

Once again, the points at issue can be best explained with a few concrete examples.[6]

---

[6] The data mentioned here are mainly based on discussions with and documents supplied by Mr. John S. Balis of USAID in New Delhi, especially his report *Farm Machinery Input in Agricultural Development—1969*. The discussions were held first in December 1969 and again in August 1972.

Both man-power and animal-power have long been used for lift irrigation. But they are being rapidly replaced by diesel engines and electric
motors which are faster, cheaper and, of course, technically more suitable
when water has to be lifted from a relatively greater depth, as shown
below.

### Low-lift Irrigation Pumps—Performance Data[7]

| Power source | Lift in ft. | Discharge rate in GPM* | Investment in Rs. | Command areas:Acres | Investment per Acre Rs. | Water Cost for 10A. in** Rs. |
|---|---|---|---|---|---|---|
| Manual | 5 | 38.4 | 360 | 2.5 | 145 | 120 |
| Bullock | 15 | 50.8 | 3,000 | 3.3 | 910 | 118 |
| Engine | 25 | 230 | 10,500 | 15 | 700 | 45 |
| „ | 40 | 200 | 10,500 | 10 | 1,050 | 60 |

*gallon per minute
**10 inches per acre

Thus the investment in a pump-set pays off handsomely. Not only that;
once an engine, diesel or electric, is introduced as a prime mover, it can
be put to a number of other uses—to drive threshers, grinders, chaff-
cutters and other machines. This is what Indian farmers are increasingly
discovering—and doing. As pump irrigation spreads, it stimulates mechanization of other farm activities.

There are compelling reasons why some of these activities must be
mechanized. The most obvious of them are harvesting and threshing.
The *deshi* varieties of wheat yield 1,000 pounds of wheat and 2,500 pounds
of straw per acre. The dwarf wheats may yield as much as 4,000 pounds
of grain and 6,000 pounds of straw. The harvest *work-load*, as measured
by the combined total of grain and straw, is thus almost trebled. But the
harvest *time* for both *deshi* and dwarf varieties is the same—10-20 days
are considered to be the optimum period. The conventional harvesting
and threshing crew cannot cope with the swollen work-load.

In Punjab, the avant-garde of the wheat revolution, farmers are rapidly
switching over to threshing machines—at an annual rate of 20,000—and
have more than doubled the wages to attract temporary labour. The
trend is gaining momentum, and, by all tokens, it will spread further in
Punjab and in other states.

Then there are the exigencies of cropping plans which are changing
fast. Particularly marked is the shift from single to multiple cropping
which has been stimulated by several factors: the HYV's which not only

[7] The Table includes irrigation from shallow-wells. Water cost includes cost of
man and animal power. Source : Agricultural Inputs Division, USAID, New Delhi,
September 1969.

give high yields, but do so within a much shorter time-period; possibility to grow two short-duration HYV's, such as dwarf rice, even in many rainfed areas; an expanding acreage assured of year-round irrigation with pumped water, where continuous cropping is increasingly adopted. In Punjab, for example, a monsoon maize followed by potato and a late wheat crop is becoming a favourite rotation with many farmers who formerly used to grow only one slow-maturing traditional wheat crop.[8]

As multiple cropping spreads, *timeliness* in harvesting, tillage and planting becomes a critical factor. The long months of fallow time, so typical of subsistence agriculture, is disappearing, and with it the leisurely preparation of the seed-bed; instead, a new rush sets in; loss of time between harvesting a mature crop and planting a new one means a corresponding loss in terms of output and income. Ways and means must therefore be found to tackle the seasonal peaks which will be far more pronounced than before. This will no doubt call for a larger farm labour force. But, as experience shows, by itself it will not be enough. The time constraint will persist even if there is no labour constraint. Farm machinery will be needed to do a number of critical jobs relating to harvesting, threshing, ploughing, and sowing. Only with such machinery would it be possible to ease the bottlenecks as they develop and to fully exploit the new opportunities for multiple cropping as they open up.

The HYV's need machinery for another reason, namely, *greater precision* in cultural practices. The first experience of many farmers with the Mexican dwarf wheats was very much of a hit-or-miss affair, and the results were at best a qualified success (see Chapter 3). It was soon realized that, to achieve optimum results, seeds and fertilizers would have to be placed at the right time, in the right depth, and in the right relation to each other. What clinches the matter is the fact that the additional yield derived from such precision cultivation is enough to pay for the machines needed to do the job. After experiments with different types and sizes, designs and specifications for planting machines were worked out and arrangements made for their manufacture in India. And some 4,000 to 5,000 units were due to be available for sale in 1970.

The same principle of precision applies also to plant protection—mechanical sprayers and other equipment enable the farmer to apply pesticides uniformly, in correct doses, and at the right time. To take one example, a farmer with a single-nozzle sprayer worked with a foot-operated pump is unable to apply pesticides uniformly. But with an ordinary knapsack duster or sprayer operated with a two-horsepower engine he can do an efficient job and cover as much as 50 acres per day.[9] That precision in timing—for planting, weeding, and harvesting—is

---

[8] The fascinating new vistas opened up by the HYV's are discussed at some length in *Reaping the Green Revolution.*

[9] *The World Food Problem*, loc. cit., Vol. II, p. 399.

important has already been noted. A farmer equipped with suitable machines is better placed to keep to optimum schedules and to maximize yields.

The crucial role of the drier for cultivating IR8 and other HYV's of rice in the monsoon season has already been noted.[10] Unless dried up quickly after harvest, the grains would sprout; the only alternative would then be to grow a slow-maturing variety which would ripen in the dry season, i.e. November-December. In short, given the drier, a second crop, probably rice, can be grown after the short-duration HYV rice; without it, this crop has to be sacrificed.

The use of farm machinery is still limited in India, and it is mainly confined to Punjab and other wheat-growing areas. Nevertheless, its trend is clearly upward, and it is bound to accelerate with the spread of other HYV crops. In particular, as soon as the pending problems of the HYV's of rice are overcome—and this should not take very long—a scramble for machinery will almost inevitably develop among the more enterprising of India's millions of rice farmers.

Clearly, machinery must be regarded as an essential input—like water, seeds, fertilizers, and pesticides—to cope with the mounting peak loads of farm work within shorter growing seasons, to ensure needed precision in the new and more demanding cultural practices, for better timing in operations, and for surer control over the plant environment in general.

## DANGERS OF BLIND MECHANIZATION

More farm machinery will call for more power to operate them. Where will it come from?

Additional man-power will be of little avail, as should be clear from the examples given above. Bullock-power would be too slow for most of the operations. Nor can it be arbitrarily augmented since the animals have to be bred, fed, and maintained in serviceable condition. Moreover, for an economy already overburdened with surplus cattle, the problem is how to cut down drastically on their number; the last thing India should attempt is to multiply them for use as draught animals. There remains only one valid option, namely, tractor power.

Calculations of tractor and bullock performance suggest that a farmer owning 15 acres of land can reduce cost by switching over from bullock to tractor power when he reaches a cultivation intensity of 150 per cent. On the same basis a farmer with, say, 11 double-cropped, and seven or even less perennially cropped, acres would be better off by switching over to tractor power.

But what about the *capacity* of tractors and their attachments and the *size* of the farms? This is where the snag lies, where a sharp conflict

[10] In Chapters 3 and 17.

emerges between the interests of individual farmers and those of the economy as a whole, between *their* costs and *social* costs.

Enterprising farmers are quick to see big profits in big farms. They know only too well that big farms offer substantial economies of scale when cultivated with large tractors and other large machines. Inevitably, a pressure develops as they endeavour to acquire more land to enlarge their own farms, almost always at the expense of the relatively small and weak farmers. This is the trend increasingly noticeable in rural India today.

"What is wrong with such a trend?"—some would be inclined to ask. Would it not be best for all concerned if land gravitates to, or is even grabbed by, enterprising and resourceful farmers and if, in the process, millions of tiny and uneconomic holdings are liquidated? After all, is it not what happened in the industrialized countries of the West, especially in the early stages of their development?

The historical analogy does not hold good. Times have changed. For one thing, the forces of an unprecedented population upsurge have been unleashed on the world, and they are working most virulently in the underdeveloped countries; and for another, spectacular advances have been, and are being, made in science and technology. To put it differently, in two hundred years, and more particularly in recent times, the developed countries, largely in the process of their own development, have radically altered the world environment, so much so that their own early experience has little practical relevance to the countries which now stand on the threshold of modernization. Yet how often is this plain fact overlooked in practice, even by experts from the developed countries who ought to know better!

In any case, today's policies must be based on today's realities, and not derived from the happenings of a bygone past in remote countries. In India's case the realities are absolutely clear, and so also are—or at least should be—their implications.

First, the arable land in India is about 340 million acres. It could, at best, be stretched by, say, another 5 per cent; on the other hand, some of the land now under cultivation is more suited to be put under forests. On a per capita basis, it is now about 0.6 acre; by 1980, it will drop further—to 0.5 acre, if not still lower.

To feed and maintain the present and the future population, India must grow foodgrains, and other crops, on every acre of land to the maximum possible extent. She cannot afford extensive cultivation. Her agriculture must be as intensive as is feasible, scientifically and economically.

Second, small farms, even of 2-3 acres, if efficiently managed, can be highly productive, and therefore viable; in fact, on a per-acre basis they can be made to yield substantially more than large farms. This is because agriculture, as a rule, is free from the lumpiness of capital, unlike most manufacturing industries, of which steel and chemicals are extreme examples. Even the most advanced science and technology can be applied as effectively to small farms as to large ones.

This offers an option regarding the economies of scale. They can be reaped either *horizontally* as modern inputs are spread relatively thinly over a large acreage, or *vertically* as the inputs are pyramided over a small area. For a profit-motivated individual farmer it is only natural to run after the economies of the first category. But it is vital for the authorities to curb this impulse in national interest and to deflect his energies and enterprise, if possible, to more constructive channels, such as input handling and distribution, and promotion of agro-industries.

And, third, there is the enormous problem of unemployment—full or partial, overt or disguised with several men doing one man's job. Slighted for decades, and vastly aggravated by the swelling population, it is fast assuming uncontrollable dimensions. Of the millions of able-bodied workers flooding the employment market, only a tiny fraction can be absorbed in industries, even if industrialization is pursued with all conceivable vigour and speed. Assuming that the adult male population is now growing at something like five million a year, it would be a miracle if industries could absorb more than a quarter of it. The bulk of the newcomers must be employed in rural areas, and primarily in agriculture in its broadest sense—on farms, in agro-industries, agri-business, and agri-supporting services.[11]

Given the mounting joblessness, the most pressing problem is how to employ many more people more productively in rural areas. The last thing India can afford, at this juncture of her economic development, is a large-scale displacement of farm labour. Should this be allowed to happen—because of misconceived ideas about agricultural development or of impotent political leadership—several disastrous consequences will ensue:

One, unemployment and poverty, already intolerable in rural India, will continue on their present dismal course. And it will not take long for them to reach the point of no-return.

Two, the disparity in income distribution will be accentuated, and with it the social unrest which has already gripped rural India. It is naive to assume that the rich can peacefully grow richer while the deprived and the starving continue to watch their yellowing bumper crops and overflowing granaries as helpless onlookers. This would be too much to expect even in India, the land of tolerance *par excellence*, more so today when militant ideologies are constantly at work to build mass movements precisely around such legitimate grievances. The grow-

[11] Problems relating to population growth, family planning and rising unemployment are examined in *Reaping the Green Revolution*.

ing agrarian unrest is already telling on development in some areas. Unless arrested, it will before long disrupt the green revolution.

And three, rural migrants streaming into the cities are increasingly turning them into slums. Large-scale displacement of farm labour will swell the tide which will submerge the cities beyond all hopes of redemption.

Thus, the dictates of economics, social justice, political tranquillity and better rural-urban balance, all converge on the same point and re-inforce the same conclusion: mechanization there must be, but on a highly selective basis; its sole purpose must be to maximize productivity *per unit of land,* not per tractor or per man-hour, nor per farm or per farmer.

How misplaced, then, is the emphasis laid by the "progressivists" in India on indiscriminate, Western-style tractor mechanization, unworried over its labour-displacing impact! They equate modernization with tractorization, look upon it as the best technique to maximize output with the lowest unit cost, minimize its social consequences in terms of displaced labour, much of which, it is assumed, will be absorbed else-where, and are in any case apt to dismiss them as the inevitable price of progress in the modern world. Such views are as erroneous as they are dangerous.

First of all, tractor mechanization is not all that cheap; it appears so only because of defective cost-accounting. There is a hidden subsidy for imported tractors because of an overvalued exchange rate and prefer-ential tariff; grain prices are kept high to provide incentives to produc-tion; irrigation and other services are supplied more or less free of charge by the government. All-in cost accounting will give a far less favourable picture of tractor economics.

It is one thing to mechanize farm work when non-farm employment expands rapidly, farm labourers get scarce, and their wages trend up-wards; this is the classic syndrome that accompanied farm mechanization in Western countries. But it is quite another matter to rush to machines, mostly at high cost, to displace labour when it is cheap and plentiful, and thus to augment unemployment which is already causing grave concern.

Even in Punjab where, with the onset of the wheat revolution, rela-tively short supply of labour and rising wages have given an impetus to the use of machines, it is a moot point if freer inter-state movement of farm labour would not have increased its supply and slowed down the rise in farm wages.[12]

Besides, small farms, as noted earlier, can outperform big ones, both in yield and in unit cost, provided, however, they are placed on a par

---

[12] There is a sizable influx of labour from UP and Rajasthan, which is mostly seasonal and unskilled, and sometimes poses a management problem.

with the latter as regards basic facilities—supply of inputs, credit, transportation and marketing, along with tailor-made equipment to suit the specific needs of small-scale farming.

This is precisely what Japan has done since the Meiji Revolution which marked the beginning of modernization in her agriculture; and more recently, it has been repeated by Taiwan. In both cases, farms have been kept deliberately small; productivity has been built up with improved seeds, fertilizers, and other inputs; machinery was devised and introduced with a good deal of thought and ingenuity to tackle peak loads, to ease bottlenecks, to ensure timeliness in operations, to help precision cultivation.

Mechanization was promoted, but with one and only one goal in view, namely, to improve yield and income. It was adapted to the needs of the small farms; what was avoided was the reverse process—of allowing the size of farms to be determined by the "needs" of unbridled mechanization. The emphasis, all along, was on saving capital, not labour.

The result is an exceptionally high output per acre, achieved with a low capital cost and nil-displacement of labour. In fact, in both countries, for a long time, the farm labour force grew in size and absorbed a substantial part of the increasing population. Only in recent years, with Japan's population stabilized and her industries booming at an unprecedented rate, her farm population has begun to show a net decline. In Taiwan, too, with a rapidly expanding non-farm sector, the same trend is noticeable, though in a milder form. Agriculture accounted for 59 per cent of the total labour force during 1952-59; by 1966, it receded to 53 per cent.[13]

How labour-intensive has been Japan's agriculture can be judged from one simple fact. According to studies made a few years ago, about 1,750 man-hours are invested in cultivating one hectare of rice. This is equivalent to about 85 per cent of one man's total working time in a whole year. Acre-yield of rice is the highest in Japan, but so also is her acre-input of labour. Yet with this intensive work a Japanese rice farmer is far better off than his Indian counterpart who can work only half as many hours a year in most cases because of his dependence on the monsoon, and grows only one-third as much rice per hectare. What he needs, and longs for, is the opportunity to work more hours more productively on his land to produce more grain, and not to surrender his

[13] *Agricultural Strategy and Industrial Growth*: A Report on Visits to Taiwan, India and West Pakistan (August-September 1969), by Bruce F. Johnston and Peter Kilby. This paper (made available in unpublished form by courtesy of Agricultural Development Council, New York) gives interesting data about the comparative problems of the three countries, especially regarding employment, yield, and mechanization.

38

land and his means of livelihood, meagre as it is, to a tractor-owning farmer.[14]

The Japan-Taiwan example stands in direct contrast to what happened in the Western countries in the early stages of their agricultural development. It is also specially relevant to—indeed, it provides a near-perfect model for—India-Pakistan, though in this vital matter they are still too much West-oriented, no doubt because of the Western tide of history that swept over them since the dawn of the modern industrial era. But the task remains: to reorient them—in this particular case, away from the West towards the Orient.

How did Japan and Taiwan avert the dangers of labour-displacing mechanization? Primarily no doubt because official policy was determined to avert them. Policy, however, proved so effective for another reason—the absence of large farmers. Differences did exist in the size of holdings, as they do also today. But they have been kept within narrow limits with an overwhelming preponderance of small farmers. The result was a fairly homogeneous farming community. This made it much easier for farmers to cooperate among themselves to protect or promote their common interests; machinery could be standardized more easily and into fewer types than would otherwise have been the case; both credit and service cooperatives could multiply and flourish in such a favourable environment.

To put it differently, absence of large farmers meant freedom from political pressures they are apt to exercise on policy-makers to further their own interests. It also helped avert the demoralizing effects a farming community invariably suffers from when it is dominated by a few big farmers or landlords. And it provided immunity from something else —the all too frequent distortions of tractor economics with propagation of the myth that large farms alone, when equipped with large tractors and other heavy machines, are the most productive and the most economical.

Taiwan's experience provided persuasive evidence, so observed Dr. Johnston and Dr. Kilby, that the "unimodel" strategy of agricultural development, associated with a labour-intensive, capital-saving approach, had a "higher rate of social return than the alternative of a bimodel strategy in which a part of the agricultural sector would have moved towards large-scale, capital-intensive production."[15]

Today strong pressures have developed in India (and in Pakistan) to

[14] For a good discussion on the importance of selectivity in farm mechanization, reference may be made to the papers by Dr. Arthur T. Mosher and Mr. Lester R. Brown in *The Green Revolution*, Symposium on Science and Foreign Policy, Committee on Foreign Affairs, House of Representatives, U.S. Government Printing Office, Washington, D.C., 1970; also to Mr. Brown's *Seeds of Change* (The Green Revolution and Development in the 1970's), Praeger Publishers, 1970, esp. Chapter 14.
[15] In the paper cited above.

go ahead with tractor mechanization without paying much heed to its overall impact—on production, employment, and social welfare. Big farmers and landlords are at a clear advantage because they wield big political influence. Yet, when agriculture is heavily supported by the state in so many ways, it would be atrocious to allow profits to be tractor-ploughed into their coffers while all they offer in return is, in addition to evading the tax-net, to serve to the state an enormous bill of social costs on account of displaced labour, of which at best only a fraction can be absorbed elsewhere in the economy.

Yet the danger is far from academic. Evidence is pouring in to show how agonizingly real it has already become in many parts of the country. Big landlords may very well carry the day unless the leadership is strong, alert, and acts with determination to counter the pressures before the damage is done.

## TASKS AHEAD

To garner the full bounties of the green revolution, it is essential to proceed simultaneously on two different fronts: to press ahead vigorously with mechanization to book the right kind of economies—those arising from the timeliness of operations, precision cultivation, better tillage, and improved technologies—to salvage sizable increments of output which would otherwise be lost; and to resist mechanization which aims at the conventional, but false economies of scale derived purely from the extensiveness of cultivation. It is as important to veto the second as it is to affirm and encourage the first.

Indian farmers will certainly need tractors, ultimately millions of them, to generate enough momentum for the green revolution. Just as pumpset prime movers, introduced for irrigation, are being used to drive threshers, grinders, chaff-cutters and other machines, tractors too can and must be used with a whole array of implements—plough, harrow, tiller, ridger, cultivator, pump, seeder, thresher, trailer, and various wheel equipment. But what is important is to keep them small in size, low in horsepower and in capital cost, to use them to aid labour to increase its efficiency, and not to displace it.

This is recognized in principle and is frequently stressed in official publications. Care has to be taken that "the process of mechanization does not result in undue displacement of labour," observed the IADP Evaluation Report.[16] The Planning Commission, too, speaks of "a selective process of farm mechanization." Besides, as mentioned earlier, it has stressed the need to make better use of the available bullock power and to harness it to improved implements like seed drills and planters.

[16] *Report on the IADP 1960-68*—Expert Committee on Assessment and Evaluation, p. 57.

But mere recognition of the principle of selectivity and non-displacement of labour is not enough. To give effect to it in actual practice is a most difficult task. Nor is there any indication, as yet, that the government has a clear idea as to how best to go about this problem. For example, the Planning Commission, after mentioning the need for selectivity in an almost casual tone, proceeds to speak about the "substantial demand for modern machinery"; there is a pending demand for about 80,000 tractors, and, by 1973-74, the annual demand should exceed 100,000; the domestic capacity for tractor manufacture is being increased; and to create additional capacity, the "wheeled tractor industry has been de-licensed," also the power tiller industry "for a similar reason"; to the extent possible, the gap between demand and supply "will be met by imports."

The facilities at the Central Tractor Training Centres, respectively at Budni and Hissar, are being expanded, and a third centre will be established in another region. Meanwhile, agro-industries corporations have been established in 15 states as Centre-State joint ventures to distribute tractors and other agricultural equipment, to supply spare parts, and to set up stations for hiring, servicing, and repairing.[17]

In all this the Commission gives no hint about the size and capacity of the tractors. Domestic tractor production has been growing at a rate of 50 per cent compounded annually. They are available in a wide range— up to 50 H.P. tractors.

Strong tractors have a valid economic role in India—to till tough soils before the monsoon, to reclaim wastelands, to make contour bunds, and the like, as was explained earlier. Custom hiring of equipment and co-operative preparation of seed beds, should the practice spread noticeably, would create a legitimate scope for relatively high-H.P. tractors. Exceptions should not, however, detract attention from what should be the rule. The vast majority of India's 50 million farmers will need low-H.P., low-cost tractor equipment.

The Allahabad Agricultural Institute, it appears, has done some valuable work on this problem through its Tractor Evaluation Project. The specifications it has developed for tractors of less than 15 H.P. recommended for use in India deserve most careful consideration and follow-up action.[18]

There is a strong presumption that tractors and other machinery of Japanese design could be readily adapted to the majority of India's medium and small farms. A good beginning has been made to experiment with them in India. What is needed now is to conduct more extensive research, experiment, and testing with different types of machinery,

[17] *Fourth Five Year Plan—1969-74*, pp. 135-36.
[18] 5 H.P. and 10 H.P. 2-wheel tractors, and 10 H.P. and 15 H.P. 4-wheel tractors, adapted to the needs of both dry and wet lands.

particularly with those which are in actual use in Japan and Taiwan, to make a judicious selection of the types most suitable to India with whatever adaptation may be found necessary, to arrange for their manufacture, distribution, and demonstration, and to build up adequate organizations and facilities for their repair and maintenance.

This is an enormous task. Nevertheless, rapid progress can be made, provided goals and policies are clearly defined and realistically pursued. For example, there is a strong case for close Indo-Japanese collaboration in this field, including joint ventures for manufacturing selected agricultural equipment in India.

As usual, there are many currents and cross-currents in India. At this moment the strongest current is flowing in the direction of rather indiscriminate tractorization of her farming. This, certainly, is ominous. The danger is exaggerated, some argue, because the inadequate allocation of funds, limited capacity of domestic manufacture, and the small number of tractors actually available would provide enough safeguards. What is overlooked, however, is that such safeguards are neither the most desirable, nor the most effective. Even a limited supply of tractors can do much damage unless they are "well-tailored" to suit small farms. Besides, a few examples of heedless mechanization can cause widespread nervousness and demoralize the countryside, as is already happening in many places. Meanwhile, in such a confused climate, progress suffers where it is most needed—in selecting, producing, and introducing the right machines to improve yields.

Moreover, mechanization, even when it starts in a low gear, creates its own momentum and tends to get out of control. This happens the more easily in a democracy where big landlords favouring big machines are also able to favour political parties of their own choice as big vote-getters at election time.

In the final analysis, the most effective safeguard would be to lower the ceilings on holdings, say, to 10 acres, and to enforce them stringently.[19] This will drastically reduce the inequalities in land distribution and will create a unimodel type of agrarian economy. Today's big farmers or landlords, once their *political* wings have been clipped by such legislation, will be left with only one other alternative: to take off on *economic* wings, to the lasting benefit of all concerned.

The tall varieties of wheat and rice had to be dwarfed to produce the seeds of the green revolution. The critical dwarfing genes came from Japan and Taiwan. To make the most of the new seeds, big farms, too, will need to be dwarfed. For the right model one can best turn, once again, to the same twin sources.

---

[19] Land reform, land utilization and related issues are examined in a separate study which also shows how small farmers can prosper (in *Reaping the Green Revolution*).

CHAPTER 21

# Rural Electrification

## THE POWER GAP

Will there be enough power, electric and diesel, to propel the green revolution? Or, will it run out of fuel? As things now stand, the chances are that it will, and probably quite soon.

Demand for power, long dormant in rural areas, has suddenly been activated in a big way. They could, even today, profitably consume many times more power if supplies were available at important centres of potential growth. Present consumption is minimal only because power is so hard to come by. Rural electrification is making progress, but still at a painfully slow pace. So far it has reached only 71,000 out of India's 567,000 villages. Thus, on an average, only one out of eight villages is serviced with electricity. And even this fortunate one cannot always count on an adequate and dependable supply at a reasonable cost.

Even the IADP districts, despite the most-favoured-district treatment they have been receiving for a whole decade, still suffer from a shortage of power. The last Evaluation Report had a pointed comment to make on the subject. Rural electrification and supply of diesel oil and engines where electric power could not be provided, it emphasized, would greatly help in modernizing India's agriculture. But present supplies "are both inadequate and irregular and need to be greatly improved."[1]

Power-consciousness is rapidly spreading in the villages. Just as the people have seen the results of the miracle seeds, they have also had enough foretaste of the benefits of power. They know that the two must go together. The demand for power, like the demand for the new seeds, is growing into a clamour. Yet official policy has so far taken only

[1] Report on IADP (1960-68), loc. cit., p. 58.

half-hearted cognizance of this trend. Power generation is expanding, but much too slowly. Transmission lines are being erected to deliver more power to more villages, but at a pace that betrays no sense of the crisis that lies ahead.

With the potential demand increasingly outpacing the projected supplies, the stage is set for a massive power famine. And unless steps are taken promptly, if not to close, at least to substantially narrow the gap, it will act as a major drag on future progress.

## POWER FOR GREEN REVOLUTION

What triggered the demand for power was the need to energize pumpsets. Minor irrigation is the backbone of the HYV programme (Chapter 16), and energized pumpsets, because of lower costs and quicker operation, are in most cases the backbone of minor irrigation projects (Chapter 20).

The figures about irrigation pumpsets/tubewells energized in the past are quite telling. In April 1951, at the beginning of the First Five Year Plan, their total stood at only 18,698; at the end of this Plan period, it was still no more than 50,097; and by the end of the Second Plan, it rose to 191,766. During the Third Plan, however, additional 322,465 pumpsets/tubewells were energized—of these 105,000 were added in the single year 1965-66. The growth thereafter continued at an even faster rate—with 137,276 energized in 1967-68, and 183,498 in the following year. By 1968-69 about 1,087,500 energized pumpsets were in operation, as against 513,000 in 1966 and 192,000 in 1961. The figures clearly reflect the powerful impetus given to pumpset energization by the droughts and the wars.

The momentum will continue during the Fourth Plan which has provided for energizing 1,250,000 new pumpsets to reach a total of 2,337,500 by March 1974. A sum of Rs. 444.69 crores has been allocated for the purpose, of which Rs. 150 crores will be channelled through the newly-established REC (see below).

This is a large increase over past allocations—the outlay during 1961-66 had amounted to Rs. 134.57 crores. The Fourth Plan provision, on the face of it, is generous. Nevertheless, in the emergency conditions prevailing in India today, it is legitimate to ask: Could she do better and proceed faster with rural electrification? The Working Group which formulated proposals for the Fourth Plan in this field observed that the main bottleneck in further extending rural electrification was lack of financial resources.

To overcome this impediment efforts have been made to pool resources from different sources, in particular from the State Electricity Boards, Agricultural Refinance Corporation, Land Development Banks, and the

Commercial Banks. A "Deposit Scheme" was introduced under which cultivators could obtain power after making, for each connection, an advance deposit of Rs. 1,000 to Rs. 2,000, to be adjusted later against electricity bills. Affluent farmers, it was suggested, should be urged to bear the entire cost from their own resources, receiving in return priority over other customers in securing power connections. As for small farmers, loan facilities were to be arranged from commercial banks to enable them to pay for the necessary installations.

All this shows that progress is being made in solving the problem of finance. But the approach still remains too narrow and old-fashioned. The commercial banks charge 7½ to 8 per cent interest on their loans, if loans are available at all, while the State Electricity Boards are reluctant to pay such a high interest. What is worse, the Boards insist on an advance assurance of a gross return ranging from 10 to 18 per cent on the capital invested in transmission lines, before they are willing to consider electrification projects.

Today cultivators, even according to official reports, are "enthusiastic" about the high-yielding varieties; they know they need power for their pumpsets, and are fretting for it; they are ready to pay the full cost either from their own pockets if they belong to the affluent few or with funds borrowed even at high interest rates if they have access to credit facilities. But the government response is still hesitant and unbusiness-like.

Installation and energization of irrigation pumpsets could, even now, proceed much faster—perhaps at twice the present rate—if official policy were not so feeble-minded. By April 1974, the total number of irrigation wells is expected to go up to 6.7 million; but the target for energized wells to be reached by then is about 2.3 million, or just about one-third of the total. The pace is still depressingly slow.

Pumpsets can, of course, be energized also with diesel oil and engines. Cultivators, however, have shown a clear preference for electric pumps since they are cheaper—by about Rs. 2,000 per piece—and also much easier to maintain than diesel pumps. It goes without saying, however, that a diesel pump and engine would be a vast improvement over the status quo, and should be provided where no electric power is available. Moreover, as the use of tractors and tractor equipment comes into vogue, supply of oil will have to be organized on an adequate scale.

A very serious weakness of the current Plan is its tendency to equate rural electrification with pumpset energization. Virtually the whole provision of Rs. 445 crores has been earmarked for this single purpose, and little attention is paid to other urgent requirements. To mention only the most obvious ones, power will certainly be needed:

1. To operate various small machines, such as threshers, grinders, chaff-cutters, etc. which, for reasons explained in the previous chapter, are increasingly coming into use.

2. To operate driers which are indispensable today for the short-duration, sprout-prone paddy crop harvested in the wet months (see Chapters 3 and 17).

3. To meet the needs of seed processing and seed storage plants, which must be multiplied fast to spread the seeds of the green revolution with their purity and viability fully safeguarded (Chapter 17).

4. To build up cold storage facilities on an extensive scale. Their importance in a tropical-humid country cannot be stressed too strongly for handling and marketing perishable and seasonal products—potatoes and other tubers, fruits and vegetables, milk and other dairy products, fish and meat. If cold storages are available, the colossal wastes, which now occur between their harvesting and marketing, can be drastically reduced, and their production greatly stimulated, which will directly lead to a substantial build-up of farm incomes.

5. To develop industries in villages, small in scale, but modern in technology and therefore in efficiency, cost and quality. In general this calls for a wide variety of tailor-made, but power-driven tools and equipment.

Such industries are needed to serve three primary functions: to provide in some instances direct support to agriculture as, for example, through workshops for repair, maintenance, and sometimes also production of farm tools and equipment; to provide productive, off-farm employment to the rapidly rising labour force; and to create an expanding local market, both for farm and non-farm products.

6. To provide some basic amenities, such as power-operated tubewells for drinking-water, street-lighting, lights for schools, clinics, community halls, and, on an increasing scale, in village homes.

7. To meet the demand for power from new or expanding towns and townships in rural areas which must be given urgent attention to build up agri-support activities, to raise the living standard in rural areas, and to secure a more rational rural-urban balance in the distribution of the fast expanding population.[2]

Even this quick listing shows how vast is the market for power. If supplies are available, the load will grow by leaps and bounds. But so far rural areas have been starved of power as will be evident from the figures on p. 306, which show the pattern of utilization of electricity energy (including consumption in self-generating industrial establishments).[3]

The bulk of the power, almost three-quarters, is consumed in industries; the offtake for traction is small, though steadily rising. The other categories relate mostly to urban consumption, the only exceptions being irrigation (item 6) and perhaps a fraction of domestic or residential light and small power (item 1). The offtake for irrigation has gone up almost

[2] Items 4 through 7 are discussed at length in *Reaping the Green Revolution.*
[3] *Fourth Five Year Plan 1969-74,* p. 276.

| Class of Utilization | 1960-61 | In billion kWh 1965-66 | 1968-69 |
|---|---|---|---|
| 1. Domestic or residential light and small power | 1.49 | 2.36 | 3.20 |
| 2. Commercial light and small power | 0.85 | 1.65 | 1.98 |
| 3. Industrial power | 12.39 | 22.41 | 30.48 |
| 4. Traction | 0.45 | 1.15 | 1.25 |
| 5. Public lighting | 0.19 | 0.28 | 0.40 |
| 6. Irrigation | 0.83 | 1.89 | 3.29 |
| 7. Water works and sewage pumping | 0.44 | 0.63 | 0.80 |
| 8. Total energy sold | 16.64 | 30.37 | 41.40 |

four times since 1960-61; however, as a share of the total it rose only from .05 to .08 per cent.

These are eloquent figures. Over 80 per cent of India's population live in villages. Yet of the total power generated and consumed, their share was barely one per cent! Even irrigation, which accounts for four-fifths of this one per cent, continues to suffer from undersupply. As for the other requirements listed above, they hardly figure anywhere in the Plan.

## A TIMID TARGET

In power development, as in practically all major fields, India constantly reveals an all too human, but nonetheless dangerous proclivity: to look back and feel elated over the ground already covered, and not to look forward at the steep, uphill climb that lies ahead. What she has already achieved starting from the dark valley of long neglect is no doubt creditable, but it is far from enough. She can, and she must, achieve a great deal more if she is to overcome the problems that confront her, and not be overwhelmed by them.

The progress made in power generation, when judged in absolute terms, is quite impressive. But it still falls woefully short of the needs of a vast country like India.

The total installed capacity of all generating plants—steam, diesel, and hydro, public and private put together—amounted to 1,070,000 kW in 1939. Eight years later, in 1947 on the eve of independence, it was somewhat higher, but still only 1,363,000 kW. Per capita consumption during that period rose from an estimated 8 kWh to barely 12 kWh a year.

After independence the government set out to make amends for the past omissions. As a result, the installed capacity grew steadily to:

5.65 million kW in 1960-61
10.17 ,, ,, ,, 1965-66
14.29 ,, ,, ,, 1968-69

And by 1974, another 9.04 million kW are expected to be added, thus bringing the total to 23 million kW, after retiring about 400,000 kW of old and obsolete plant.

Consumption of power, on a per capita basis, which stood at 38 kWh at the end of 1960-61, rose to 61.4 kWh at the end of the Third Plan, and to 79 kWh by March 1969. It should reach, or somewhat exceed, 100 kWh by March 1974 after making allowance for population growth, provided the programme envisaged in the Fourth Plan is implemented in full.

An Energy Survey Committee was appointed by the Government of India to assess the future needs of installed capacity to help formulate proposals for the Fourth Plan. The projections it made in 1965, on alternative assumptions of six per cent and seven per cent growth in the national income, were as follows:[4]

| Period ending March | Million kW for growth of national income | |
| --- | --- | --- |
| | 6% | 7% |
| 1961 | 5.6 | 5.6 |
| 1971 | 19.2 | 21.41 |
| 1976 | 28.7 | 33.90 |
| 1981 | 46.2 | 55.70 |

The assumption about the GNP growth could not but be arbitrary. Nevertheless, the figures did provide some indication of the magnitudes involved. The Planning Commission, after taking note of what it implicitly regarded as theoretical estimates, argued that the actual power target for a Plan had to be worked out "by a detailed examination of the load requirements of various categories of demand, *especially in the industrial sector*."[5] The Commission then fixed, in its own wisdom, a target of 20.0 million kW of installed capacity for the Fourth Plan, based on "various considerations."

What these considerations were the Draft Plan did not indicate. Nonetheless, the words "especially in the industrial sector" are sufficiently revealing. They show how easily the planners can bypass the power requirements for agriculture, how completely they fail to see the vast potential load in rural areas, and how grossly they underestimate the growth-generating capacity of this load, once it is systematically stimulated. This failure has been, and still remains, one of the weakest features of India's Five Year Plans. But for it, there is every reason to believe that her economic growth would have far exceeded the artificially pro-

[4] *Fourth Five Year Plan—A Draft Outline*, 1966, p. 226.
[5] Ibid., italics supplied.

jected rates of five to six per cent which were seldom attained in reality.

The target of 20 million kW proposed in the Draft Fourth Plan was to be reached by 31 March 1971. It was not officially adopted however, as the entire Fourth Plan was held up for three years. Meanwhile, actual installed capacity lagged behind the earlier targets by some 4 million kW owing to delays in implementing several major power projects and the general slowdown induced by wars and droughts. The Fourth Plan, with a provision of 9.4 million kW of *new* capacity, in part seeks to make good the earlier shortfalls. Its overall target of 23 million kW, it will be noticed, lags far behind what was recommended by the Energy Survey Committee.

India has already experienced several spells of power shortages when substantial power cuts had to be imposed in several regions with a staggering of loads. More of them clearly lie ahead as the gap between potential demand and actual supply continues to widen from year to year. And the brunt of the future shortages, one can confidently predict, will fall on the rural areas where the demand for power has been growing fast as a direct result of the green revolution.

### THE LOADED QUESTION

"But where is the load?" For a long time this loaded question was enough to hold up power development in India on a significant scale. Since there was no load, investments in electricity, it was promptly assumed, would not pay. Power, in other words, was a costly luxury that India could not afford. That such logic was flying in the face of historical facts troubled very few people. That a densely populated resource-rich area *ipso facto* contains a large market for power, that the purpose of development, among other things, is to activate and to serve this demand, that in such an area injection of power is the most effective means to create a demand for it, and that the load mostly feeds on itself in a process of self-acceleration—all these are well-established axioms of modern economic life, yet they found little recognition in India. And they could be missed, or ignored, the more easily because of the attitudes of the national leaders who, mostly steeped in Gandhian teachings, idealized manual labour and bullock-power.

After independence things began to change, but only very slowly. For example, in 1948 when orders for the heavy plant and equipment were placed for the Bokharo Thermal Power Station of the DVC, charges of extravagance were levelled against the Corporation. The station was to consist of three generators of 50,000 kW each (the rated capacity was higher—57,500 kW each), with provision for a fourth unit to be installed later.[6]

[6] The primary order was placed with the International General Electric Company

A power station of 200,000 kW, costing about $30 million! Could the country afford it? And where on earth was the load? To convince cynics in such matters is one of the hardest tasks in life. For they can be convinced only in one way—through actual demonstration, not in a remote land, but under their very eyes, and that takes time. Even in the best of circumstances one needs four to five years to plan, erect, and operate a power station with the related transmission system. What helped silence the critics was a World Bank loan of $19.5 million extended to the Bokharo project in 1949—one of the first three loans given by the Bank to India. The load projections made by a handful of forward-looking Indians were found more acceptable once they received the Bank's authoritative stamp of approval.

The first units at Bokharo were commissioned early in 1953, and immediately the load began to pick up. More stations, both thermal and hydro, were added, but the demand for power outpaced its supply. By the early 1960's, the Valley was in the grip of a power shortage, aggravated by occasional plant breakdowns. Criticism now took a different turn: Why did the DVC not foresee the rising demand, and plan ahead? This was a refreshing reversal of the earlier charge. It betokened, first, that India was learning, though the hard way from her own experience; and, second, that she had begun to realize, at long last, the value of electricity.[7]

This realization did not, however, dawn for a good many more years when it came to the question of rural electrification. Here, strangely enough, the old views continued to hold unabated sway: the power market in rural areas was much too limited; the villagers could not, or would not, pay an economic rate; supply to them would, therefore, have to be heavily subsidized; and such subsidies would impose an undue burden on the exchequer. This was the standard line of reasoning, and it was accepted by the policy-makers as flawless. And so, though the generating capacity increased, rural areas were more or less bypassed, and most of the power continued to flow, as before, to large consumers—existing industrial establishments and urban areas, and the numerous public-sector industries which were emerging, mostly with new townships.

Oddly enough, even the DVC did, or could do, very little for rural electrification. Its rates were high—they were much higher for rural areas than, for example, for the city of Calcutta. Besides, under its charter the Corporation was required to sell power only in bulk at a voltage not below 32 kV, which ruled out direct supplies to village consumers. Nor

---

of the USA for $13,362,000. The contract was signed, on 28 December, 1948, by the writer as the Chief Executive Officer of the DVC. This was the largest steam power plant in South-East Asia in those days. Since then India (also DVC) has built much larger plants.

[7] The DVC's installed capacity now exceeds 1,000,000 kW, yet it is unable to catch up with the growing demand.

did the DVC feel unduly concerned about this handicap—it showed no anxiety to overcome it and, as an agency for regional development, to promote rural electrification. Instead, it was content to sell power in bulk—to Calcutta, old and new industries, collieries, and to other large consumers, and to collect handsome revenues to improve its financial balance-sheet.[8]

Irrigation water, it is interesting to note, has always been heavily subsidized in India, and in many cases it is provided free of charge. The justification of such a policy is now being increasingly questioned. In fact, the consensus of enlightened opinion at present is that irrigation water should be charged more adequately to enable irrigation projects to pay their way, and to provide the government with more revenue to finance new projects for agricultural or rural development. As farm prosperity grows in irrigated areas, the case for higher water rates and taxation of agricultural incomes becomes unanswerable. But attempts to restore better fiscal equilibrium through such measures have consistently foundered on the political rock. Wealthy landowners in a democracy can easily veto such proposals; and so far they have successfully done so.

Should power for rural areas be treated differently from irrigation water? There is no inherent reason why the government should be ultra-commercial about power and ultra-lenient about water, no reason, that is to say, except the force of tradition. For, the fact is that subsidized power will yield large indirect benefits in terms of employment, production, incomes, and taxable wealth, which will more than justify itself. There is thus an excellent case for supplying power at preferential rates to rural areas, and more particularly in the early promotional stage.

Today, however, there is no longer any need to press this case. The high-yielding varieties have greatly strengthened the economics of rural electrification. Power is an essential input for intensive agriculture based on the new seeds. Farmers, in increasing numbers, now recognize this fact; they are demanding more and more power; and, most significant of all, they are ready to pay for it the full economic price. This has clinched the old issue once and for all. It is no longer possible, even for the most confirmed cynic, to deny electricity to the rural areas on the ground of non-existence of load. The load is already there for all to see, and is rising sharply. It is now for the government to step up the supply rapidly enough to meet it.

[8] The record regarding India's post-independence electrification policy under the several Plans, observes an expert study, is "quite clear; the larger cities or towns were favoured and the smaller communities were quite consistently discriminated against in almost direct proportion to their size." *Market Towns and Spatial Development in India*, National Council of Applied Economic Research, New Delhi, 1965, p. 116.

## ELECTRIFICATION OF VILLAGES

Villages or pumpsets—which should be electrified? In recent years this question has come to occupy much attention, with pumpsets more and more gaining the upperhand. Yet today, they can no longer be regarded as alternatives. Rural India needs, and must have, both.

The first steps to electrify villages were taken, in the early 1930's, in Madras Province (now Tamil Nadu), followed by Mysore and Travancore (now the bulk of Kerala) which were the most progressive of India's 700 princely states. Power was supplied from Mettur and Krishnarajsagar dams, the first multi-purpose projects constructed in India to provide irrigation, generate electricity, and supply drinking water. As a result, even before independence hundreds of villages were electrified in this area.

For the country as a whole, however, progress was negligible—in 1951, on the eve of the First Plan, the number of villages electrified was 3,619 out of a total of 567,217. The states of Assam, Jammu and Kashmir, Madhya Pradesh, and Orissa did not have a single electrified village; Bihar and Rajasthan had three or four each.

The all-India figure for electrified villages rose gradually to: 9,886 in 1956; 25,358 in 1961; 44,380 in 1966; and 71,280 in 1969. The Fourth Plan has set a specific target for energizing irrigation pumpsets as seen earlier, but apparently none for electrifying villages. However, electrification of pumpsets, it may be presumed, will lead to electrification of villages as well in many instances.

The Fourth Plan reflects a policy shift which began in 1966. Until then, the main focus of the rural electrification programme was on the social objective, namely, provision of domestic and village street lighting. And except in a few states, particularly Tamil Nadu, Maharashtra, and Punjab, little attention was paid to its economic function, that is, stimulating production in the two principal sectors of the rural economy—agriculture and small industries. In fact, it is this failure to harness power for productive purposes which made the programme dependent on heavier subsidies and therefore financially more burdensome than need have been the case.

The new policy came in the wake of the drought, the food crisis, and the just-introduced high-yielding varieties. With its emphasis on energized pumpsets and minor irrigation, it sought to cash in quickly on the dwarf wheat and rice. This was the only course India could follow, once she was caught in a grave national emergency. But as a longer-range policy it is utterly inadequate. There is room, and need, to speed up pumpset electrification. Besides, electric power is needed for a good many other activities which must proceed side by side to sustain the green revolution, and, beyond that, to stimulate development in other sectors of the rural economy.

The present hand-to-mouth approach to power supply falls dangerously short even of the most pressing requirements, not to speak of the very substantial potential loads which, though now invisible to the naked eye, are bound to surface before long. The Fourth Plan targets, it is now quite obvious, must be revised upwards, promptly and boldly, to provide for rural electrification conceived in far more comprehensive terms. Otherwise what can be a most potent growth-generating force will, to the misfortune of all concerned, turn into one of the worst growth-inhibiting factors.

In August, 1969 the government of India created a Rural Electrification Corporation (REC) with a capital of Rs. 150 crores. This was a significant event, though it certainly did not come too soon. Indeed, it would have been far more appropriate if it had been established twenty years earlier with adequate funds and a clear mandate to bring electricity to India's villages as fast as possible, and to encourage its use on a broad front—in agriculture, in small industries, for small town and village electrification, in private homes—allowing initial promotional rates where warranted. This single factor alone would have made a world of difference not only to rural India, but to the country's economy as a whole.

What cannot but be deplored is that, even today, the REC has been given no such mandate. Its functions are still conceived in surprisingly narrow and timid terms—all it is required to do, at least in the foreseeable future, is to push ahead with the programme for energizing irrigation pumpsets. This simply is not good enough. It is high time to pump into the REC more courage, more funds, and more imagination.[8a]

## TASKS AHEAD

Put briefly, the most urgent needs of India now are twofold: a much bolder programme for power development and an aggressive policy for rural electrification.

The overall installed capacity, as seen earlier, rose from 5.65 million kW in 1960-61 to 14.5 million kW in 1968-69, or at an average rate of over one million kW a year. This was the case in spite of two wars and two droughts which, for a considerable length of time, threw the economy out of gear. In fact, almost half of the new capacity was added in the three years 1966-68 at an average annual rate of 1.3 million kW. The

[8a] In its first 30 months—through August 1972—REC had granted 274 project and 19 non-project loans for a total of Rs. 167 crores. The former would cover some 26,000 villages, 360,000 pumpsets (against its Fourth Plan target of 500,000 sets), and 56,000 rural industries. A sanctioned project takes three to five years for completion.

overall target of 23 million kW projected for March 1974 will give an average increase of 1.8 million kW per year. This grossly underestimates even the *actual* demand as it exists today, not to speak of the vast *potential* needs which, one may assume—and hope—will increasingly emerge out of their present dormant state.

Symptoms of a power shortage are already developing in many parts of the country. The spreading agricultural revolution will create new demand on a wide front; so also will the work of the REC if it pursues its tasks unflaggingly and in a business-like fashion. Industries—large, medium, and small—are expanding both in the public and the private sector; they must, if anything, continue to do so at a faster rate. To this should be added the rapid growth of population, especially in urban areas, which in many ways adds to the overall demand.

By all tokens, the Indian economy has, at long last, entered a phase where an all-round acceleration of its activities over the coming years can be confidently reckoned with, and this is bound to be reflected, both directly and indirectly, in a steeply rising demand for power. Not only that; a stepped-up programme of power generation and its countrywide distribution will give a tremendous impetus to India's overall economic development, just as, conversely, failure to do so will effectively frustrate the hopes of accelerated growth.

The value of rural electrification has, all along, been grossly underestimated in India. It has been, and to a large extent it still continues to be, one of the worst examples of penny-wise pound-foolish attitude. The pennies received for the kilowatt-hours of power sold were diligently counted while the pounds of wealth and income generated by the same kilowatt-hours were consistently ignored.

Rural electrification is a crucial component of rural development. And as such, it deserves the same high-priority treatment as irrigation canals, roads and communications, education and health services, on which the government readily makes heavy investments without insisting on an immediate economic *quid pro quo*, but knowing very well that they will, in due course, bring adequate rewards, both directly and indirectly. Yet hitherto rural electrification has been heavily discriminated against. For this the country has already paid a heavy penalty in terms of retarded growth.

If the past policy was shortsighted, it will be incomparably more so today. The high-yielding varieties have revolutionized the economics of rural electrification—they have made it an exceptionally high-yielding investment. Today it can more than pay its way, even by the conservative, "penny-counting" approach, while its multiplier effects are further multiplied. And here is the other side of the coin: without rural electrification and adequate supply of power to meet the steeply rising needs of the villages, the benefits of the high-yielding varieties will be largely lost,

40

and the green revolution will at best grind slowly, even if it does not come to a premature halt.

What, then, should be the targets for the Fourth Plan? As a late-starter in economic development, having lost much precious time through faulty planning in the last two decades, caught in a remorseless demographic spiral, and with the exciting possibilities opened up by the HYV's, India must raise her sights far above what she has so far aimed at. A doubling of her generating capacity—to 28-30 million kW within five years, and a quickening of the pace of electrification—to about 30,000 villages a year, compared with about 10,000 electrified in 1969—this is the order of magnitude that would answer India's needs today, and this is what she must plan for and work for. At this rate she will be able to electrify, within the next fifteen years, virtually all the 567,000 villages of India, and in any case the more densely populated ones which constitute the vast majority of them.

Luckily, India is well endowed as regards energy resources. She has coal deposits in abundance, though mostly of low grade; large water resources which can be harnessed for electricity—by March 1969 only seven per cent of the potential had been developed; and substantial deposits of thorium which can be used as nuclear fuel. Exploration for oil, begun in the fifties, has yielded some good results, and more should follow in due course. Lignite, natural gas, and refinery gas are being used, where economically feasible, for power generation.

The net installed capacity of 23.0 million kW, to be achieved by the end of the Fourth Plan, will consist of 9.42 million kW from hydro, 12.75 million kW from thermal, and 0.98 million kW from nuclear stations. Capacity, in all the three categories, can be expanded more rapidly; and the *known* energy resources should be adequate, for decades to come, to support a programme of vigorous expansion. In this respect India need fear no natural or physical constraint.

For the next ten years the requirements of electric power as assessed by the Energy Survey Committee, that is, 33.90 million kW in 1976 and 55.70 million kW in 1981, appear quite realistic in the sense that they are in line with India's pressing needs, and they also lie within her capacity to achieve.

The only caveat to be entered is that they should not be dogmatically tied down to a seven per cent growth in national income. The actual percentage growth may be, and will be, much higher: if the installed capacity is fully and efficiently utilized, which is even now not the case; if the energy generated is widely, and wisely, distributed throughout the country, with special emphasis on production, which is far from the case at present; and if power, like machinery, is used, especially in the countryside, to aid labour and augment its productivity, but in general not to displace it. A little power must be made to go a much longer way than in developed countries. Though an essential input for agriculture, industry, and a great many other activities, it must, in the vast majority of cases, be administered in small doses to drive small machinery as part of predominantly labour-intensive methods of production.

The Fourth Plan has drawn pointed attention to the need for better utilization of the existing capacity, which "is at present low. There is scope for improving efficiency of operation."[9]

Better capacity utilization, among other things, calls for integrated operation of state grid systems utilizing inter-state lines. In recent years much progress has been made in that direction. A Bihar-DVC-West Bengal grid has been established; the Mysore grid has been linked up with Tamil Nadu, Andhra Pradesh, and Kerala grids; Mysore-Maharashtra, Madhya Pradesh-Maharashtra, Kerala-Tamil Nadu lines were constructed in 1969. These and a few other interconnections have made better utilization of surplus power possible through inter-state transfers.

But there is still a long way to go. All power stations have to be interconnected to form state, zonal or super-grids, as was envisaged in the Third Plan, to pool capacities and to use them to the best possible advantage. And for this purpose the country has been divided into five regions, each with a Regional Electricity Board.

Progress with the transmission network has been rather slow, though it has picked up some speed in recent years. The network of 11 KV lines and above added up to only 58,400 circuit kilometres in 1955; it rose to 134,400 km in 1960-61, to 290,800 km in 1965-66, and then jumped to an estimated total of 485,200 km by March 1969. Clearly, the transmission systems need to be strengthened and improved, as emphasized in the Fourth Plan, though the Plan did not lay down any specific targets. It is essential, however, to achieve much faster progress than hitherto.

There remains the other task, namely, to bring power to India's 567,000 villages scattered over the whole country. This will call for the construction of a vast mileage of low-voltage transmission lines. The task is stupendous, but there is no escape from it. It must be tackled courageously with the maximum possible speed. Given the right policy, it should be possible to accomplish it in about fifteen years.

It takes time to build up the installed capacity. Neither the green revolution, nor rural India can any longer mark time. Both must be kept on the march. It is therefore of the utmost importance to make-do with

[9] *Fourth Five Year Plan*, p. 272. Clearly, the Plan has glossed over a dismal fact. The utilization of the installed capacity of power in the public sector averages at a miserable 50 per cent, or thereabouts, largely because of bad maintenance of plants resulting in frequent breakdowns. Contrast this with a utilization rate of 80 per cent or more achieved, for example, in Tata's power plants.

diesel oil and engines in many places until electric power is available. Such an interim solution, if adopted in a big way, can considerably hasten progress.

## THE FINANCIAL CONSTRAINT

But where is the money to finance a power programme of such dimensions? Can India really afford it? Planners are eternally tortured by these questions. Yet it is hard to extend to them the sympathy they so ostentatiously crave for if only because the torture is largely self-inflicted. What we are faced with is primarily not a *financial*, but a *planning* constraint, what is lacking is not money, but vision. The imperatives of the case are quite plain:

1. *Reorder priorities.* Power and rural electrification are, at this stage, perhaps the most important determinants of the future rate of development in India. To deny power to the villages is as good as to cut down on economic growth. From this follows the motto to guide the planners: Stint elsewhere if you must, but not on power development and certainly not on rural electrification.

2. *Mobilize private enterprise.* Private parties may be encouraged to come into the power business—for distribution, even generation. The public sector, instead of loading itself with more industries, could throw at least part of the burden on the private sector and devote to the power programme the resources thus released.[10]

3. *Use international programmes.* Both bilateral (especially USAID) and multilateral (IBRD, IDA, and UNDP) resources could be used to a greater extent for power development, curtailing, if necessary, other activities financed from these sources.

4. *Use suppliers' credit.* All power projects, if properly planned and managed, should more than pay their way in India today. Increased use of foreign suppliers' credit for building or expanding power stations would be fully warranted. And given the slacks in foreign economies—in the USA, for example, the industrial plant is operating at the abnormally low level of 72.3 per cent (in January 1971)—it should not be hard to negotiate such credits on a substantial scale and on reasonable terms.

5. *Expand credit.* The loud sighs about shortage of finance for energizing pumpsets are wholly unrealistic; and the "deposit scheme" now insisted upon as a precondition for giving electric connections is both unnecessary and cumbersome. They can all be financed by full-blooded expansion of credit at reasonable interest and subject to normal safeguards. The same mechanism can be used for a great many other productive projects—and this should definitely include electrification of

[10] See also Chapter 29, "Road to Survival."

villages—when credits are needed for short or medium terms not exceeding, say, 24 months.[11]

6. *Use PL480 rupee funds.* The REC has been funded with Rs. 150 crores, of which the Government of India provided Rs. 45 crores and the balance of Rs. 105 crores came from the PL480 funds. This can serve as a useful precedent. Most of over 4 billion dollars worth of rupee funds, accumulated by July 1968 under PL480 agreements, is available for economic development in India. The financial purists who feel scared at the very thought of credit expansion may find less objection, on grounds of legitimacy, in making liberal use of these massive funds.[12]

To conclude, the shortage of finance is a figment of imagination. There may be a real shortage, though—of material and equipment, of trained man-power, i.e. experts, technicians, and administrators, and of the right kind of organization. What is necessary is to mobilize the *real* resources now available to make the best possible use of them, and to expand them further so as to achieve the required targets. It is time to start worrying about *these* resources, just as it is time to stop worrying about lack of finance.

## LET THERE BE LIGHT

What Lenin called his "dream of electricity" has become a folklore of history. In the developed countries the use of power has long been widespread; and consumption per head has been mounting, sometimes at a spectacular rate. In the USA, for example, where per capita power consumption is the highest in the world, it is growing at a compound rate of 7 per cent a year, thus doubling in ten years.

In the underdeveloped countries, however, electricity still remains very largely a dream. In this respect India has been no exception. True, villages in South India were electrified even before independence, and more have been added since then. But the general picture in the country—for seven out of eight villages—is still dark.

One of the main reasons for India's economic backwardness lies right here. To argue that power-operated irrigation pumpsets had to wait until the arrival of the HYV's, and until the country was plunged into a disastrous food crisis, is sheer nonsense. To overlook what powerlooms and a host of other electrified tools and equipment for small industries could do to spur the rural economy in the last fifty years, or even in the two decades since independence, is to betray a rare economic myopia, a phenomenon all the more baffling because of the striking contrast it presents to the sparkling example of Japan.

Historically, electricity has been the most important single lever of economic progress. That is because its benefits radiate far and wide, and

[11] and [12] Discussed further in Chapter 27. "The Credit Shackles."

penetrate into every nook and corner of life. It not only alleviates manual labour, raises man-hour output, and builds up earnings; it also demonstrates, in the most compelling fashion, the fruits of modern science to the simple village folks, switches their minds from traditionalism to modernism, and sparks the desire for better living—with better food, more adequate clothing, and healthier children in a more decent home. Rural electrification has a tremendous psychological value. It invariably produces an electrifying effect on traditional society.

This magic power of electricity has, to some extent, been pre-empted by the miracle wheat and rice. The dwarfs, preceding large-scale electrification, have baptised rural India in modernism; under their impact the barriers of traditionalism have begun to crumble. This, however, is only the beginning of the process. Rural electrification is needed today to reinforce it, to continue the transformation the dwarfs have begun, and to realize the promise of abundance they have brought with them.

Of the multiplier effects of rural electrification not the least important is the impact it can make on the multiplying population. By the kind of alchemy referred to above, the mind is attuned to better planning for modern living. The value of electricity thus transcends its value as a production input for agriculture, industries, and what not. It can serve as an invaluable family-planning input.

The twin programmes—for high-yielding varieties (HYVP) and for rural electrification—hold out the best hopes for India to overcome her twin problems—of food and population. They are not only complementary, but can greatly reinforce each other. Both must therefore be pushed ahead vigorously.

The Planning Commission recognized, though rather lamely, the "special significance" of rural electrification in the development of rural economy. Apart from providing power for agricultural purposes, small-scale industries, and domestic use, "it helps in modernizing the outlook of people living in rural areas," and has therefore been "accorded importance in the Plan."[13]

The Commission did suggest a target of 110,000 villages to be electrified during 1966-71, which was subsequently scrapped, while the final version of the Fourth Plan laid its primary emphasis on energizing pumpsets. This target should be revived, stepped up to 30–35,000 villages a year, and rapidly implemented, without prejudice, however, to the pumpset programme.

The Commission also laid down a price policy for electricity undertakings which was solemnly reactionary and treasury-oriented. This should be scrapped and replaced by a frankly development-oriented approach.

[13] *Fourth Five Year Plan—A Draft Outline*, 1966, p. 228. These words, perhaps significantly enough, were deleted from the Fourth Plan's final version.

Let there be light, at long last, in India's villages. It will dispel darkness —of the mind as well. It is time for the Government to see light, and for the Planning Commission to be energized.

## POSTSCRIPT ON POWER FAMINE

This Chapter was written about three years ago (in fall 1969). The "massive power famine" predicted therein has, it seems, already arrived. "Load-shedding," a euphemism for power cuts, is gaining both in frequency and in duration, especially in the north-eastern states. And it means "shedding" of industrial production, of amenities like lights and fans, and of food.

In summer, 1972 drought once again hit many parts of India. Perhaps its most tragic, and paradoxical, consequence could be seen in West Bengal. Tens of thousands of acres could not be planted to rice in time for lack of water, and there was no water because the unlimited underground supply could not be tapped for lack of wells, pumps, and power!

Even in Punjab-Haryana, as the writer found during a visit, existing pumps worked fitfully with too many stoppages at arbitrary hours because power had to be "rationed"!

That the fate of the green revolution hinges on assured irrigation is now better appreciated in India. But she has yet to see more clearly how assured irrigation hinges on assured power supply. The only way India can combat the vagaries of the monsoon is by systematically exploiting the vast supply of water stored underground at varying depths. And the only way she can do so is through millions of wells dotting the countryside and operating with energized pumpsets.

In addition, power, as seen above, is needed for a great many other things to propel the green revolution. In short, in today's India power, like water, means food.

CHAPTER 22

# Education, Research, Extension

## 1. TOWARDS AGRICULTURAL UNIVERSITIES

### A MINDLESS SYSTEM

Thoughtful people have long bewailed the system of education as it has developed in India. Its hallmarks are common knowledge: heavy emphasis on liberal arts, little science at school and college, very little research even at university level, outdated curricula, outmoded tools and methods of teaching, high premium on rote learning, little concern for creative thinking. It is a mindless system divorced from life, and therefore incapable of improving the quality of life. In a scathing parody, Tagore called it "the parrot's learning."

The design was not an accident. The central purpose of education, as officially declared at its inception, was "preparing natives for public employment." The shortest, and cheapest, route to that goal was a few universities, each with a large number of widely-scattered colleges affiliated to it, and each college dedicated to one solemn objective: to prepare its students for university examinations, mostly by massive cramming which was treated as synonymous with teaching and learning.

Incidentally, this method fitted easily with India's own tradition. After all, her priceless scriptures, such as the Vedas and the Upanishads, had been carried, literally, from head to head for a thousand years or more in what was history's most gigantic feat of memory. From memorizing Sanskrit it was but a short step to memorize English when this was made the medium of education and was badly taught everywhere except in a handful of British-run schools.

What the students coveted most was the degree, the only recognized passport to jobs in government offices; and what they dreaded most was the examination—for it was all a one-time affair, and they knew that the marks they obtained would make or mar their whole career. The one "big examination" method was always a big gamble. Students by tens of thousands were drawn into it every year, and a great many of them became casualties for no fault of theirs.

Some vintage universities—that is, of the residential type—were subsequently established at Dacca, Aligarh and Banaras, but the few swallows could not usher in a summer in India's education. The University Education Commission of 1949[1] had few complimentary things to say about the system. In particular, it singled out the university examinations, as they had been functioning for almost half a century, as "one of its worst features." The external examination system, in the Commission's view, was unreliable, inadequate, inappropriate for measuring what it was supposed to measure, not objective enough since the marks awarded were influenced by the examiner's personal bias; it subordinated teaching to examination and was therefore unable to provide true education and to stimulate wider interests; and it opened the door to cheating, corruption and favouritism. The fact that a university degree was treated as the minimum requirement even for petty clerical posts had a degrading effect on university education, apart from other evils for which it was directly responsible.

Two conspicuous victims in this sterile environment of non-education were social sciences and agriculture. For both require a great deal of local research, at least of an adaptive type, and research was the last thing Indian education provided for or cared for. In economics, for example, the principles copied from prescribed textbooks, however sound they might be, could not by themselves dictate sound policies for development; their underlying premises needed to be carefully examined in every specific instance and consciously adapted to an entirely different local environment. Of this there was not the slightest suggestion. As a result, economic policies were, only too often, trapped in fallacies of false premises borrowed from abroad and thoughtlessly applied to a totally different set of circumstances. Some theoreticians, at least by implication, blamed the realities for being different and not fitting their pet premises!

India's political leaders, especially under Gandhiji's inspiring leadership, instinctively sensed this grave weakness. But instead of correcting it by insisting on a strictly scientific approach to the problems of the day, they chose to turn their backs on science itself, and sought the future of the nation in its outdated past.

Similarly, in agriculture, which is a biological industry, no progress can

[1] Apart from its Chairman, Dr. S. Radhakrishnan, later President of India (1956-67), the Commission consisted of nine outstanding educationists—six from India, two from Britain, and one from the U.S.A.

41

be made without extensive local research, if only to adapt available knowledge to local conditions, and this involves a broad spectrum of sciences—plant genetics, soil chemistry, agronomy, plant pathology entomology, to mention only the most obvious, If agriculture can get nowhere without research, research can get nowhere without a well-organized system of education to produce competent scientists who would undertake the needed research and would, among other things, evolve improved strains of plants and animals, better cultural practices and better methods of animal care, and would relay them persuasively to the farmers through effective field demonstration. For this India's education made no provision. Indeed, the very idea remained foreign to her for a long time.

In 1928, the Royal Commission on Agriculture deplored this omission and underscored the importance of research in emphatic terms: However efficient might be the organization built up for demonstration and propaganda, it observed, "unless it was based on the solid foundations provided by research, it was merely a foundation built on sand." An identical view, it may be noted in passing, was expressed about Mexico in 1941 by the Survey Commission of the Rockefeller Foundation (see Chapter 3).

In 1937, Sir John Russel, Director of Rothamsted Experimental Station, after reviewing the state of India's agriculture, observed that "in general, the men who actually till the soil are scarcely touched by the national programme of agricultural education."[2]

The Royal Commission gave an impetus to an expansion of facilities for education and research in agriculture. On the eve of independence, India had 17 agricultural colleges with about 1500 students enrolled annually. In addition, there were several institutions, commodity committees, and ad hoc bodies. But education, and also research to the extent it existed, remained too fragmented and disjointed; in general, they made no impact on farming to increase production.

There were, of course, exceptions, and some outstanding ones, all in the field of commercial crops which happened to be of special interest to particular industries. Among the leading beneficiaries of research were jute and tea, the two leading commodities for export. Sugarcane was another; its famous CO varieties rapidly spread over the country and became the backbone of an expanding sugar industry. Other crops to benefit from research in varying degrees were lac, coffee, rubber and tobacco.

But the exceptions only proved the rule. Food crops, which accounted for 85 per cent of India's agricultural production, suffered from con-

[2] Quoted by Dr. K. C. Naik, Vice-Chancellor, University of Agricultural Sciences, Bangalore, in *A History of Agricultural Universities*, USAID, New Delhi, 1968. The writer has relied on this excellent study for much of the historical facts used in this section,

spicuous neglect—even in the face of widespread starvation, fast-rising population, and a widening food deficit. The University Education Commission of 1949 found the trend disconcerting. The country's food situation, in its view, was "pathetic."

In sum, education and research, as developed in India over the years, were wholly inadequate in quantity, mostly poor in quality, badly organized, and, in general, divorced from production. The imprint of all this was writ large, above all, on one simple fact—the low productivity of India's agriculture. Almost all along the line, it was—and still is—one of the lowest in the world.

## THE SEEDS OF REFORM

The year 1960 marks the beginning of a revolution in India's education. The first Agricultural University, established in that year at Pantnagar in Uttar Pradesh (UPAU), introduced a new breed of educational institution which is destined not only to spur agriculture, but also to blaze a trail to creative education in general.

The UPAU was followed, in quick succession, by six similar universities, planted respectively in Rajasthan, Orissa, Punjab, Andhra Pradesh, Madhya Pradesh and Mysore. In addition, the Indian Agricultural Research Institute assumed much of the function of an agricultural university, and so did the Kalyani University in West Bengal.

All this was achieved within the brief space of six years, by 1966. That year another Education Commission, headed by Dr. D. S. Kothari, gave strong support to the concept of agricultural universities, and recommended that the minimum goal should be to establish at least one such university in every state.

The new institutions, needless to say, did not mushroom on unprepared ground. Behind them lay at least a decade of intellectual ferment characterized by intense debate, and of relentless effort and hard struggle, especially to overcome the entrenched forces of status quo.

In this case the seeds of change were sown, in 1949, by the University Education Commission referred to earlier, or more precisely, by one of its most rebelliously creative members, Dr. Arthur E. Morgan, the first TVA Chairman. It was his impassioned plea that swayed the Commission to accept his proposal to establish a series of Rural Universities in India, modelled on the Land-Grant colleges of the USA, to bridge the gulf between the universities and the realities of life, to break down the isolation of rural India, to bring the benefits of science and technology to the farming community, to free education from its deadweight, and to turn it into a vehicle of progress.

The idea bore the distinctive stamp of Dr. Morgan's sharp intellect and his fiery social conscience. But it was too novel, and too exotic, to find favour with people wedded to a rigid past. Veteran educationists of India frowned upon the very concept of a single-faculty university devoted, of all things, to agriculture. Others were ready to reject outright the proposal to bring under one roof agricultural education, research, and extension which languished, futilely, in the cosy corners of numerous ill-equipped and poorly-staffed institutions scattered over the country. The state agriculture departments, in particular, were loath to shed the functions they had long been inured to; most of them resented the thought that their extension wing might be clipped.

At the same time, the Congress Party had come to power with a long and loud commitment to rural development. After independence, it was anxious to translate it into action in accordance with its party plank. Dr. Morgan's concept of rural universities appeared too radical—perhaps also too ambitious—to evoke wholehearted enthusiasm. And so its "rural" part was warmly acclaimed, but its university-based approach was quietly ignored.

The result was a massive commitment, starting with 1952, to the Community Development Programme with CD blocks and a National Extension Service.[3] Then came the decision, in 1955, to establish a series of "Rural Institutes." The initiative, in this case, was taken by the Central Ministry of Education. In designing the new institutes it sponsored, the Ministry, strangely enough, paid no heed to the recommendation the high-level Education Commission of 1949 had made about rural universities modelled on the Land-Grant colleges of the USA. What the Commission had urged was to set up institutions in rural areas to channel science and technology in order to build up India's agriculture. What the CDP and the Rural Institutes sought to achieve was rural development *sans* science and *sans* technology. And so they ended up by creating low-yielding programmes and activities backed by sprawling bureaucracies.

## A MONUMENTAL STRUGGLE

The seeds of reform sown by the University Education Commission failed to germinate; even to start with, they needed a good deal of groundwork which was not forthcoming. Instead, the task was vastly complicated by the high-spirited, but ill-considered commitments made on a grandiose scale.

However, luck favoured India in this case. The vision, coupled with almost passionate concern, of some outstanding scientists from the USA helped rescue the original Morgan concept—they shaped and moulded it, and piloted it skilfully through shoals of misconceptions and barely submerged hostilities, until a series of agricultural universities was firmly established in the country. The yeoman's service they rendered has been

[3] See Chapter 8.

ably described by Dr. Naik and others, and only its highlights need be noted here.

A major turning-point was the arrival of Dr. Frank W. Parker, in 1953, as chief agricultural advisor to the US Embassy in New Delhi. A staunch believer in the US land-grant system, Dr. Parker became a pillar of support for the proposal to establish agricultural universities on similar lines. The ice was broken with the execution of Operation Agreement No. 28 between the TCM (now AID) and the Government of India, which bore the title "Project for Assistance to Agricultural Research, Education and Extension Organizations," and was signed on 30 April, 1954.

Following this, a Joint Indo-American Team was set up, in November 1954, with three Indian specialists in addition to its chairman, and three specialists from the USA. The Indian members toured extensively in the USA studying research and educational activities there, while the US members surveyed and evaluated the situation in India. In September 1955, the Team submitted its report with comprehensive recommendations, in which it endorsed the 1949 proposal for agricultural universities and spelled out at length their functions and organizational pattern. The Team's report became the foundation for future development in this field.

In this long and uphill path the next milestone was a supplement to the Operating Agreement No. 28, under which TCM entered into contracts with five US land-grant universities, all intended to strengthen agricultural institutions in India and to promote cooperation and coordination in research and education.

At first the five advisory teams drawn from American universities were assigned to five regions with the broad responsibility to work with the agricultural and veterinary colleges located within each region. This led to a diffusion of effort since the areas were too large and the institutions were too many and too scattered. The situation was soon remedied; when India decided to set up agricultural universities, the teams were concentrated on them to provide support on a continuous basis.

In 1956, Dr. H. W. Hannah, associate dean of the University of Illinois, drew up a blueprint for a rural university, "rural" in this case being treated as virtually synonymous with "agricultural." This became the basis for formulating the first detailed proposal to establish an agricultural university in Terai, U.P.; and it also stimulated interest in other states for similar institutions. But the Government of India, still inclined to move slowly, decided that only one such university should be established, on an experimental basis, during the Second Plan period. And since UP was the first state to submit a complete plan for one, it was also the first to get it, although the actual establishment of the UPAU was delayed until 1960.

But things did not rest there. Other states began to stake their claims for agricultural universities; soon there was a groundswell for the new institution, and this induced the government to move faster. A second Joint Indo-American Team was set up, in 1959, with four US experts (three deans of land-grant universities and a representative of the US Department of Agriculture) and eight Indian members, mostly agricultural scientists. Its main terms of reference were to assess the progress made in agricultural education, research and extension in India over the preceding five years and to make specific recommendations to strengthen them further during the Third Plan period (1961-66).

In its report, submitted in July 1960, the Team made three major recommendations. First, pressure was building up in the country for agricultural universities, but most states had only a nebulous notion about their structure, aims and *modus operandi*; some, at least, treated it as a quick panacea for the prevailing ills. While favouring a positive response in principle, the Team also urged that approval should be withheld until some basic conditions were satisfied, in particular: autonomy of the new institution; concentration of agricultural, veterinary and animal husbandry, home science, technological and science colleges on the same campus; and integration of education, research, and extension.

Second, the Indian Council of Agricultural Research (ICAR) should be greatly strengthened, and for this purpose it should be given full control, both technical and administrative, over all agricultural research activities. More specifically, all Central Research Institutes and all Commodity Committees should be brought under its direct control.

And, third, all the US advisory teams provided by USAID under the Inter-University Contract Programme should be concentrated in fewer institutions, more particularly those that showed the best prospects to grow into universities.

These recommendations were officially accepted as a basis for further action. Meanwhile, some senior Indian specialists, sponsored by USAID and the Rockefeller Foundation, visited land-grant institutions in the USA and prepared studies highlighting the vital role they played in US agriculture. These studies reinforced the general interest in agricultural universities and helped further crystallize the fundamentals about their structure and operations.

### THE FIRST HARVEST

By 1961, India had espoused the idea of land-grant type of institutions. Proposals for them flowed in from the states. And it was also time to prepare the Third Plan. The government therefore decided to set up a few more agricultural universities. But it had to choose from among competing proposals sponsored by the states, and it was also necessary to process them and to cast them in the right mould. This sensitive task was entrusted to a small Committee headed by Dr. Ralph W. Cummings, then Field Director of the Rockefeller Foundation programme in India.[4]

The Cummings Committee, as it came to be called, did a magnificent job of persuasion. It held discussions at the Centre and in the states; reviewed critically, but constructively the state governments' draft legislation for agricultural universities; and sought to salvage their basic principles, particularly the concentration of research in the universities and its integration with teaching and extension.

The task was unusually difficult because of a hardened tradition; but it was desperately urgent if India's agriculture were ever to escape from an old rut. There were, at that time, 53 agricultural colleges and 17 veterinary colleges—all under state governments except a few privately-managed colleges in the first category. Training of agricultural graduates rested with the existing universities, but research and extension activities were in charge of the departments of agriculture and community development. The link between the two was tenuous, and the exchange of ideas and experience virtually nonexistent. A system based on such an artificial dichotomy was incapable of serving the farmers.

The Cummings Committee succeeded, to a great extent, in remedying this structural defect, while facilitating the groundwork for the first batch of agricultural universities, which have been established at Ludhiana, Udaipur, Jabalpur, Hyderabad, Bangalore, and Bhubaneswar respectively. In addition, the Kalyani University of West Bengal, which was set up by a special Act in 1960, has been recognized by the Centre as equivalent to an agricultural university. And all of them were preceded by the elevation of the Indian Agricultural Research Institute (IARI) to the status of a university, with effect from 1958, when a large post-graduate school was established there with a training programme patterned largely on the land-grant system (see below).

The universities now in operation are listed below,[5] along with the US land-grant universities which, under USAID's Operation Agreement 28, are providing continuing assistance to them:

| Name | Operative since | Aided from US by |
|---|---|---|
| 1. Uttar Pradesh A. U., Pantnagar | July 1960 | AID/University of Illinois |
| 2. University of Udaipur, Rajasthan | October 1963 | AID/Ohio State University |
| 3. Orissa University of Agriculture and Technology, Bhubaneswar | August 1962 | AID/University of Missouri |

[4] The other members of the Committee were: Dr. Ephriam Hixon of USAID; Dr. L. Sahai, Animal Husbandry Commissioner, India; and Dr. K. C. Naik, now Vice-Chancellor, University of Agricultural Sciences, Bangalore.

[5] To the family of India's AU's should be added the recently established Haryana Agricultural University at Hissar, which is developing into an impressive institution.

| Name | | Operative since | Aided from US by |
|---|---|---|---|
| 4. Punjab A.U., Ludhiana | | October 1962 | AID/Ohio State University |
| 5. Andhra Pradesh A.U., Rajendranagar | | May 1964 | AID/Kansas State University |
| 6. Jawaharlal Nehru A.U., Jabalpur, Madhya Pradesh | | October 1964 | AID/University of Illinois |
| 7. University of Agricultural Sciences, Bangalore, Mysore | | August 1964 | AID/University of Tennessee |
| 8. Kalyani University, Kalyani, West Bengal[6] | | 1960 | AID/University of Missouri (occasional) |
| 9. Assam A.U., Jorhat | | 1969 | — do — |
| 10. Maharashtra A.U., Poona | | 1969 | AID/Pennsylvania State University |
| 11. IARI, New Delhi, elevated to A.U. with Graduate School | | 1958 | The Rockefeller Foundation |

The Kothari Commission on Education, which submitted its report immediately after the drought years, in June 1966, was eloquent in its support of the agricultural universities. Their role, it emphasized, should be: to increase and disseminate knowledge related to agriculture, based on both basic and applied research; to undertake teaching and research primarily to solve immediate economic and social problems of the rural areas; to develop and teach a wide range of sciences and technologies in order to build up the rural economy; not only to teach undergraduate, postgraduate and research students, but also to give technical training to young people not aiming at degrees, and to provide education, on a continuing basis, to adults and others not enrolled as students. Finally, as noted before, the Commission urged that at least one such university should be established in every state.

The last recommendation has been accepted by the government in principle. The Fourth Plan provides for six additional universities to be established during the Plan period so that, by 1974, every state may be equipped with one agricultural university.

India has come a long way, almost at a breakneck pace, with her new institutions. A decade of floundering has been followed by a decade of progress that is truly phenomenal. Problems, of course, persist—problems of staffing and funding; of upgrading the quality of teaching, training and research; of further streamlining the organizational structure; of working out the right kind of relationships between the new universities and the

---

[6] The weakest of the AU's is the Kalyani University of West Bengal. Should it be a composite university or a straightforward AU? The controversy still remains unresolved. The absence of a dynamic AU is another potent factor contributing to the deplorable state of West Bengal's agriculture.

concerned ministries and departments, and between the scientists and the administrators; of strengthening their autonomy; in short, of clinching the victories the new system has won over a static and chaotic past.[7]

However, the foundations of the land-grant type of institutions have been solidly laid. Some of them have forged ahead and have already established brilliant records of performance. The utility—nay, the indispensability—of the system has been abundantly demonstrated. The whole trend has been immeasurably strengthened by the glittering successes achieved in producing new varieties with astoundingly high yields.

India's agriculture has been finally caught in the dynamics of the scientific age. There can be no more turning back. It is now destined to move forward despite adverse factors. The pace can be considerably quickened if the directions already set are unswervingly adhered to and the basic policies already laid down are unflinchingly carried out.

## II. REORGANIZATION OF RESEARCH

### ROCKEFELLER FOUNDATION'S INDIA PROGRAMHE

Soon after Dr. Frank Parker had dusted off the proposal for rural universities and given it the first big push with a Joint Indo-American Team, another memorable step was taken in a cognate field to propel India's agriculture in the same direction.

The India-Rockefeller Foundation programme was signed in April 1956 with a twofold object in view: to develop a post-graduate school at IARI and to improve maize, sorghum and millet production in India. The second part was broadened later to embrace wheat, rice and other crops.[8]

The first task was entrusted to Dr. Ralph W. Cummings who, from January 1957, became the field director of the Foundation's India programme; and in that capacity he played a dominant role in modernizing agricultural education in India. The goal set for IARI was refreshingly high—in due course it was to equal the best post-graduate agricultural institutions in the world. Plans were drawn up accordingly; the first batch of students—150 in all—were admitted, in 1958, to what was India's first graduate school in agriculture; Dr. Cummings headed it for a year as acting dean during its formative phase. Since then IARI has been turning

[7] For detailed analysis of the outstanding problems, see: K. C. Naik, op. cit., and Roger Revelle, "Education for Agriculture in India," in *The World Food Problem*, President's Report, loc. cit., Vol. III, Chapter 5. Dr. Revelle also gives an assessment of India's manpower needs for agricultural development, as follows: university graduates, postgraduates and doctoral level in 13 specified categories—256,000; and persons with training at diploma level—300,000 to 600,000.

[8] For a detailed account of the contributions made by the Rockefeller Foundation to India's agriculture, see Carroll Streeter's *India : A Partnership*, op. cit.; also Dr. Naik's study, ibid.

out some 100 students a year on an average with advanced degrees in agriculture.

As for crop improvement, the main attention, to start with, was focussed on maize (corn). Though nowhere near rice and wheat in importance, corn is nonetheless a significant food crop in India, fourth in acreage—currently over 12 million acres, and eighth in production—around 5 million tons a year. Moreover, there was the example of the USA which had achieved tremendous success with hybrid corn. It was therefore widely assumed that in India, too, hybrid corn would flourish readily and provide the quickest route to a big increase in food production.

After the Bengal famine of 1943, maize had, in fact, been given somewhat more attention. A breeding programme was started under ICAR auspices; its results were, however, much too modest, giving yield increases of some 20 per cent. Later, TCM attempted, as one of its earliest projects in India, to breed hybrid corn from material imported from the USA, but once again little real headway was made.

Meanwhile, IARI experimented with hybrids imported from the USA and Australia, and obtained yields about double those from locally-developed varieties. But to move the hybrids from the research station to the farmers' fields proved an impossible task.

The biggest obstacle was the lack of a seed industry, and hybrid corn happens to be particularly demanding in this respect: its seeds have to be reproduced every year under strictly controlled conditions to ensure the purity of the inbred lines the hybrid is derived from, a condition India was totally unable to comply with.

There were, of course, other obstacles relating in particular to field-testing of the new varieties, determination of cultural practices for specific locations, extension work, input supplies, and price support.

A new chapter in corn-breeding—indeed, in plant-breeding—began with the arrival, in 1954, of the two leading corn specialists of the Rockefeller Foundation, Dr. Edwin J. Wellhausen, and Dr. U. J. Grant, then working in Mexico and Colombia respectively. The conclusions they arrived at after extensive surveys and consultations were: the native varieties had genetic limitations, and the spectrum they covered was not broad enough; they were not fertilizer-responsive; they were, in addition, susceptible to numerous diseases; the hybrids bred from imported US materials suited at best the more temperate climate of the hilly north, but not the plains down below.

These findings dictated the next step. To develop an effective corn-breeding programme India needed new germplasms of tropical and subtropical origin. Accordingly, germplasms were imported from Mexico, Central America, the Caribbeans, and, to some extent, also from the southern region of the USA. The breeders, now well armed with a richly diversified germplasm bank, set about their work.

But the breeding work needed a broad enough base; it had to be organized on a country-wide basis, with facilities for varietal testing in different regions; at the same time, it had to be effectively coordinated, with provision for careful scrutiny and evaluation of the results. And so, in 1957, at the suggestion of the Rockefeller Foundation, the Indian Council of Agricultural Research (ICAR) established an All-India Coordinated Maize Breeding Scheme (AICMBS). Four main research stations and nine substations were set up so as to cover all major variations in the conditions obtaining in the maize-growing areas.

IARI, as one of the four main stations, also became the coordinating centre for the whole project. The Rockefeller Foundation was requested to provide a Joint Coordinator. The first corn specialist to serve in that capacity was Dr. Grant who was succeeded, in 1959, by Dr. Ernest W. Sprague.

AICMBS brought together all the maize scientists of India for exchange and cross-fertilization of ideas and experience, all directed towards one central purpose, namely, to improve a single crop of major economic significance to the country. Such a nationwide pooling of talent and experience bred a new spirit of teamwork among the scientists, and this, in turn, made the breeding programme vastly more effective—in scope, quality and speed. Because of the outstanding success it achieved, AICMBS became the harbinger—and the model—for a whole series of all-India coordinated projects for crop improvement—for wheat, rice, sorghum and millets among others.

It took about eighteen months of crisscrossing with germplasms before the breeders were able to make a preliminary selection of four hybrids. Two of these—Deccan and Ganga 101—have stood the test of time, and they still figure among the leading hybrid corns of India.

To breed better varieties is one thing, to propagate and disseminate them is quite another. Once the four hybrids were selected and officially released for cultivation, the need for a modern seed industry suddenly loomed large. It was absolutely essential to overcome this bottleneck if India were to make any progress at all with hybrid corn and improved varieties of other crops. A committee was therefore appointed to work out a detailed plan for developing an adequate seed industry in India. The plan it prepared[9] became the blueprint for the National Seeds Corporation (NSC), which was established, in 1961, as a Central Government agency. Since then NSC has been the driving force behind this vital industry.

[9] The Committee worked about a year on the project, and as noted in Chapter 17, it received valuable guidance from the late Dr. Will M. Myers who, prior to his death, was Vice-President of the Rockefeller Foundation, and, on a more continuous basis, from Dr. A. A. Johnson, who later became Director of the Ford Foundation's agricultural programme in India.

The maize hybrids bred in India could claim a truly international parentage. Genes of Mexican and Central American origin supplied the capacity to stand high temperatures along with resistance to insects and diseases; genes from the small island of Antigua reduced the vulnerability to stem borers; Cuba's contribution was a bright orange colour and a hard, flinty type of endosperm; the US corn boosted the yield. As with wheat and rice, the breeders' primary objective was to combine high yield, strong resistance to insects and diseases, and good grain quality. As for the last attribute, India's preference was for orange or yellow colour and flinty endosperm, but the white colour, dent-type varieties are also coming into vogue.

To increase the yield further, the maize-breeders are now working on a different plant-type, similar to that of wheat and rice, and, for the same reasons. It should be short-statured, sturdy and non-lodging, erect-leafed, and able to absorb large doses of fertilizers. Apparently, such varieties are now in an advanced state of development and are due to be released before long.

Meanwhile, attempts to increase disease-resistance have continued unabated. Stalk rots and downy mildew have posed some tough problems. However, the scientists are confident that the problems can be overcome —through a combination of better agronomic practices and continued breeding effort with new and more resistant strains.

On the quality side, the breeders are endeavouring to increase the protein—particularly the lysine—content of the grain. Here again, success seems within reach. The two genes—opaque-2 and floury-2—isolated by scientists at Purdue University have made it possible to breed high-lysine varieties of corn.[10] Indan corn-breeders are now working towards that goal, and it should not be long before they are able to release some suitable varieties with higher protein content.

Hybrids, as noted earlier, must be grown from new seeds every year; and the seeds must be produced under stringent scientific control; otherwise they will lose their hybrid vigour. This is a difficult condition to satisfy in the present state of India's seed industry. The task is further complicated by the fact that there is no corn-belt *per se* in India; corn cultivation is spread rather thinly over the whole country, which tremendously aggravates the problem of seed distribution. To get over this hurdle, scientists are aiming at a somewhat different objective—to breed the so-called composite or synthetic varieties which will have a twofold advantage: their seeds can be multiplied much more easily, while farmers can save and use the same seed for four to five years without sacrificing much of the yield potential. Several composites have already been devel-

---

[10] For a discussion of the importance of this nutritional breakthrough, see President's Report, loc. cit., Vol. II, esp. pp. 224, 329-30.

oped, and some (Vijay and Kissan) have met with outstanding success under field conditions.

During the 1960's, ten home-bred hybrids were released in India. In terms of actual production, however, the record so far has been rather mixed. Over a 10-year period corn production has gone up by 75 per cent; of this, 30 per cent is attributed to increased acreage, and 45 per cent to higher acre-yield. In general, farmers have been willing, even eager, to cultivate hybrid maize where conditions are favourable, physically and economically. In Mysore state, for example, practically no maize was grown until about the mid-sixties. Then, in four years, it spread over 200,000 acres.

Nevertheless, there is no denying the fact that, in overall terms, hybrid maize is nowhere near redeeming the high expectations it had originally aroused. The factors already noted should be enough to explain the slow progress, namely, the problem of hybrid seed supply, scattered cultivation in what are often inaccessible areas, weak extension service, and, last but not least, an uncertain price policy.[11]

There was yet another factor, perhaps even more decisive: the arrival of dwarf wheat followed by dwarf rice. As crops, both are far more important in India than corn; they also posed fewer problems, and gave far bigger yields; and so it was easy for them to steal the limelight from hybrid corn. Dwarf wheat, in particular, was most favourably placed—in terms of yield potential and of the number and character of the problems to be resolved; and this enabled it to stage a stormy progress.

Yet the contribution hybrid corn has already made to India's agriculture should not be overlooked, nor its future underrated. It has, for one thing, scored a number of thumping firsts. It has been instrumental in bringing together outstanding US scientists and their Indian counterparts; it has set an inspiring example of genetic engineering based on diversified germplasms collected from far afield; it has ushered in an era of co-ordinated crop improvement projects on a countrywide basis with intimate teamwork among the specialists for each crop; it has spurred the establishment of a seed industry in India based on modern science and technology.

Another valuable offshoot of the work on hybrid corn done in India is the Inter-Asian Corn Programme which has spearheaded corn improvement in the entire region, with collaboration among scientists from about a dozen countries. Corn growing is expanding in the region, and a boom in corn is clearly in the making.[12]

Hybrid corn has, in many ways, blazed the trail for dwarf wheat and rice; this has, no doubt, helped them to come so far and so fast. The process, it seems, has now been reversed; the dwarfs, very much in the

[11] See Chapter 23 on Price Support.
[12] Carroll Streeter gives some interesting details, ibid., pp. 45-46.

lead for some time, are paving the way also for hybrid corn which is sure to come more vigorously into play, often as part of multiple-cropping cycles,[13] to produce more food for humans as well as for animals.

All in all, the future of hybrid corn in India's agriculture seems fully assured. And the current decade may very well see a spectacular rise in its acreage and production, thereby redeeming fully, though somewhat belatedly, its earlier promise.

## RESTRUCTURING ICAR

The Second Joint Indo-American Team had emphasized, in 1960, the need to strengthen the Indian Council of Agricultural Research. As mentioned above, it wanted full control, both technical and administrative, over all agricultural research activities to be vested exclusively in the Council; and so it urged, *inter alia*, that all the Central Research Institutes and the Commodity Committees, including the Central Sugarcane Committee, should be placed directly in its charge.

About three years later the problem was investigated, more incisively and comprehensively, by the Agricultural Research Review Team, often referred to as the Parker Committee since it was headed by Dr. Marion Wesley Parker of USDA. The Committee, under its terms of reference, was required to suggest measures to improve the organization and administration of research, to ensure Centre-State coordination in this field, to make research more effective as a means to achieve substantial and sustained improvement in agricultural production, and to establish close contact with the extension worker and, through him, to develop a two-way relationship between the farmer and the research institution.

The Committee came out forthrightly in favour of strengthening the Council and overhauling its structure, while placing all agricultural research programmes squarely under its unified guidance and control. At the state level, it reaffirmed that agricultural universities provided a better environment for research than the departments of agriculture. As for Centre-State coordination, this could, in the Committee's view, be best achieved through teams of specialists located mainly at these new universities.

Following these recommendations, ICAR was reorganized (in 1965). The Commodity Committees were disbanded; the Central agricultural research stations were brought within its jurisdiction; rules of recruitment and personnel management were rationalized; and the top position of the Council was given to a scientist, rather than to an administrator as had hitherto been the case. The Council thus emerged as the apex body

---

[13] The vast scope for multiple cropping is discussed in *Reaping the Green Revolution*, esp. in Chapters 2 and 9.

of scientists responsible for coordinating and guiding research and higher education in agriculture all over the country.

As a result, it now has 25 research institutes and eight soil conservation research and training centres functioning under its authority. Their programmes have been reviewed and redirected to serve approved objectives of national importance. In addition, the Council examined the entire research field which had been cluttered with numerous ad hoc projects, and redesigned it with a deliberate thrust towards solving practical problems to increase production and accelerate economic growth.

A major outcome of this reorientation was a series of All-India Co-ordinated Projects. The "philosophy" of the new approach was derived from its two forerunners—the Coordinated Maize Breeding Scheme established in 1957 and the Accelerated Sorghum Improvement Scheme initiated in 1961, both of which, as already noted, were largely inspired by the scientists of the Rockefeller Foundation. The same approach, it was soon realized, could be profitably extended not only to other crops, but also to other fields of agri-related research. As a result, coordinated projects have been set up to cover the whole gamut of food and fodder crops, commercial crops, animal sciences, dairying, also soils, agronomy, and engineering. "This problem-solving, production-oriented, multi-disci-plinary approach in research," observed Dr. B. P. Pal, Director-General of ICAR, "was indeed a unique break with the past, and is now looked upon as a model."[14]

CROP RESEARCH—THEN AND NOW

How much of a break it was with the past can be best judged when it is recalled how little had been achieved until then by research on India's two most important food crops—rice and wheat.

To take wheat first,[15] steps to improve this crop were taken in the early years of the century, under the guidance of Sir Albert Howard, at what was then the Imperial (now Indian) Agricultural Research Institute at Pusa, Bihar. New varieties were evolved beginning with Pusa 4 (later re-named N.P. 4), others followed in the same series with increased yield and better grain type. But they made little difference to the acre-yield realized by farmers.

In the mid-1930's, the emphasis shifted to greater disease-resistance, mainly under Dr. B. P. Pal's guidance, which resulted in two new series —N.P. 700 and N.P. 800. Because of their greater resistance to rusts, they

---

[14] In "New Approach to Farm Research," *The Statesman*, Calcutta, 8 November 1969.

[15] Indian Agricultural Research Institute 1905-1965—*Diamond Jubilee Souvenir*. The pamphlet gives an overview of the research done by IARI.

became popular among farmers who could harvest some grains even in years of rust epidemics.

In addition, there were state (or provincial) programmes, though notable results were achieved mainly in the Punjab, with the so-called "C series." The strongest feature of the Punjab-bred varieties was their grain quality—their bold, hard, amber and lustrous grains set the pattern for consumer preference in India.

This early wheat-breeding programme is revealing in many ways. It shows that considerable scientific talent did exist in the country; the varieties evolved testify to this fact. But research was treated as a matter of scientific hobby, as an ivory-tower pursuit; it lacked the pulse-beat of a social conscience, and reflected little concern for the farmer's plight. For example, N.P.4 and N.P.54 could reportedly yield about 3 tons/ha, but the high yield was achieved in experimental plots, and there never was any suggestion of achieving anywhere near these yields in the farmer's field. Indeed, the whole idea was ruled out almost *ex hypothesi*; for, fertilizer-using agriculture, it was consistently assumed, was not meant for the Indian farmer.

This attitude was enough to explain why little or no attention was paid to evolve fertilizer-responsive, high-yielding varieties for farmers' use. The breeders' primary emphasis was therefore laid, first, on protecting the low yield by developing more resistant varieties; and, second, on improving the grain quality which would fetch a better price.

Much progress was made in both respects. However, susceptibility to rusts still remained high; lodging continued to be a severe problem even without fertilizers, thus cutting further into yield and delaying maturity. And worst of all, wheat remained a hostage to weather; the wheat cycle in India ran from October-November when the crop was sown to March-April when it was harvested; but from March the temperature would shoot up to 30°C and beyond; drought conditions would develop at the grain-formation stage; even irrigation, if at all available, could not help much, for by February the plant was already much too tall to withstand irrigation which only induced more severe lodging. This syndrome had impelled Sir Albert Howard, some six decades ago, to the remark: "Wheat yield in India is a gamble in temperature."

The observation was apt. However, breeding to conquer weather, and other handicaps, had to wait until almost the mid-sixties. It came finally with the sturdy dwarfs, which ended the long tale of woes India's wheat had suffered from. Thereafter things changed rapidly—and radically (see Chapter 4). Said Dr. Norman Borlaug in November 1971:

> The All-India Coordinated Wheat Improvement Programme, which is largely responsible for wheat revolution in India, has developed one of the most extensive and widely diversified wheat research programmes

in the world. Its success has generated confidence, a sense of purpose, and determination. The current agronomic research on wheat in
India equals the best in the world. The breeding programme, also one
of the world's best, is huge, diversified, and aggressive; already it has
produced several varieties which surpass in performance those originally introduced from Mexico in 1965. Two newer groups of Indian
varieties are already being grown extensively in commercial production. ... The rapidity of creation and distribution of these new varieties has already diversified the type of resistance to diseases and therefore minimizes the menace of destructive disease epidemics if and
when changes occur in parasitic races of the pathogens.[16]

No compliments could be more eloquent, none more authoritative.

As for rice research,[17] the situation, at least until 1945, was perfectly
chaotic. There was no Central initiative; breeding was left, almost
entirely, to the state experimental stations; it was pursued solely by pure
line selection; and each selected variety was dedicated to a small local
niche. It was implicitly assumed that the adaptability of rice was, by
nature, extremely limited so that every locality, however small, had to
have its own variety. This view was staunchly upheld by the rice scientists almost as an axiomatic truth; they did not contemplate even the
need to put the hypothesis to field tests.

In this atmosphere of laissez-faire *par excellence*, each scientist tended
to go his own way, and pursued his own objective, even whim, such as
developing aromatic rice or rice with special grain types. Yield increases
were, at best, of marginal concern; nor did plant protection receive much
attention. In short, for decades India's rice scientists indulged in precisely
what Norman Borlaug, in 1943, had enjoined Mexico's wheat scientists
from doing: to get busy on "a lot of splinter programmes," on "scientific
sideshows," on "chasing academic butterflies."[18]

No wonder that the "improved" varieties listed in different parts of
the country numbered over 500! They were all tall, and, like the tall
wheat, were prone to lodge even in unfertilized fields; they were particularly unsuitable for intensive agriculture; and most of them fell easy
prey to insects and diseases. And if India's wheat was a gamble in temperature, her rice, mostly grown as a kharif crop, was a gamble in the
monsoon which usually brought either too much or too little water.

The ICAR role was confined to ad hoc support extended to some
isolated projects, such as for breeding varieties with resistance to flood

[16] 1971 McDougall Memorial Lecture (8 November 1971), FAO, Rome, mimeo.,
p. 30.
[17] The facts about rice research are based largely on personal briefings by Dr
S. V. S. Shastry—see footnote 8, p. 49.
[18] For the context see Chapter 3, p. 34.

43

or drought, or suitable for upland conditions, and, to a small extent, also for plant protection, especially disease and insect control.

The need for some Central initiative was too obvious to be indefinitely ignored. It came finally in 1945 when the Central Rice Research Institute (CRRI) was established at Cuttack, Orissa. Under the able leadership of its founder Director, Dr. K. Ramiah, the Institute assembled rice varieties cultivated all over the country, though it stopped short of inter-state coordination of research; while the studies it initiated contributed much to the knowledge about diseases and insects that habitually invaded the rice crop.

Of great significance was the step Dr. Ramiah took to hybridize japonica and indica rice. He was intrigued by the high yields of rice in temperate zones, felt the need to evolve varieties suitable for high fertilizer application, and proceeded on the hypothesis that japonica-indica crosses might provide the answer. He was, as subsequent history has proved, on a surprisingly right track even though it fell short of the desired goal.

The hybridization programme was started in 1950 as a regional project under FAO auspices with participation of the countries of South-East Asia. Burma, Thailand, Indochina, Malaya and Indonesia offered two to four of their improved strains to be crossed with eight japonica varieties; CRRI implemented the programme, and ICAR, too, promoted a similar project involving different states of India. As a result, large quantities of breeding materials were distributed both within India and to other countries.

However, in terms of immediate, tangible results, the programme proved a disappointment. For this negative outcome various explanations were given, such as lack of qualified personnel and organizational deficiencies. However, the real reason was much more fundamental. The fertilizer-responsiveness of the japonica varieties was, at that time, looked upon, to quote Dr. Shastry's words, "as a mysterious phenomenon associated with the varieties." What was still lacking was the knowledge of the proper plant-type and its influence. It was only IRRI that established, in 1963, the proper plant-type concept; and once this key was found, it immediately opened the door to the miracle rice.[19]

The japonica-indica hybridization programme, though deemed a failure, did yield some by-products. It stirred the scientists' minds and set them athinking in quest of higher-yielding varieties. Besides, it did lead to the evolution of a new variety, ADT-27, in Madras state. Even though it fell far short of the post-IRRI standards, it induced inter-state coopera-

[19] See Chapter 3. Dr. Shastry's remarks were made in some personal notes he was kind enough to prepare for the writer. For an overview of CRRI's achievements, see *Indian Farmer*, October 1971, Central Rice Research Institute Silver Jubilee Number.

tive trials in India, and in that sense, despite its shortfalls, it was a kind of forerunner of the All-India Coordinated Rice Improvement Project.

With the setting up of AICRIP and the arrival of TN-1 followed by IR-8, there began a new and dramatic phase. After dillydallying for decades India's rice-breeders suddenly marched at a galloping pace to occupy a commanding position in rice research. And within a few years, they have made her, to recall Dr. Chandler's words, the "most exciting place in the world today" so far as rice is concerned.[20]

The all-India coordinated programmes brought about, as their logical concomitant, another change of great significance—in the variety release procedure. The old practice, as indicated in Chapter 17, was to release a few kilograms of seed of a new variety to interested farmers; if it proved satisfactory to them and spread to a noticeable extent on a farmer-to-farmer basis, then and then only the official seal of approval was given to it *ex post facto*.

This process was much too slow; it invariably brought too many varieties into the field which confused the farmers;[21] and it left their crops vulnerable to pests and diseases, since the varieties were not accompanied by instructions about cultural practices and plant protection measures. There was no active promotion of new varieties; they were left to their own fate, and fate, needless to say, did not treat them kindly.

All this has now completely changed. As an adjunct to the all-India coordinated approach, Variety Release Committees have been set up; and each Committee now officially approves and releases new varieties, once its members are collectively convinced of their worth after thorough technical scrutiny and evaluation. Seeds are then multiplied by, or under the direction of, the National Seeds Corporation. Thereafter it is the task of the extension service to spread the varieties among the farmers through demonstration and other promotional work.

Teamwork among the scientists and activism all along the line have now become the order of the day. This has greatly accelerated the pace of research work in India. For example, formerly it used to take eight to twelve years to complete the researches involved in breeding and testing newer crop varieties and to bring them to the point where they could be released for general cultivation. Today, the whole process takes one-half of the time, or less.

## RESEARCH TAKES OFF

Apart from wheat, rice and maize, the 1960's have brought notable

---

[20] See Chapter 4, pp. 55-59.

[21] According to the Ford Foundation's Crisis Report, there were, in 1959, about 300 "improved varieties" of rice, more than 50 for wheat, about 40 for jawar, 18 for ragi, and some 20 for gram. Report, p. 207.

achievements in several other fields. An Accelerated Sorghum Improvement Scheme was established in 1961 with support from the Rockefeller
Foundation. A sorghum germplasm bank with a highly diversified collection has been created at Rajendranagar, the seat of the Andhra Pradesh
Agricultural University (APAU) near Hyderabad; breeding is proceeding apace, and as in the case of maize, it has been expanded into a cooperative programme embracing several other countries of the region.

The first hybrid sorghum produced in India was CSH-1, shortened
from Coordinated Sorghum Hybrid No. 1. Introduced in the midst of a
raging drought (in the 1965 crop season), it remarkably vindicated itself
—even in drought conditions, its yield amounted to 2,000 pounds per
acre, or four-to-five times the average yield in normal conditions. A
second hybrid, CSH-2, followed after a brief interval; it yields slightly
more and matures slightly (10 to 15 days) later, and therefore better
suits certain areas.

In 1968 came Swarna, a high-yielding, but non-hybridized sorghum
which has simplified the problem of seed supply. Farmers need not buy
the Swarna seed fresh from the industry every year; it is enough for
them to do so once in three to five years, using in the interval the seeds
saved from their annual harvests.

There are still problems of disease control for all the HYV's of sorghum—in particular, of protecting them from shootfly, their worst
enemy. The breeders are, however, hard at work on this and other problems, and are quite confident about resolving them fairly soon. That
sorghum has a great future in India's agriculture is already clear. Its
yield is now most attractive, thanks to the new varieties—the average
yield of 500 pounds per acre could be boosted to 3,500 pounds simply by
adding 100 pounds of nitrogen, and to 7,500 pounds by applying 125
pounds of nitrogen coupled with 40 to 80 pounds of phosphorus; it can
be grown easily in drylands or rainfed areas which account for four-
fifths of India's arable lands; it ratoons and fits perfectly into multiple-
cropping cycles, especially with the new short-duration varieties like
IRRI rice;[22] grains can be used as human food, while its grains and stalks
make excellect feed and fodder for livestock.

By and large, the same remarks hold good also for *bajra* (pearl millet)
and for *ragi* (finger millet). Much progress has been made with them.
Germplasm banks, with rich collections from domestic and overseas
sources, have been established for both millets; and several high-yielding
varieties of them have been developed and released.

The work done on bajra at the Punjab Agricultural University under
the leadership of Dr. D. S. Athwal has been widely acclaimed in India,
and beyond. Hybrid Bajra No. 1 (HB-1) was released in February 1965,

[22] IRRI has done some highly promising experimental work on multiple cropping
with sorghum and sorghum ratoons included in the annual cycle.

and even in a year of extreme drought, it performed extremely well. With irrigation and fertilizers, demonstration farmers were able to reap 3,500 to 6,000 pounds per acre, against a national average of 350 to 400 pounds. And bajra needs only 80 days from sowing to harvesting. Three other varieties have been subsequently released in the HB series, all with a parentage derived from Tift 23A produced at Tifton, Georgia (USA).

Ragi normally yields about 800 pounds per acre, but with an improved variety called S.929, yields up to a maximum of 7,000 pounds have been obtained. Its all-India coordinated programme is centred at the University of Agricultural Sciences in Mysore, which is the leading ragi-growing state.

The immediate objectives the millet breeders have in view are two-fold: First, to produce dwarf hybrids since the shorter plants—like the dwarfs of other cereals—will have an even greater yield potential; several short varieties have already been developed, and are now apparently in the pre-release state. And, second, to control pests and diseases—bajra, in particular, is a regular victim of bird pests which cause heavy damages; and, in addition, it is susceptible to a deadly disease called ergot. No germplasm to neutralize ergot has yet been discovered, but the quest continues.

And with the genetic wealth already accumulated in the germplasm banks, it cannot be long before this problem is resolved. For the same reason one may well assume that even better varieties of sorghum, pearl millet and finger millet—in terms of both disease-resistance and yield capability—will be ready for release in the near future.

The reorganization of research has yielded several other significant results. An All-India Coordinated Research Project has been established for improvement of pulse crops. In particular, work is proceeding to evolve early-maturing and disease-resistant varieties of arhar. Another crop of great possibilities is soyabean; it has been introduced in India for the first time, and a variety, called Bragg, has been released for cultivation in northern and central India.[23]

Research on potatoes has made much headway; several new varieties have been released, and two of them—Kufri Sindhuri and Kufri Chendramukhi—are given the highest rating. Some hybrids of tapioca and of sweet potatoes have been developed by the Central Tuber Crops Research Institute at Trivandrum and were close to the release point in 1971. They are capable of yielding twice as much as the local varieties.

Some hybrids of mango developed at IARI are considered to be promising in quality and yield. The Institute's research on vegetables has

[23] The establishment of ICRISAT in May 1972 at Hyderabad, India should give an impetus to research for improvement of crops grown in semi-arid tropics. See Chapter 31 under "A Momentous Step."

apparently produced some good results, examples of which include Pusa Drumhead cabbage, Contender French beans, and Pusa Early Dwarf tomato.

In cotton, the raw material for India's biggest industry, IARI has released a new variety, called "Sujata" (literally, "well-bred"), which combines good yield with good quality of fibre and can be used for spinning fine yarn up to 99 counts. Cotton research is currently directed towards evolving new varieties which would be short and more compact in growth, early-maturing, and yielding large bolls of high-grade fibre.

The Indian Grassland and Fodder Research Institute at Jhansi has demonstrated how green fodder production can be increased with intensive cultivation of Hybrid Napier grass intercropped with berseem.

Much research is now going into relay cropping or multiple-cropping cycles to maximize production per unit of land per unit of time. Research under ICAR is also concerned with a number of other areas, such as soil, agronomy, engineering, animal sciences, dairying. And the pattern of all-India coordinated research has been adopted in most cases.[24]

Clearly, agricultural research has come out of the doldrums and is now impressively on the march. The progress it has already made would have been inconceivable only a decade ago.

## SOME NEW TASKS

As research proliferates, new tasks loom. There is now a whole array of all-India coordinated projects. This is all to the good as it adds a new dimension to research, gives the results a guaranteed breadth of adaptation, and speeds up countrywide progress. At the same time the coordinated projects need to be coordinated so as to ensure the right priorities, to resolve possible inter-project conflicts, and to integrate two or more of them when they critically impinge on one another. The more obvious questions pressing for early attention are mentioned below.

Breeding high-yielding varieties of pulses like arhar has been apparently given a fairly high priority. Can the programme be broadened, and quickened, with greater concentration of scientific talent and financial resources? The question has a special urgency since the HYV's of wheat and rice are cutting deeply into the acreage under pulses, a major source of protein in the national diet. This situation will continue as long as pulses lack HYV's of their own to compete with those of wheat and rice.

Only about one-fifth of the cultivated area is under some sort of irrigation. Yet it seems there is a marked tendency to slant breeding, and

---

[24] In 1972, as many as 69 all-India coordinated research projects were in operation under ICAR auspices in agriculture, animal husbandry, and fisheries.

development effort in general, too much towards "wetlands", and not sufficiently towards drylands or rainfed areas.[25]

To take one example, castor seed is an excellent crop for arid and semi-arid soils. Improved varieties coupled with better agronomy can substantially increase its yield from such soils. Is it wise to breed castor away from them towards irrigated areas, as has been done with NPH-1 (Aruna) and the hybrid castor GHC-3? It is not enough to consider only the extra yield high-yielding varieties of castor can give from irrigated lands. This must be weighed against two other factors—the yield of alternative crops, such as wheat, rice and tubers, displaced by irrigated castor, and the yield of unirrigated castor displaced from arid and semi-arid lands. *Prima facie*, the opportunity cost of irrigated castor can be too high.

The newly-bred varieties of maize, sorghum, and millets have created an enormous potential to increase grain production from unirrigated lands. But so far only a tiny fraction of it has been actually exploited. True, these varieties are not yet free from problems, but this can only partly explain the utilization lag. In any case, there is clearly need for far greater effort in this field. With such effort it should be possible, here and now, to vastly increase the production of maize, sorghum and millets at very small additional cost.

An urgent need in the rainfed areas is to combine better agronomy with improved varieties. And in most cases, better agronomy implies, first and foremost, skilful harvesting of rainwater.[26] If the available moisture is carefully conserved and stretched out, it should be possible to grow in these areas two, sometimes even three, short-duration high-yielding crops. There is a clear need for vigorous ICAR initiative in this field to develop moisture-conserving methods of cultivation, to work out appropriate multiple-cropping systems, and to organize effective field demonstrations for the benefit of farmers.

Some kind of initiative is needed also in irrigated areas to cut down on the waste of water and to regulate its supply stringently to meet the exact requirements of crops, in short, to turn "wild flooding" into proper irrigation.[27] Some action has been taken in this field, but a great deal more remains to be done.

Then, there is a related field—consolidation of holdings; for, improved agronomy based on better water husbandry is feasible only when holdings are compact. What India's farmers need today is a countrywide demonstration of these facts. This, by itself, will go a long way towards triggering a consolidation movement, which can be tremendously spurred

---

[25] The newly-established ICRISAT should help counteract the excessive orientation of plant-breeding towards irrigated lands.

[26] and [27] See Chapter 16.

if it is accompanied by effective land reform, that is, a genuine land-to-the-tiller programme.

Another urgent field waiting for ICAR initiative relates to the size of holdings and the intrinsic productivity of small versus large holdings. Misconceptions, in this field, are still profound; in some quarters there is a strong bias in favour of large-scale, mechanized farming, while others are emotionally committed to support the small farmer's cause. Only scientific research can resolve this tangle. And if it is carried out properly, it can convincingly demonstrate why India must be a land of small farmers, even more than she is today, very much like Japan and Taiwan, in order to extract maximum food and fibre per acre of land through very intensive cultivation, also to maximize job opportunities and income from land. Objective research can still give the right lead to the policy-makers before the irrational pull of political pressure becomes irresistible.

This ties in with another question: farm machinery. The ICAR research programme does embrace the important field of agricultural engineering. Now, farm machinery is largely a function of the size of holdings, which, in turn, directly depends on land reform. The economic determinants of the size of holdings, as suggested above, must be productivity, income, and job potential per acre; and given the right size of holdings, machinery should be custom-built to meet their specific needs, such as to ease seasonal bottlenecks and to improve efficiency of cultivation. What is absolutely essential, however, is to hold mechanization firmly in leash, and not to allow it to bulldoze small farms out of existence to create fewer and larger ones in their place. Here again, scientific research under ICAR auspices is urgently needed to protect national, as against sectional, interest.

Finally, research must look beyond production and come to grips with the problems of storage, transportation, markets. Absence of these facilities, perhaps more than any other factor, has long paralyzed India's agriculture. Even today, in most parts of India, these facilities are woefully inadequate. It is essential to overcome this limitation with more vigorous effort. For this the leadership can come, most appropriately, from ICAR. Otherwise the high-yielding varieties it has been at pains to develop, and all its other research efforts, will yield limited results.

From the foregoing it should be clear that ICAR has already grown into a powerful engine of progress. But it is equally clear that research is yet to be fully harnessed to India's agriculture.

## III. EXTENSION SERVICE

### THE WEAKEST LINK

In harnessing research to agriculture, the weakest link remains the extension service. This is due to the fact that the service owes its origin to idealistic impulses and was therefore staffed mostly with well-meaning amateurs, not with scientifically trained workers. Born under different stars, it cannot tackle today's vastly more demanding and complicated tasks.

The extension service in India, it has been said, had nothing to extend in the absence of creative, farm-oriented scientific research. This contains an element of exaggeration; much could have been done, for example, in improving irrigation, and in organizing marketing, transportation, warehousing, and agricultural credit. Nonetheless, the observation is largely correct so far as the purely scientific—that is, biological and chemical—side of agriculture was concerned.

Today it is an entirely different story. Expanding research is rapidly stockpiling exciting results, especially as high-yielding varieties of crops with related cultural practices including plant protection measures. But the extension service—the so-called conveyor-belt—is unable to deliver them to the farmers. Dynamic research and a ramshackle extension outfit do not pair well. The pace of future progress in India's agriculture will depend very largely on the rapidity with which this incongruity is rectified. Extension must keep step with research.


## FROM AMATEURISM TO SCIENCE

The Community Development Programme (CDP), launched on a small scale early in 1952, broadened into a National Extension Service (NES) after October 1953. The mainstay of both was the multi-purpose Village Level Worker (VLW or "Gramsevak"), though NES laid much greater emphasis on agriculture and irrigation, and less on education and health, than CDP.

A separate training programme was subsequently instituted with 100 special training centres; 20 of them were upgraded and oriented more directly towards agriculture in the Third Plan period, and the remaining 80 were to be similarly upgraded during the Fourth Plan. Future Gramsevaks, it is now stipulated, should spend almost all their time on agriculture.

Will this approach produce an effective extension service? It is an illusion to think that it will, or that it can. Intensive agriculture that India has now embarked upon involves, above all, intensive application of science; it therefore needs well-trained scientists to serve as extension workers. The VLW's, on the other hand, were educated, as a rule, in liberal arts and quite often rather perfunctorily; they cannot blossom into qualified scientists, even when subjected to intensive training courses. The policy of "employ first, train later," as hitherto pursued, is enormously cumbersome, time-consuming, and inefficient. And, inevitably, it has become a heavy drag on India's agriculture.

44

In all the Western countries where agriculture has prospered—and they, of course, include Japan—the extension worker, or the so-called agronome of the non-English-speaking countries, invariably plays a vital role alongside agricultural research and education. And in all of them, he has, unlike India's VLW's, a thorough scientific background even to start with, which is supplemented with considerable practical training. This is also the path India must travel. Her agriculture will begin to move much faster when her extension service is freed from the albatross of amateurism.

The analogy of the health service is sometimes evoked to drive this point home, and rightly too. For, the problems of health and agriculture are in many ways similar and, therefore, call for the same kind of treatment. In building a health service, for example, the need for high-quality medical education, professionally qualified staff, and well-equipped hospitals and clinics is taken for granted; and it is also assumed that the medical personnel all along the line—from the top-level doctors down to the nurses—must have the needed expertise and must, therefore, be professionally trained according to prescribed courses. Now, plant and animal health and nutrition require the same kind of professional competence. No one in his senses would entrust the case of human health to quacks or amateurs. It would be no more sensible to rely on them for agriculture and livestock.

The root cause of the dilemma India is now faced with in her extension service should no longer be in doubt. She erred in that she decided to start at the bottom and work towards the top, which is just the opposite of the "basic philosophy" the farsighted architects of the Rockefeller programme in Mexico had propounded, namely, that "most rapid progress can be made by starting at the top and working downward," and not the other way round.[28]

Incidentally, the principle of starting at the top and working downwards has, in more recent years, been accepted by India in agricultural research and education. And this largely explains the very rapid progress she has been able to make in these two fields.

There is the ever-present temptation—and India is ever ready to succumb to it—to assume away the problems involved in training and upgrading workers, once they are recruited to serve at the bottom of the ladder, like the VLW's, and are given permanent or long-term job contracts. They may, as they often do, lack the minimum academic background on which to build further; lay recruits, even when they are of good timber, cannot be shaped into qualified scientists through short-term training courses; such courses, even when well-conceived and run by competent specialists, a condition not always satisfied in India even today, can be no substitute for several years of science learning at col-

[28] See Chapter 3, pp. 31-34.

leges and universities. To these should be added the all-too-common human failing—the trainees, especially when armed with job security, may simply lack the motivation to submit themselves to fresh academic exertion to process their own talent.

Building a competent extension service for agriculture would, in any case, be an uphill task in any developing country. There is no denying the fact that, by starting at the bottom with wrong men, India has made it immeasurably more uphill.

## REBUILDING THE SERVICE

But the folly must be undone. India's agriculture cannot be left a permanent hostage to CDP-NES amateurism. It must be rebuilt on the foundation of science. And there is only one way to do this—through massive restaffing.

A sensible approach would be to set up a small committee of outstanding scientists under Central auspices to act somewhat like the Cummings Committee (see above), both at the Central and the state level, to bring about this reorganization. Obviously, it will be necessary to set up a suitable machinery, again primarily under scientists of proven ability and integrity, to review the qualifications of the existing VLW's and other CDP-NES staff and to decide, on a case-by-case basis, who should be retained in the service with or without further training, and who had better be transferred elsewhere, in their own interest as well as that of extension work.

It is not suggested that individual workers, even when considered unsuitable for this particular service, should be unconditionally discharged. Such a policy would be inexpedient, unjust, and unnecessary. It will immediately run into political opposition; nor should the staff be penalized for a faulty recruitment policy pursued in the past. Besides, though misfits in the extension service, they should very well fit into numerous other jobs, of administrative and business character, which are bound to be created as agriculture becomes more intensive and as the rural economy develops, accompanied, one must hope, by an expanding public works programme.[29]

The thinned-out extension service will, of course, have to be strengthened with fresh recruitment. Not only that; India needs a far larger number of extension workers than is the case today—for, the existing organization is weak not only in quality, but also in quantity. Its quantitative inadequacy can be best judged when compared with the size of the clientele per extension worker in a few other countries. On an average, one such worker serves 157 clients in Israel, 403 in Greece, 728

[29] Discussed more fully in *Reaping the Green Revolution.*

in Japan, 1,698 in Taiwan, and 2,696 in India.[30] Clearly, the VLW's are too few in number. To cover the needs adequately, India will need three to four times more extension workers in the immediate future.

What should be the qualification of the new recruits? To ensure best results, they should all be science graduates with special emphasis on agricultural sciences, and with practical training in extension work at the agricultural universities, preferably ending up with a special diploma certifying their professional competence to serve as extension workers or agents.

This, then, is the magnitude of the task. It is gigantic, but there is no escape from it. Agricultural progress is a three-legged affair, based on education, research, and extension. All three must march in mutual harmony. At present research is ready for a race, education is well poised to get into the stride, but progress is hobbled by a malfunctioning extension leg. This imbalance must be urgently rectified. Today, this tops all other priorities in India's agriculture.

Reorganization of the extension service on such a scale and intensity will no doubt take time. However, with a well-planned action programme, based on mobilization of the available scientific manpower, an accelerated training programme, and increased output of graduates from the agricultural universities, it should be possible to accomplish most of the task in about five years.

In the transitional stage it would be essential to continue the National Demonstrations programme which was first introduced in 1965. This was an imaginative act which, at a lightning speed, awakened millions of farmers to the seed-fertilizer revolution that had suddenly broken out in tropical agriculture.[31]

Previously, the so-called demonstration work, confined mainly to the government's experimental plots, had demonstrated little of practical interest to the farmers and had, as a rule, evoked from them only a cynically indifferent response. What the new programme did was to bypass these meaningless rituals and to strike out on an entirely new course. Its sole purpose was to establish, through a series of national demonstrations and beyond all shadow of doubt, one single fact: that the high yields of the new varieties—some five times more than those of the old varieties—could be attained not only in the experimental plots, but in the farmers' own fields as well.

To do so, the programme fixed stiff yield targets, such as 3,500 kg per hectare, and then geared all efforts to fulfil—and overfulfil—them. The "control plot" technique that had routinely accompanied earlier demon-

[30] Figures quoted by the Extension Service, The University of Agricultural Sciences, Bangalore.

[31] For this the nation should be grateful to the IARI Director, Dr. M. S. Swaminathan, the originator of this idea, who is now Director-General of ICAR.

strations was dispensed with as a useless encumbrance. After all, farmers' lifelong experience with yields and those currently obtained in surrounding villages provided ample "control" for purposes of comparison.

Each demonstration was organized on a sizable plot—of about a hectare—to make the results sufficiently striking. And what is even more important, the demonstrations were laid in the fields of actual cultivators with small holdings in order to eliminate the suspicion that high yields had anything to do with the affluence of individual farmers. Finally, they were carried out by competent scientists in strict accordance with the cultural practices prescribed for each high-yielding variety. This, in short, was the first time India saw a large-scale infusion of science in her extension work.

The National Demonstrations programme has rendered two extremely valuable services: it gave the first big push to spread the high-yielding varieties all over the country; and it demonstrated how demonstration work ought to be organized. These tasks have been largely accomplished. As Dr. Swaminathan puts it, the programme "served as windows into the world of plenty," dispelled doubts about the feasibility of getting high yields in cultivators' fields, and generated "a hunger for seeds and fertilizer."[32]

Millions of farmers are now ready to accept the new seeds along with the new technologies. What they need today is not more inspiration, but the physical inputs and facilities.

While this programme may continue yet for some time, it cannot, from its very nature, be a substitute for a permanent extension service built on the lines outlined above. The task today is to service the farmers—50 million of them—individually and on a continuous basis. It is this task to which the nation must address itself.


## IV. THE IMPERATIVES

The tasks still confronting India in education, research and extension should be clear from what has been said above. There are, briefly, five imperatives:

1. *Stay the course.* The hard-won victories of recent years must be jealously safeguarded. The most important of them are: the preeminence of scientists over general-purpose administrators; the all-India approach to varietal breeding and testing; integration of education, research, and extension; and concentration of all these in the agricultural universities, away from government departments.

There are still too many old-timers unable to comprehend the reasons

[32] *National Demonstrations*, Indian Institute of Agricultural Research, New Delhi, 1969, p. (iii).

underlying these fundamentals, who find it hard to accept, and to get used to, the changes and would therefore revert to the *status quo ante*, if at all possible. Such atavistic tendencies must be resisted until the hard-won ground is fully consolidated.[33]

2. *Build science-based extension.* To wean the extension service from its ingrained amateurism and to reorient it towards science has an urgency that cannot be overstated. And this should be accompanied by vigorous effort to build it up to the requisite strength.

It follows that the agricultural universities already established should be strengthened and expanded; and that new universities should be established, especially in the states which at present have none. At the same time, the utmost possible care should be taken not to compromise with the quality of teaching, training, and research.

There is also a clear need to attract to these universities a much larger number of topgrade students graduating from schools, with well-conceived inducements such as fellowships and assured job prospects on attractive terms. The cream of the graduating student community has, in the past, gone disproportionately to other fields such as public administration, business, engineering, medicine and law, which offer better earning prospects. Agriculture must effectively compete with them.

3. *Give scientists a better deal.* The high priests of the green revolution are the scientists. This should be quite clear from the foregoing. India's administration has yet to grasp this truth more fully and to give her scientists a better deal—in terms of salaries and emoluments, of work facilities, of the budgets they are offered, and, last but not least, of the authority they are allowed to exercise over their own budgets and their own departments. The present system is a relic from a bygone past, diligently kept alive by a rule-ridden administration. But it has no place in this scientific age and deserves early liquidation.[34]

All this has acquired a special urgency for another reason. India has been suffering from a scientific brain drain she, most certainly, cannot afford. Quite a few of her outstanding plant geneticists and other agricultural scientists have left the country in quest of jobs abroad. This is the last thing that should happen at this crucial moment of India's agricultural research and development. The nation desperately needs their service. It must make every effort to keep them at home, not by an administrative fiat, but by a readiness to meet all their legitimate needs and wishes, coupled with a strong appeal to their sense of duty and responsibility to the nation.

4. *Nourish the Golden Goose.* Agricultural research is not immune from standard talks of financial constraint and budget-pruning. Yet this

---

[33] See Chapter 28, especially the interim recommendations of the National Commission of Agriculture on education, research, and extension.

[34] See also Chapter 28.

is the most myopic exercise in finance one could think of. For, agricultural research, when properly conceived and directed by competent men to solve practical problems to increase production, yields truly phenomenal dividends. It is the most prolific golden goose that has ever existed. It should be fondly nourished, not starved of the essential wherewithal.

For example, in the USA, it is estimated that the accumulated research expenditures on hybrid corn research, private and public, until 1955 amounted to $131 million; for each dollar of this expenditure the social return worked out to $7 annually, giving a 700 per cent rate of return. Comments Dr. Theodore Schultz after quoting these figures: "Costly? Yes. Payoff? High indeed."[35]

Mexico provides an even more striking example. According to an estimate made at the University of Chicago, the money value of Mexico's increased wheat and corn production resulting from research worked out to 400 per cent annual interest or return on the total amount spent on all research under the cooperative programme in the decades from 1943 to 1962. For wheat alone, the return on wheat research expenditures is at least 800 per cent per year.[36]

And as Dr. Wortman rightly points out, the returns should be "many fold higher" than the dramatic figures cited above for the USA or Mexico, when all a country needs to do is "a minimum of adaptive research" to utilize quickly a technology already developed elsewhere, as has so conspicuously been the case with dwarf wheat and rice in India and Pakistan.[37]

It would, of course, be rash to assume that all agricultural research would assure a high payoff. Here, as elsewhere, good money can be frittered away on a good cause unless it is well planned and well executed. Research in India, as seen earlier, consumed sizable sums of money without giving any noticeable return on it.

As for the prerequisites of high-quality research guaranteeing a high payoff, Dr. Wortman's guidelines are virtually foolproof: research must be directed against all technical barriers to productivity of a given commodity; it must be led by highly competent and dedicated scientists; it must be conducted by interdisciplinary teams of scientists with simultaneous attacks on all major problems; and it must be adequately supported with men and money.

It follows that money should not be a constraint at all. The real con-

---

[35] Quoted by Dr. Sterling Wortman in "The Technological Basis for Intensive Agriculture," *Agricultural Development—Proceedings of a Conference*, The Rockefeller Foundation, New York, 1960, pp. 25-26. The estimates quoted by Dr. Schultz were extracted from a study by Dr. Zvi Griliches. Dr. Wortman's paper gives a thorough analysis of the role of research, education and extension and contains many valuable insights.

[36] Stakman *et al.*, op. cit., p. 91 footnote.

[37] Ibid., p. 27.

straint is the capacity to find able scientists, to design the right kind of production-oriented programmes, and to ensure teamwork to attack all interrelated problems. Once these preconditions are satisfied, money should be made readily available and treated as a most remunerative investment of public funds.[38]

5. *Expand Indo-US Collaboration.* The cooperative programmes with the USA have been outstandingly productive; the Rockefeller Foundation in plant-breeding, in agricultural education, and in developing a seed industry; the USAID in building up agricultural universities on the lines of the land-grant institutions, with valuable assistance in such key areas as seed multiplication and distribution, formulation of a sound fertilizer policy, and farm mechanization; the Ford Foundation in intensive agriculture based on package approach with special emphasis on farm planning, farm credit, administrative organization, and more recently on plant protection and water management. It would be wise to continue the programmes in their essentials for another decade or so, also to expand them further in some important respects. This will help maintain, and increase, the current momentum and will thereby speed up the rate of progress.

It is worth remembering in this context that the supply of experts in tropical agriculture is still extremely limited; that the developing countries are waking up only now to the enormous potential it contains; that, as this realization spreads, the demand for the available specialists will grow and may well turn into a scramble. Yet India can, if she plans and acts with imagination, build up a large reservoir of competent scientists within a short time, and use them to help herself and also others. She can help train people from other developing countries at her newly-built institutions, and also send out to them her own scientists, as and when she is able to do so, to render to them the kind of service both she and Mexico have received from the Rockefeller Foundation. It would be most logical for her to assume a leadership role in this field, for which she is admirably cut out by virtue of her size and geographic location, the latent intelligence of her people, and their general aptitude to acquire and apply scientific knowledge. This is the role she should aim at and qualify herself for with a clear-sighted policy backed by sustained effort.

## USA'S HISTORIC CONTRIBUTION

The review given above should leave no doubt about one thing—the momentous contribution the USA has already made to India's agricultural development through a remarkable band of scientist-idealists fielded by two US Foundations and USAID. Its full import is not yet appreciated except by the prescient few in both countries, partly because

[38] See also Chapter 27 on "Credit Shackles and Deficit Financing."

people in general see things more clearly only in hindsight, but largely because of the political mist that has obstinately overhung Indo-US relations almost since the dawn of India's independence. When that mist finally lifts—as no doubt it will some day if only because the two countries have too much of human values in common to concentrate on fleeting differences, fancied or real, and to keep alive indefinitely a policy of sullen estrangement—the Indo-US collaboration in the agricultural field will stand out as an epoch-making event in India's history, also as an object lesson to other developing countries. For this there are several solid reasons:

*One.* It has set India on the road to victory in her grim race between food production and population growth. The direction she must follow is no longer in doubt. Nor can there be any more turning back from the course she has already embarked upon.

This assurance stems from two heartening developments: India's agricultural scientists are now, by and large, firmly committed to a new creative effort to build up her agriculture through concerted, sustained, and purposeful research. Besides, millions of farmers have now formed a surprisingly solid alliance with the newly-established agricultural universities in expectation of a steady flow of "miracles" from them. They have tasted progress and have instinctively built up a kind of farmers' lobby with considerable political muscles to ensure that more progress will be made more rapidly.

The direction is firmly set; scientists and farmers are ready to forge ahead; it is now for the planners, policymakers, economists, irrigation engineers, and administrators to update their thinking, and to fall in line with them in order to quicken the tempo and to win decisively the food-population race.

*Two.* It has shown how India can accelerate her economic growth far beyond the present rate, and thereby conquer not only hunger, but also poverty. For, it has revealed—even for the most cynical eyes to see—the unlimited wealth that lies buried in tropical agriculture. Once a systematic effort is made to mine it on an optimum scale, it will turn out not only enough food, but also enough jobs and incomes for the masses of people, and this will propel the economy forward at a rate hitherto undreamt of in India.

*Three.* It has injected a new sense and purpose into India's education by forcing her to apply her mind, first and foremost, to her own problems and potentialities. Thus, at long last, the mindless system is becoming mindful of the realities around. As this trend continues, it will more and more throw the parrot's learning on the defensive, which should soon be definitely on its way out; and this will rid India of the worst malaise she has been stricken with in her long history.

*Four.* It has opened up other avenues for creative work which should

45

spur all-round progress. Western renaissance, which arrived in India packaged in colonialism, could not penetrate very far. It proved much too fragile, and, like an exotic plant insufficiently acclimatized with local research and culture, it wilted and withered after a while.

Today, as the agricultural revolution spreads through the country, it is bringing in its wake a new renaissance—vibrant, dynamic, pervasive— and since largely home-bred and people-oriented, it has, this time, all the promise to be robust and durable—unless extinguished by doctrinaire ideologies uncritically imported from abroad.

*Five.* It has demonstrated, as in Mexico, that agri-centred development provides the shortest and quickest route to a high-growth economy, that it can be achieved with an astoundingly high output-input ratio, provided it is fully science-oriented and is firmly geared to high-quality education, research, and extension.

It has further shown how the government of a developing country can be persuaded to adopt the right strategy for agri-centred economic development when top-grade scientists are assigned to serve in intimate cooperation with its own nationals, and how quickly persuasion is followed by enthusiastic government response, once the first few solid successes have been booked. Like farmers, governments too need successful demonstration if they are to be fully sold on a new idea or a new project.

Here, then, is a model—indeed, the only valid model for most developing countries—which all aid programmes, international and bilateral, will do well to emulate if they are to be true to their *raison d'être*.

## A FOOTNOTE TO HISTORY

This chapter can perhaps best end with a footnote to history. For, it shows how, in its wayward course, history is apt to take unexpected turns, at times even to repair the damages inflicted by its own turbulence. There is, surely, a special poignancy in the fact that the first large colony to break away from history's mightiest empire came—some 175 years later—to assist the last large colony once it cut loose from the same imperial moorings, to lift as it were the curse of sterility it had been stricken with since the dawn of modern industrial civilization. The impact of this unique salvage work is still rather muffled. But it is safe to predict even today that, as the century marches to its end and well beyond that, its echo will resound, ever more loudly, through the corridors of time.

CHAPTER 23

# On Price Support

## A DELAYED REALIZATION

The modern farmer is a kind of businessman. He buys manufactured inputs, grows crops with them, and sells the produce in the market. The margin between the costs he incurs—for the purchased inputs, for his field operations, and for post-harvest handling of the produce—and the proceeds he realizes from its sale represents his profit or income, the wherewithal he must rely on for the livelihood and welfare of himself and his family.

The margin must be *attractive*; otherwise the farmer would be unwilling to put in the extra effort to produce a marketable surplus. It must be *dependable*; he cannot afford to gamble on a price that might sag when he markets his produce. And it must be *known well in advance*; only then he would be able to do his cost calculations, take the production decisions, and make the necessary commitments. This is the *raison d'être* of guaranteed price support for commercial agriculture, the pillar without which it would collapse to a subsistence level.

It has taken ages to realize these simple truths. In hindsight, it is amazing to reflect how they were missed both by experts and laymen, in both developed and underdeveloped countries. Yet this is only one aspect of the stubborn misconceptions which have long dogged tropical agriculture and, to a large extent, continue to do so even today. Its true potential has been grossly underestimated; the preconditions for its modernization have been misunderstood; the critical role of government in relation to it has been overlooked; the farmer's behaviour has been misjudged, and the blame for backwardness has been placed on him rather than where it belongs—the limitations he has to work under and which would be enough to paralyze farmer initiative in any country.[1]

Price incentives, it was widely believed, did not work in the case of an Indian farmer. With higher prices he would prefer to work less, not more, and would rather add to his leisure than to his income. Or, he would consume more to make up for his normal under-consumption, and sell less—a smaller quantity sold at a higher price would give him enough cash to pay for such essentials as salt, sugar, kerosene, matches, and a few yards of cloth. His needs were few and inelastic; his living standard was low, but he lacked the urge, or "motivation," to alter it.

These views have long held the ground among experts, both Indian and foreign, in the face of accumulating evidence to the contrary. What the farmer lacked was, almost always, not motivation but opportunity; and when real opportunities opened up, as a rule he did try to seize them, sometimes with surprising skill and success.[2]

The much-publicized failure of price incentives in his case was more apparent than real. For one thing, the incentive only too often failed to touch the farmer; instead, it benefited the landlord, the moneylender, and the middleman. His unwillingness to exert himself more in such cases is precisely what one should have expected. He responded negatively to what, for him, was zero-incentive.

That, with higher prices, the farmer would increase his own consumption of foodgrains was in itself another evidence of perfectly rational behaviour. Given his subnormal standard of nutrition, this is both natural and desirable. It is equivalent to spending, in kind rather than in cash, the extra income on his first essential, namely, food.

His apathy for consumer goods, too, was grossly exaggerated. Quite often their supply happened to be inelastic, not his demand—goods likely to evoke his interest were just not available within his easy reach or at prices he could afford. However, the situation has been changing rapidly, thanks to the expanding domestic industry, growth of communications, and rise of rural incomes. Many farmers today consume a range of manufactured articles which would have been unbelievable only a decade ago.

The truth is that the "economic man" has always been present in the Indian farmer, as in his prototypes in other developing countries; but he lay dormant—like the dormant productivity of his farmland. Once the latter explodes, the economic man, too, instantaneously springs to life. This is exactly the phenomenon the world is experiencing today, in India and in a good many other developing countries.

"Price policy is of great importance at this stage," observes an authori-

---

[1] Discussed in Chapters 2 and 9; see also Chapter 24.
[2] For examples, see Chapter 9.

tative group of experts. "At the very least, a farmer must remain solvent. He cannot be expected to produce for the market at a loss."[3]

This does not mean that incentive price is all that the farmer needs; he must obviously be in a position to take advantage of it. And this he can do only when he has, at his disposal, all the other essential elements that go to make successful commercial farming—manufactured inputs, technical services, transportation and marketing facilities, credit. If any one of them is lacking, or seriously lagging, his whole operation will be jeopardized, despite the price incentive. This, as was seen earlier, is the essence of the package approach. Price alone will not do, but without remunerative price agriculture will get nowhere.

### "BON PRIX" OR "BON MARCHE"

Before independence, agricultural prices were left to the free play of market forces. For cultivators the result was disastrous. As a rule, they had no holding power, and so they had to dump the produce on the market immediately after harvest. The resulting slump in prices benefited traders, manufacturers and, to some extent, urban consumers at their expense. This cruel pattern continued year after year. It would, by itself, have been enough, at any time and in any clime, to kill farmer initiative and to ruin the prospects of modernizing agriculture.[4]

A great deal had been said and written, often backed by telling statistics, about the woes of Indian cultivators and their exploitation under the colonial regime. Yet the change of regime made little real difference to their fate. Despite voluminous concern for them, the government of free India—whether out of inertia or of expediency—hardly deviated from the beaten track.

How to make agriculture serve the manufacturing industry and feed the urban population became its dominant concern. The result was ironical. After independence, rural India, for all practical purposes, only changed masters: economically, it became a *colony* of urban India, and official policy came to bear the hallmark of this *neocolonialism*.

It is, of course, not suggested that such a policy was deliberately pursued or that rural exploitation was consciously tolerated. Such a view would be both cynical and wrong. What happened was more complex: an unwary government, misreading the signposts of history, took to a

---

[3] *The World Food Problem*, Report of the President's Science Advisory Committee, Vol. II, p. 505. The Committee has demolished much of the misconceptions about farmer response to incentive prices in a developing economy (in Chapter 9).

[4] Even in an advanced country like the USA, farmers were at the mercy of organized industry. To remedy this imbalance in bargaining strength, the government stepped in with price-support programmes. By now, the practice has become universal in the developed world. See Chapter 30.

wrong policy route and, after some adventurous detours, hastily back-tracked in a dazed and confused mood.

It is useful to recall at this point the ideological tussle which took place in Europe, about two centuries ago, between two dominant schools of economic thought. Britain had begun to shed the cruder tenets of mercantilism, especially its emphasis on a perpetually favourable balance of trade and accumulation of precious metals. But the neo-mercantilism she came to embrace and practise continued to extol manufacture and trade, while minimizing the role of agriculture. As a result, even in the days of her spectacular economic upsurge, her agriculture remained an interesting sideshow, a classic example of "gentleman," rather than com-mercial, type of farming.

Across the channel, the physiocrats were busy preaching the reverse article of faith. France, they urged, must give her primary attention to agriculture, more so since she had been less successful than England in capturing overseas markets. They constructed something akin to an economic cult with their nebulous concept of "the rule of nature," a one-sided view that agriculture alone was productive, and rather puerile rejection of trade, commerce, and professions as sterile.

As a corollary to this cryptic philosophy, some physiocrats argued that agricultural products were to be sold at *bon prix* (good price) whereas manufactured products should be sold at *bon marché* ("good bargain" or low price).

It was easy to dispose of the physiocratic fallacies, and this was done quite thoroughly by later economists. But the job was done too well, to the point where the baby was thrown out with the bathwater.

For, after the palpable illogicalities and the mystifying excesses were stripped off, there still remained a hard core of truth in the physiocrats' teachings, namely, the vital role agriculture must play in a nation's eco-nomic life, especially when it is blessed with reasonably rich land re-sources like France, and not so highly blessed with overseas trade pros-pects like Britain.

After independence, the wisest course of action for India would have been to concentrate national effort on agriculture to the utmost possible extent. The reasons were unmistakable. The population was growing fast—faster than was realized at that time; it had to be checked. Rural misery had accumulated to an appalling level; it had to be remedied. Vast land resources were lying idle or quasi-idle; they needed to be put to productive work. Productivity per acre was dismally low; it had to be built up. Consumer goods industries, particularly textiles, were short of raw materials; the demand had to be met. Agricultural sciences were making rapid strides in the West; much of it could be imported and adapted to raise output and income from land. For developing essential industries and services India needed vast resources; these had to come very largely from her agriculture.

Thus, what India needed was a large infusion of the physiocratic spirit. But the blind pull of history proved decisive; and, without further thought, she took to the neo-mercantilistic track chalked out in the days of British rule. The primary emphasis, after independence, was laid on industry. Not that agriculture was consciously ignored; indeed, in terms of Plan allocations it did not fare too badly.[5] Its fate was, however, left in the hands of dam-building irrigation engineers and community-developing amateur-workers, to which was later added a third category, self-serving panchayati-raj politicians. And as seen earlier,[6] together they underwrote high-cost stagnation.

Agricultural prices were, in general, left to the market forces. The government did intervene, though rather halfheartedly, to control or regulate prices. And when it did so, it was not to help the producer, but to keep the prices down for the benefit of the industry and the urban consumer. The physiocratic formula was reversed: agricultural products were sold at *bon marché*, and manufactured products at *bon prix*.

The farmer was obliged to accept low prices, as before, to help keep down the cost of manufactures and make them more competitive, even though they were mostly sold in a sheltered domestic market and fetched handsome profits. This was duly hailed as industrial progress. Thus, for the farmer, the net effect of the change from colonialism to independence was hardly noticeable. Essentially, it was another case of *plus ça change...*

## CONSUMER-ORIENTED PRICES

There have been three fairly distinct phases in India's agricultural price policy.[7] The objective was the same all along, namely, to solve the problem of food shortage in the country, but the method adopted showed sharp differences.

Around 1943, when the symptoms of an absolute shortage of foodgrains became abundantly clear,[8] the government initiated the policy of procurement of foodgrains in surplus areas and their distribution in deficit areas through official channels. Rationing of foodgrains and other essential articles was introduced in large urban centres, such as Calcutta and Bombay, which were hardest hit by the shortages. This system of

[5] See Chapter 6.
[6] Chapters 8 and 9.
[7] This may be treated as virtually synonymous with the price policy for *foodgrains* which account for the bulk, about 85 per cent, of India's total agricultural production.
[8] For the background facts, see Chapter 10.

domestic procurement cum regulated distribution lasted more than a decade, until mid-1954.[9]

The principle was sound if only because, given the shortage, it was inescapable. But the system worked fitfully and none too efficiently. It could not be otherwise in view of the manifold obstacles, such as: lack of transportation in rural areas, inadequacy of storage facilities, lack of firm statistics about city-dwellers resulting in large-scale falsification of ration-cards, and, perhaps worst of all, the ingenuity of traders seasoned in evading laws, and in hoarding and black marketing. Prices were officially pegged for the benefit of the consumers. But they constantly tended to shoot up, especially in years of a serious shortfall in overall production. No wonder that the policy should have met with considerable opposition from critics who vigorously pleaded for decontrol and derationing with unrestricted internal movement of grains, which they regarded as the lesser evil. In fact, the government, too, tended to relax in years of good production, when the procurement drive slackened and, as a result, no sizable buffer-stock could be built up.

During 1952-54, India enjoyed two successive years of favourable monsoon. Production reached a relatively high level, supplies looked plentiful, and prices of foodgrains declined appreciably. These events reinforced the hands of the decontrol school. The policy adopted in the closing years of the war was finally abandoned; and, by mid-1954, the administrative machinery built up for the purpose was completely dismantled.

This policy switch was made without much firm conviction. Fear lingered in the official mind that large deficits could reappear any time to upset all calculations. As usual, much depended on the monsoon, and there was no reason to assume an unbroken chain of good years. Demand was rising, more sharply than was yet visible on the surface, owing to a higher-than-assumed rate of population growth and some absolute rise in average per capita consumption. Moreover, the country was about to embark upon the Second Plan to accelerate economic development, with heavy emphasis on heavy industries and a large dose of deficit financing. That this would tend to feed inflation was not overlooked. Thus, the food problem was very much there, despite an apparent lull. And it needed to be tackled not on a hand-to-mouth, but on a more durable basis. This time the search for an adequate solution led the government far afield.

India began to cast wistful eyes on the surplus food stocks of the USA as soon as they were thrown open to the outside world under the Public Law 480.[10] As passed in 1954, the Law aimed at several objectives in the field of foreign economic relations, namely: to make "maximum efficient

[9] Except for a short break. Foodgrains prices were decontrolled in 1947, but the controls were reimposed the following year.

use" of the USA's surplus agricultural commodities to further its foreign policy; to expand its trade with friendly countries; to facilitate currency convertibility; to stimulate and expand foreign trade in agricultural commodities; and to encourage economic development.

Of particular interest to India was Title I of P.L. 480 which provided for the sale of surplus agricultural commodities for foreign currencies and the utilization of these currencies within the recipient countries for their economic development. India's policy-makers saw in it an easy way out of their own dilemma, and eagerly seized the opportunity.

In 1955 the position of domestic food supplies happened to be markedly better than almost in a whole decade; the prices, too, had receded to a more tolerable level. But the government decided not to undertake any procurement within the country and turned, instead, to the USA to arrange for imports under P.L. 480. The negotiations initiated in May of that year culminated in the first agreement signed in August 1956. This was followed by a series of agreements, all under Title I of the Law. By the end of December 1962 altogether eight of them had been signed, authorizing India to receive agricultural commodities worth Rs. 1,156 crores.[11]

Thus began the second phase of India's food policy, based not on domestic procurement, but on US food aid. The quantities involved were staggering, especially by earlier standards. For example, by the end of December 1962, or in just about six years, India had imported 16.6 million metric tons of wheat, valued at 1.6 billion US dollars.[12]

What were the reasons for such a radical policy change? They were many and, *prima facie*, appeared quite plausible to a lot of people—at least at that time. Domestic procurement had proved a major headache —grains had to be purchased in small quantities mostly in remote areas, and had to be assembled at selected centres for distribution. Imports provided a neat solution—all the grains coming from abroad went straight under government control, the entire quantity was available for distribution, and they could be shipped direct to the large deficit areas like Calcutta and Bombay. From food administration's angle, this greatly simplified the tasks.

The wily grain merchants had often proved more than a match for the government; they were constantly trying to push up prices with

[10] Its full title was: The United States Agricultural Trade Development and Assistance Act of 1954.

[11] For a thorough factual analysis of the subject, see *Impact of Assistance under P.L. 480* by Nilakanth Rath and V. S. Patvardhan, Asia Publishing House, Bombay, 1967.

[12] Other imports made by the same date were (in million metric tons): rice—0.84; corn—0.60; plus (in 1,000 m. tons) milk powder—20.70; soyabean oil—3.00; tobacco— 3.86. Cotton imports amounted to 1.3 million bales (480 lbs. each). These items (excluding wheat) were valued at Rs. 301 crores. Ibid., Table on p. 40.

hoarding and black marketing; the resulting scarcity induced hoarding also by consumers and thereby further aggravated the situation. The new policy, it was hoped, would help counteract these tendencies by creating what was called a "psychology of abundance."

The authorities were well aware that the Second Plan, as then conceived, would almost certainly kindle inflation. The new food policy, it was assumed, would help quench it by keeping down foodgrain prices.

The Plan was not adequately funded. The P.L. 480 imports, it was felt, would provide a twofold relief—they would help partly meet the immediate foreign exchange needs, and they would build up a substantial rupee fund which could be drawn upon to meet part of the Plan expenditures.

And, finally, the P.L. 480 imports would give the government a much-needed breathing-space to seek a lasting solution of its own food problem. A substantial buffer-stock built with these imports would help iron out temporary deficits, and this would give time to step up domestic grain production to a substantially higher level.

A Foodgrain Enquiry Committee, appointed in 1957, wholeheartedly endorsed the new policy; and among other things, it particularly stressed the importance of the last point, namely, of using the opportunity created by P.L. 480 imports to work out a "stable and long-term food policy" for India.

Thus, the new policy sought to kill several birds with one stone. But was it also going to depress domestic prices, discourage production, perpetuate food deficits, and kill India's own agriculture? The question was too unpleasant to be raised, far less considered, in the euphoric atmosphere that prevailed at that time. The answer came, a decade later, in a most brutal form from the chastening school of experience.

To give effect to the new food policy, over 50,000 fair price shops were set up covering the entire country. It took seven years to do so; and by then, India was equipped to absorb some 4,000,000 tons of imported wheat every year. All this was done to combat profiteers and black marketeers, to bring down domestic prices of foodgrains, to protect poorer sections of the population, and to promote economic development.

And all this did create a psychology of abundance, which stalked the land, but only for a while. The new strategy was hardly in full operation when it began to crumble. It was bound to do so. In bad monsoon years —and there were several of them—domestic production receded, the food deficit widened, and larger imports were needed to close the gap. Prices shot up in areas of pronounced shortfall; the impact of the imported wheat was not strong enough to dampen them.

Meanwhile, demand for grains rose sharply, spurred by population growth and low-priced wheat sold from fair price shops. Production of food within the country inched ahead, aided by the extension of irrigation and of the acreage under crops. Per acre yield remained deplorably low, as before.

Matters came to a head when, following two poor harvests in succession, prices began to rise from mid-1963 and continued on the uptrend through 1964. More and more people turned to the fair price shops for cheaper foodgrains, and soon the demand began to outrun their supplies. To meet the situation, a desperate government hurriedly set up more fair price shops—by the end of 1964, their total number had almost doubled to over 100,000—and released imported stocks on a staggering scale. In that single year India absorbed seven million tons of imported wheat! Even this massive tonnage could not make a dent in the domestic prices of foodgrains. It was, however, enough to bury, several fathoms deep, the naively contrived psychology of abundance.

The imported grain sold through the fair price shops at low prices did, for a while, serve a social objective—it helped protect the "poor and vulnerable" sections of the population at a time of rising prices. But, in the process, it left the entire economy poor and vulnerable, how vulnerable was dramatically brought home only a year later—in 1965—when, in the midst of an emergency that erupted in the subcontinent, the inflow of transatlantic foodgrains India had unquestioningly relied upon came to an abrupt halt.

And as if this was not enough, she was dealt a second blow quickly thereafter, this time by nature descending remorselessly like a nemesis to inflict on her a maximum of punishment. The droughts bared the stupendous folly of the past policy, the folly of cultivating dependence on the outside world for food and of not cultivating her own fields more fully to grow it at home.

India had learnt a costly lesson: No nation can comfortably live with an economic heart transplant, however generously donated.

## THE TURNAROUND

The food policy based on concessional food imports proved a near-complete failure. It could not hold down the prices, which was one of its primary objectives; the inflationary pressures abated for a while, but only to reappear later in a more virulent form. Demand for foodgrains, it soon became clear, was rising much faster than the imports could cope with. In fact, it was further stimulated by the very policy of selling grains through fair price shops at prices much below the prevailing market rates.

A buffer-stock built with P.L. 480 imports, it had been assumed, would give a sorely needed respite to tackle the problem on a durable basis. It was also hoped that while the Second Plan, with its deliberate thrust towards industrialization, forged ahead, domestic grain production would catch up with the rising demand. Nothing like this, however, happened in practice. An expanding public sector quenched the thirst for state capitalism, more with losses than profits. Food production crawled ahead, but lagged far behind the desired level. And a hungry nation ate up the buffer-stocks in no time.

The worst feature of the policy was even more fundamental, a fact that no longer admits of any doubt. Food was imported on a colossal scale when it could—and should—have been grown at home to build up rural income, to provide employment, and to strengthen the national economy.

It is tempting to speculate what might have happened. If irrigation were less obsessed with high dams and were, instead, more crop-oriented with a rapid extension of wells, tanks and other minor projects; if agriculture were not left at the mercy of community development with its army of untrained workers, but were actively stimulated along modern lines with the help of the sizable corps of qualified scientists who were eager to make their contribution to nation-building work; and if agricultural prices were left even to the free play of market forces, instead of haphazard attempts to control them artificially, and often vainly, for the benefit of the consumers to end up in practice by benefiting mainly the middlemen at the expense of the farmers—there can be little doubt that India would have moved much faster towards, and beyond, the point of self-sufficiency in food. In addition, the ground would have been prepared well in advance for the new seeds which would have blossomed more readily into a vigorous green revolution.

It is strange to reflect that a government which worried so much about ensuring a fair price for consumers, cared so little about giving a fair price to the farmers who comprised three-quarters of the population and included its most depressed classes. And as if to add a needlessly cruel touch to an inherently callous policy, it was bolstered with the wrong-headed notion that the Indian farmers were price-insensitive.

In fairness, it must be admitted, however, that there *were* some keen and sensitive minds within the central food and agriculture administration, which protested against this policy as wrong, both economically and socially. Some of them recalled how, in the latter part of the war, the realization grew that, in many fertile areas of the country, production suffered simply because of remoteness from markets and transportation difficulties, and how spectacularly it spurted as soon as a minimum price had been guaranteed by the civil supplies administration.

Armed with this hard-won experience, they pleaded, ever since independence, for a policy of guaranteed minimum price for the principal cereals. This, they argued, was the first and most important single step needed for an effective solution of the food problem. But such views cut no ice with the policy-makers. The country was not yet ready to heed this voice of reason. Instead, it muddled along to pick up this truth, years later, from the pit of disasters.

Decontrol of foodgrain prices in 1947, according to the First Five Year Plan, had resulted in a 30 per cent rise in wholesale prices. After reimposition of controls in 1948, the situation improved temporarily. Thereafter prices moved up and down, but the ground lost was never regained, which caused "serious hardship to the middle classes." The Plan therefore stressed the need for a disinflationary price policy. In doing so, it also recognized that a stabilization policy should have not only a ceiling, but also a floor to safeguard the producer's interest by preventing prices from falling unduly. The primary concern of the Plan was, however, with the cost of living and how to prevent it from rising. No concrete action was proposed to protect the producer's interest, nor was there any suggestion for an *incentive* price.[13]

The Second Plan spoke of "an appropriate price policy," but the emphasis was on counteracting inflationary pressures with buffer-stocks of foodgrains and other strategic commodities to mitigate sharp fluctuations in prices, and with physical controls, should this prove necessary. With the decision to import P.L. 480 foodgrains the Plan had moved even most sharply away from the concept of a guaranteed fair price for producers.[14]

The Third Plan broke no fresh ground. It reiterated the need for relative stability of prices, especially of essential consumer foods, and stressed the dual role of P.L. 480 imports—to bridge the current gap between demand and domestic production, and to build up buffer-stocks as a hedge against future contingencies.[15]

In 1960, while preparing the ground for launching the IADP, the 10-Point Pilot Programme emphasized the need to provide "price incentives to participating cultivators through assured price agreements for rice and wheat and millets announced two years in advance."[16] The government was, however, unable to concur on the ground that it would be difficult to operate any guaranteed price scheme "in isolated pockets of the country." By implication, it was not ready to consider such a scheme on a nationwide scale.

In fact, one could hardly expect any other official reaction at that time; for, the food-aid-based food policy was then in full swing, and prices were explicitly consumer-oriented. As a result, the IADP had to be launched without an all-important support—a system of minimum guaranteed prices.[17]

[13] *First Five Year Plan, A Summary*, 1952, pp. 57-58.
[14] *Second Five Year Plan*, 1956, pp. 38-40, 86.
[15] *Third Five Year Plan*, pp. 119-32.
[16] See Chapter 12.
[17] *Report on the IADP (1960-68)*, Expert Committee on Assessment and Evaluation, Vol. I, New Delhi, 1969, p. 26.

This negative stance could not, however, last long. A decisive turn-around came when in one single year, namely 1964, consumption of imported wheat reached the dizzy figure of seven million tons. The old policy foundered on this *reductio ad absurdum*.

The Fourth Plan, in its Draft Outline, recognized the past error rather candidly. The absence of "an effective price policy," it observed, had contributed to "slow growth in agricultural production." Price support policy in the past "was aimed at eliminating distress," and this did not provide "the incentive needed for dynamic agricultural growth."[18]

The breakthrough in price policy came in 1964 when the government formally accepted the principle of fixing, on an all-India basis, support prices for some foodgrains. To start with, it announced minimum prices for rice and wheat. In January, 1965, an Agricultural Prices Commission (APC) was established to provide advice, on a continuing basis, on agri-cultural price policy and price structure with a twofold objective in view—"to raise agricultural production and give relief to the consumer."[19]

A policy of guaranteed minimum price must go hand in hand with an effective procurement policy. For, the concept of a minimum price would be meaningless unless the government steps in to buy up, at that price, all surpluses as soon as they begin to exercise a downward pressure. Accordingly, the Food Corporation of India (FCI) was established, almost at the same time as the APC, to discharge this cognate function.

The Corporation was given a comprehensive mandate. It was called upon not only to undertake all procurement-related functions—purchase, storage, movement, transportation, distribution, and sale of foodgrains and other foodstuffs—but also to promote production of foodgrains, and to set up, or assist in setting up, rice mills, flour mills, and similar enter-prises for processing foodgrains and other foodstuffs. On 1 January 1965, it formally came into existence.

The APC and the FCI became the twin pillars of the new price policy which, in turn, became the foundation of the new agricultural strategy.[20] Both of them, however, had to mark time for a while. The droughts made their work practically redundant during 1965-67. The FCI had a dual purpose to serve—to undertake procurement of foodgrains in times of shortage, and to provide price support in times of plenty. During the two drought years it could do neither—acute shortages prevailed in most areas so that practically all the procurement had to be made abroad; and prices ruled so high that talks of price support became irrelevant.

But things changed abruptly with the bumper crops, particularly of wheat, in 1967-68. The FCI swung into action and undertook purchases on a large scale, especially in Punjab and Haryana, assisted by the Punjab

[18] *Fourth Five Year Plan—A Draft Outline*, 1966, p. 174.
[19] Notified in the *Gazette of India, Extraordinary*, on 8 January 1965.
[20] See Chapter 15.

Cooperative Marketing Federation. The FCI's procurement prices were kept *above* the minimum support prices, and this was done as a matter of deliberate policy to give the farmers adequate incentive.

Meanwhile, on the APC's recommendations, the Government of India began to announce, from time to time, minimum support prices for foodgrains and other commodities well in advance of the growing season. For the 1967-68 season, for example, prices were fixed for paddy (Rs. 42 to Rs. 44 per quintal for different states), wheat, jowar, bajra, maize, and gram among foodgrains, and for cotton, jute, and sugarcane among cash crops. In general, they were fixed at levels higher than those of the preceding season; an element of incentive was thus frankly built into them. The statutory ceilings on the prices of raw cotton were removed with effect from the 1967-68 growing season. Though minimum prices were set for jute, they could not be enforced in the absence of an adequate purchase organization.

In the intervening years the FCI has expanded its operations. The APC, too, has continued in its role of determining minimum prices for major crops. It is, however, not necessary to go into the details of their activities.[21]

What is particularly important in the present context is the policy change, the adoption by the government of the principle of minimum support prices backed by systematic procurement, warehousing, and distribution of foodgrains. It was a great victory for common sense. And though it came late, it nonetheless marked a watershed in the history of India's agriculture.

This reversal of earlier official policy was by no means a smooth process. Behind it lay much tough fighting among policy-makers. Beyond that there was the inescapable logic of events which prevailed in the end. Stagnating acre-yield and unused potential at a time of rising population pressure, growing demand, looming shortages, mounting food imports entailing crippling foreign exchange expenditures—all these factors, as seen earlier, played their part in spreading the realization of the need for a basic reorientation of India's agricultural price policy, even before she was struck by a war and two droughts in quick succession as if to vindicate it *ex post facto*.

In addition, the IADP philosophy, with its intensely practical approach, the tenacious pleading of its devoted followers, and the actual demonstration of the pros and cons given in the IADP districts, must have significantly contributed to the same end.

Here, then, is an interesting fact which those with a love for paradoxes will find particularly delectable. While the benevolence of the US author-

[21] This information is readily available from the annual reports of the Central Ministry of Agriculture and other official documents. The yearbook called *INDIA* gives an annual resumé.

ities, as embodied in P.L. 480 food aid, was flooding the Indian grain markets and thereby setting up formidable price deterrents for Indian producers, a non-governmental US institution, combining service with science and tempering altruism with realism, worked in the opposite direction—to persuade the Indian authorities to give effective price incentives to their own farmers. And thus, it helped undo much of the unintended damage caused by unwary humanitarianism.

## FARMER RESPONSE

What has been the impact of higher prices on farmers in terms of production? There can be no more doubt on this score today.

Agricultural prices in India have tended upwards since 1939-40, and at a quicker pace since the late fifties. Initially, the response of farmers was blurred, often neutralized, by several factors. The rise, to start with, was not enough, especially since it began to climb from a traditionally depressed level; costs, too, went up simultaneously; fertilizers, if at all available, were far too expensive while other inputs were as yet unknown. Meanwhile, the bias of official policy was to keep prices down, which could not but act as a psychological deterrent.

Worst of all, even when prices were relatively high, there was no guarantee that they would remain so. On the contrary, the post-harvest slump and off-season jump in prices were annual phenomena. The former invariably hurt the producers while the latter usually meant a handsome windfall for the traders.

A dramatic breakthrough on the production front had to wait for a dramatic rise in prices. This happened around the mid-sixties. The almost simultaneous arrival of the dwarf varieties and the adoption of a price support policy reinforced the trend.

The really steep rise in fertilizer consumption began in 1965-66,[22] and reflected a corresponding rise in prices. This was the time when grain prices began to outpace fertilizer prices by an attractive margin, as will be evident from the following comparison of wholesale prices for wheat, rice, ammonium sulphate:

WHOLESALE PRICE INDEXES  (1960 = 100)[23]

| Year | Wheat | Rice | Ammonium Sulphate |
|------|-------|------|-------------------|
| 1955 | 77    | 70   | 82                |
| 1960 | 100   | 100  | 100               |

[22] See Chapter 18.

[23] Extracted from *Background of Indian Agriculture and India's Intensive Agricultural Program*, mimeographed report by Dr. Carl C. Malone, Consultant on Agricultural Development, The Ford Foundation, New Delhi, May 1969, p. 15.

| Year | Wheat | Rice | Ammonium Sulphate |
|------|-------|------|-------------------|
| 1961 | 98 | 95 | 98 |
| 1962 | 101 | 100 | 95 |
| 1963 | 100 | 112 | 95 |
| 1964 | 136 | 122 | 95 |
| 1965 | 154 | 124 | 97 |
| 1966 | 158 | 151 | 106 |
| 1967 | 218 | 183 | 131 |
| 1968 | 205 | 196 | 134 |

Until 1964 fertilizer was quite expensive in terms of wheat and rice, but thereafter its relative cost declined appreciably.

According to a study based on IADP, the incentives for fertilizer use are weak if the value of the additional output is less than twice the cost of fertilizer; it is moderate to strong when the ratio ranges between 2.0 to 2.5; and it is very strong when the relationship exceeds 3.0.[24]

Consumption of nitrogenous fertilizers (N) more than quintupled—from 210,000 to 1,145,00 tons—in eight years, between 1960-61 and 1968-69. During the same period, consumption of phosphates ($P_2O_5$) rose from 70,000 to 391,000 tons, and of potash ($K_2O$) from 25,000 to 160,000 tons. In the USA total plant food use, recalls Dr. Malone, increased by about 1.3 million tons in 40 years—from 1900 to 1940; whereas India has been able to make "this much increase in five years."[25]

The relevant question is, as it always has been, not how favourable is the farmer's response, but how effective is the government's price policy. In this respect an uphill task still lies ahead.

## IMPLEMENTING THE NEW POLICY

In recent years, says the Fourth Plan, the policy of minimum prices as an incentive to agricultural production has been given "pointed recognition."[26] A great battle of principle has been won. The task now is to apply it effectively on a countrywide basis.

The prerequisites of an adequate support policy were restated by the Foodgrains Policy Committee (1966) as follows: Advance announcement of prices well before the growing season; holding them "fairly stable over a long period" to help create a "favourable climate for long-

[24] Dorris D. Brown and Harold Dunkerley, Development Advisory Service, Harvard University, USA—*Fertilizer News*, Dec. 1968. Quoted in *Report on the IADP (1960-68)*, Expert Committee on Assessment and Evaluation, Vol. 1, New Delhi, 1969, p. 26.

[25] Ibid., p. 3.

[26] *Fourth Five Year Plan, 1969-74*, p. 144.

term investment"; wide publicity of the minimum support prices by the government; its readiness to purchase all the quantities offered to it at those prices; and adequate arrangements at important markets for making such purchases whenever the need arises. These are inescapable conditions, and they were also recognized as such in the Fourth Plan.

A policy of extending minimum support prices to foodgrains, sugarcane, jute and cotton has already been announced. It is now necessary to translate the policy more fully into action, and also to extend it to a few other commodities, especially oilseeds.

For implementing a price support policy a great deal depends on the purchasing machinery. Despite recent progress, this machinery is still inadequate, both in scope and in effectiveness, and needs to be strengthened and expanded on many fronts. Separate corporations are due to be established, during the Fourth Plan period, to handle price-support purchase operations respectively for cotton, jute, and oilseeds. For foodgrains, such purchases are currently made by the Food Corporation of India; the State Trading Corporation, and the cooperative marketing organizations. But together, they are so far able to tackle only a small fraction of this huge task. Millions of grain producers in most of the states are yet to be brought within the ambit of their operations.

The fact is that if the quality of the price support administration depends on the adequacy of the purchasing machinery, the latter, in turn, can be effective only when the country is properly equipped with transportation, marketing and warehouse facilities. These essential concomitants of modern commercial agriculture have hitherto been woefully lacking in India. Progress in these fields must be greatly speeded up if a price support programme is to be successful.[27]

Above all, there is the question of long-term stability of prices, also of the *levels* at which they are held stable. Obviously, prices must be both stable and remunerative if they are to serve as incentives to production. In neither respect are the current signs sufficiently reassuring.

Minimum support prices constitute the very foundation of modern high-technology agriculture. But the concept is still new to India; there are, as a result, too many people—businessmen, industrialists, economists, and political leaders who have not yet been able to grasp it firmly enough. Moreover, the memories of cheaper food are still vivid in the public mind; and as the cost of living soars, the demand for lower food prices gains in strength. The recent improvement in the food situation tends to lend fresh weight to it. How to reconcile the apparently conflicting interests of producers and consumers has become a major issue which is yet to be resolved.

The Agricultural Prices Commission, in making its recommendations, was explicitly asked to bear three considerations in mind: *first*, the need

[27] Discussed in the next chapter.

to provide incentive to the producer "for adopting improved technology and for maximizing production"; *second*, the need to ensure "rational utilisation of land and other production resources"; and *third*, the likely effect of price policy on "the rest of the economy, particularly on the cost of living, level of wages, industrial cost structure, etc."[28]

This was a tall mandate. The sensitive task of harmonizing conflicting interests was entrusted to the Commission which was thus directly exposed to political pressures in formulating its price recommendations. This cannot but inhibit longer-term stability of prices. Even the brief experience of the few years the Commission has been at work shows that the danger is very real.

Worse still, the third condition implies that the impact of the first two on the economy could be adverse. This assumption, in India's present condition, is at best academic. By far the most important task today—and for the foreseeable future—is to fix prices at levels which will assure farmers of a *stable and sufficiently attractive margin of profit* from the cultivation of the main crops. Without this, the first two conditions will never be satisfied, production will suffer, and, as a result, the whole economy will be worse off.

That a manufacturer must have a reasonable margin of profit is accepted as an axiom. What is frequently overlooked is that a farmer, too, must make sure of a similar profit the moment he turns away from subsistence agriculture—that is, producing for his family—to commercial agriculture—that is, producing for the market.

To put it differently, modern farming with intensive use of manufactured inputs and market-oriented production is an industry; the farmer engaged in such operations, no matter on what scale, is an entrepreneur; and, like his manufacturing counterpart, he, too, must have a fair margin of profit. A state that wants him to come out of his traditional stronghold and to produce for the market must also assure him of such a margin. This is absolutely essential. Any compromise here would be fatal and defeat the objective.

But what about the cost of living and the cost of manufactured goods, which are directly affected by the prices of foodgrains and industrial raw materials? These are, of course, vitally important questions. That agriculture must serve the public and the manufacturing industry to the utmost possible extent goes without saying. It can do so, however, only when its *capacity* to serve has been built up first. The worst policy for India today would be to deny to the farmers price incentives to produce marketable surpluses, which will push them back towards the subsistence-type of farming and push the country back into the throes of food deficits.

For a long time India's undeveloped agriculture was milked too hard,

[28] Notification in the *Gazette of India, Extraordinary*, 8 January 1965, cited earlier.

the effects of which are writ large all over the economy. A repetition of that folly will help none. It will, instead, once again turn what is a vast potential asset into an intolerable liability.

Luckily, the conflicts of interests in this case are more apparent than real. They can be easily reconciled if the issues are seen in the right perspective. One might, broadly speaking, distinguish three different phases in the evolution of an adequate price support policy.

Initially, as the farmer ventures out of his traditional shell and takes the first cautious steps towards modern farming with purchased inputs, he must be protected with minimum support prices guaranteed for a fairly long period. The prices should be liberal enough to cover the normal risks of farming; in addition, they must also give him a definite incentive to move faster towards market-oriented production.

That an industry must be protected in its infant stage, especially with import duties, has long been taken for granted. Commercial agriculture, too, has its period of infancy with all the attending troubles. Consequently, it is entitled, during this vulnerable phase, to the same kind of protection which is readily extended to a manufacturing industry under the umbrella of infant industry argument.

However, support prices need not, indeed must not, be frozen permanently at fixed levels. For, what matters from the farmer's angle is not the *absolute level* of a support price, but the *net margin* between his total costs and his gross sale proceeds. It is this margin, or his profit, which must be protected. Subject to this, lowering of the support price level would be perfectly justified. In short, *price-cutting must come not via profit-cutting, but via cost-cutting.* Here, again, the farmer's position is essentially no different from that of a manufacturer.

The all-important task, in the second phase, is to explore opportunities for reducing costs all along the line. For this a modernizing agriculture in a developing economy offers enormous scope. To mention only the more obvious:

> Costs of fertilizers and other inputs, at the farm level, are very high. They can be brought down substantially if the industries now producing them in India are run with greater efficiency, and if their distribution through wholesale and retail trade channels is better organized.
>
> Irrigation can be greatly improved, and this is true of farm planning, farm operations and management in general; with intensive effort, acre-yield can be raised, sometimes several times, with a sharp lowering of unit costs.
>
> Transportation, warehousing, and marketing facilities are still in a primitive stage; there is great urgency to expand and improve them, and as this occurs costs will come down; refrigeration, too, can solidly contribute to the same end.[29]

The proportion of wastage due to pests, insects, rodents, and weather is exceedingly high; there is a vast scope for improvement here—for lowering unit costs by cutting down on wastage.[30]

Genetic research and plant-breeding hold the key to high yield; they can and should be greatly expanded to ensure a steady flow of high-yielding varieties of different crops.[31]

Here, then, is a never-ending task, all directed to raise production, improve quality, and lower costs. As costs come down, the support prices, too, can be lowered, without unduly impairing the farmer's profit margin and his incentive to production.

What India now needs is unflagging effort along these lines to usher in the third phase when agriculture will be in an advanced state of development, and when, as a result, farmers will be more efficient, more self-reliant, also better organized in cooperatives and other institutions. They will still need, and demand, support prices, at least for their main crops. But they will be better placed to defend their own interests, and also to serve the consumers and the manufacturing industries.

Such an approach will make for a more prosperous economy with a healthier balance among its different sectors. This is the goal today's price support policy should constantly keep in view and try to achieve as fast as possible.

## A FATAL HESITANCY

After a long struggle, India's major foodgrain and a few other prices have become, or are becoming, producer-oriented. With this the foundation has been laid for building up a strong, modern agriculture. But the foundation itself is still shaky; it rests on a weak conviction of the policy-makers, whose conversion to the new policy has been half-hearted, if not reluctant. Many of them would, if possible, set the clock back and revert to the good old days of depressed agricultural prices.

What is the reason for this fatal hesitancy? There is no doubt the conflict of interests inevitable in any human society. There is also a genuine difficulty to understand why price support must be built into the system and used as the lever for turning family-oriented primitive farming into market-oriented modern agriculture. Beyond all this, however, there is an ingrained intellectual inertia.

India's educated elite still relies heavily on the "neo-mercantilistic" ideas to which it has long been inured. It overlooks the plain fact that what was good for Imperial Britain is not good for free India. The

---

[29] See next Chapter.
[30] Discussed at length in *Reaping the Green Revolution*.
[31] See Chapters 3, 4 and 22.

realities of the two situations are completely different. For an insular maritime country like Britain which had pioneered the industrial revolution, built up farflung global interests and acquired an entrenched position in world trade, it made a great deal of economic sense to import cheap food and raw materials and to sell in return manufactured goods in the overseas markets. This is a most inappropriate model for India to follow, more so at a time when a non-imperial Britain is busily reshaping and readjusting it to the radically altered conditions of today.[32]

One of the world's largest potential markets, India must realize, lies right within her own frontiers, in the rural areas inhabited by 80 per cent of her 575 million people. No market she can ever expect to command abroad for her manufactures will be remotely comparable to it—even at its best it will be only a tiny fraction of what she can readily command at home. This is the market she should develop, the market her domestic industry must learn—or be taught—to nurse with care, and affection, in its own long-range interest.

To develop this market India must build up her long-neglected rural economy, and, above all, exploit the vast potential of her tropical and sub-tropical agriculture and multiply the purchasing power of the farming community. In the process she can also promote agri-based exports. Jute and tea figure even now as her best foreign exchange earners. It should be possible to add many more items to the list.[33]

India's manufacturing industries, too, will then be in a far better position to venture into the overseas markets. A strong domestic market will enable them to reap the economies of scale, which will often give them the needed competitive edge in world trade.

If India must look for a model abroad, she must turn her eyes away from pre-war Britain, and turn them towards the USA where agriculture has spearheaded her economic growth in the past, where even today it accounts for a very large part of her overall exports, a fact that is frequently overlooked.

What India needs is primarily agri-centred, home market-oriented industrial development. Failure to realize this has brought her economy to the present impasse. Chronic food deficits have greatly damaged it. There never was any justification for them, and certainly there is none today. She can liquidate the deficits, even become a food-surplus country and a major exporter of agricultural products, if she can bring to bear the requisite will and realism on her economic policies.

The manufacturing industries have been demanding, and commanding, high prices from the public, aided by a producer-oriented industrial policy and a virtually sheltered domestic market. Though high food

[32] For further comments on these points, see Chapter 30: "Challenges and Opportunities."

[33] Discussed further in *Reaping the Green Revolution.*

prices are frequently blamed for high cost of living, industries' contribution to it has been no less conspicuous. For example, the price of cotton textiles, next only to food in importance, has skyrocketed in recent years.

India must resist the whisperings—the siren lure—of neo-mercantilism. She must stick to a policy of *bon prix* for agricultural goods, despite the hue and cry raised from time to time to make them available at *bon marché*, and forge ahead with the development of her agriculture. The entire economy will stand to gain from such a policy. And, all sections of the public will then be assured of adequate supplies of essential articles —both food and non-food—at *meilleur marché*, or lower prices.

# CHAPTER 24

# Marketing, Transportation, and Storage

## POST-HARVEST UNDERPINNINGS

A modern farmer, as explained in the preceding chapter, is an entre-preneur; and as such, he resembles his manufacturing counterpart. There are, of course, significant differences between the two types of entre-preneurial activities because of differences inherent in the nature of their business.

A manufacturer has considerable flexibility in making his initial deci-sions. He chooses his line of business with care, usually from among many alternatives, carries out feasibility studies in advance, and picks the best possible location, bearing all cost factors in mind. Accessibility and proximity to raw materials and markets weigh most heavily in his calculations. His production is market-oriented and, in general, also prof-itable from the start. In addition, he has normally a lot of political muscle, which often serves him as a second line of defence. Should he, for example, run into unexpected troubles, he can run to the government which, as a rule, is understanding enough to help him tide over his diffi-culties with tax rebates, depreciation allowances, import duties, and similar relief measures.

Agriculture, in all these respects, is far less fortunate. As one of man's oldest occupations, it has an entirely different origin. It was born as nature's prisoner, and, to a large extent, it remains so even today. It is place-bound—being tied to a farmland, it offers no locational choice; it is also family-bound, at least initially when almost the whole production goes to maintain the farmer's own family. The primary task of modernization is to alter the second feature, that is, to give farming a commercial or market-oriented slant. At this stage agriculture, too, would need its own "feasibility study" with assurance of a reasonable margin of profit, which, as seen in the previous chapter, would be possible only with adequate price support.

But there is no escape for agriculture from the first feature—its locational limitation. Unlike a manufacturing industry, it is stationary—even when it produces for the market, it cannot move any closer to it. The movement must, therefore, be reversed—like the mountain going to Mohamet, the market must move close to the farmland.

This has three major implications for traditional agriculture. First, since markets are nonexistent in most areas, they must be created from scratch and suitably located so as to be within easy reach of the surrounding farmlands. In addition, the existing markets will often need to be enlarged and modernized. Second, farms must be provided with outlets to markets, which will require village-to-market roads to be built all over the country. And, third, there must be adequate facilities, again within easy reach of the farmers, for storing grains and other crops, so that they may be placed on the market in an orderly manner, and not dumped all at a time after the harvest, causing a slump in prices and heavy losses due to wastage.

It is not enough to produce a green revolution with dwarf seeds and modern inputs. Its fruits must be harvested and spread over the country. This can be done only when there are enough markets, link roads, and warehouses.

## SCARCITY OF MARKETS

Markets in India have been, and still are, too few in number and too remote from the farms, mostly without any means of access to them. This, undoubtedly, has been a major factor responsible for the backwardness of her agriculture.

The shortage of market-towns can be judged from a few broad figures. According to the 1961 census, India had, all sizes taken together, 564,718 villages, whereas towns and cities numbered only 2,690. In the second category were 248 large urban centres, each with a population ranging from 50,000 to 4 million, and another 515 urban centres, or small cities, with 20,000 to 50,000 people each. This left a balance of 1,927 small and medium-sized towns or, on an average, one town for 293 villages. Obviously, the proportion of towns was far too low.

In the background of these facts, the National Council of Applied Economic Research (NCAER) made a special study a few years ago, in which it tried to assess India's needs for market-towns to stimulate her agricultural and spatial development.[1] Most villages, the study emphasized, cannot be "transport-linked" with the existing urban centres which are at present too few and too remote. Between the burgeoning cities and the primitive villages, there is no organic link, no real give-and-take— except the formidable "take" of the rural population which now swamps the cities. There can be no significant development as long as this "dual economy" lasts. It must be broken down to achieve a new rural-urban integration. This underlines the urgency of planting, in the heart of rural India, a great many more market-towns which will hasten this end and will, at the same time, both promote and support the growth of her agricultural economy.

How many more cities or market-towns would meet India's current needs? The NCAER recognized the difficulty of offering a clearcut answer without further field investigations, since geography, agronomy, climate, population density, communication and other factors would influence the number. However, it did try to work out a "very rough approximation" based on some hypothetical premises. Assuming that villages are located at three-mile intervals on an average, and that a 12-mile radius is the maximum practical extension of a market-town, India would then need one market-town for every 40-45 villages. This would work out to 12,500 to 14,000 market-towns for the whole country, or a six to seven fold increase over the present number.

The study rightly rejected the Community Development Block as a possible market-town unit. The Block, it argued, was an artificial creation, mechanically uniform, but functionally meaningless; it was also much too large; at best, it could serve as an administrative unit. On the other hand, rural India's real need was a large number of newly created, spatially dispersed semi-urban communities, relatively small in size but highly functional.

The NCAER study was made before there was any suggestion of a green revolution. The yield explosion that followed and the population explosion which has continued unabated have greatly increased the total number of market-towns India would need today. It may therefore be more appropriate to double the NCAER's estimate to, say, 25,000 to 30,000 market-towns.

Moreover, the study had outlined a plan for the future. The future has already arrived. With a green revolution already on hand, there is no time to lose. The task of building market-towns must now be tackled as a matter of high national priority.

[1] *Market Towns and Spatial Development in India*, National Council of Applied Economic Research, New Delhi, 1965. This is a path-finding, pioneering study for India with constructive proposals which deserve much greater attention than they have received so far,

An example will illustrate the urgency.[2] In Punjab, the cradle of India's green revolution, wheat yield shot up by 52 per cent in 1967-68 over the previous three years' average, as a direct result of the large-scale adoption of dwarf wheats imported from Mexico. The post-harvest arrivals in the market, however, rose far more sharply—by as much as 150 per cent as compared with the preceding three-year average. The result was an unprecedented glut. Caught unprepared, the markets were choked and swamped.

Why should a 52 per cent increase in grain output cause a three times larger flow to the market? The main reason of course was that most of the increase, being an excess over the growers' own consumption requirements, represented a marketable surplus. Two other factors helped build up the glut. Mechanized threshing and winnowing had eliminated the customary fortnight's lag between harvesting and readying the grains for sale. And, with a huge crop on hand, the growers were apprehensive of a price crash, and rushed their surplus to the market.

Incidentally, those sceptics who still look askance at the concept of support prices should do well to ponder this phenomenon and the disaster that would ensue in a situation like this without such support.[3]

The PAU study on the subject vividly describes the effects of this sudden flood on the market. The yards were soon all crammed; stocks were unloaded around the markets, even in roads and lanes; some growers did the cleaning and dressing of the produce in the marketplace, and thereby further accentuated the shortage of space. During the study it was found that in two major markets—Ludhiana and Khana—23 and 29 per cent, respectively, of the wheat transactions took place outside the market yards—in roads, lanes and fields, and this resulted in pilferage and spoilage, in addition to causing traffic jams and inconvenience to the public.[4]

The situation was indeed chaotic, yet it was only a curtain-raiser. It revealed what would happen with the spread of the high-yielding varieties—what is perhaps already happening in several other places—unless the problems of marketing are tackled promptly and adequately.

The study points out some ameliorative steps which could be taken forthwith. Cleaning grains in the market should be banned; this job can and should be done in the villages. Wheat supplies to local flour mills on state government account should be purchased direct from the market; they need not pass through the procurement agency. This agency, in its

---

[2] The facts cited here have been drawn from *Wheat Market Behaviour in Punjab —Post-Harvest Period 1968-69* by K. S. Gill, Punjab Agricultural University, Ludhiana. The study gives a thorough analysis of the problems and suggests practical steps to tackle them.

[3] See the previous chapter.

[4] Ibid.

turn, should make its procurement increasingly in the villages, rather than in the markets; this will help reduce the strain on the available storage, transportation, and market facilities. The structure of procurement prices, too, should be improved allowing, in particular, a reasonable price premium for the "lean months." The absence of this premium induced the growers to dump their produce on the market to the maximum possible extent right after the harvest.

These steps will help improve matters in so far as they will take some of the pressures off the markets. But the relief they will provide, welcome though it is, will not touch the heart of the problem. For an adequate solution, markets must be multiplied in number, suitably located, and properly equipped, with a large increase both in storage and transportation facilities.

## REGULATED MARKETS

The first attempt to regulate agricultural markets in India was made in 1897. An Act passed in that year authorized the then British Resident in Hyderabad Assigned District to declare any place within his jurisdiction a market for sale and purchase of agricultural produce, and to constitute a Committee to supervise and regulate the markets.[5] The law did help improve the buying and selling of cotton. But it suffered from three major limitations: The market committee consisted solely of traders, and this tended to defeat the declared objective of benefiting the cultivator-seller. In practice, the law was applied only to cotton, the main cash crop of the region, and, despite its title, did not include grain. Any net income derived from the market, it was explicitly stipulated, would go to the local municipal authority, instead of being ploughed back into the market for further development.

The next step came, thirty years later, with the passage of the "Cotton Markets Act" (1927) in Bombay. Once again, the law was concerned only with a single crop. However, in an important departure from the Berar Law, it gave the cotton growers a majority on the market committee.

The Royal Commission on Agriculture, reporting a year later, urged that *all* provinces should establish regulated markets to help orderly marketing of *all* agricultural produce. It deprecated the practice of treating regulated markets as a source of municipal revenue, and insisted that surplus incomes, if any, must be used solely to develop and improve the facilities and services for the benefit of the producers.

Hyderabad, Central Provinces, and Madras promptly acted on the Commission's recommendation and passed appropriate legislation. Others

[5] "Cotton and Grain Markets Act of Hyderabad Assigned District" (1897), or the so-called Berar Law.

followed with longer intervals—Punjab in 1939, also Mysore the same year, though its Act was not operative until 1948, Madhya Pradesh in 1952, Kerala and Orissa in 1957.

At the beginning of the Third Plan, legislation for establishing regulated markets was in force in nine states. Four more states enacted the Agricultural Produce Markets Act by 1968, and the remaining states—Assam, Nagaland, Kerala, and Jammu and Kashmir—are expected to do so during the Fourth Plan period.

The number of regulated markets and submarket yards, on the eve of the Fourth Plan, was 1,616. Some 2,100 markets and submarket yards were yet to be brought under regulation, a task which has been earmarked for the Fourth Plan period.[6]

The regulated markets established in different states show much similarity today, both in law and in actual practice. This is due largely to the fact that their state laws were patterned on the same model, specially on a model Bill prepared by the Central Government in 1938. But the actual growth of regulated markets and their geographical distribution have been highly uneven. They are well developed in Maharashtra and Gujarat, followed by Mysore, Punjab and Madhya Pradesh. Another significant fact about them is their heavy concentration in the cotton-growing states. This largely explains why, in 1964, 80 per cent of a total of 1,000 regulated markets then in existence were located in the five Western states although, together, they accounted for only 30 per cent of India's population.

Thus, despite the expostulations of the Royal Commission of 1928, the progress made with regulated markets in the intervening decades has been slow and fitful, while they are still wholly inadequate in coverage. They are largely confined to cotton and do not embrace other agricultural produce. Until recently, U.P., West Bengal, and Assam hardly had any regulated markets. And only now the omission is being made good.

The inadequacy of the marketing system can be judged from another key index—the facilities available for grading agricultural produce. In 1969, there were only 450 grading units operated by different agencies, such as regulated markets, cooperative societies, and central and state warehouses, and together they could grade just about 1 per cent of the total value of the agricultural produce entering the trade. As a step towards overcoming this deficiency the Fourth Plan has provided for another 600 grading units.[7]

The regulated markets naturally had some spread effect. Once they gained in reputation as centres for more orderly transaction of business, they attracted producers from a wider area. However, as their name implies, they are concerned with *better* regulation of *existing* markets,

[6] *Fourth Five Year Plan 1969-74*, p. 143.
[7] *Fourth Five Year Plan 1969-74*, p. 143.

not with creation of *new* ones. With regulation, the markets improved in capacity and serviceability, but their total number remained unchanged.

Since the early sixties a new trend has set in, and subyards have been established in "unserviced" areas linking them with the regulated markets. However, as is to be expected, most of them are concentrated in a few states led by Maharashtra, Gujarat, and Mysore where the markets are best developed and have a relatively good coverage.

As this brief review clearly shows, the number of markets in existence—3,716 in 1969, inclusive of submarket yards, and giving a ratio of one unit for 150,000 people or more—is totally inadequate to meet India's needs. Lack of markets has long inhibited her agricultural progress. Today it is jeopardizing the spread of the green revolution.

The tasks are obvious and urgent; they are also stupendous because of the need to make amends for a long record of gross omissions and to cash in on the unparalleled opportunities which have suddenly opened up. The market-density in India must be rapidly raised—a tenfold increase over the next fifteen years would, on a rough estimate, more closely correspond to her real needs.

The need, however, is not simply for more, but also for better, markets. For example, the so-called submarket yards are little more than single-purpose assembly points, usually for handling one or two cash crops. They must grow into full-fledged markets with modern facilities and other ancillary functions to promote not only the marketing of agricultural produce, but also exchange of goods on a wide scale.

The existing markets, as seen above, are very unevenly distributed. The new markets must therefore be more rationally spread to achieve optimum "saturation" of all the states. They must also correspond, even if approximately, to the productive potential and population density of individual areas.

And, finally, the market centres should be given the facilities and inducements to grow into townships, towns, and medium cities with processing and other industries, and essential services, as hubs of economic and social activities. Markets, in short, should serve as the vanguard of urbanization in the rural hinterland.[8]

## A ROADBLOCK TO PROGRESS

Just as a power station must be provided with a transmission system, and an irrigation project with a canal system, a market, to be functionally meaningful, must have a network of roads serving a sufficiently large number of producers and consumers. But whereas for a power or an

[8] Town-building, urbanization, spatial distribution of population and related questions are discussed in *Reaping the Green Revolution*.

irrigation project the delivery system works only one way, market roads serve as a two-way conveyor-belt—to carry inputs and extension workers to the farms, to bring back the farm produce to the market, also to distribute consumer goods to the rural community. And since not only goods, but also ideas and information accumulate at market centres, they travel along the same routes into the villages.

Roads, in short, are like the veins and arteries of an integrated rural economy. This is no doubt the meaning of Dr. Ashby's remark, quoted in Chapter 2, emphasizing that he would accord not only the first, but also the second, even the third priority to roads in any programme of agricultural development. For traditional farming the first breakthrough occurs when it is given a market-linked road. And for the same reason, its absence remains the worst roadblock to progress.

The President's Science Advisory Committee, in its study on the World Food Crisis, singled out transportation as the most critical factor in any attempt to increase agricultural production. "It has never been possible," reminded the Committee's Panel of Experts on Transportation, "to exchange traditional methods of cultivation and patterns of production until transport is adequate because transport is a means of moving ideas and information as well as goods."[9]

An adequate transportation system, the Panel goes on to say, has three general features: "a fine-mesh network of low-capacity routes blanketing each food-producing and food-consuming area"; "focal points" scattered within each of these networks to serve as collection and distribution centres; and "a loose network of high-capacity routes" that connects the collection-distribution centres with major cities and seaports. Together, they build up a national transportation system; each of them is an essential ingredient so that the system's effectiveness is no greater than its weakest link.

"The critical importance of a fine-mesh transport grid," the Panel observes, "is universally recognized for the population-dense, food-consuming areas but is completely ignored for the rural, food-producing areas." Yet in both cases the objective is the same—convenience in marketing or acquiring products; in one case the commuter goes to the working-place to sell his services, while in the other case the farmer takes his produce to market and picks up his supplies.

The farmer must be in a position to exchange his surplus crops for consumer goods with reasonable convenience. Otherwise he will lack "an important incentive to exploit the full potential of his land." The absence of "an efficient rural transport net," in the Panel's view, may be

[9] *The World Food Crisis*, A Report of the President's Science Advisory Committee, The White House, May 1967, Vol. II, pp. 573-4. Policy-makers in developing countries—and international aid-givers—will do well to ponder over the ideas presented in Chapter 11 on Transportation, Vol. II, pp. 569-92.

"the real limiting factor" in any programme to raise agricultural productivity.

## THE ROADBLOCK IN INDIA

Developing countries have been spending a large part of their limited resources on transportation. The proportion, according to the Panel, ranges from 20 to 40 per cent of the investments made in the public sector. But planners have been preoccupied, almost everywhere, with the inter-city traffic in industrial goods; rural transport and, in particular, the specific needs of agriculture have been almost consistently ignored. The result has been poor return from the heavy capital investments, along with continued poor return from land.

India is a conspicuous example of this general failing. The total road mileage shows a substantial increase since independence:[10]

### (*In 1,000 kilometres*)

| Type | 1947 | 1961 | 1969 |
|---|---|---|---|
| Surfaced | 1.46 | 2.31 | 3.25 |
| Unsurfaced | 2.42 | 4.48 | 6.47 |
| Total | 3.88 | 6.79 | 9.72 |

In 22 years the total has gone up by 187 per cent. Even then it is small for a country of India's size and population—the 1969 mileage works out to about 30 km. for every 100,000 of people.

What is worse, the most critical shortage is in rural areas, especially in terms of village-to-market roads. According to the President's Science Advisory Committee,[11] the agriculturally advanced Western countries have 3 to 4 miles of farm-to-market roads per square mile of cultivated land. In grain-producing areas the mileage varies somewhat, depending on the size of the farms and the nature of the topography. Britain, France, Japan, and the United States have an average of about 4, while in Taiwan and Denmark it is closer to 3.

In India, the figure is only a fraction of this average—per square mile of cultivated land she has only about 0.7 mile of road. And only 11 per cent of India's 580,000 villages, according to the Committee, have "reasonably adequate" roads, while one out of three is more than five miles from a satisfactory road. To meet the access requirements of these villages. India will have to build 1,000,000 miles of roads. The size of the road-building task is "staggering." And this underlines the need for con-

[10] Source: *India 1970*, p. 402.
[11] Loc. cit., Vol. II, p. 582.

centrating efforts, in the first place, in areas showing the greatest promise of increased productivity.

Expenditures on roads in India under the different Plans have been as follows (in crore Rs.): First Plan—155; Second Plan—250; Third Plan —440; 1966-69 (estimated)—307; Fourth Plan (provision)—871. This is a big increase, even after allowance is made for the rise in prices.

The Fourth Plan allocation consists of an outlay of Rs. 418 crores for Central road programmes, and the balance of Rs. 453 crores for road development in the states and Union territories. Thus, close to one-half of the funds is earmarked for Central projects. Even in the second category, priority is given to: completion of works in progress; removal of deficiencies in the existing road system, such as missing links, unbridged river crossings, and improvement of low-grade sections; reconstruction of weak bridges and widening of roads; some strengthening of the road system to meet the requirements of the metropolitan cities, industrial and mining areas, and hilly and backward regions; and a rather small increase in surfaced roads during the Plan period—from 325,000 to 385,000 kilometres.

What about rural roads? Special emphasis "is being laid" on their development, observes the Fourth Plan. They are "necessary" for the growth of the rural economy and for increase in agricultural production. State governments "have agreed" to set apart about 25 per cent of their outlay on road development for rural areas. Local resources, too, will be mobilized. And priority will be given to roads leading to market-towns.[12]

Thus, there is at last some recognition of the importance of rural roads. But it is made in a tone that sounds casual; the allocation made is much too modest; worst of all, the Plan postulates the simplistic view that the essence of the task consists of allocation of funds, although this has been repeatedly belied by experience. There are already complaints that roadbuilding is lagging seriously behind the schedule, and that the funds allocated are not being spent in practice.

Another evidence of misplanning in this field is the 20-year plan (1961-81) prepared some time ago for road development. Its declared aim is to bring every village (a) in a developed agricultural area within 6 km. of a metalled road and 2.5 km. of any road, (b) in a semi-developed area within 13 km. of a metalled road and 5 km. of any road, and (c) in an undeveloped and uncultivable area within 19 km. of a metalled road and 8 km. of any road.[13]

The plan is obviously based on the assumption that half a road is better than none. It is ideally suited to ensure zero return on the investment for

[12] *Fourth Five Year Plan 1969-74*, p. 345.
[13] *India 1969*, p. 391.

49

a maximum length of time. Luckily the plan, it seems, did not get much beyond the ink-and-paper stage.

There is a widespread feeling in India, among both policy-makers and the general public, that roadbuilding is an expensive proposition; that though desirable from a national angle, highways are often uneconomic; that rural roads would not pay their way, and that one can, somehow or other, make-do without them. And in support of these views evidence is cited from recent experience, which, *prima facie*, looks quite plausible.

For example, on most long-haul inter-city highways traffic growth has been exceedingly slow, so that their economics, in most cases, look highly dubious. The same remark applies to the rural roads built under the Community Development Programme.[14] Sizable mileages were built under their auspices in some regions. But they made little impact on production, and most of them quickly fell into disrepair.

Yet the evidence is misleading. The facts cited are correct, but the conclusions drawn are wrong. They prove, first of all, that not all roads are economic. There is the important question of timing—they may be built too far ahead of traffic growth, just as they may not be built soon enough. Construction costs are another important factor; the initial outlay can be kept down by proper staging aimed at progressively improving the quality and capacity of roads. Construction schedules are often too slow and pile up overhead costs; missing mileages, narrow and weak bridges, lack of culverts and the like may cause disproportionate delays in bringing a highway into use.[15]

Another set of cost-push factors relate to road transport policies: high cost of vehicles, tyres, and spare parts often due to import duties; multiple taxes on motor fuel—import duty, excise, and sales taxes; licensing fees for vehicles and drivers; arbitrary restriction on inter-state trucking and its absurd effect as reflected in the transhipment of goods at some state boundaries to avoid double taxation. More rational policies could substantially reduce road transport costs and thereby help stimulate traffic growth.[16]

The greatest weakness of India's roadbuilding programme lies in the neglect of rural, or feeder, roads linked to the farms, though they are by far the biggest generators of traffic. It is like setting up an expensive conveyor-belt without paying much heed to the flow of supplies to be

[14] For example, the progress made under the C.D. programmes during the year ending September 1969 was as follows: new *kacha* (unsurfaced) roads constructed —29,774 km., culverts constructed—16,672, and existing *kacha* roads improved— 46,732 km. See *India 1970*, p. 275. The CDP-built roads are included in the all-India totals given earlier.

[15] The *Fourth Five Year Plan 1969-74* lists some of these factors (p. 344).

[16] For a good discussion on the economics of road transportation, see "The Role of Transportation in the Process of Economic Development" by Daniel G. Sisler, *Some Issues Emerging*, etc., Kenneth L. Turk, ed., loc. cit.

fed into it. Or, to change the analogy, building highways to the neglect of rural roads is like concentrating on high dams for irrigation to the neglect of minor projects, although the latter are cheaper, quicker, and more productive. In both cases, maximum benefit can be achieved only through a conjunctive approach comprising small as well as large projects. And in both cases, the most economic route leads from the small to the large, and not the other way round, as has been the case in India.

But what about the CDP-built village roads which, for years, received so much attention? They suffered from several weaknesses. Only too often, they were hastily conceived without proper layout and design. They were treated as part not of a productive, but of a welfare package; not as a means of raising farm output and delivering it to the market, but as a rural amenity. And so they were not backed by greater use of productive inputs, not even by minor irrigation projects except in isolated instances.

Nor were they, in general, linked to markets. In fact, markets were too few and in most cases too far away to be joined by the CDP-built roads. And, finally, the whole agri-climate was still too confused and too inhospitable to stimulate production. The cheap-food policy acted as a price depressant, and farmers were denied not only the benefit of a price support policy, but even the normal inducement of higher market prices at a time of rising demand from a fast growing population.

Rural roads, like others, must be economically functional. The function they have to perform is similar to that of roads carrying, say, coal from the mines to the market. The CDP roads did not deliver the goods primarily because they were not planned to do so. This, in itself, was a major error. It should not be further compounded now by drawing a wrong conclusion, as some policy-makers are still prone to do, namely, that rural roads do not pay and that the rural economy can be developed without a network of market-linked roads.

The fact is that India has not yet grasped the vital importance of a "fine-mesh, low-capacity" system of farm-to-market roads, the arms which alone can rescue the rural economy from its age-old isolation and provide the leverage to lift its primitive agriculture to a higher level of productivity. In designing a system of transportation to promote agricultural development the planners can learn something valuable from plant breeders, suggests Dr. Sisler. They should "concentrate on a good root system of farm access roads" to help convert inputs into grain, and shun the "showy straw" which is subject to lodging.[17]

Of all India's states Punjab has the best "root system of farm access roads." In 1969, as much as 66 per cent of its villages were located on or within one mile of the roads, another 22 per cent at a distance of one to

---

[17] Loc. cit.

two miles, and only 4 per cent were more than three miles away from the roads.

The Punjab Government has shown commendable awareness of the critical role rural link roads must play in agricultural development. Accordingly, it has drawn up a bold programme which should before long link *all* the villages with *pacca* or metalled roads. The correlation between Punjab's progress in rural roads and its advancing green revolution should not be overlooked.[18]

## STORAGE AND WAREHOUSING

Transportation, by itself, may not catalyze traditional agriculture. It certainly will not, if it is confined to inter-city industrial traffic and by-passes the farming community. It is equally certain, however, that without markets and roads there can be no progress; they are indispensable to liberate captive agriculture from its traditional bondage. Even they cannot, however, do the job by themselves. To be effective they must have another component—storage and warehousing facilities.

For this there are three overriding reasons. First, since agricultural production is seasonal in character, ways and means must be found to spread the harvested produce over longer periods—to bridge the gap from one season to another, also to carry stocks as a hedge against lean years. Second, the seasonal produce must be released to the market in an orderly fashion to avoid a feast-and-famine situation which would play havoc with prices. And, third, proper storage is essential to cut down on losses of food and other crops.[19]

The importance of storage and warehouses was recognized in India long ago, but for decades there was little sign of action. The Royal Commission on Agriculture urged the government, in 1928, to establish a warehousing system. The need was underscored by the non-official National Planning Committee in 1939. The Reserve Bank of India emphasized it in 1944 and suggested to the provincial governments to pass legislation to that effect, but only Bombay did so, in 1947. The Rural Banking Enquiry Committee made a strong plea, in 1950, for creating a network of warehouses for agricultural produce. And, in 1954, the All-India Rural Credit Survey Committee made the same plea,[20] in even stronger terms, as part of its integrated rural credit scheme. Action came in 1956 when Parliament passed "The Agricultural Produce

[18] The state of Haryana recently created by a spin-off from Punjab is also fairly well equipped with rural roads. According to present plans, all its villages should be linked with good roads by 1974 or thereabouts.

[19] The question of reducing losses through better storage is discussed in *Reaping the Green Revolution*.

[20] See Chapter 25, also Chapter 9.

(Development and Warehousing) Corporation Act." It authorized the creation of a Central Warehousing Corporation (CWC) in the public sector with powers to acquire, build, and operate godowns and warehouses. And it combined this, somewhat mechanically, with the development of agricultural cooperatives.

The incongruity of the two functions, however, became evident before long. Accordingly, an amendment of the Act, passed in 1962, restricted the Corporation's activities entirely to warehousing. At the same time, its functions and duties were defined in sharper terms, all purporting to turn it into a more specialized body for competently rendering an essential technical service.

The Act of 1956 had also provided for the establishment of warehousing corporations in the states, which were, however, placed under a single Central Board of Directors for policy supervision. The states acted rather promptly, and, by 1960, virtually all of them passed the necessary legislation setting up their respective warehouse corporations.

The CWC was authorized to subscribe to their share capital on a 50:50 basis. Its functions, as laid down in the Act, were quite comprehensive: to store agricultural produce and farm supplies; to arrange for their transport to and from warehouses; to act as agent of the government for their purchase, sale, storage, and distribution; and after the 1962 amendment, also to acquire and build godowns and warehouses at such suitable places as the Corporation deemed fit.

The progress since the passage of the Act has been quite remarkable. In 1957, there were only seven Central warehouses with a capacity of 7,020 tons. In 1968-69, on the eve of the Fourth Plan, the position was as follows: [21]

*(In million tons)*

|  | Owned | Hired | Total |
|---|---|---|---|
| At Central level | 3.27 | 1.57 | 4.84 |
| At state level | 1.63 | 1.86 | 3.49 |
| Cooperatives | 2.60 | — | 2.60 |
| Total | 7.50 | 3.43 | 10.93 |

The Fourth Plan provides for a substantial capacity expansion: 3.4 million tons of additional storage to accommodate buffer stocks totalling 5 million tons; 200,000 tons for fertilizer storage; 1 million tons to be added to the Central and state warehousing corporations; and another 2

[21] *Fourth Five Year Plan 1969-74*, p. 145. The capacity is owned or hired by the Food Dept., FCI and CWC at the Centre and by state governments and state warehouse corporations in the states.

million tons in the cooperative sector. A public sector outlay of Rs. 94 crores is foreseen in the Plan, most of it, or Rs. 87 crores, being in the Central sector. The cooperatives would rely mainly on bank finance, including the ARC, to build up their capacity.

The progress made in storage and warehousing since the mid-fifties is no doubt impressive, especially when judged in absolute terms. Unfortunately, it is snagged by several factors. A substantial part of the total capacity is earmarked to carry buffer stocks of foodgrains, another part is needed for the operation of these stocks. The high priority given to them in the storage programme is only natural since warehouse-building had received the first big impulse from the large imports under P.L. 480 and the need to carry large stocks on a year-to-year basis. And it is also indispensable—without buffer stocks India's economy would be even more vulnerable in years of poor monsoon. The point to note, however, is that much of the total capacity is immobilized to carry these stocks and is therefore normally not available to support current agricultural operations.

Besides, the utilization of the capacity built so far has not been up to the mark, and this has caused some legitimate concern. The NCAER study, cited earlier in this Chapter, showed that between March 1963 and June 1964 the rate of utilization of the capacity, owned and hired by the CWC, had sharply declined—from 70 to 45 per cent. What was the reason for this? The explanation given in the study is revealing. Many warehouses were "improperly located so that they are excessive in terms of market isovectures," that is, in relation to market-town and spatial development.[22]

For the entire state warehousing system the utilization rate, according to this study, worked out to about 55 per cent. It found "a startling contrast" between the low utilization of government warehouses, both Central and state, and "the consistently high utilization rates of privately-owned cold storage facilities throughout India."

There were examples of competently operated public-sector warehouses, but they were wrongly located; in contrast to this, the private-sector warehouses were better located, concluded the study. Its analysis further showed that four-fifths of the space in both Central and state warehouses were utilized by merchants, while producers accounted for only 10 per cent in state warehouses and even less in Central warehouses.

[22] Loc. cit., p. 133. The problem of low utilization rate, observed the Fourth Plan in its Draft Outline, "needs to be watched." The CWC's occupancy rate improved from 53 in March 1965 to 87 in March 1966 through special measures including concessional rates. That such action did prove necessary seems to confirm the NCAER's conclusion. Significantly enough, the utilization rate for state warehouse corporations was 55 per cent even in September 1965. (Draft Outline, Aug. 1966, p. 208).

The final conclusion it reached is even more significant: the planners of this "very elaborate network of warehouse and storage facilities" had located almost all of them "in sizable cities" and had thereby "failed to place the storage space within easy reach of Indian farmers."[23] Thus, merchants, rather than producers, were benefiting from the *non-profit* warehouses.

Not that this meant a dead loss to the national economy. Certainly not, for wealth has been saved through better storage; and given competition among merchants, this should also help lower costs. The trouble, as the NCAER rightly stressed, was not that the merchants were using the facilities, but that the farmers were not doing so.

And this is all the more disappointing since the legislation explicitly wanted not traders, but producers to be its primary beneficiaries. It was intended, among other things, to help farmers obtain credit facilities, distribute their sales more evenly over a crop year, protect their crops against rodents, etc., improve farm incomes, and thereby raise the farmer's living standard. These objectives were, at best, only marginally fulfilled.

## THE MISSING LAYER

Thus, despite all the progress made in recent years in expanding storage and warehousing facilities, the farmer's position has not materially changed. He is still compelled to follow the traditional methods of storage—in village cisterns or in mudwall sheds, even though they are known to be highly wasteful.[24]

In recent years encouraging experiments have been made to develop metal storage bins to protect grains from rodents and insects at farm level. The Fourth Plan has provided for a pilot scheme, under which metal bins will be supplied to farmers on instalment basis, along with necessary technical guidance for their installation and maintenance. In addition, over 10,000 metal storage bins have been introduced in certain areas, including Punjab.[25]

The metal bin promises to cut down substantially on storage losses at farm level, and on this ground the innovation merits support. However, its utility should not be exaggerated. It would be useful mainly for storing the grains farmers would need for their own consumption. In any case, it must not be regarded as a substitute for large-scale scientific

[23] Loc. cit., p. 135.

[24] Storage losses due to various factors, along with their quantitative estimates, are analyzed in *Reaping the Green Revolution*.

[25] *Fourth Five Year Plan 1969-74*, p. 147. The metal storage bin developed by the Indian Agricultural Research Institute at Pusa is commonly known as the "Pusa bin."

storage and warehousing which constitute the backbone of commercial agriculture.

The more farmers switch to intensive cultivation with modern inputs, the more they will produce for the market. They cannot very well carry large marketable surpluses on the farms. For one thing, this will often mean diverting much of their time and attention away from more productive farm operations. Besides, large-scale storage is a specialized job in its own right, and many farmers will find it hard to acquire the needed technical competence.

What is even more important, perhaps decisive, is the fact that farm-stored crop will not be "bankable," unlike when it is warehoused. Yet most farmers will need cash once the crop is harvested, to repay the debts incurred for credit-purchased inputs at the beginning of the growing season. They must, therefore, either sell or warehouse most of their marketable surpluses soon after the harvest.

Nor should too much be expected from warehouses in the cooperative sector. Conditions are not yet ripe in rural India for genuine cooperation. Most of the existing cooperatives are more so in name than in reality;[26] and they are prone to leave in the lurch just those who need them most—the small farmers who constitute the great majority in India's agriculture.

There is yet another factor, of a different but no less compelling nature, which today would severely limit the usefulness of most cooperative warehouses, namely, the isolation of India's villages. The markets are too few; in most cases they are too remote; access roads with tolerable means of transportation are still the exception rather than the rule; village-centered warehouses, cooperative or otherwise, cannot function economically in such conditions.

This space-induced limitation has to be overcome as a matter of utmost urgency. This can be done only in one way—by moving markets closer to the farms and linking them with a network of access roads. In practical terms, this means new markets must be created, by thousands, and located at strategic points in rural areas so as to reduce the farm-to-market distance to a manageable level.

When farm productivity rises steeply, and the acre-output trebles or quadruples, as is now clearly happening in many areas, the spatial density of markets must also rise, and the capacity of each suitably stepped up. In areas already caught in the green revolution, the market radius should be no more than, say, ten miles. This is about the maximum bullock-cart distance which a farmer can negotiate, both ways, in a single day and over a reasonably good road, with enough margin of time to transact his business in the market.

Spatial dispersion of markets and warehouses, as the NCAER has

[26] See Chapter 9.

correctly diagnosed, holds a major key to India's future development. But its analysis also shows that the three-layer system she has developed since the passage of the 1956 Act does not satisfy this condition.

At the village level, there are the *cooperative storage* facilities, mostly small godowns with an average capacity below 1,500 tons. They are still small in number, and eventually India will need tens of thousands of them.

The second layer consists of *state warehouses* which are larger in size, with capacity up to 5,000 tons each. Normally located in important market-towns, though not necessarily at district headquarters, they are provided with modern facilities and staffed with trained personnel.

And, finally, there are the *Central warehouses* established at important market centres, with capacity exceeding 5,000 tons each. Among other things, they are provided with specialized storage facilities needed for sensitive or perishable commodities.

The system has several strong features. A powerful policy board at the Centre and 50 per cent CWC's participation in the state corporations have ensured frequent state-Centre consultations, facilitated coordination of their activities and helped avoid duplication of effort. In general, the system, it appears, has an able management with qualified specialists on its staff.

Yet the results so far achieved cannot be rated as satisfactory, mainly because warehouses were overbuilt in larger towns, and were too far removed from producers; on an average, there was only one warehouse for every 775 villages. In short, the existing system suffers from spatial inadequacy, which has distorted its economics and detracted from its usefulness.

This also points up the remedy needed in this case. As the NCAER emphasized, "A fourth layer of storage infrastructure is urgently needed."[27] New warehouses must be set up at "growth-point locations." They may be relatively modest in size, but must nonetheless be modern and well-equipped to provide scientific storage; and they must be within easy reach of the growers.

The four layers of warehouses—in the village, at new growth points, in larger towns, and in the cities, respectively—make a kind of spatial package. Here, too, the principle of complementarity holds good. The whole system has been disproportionately weakened by the missing layer between the village and the large town. Once this omission is remedied, it will grow many times more in effectiveness.


## HOW TO ACCELERATE PROGRESS

Agricultural development must go hand in hand with spatial develop-

[27] Loc. cit., p. 116.

50

ment. There is no escape from this; for, the basic raw materials of agriculture—soil and sunshine—are diffused over the whole expanse of the country.

The package of production inputs, coupled with the package of cultural practices, has incubated a green revolution. What is still lacking are the *spatial inputs*—the post-harvest package of conveniently located markets, scientific warehouses, and all-weather roads between farms and markets. Without it the green revolution will tantalize the nation for a while, then flounder in the fields and fade away from most areas.

India must plan to build thousands of new markets, hundreds of thousands of miles of rural roads, and thousands of warehouses, especially at the new marketplaces. Can she do so fast enough to feed and spread the green revolution? And has she the resources—scientific personnel, manpower, and finances—to carry out such a vast programme? The answer, in both cases, is an unequivocal affirmative, provided she can bring enough will, vision, and realism to bear on the tasks and proceeds to mobilize the vast resources she already has at her disposal. The imperatives, both negative and positive, are briefly indicated below.

The approach hitherto adopted in the Plans has not been conducive to progress in this field. It has been concerned solely with how much money could be allocated in a given Plan; all concerned have usually marked time pending this central decision, putting off the difficult and time-consuming tasks of physical planning, such as the location of the facilities and the preparation of blueprints. The inevitable result has been late start, slow and haphazard planning of facilities, inability to spend even the modest sums allocated for them, halting progress.

The first task is to rescue development from this mockery of planning. It is therefore essential to launch, as a matter of foremost priority, a comprehensive programme for preparing physical plans for the whole country with location of markets and warehouses, and alignment of access roads.[28] Though the states will have to carry out the programme, clear policy directions from a competent Central body will be essential, with periodic review and evaluation of progress. The actual planning work can be best conducted at the district level, for which the development staff will need to be suitably strengthened.

Will there be enough technical personnel available for the purpose? There are thousands of young engineers and scientists now lying idle, who could be mobilized and, with or without a little initial training, could be fitted into the job. Some phasing of the work will in any case be necessary, with preference given to the areas already caught or about to be caught in the green revolution. Part of the work may be entrusted

[28] For a good example of the kind of physical planning needed for rural roads, see *Roads in the Rural Punjab* by Harpal Singh Mavi, Punjab Agricultural University, Ludhiana, 1969.

to private firms. Where necessary, technical assistance may be sought from abroad under different programmes.

In recent years, a great many agencies have been established, mostly as Central and state corporations, to speed up progress in agriculture. Two new agencies need to be added to complete the galaxy—for market and road development respectively—in rural areas. The Central Warehousing Acts of 1956 and 1962 could serve as a good model for them, particularly in respect of Central guidance and state-Centre coordination. To achieve the best results, however, it would be necessary to ensure proper coordination not only among these three bodies, but also between them and other agri-business institutions.

Where should the new markets be located? The so-called "growth points" will no doubt be the best locations for them. What cannot be overstressed, however, is that, in today's India, it should not be necessary to waste time by employing over-sophisticated methods for identifying them—to grope around for growth points. A great many of them can be readily pinpointed in high productivity and high population-density areas. Planning and construction of facilities should be initiated in these places with the least possible delay.[29]

Road building in rural areas must be treated as a public-sector responsibility and directly handled by the government. But it is too important to be left to community development and panchayati raj institutions which lack the needed expertise, administrative competence, and financial support. Instead, it calls for sustained effort from the highest levels on a nationwide scale. And as indicated above, only a separate agency—a Central Roadbuilding Corporation patterned on the CWC with a strong policy board at the Centre and backed by a family of corporations at the state level—would be equal to this mammoth task.

In planning a network of rural roads two principles would deserve special attention. First, its layout should be dictated not by the ease of land acquisition, but by the ease and cost of transportation, both now and in the future. Contrary to the all too common tendency, it should not, therefore, follow the line of least resistance and settle for meandering routes, along already existing footpaths or over other readily-available property, just because they would pose the least difficulty for securing the rights-of-way. An adequate grid of access roads is so important to the future development of an area, observes the President's Science Advisory Committee, that early consideration should be given to a "total plan," and the right of eminent domain should be evoked "to locate roads properly rather than to locate them haphazardly along old trails or where landowners are willing to donate a route."[30]

[29] The points mentioned here are discussed more fully in *Reaping the Green Revolution*.

[30] Loc. cit., p. 533.

The second principle relates to phasing of the work. There is a pervasive temptation, in India as in other developing countries, to ask for the best and nothing but the best when it comes to a matter like road-building, and to move, in one big leap, from a mud road, or no road, to a 20-feet wide concrete road. This tends to make roadbuilding forbiddingly expensive.

Yet what rural India needs today are not a few fancy roads built at exorbitant cost, warranted neither by the volume of traffic nor by the still most widely prevalent bullock-cart mode of transport, but countless, inexpensively built, yet fully serviceable utilitarian-type of access roads, all over the country. A more rational, indeed the only practicable approach, would be to build roads of, say, 10-feet width to start with, using local material—stone from rock outcrops, tarred gravel, even locally-made hard bricks where necessary—as the basic material, and to undertake further widening and surface improvement in stages as and when justified by traffic growth. "What the traffic will bear" is a sound criterion also in making investments in roads.

In warehousing, private enterprise can, and will, play a major role, once the government has established markets and built the access roads. Indeed, the government would be wise to adopt a policy of actively encouraging the growth of warehousing in the private sector to the maximum possible extent and to supplement it to the extent entrepreneurs are either unable or unwilling to do the job. Such a division of labour will save the government a lot of headaches, in addition to saving substantial resources which can be used elsewhere, while profit-motivated private owners would, in their own interest, search out the best locations for their warehouses and develop a wide range of services to ensure full utilization of space and thereby to maximize their own earnings.

Even then, a large measure of responsibilities will continue to devolve on the government. It will have to ensure that adequate facilities are created and to provide the needed services including utilities. In addition, it will have to regulate privately owned warehouses, enforce requisite standards, and ensure fair price to the customers, especially the producers.

Such regulation will call for a competent corps of government inspectors to serve as watchdogs on behalf of the public. Logically, the corps should form part of a broadbased market regulation service in every state to enforce predetermined standards laid down on an all-India basis. This is the most practicable way in which the government can expect to cope with the vastly increased regulatory functions it will be faced with, once markets begin to multiply rapidly as they must do before long.

The tradition of regulated markets, as it has developed since the Berar Law of 1897 and the Royal Commission's Report of 1928, is no longer in line with today's expanded needs. The elaborate machinery provided by this legislation, with a sizable regulating committee in each case, may be appropriate when markets are limited in number and quite large in size, but not when the whole country is dotted with small and medium-sized markets. This will call for a simplified approach with a streamlined organization and a centralized staff of qualified specialists for periodic market inspection.[31]

Construction of markets, roads and warehouses will provide jobs to millions of people in rural areas for years to come. The markets, in their turn, are bound to grow into hubs of agro-urban communities while the great majority of them, it may be safely assumed, will develop into sizable towns and cities, more so if the process is actively aided by government policy. Once these trends are set in motion, manysided benefits will follow, not only for rural areas but for the nation's economy as a whole.[32]

In the name of planning, India has hitherto made tremendous fuss about funds. It is time to turn to the real tasks, the tasks of physical planning, and to prepare the blueprints for markets, roads, and warehouses. Building should begin as soon as they are approved, both technically and economically, by a competent body of experts at a sufficiently high level. These underpinnings of the green revolution must be created just as fast as is physically possible. This is a matter of the utmost urgency. Lack of funds must not be allowed to hold them up. When necessary, they should be boldly financed with credit, or created money.[33]

[31] As for the proper role of government in relation to modernized agriculture, see Chapter 22, also the section on "Agricultural Administration" in Chapter 28.

[32] Discussed more fully in *Reaping the Green Revolution.*

[33] See Chapter 27.

# CHAPTER 25

# Agricultural Credit

## I. FROM COOPERATIVE MONOPOLY TO MULTI-AGENCY APPROACH

### NEEDLESS GYRATIONS

Agricultural credit in India has long been in need of a drastic overhaul and of a bolder, yet more down-to-earth approach. This realization has at last begun to dawn on the authorities, but still too slowly and too dimly.

False starts, hasty commitments, frantic institution-building based on faulty designs—these, as seen earlier, have characterized India's rural scene for the last twenty years.[1] And, inevitably, they have left a legacy of great confusion and entrenched vested interests.

The most disturbing fact today is that precious little has been learnt from the long period of brave experimentation with fancied panaceas. There is a strong penchant, even today, among the policy-makers to draw wrong lessons from past failures, to write more hasty remedies on their basis, to attempt to cure past errors with new ones.

Not that the bewildering policy gyrations were really necessary. The problems involved in rural credit had been pretty clearly identified, so also the practical measures needed to tackle them. For example, on the eve of the Second World War, they were thoroughly analyzed by the National Planning Committee, of which Pandit Jawaharlal Nehru was

In Chapters 25-26 the writer has used an article published in a Supplement to *Capital*, Calcutta, on 25 December 1969, under the title: "Revising Agricultural Credit Policies to Sustain the Green Revolution." Permission to use it here is acknowledged with thanks.

[1] See Chapters 8 and 9.

the Chairman. The NPC's Subcommittee on Rural Marketing and Finance[2] submitted a comprehensive report in March, 1940, in which it referred, among other things, to the "plethora of funds" at the bigger money markets while rural areas suffered from a scarcity of liquid capital, and pleaded for what it called a system for "better financial irrigation."

It examined the causes of this "mal-distribution of credit facilities"; frankly recognized the reasons, historical and institutional, which had led to a lopsided growth of the commercial banks with their operations almost exclusively confined to the supply of short-term capital in the urban centres; argued that the government should float long-term bonds, raise funds in the money markets, and make them available, through suitable machinery, to the cultivating classes as loans for productive purposes on reasonable rates of interest.

The simplest and most effective method of rectifying the maldistribution of credit, the Report emphasized, would be "to induce the joint-stock banks to participate actively in agricultural credit." To stimulate the growth of branch banking it urged several concrete steps aimed at creating some first-class agricultural bills. Railway receipts, it recommended, could and should be turned into negotiable credit instruments. It stressed the need for better marketing and storage facilities, and pleaded for a rapid expansion of regulated markets. It spelled out how crop bills and warehouse receipts could be developed into first-class agricultural paper. And it discussed, at considerable length, the problems of cooperatives and how to develop efficient and viable units in India.

No action was taken on this report. For one thing, the time was not ripe for it—the country had yet to go through the war and the post-war turmoil, also the period of uncertainty that marked the dawn of independence. There was a second and even more fundamental reason as well: Prime Minister Nehru, inspired by his never-failing "dynamism," jettisoned all the NPC reports and turned to the old establishment to solve the problems of new India.

### "CREDIT AGRICOLE"

In Bengal, after the 1943 famine, development of agriculture became a more lively subject and, for a while, received increased attention from the Government, particularly from the then Governor of Bengal, Sir Robert Casey. On his invitation Mr. Leonard K. Elmhirst came to serve as a short-term Agricultural Adviser, and the writer was assigned to

---

[2] The Subcommittee's membership included such veterans of rural credit as Ramdas Pantulu (Chairman), Vaikunth Lal Mehta, and R. G. Saraiya. The writer served it as Member-Secretary. The report, like the rest of the NPC studies, was published in Bombay in book form after the war,

work closely with him. Various proposals emanated from this office, such as the Haringhata Scheme for Livestock Improvement, which, after a good start, suffered delays and interruptions, but in the end grew into a successful enterprise. It now serves as a major source of milk supply to Calcutta.

Of special relevance in the present context was the proposal submitted for establishing an agricultural credit bank in Bengal on the lines of "Crédit Agricole d'Egypte."[3] As in the NPC study referred to above, pointed attention was drawn to the anomalies that were so conspicuous in the field of credit.

The interests of the peasantry in Bengal, as in other parts of India, had hitherto gone largely by default. The farmer had derived little benefit from the expansion of modern banking facilities in the country; on the contrary, the commercial banks continued to drain liquid money from the countryside into the main money market centres. Even the pull of the Post Office Savings Banks, though the scale of their operations was relatively small, worked in the same direction.

The unprecedented expansion of currency—the note circulation increased from Rs. 179 crores in August 1939 to Rs. 1,000 crores by December 1945—had made little impact on rural credit; and in an era of cheap money, usurious rates persisted in rural areas. Vast sums of money went abegging in large urban centres for lack of remunerative investment opportunities, yet the farmer and his land continued to be starved of short- and long-term capital.

This was a wholly untenable situation, the study emphasized. It was therefore essential "to cut a canal," so to say, which would carry an adequate flow of funds from the big money market "reservoirs" into the rural areas and thereby ensure a better financial irrigation of the country.

This, it was argued, could be best achieved by creating a new institution on the lines of "Crédit Agricole" of Egypt, which, established in 1931, already had behind it thirteen years of outstanding performance. Of its main features four were emphasized in particular. First, the Bank was set up as a joint-stock concern of a hybrid type—the Government owned one-half of the share capital, and the balance was contributed by 20 leading banks including a 20 per cent share of the National Bank of Egypt. The secret of the Bank's success lay, above all, here—in a happy blending of state enterprise and policy guidance with business experience and management.

Second, the Bank was required to provide short, medium, and long term loans for periods not exceeding 14 months, 10 years, and 20 years respectively. They covered all the essential needs of farming—from

[3] For the historically minded it may be noted that the proposals were published by the Government of Bengal in 1945 as "Collected Notes on Agricultural Problems in Bengal" (203 pages). The proposal for rural credit was made in pages 103-23.

credit purchase of seeds and fertilizers, agricultural machinery and cattle to better irrigation and drainage.

Third, the Bank created an extensive network of branches, with storage and godown facilities. What was even more important, it took special care to recruit competent expert staff, not simply to appraise the loan applications, but to help the farmers with technical advice and guidance in preparing sound cropping plans; and to supervise the use of credit from the time it was granted through different stages of its utilization to its final repayment. Thus, provision of credit went hand in hand with provision of valuable technical services and effective supervision.

And, finally, Crédit Agricole was specifically required to finance essential agricultural institutions to facilitate their creation or development, and these included cooperative societies. In fact, the Bank was given a special mandate under its statute to assist and stimulate in every possible way the cooperative societies, since the *raison d'être* of both was virtually identical, namely, faster development of agriculture and the promotion of farmers' welfare. A number of special concessions were extended to the cooperative societies, such as advances at 4 per cent interest as against 5 per cent charged from individual farmers; a 5 per cent discount on prices of seeds; no ceiling for advances made to cover expenses of cultivation and harvesting or against the security of grains deposited with the Bank; no-mortgage loans up to 10 years when needed for purchasing agricultural machinery or cattle or for land improvement; and only cooperatives were allowed loans for purchasing fuel and gunny bags, for payment of freight, for transport of onions and potatoes, for packing and exporting fruits.

Thus, Crédit Agricole became a pillar not only of agriculture, but also of the cooperative societies. It extended to them tangible, carefully thought-out concessions as incentives, and it provided them with much needed expert guidance and technical services. All this gave them a business, as opposed to a bureaucratic, orientation and helped develop them into viable and profitable enterprises. What a refreshing contrast does this present to India's attempt to unfold a cooperative movement without considerations of business efficiency, without the supporting technical services, and without the needed incentives!

Once again, nothing came out of the proposal for a Crédit Agricole in Bengal. In accordance with the long established tradition, it was duly filed and consigned to oblivion.

Incidentally, information received in Cairo early in 1970[4] indicated

[4] On 10-11 January, 1970 in discussions with Mr. Mustafa Kamel El Far, Chairman, Agricultural Credit Bank; Mr. Mahmud Fauzi, Chairman, General Organization for Agricultural Credit; Dr. Kamel Hindi, Chairman, Economic and Statistical Department, Ministry of Agriculture; and Mr. Abdalla Shafie, Director, Foreign Relations Department, Ministry of Agriculture. The writer is indebted to them for the up-to-date information readily supplied to him.

that the old Crédit Agricole had undergone several changes in keeping with the change in Egypt's political and economic climate. After the revolution and nationalization of banks it become a fully State-owned enterprise and was renamed "Egyptian General Organization for Agricultural and Cooperative Credit." The Agrarian Reform Law of 1952 broke up the large estates and broadened the base of agricultural ownership. The old cooperatives were dominated by a handful of big landowners who virtually monopolized cooperative credit and other benefits. After the land reform small farmers became the backbone of Egypt's agriculture; cooperatives grew in number and participation, and their benefits spread among millions of small farmers who had previously been left more or less in the lurch. The result has been a double gain: higher productivity of agriculture and greater welfare of peasant communities.

The Egyptian experience, first under the Crédit Agricole and later under its metamorphosed version, underlines the need for a *national* organization for agricultural credit, qualified staff to render technical services to farmers, an integrated approach from crop planning and crop loans to storage and marketing, land reform to eliminate the grosser inequalities in land ownership, and incentives to build strong, well-managed cooperatives. Thanks largely to these factors, Egypt's agriculture—which has been ahead of India's in many respects, such as multiple cropping, input-intensive farming, cultural practices, supply of supervised credit, and marketing—has successfully maintained its forward thrust.

### "INTEGRATED RURAL CREDIT" IN RETROSPECT

If the pre-independence regime was reputed for its inaction, the post-independence years have been distinguished mainly by wrong action. A giant stride in wrong direction was taken way back in 1951-52, on the recommendations of the All-India Committee on Rural Credit Survey. The commitments then made set the stage for today's widespread disillusionment.

How spurious were the premises underlying the Survey Committee's analysis has already been pointed out.[5] Old obsessions, however, die hard, and they have continued to vitiate all attempts to analyze and evaluate the past objectively. Even realities are blamed for refusing to conform to those premises! This is well illustrated by the most recent Report of the All-India Rural Credit Review Committee (AIRCRC).[6]

[5] See Chapter 9.
[6] Published in 1970. The Committee was chaired by a senior administrator who had also served as a member of the three-man All-India Rural Credit Survey Committee of 1951-52.

Successful working of a cooperative institution depends on "leadership of competence and integrity." This is an "important" condition; but, by and large, there has been "a paucity of leadership" in most states, especially at the base, so laments the Report. But should it have been all that hard to foresee this paucity even twenty years earlier? What justification was there to assume that leadership of a high calibre would spring up all over the country to build a cooperative paradise?

At the primary level, cooperatives have often been organized "hurriedly and casually," and almost always "under official auspices." This, the Report holds, is hardly conducive to the "emergence of leadership." Besides, the superstructure of apex and central banks has, by and large, come "in advance of the development of sound primaries," a fact that partly explains the "hiatus in leadership." Some state governments, the Report regretfully adds, are so keen to maintain their hold on cooperative institutions—with official chairmen, nominated boards or departmental control over their day-to-day working—that cooperators "do not find much scope for their initiative," so much so that they do not "feel involved" in the working of these institutions. And, finally, there is the "complexity" of running a cooperative in conformity with "various statutory regulations," and this, too, has sometimes acted as "a deterrent factor" in attracting good leadership.

Are these developments surprising after all? The Survey Committee of 1951-52 had exuberantly proclaimed the slogan: "Not by cooperation alone, but by cooperation in conjunction with the State." And then it proceeded to bring the government into all the three tiers of cooperation as the major shareholder. Was it realistic to assume that the government would pour money into the cooperatives and then stand aloof, that it would pay handsomely and yet not call the tune? Once the State came in as the big brother with big money, could big bureaucracy be far behind? It is strange that even seasoned civil servants should fall into such easy traps.

Today's lament about the lack of cooperative leadership is likely to evoke not sympathy, but a cynical smile. For, what the authors of the "integrated rural credit" had produced was only a progeny of the State, though it was enthusiastically hailed as cooperation. And the kind of leadership they opted for, even if unknowingly, was not entrepreneurial or managerial, but bureaucratic. This they did receive in plenty; and soon it spread all over the country, leaving little room for real cooperation to grow.

The Report goes on to explain other adverse factors. The socio-economic background of the Indian village, especially in areas with long feudal traditions, is not conducive to the functioning of a cooperative institution which is based on "democratic and egalitarian principles." Leadership in such conditions is determined not so much by popular will as "by status and position in the rural hierarchy." The caste system, inadequate spread of literacy, the type of land tenures prevailing in certain areas, large disparities among members in terms of wealth, influence, authority, and social status—all these impede the working of cooperative and other self-governing institutions postulated on democratic principles. As a result, "the impact of vested interests . . . is in evidence in a large number of these institutions."

These are melancholy facts no doubt, but they are certainly not new. They were, at least, as much a part and parcel of India's rural society twenty years ago as today. It is odd to reflect that the official world should have taken all these years to discover such eye-catching phenomena.

The list of cooperative woes is long, but the rest are more like symptoms reflecting the root causes mentioned above. Field studies conducted by the Committee led, *inter alia*, to the following conclusions: the same individuals had an "unduly long tenure" on the management committee of a society, and this led to various abuses; credit limits were not fixed realistically in many instances for lack of authentic data regarding the areas owned and cultivated by individual members and their cropping pattern; in several states bigger cultivators obtained larger credit per acre than the smaller ones; sometimes members and secretaries of the managing committees took undue advantage of their position to draw loans and other benefits from the societies' funds; multiple membership by persons belonging to the same family was a common occurrence for many societies; to fulfil official targets, societies sometimes allocated more fertilizers to well-to-do farmers than could be used on the lands they cultivated; in the distribution of scarce commodities like sugar vested interests had grown up among the members of primary societies; there were also cases of manipulation of accounts by the officer-bearers of some societies.

Can there be any doubt that the past policy has led rural India not towards the lofty goals it had been tantalized with, but downhill into a deep and unsuspected morass? The government went out of its way to establish a cooperative monopoly of rural credit; to it were subsequently added other monopoly functions, such as distribution of fertilizers, sugar, and other commodities. And the cooperatives, in their turn, were monopolized by the small but powerful vested interests in rural communities.

There have been other symptoms of the same malaise. The Review Committee mournfully speaks of "the lack of a sense of responsibility" on the part of its members, and, with unusual frankness, attributes it largely to the fact that the local people have "little stake in the cooperative when resources come largely from outside." Cooperatives are often looked upon "not as farmers' institutions, but as part of government." And their members show greater awareness about their rights in matters of membership and credit than about their obligations, such as about the proper use and prompt repayment of credit.

All this is wisdom by hindsight. How much better would it have been for the country if it had been anticipated, and acted upon, in the early fifties! Surely, no prophetic quality should have been needed to visualize such eventualities which, after all, sprang from entirely predictable human frailties.

The same remark applies to the Committee's complaint that "too few cooperatives think in terms of cost and efficiency"; that they are getting "so used to subsidies and protection of various types" that cost considerations hardly matter with them. This, the Committee goes on to say, is clearly reflected in their indifference to the collection of overdue loans, in staff recruitment, salary scales, and overheads in general, and, above all, in their refusal to charge economic rates of interest on loans sanctioned by them. Their emphasis is on artificially low interest, so much so that the rates they charge on their loans do not even cover their actual cost of raising funds and rendering services.

In many areas the Committee found the cooperatives were content "to make do with low paid and non-professional staff," the efficiency of the staff was not equal to their tasks, their selection was "often influenced by considerations of local patronage or personal favouritism." All this, in the Committee's view, was "one aspect of the lack of a businesslike approach."

Training is being provided through various programmes, both in government departments and in institutions. But can such deep-seated malaise be cured by such *ad hoc* training?

Moreover, as the Committee itself admits, the malaise starts right at the top. In a large number of cases, the chief executives of central banks have not been "suitably trained," and their management is often either not independent enough or not competent enough to ensure efficient working. The government has been ready to pay for staff of the requisite quality and in adequate strength; nonetheless, the standards of recruitment have remained low.

Field investigations as well as inspections by the Reserve Bank, the Committee reminds, have confirmed the poor quality of management, both at the primary and central bank levels. This was true of most states and was evident from the way books were kept, the public was served, instructions were complied with, and primaries were supervised.

Finally, the Committee observes, with apparent regret, that the role of state governments has, in several instances, "not developed as expected." For example, a Committee on Cooperative Credit had recommended, in 1960, that certain quasi-government bodies should be permitted to keep their funds with cooperative banks; but no action was taken in this matter. Some state government officials have instructed the marketing cooperatives not to recoup cooperative credit dues before passing on the proceeds of the foodgrains delivered to them under the government's procurement operations. *Taccavi* loans[7] have been provided on more favourable terms than cooperative credit, at times even to defaulting members of cooperatives, though this could not but weaken the sense of discipline in dealing with cooperative credit. The top positions in state and central cooperative banks have been frequently filled by government officials; and this has been inimical to the emergence of non-official cooperative leadership. In certain instances, cooperative banks have been instructed, formally or informally, by government officials or others, "to make particular loans."

There has no doubt been some lack of *coordination* within a state government between the cooperative wing and its other departments. One suspects, however, that there has also been a lack of *cooperation* between the two. The cooperatives, as they have developed over the years, have failed to inspire confidence even among government departments. Most officials have anything but a high opinion about their performance and their capacity to deliver the goods. When it comes to transacting business in rural areas, whether credit or distribution of inputs and scarce commodities, quite a few, left to themselves, would therefore like to bypass them quietly. In view of what has been said above, should this cause any surprise?

The Review Committee of 1969 has illumined, once again, the failings of the system of cooperatives India has erected with great effort and at high cost. The facts it has assembled add up to a devastating charge-sheet, also to an unequivocal confession that the vast experiment in State-backed cooperatives launched in the early fifties was a colossal *faux pas*. Yet the most lamentable fact about it is not that it has failed, but that it should have been tried at all, in the face of a formidable array of adverse factors which had foredoomed it to failure.

The Committee's analysis is marked by a candour which is particularly refreshing for an official document. But it has stopped short of admitting any conceptual flaw in past policies. On the contrary, it strains itself, though futilely, to defend the concept of State-backed cooperatives as envisioned in the integrated rural credit scheme. And because of this unyielding allegiance to the original design, even though it was gravely flawed by its inner contradictions, the Committee has been unable to help rescue rural credit from its present impasse. The whole system badly needs radical redesigning and restructuring. Of this there has so far been no sign.

Not that the public has been unaware of this need. Consider, for example, the following observations made by a high executive, now retired, of the Central Government with long experience in agriculture,

[7] That is, loans directly given by the government, usually to small farmers.

particularly cooperative credit: "...no one has had the courage to say that the rural cooperatives have been a dismal failure and that a more competent and businesslike agency should be constituted for this purpose. The magic word 'cooperation' is still a lure to the politician," because of its "pseudo-democratic implications," although cooperatives have proved to be "breeding grounds for petty corruption and favouritism." He then puts his finger on a most important point which has hitherto been systematically ignored: "No credit institution can flourish which does not attract its own deposits and no deposits will be attracted unless it is part of a well-established Bank and invites confidence. The theory of the village cooperative is outmoded and has to be scrapped."[8]

It is more than time to recognize the past blunder, to retreat from the blind alley, and to make a fresh start with a foolproof plan, boldly conceived and firmly anchored in realities.

## MULTI-AGENCY CREDIT

The process of retreat has begun, slowly and unavoidably, mainly under the stress of circumstances. As yet there is no clear vision of the future goals, and no sure sign of the direction the country should take.

Until the end of 1966, practically no distinction was made between cooperative credit and agricultural credit; the two were used interchangeably, almost as synonymous. As a result, agriculture continued to be credit-starved although hundreds of crores of public money were pumped into the cooperative system.

Such a situation could not be ignored indefinitely even by purblind "cooperators." And it became intolerable as intensive agriculture spread and the demand for credit surged. The package of inputs—seeds, fertilizers, pesticides, essential implements—must be financed adequately, and in time. Credit is thus an indispensable input. Not only that; it is so crucial in its role that it determines the fate of the rest. Without it the whole package falls apart.

The programme for intensive agriculture in India was born in the shadow of a credit crisis, and it has been haunted by it ever since. The Expert Committee on IADP has harped on this theme, in a clear crescendo, in all its four evaluation reports. It was envisaged, says the latest report published in 1969, that the cooperatives would be "geared up to meet fully the credit and input needs of the farmers." The pace of the programme was thus linked with the performance of the cooperatives. But experience shows that, in general, they "had not been developed enough to carry their part of the load."

[8] Mr. S. Y. Krishnaswamy in a paper on *Management in Agriculture*. A typed copy was given to the writer in Madras on 25 December, 1969.

The report points out how credit institutions can quicken the adoption of new technologies, but also emphasizes that in order to render this valuable service, they must themselves be "dynamic and responsive to the needs of fast moving technology."[9]

The cooperatives in the IADP districts, it should be recalled, were substantially strengthened with several *ad hoc* measures when the Package Programme was first initiated.[10] Yet its operations have been impeded by a persistent credit shortage. From this it is easy to imagine the fate of the other and less fortunate areas which were left at the mercy of the run-of-the-mill type of cooperatives as the sole means of credit supply.

The crisis in agricultural credit, dormant for decades, first surfaced in the IADP districts and then exploded all over the country. Fuelled by IADP, IAAP and HYVP, the demand for credit has far outpaced its supply. Yet this is only the beginning of a strong trend. For the coming years big increases are foreseen in many directions: in the areas under HYVP, in irrigation facilities and multiple cropping, in the use of fertilizers, pesticides, pumpsets, and farm machinery, in the development of livestock, poultry and fisheries, and in a host of agri-services.

The All-India Rural Credit Review Committee (1969) has estimated that the short-term production credit requirements will rise to an *annual rate* of Rs. 2000 crores in 1973-74. To this should be added the medium and short-term credit—for the *whole plan-period* the Committee put them at Rs. 500 and Rs. 1500 crores respectively.[11] These estimates, which have been embodied in the Fourth Plan, are conservative, if not restrictive, although much will depend on how smoothly and competently production-stimulating policies are adopted and implemented.

How much of this demand can be met from the cooperative sector? The short and medium term credit available from this source will, it has been assumed, rise from an annual rate of Rs. 450 crores to Rs. 750 crores in the final year of the Fourth Plan. This means that cooperative credit can, at best, supply just about one-third of the annual requirement; the remaining two-thirds must come from other sources. These figures are eloquent. They have highlighted the folly of a cooperative credit monopoly in a way nobody can ignore any longer.

The rapidly widening credit gap, along with the besetting problems of an ailing cooperative sector, has, at long last, forced on the government a reorientation of its rural credit policy. But the dawn of this hard-won realism is still shrouded in too much mist.

The emphasis has now shifted from cooperative to "multi-agency"

[9] Report on IADP (1960-68), Expert Committee on Assessment and Evaluation, New Delhi, Vol. I, p. 54.
[10] See Chapter 12.
[11] *Fourth Five Year Plan 1969-74*, p. 140.

credit. The underlying idea is that *all* credit institutions should be brought into the picture so that they may *collectively* bridge the gap between the supply and demand, very much like the "conjunctive" approach recently adopted for irrigation, embracing large, medium, and minor projects to utilize surface, subsurface and ground water.[12] There is, however, too much concern for the purely *quantitative* aspects of credit, and not remotely enough for those interrelated problems of agriculture which will determine its *quality*. From a cooperative monopoly the country is now moving to the other extreme—with too many agencies, too few qualified experts, and too little coordination. Nor has enough thought been given as to how best one could provide legitimate under-pinnings to the deserving cooperatives.

That the supply of credit must be adequate in quantity goes without saying. But this is not enough. It must go, hand in hand, with the smooth flow of inputs, preparation of technically sound and economically prof-itable farm plans, supervision of credit to ensure its proper use, and repayment according to schedule, also adequate facilities for transporta-tion, storage, and marketing. Without the essential supplies, services, and safeguards, plans for rural credit can never succeed and will, sooner or later, come to grief. To satisfy these preconditions, organizations must be built up and equipped adequately with trained staff; and all the func-tions must be closely coordinated even if they are not placed under a single unified control in each district or region. What must be avoided at all costs is a multiplicity of agencies and institutions working more or less independently and often at cross purposes, thereby sowing the seeds of new frustrations.

The shift towards multi-agency credit has, understandably enough, created a flutter in the cooperative dovecot. The societies are afraid of losing their good business to the bigger and more efficient commercial banks. Some cooperative vested interests are nervously trying to avert the threat and, in self-protection, are planning for a special brand of "co-ordination" with other kinds of credit.

Clearly, what the cooperatives need today is not "co-ordination," but competition; not the sheltered, anaemic existence in a murky rural environment, but an infusion of fresh blood from outside; not tradi-tional crutches, bureaucratic or political, but firm and competent pro-fessional guidance to stir them out of their inertia and to spur their management so that they may grow into real cooperatives—self-reliant, progressive, businesslike, and profitable.

Significantly enough, the All-India Rural Credit Review Committee (1969) has, willynilly, veered round to the idea of creating competition for the cooperatives rather than continuing the old policy of pampering them with onesided protection, though it is unable to shed old dogmas

[12] Discussed in Chapter 16.

52

on which the present shaky cooperative structure has been built. There has been progress, but it is still too meagre and piecemeal.

## A DUBIOUS STEP[13]

The old panacea has failed, as it was bound to. The search for a new one has begun, and with it also for a scapegoat for past failures. The finger of accusation is now pointed at the commercial banks. Yet, in fairness, it should be pointed at the past policies which erred so egregiously.

The nationalization of fourteen leading commercial banks, in July 1969, has been justified mainly in terms of the need to meet the growing crisis in agricultural credit. Yet in actual fact it can, by itself, solve nothing. So far as rural credit is concerned, it remains largely an irrelevant act.

The assumption that vast sums of money are diverted by the banks to speculative and unproductive channels is vastly exaggerated. In any case, the Reserve Bank had enough powers to rectify whatever anomalies or "anti-social" behaviour there might exist.

Nor is it correct to assume that there is an absolute shortage of financial resources for agriculture. Not enough has been done to mobilize the surpluses available in rural areas and to plough them back into agriculture. The government has failed to evolve the right institutions and right policies for the purpose. Even in these days of high interest, the rates allowed on savings, both in rural and urban areas, are much too low to attract surplus funds.

Moreover, by far the most important task in India's agriculture today is to produce sound, high-payoff farm plans with the help of fully qualified extension workers. Given such plans, credit can and should be *created*. Such credit will, in effect, prove to be the most remunerative form of working capital.[14]

Furthermore, rural banking, to be successful, must be backed by a wide range of *non-banking* services—for the supply and distribution of inputs, formulation of farm plans, supervision of credit, for storage, transportation and marketing, as discussed in the preceding chapters. In a modern state it is the task of the government to organize these services efficiently with competent specialists and administrators. It is precisely here that the government has hitherto grievously defaulted.

Once the non-banking services are effectively organized, farming will prove many times more remunerative, and with it also rural banking. And prompted by the prospects of profitable business, commercial banks

[13] This section contains some of the comments which were made in 1969, soon after the bank nationalization ordinance was announced. They are reproduced here to set the perspective right.
[14] See Chapter 27 on "The Credit Shackles."

will then run after the farmers and set up branches in rural areas. It will not be necessary for the government to run after the banks.

What India's agriculture needs most urgently today are the facilities and services discussed in the preceding chapters. Modern banking can flourish in rural areas only when farming itself is modernized. Lack of banking facilities is a symptom, rather than a cause.

# CHAPTER 26

# Agricultural Credit

## II. FROM MULTI-AGENCY APPROACH TO A UNIFIED SYSTEM

### TWO FUNDAMENTALS

The search for an adequate policy must begin with unqualified acceptance of a simple axiom: *Modern agriculture needs modern banking.*

If properly developed, banking services can impart a strong upward push to agriculture and accelerate the adoption of yield-raising technologies. But the converse is equally true: Agriculture will be held back, and the dissemination of new technologies will be impeded, in the absence of a forward-looking banking service that could both promote and sustain them. Banking, in short, can be an *engine* of progress, or it can act as a powerful *brake.*

This is well understood in the case of industries even in India despite all her *charkha*-based ideological encumbrances; but for agriculture it has been completely ignored. What she has done so far is in effect to tailor rural banking to a static village economy with its subsistence agriculture, and has thus used it as a brake.

Essentially, this is also what happened in the aftermath of the all-India Credit Survey of 1951-52. The emphasis it laid on linking credit with crop loans, storage, and marketing, also on the need for stabilizing agricultural prices, was sound. But it showed no understanding of the nature of modern banking business; what it created was in essence only a kind of *departmental* banking, though hallowed in the name of cooperation. It paid little attention to the requirements of improved farming and higher productivity, though this is the primary objective of agricultural credit and also the foundation of prosperous rural banking. It readily assumed that the village was a viable economic unit and could support a viable banking unit, while both assumptions were belied by realities. And so, though *prima facie* engaged in designing an engine of progress, it, too, ended by forging powerful new brakes for rural India.

There is a second axiom which is somewhat more subtle, but no less vital: *Agricultural banking differs from commercial banking; it must therefore be treated differently with due regard to its own specific needs.*

This difference mainly reflects the difference between agriculture and manufacturing industry, as discussed in Chapter 2. Unlike the latter, agriculture is, first, a biological industry; and, second, it is location-specific. As a result, production inputs must be hauled to every farm; the harvested output must be hauled out of every farm; it must be processed, stored, transported, marketed; and it must be protected against damage or deterioration. Credit is needed at every stage of this long chain—from supply of inputs to the marketing of output. Moreover, credit, once supplied, will need to be monitored to ensure that it is not diverted away from the purpose for which it is granted.

Add to all this the fact that there are some 50 million farmers, mostly with small holdings, scattered all over the country, and the complexities of the tasks involved will become clear. What is not yet realized in India is that agricultural credit is not simply a function of adequate funds for loan giving, but of funding linked inseparably to a whole package of expert services, including loan supervision.

From this it follows that forcing commercial banks into agricultural credit does not make much sense. They have been evolved, over a century or more, to cater to the short-term credit needs of industry and commerce, which are vital functions in any modern economy. They have not been set up, nor are they equipped, to handle agricultural credit. For one thing, they lack the expert staff to render the technical services which must go hand in hand with farm loans. For another thing, even if they have the staff, they would still be unable to render these services unless rural areas are provided, on a much more adequate scale, with roads, transportation, regulated markets, storage facilities, power supply, reasonable price support, a competent extension service. These are vital underpinnings of modern agriculture and of agricultural credit. They fall, almost entirely, within the sphere of a modern government. Thus, what the commercial banks can do depends directly on how far the government fulfils its own elementary responsibilities.

Nevertheless, in the present grave crisis which has developed in agricultural credit as a direct result of past misjudgements, commercial banks can do a great deal to relieve the immediate pressure. They can help meet, at least in part, the spiralling credit needs in support of the green revolution, and they will bring modern banking to the rural areas with managerial ability, big resources, and the economies of scale, so essential to inspire confidence, particularly among prospective depositors. There is a good case for persuading them to help the country, as far as they can, out of its present credit bind. There is none, however, for chastising or browbeating them, certainly none for forcing them prematurely into areas where they can at present only incur losses because the government has not yet built the minimum agri-supporting facilities and services.

As long as the present critical situation lasts, direct government credit —the so-called *taccavi* loans—may well have to be extended in many areas, particularly for the benefit of small farmers who are otherwise likely to be starved of credit. This, again, would be warranted only as a kind of emergency operation, not as an ideal solution. Government banking can never be satisfactory. It is bound to be entangled in rigid bureaucratic rules; it can never develop enough person-to-person contact, nor gain the insight into individual credit needs and creditworthiness, so essential for success in these operations; it can serve only as an additional source of loan funds without, however, the technical services needed to ensure the best use of those loans.

Commercial banks and *taccavi* loans are both needed in the present emergency, but only as a *pis aller*, not as a lasting solution. They are inadequate both in quantity and in quality.

### INADEQUACIES OF MULTI-AGENCY APPROACH

In recent years there has been an explosion of agricultural institutions in India. Though well-intentioned, they have not always been well-conceived. And they have greatly aggravated the problem of coordination or, rather, of integrated handling of interrelated functions.

As for agricultural credit, reliance is now placed simultaneously on several agencies. This is best illustrated by the provisions made in the Fourth Plan for meeting the estimated credit requirements during the five years ending on 31 March, 1974:[1]

a. *Cooperative credit*. As mentioned earlier, the supply from this source, it is assumed, will rise to an annual rate of Rs. 750 crores in the final year of the Fourth Plan. This will represent an increase of Rs. 300 crores over the 1969 level.

b. *Land Development Banks*. They have made significant progress in recent years and now serve all the states with a network of 1,250 primary banks and branches. According to the Fourth Plan, they are capable of handling Rs. 1,000 crores as long-term loans over the five-year period. However, "on the basis of financial resources now in sight," a target of Rs. 700 crores has been fixed for them. This is less

[1] *Fourth Five Year Plan 1969-74*, pp. 139-42.

than half of the total long-term loan requirements estimated at Rs. 1,500 crores for the period.

c. *Government Loans.* They have been resorted to especially where cooperatives have been conspicuously weak. The Plan, however, does not favour direct loaning by the government and wants it to be reduced to a minimum, while "institutionalizing" agricultural credit to the maximum possible extent.

d. *Agricultural Credit Corporations.* One way to institutionalize credit, it is suggested, is to set up such corporations, under a law enacted by Parliament, in those states where the cooperative credit structure is "weak" and is "unequal to the task of providing adequate agricultural credit." One, however, wonders how many states can really boast of robust cooperatives. The findings of the last AIRCRC, as seen in the preceding chapter, should demolish any lingering illusion on this point.

e. *Agro-industries Corporations.* Fifteen states have already set up such corporations, under the Companies Act 1956, as joint ventures of the Central and state governments to facilitate the supply of farm machinery and improved implements, to develop processing and storage facilities, and to promote similar agri-related activities. These corporations are expected to provide finance for hire purchase of agricultural machinery and pumpsets. In that sense they, too, constitute an additional source of longer-term agricultural credit.

f. *Agricultural Refinance Corporation.* The ARC was established, under an Act of 1963, to provide medium and long-term credit, mostly by way of refinance. In the last few years its business has expanded more rapidly. By 31 March, 1969, the Corporation had sanctioned 233 projects with a total outlay of Rs. 182 crores, of which the ARC's share amounted to Rs. 156 crores. Minor irrigation accounted for the bulk of the projects—for 125 out of the total. The Corporation is now trying to diversify its refinancing portfolio in order to include projects for poultry, dairying, fisheries, even warehouse construction. For the Fourth Plan period, the ARC is expected to provide some Rs. 200 crores as refinance.

g. *Commercial Banks.* After the introduction of "social control," commercial banks began to take greater interest in the agricultural sector. Direct agricultural finance outstanding on their account amounted to only Rs. 5 crores during 1966-67, but in the following two years it went up to Rs. 53 crores. A consortium of commercial banks set up, in 1968, an Agricultural Finance Corporation to coordinate the activities of the constituent banks and to assist them with consultancy services.

After their nationalization some action has been taken to speed up the extension of commercial banking into rural areas. It has been assumed that, as a result, direct lending from the commercial banks to farmers will rise rapidly to reach Rs. 400 crores by the end of the Fourth Plan from a level of Rs. 53.59 crores in June 1969.

h. *The Reserve Bank.* To complete the picture, one must mention India's Central Bank which, in one form or another, has been a major source of supply for rural credit. In particular, it has, over the years, helped pump substantial credit into the cooperative system.

This, then, is the multi-agency system India has now adopted to keep pace with the swiftly rising demand for credit. It represents a big step forward; indeed, without it the green revolution could hardly take off the ground. However, it would be a dangerous illusion to assume that it provides an adequate or durable solution of the problem. Even at its best, it is no more than a makeshift arrangement and is vulnerable for several reasons.

*First*, there is still an almost exclusive preoccupation with money. The so-called financial resources are still treated as the essence of rural credit to the neglect of those critical services which are as much a precondition for success in agricultural banking. The second of the two axioms mentioned above continues to be ignored almost completely.

Take, for example, the case of the nationalized commercial banks. A major objective is to spread banking, and, in particular, to bring it into "unbanked" towns or centres. With this object in view each district in the country has been allotted one of the fourteen nationalized banks. This "lead bank" is required to assume a major role within the district, and, for this purpose, to survey the resources, assess the potential for banking development, offer advice to small borrowers—particularly small farmers, assist the other primary lending agencies, maintain liaison with the government and quasi-government agencies. This leadership role does not, however, give it a monopoly of banking business in the area.

All this has been greeted as solid progress, especially since the urban-oriented commercial banks are now being forcibly given a more rural orientation. Jubilation may, however, very well prove premature. A great deal will depend, now as before, on the traditional arms of the government—how fast they move to create modern underpinnings for modern agriculture. If these are provided on an adequate scale, the banking potential will multiply fast; without them, it will continue to stagnate.

To put it differently, what was needed in the past, and what is needed now, is for the government to grab the "leadership role" in every district, and to provide the vital services listed above, which would have automatically attracted the commercial banks into the field. What was not necessary for the government was to impose, by an impetuous fiat, this leadership role on the banks before it had seriously begun to fulfil its own prior obligations. Nothing has been gained by this refusal to put first things first, except some fleeting euphoria ending in further obfuscation of the main issues.

The banking potential in a district, to repeat, is a function of government-created infrastructure. The task, in a sense, is to semi-urbanize rural areas with modern facilities and services rather than force modern banks into a stagnant rural economy. Given the right strategy, agricultural credit from commercial banks would rise much faster than what has been envisaged for the current plan-period. Without it, the target of Rs. 400 crores by March 1974 will be hard to reach.

*Second*, under the multi-agency credit system the problems of coordination have multiplied and assumed formidable dimensions. The Fourth Plan glibly talks of "close coordination" between the cooperative sector and the commercial banks, that the various institutional agencies catering to the requirements of rural credit will have to function "in an integrated and coordinated manner"; but it shows little awareness of its practical implications. The multi-agency system has grown in a purely *ad hoc* fashion, mainly in response to emergency conditions. It has not been based on a coherent design, and the greatest weakness in the structure as it now stands is that it lacks an arch.

It is absurd to think that this weakness could be remedied by the Credit Cell which was created in the Central Ministry of Agriculture at the end of 1966, as has sometimes been suggested. Such improvised tinkering can never rectify a fundamental structural defect.

Nor is the Reserve Bank of India the right agency to look after agricultural credit. The Bank has been saddled with large and direct responsibility for cooperative credit. It is, however, much too preoccupied with other matters of great national importance to do anything like justice to this extraneous function, which was entrusted to it not on any rational calculation, but by some purely historical accident. In any case, money management, including regulation of banking and foreign exchange administration, in a vast country like India should be enough to tax its capacity to the hilt.

Clearly, the Bank cannot, in addition, attend to the gigantic and intricate tasks of agricultural credit in a country of 570 million people with 568,000 villages and 50 million farm households of varying sizes. Its unsuitability is becoming more glaring every day as intensive agriculture spreads and the demand for farm credit mounts, highlighting the urgency of giving correspondingly intensive attention to individual farmers. This inexorably leads up to the need for creating a separate, Crédit Agricole type of institution at the national level, with overall authority to coordinate the activities of all public and quasi-public agencies engaged in agricultural credit, to guide them with policy directions, to serve them with credit accommodation, and also to help actively in creating essential agri-related services.

*Third*, the realization of the other axiom—that modern farming needs modern banking—is still too nebulous. This is true despite the fact that

53

commercial banks have been drafted overnight into agricultural credit after they had been deliberately kept at an arm's length for almost two decades. For, this action was prompted not by an irrepressible urge to modernize rural banking, but by sheer expediency. The cooperative credit available in India works out, on an average, to only Rs. 30 per acre, whereas *one single intensive crop* of a high-yielding variety may need as much as Rs. 200 per acre *for fertilizer alone*. The resources of the commercial banks were nervously commandeered in an anxiety to bridge an alarming gap. It is not the managerial ability they possessed, nor the economies of scale they could bring to bear on the banking operations, nor the technical services they could render that led to their nationalization, but the financial resources they had at their command. Such motivation cannot advance the cause of modernization of rural credit.

And, *fourth*, which only confirms the last point, the fetish of hothouse-produced pseudo-cooperatives continues to cast its withering spell all around.

"Our policy has been and continues to be to arrange for the supply of agricultural credit through cooperatives." This unequivocal pronouncement was made as late as mid-1966, in the draft outline of the Fourth Plan.[2] The only reservation it made was that where the cooperative machinery was "too weak to undertake the work" involved in the production programme, "a supplementary line of credit" might have to be provided through the establishment of agricultural credit corporations in some of the states, while *taccavi* loans would have to be continued as "an interim measure." The cooperative structure, it recognized, also needed assistance—for extension of its coverage and for "improvement in its functioning."

Four years later the Planning Commission, in the final version of the Fourth Plan, quite perceptibly shifted the emphasis. Cooperatives, it observed, would have to be "strengthened" and treated as the "principal agency" for agricultural credit. And then it added that the approach in the Fourth Plan would be to ensure that "agricultural production is not inhibited by the weakness of the cooperatives."[3]

This is reassuring as far as it goes. But it still begs the main question: How will the cooperatives, vaunted as the principal agency for agricultural credit, be strengthened and improved? The only answer one finds is obscurantism. The Commission, as will be seen in the next section, contents itself with a mindless reiteration of outworn clichés.

## EVASIVE PALLIATIVES

"One of the basic weaknesses of the cooperative credit system is the

[2] *Fourth Five Year Plan—A Draft Outline*, August 1966, New Delhi, p. 177.
[3] *Fourth Five Year Plan 1969-74*, July 1970, p. 140.

non-viability of a large number of primary agricultural credit societies," so says the Fourth Plan.[4] This is an amazing clinical bulletin on cooperative health, and a devastating admission, though made in a casual tone: for it is tantamount to saying: The patient is all right except that he is —dying.

To tackle the problem, a programme of rationalization has been initiated at the primary level. As a result, the number of primary agricultural societies dropped from 212,000 in fiscal 1961 to 171,800 in fiscal 1968. But a number of non-viable credit cooperatives, it is stated with some impatience, still continue "to clutter up the credit system." Reorganization should yield about 120,000 viable credit cooperatives, the Commission estimates; and the process, it urges, should be speeded up.

Thus, the concept of the village cooperative is at last being abandoned. A merger of primary societies is under way, though progress is slow mainly because of footdragging by entrenched interests. Nor should too much be expected from mergers and the creation of larger units. Size helps, but much more is needed for successful cooperative business.

Weak district central cooperative banks are called a "bottleneck" in many areas; and even according to the official count, over one-third of them fall in this category. It is intended to undertake "suitable programmes" for their rehabilitation. To judge from past experience, the outcome of such programmes, whatever their precise character may be, cannot but be problematical. In any case, these banks will be bypassed in the interim period; and primary credit societies falling within their jurisdiction will be financed directly by the "apex banks" of the states.

Another major symptom of cooperative sickness is, to put it in the words of the Fourth Plan's Draft Outline, "a high level of overdues and inadequacy of owned resources, especially deposits." In 1963-64, overdues of primary credit societies totalled Rs. 77.31 crores, or 22.5 per cent of the outstanding loans; their deposits amounted to Rs. 26.06 crores, or only 5.9 per cent of their working capital; average deposits per society worked out to Rs. 1,243 and per member to Rs. 11.[5] The picture has not much changed since then.

Slackness in recovery of loans with mounting overdues, bemoans the Fourth Plan, is "undermining the soundness" of the cooperative structure in many areas; it has led to the "stagnation, if not recession of cooperative credit"; and this is the case not only in less developed, but also "in relatively advanced States." This, the Commission goes on to say, points to the "deficiencies in loaning policies..., inadequate arrangements for supervision and weakness of internal management."[6] After an authori-

---

[4] Ibid., p. 217.
[5] *Fourth Five Year Plan—A Draft Outline*, 1966, p. 137.
[6] *Fourth Five Year Plan 1969-74*, p. 217.

tative evaluation of this kind one is indeed entitled to wonder how much has, in fact, gone right with cooperative credit so far.

What, then, are the remedies? Again, a few palliatives are prescribed in an off-the-cuff fashion. Systematic efforts should be made by the state governments and cooperative banks to reduce the overdues substantially; the primary responsibility for taking legal action against "wilful defaulters" rests with the primary credit societies; but where the societies themselves are defaulting, the central cooperative banks should step in and take action against them. Some state laws contain provisions enabling the banks to take such action. Other states should enact similar laws.

But has the law worked in the states where it is already in existence? And what about those central banks which are themselves sick? Is it not far more likely that the primary societies are often inefficient and callous because the central banks, which are supposed to guide and supervise them, are at least equally and often much more so? These questions are not even touched.

The "recovery staff" should be strengthened, both in the department and the district central banks, for which budgetary provision has been made. Here is a typical bureaucratic illusion, an attempt to cure managerial weakness with staff extension.

Overdues may not be wilful, but due to natural calamities. In such cases short-term loans should be converted into medium-term loans, for which the mechanism already exists in the agricultural credit stabilization funds maintained by cooperative banks and the National Credit Agricultural Stabilization Fund established by the Reserve Bank. Such conversion is quite legitimate and must be a part of any adequate system of agricultural credit; and it acquires a special urgency after such disasters as the droughts of the mid-sixties. The only way to minimize the need for such conversion is to build up productivity and income of farmers so that what they earn, and save, in normal years may help them tide over lean ones.

After these specific palliatives, the prescription suddenly becomes bold, and too general to be useful. Greater effort to collect overdues must be accompanied by greater effort to prevent their recurrence in future. But how? Through "more rational loaning policies" relating the size of credit to production outlay, effective linking of credit and marketing, strict supervision of loan utilization, and, "above all the education of members of cooperatives." All these are unexceptionable. The only question left unanswered is what chances are there that they will prove effective in the future after they have ignominiously failed in the past.

Finally, the Plan stresses the urgency of "a substantial increase" of deposits at various levels, and lists the reasons as if they were not known —to help absorb overdues, to keep up the flow of credit, to facilitate increase in loanable resources to meet the growing credit demand for intensive agriculture, "to mop up" a part of the increased rural income by "deposit mobilization" in order to use it for productive investment. What methods should be applied to bring about this happy consummation? Two steps have been suggested: extension of the Deposit Insurance Scheme to cover the deposits of cooperative banks, evidently to reassure depositors against risks of loss, and opening new branches of these banks to attract more deposits. But will the rural rich entrust their money to the cooperative banks which are demonstrably ill-managed, a fact that stares out of the government's own analysis? Will they do so, even if they are guaranteed against loss, when they can manage their own savings with perfect safety and far more efficiently to earn a much higher return? It is idle to think that they will.

Figures about the growth of cooperative credit are often flaunted as a great achievement. The total rose from about Rs. 23 crores in 1951 to Rs. 244 in 1961 and Rs. 450 in 1968. *Prima facie*, this is no doubt a big increase. But the sense of gratification must be tempered by some sober thoughts. Much of the so-called cooperative credit is nothing but government contribution, or subsidy, channelled through the system in one form or another; and much of the loans given, as seen above, are "overdues" which, in most cases, is only a euphemism for bad loans. And, finally, this progress has been achieved after the cooperatives have enjoyed two decades of monopoly in rural credit.

There is not the slightest doubt that this record could have been vastly improved if the government had opted, right from the start, for what was obviously the only rational course of action—to bring modern large-scale banking to rural areas with agriculture-oriented services. In that case the banking habit would have spread faster in these areas, deposits would have grown rapidly, large sums of money would have been saved to the public exchequer, and agriculture would have benefited from the presence of a powerful modernizing force.

No, the record of cooperative credit in India is nothing to be proud of; on the contrary, it is one of pathetic performance. No less so is the government's own record. Most disheartening of all, however, is the fact that, even in face of the excruciatingly poor results, it proved itself unable to evaluate the record objectively; instead, it has been satisfied with tortured rationalizations of past policies. The remedies it continues to prescribe cannot stand up even to a cursory scrutiny. They are, as seen above, more legislation, more financial aid, and more bureaucratic rules when the real needs are able management, competent business judgment, highgrade expertise, efficient technical services.

The country has paid a staggering price for the hasty commitment made in 1952. Whatever may have been the excuse for the initial error, there is absolutely none today to persist in it.

## THE IMPERATIVES

What, then, are the essentials of a sound agricultural credit policy in India? There should be no more doubt on this score. Past experience has made them abundantly clear. They are also implicit in the foregoing analysis. Nevertheless, it would be worth putting them together in unmistakable terms, particularly for the benefit of the still wavering souls who, even today, crowd India's political and bureaucratic leadership. The imperatives are:

*First*, dismantle the cooperative monopoly. It has been holding the much publicized new agricultural strategy to ransom. The puny cooperative tail has been wagging the giant dog—the Green Revolution. This is an intolerable situation and must end soon.

*Sceond*, free the IADP districts from the cooperative shackles. It was a blunder, in the first place, to make this historic experiment completely dependent on cooperatives for credit and supply of inputs like seeds, fertilizers, and pesticides.[7] This initial blunder should be rectified without delay. Branches of the State Bank of India or of the leading commercial banks, or, better still, of a newly created all-India credit institution (see below) should be set up immediately in the IADP districts.

*Third*, establish similar branch banks, as fast as possible, in the IAAP districts to ensure that the High-Yielding Varieties Programme will not fail for lack of credit. The longer term objective must be to introduce the Package Programme with the full complement of services in all the districts, 320 or more, of India. And all of them must be served by branches of modern banks.[8]

*Fourth*, launch a massive training programme for agricultural extension workers and other specialists. The present pace of progress in this vital field is still dishearteningly slow and must be stepped up many times. The importance of competent professional staff cannot be overstressed. On them will depend the quality of the farm plans and of farm supervision, which, in turn, will determine the success or failure of rural credit and of agricultural development.[9]

*Fifth*, multiply efforts to organize transportation, storage, and warehousing, and marketing of farm products much more adequately, also more efficiently. Among other things, this implies construction of village-to-market roads, modern warehouses and godowns, establishment of many more regulated markets, and maintenance of reasonable price stability. Progress has been made in all these directions, but a great deal more remains to be done.[10]

[7] See Chapter 12.   [8] See Chapter 15.   [9] See Chapter 22.
[10] See Chapters 23 and 24.

*Sixth*, decentralize, debureaucratize, and depoliticize the cooperative movement, and make a new start to place them on a sound business footing along the lines indicated below.

And, *seventh*, there remains the super-imperative, the need for creating a superstructure overarching the multiplicity of institutions now engaged in providing agricultural credit in one form or another.

## AN ALL-INDIA AGRICULTURAL
## CREDIT CORPORATION

It is not possible nor necessary here to deal at length with the structure, functions, and methods of operations of such a Corporation. Some comments on the broad principles and the prerequisites for its success should, however, be worthwhile.[11]

a. *Decentralized Corporate Body.* The apex body, to be really effective, must be set up as a government-owned public corporation, but with a large degree of autonomy to give it both flexibility and freedom of operation. Like well-conceived public corporations, its charter should clearly define its objectives, lay down a broad policy framework for the purpose while leaving it free to operate within this framework, provide for independent auditing of its accounts every year, and judge its performance by the results achieved after a reasonable period of time.

b. *Policy Board.* The Corporation will clearly need a high-powered board, meeting, say, three times a year, to formulate policies in concrete terms within the provisions of its charter, to review the progress made, to take cognizance of and help overcome any major problems it may be faced with. In view of the peculiar nature of the Corporation's business, it would be desirable to set up a mixed board representing the government, banking, industry and commerce, and agricultural sciences.

To suggest a more specific, though tentative, composition, the board may consist of: representatives of the Central Ministries directly concerned (Food and Agriculture, Community Development and Cooperation, Irrigation and Power, Finance); representatives of the State Department of Agriculture, Reserve Bank, State Bank of India, Agricultural Refinance Corporation, Food Corporation of India, two members on behalf of the nationalized commercial banks; two members from the private sector; and Director-General, Indian Council of Agricultural Research (ICAR), and Director, Indian Agricultural Research Institute (IARI).

[11] A proposal for an All-India Agricultural Credit Corporation on substantially the same lines, though with some differences in emphasis, was made in 1965 by Dr. Harold A. Miles, then Leader of the Ford Foundation's IADP Team. The writer had a very useful discussion in New Delhi with Dr. Miles and his colleague on 10 December 1969, for which he records his appreciation and thanks.

The representatives should, in general, come from the highest echelons, subject to their special interest in or aptitude for agriculture. The Minister of Food and Agriculture would be the most appropriate chairman of the board, with his Secretary of Agriculture serving as its secretary. This will lend authority to the board and will facilitate the Corporation's work.

c. *Executive Committee.* Such a Committee, consisting of half a dozen members appointed by the board mainly from among the state representatives and meeting fairly frequently under a high-powered chairman, would be most desirable for several reasons. It could work out the board's policies in detail and help implement them on a continuous basis; deal, on behalf of the board, with important issues which might arise between board meetings; provide an effective link between the Corporation and the Central Government and help resolve a host of problems, including those of inter-departmental, inter-state, and inter-agency coordination, which the Corporation may be faced with from time to time.

The membership of the Committee should be suitably rotated among the states while maintaining continuity in its work.

d. *State Corporations.* In a vast country like India it would be absolutely essential for the all-India Corporation to set up a branch organization, or a state corporation, in each state and to allow it to function with a large delegation of authority, but within the framework of policies and standard regulations laid down from the headquarters. Each corporation should have a small executive committee, as a prototype of the one at the Centre, for policy-making and coordination at the state level.

These state corporations, it should be noted, are quite different from what is now envisaged in the Fourth Plan, as mentioned earlier. The Plan proposal is to set up such corporations only in those states where credit cooperatives are too weak for their jobs; they have also been conceived in very narrow terms, almost exclusively as an additional source of credit. The proposal made here is much broader—*every* state will be provided with a corporation, as a branch of the all-India institution, and it will render the whole gamut of services directly bearing on agricultural credit and will, in addition, provide both props and prods to build up well managed, profitable cooperatives.

e. *Management.* The Corporation should be headed by a Managing Director, and each state corporation by a Manager. Only men of high competence with adequate understanding of agricultural operations should qualify for these key positions. Once selected, they should be given large freedom in their day-to-day operations.

f. *Funding.* The Corporation should be set up with authorized and paid-up capital, mainly or exclusively contributed by the Central Government. This will, of course, need to be supplemented with liberal borrowings from designated sources, such as the Reserve Bank, the State

Bank of India, Agricultural Refinance Corporation, Life Insurance Corporation, nationalized commercial banks.

Since crops and growing seasons vary widely within the country, an all-India body could achieve a substantial turnover of the resources for short-term crop loans by rotating them among different regions.

Should PL-480 funds be used as an additional source? There is a good case for doing so. If the demand for credit mounts steeply—and this is what is devoutly to be wished under the new agricultural strategy—it would be shortsighted to stint on credit rather than use these funds.[12]

g. *Functions.* The primary function of the Corporation would be to provide short, medium, and long-term loans for agriculture. They should closely resemble those of the Crédit Agricole of Egypt mentioned in the previous chapter, and need not therefore be repeated.

Each state corporation will have to build up a state-wide organization in adequate strength. It will need trained, or easily trainable, staff to process loan applications and to serve in its "extension" wing to establish close contacts with individual farmers, to ensure the timely availability of loans, to supervise their utilization, and to see that they are repaid after crops have been harvested and marketed.

A major objective must be to see that *all* farmers, particularly the small ones who are the first to be ignored, are provided with sound crop plans and reasonable short-term credits. The Corporation's task will be facilitated to the extent the government succeeds in building up an effective agricultural extension service. The two will obviously have to work in close cooperation with each other.

The declared official policy is "to institutionalize" the *taccavi* loans in order to free the government from this responsibility. The most sensible course would be to entrust this function completely to the new credit corporations, and this should include not only future loans of this type, but also the management of those already granted but not recovered.

Incidentally, on a realistic view, there is no escape from having much greater recourse to *taccavi* than in the past—there is simply no other conceivable way to extend the credit service to millions of small and medium farmers. Ideally, they should be approached not individually, but through cooperatives. But it will take time to build real cooperatives with comprehensive membership including the smaller cultivators. Till then, there is no alternative to *taccavi* if they are at all to receive the credits they sorely need.

If the Corporation and its state branches work in businesslike fashion, the management of *taccavi* will prove far more efficient than it is today. As a result, the government will be relieved of a major headache, countless more farmers will benefit from the system, and the burden on the

[12] See Chapter 27. The Credit Shackles and Deficit Financing.

54

exchequer, due to bad or overdue *taccavis*, will be minimized, even if not eliminated.

It would be necessary for the Corporation, especially at the state level, to take active interest in building up essential non-credit agri-support facilities and services—from the inflow of inputs to the marketing of the produce—since all the links in the chain must function smoothly if the credit operations are to succeed. More concretely, it will need to watch closely the activities of other agencies—wholesale and retail suppliers of inputs, agro-industries corporations, warehousing corporations, regulated market authorities, Rural Electrification Corporation, Land Development Banks, the Food Corporation of India, also road, transport and communication authorities—and intervene persuasively in the interest of speed in construction of facilities, their quality and management. It can and should act as a powerful catalyzer when the situation so demands.

h. *Building Real Cooperatives.* This is a function of overriding national importance. The Corporation would be an ideal agency to shoulder this responsibility. It should therefore be given, through its charter, a clear mandate to that effect along with wide powers. For best results action will be needed on several fronts:

1. The government departments should withdraw from direct dealings with cooperative business. All the government assets and liabilities in the district central banks and primary societies, along with the official staff employed in these two tiers, should be transferred to the Corporation, mainly at the state level. And the cooperative departments, as they now exist, should be liquidated.

2. A small cell may be created in the agriculture department to keep watch over the reorganization of the cooperatives and to extend from the government such assistance, including legislation, as may be found necessary.

3. The Corporation should be given a completely free hand to build new businesslike cooperatives with lively farmer participation to replace the inert, rule-ridden "non-cooperatives" which now impede progress, and therefore to remould, recast and restaff them, also to amalgamate or eliminate them as may prove necessary. The present staff may be retained when considered "usable" or "trainable." A good part of it will, almost certainly, have to be discharged.

4. A major weakness of cooperation in India, which goes back to the British days, has been its exclusive preoccupation with credit, although success in cooperative credit is the hardest to achieve if only because the vast majority of the rural people are too poor to be creditworthy. Service cooperatives—for tubewell irrigation, marketing of food crops and livestock produce, processing industries, even purchase and sale of essential consumer goods—are inherently easier

to organize and operate because they offer obvious economies of scale. Greater emphasis on this type of cooperatives would be eminently desirable. They will also help build up a much needed psychology of success in a field where it has proved particularly hard to come by.

Some marketing and processing cooperatives, especially for sugar-cane and oilseeds, have achieved excellent results in Maharashtra, Madras, Punjab, and Gujarat. They have convincingly shown how much can be achieved with Indian farmers when due attention is paid to the scale of operation, quality of management, market demand, and adequate capitalization.

5. The Corporation can and should extend concessional terms to *well-run* cooperatives in such matters as the amount of advances allowed and the rate of interest charged on them. It may also help negotiate special discounts on purchases of inputs and price premiums on sales of farm produce, when the transactions are made through cooperatives. Some concessions of this type would be quite legitimate because of the economies arising from larger-scale transactions. It would also be justified, particularly in the early stages, to go even beyond these economies and to add to them a modest element of subsidy as an incentive to stimulate the growth of cooperatives. In business terms, this would be a very desirable type of promotional cost which should in due course bring solid gains. The Corporation, it need hardly be added, must be left free to exercise its unfettered judgement as regards the specific form and extent of these concessions and whether or not individual cooperatives would be entitled to them.

6. Special effort should be made to form small farmers' cooperatives because, being small, the farmers need even more urgently the benefits and the protection to be derived from them. The Corporation, in its turn, will find it easier, and cheaper, to serve them through effective cooperatives rather than individually.

i. *Land Reform.* It may appear out of context to bring in land reform while dealing with credit and cooperation, but it is not so. Effective land reform—that is, a land-to-the-tiller programme—is an indispensable precondition for building real cooperatives. Gross inequalities in land ownership and, consequently, in economic and political influence are inimical to the germination of a cooperative spirit. This is the costliest lesson India has to learn from her twenty years of experience, during which a placid bureaucracy routinely continued to sow the seeds of cooperation on sterile ground, unperturbed by the bitter harvest it reaped year after year.

This is also the lesson to be learnt from the experience of other countries, such as Mexico, Egypt, and Taiwan. In all these cases, radical land reform preceded an effective cooperative movement. It broke down large estates, greatly reduced property and income disparities, and thereby created a favourable environment in which both cooperation and agriculture could flourish. It cannot be different in India.

j. *Deposit Mobilization.* Should the Corporation receive deposits like a commercial bank? Rather not. Its hands will be more than full with the tasks directly related to agricultural credit—making loans, supervising and servicing them, ensuring their repayment—in a country teeming with small farmers. These are services of seminal importance; how to discharge them efficiently, and at the least possible cost, to the farmer and to the public should be its sole concern; it would therefore be unwise to distract its attention away from them or to saddle it with additional tasks like receiving and handling deposits.

There is a second reason no less relevant. If the Corporation were to serve as a deposit bank as well, it would have to pay special attention to the interests of the depositors, which may very well clash with those of its principal clientele, the farmers, for whose benefit it is proposed to be established.

However, the Corporation can, as a little reflection will show, make a most significant contribution to deposit mobilization even without being itself involved in deposit banking, provided it handles its primary business with the requisite imagination, care, and skill. It will, through its day-to-day work, give the farm business a more monetary orientation, make the farmers more conscious of thrift and savings, and thereby help spread the banking habit among them. As a result, their savings should flow more readily into the commercial banks, assuming that their branches are located within easy reach, also into the cooperatives if they are remoulded into larger and more efficient units on the lines indicated above.

With the spread of the banking habit, the farmers, it may be safely assumed, will increasingly turn to the Corporation, to commercial banks and cooperatives, since loans from these sources will be available on much more attractive terms than in the past. The rural money-lenders and the rich agriculturists who have hitherto been catering to their credit needs on a substantial scale, will more and more loosen their stranglehold. And once the path of easy and exploitative money-making is definitely blocked for them, their surplus resources—it may be presumed, and hoped—will spill over into more productive channels, such as rural industries, various types of agri-business, and into new growth centres.

The process of deposit mobilization can be greatly stimulated if, in addition to the steps indicated here, the interests allowed on savings and deposits are raised to much more attractive levels while charging a correspondingly higher rate on loans. The concept of cheap money has come to rural India too soon; it is, in fact, cheap judged even by Western standards (the real interest in the USA on instalment loans, for example, amounts to something like 12 to 18 per cent); and its net effect has been to discourage savings, to hinder deposit mobilization, and thus to make money scarce.[13]

*A Warning.* It is necessary to sound a note of warning at this stage. A public corporation to minister to agricultural credit will undoubtedly be the best institutional device subject, however, to one obvious condition: that it is really worked as a public corporation, which will be the case only if

a. Its autonomy is respected in practice;
b. it is allowed to function as a non-political body and is shielded from the pressures of democratic politics;
c. the managing director and the managers are chosen with great care and solely for their ability, professional competence, and integrity of character;
d. they are given the requisite freedom to choose and manage their personnel, based on a merit system rather than on the rule of seniority;
e. its finances are completely freed from treasury control; and
f. its accounts are subjected to commercial audit, and not to the traditional government audit.

These, in a nutshell, are the quintessential characteristics of a public corporation. Together, they invest it with a dynamic quality, thereby distinguishing it from a rule-ridden pedestrian government department. And, together, they make it incomparably superior to the latter for handling dynamic business functions on public account.

Hitherto India has shown a genius for setting up public corporations because they are believed to be intrinsically superior for handling government business, but only to turn them, by the back door, into the very government departments from which they were supposed to provide an escape. She has thus produced what is a peculiar brand of *departmental public corporations*, sometimes making the worst of both worlds, to match, as it were, the *departmental cooperatives* she has zealously planted for the economic uplift of rural India. There would be absolutely no justification to re-enact this dreary scenario with the credit corporation proposed above.

## THE STAKE

Past policies in rural credit have done incalculable damage, though the

[13] The IADP Evaluation Reports have, on several occasions, stressed this anomaly. "In both the cooperative and commercial banking systems," says Dr. Harold A. Miles, "rates of interest paid on deposits and rates charged borrowers are consid-

full extent is seldom realized. The usual view runs somewhat as follows: cooperation is a highly desirable objective—indeed, in a land of mostly small farmers, it holds out the best hope for progress; true, it has faltered in the past and has yielded very mixed results; this, however, is a case not for giving up the pursuit of the goal, but for trying even harder.

The reasoning sounds plausible, but it contains some serious pitfalls. For, it is based on a misleadingly superficial view of what has actually happened, and is still happening, in India.

Credit, like irrigation water, is a most essential input for agriculture. Whatever system is built, it must ensure a smooth flow to reach individual farmers. What India has done hitherto is, in effect, to insist that the credit, instead of flowing smoothly and easily through wide open institutional channels, must trickle to them through an ill-functioning cooperative filter. This was a stupendous folly. Starved of credit, agriculture stagnated; and stagnating agriculture and farm incomes deprived cooperation of the only real chance it had to sprout and flourish.

Or, to look at it from a slightly different angle, economic development, or the rate of growth, depended overwhelmingly on agriculture, by far the greatest potential generator of wealth; the fate of agriculture depended, among other things, on a plentiful supply of credit for productive use; the supply of credit was made wholly dependent on the growth of cooperatives; and cooperatives could not strike root in the bleak milieu of rural India. And so agriculture, instead of turning out a large surplus to feed and support other sectors of the economy, itself turned into a crippling economic burden.

To crown it all, there appeared on the scene formidable theoreticians, armed with fallacious doctrines, to propagate the fatal thesis that agriculture was intrinsically unprofitable; that, as a result, it would always have to depend on generous subsidies, direct or indirect.[14] Few realized that, in reality, neither agriculture nor cooperation had been given in India a real chance to grow; that, instead, both had been victims of policies which could only stabilize a miserable *status quo*.

The root cause of the trouble lies somewhere else. For too long India has relied on impassioned declarations of high ideals as the highway to their realization. In the case of the freedom movement, it did work— repeated declarations of the goal, the tumultuous upsurge of emotion, a mass movement rising to tidal proportions, all hastened the day of national independence.

But it does not, and cannot, work for realizing the ideals of democracy, cooperation, community development, panchayati raj, or for achieving higher levels of national well-being—any more than the Everest can be

erably lower than the capital supply-demand warrants." *The Outlook for Farm Credit in India*, Ford Foundation, New Delhi, June 1969.

[14] For further comments see Chapter 29, the section on "Some Glittering Fallacies."

climbed by proclamations. However exciting the goals may be, they call for cool headed, scientific analysis, a well-thought-out strategy, and sustained, painstaking effort. Emotion is still needed as the propelling force, but only to direct effort into the right channel, and not to deflect it wilfully.

The analysis given above shows how to resolve the problems of agricultural credit, and to realize the ideals of cooperation in rural India. This is the only way. It is a delusion to believe there is, or could be, any other.

# CHAPTER 27

# The Credit Shackles
# and Deficit Financing

## A GOLD MINE

Where is the money? The anguished cry rends the air in New Delhi, and echoes and reechoes around the country. Yet the fault, in this case, lies not in the stars. It reflects an astounding lack of imagination, and commonsense.

The issues can be best clarified with some analogies.

Suppose, by a rare good luck, India suddenly struck a rich oil well or discovered a gold mine somewhere in her domain. It is easy to visualize how the nation would beam with joy and treat it as an appropriate occasion for countrywide celebration. Some believers might even start making prayerful offering to some divinity for such a lifesaving piece of serendipity. In any case, steps would be promptly initiated to exploit this precious resource.

Would finance stand in the way? The very thought would be ridiculed. How could there be a shortage of money to make money from an investment where the payoff is high, and foolproof? Finance would be found from the public exchequer, or from public and private sources at home and abroad, or from deficit finance perhaps through an overdraft, probably from a combination of several sources. What is certain is that the project would be funded promptly and adequately.

The next steps are also fairly easy to predict. The authorities would proclaim a new public-sector project; its blueprint would provide for the construction of a colony on a rather lavish scale with access roads, utilities, office buildings, staff quarters and houses for workers; orders would be placed for machinery and equipment, costing large sums of money and involving, in all probability, substantial foreign exchange; actual construction work would perhaps be undertaken departmentally, and would, as usual, proceed slothfully—piling up overheads and capital costs, and cutting into future profits. In due course the operation would start, the underground wealth would be mined and marketed, and the project would be hailed as a success.

Now, *tropical agriculture, based on Borlaug seeds, is a gold mine. It provides solid backing for all the cash and credit that may be needed to dig out the treasures.*

The analogy is not perfect, but mainly because it understates the intrinsic worth and the profitability of our figurative gold mine on four important counts:

*a.* The subsurface and underground water, which can largely supplement the monsoon rains, has a fabulous wealth-creating potential. But whereas an oil well or a gold mine is an *exhaustible* resource, the underground water, in a great many cases, is replenished by nature year after year and is virtually *inexhaustible.*

*b.* The waiting period between investment and benefit in the case of tropical agriculture is surprisingly short—a bumper crop can be raised in about 100 days. In the other case, some four years or more will be needed to bring the project to the point of production.

*c.* The capital needed for crop-raising is minimal, whereas the mining project, from its very nature, will be highly capital-intensive.

*d.* The biology and chemistry of agriculture offer vast scope for improvement through imaginative scientific research. As a result, its value is not static, but can be augmented, often severalfold.

How unreal it is, then, and how shortsighted to complain about the lack of financial resources, to treat this as an unbreakable constraint, and to slow down the green revolution nervously on such a fictitious ground!

There is another analogy, much less edifying but no less compelling, which one could evoke in this context. Suppose, by some misfortune, a war were to break out involving India, as happened during World War II, and was repeated twice—though on a smaller scale—in the sixties. The canons of financial orthodoxy would be immediately suspended; budget-balancing would lose all relevance; printing notes, minting money and granting overdrafts to the government would become the order of the day. Survival of the nation would be proclaimed as the sole concern in such an emergency. And on this rationale, finance unlimited would be made available for activities where the output-input ratio would be nil, probably lower.

What about the other war, one might ask, the war on poverty which has engaged India for decades, which, too, has grown into a desperate struggle for survival? Must financial orthodoxy hold unbridled sway in

55

this case? Must it be allowed to veto projects with amazingly high output-input ratios, to cripple development, and thereby to make the war unwinnable from the start? Nothing could be more absurd and irresponsible.

## CREDIT-FINANCING

When yield per crop jumps five to six times and the number of crops per acre doubles or trebles, the need for finance, too, goes up sharply in order to capitalize on the production breakthrough. The bulk of it, however, is needed as working capital—in the form of seasonal or medium-term loans—and can therefore be easily met by straightforward credit expansion.

The activities that should fully qualify to be "credit-financed" have been indicated in other chapters.[1] They cover an extraordinarily wide range as will be clear even from the brief listing given below.

*Crop loans*: Seasonal loans for farm plans constitute the largest single item in cultivator financing; and they have grown tremendously in importance and urgency. Yet as seen earlier, even the IADP districts have all along suffered from a serious credit shortage which has greatly hampered their operations.[2] This is as unfortunate as it is uncalled for. Once farm plans are prepared by the extension workers and certified as sound by the IADP authorities, credit ought to be made available straightaway.

The risks involved in such short-term farm credit for what, by any standard, are exceptionally high-yielding plans would be negligible; and they would be no more than a fraction of the risks now involved in cooperative credit in general. In any case, as an additional safeguard arrangement can be made to have these risks underwritten by a suitable government agency.

The same principle should be applied to the other districts as well. Formulation of high-quality farm plans must be given the foremost priority. Once formulated, they must not suffer for lack of funds.

*Irrigation.* Demand for credit to finance minor irrigation projects of all kinds—shallow wells, tubewells, tanks, tiny dams, lift irrigation from rivers and lakes—has been on a steep uptrend. But programmes have been repeatedly slashed for lack of funds. Such axe-wielding is utterly senseless. What the government should do today is, first, to make an all-out effort to promote low-cost minor irrigation projects all over the country to the utmost possible extent; and, second, once their econmic soundness is fully assured, to make credit immediately available *without limit*.

The same approach should be applied to other urgent irrigation-related

---

[1] Especially in Chapters 16 through 23, also a good many other activities discussed in *Reaping the Green Revolution*.

[2] See Chapters 12-13.

activities, such as groundwater exploration and development, remodelling of major irrigation projects and creation of irrigation grids with field channels and controls, drainage works to go hand in hand with irrigation, repair and maintenance of all existing and future works, and energization of pumpsets.[3] Such activities must not be held up for lack of credit. Whenever necessary, credit should be boldly created to finance them.

*Seed programmes.* Production and distribution of inputs call for a large amount of short and medium term finance. The urgency is obvious. Without a smooth and assured inflow of improved seeds of guaranteed purity, it would, for example, be idle to talk of modernizing the agriculture. Yet this inflow is still fitful and precarious owing largely to a credit shortage.

As early as 1964, the Rockefeller Foundation identified this as a major problem while dealing with the question of propagating hybrid maize. The provision of capital resources, including both intermediate term and short term credit, it observed, "is emerging as one of the most critical limiting factors" for production and distribution of improved seeds on an adequate scale in India. This was being "brought into sharp focus" in relation to the commercial production and distribution of certified seed of maize, jowar, and bajra hybrids, but it would "have a broad applicability of all crop seeds for Indian agriculture."[4]

The constraint shows no sign of easing; in fact, it is now felt even more severely than before. With the arrival of miracle wheat and rice, the need for capital to multiply and distribute certified seed on a commercial scale has gone up rapidly; the supply of funds, too, has increased but not fast enough; and the net result has been a widening gap between the two.

How can there be a green revolution if its seeds cannot be multiplied and distributed to the farmers? This would be like killing the golden goose, or, to be more precise, refusing to hatch it. That money must be found to finance an adequate seed programme in all its phases goes without saying. And this must, among other things, include seed farms, well-equipped seed storage plants, drying-and-processing plants for rice, seed-testing laboratories, credit for seed distributors, both wholesale and retail.[5] Where money is in short supply, it will simply have to be created.

*Fertilizers and pesticides.* Broadly, the same principle holds good for financing other inputs. The credits required for fertilizers are large, and they have been rising steeply as shown by the following figures (millions of rupees):[6]

[3] See Chapters 16 and 21.
[4] In an unpublished paper of the Rockefeller Foundation, New Delhi, 1964.
[5] See Chapter 17.
[6] Report of the Fertilizer Credit Committee of the Fertilizer Association of India, New Delhi, 1968.

| Year | Distribution credit needs | Credit needed at farmer's level |
|---|---|---|
| 1967-68 | 1,650 | 2,519 |
| 1968-69 | 2,085 | 3,381 |
| 1969-70 | 2,457 | 4,153 |
| 1970-71 | 2,970 | 5,200 |

The credit needs, which are mostly short-term, virtually doubled in four years. They should grow even faster over the coming years if, as is assumed, concerted effort is made to spread the green revolution at a fast enough rate. The Fertilizer Committee underscored the inability of the cooperatives to cope with credit requirement of this magnitude and stressed the urgency of tapping other sources. It estimated that, under favourable conditions, and if reinforced with government participation, the cooperatives could meet about one-half of the credit needed for fertilizers at the farmer's level. And so for some time a frantic search has been going on for the balance to fill the credit gap.

Some people are apt to speculate, almost despairingly, how much more India could have achieved if only she were not in such a tragic financial bind. Yet the headaches are needlessly exaggerated. This particular Gordian knot should be dealt with in a more straightforward fashion—it should be neatly cut by creating credit on the required scale.

Fertilizer credit, at the farmer's level, is the biggest single component of crop loans. These, as suggested earlier, should be financed by credit expansion. Distributors' credit can—and should—be dealt with precisely the same way.

And the same approach should be applied also to pesticides.[7] The State Bank of India and the Agricultural Refinance Corporation, a consortium of 36 member banks, are reportedly working on the problem to find enough finance to cope with the mounting demand at all stages—from the manufacturing point through the long chain of suppliers and distributors to their actual use on the farms. This is commendable provided two guiding principles are strictly adhered to: first, the supply of pesticides must not suffer for lack of credit; where such a situation threatens to develop, it should be eased forthwith, if necessary by creating extra credit with central bank overdrafts.

And, second, credit must be available in order to enable farmers to procure the right kind of pesticides at the right time from wherever they may be available. Timeliness, in this case, is particularly important. The Pesticides Association of India has therefore suggested that the cooperatives or commercial banks should issue to the farmers credit coupons against which they could draw the needed supplies from local distrib-

[7] See Chapter 19.

utors who, in their turn, could cash the coupons at commercial banks. Some such mechanism is essential under existing conditions. Pesticides remain the best means of crop insurance, next in importance only to the breeding of disease-resistant varieties.

*Farm machinery.* The kind of machinery needed to support intensive agriculture has been discussed at length in an earlier chapter.[8] Substantial credit will be needed both by distributors and farmers, mostly for short or medium term. Small farmers in particular will need facilities to purchase equipment on instalment basis. Here again, it would be perfectly legitimate to meet such requirements by *ad hoc* credit creation whenever found necessary.

*Rural electrification.* Power shortage, in many cases, is aggravated by a credit shortage.[9] Construction of feeder lines and energization of irrigation pumpsets are frequently delayed or suspended for lack of funds. Such intolerable situations arise only because of an implicit refusal to create credit on an adequate scale. In such instances, power shortage can be quickly remedied—simply by exercising a little more will power.

*Land and soil improvement.* There are countless activities which fall in this category,[10] but it would be shortsighted to hold them up for lack of finance. The great majority of them can and should be financed simply by creating short-to-medium term credit. This holds good for small-scale reclamation and drainage projects, for erosion control and soil conservation activities in general, and for consolidation of holdings.

There is no warrant whatever to put off such pressing, quick-maturing, high-payoff projects on the familiar plea of financial stringency. They should be credit-financed; and when needed, credit should be readily expanded to finance them.

*Agri-support facilities.* Village-to-market roads, storage godowns, warehouses, regulated markets with proper facilities—all these are indispensable for post-harvest handling and marketing of farm output. Without them no commercial agriculture would be possible. Despite the progress made in recent years, the existing facilities are only a small fraction of India's total needs.[11] Massive investments are necessary to expand them rapidly, and large-scale deficit finance must be resorted to when enough means are otherwise not available.

*Research and extension.* They belong to the very heart of modern agriculture. Money pumped into them imaginatively will pay rich, even spectacular, dividends.[12] They, too, fully qualify to be credit-financed. In any case, they must not be starved of funds.

[8] In Chapter 20.
[9] See Chapter 21.
[10] The activities falling in this category are discussed in *Reaping the Green Revolution.*
[11] See Chapter 24.
[12] See Chapter 22.

To conclude: Agriculture in India, despite the professed concern for it, has long been discriminated against in actual practice, though mainly out of a failure to grasp its real needs. Without essential scientific services, without roads and other elementary facilities, and without much concern for the investments needed to create them, it has for generations been condemned to a stagnant, poorly-performing existence. It is, in any case, past the time to make amends for these accumulated omissions.

To India's good fortune, the miracle seeds have created a golden opportunity to come to grips with these tasks. But, alas, the yield breakthrough they have brought about has not been able to break through the encrusted conservatism of nineteenth-century-style financiers. They are still unable to comprehend how dramatically the cost-benefit relations have improved in India's agriculture; how short-term working capital, by rapid turnover, can do an incomparably better job for producing income increments than what one could expect, only a few short years ago, from large investments of long-term capital; how, as a result, a farmland, cultivated with the new seeds, has turned into a priceless asset; how this process can be both extended and accelerated as more and more miracle seeds of different crops emerge out of the research pipeline. It is, to say the least, ironic that the authorities, in particular their planning experts, should be throwing up their hands in despair for lack of finance, that is to say, for lack of *the means to rake in the unprecedented bounties the dwarfs are throwing up before their very eyes!*

India's agriculture must be rescued from the stifling grip of a mindless orthodoxy. This means three things today: First, every farm must be equipped with the basic facilities in every possible way. Second, projects for doing so should be quickly prepared, all over the country, with proper input of science and economics to ensure their fundamental soundness. And, third, once properly prepared, they should be promptly funded. No financial stringency should be allowed to develop, certainly not to stand in the way. Credit should be stretched as far as necessary to meet all legitimate needs. It should, so to say, be *available on tap.*

*Not from funds to projects, but from projects to funds*—this is the about-turn India needs today for the categories of agri-support activities listed above.[13] There should be no hesitation *to create* funds for them with a full-blooded expansion of credit.

The credit shackles must be shattered. This is the foremost task India is faced with today to liberate her agriculture—nay, her entire economy —from a financial stranglehold. And when this happens, her green revolution will rapidly pick up momentum and roll over the country.

[13] The writer believes the same principle should be applied to a number of other fields, such as rural public works, many rural industries, hospitals and clinics as part of the family planning programme, even rural schools. As for the scope of deficit finance in general, see below.

**PL 480 FUNDS**

Large funds have accumulated in India as the rupee counterpart of the US aid under Public Law 480 (Food for Peace) Programme. Could they be utilized for developing India's agriculture? Would this alleviate the credit shortage? And would such a policy aggravate inflation? These questions have been, and are still being, debated in an atmosphere of mixed feelings and confused logic. A brief look into their broad implications should be of interest in the present context.

The nature and magnitude of these funds can be judged from a few simple facts. India has received substantial quantities of agricultural commodities, mainly wheat, under PL 480.[14] The original legislation, enacted by the U.S. Congress in 1954, expired in December 1966. But an Amending Act passed prior to that date extended it for two years with some important modifications. The amended Act was given a fresh lease of life for another two-year period by legislation passed in 1968.

Under the ten PL 480 agreements concluded between the two countries, India had received, by July 1968, commodities valued at $4,221.2 million, equivalent to Rs. 2,240 crores.[15] Of this, a sum of $90.1 million is repayable in rupees convertible into dollars at the option of the US Government, as laid down in the Amending Act of 1966. The balance of $4,131.1 million should, according to the provisions of the agreements, be disposed of as follows:

> 80.2 per cent should be returned to the Government of India—19.8 per cent as grant, and 60.4 per cent as loans;
> 13.2 per cent is earmarked for US Government uses; and
> 6.6 per cent is reserved for loans to private enterprise—the so-called "Cooley loans."

The counterpart funds, some have argued in India, constitute a serious threat of inflation. In view of the growing controversy the Government of India decided, in 1968, to have the whole matter investigated by an Expert Panel.[16]

The experts took some pains to demonstrate that the way PL 480 transactions had been effected produced no inflationary effect, and that their actual impact on money creation was neutral.

At the same time they hoisted a danger signal for the future, that is, after the cessation of PL 480 imports. The funds did constitute a potential source of inflation, the Panel argued, and considered several alter-

[14] See also Chapter 23.

[15] Converted into rupees mostly at the pre-devaluation rate of $1 = Rs. 4.75, since most of the transactions had taken place before the rupee was devalued, in June 1966.

[16] The panel was headed by Professor A. M. Khusro.

natives to forestall the risk. American expenditures on US uses, it hoped, "would be properly phased" in agreement with the Government of India; the latter, it urged, should have previous knowledge about the annual expenditure flows from this source so that it could plan its own budget deficits and surpluses appropriately. "But there is no denying," added the Panel, "that, other things remaining equal, the impact of the expenditures will clearly be inflationary."

Other things, however, should not remain equal, and so the Government, the Panel urged, should try and obtain a grant from the USA to insulate the economy from an eventual inflationary effect. As a last resort, it suggested "a mutual agreement to freeze the funds permanently." In this way "the accumulated amounts or agreed parts thereof can be annihilated and the economy cushioned from the impact." This, the Panel observed, would be "akin to the burning of currency notes at retirement."

These conclusions need to be qualified in some important respects. It is true that PL 480 imports did not produce inflation via money creation. They did, however, have an inflationary effect in another and more subtle sense—via retardation of domestic production. The imports, as seen elsewhere,[17] helped peg wheat prices to an artificially low level; this price deterrent kept down India's own production of wheat even at a time of rising demand, and thereby in the end contributed to higher wheat prices.

As for the future, everything will depend on *how* the funds are used. If used to finance the items listed earlier in this chapter to support India's agriculture, especially to accelerate the spread of the green revolution, they will help boost production and check inflation. This, indeed, would be the most desirable kind of utilization of the counterpart funds.

In this respect, the Rural Electrification Corporation can serve as an excellent example. As mentioned earlier,[18] it has been funded with Rs. 150 crores; of this, Rs. 45 crores came from the Central Government while the balance of Rs. 105 crores was drawn from PL 480 funds, with a tacit understanding that fresh financing from the same source would be permissible should this be deemed necessary. The same principle could be extended to meet many of the other pressing needs for rural development.

A permanent freeze on the US holdings will no doubt neutralize the threat of future inflation they pose, but such a policy is unlikely to find favourable response in the USA. The accumulation of these funds has already become a source of some embarrassment to the US administration; it is therefore understandably reluctant to see them grow further

[17] See Chapter 23.
[18] In Chapter 21.

in size and would much rather have them drawn down to a substantially lower level.[19]

On the other hand, it would be extremely difficult to persuade the U.S. Congress and public to bless the idea of a permanent freeze, which is only another name for writing off the funds for good. It would not only neutralize the threat of inflation, but would, to all intents and purposes, also nullify a major provision of the original agreements. The USA, it may be assumed, will ask for and, in all probability, also insist on a reasonable *quid pro quo*.

However, the US authorities have clearly indicated that they have no intention to interpret this last phrase in a narrow sense; that if the funds are demonstrably used to serve the best economic interests of India, this will be treated as an acceptable *quid pro quo*. Significantly enough, the amended law contains an explicit provision authorizing their use more liberally for agricultural development.

Can the example set by the REC be followed for other agri-support programmes enlarging the use of the counterpart funds in a really big way? There are some unmistakable snags, both legal and political. Specific Congressional authorization would be required for wider use of the funds. And Congress has apparently been chary about fresh legislation to that effect in order, one suspects, not to upset Indian feelings on what has become a rather sensitive issue. The Indian Government has hitherto sought to put tight restrictions on the use of the funds out of fear that they would kindle inflationary fires.

To some extent the fear may be, and probably is, politically motivated, but with a lot of people the fear is genuine, though it is mainly based on emotion rather than reason. What they are unable to realize is that the counterpart funds, if injected in large doses into the productive activities indicated earlier, would not only cause no inflation, but would be definitely salutary, and counterinflationary.

Clearly, from India's angle, the wisest course of action would be: first, to prepare an inventory of high-yielding and quick-maturing agri-support projects, particularly those mentioned above; and, second, to persuade the U. S. administration to seek specific legislative authority to use up the counterpart funds almost exclusively for these projects.

Such a policy, if successfully initiated. would have several advantages. It would kill, not kindle inflation; it would speed up the spread of the green revolution, increase production, and raise living standards; and it would meet India's commitments under the PL 480 agreements in full. The last point should not be ignored. India has a proud record of meticulously

---

[19] According to a G.A.O. study made in the USA in February, 1971, the holdings of Indian currency would last 19 years at the present rate of their disposal. And they are expected to rise to $ 3.5 billion over the next 40 years through the restricted spending, new accumulations, and repayments of principal and interest on loans.

honouring her international obligations. That record should not be tarnished.

From the U.S. angle too, nothing could be more desirable than such a policy. It would liquidate what has become almost a chronic problem—the massive build-up of soft-currency counterpart funds can hardly be rated as an economic asset while it has definitely turned into a political liability. It would eliminate a potential source of inflation in India, and also a potent source of ill-feeling between the two nations. Above all, it would confer lasting benefits on the Indian economy and would thereby do justice—even more convincingly than the annual deliveries of foodgrains—to that altruistic impulse which had given birth to a food-for-peace programme to share the abundance of America with an impoverished third world.

## DEFICIT FINANCE

The use of PL 480 funds for a rural development programme remains speculative at this stage. And even if wisdom prevails, it will take time for the idea to materialize. Besides, the funds, large though they are, can meet only a part of India's total needs. There remains, in effect, only one practical alternative, namely, to have recourse to credit creation or deficit financing on a massive scale.

The role played by deficit finance in India's Plans has been highly erratic, as will be seen from the following figures:

DEFICIT FINANCING IN INDIA (*In crores of Rs.*)

| | Public-sector Outlay | | Deficit Financing[20] | |
|---|---|---|---|---|
| | *planned* | *actual* | *planned* | *actual* |
| First Plan | 1,793 | 1,960 | 290 | 333 |
| Second Plan | 4,800 | 4,600 | 1,200 | 948 |
| Third Plan | 7,500 | 8,577 | 550 | 1,133 |
| Annual Plans | | | | |
| for 1966-69 | 6,665 | 6,756 | 335 | 682 |
| Fourth Plan Provision | 15,902 | — | 850 | — |

In the First Plan, deficit finance was given a nodding recognition. The Plan itself was comparatively small in size, and about 17 per cent was

[20] The First Plan included short-term treasury borrowing—from the Central Bank, commercial banks and the public—in the totals for deficit finance; but starting with the Second Plan, they were excluded. (*Second Five Year Plan*, 1956, p. 84). Thus, the jump from the First to the Second Plan under this head was even bigger than is shown by the figures.

expected to come from this source. The actual figure turned out to be somewhat higher.

The Second Plan warmly embraced the concept, relied on it heavily, and rationalized it in almost defiant terms. It was going to strain the country's financial resources, but then "a plan is an attempt to raise the rate of investment" above what it would otherwise have been. True, there was the risk of inflation, but "no amount of prudence" could eliminate it completely. The best defence against inflation "is, in a sense, to keep clear of it, but a policy of 'playing safe' is not always conducive to development."[21]

The Second Plan was almost three times bigger than the first. Of this, deficit finance was to supply a full quarter. Its actual performance, however, fell appreciably short of this target.

As the economy heated and prices climbed, there was a distinct cooling off of the initial fervour for it. The Third Plan was as explicit on this point as official decorum would permit. In view of the rise in prices that had occurred during the Second Plan period and the fact that, unlike in the Second Plan, there was "no cushion of foreign exchange reserves" which could be drawn upon as an "offset to deficit financing," it wanted to limit it in the Third Plan "to the minimum warranted by the genuine monetary needs of the economy."[22] In plain prose, prices were sharply up, the sterling balances were steeply down, the authorities felt nervous over the trend, they discovered the virtue of prudence, chose to "play safe" and, therefore, to minimize deficit financing.

But the choice was no longer theirs; for, by then, the situation was already getting out of control, thanks to the momentum of the earlier expenditures, quicker growth of population than anticipated, misbehaviour of the monsoon, a widening food gap, and dwindling reserves of foreign exchange. This grim scenario, it was felt, left little elbowroom for deficit finance as understood earlier.

How to make the budgetary ends meet now became the main—and largely also a vain—concern. The Finance Ministers struggled to balance their budgets, vied with each other in practising fiscal prudence, raised taxes even where they made little fiscal sense, and ostentatiously reinforced austerity, but deficits continued to pile up obstinately year after year.

The deficits had to be met of course, and they were met mainly with created bank money; and this, too, duly took its place under the handy rubric of "deficit financing." Yet the meaning of the phrase had changed radically, though imperceptibly. The deficits were no longer incurred purposefully to promote development, but for the more prosaic purpose of filling the gaping holes in the Central and state budgets. They no

[21] *Second Five Year Plan*, 1956, pp. 81 and 86.
[22] *Third Five Year Plan*, 1961, p. 99.

longer represented an act of volition, but had become a measure of helplessness.

After the experience in the Second Plan period, provisions for deficit financing were drastically pruned, yet the actuals continued to exceed them by a wide margin. In mid-1966, the Fourth Plan in its Draft Outline expressed visible concern over this trend. Despite sizable increases in receipts over the budgeted estimates, the total deficits of the Central and state governments amounted to Rs. 1150 crores for the five-year period covered by the Third Plan. "Deficit-financing was particularly large in 1965-66, when it amounted to Rs. 385 crores."[23]

The Fourth Plan, in its final version, includes a provision of Rs. 850 crores for deficit finance during 1969-74. The "stipulated growth in real income," it observed, would warrant a corresponding expansion in money supply. Then it added rather blandly: "Deficit finance may also be necessary for further activation of the economy."[24] Once again, the basic principle was accorded some legitimacy, but rather weakheartedly. One could hear in this remark only a faint echo of the robust faith that had breathed through the Second Plan.

Thus, India has doubly erred. To start with, deficit finance was misconceived, mishandled, even abused. And once it backfired, as it was bound to, she declared it almost as a kind of moral dereliction, swung back hurriedly to a soulless austerity, and began, almost in an expiatory mood, to practise financial masochism.

That mood persists even today. Bitten by her own past mistakes, it seems she has become ten times shy. This explains why, despite the dazzling performance of miracle rice and wheat, she is unwilling to go all out to capitalize on the exciting opportunities, why she timidly seeks false safety in the cosy shelter of archaic financial dogma, why she refuses to use the key she still holds to her own prosperity.

## THE GRAND FALLACIES

The wide swings in the attitude towards deficit finance are a symptom of something deeper. They point up some of the basic flaws in India's economic planning, the grand fallacies which have been embedded in it from the start.

*First,* there is what the writer has called the *Capital Error.*[25]

Resources are equated to *financial* resources, which are estimated for a given five-year period and are then used to determine the size of the Plan. Since financial resources, in an underdeveloped economy, are inevitably scarce—for the very reason that the economy is underdeveloped

---

[23] *Fourth Five Year Plan—A Draft Outline,* 1966, p. 79.
[24] *Fourth Five Year Plan, 1969-74,* p. 83.
[25] In Chapter 2.

—this approach immediately puts the Plan in a straitjacket. The purpose of planning is, above all, to develop and utilize the idle *physical* resources as rapidly as possible, wisely using the tools of modern science and technology, in order to produce food and other essential goods to the maximum possible extent. The approach actually followed poses a maximum obstacle to the realization of this goal.

It is no secret that the main concepts used in India's planning have been copied almost in toto from "the West," though more from the abstract economic theory currently in vogue there than from its concrete applications. In any case, it ignores crucial differences in the two sets of conditions. In an advanced Western economy, the natural resources have, by and large, been already developed; employment persists at a high level, though it may occasionally slip from its full potential; the economy is highly money-sensitive; as a result, financial resources represent real assets which, so to say, have released their cash counterparts into the mainstream of economic life.

How different it is in India and other underdeveloped countries where natural resources are unused or underused, manpower is unemployed or underemployed, vast areas are "unbanked" and "unmonetized," barter and hoarding of cash and precious metals are still largely the order of the day! In such a situation the savings-based approach to development planning has little relevance. It can only be self-defeating.

*Second*, macro-economic planning, especially in an underdeveloped country, is largely an exercise in abstractions and futility.

India's statistical data, in general, are of better quality than those of most developing countries, and in recent years they have shown a distinct improvement. Nevertheless, those with first-hand knowledge of the actual situation are painfully aware of their imperfections.

Income and savings data, the raw materials used in macro-planning, are completely unreliable. The extent of savings, hoarded at home and abroad, is unknown, and no means have yet been devised to estimate them even with reasonable accuracy. Large farmers, in recent years, have piled up wealth; again, nobody knows how much of it they are saving except that it must be large, and no fiscal means have yet been thought out by the government to tap their savings for development. In other sectors, the tax laws are stringent, but tax evasions are pervasive. And so the savings the planners depend upon for their plan are, to a great extent, unknown, invisible, and unavailable.

Nevertheless, a macro-plan, because of its grandiose concept, its all-embracing sweep and its econometric mystiques, duly impresses the country. Its very size flatters the national ego; the grand vision it conjures up for the future arouses great expectations. People, in short, are both intimidated and inspired; they acquiesce and applaud. The grand fallacies the macro-plan is built upon remain concealed in its foundation.

A jubilant nation defiantly celebrates the planned achievements—until the structure reveals the first cracks and the day of reckoning inexorably begins to dawn.

It is curious to reflect that the fundamental idea of a Five-Year Plan for national development has been borrowed from Soviet Russia where planning is conceived in *physical* terms of resource development with overwhelming emphasis on science and technology, and on health, education, and employment; whereas in India it has been cast in an artificially contrived, *money-based* macro-economic mould. The basic incongruity of the two concepts has made India's planning largely a meaningless exercise.

*Third,* deficit finance can play a vital role in all economics—as a *tool of economic management* in a developed country, and as a *vehicle of development* in a backward economy.

An example from contemporary U. S. experience will help explain the points at issue. Until late 1970, the Nixon Administration resolutely adhered to the principle of budget-balancing and insisted on producing at least a token surplus as part of its strategy to fight inflation, and it did so in the face of a faltering GNP, rising unemployment, and accumulating symptoms of a recession. In September 1970, Professor Heller estimated that a "$40-billion gap" had opened up between actual and potential GNP.[26] Other well-known economists, too, were sharply critical of the official fiscal policy.[27]

Then, all on a sudden, the Administration veered round, embraced Keynesianism, and boldly unbalanced the budget, so much so that, in fiscal 1972, it will probably show the largest peace-time deficit in U.S. history, variously forecast between $20 and $25 billion. The word "deficit" is, however, carefully deleted in view of its unwelcome connotations, and the budget is given a more respectable label—the so-called "full employment budget." In other words, the higher expenditures are justified in terms of the revenue *potential* of the economy on the plea that the budget would be balanced when the economy is at full employment.

The veteran Keynesian economists would like to go even further than the Administration—they would temporarily unbalance the budget even at full employment to make it somewhat more stimulative and thereby to bring unemployment more swiftly under control. Meanwhile, the GNP gap—the difference between the actual and the potential output of the economy—continues to widen; some estimates put it at $60

[26] Walter W. Heller, Chairman of the Council of Economic Advisers under Presidents Kennedy and Johnson.

[27] For example, Gardner Ackley and Arthur Okun, both former CEA chairmen, and Paul Samuelson, 1971 Nobel Prize winner in economics.

billion or more around mid-1971. And President Nixon will probably have to plunge deeper into deficit, well beyond the theoretical point of a budget balanced at full employment. What is significant, however, is that even a normally unbending conservative Government has found it necessary to stoop to conquer and espouse the Keynesian doctrine of deficit finance.

The concepts of "a GNP gap" and "a full employment budget" are no less relevant to an underdeveloped economy like India's. Her potential GNP is vastly greater than what it is today. Mechanical budget-balancing in traditional fashion would be wrong since it would needlessly throw away sorely-needed growth.

How should one compute the potential GNP? The answer is fairly simple in a developed economy. In the U.S., for example, utilization of plant capacity and the level of employment are accepted as the two main determinants. In the first quarter of 1971, utilization of capacity was only 73 per cent, some 20 points down from its post-war peak level; and the jobless rate rose to over 6 per cent, up from about 3.5 per cent when the economy runs on full steam. The goal of deficit budgeting is to help the two indices back to their respective full-employment levels.

Clearly, it would be absurd for a country like India to define its "plant capacity" so narrowly because its plant, in the main, is yet to be built. This takes one back to the starting point, namely, India's productive capacity must be measured not in terms of the small number of factories now in existence in a few industrial centres, but in terms of her vast natural resources yet to be developed. Similarly, joblessness is so pervasive that any specific target for employment would, at this stage, be quite meaningless.

The GNP gap in India, it follows, cannot be realistically computed. That it is enormous and will continue to be so for years to come goes without saying. The only sensible course, then, is to put idle and quasi-idle resources and manpower to work so as to achieve the best possible rate of growth.

*Fourth*, deficit-finance used as a gap-filler in macro-economic calculations in a developing country is not only senseless, but positively harmful.

In a developed economy, say, of the U.S.A., the budgetary deficit means a corresponding cash infusion into the main arteries of the economy, which quickens its pulse and, after a short lag of, say, six to nine months, shows up in a higher GNP and lower unemployment.

This does not, and cannot, happen in an underdeveloped economy like India's. For one thing, her economy is still largely money-insensitive—the additional money will not circulate freely, but will be clogged up in the few developed pockets, that is, the urban centres where it will tend to push up prices. What is even more important, money supplies might help put idle plant capacity in existing factories back to work, but they cannot, by themselves, activate idle natural resources. For this, more than money is necessary.

This is where the macro-economic planners have made another macro-error. As seen earlier, they filled the overall gap in the Second Plan with a very large dose of deficit finance and did not stop to do any worth-while micro-planning to ensure that the deficit would be used on projects, or sectors, which would give at least an acceptable output-input ratio. As it happened, it went mostly into capital-devouring long-gestation projects like high dams and steel mills. Thus, unwittingly it produced far more inflation than development.

Incidentally, many U.S. economists are increasingly critical of the theoretical model-builders to the neglect of fact-oriented micro-economic studies. At the vanguard is Professor Wassily W. Leontief of Harvard, who deplores the current domination of economics by abstract theorists at the expense of the empiricists.[28]

Professor John Kenneth Galbraith is critical of the abstractionist school of economists for a somewhat different reason—for their preoccupation with the *rate* of economic growth *per se*, and for making a fetish of it while neglecting the *quality* of growth and of life.

India's most immediate economic needs are unmistakable: to produce food for the hungry and to mitigate dire poverty. They call for intensely practical programmes based on an uncompromisingly down-to-earth approach. Abstract theories copied for economic planning from the West where they have been under challenge are a costly irrelevancy she cannot afford.

*Fifth*, deficit finance, contrary to the misconception now widespread in India, need not fuel inflation. In fact, it is the best conceivable antidote to inflation *if properly used*.

The last three words are extremely important. As seen above, the Second Plan did not satisfy this condition; indeed, it handled deficit finance in an utterly amateurish fashion. The Plan recognized the problem of "regulating" inflationary pressures, and went on to say, "Generation of new demand somewhat ahead of supplies is part of the strategy of development."[29] It is a great pity that the implications of the words "somewhat ahead" were not further explored. If the deficit finance were tied to high-yield projects maturing quickly, say, in a matter of months, the "strategy" would have definitely succeeded. But it was not tied to any such projects; in practice, it was used on large capital-intensive projects requiring five to ten years to mature. And so the strategy failed.

Deficit finance, as used in India under the Second Plan, resembled in

[28] For further comments on these points see "Some Glittering Fallacies" in Chapter 29.
[29] *Second Five Year Plan*, 1956, p. 38.

some ways irrigation from her high-dam projects, that is, "wild flooding" without field controls. In fact, it was even worse; for, in this case, the "liquid" released from a high level did not even reach the points of production. It was dammed up in remote areas.

Today India, like other countries, is deeply concerned about rampant inflation, but she is fighting it the wrong way. Her worst inflation is caused not by excess money, but by excess population; and not by excess demand, but by miserably low production—per acre of land, per man-hour, per unit of investment. Nor is her "stagnation" a temporary phenomenon; it represents a secular trend, with all the indicators pointing to an even faster rate of deterioration. Financial austerity, however energetically practised, can be of no avail to her. It cannot sweep back the rising tide of misery and privation. It can only inflict further loss of time while the tide continues to rise, threatening to engulf the nation.

The only way the trend can be effectively countered is via vastly greater production. The only way India can achieve this today is to quicken the pace of her green revolution and to keep it rolling fast all over the country. And the only realistic way she can hope to do so is to create credit and expand deficit financing without inhibition, and to inject them purposefully at all key points in her laggard agriculture.

## CREATE GREEN-REVOLUTION CREDITS

Scientific genius, engineering the miracle seeds, has flung the door wide open to a bright future for impoverished nations. But yesterday's financiers stand astride it blocking the escape from the poverty trap. The archaic postulates they operate with must be quickly updated. The production breakthrough will be set at nought unless it has, as its counterpart, an immediate breakthrough in financial thinking and practice.

Budget-balancing, old style, and unflinching austerity—these have been announced as the proximate financial goals. And the public has been treated, off and on, to homilies on their virtue. Yet the budget has never been balanced—for 1971-72, the estimated deficit amounts to Rs. 250 crores. Meanwhile, expenditure prunings have mostly tended to curtail essential productive programmes. The end-result has been the worst of both worlds—a combination of austerity on the development front and laxity in low-yield and no-yield activities.

Oddly enough, the government finds itself today essentially in the same quandary as the indigent Indian cultivator—burdened with debt, owning underused productive assets, yet lacking the means to work them fully and thereby to earn enough to escape from the bind. There is one difference, however: the cultivator is a victim of circumstances; trapped by fate, he can, by himself, do very little to improve his lot. The government, on the other hand, is the victim of its own policy; it has vast

57

power and large resources at its disposal; it can summon them to its aid at any time it wills to work its way out of the self-inflicted dilemma.

What, then, should be the policy? Once again, the analogy of the farmer gives the best clue. A major task in India's agriculture today, as is now recognized on all hands, is to wean the farmer from the practice of lumping together productive and consumptive loans; to equip him with technically sound farm plans; to give him, on their basis, ample loans to raise crops; to supervise the loans to ensure that they are strictly used for the purposes for which they have been granted and that, above all, the farmer, succumbing to a very human failing, does not divert it even partly to his everyday consumption; and, finally, to recover the loans from the sale proceeds of the crops after they have been produced, harvested, and marketed.

The government, too, needs to follow the same procedure. It must learn to distinguish, far more sharply than hitherto, between budget deficits to finance consumption and those devoted to production. It must draw up sound programmes for optimal increase in agricultural output, raise enough funds or create enough credits, and use them strictly to finance these programmes. To put it more specifically:

1. There is absolutely no reason today for the government to grope around helplessly for the "resources" needed to spur agriculture to capitalize on the miracle seeds. *These seeds contain, within themselves, the resources it is frantically looking for.* It should go ahead and boldly create, to the extent deemed necessary, *green revolution credits* with Reserve Bank overdrafts.

It follows that the Agricultural Credit Corporation recommended elsewhere[30] and virtually all other agri-related public corporations now in operation in India can be funded almost wholly the same way.

2. Practically all the items listed earlier in this chapter can be financed with created credit. Since the bulk of it will be short-term, this method of financing should not put any extra strain on the economy. This was indirectly recognized in the Second Plan when it decided to exclude short-term borrowings from its computation of outstanding deficit finance.

3. Many projects will require long-term capital extending from three to, say, 15 years, such as large-scale irrigation and land reclamation works, power plants, high-voltage transmission systems, refrigeration plants, drying-and-processing plants, soil-testing laboratories, factories for fertilizers and pesticides, for farm machinery and equipment. Many of them can be "deficit-financed," especially if the high-yield short-term projects are aggressively pushed through and credit-financed without stinting. One may confidently count on these projects to

[30] In Chapter 26.

throw up large increments of production fast enough to dampen the inflationary pressures which large-scale deficit-financing would tend to generate.

The policy suggested above will rapidly build up production and income, yielding surpluses which could be ploughed back to vastly speed up India's development. Ever since her misadventure with deficit finance in the late fifties, she has been haunted by the spectre of inflation. To counter the threat, she has nervously embraced an ultra-conservative fiscal policy and has greatly aggravated the ill she was anxious to cure. From abuse and non-use of deficit finance she must switch over to its right use on a massive scale. This is the only way she can effectively lay the spectre, the only way she can simultaneously strike at the jugular vein of the multiple malaise her economy has been afflicted with—stagnation, inflation, unemployment, poverty.

CHAPTER 28

# On Administrative Reform

## THE BACKGROUND

"I give credit to India's civil servants for holding the country together; and I also give them credit for holding it back," so observed a senior U.S. expert after serving in India for several years.[1] No one with an intimate knowledge of India and her development problems will disagree with this remark. It epitomizes what has been a primary source of her woes.

Meanwhile, holding the country back has made it incomparably more difficult to hold it together. For, in these restless times when people multiply at a dizzy rate, when their expectations for material well-being run high, and when these are constantly fed by competing ideologies, stagnation cannot but sap the foundations of national unity.

The present system is deeply rooted in a remote past when the functions of government were kept down to a minimum. The laissez-faire ideology which held sway in Britain in the nineteenth century dominated the Indian scene almost completely down to the end of the British rule. Ideology, in this case, was reinforced by political expediency; an alien regime was loath to tamper with a social system for fear of arousing resentment, even when it was seething with injustice and crying out for reform. For it the safest course was non-intervention, and this also meant non-development.

In such a situation it was inevitable that the functions of government would be few, and consist overwhelmingly of defence of the realm, maintenance of internal law and order, and collection of revenue. Commerce followed the standard pattern of colonialism with exports of raw

[1] This, in essence, is also the view expressed by Gunnar Myrdal in *Asian Drama*, Pantheon (Random House), New York, 1968, esp. pp. 260-73.

materials and imports of manufactures within the framework of "free trade". Other functions grew up largely as corollaries to these, such as railways, posts and telegraphs, currency management. Economic development *per se* received, at best, only peripheral attention.

Since independence all this has changed beyond recognition. The tasks of government have expanded at a frantic pace; economic development has been pushed to the forefront of all activities; ambitious five-year plans have been the order of the day. What has not changed, however, is the administrative system. The old machinery designed to uphold the status quo is still relied upon to do the dynamic job of development. This incongruous approach has subjected the economy, and the nation, to enormous strains. And because of it development itself has largely become a casualty.

The pillars of the system were—and still are—the Indian Civil Service (ICS), a remarkable institution consisting of high-IQ individuals, screened in their early twenties by a tough competitive examination, tempered for the Service through a period of intensive "probation," then posted in the field mostly in charge of a subdivision, on what in the pre-inflationary days used to be an exceedingly attractive salary scale, and endowed right from the start with authority over a large cross-section of the population. Self-confident, authoritarian, often supercilious, they served remarkably well the cause for which they were recruited. They, certainly, have held the country together.

How well they have served the people is, however, another matter. For this it would be unfair, if not wrong, to blame the Service. After all, it was designed primarily as a pillar of the Empire, not as an instrument to build a Welfare State. In fact, service to the people was treated as virtually synonymous with maintenance of law and order.

Moreover, by training—and indoctrination—the ICS was detached, mentally as well as physically, from the surroundings. It was placed above the people, not among them. Fellow-feeling was implicitly discouraged; it was, if anything, regarded as a weakness unbecoming of a civil servant; he was, at least by implication, expected to stamp it out in order to discharge his duties more worthily. In extreme cases, insensitivity to popular feelings or needs was extolled as a virtue.

On the eve of independence there was, understandably enough, much nervousness in the Service. What would be the future shape of things? And in particular, would the government of free India honour the commitments that had been entered into under the British regime to safeguard the interests of a Service which had loyally served that regime, even at the height of the national movement? The misgivings did not last long. Prime Minister Attlee, in a statement made in Parliament prior to the transfer of power, pleaded that "honourable obligations should be honourably met." And how could Gandhi's India, born in nonviolence and taught to practise "charity towards all," act differently? It decided to honour, in letter and spirit, what it regarded as inherited obligations. The Service was given an unequivocal assurance to that effect; the old terms and conditions of employment were fully protected, and with these also their position of prestige and power.

This was a watershed decision. From it flowed some far-reaching consequences which have decisively affected India's development in the last quarter century. And since the Indian Administrative Service (IAS) has been moulded by old ICS hands after its own image in most of its essentials, its spirit bids fair to dominate vicariously the administration for a long time to come, barring a radical change in the political environment.

### AN ANACHRONISM

What, then, are these consequences, and how have they, in specific terms, affected India's economic and social progress? It is not necessary in the present context to examine this question at length. Yet it is most important not to overlook the main deficiencies India's civil service has revealed over the years.

1. *It has tended to rule rather than to serve.*

Given its long tradition of authoritarianism, this was perhaps inevitable. It was not only cool-headed, but also cold and aloof. After independence, many of its members gallantly tried to adjust themselves to the new political climate, but only with varying success. The old habit died hard; in general, the attitude of standoffish superiority prevailed.

This, needless to say, was hard to reconcile with the spirit of the democratic constitution India had adopted after independence. The incompatibility was too glaring to be ignored for long. How to remedy this situation and open the door wide enough for people's participation not only in election, but also in the government became a dominant issue. The community development programme, it was assumed by many, would provide the answer; and when this assumption was belied, panchayati raj was introduced, again in the hope that it would actively involve the masses of people on a broad front. Both were prompted by a concern for people's welfare, but both were conceptually faulty and administratively inept.[2] In addition, they created a kind of parallel government which resulted in new stresses and strains.

What India needed was an administration that was both efficient and people-oriented. Instead, she had to settle for either the one or the other. How to end this schizophrenia and develop a more wholesome system is a problem that has dogged her ever since.

[2] See Chapter 8, also Chapter 11, pp. 154-55.

## 2. *It has dominated scientists and professional experts.*

Modern development is, above all, a function of science and technology. It can proceed unhampered only when competent experts and technicians are allowed to play a leading role. In India, however, they have so far been overwhelmingly subordinated to the generalist civil servants.

Under the successive five-year plans India's public sector has expanded rapidly. And nationalization—of banks and insurance companies—and, more recently, the spate of "take-overs" of industrial concerns have further inflated its size. Once this trend set in, the top civil servants moved over to occupy the top positions in the public-sector undertakings. And so they began to run multi-purpose river valley projects, steel mills, shipping, ship-building, civil aviation, banking, insurance, export trade and what not, in addition to numerous embassies especially in the leading capitals of the world.

Thus, a Service that had been created primarily for regulatory functions—maintenance of order, enforcement of law, collection of revenue, administration of land-tenure systems—suddenly assumed a managerial role to operate large-scale public projects. What was the reason? The prestige, the power, and the extra emoluments these projects offered were too attractive to be overlooked by the top civil servants. What *was* overlooked, however, was the high level of specialized experience and technical competence they demanded for their successful operation.

In 1946, when the DVC Bill was still on the anvil, the writer had occasion to discuss with a senior British member of the Indian Civil Service what would be the best composition of the DVC Board.[3] An ICS chairman of a public corporation of this nature? No, this would be completely wrong. "It is not a civil service job," he said categorically. The British had a clear notion as to what was, and what was not, a civil service job; it is the job content—the nature of the responsibilities—that was decisive in their eyes. Such objectivity—and self-denial—was conspicuous by its absence in their Indian counterparts after independence. Only too often they allowed the temptation of prestigious jobs to run away with their better judgment.

The British, it is safe to assume, would never have allowed the powerful instrument of administration they had created to be diverted, in such wholesale fashion, away from its primary purpose. If anything, many of them must have been shocked to see it saddled with technical-cum-business responsibilities on such a large scale.

Even in Soviet Russia where Party managers tend to dominate business managers, such a development would have been inconceivable. For what-

---

[3] Prior to independence he happened to be the Home Secretary in the Central Government.

ever damage the induction of politics might do to public business is held in check by another cardinal dogma unflinchingly pursued in Soviet Russia: technical jobs must be done by competent technical people. After all, the Party believes in, even worships, science and technology, which is an antidote to dilettantism.

### 3. *Its management has been riddled with divided responsibility.*

A civil servant, anywhere in the world, seeks above all his own safety. His foremost urge is to save his own skin; his standard technique is to divide responsibility for decisions, and thereby to cover himself with alibis. This enables him to share with others the blame for eventual failure or poor results and thus to escape accountability.

The first principle of good management is to counteract this tendency, to plug the loopholes, to minimize—and, if possible, to eliminate—the room for alibis. This can be done in one, and only one, way—by concentrating authority, responsibility, and accountability in the hands of a single executive.

This principle has been grossly violated in all public businesses of India. The public sector has grown enormously in scope and size, and so also has the evil of fragmented responsibility. In too many places, and on too many occasions, everybody's business has become nobody's business.

There is, first of all, the pervasive, antediluvian method of financial control. The deadening hand of the treasury stretches over all public-sector activities to stifle initiative and to cripple management. Even where public corporations have been set up to get away from an obsolete system, things have not much improved in practice. For they are still subjected, in one form or another, to *independent*, financial control.

In the early years of the DVC, the writer had occasion to examine at some length the problems of public corporations in India. "*Financial judgment*," as he then remarked, "*is no more separable from decisions than flesh from blood or body from soul.*" Under orthodox treasury control, "the distinction between finance and audit is often blurred. Yet as every commercial concern knows, there is an important difference between the two. A financial expert advises on proper spending, his function is positive. He checks, but does not checkmate; he vets, but does not veto; for he knows that jobs are done by wise expenditure, not by witholding it."[4]

Freedom from antiquated treasury control—this is what India needed in the early 1950's when she boldly launched out on five-year develop-

[4] In "The Future of Public Corporations," *Supplement to "Capital"*, 17 Dec. 1953, Calcutta; italics in original. The article also dealt with other related issues, e.g. functional or policy board, board-minister and minister-parliament relations, and the need for periodic investigations by competent, independent parties.

ment plans. And this is what she needs no less urgently today if her development projects are to be efficiently managed.

The principle of undivided responsibility has another major facet: a large degree of freedom to manage personnel. This means freedom for recruitment, placement, promotion, retirement, and, in extreme cases, even dismissal. To deny this freedom to an executive is to deny him the most essential tool he needs to do his job.

Yet the existing rules militate against this principle all along the line. The recruitment procedures are slow and cumbersome; financial checks are formidable, and often add up to a unilateral veto power; promotion is based almost exclusively on seniority, not merit; there is little incentive to superior performance; salary scales for many key categories of professional jobs are often too low to attract, and retain, competent people; the penalty for delinquency is weak, if not nonexistent.

The financial and personnel policies of the government have long been in need of a radical overhaul. Yet nothing has been done so far in that direction. In fact, the civil service heads of India's public-sector undertakings have not only put up with, but have often aggravated, the anomalies of the old system. They have exercised wide powers, protected themselves in a jungle of divided responsibility, and have diluted their accountability for results.

In every business risk-bearing is an essential function, and this also means risk-covering. The civil servants have proved past masters in this art. But the risks that mattered most in their eyes were those not of the businesses they ran, but of their own service careers.

### 4. It has indulged in excessive job rotation.

Generalist heads for scientific-cum-technical enterprises—this has been the besetting weakness of India's administration. Its effects have been aggravated by another factor—job-to-job rotation at short intervals.

The civil servant heads placed in charge of capital-intensive public-sector enterprises have received what is perhaps the world's most expensive on-the-job training. True, as highly gifted individuals, they were quick learners. But even the most brilliant of them could not learn remotely enough on the job to grow into experts in technical matters that required disciplined study of many years and almost life-long practical experience.

To crown it all, they stayed on the jobs only for short periods, at times for a year or two; and frequently they used them as springboards to something more attractive, within the country or abroad. Quite a few queued up for jobs in international organizations to earn high salaries in hard, or semi-hard, currencies along with tax benefits, to do work which involved only a fraction of the responsibilities they were used to shouldering on their domestic assignments.

58

The ministers, both at the Centre and in the states, often made a solid contribution to the crazy turnover of top personnel. Frequently, they wanted to have civil servants of their own choice for high-level jobs that fell within their jurisdiction. "The Rourkhela steel mill has produced more managers than steel," once quipped an outstanding steel-maker who had spent a whole lifetime in the industry. It typified a gross anomaly.

*5. It has an outstandingly poor record in office management, personnel-training, and morale-building.*

The civil service has ruled the roost, and has done little to improve it. It has perpetuated old procedures almost with a vengeance—with elaborate note-writing and a dismal filing system, with too little delegation to subordinate officers, with too many clerks producing too little per man-hour. It has applied old rules to do new jobs, equated subservience with discipline, and done little to build up the personnel in ability and stature. It has shown no concern to encourage initiative from below and to promote creative thinking.

In general, its attitude has been one of callousness, and this had a withering effect on that intangible asset called morale without which no enterprise can give outstanding performance.

It is true that, in recent years, morale in many enterprises has suffered, often grievously, because of labour insubordination instigated by interested parties. But the point not to be missed is that discontent flourished the more easily because its seeds fell on fertile ground long characterized by low morale.

As for technical personnel, the remark made to the writer in July, 1972 by an executive of the Heavy Machinery Corporation is worth noting. In all countries as development proceeds there emerges an expanding corps of able technocrats ready to shoulder ever-greater responsibilities. In India, he lamented, the trend had been in the reverse direction with technocrats not growing, but sinking in stature and influence. He had no doubt in his mind about the reason. It was due to civil service domination of technical functions in the public-sector undertakings.

### DIAGNOSIS BY EXPERTS

The need for administrative reform was felt quite early after independence. The old system had to be adjusted—both in organization and in spirit—to fit the new India that emerged with a new democratic constitution and embarked upon development on an unprecedented scale.[5] Yet this was one of the toughest tasks she had to grapple with. Restructuring

[5] Prime Minister Nehru was instinctively aware of this need. See, for example, his remark quoted in Chapter 8, footnote on p. 110.

an administrative system is an enormously difficult task in any country, if only because of the determined resistance it inevitably encounters from status quo forces. It was much more so in a "soft state" like India. The search for reform began in the early fifties, and has continued to this day. But, unsurprisingly enough, it has ended every time with peripheral tinkering.

In 1951, at the request of the Planning Commission, Mr. A. D. Gorwala examined the problems of public administration and made a number of recommendations, especially for efficient conduct of public businesses.[6]

About two years later Dean Paul H. Appleby was engaged by the Government of India as a short-term consultant in public administration. The report he submitted at the end of his mission[7] contained valuable insights and much wisdom, also some serious omissions and a few hasty judgments; above all, it was an intricate mixture of compliments and criticisms which made it hard to separate the one from the other, and enabled both critics and apologists to use it with almost equal effect.

Dean Appleby preambled his criticisms with a loud pat. He had gradually arrived at the "general judgment that would now rate the government of India AMONG THE DOZEN OR SO MOST ADVANCED GOVERNMENTS OF THE WORLD." The capitalized words, oddly enough, figured in the report itself. They easily overshadowed all the critical comments that followed —printed in small letters, these were treated as relatively small matters.

Having made this sweeping observation, the Dean proceeded to hedge it by playing on the word "now," expressed concern about the "still unfolding" future, entered numerous caveats about the existing system, and urged several remedial measures. Though these were lost in the loud acclaim that greeted his general verdict, some of them at least are worth noting.[8]

The system was "conceived in pre-revolutionary terms"; what had been its strength would have "its own peculiar weaknesses in the face of new dimensions and needs." Though not explicitly stated, its major weaknesses were lack of flexibility, and a lack of that "democracy *within administration*" which, in his view, was a prerequisite to democracy in citizen-government relationships.

It suffered from diffusion of administrative responsibility. There was "excessive coordination before the fact of action, slowing and retarding action," and this in turn diffused the responsibility and accountability for whatever action was taken.

---

[6] Mr. Gorwala, himself a member of the Indian Civil Service, had resigned from it, in 1948, in protest against certain official policies, a rare phenomenon, indeed, in India.

[7] *Public Administration in India—Report of a Survey*, by Paul H. Appleby, Cabinet Secretariat, Government of India, New Delhi, 1953.

[8] Ibid., see especially pp. 8-15.

Its emphasis, barring a few fields like defence, revenue collection, internal order, and external affairs, was on "coordination" rather than on administration. The Centre held conferences, made studies and plans, issued pronouncements, but was fundamentally lacking in administrative authority. It was all "staff," with no administrative "line."

Personnel administration had "too much feudalistic heritage, too much academic and 'intellectuality' orientation, too little administrative action and human-relations orientation, and is too defensive of the 'rights' of existing personnel." These characteristics were reflected in recruitment policies and methods, in assignment methods, in the attention and lack of attention given to developing the potentialities of personnel.

The criteria for selecting the personnel were "not up to date," examining and appraising techniques were "far from modern." Selection tended to be by "one type of person, which naturally perpetuates its own type." Selection was too much in terms of academic methods, and too little in terms of other considerations highly important in public administration, with too little attention paid to the "capacity for growth." Recruitment was not "imaginative or aggressive enough," was too much limited by concern for persons already employed, and was governed too easily "by an underestimate of the personnel potentialities in the society."

Selected personnel were arranged self-consciously in too firm "classes," and too firm and too many special "services," with barriers between classes and services too high. As a result, there was too little sense of one public service, and "too much jealousy." For these and other reasons, too little attention was given to "the important matter of developing the potentialities of subordinate employees already in service of government."

The administrative procedures, including the filing systems and the hierarchal movement of paper, left a great deal to be desired. The Rules of Business, Secretarial Instructions and Office Manuals were "too didactic and confining, too detailed and unimaginative." They encouraged a "literal-mindedness which damps the spirit, imagination and judgment" essential to good administration. Their basic pattern "undoubtedly originated in colonial administration."

All these added up to a devastating charge-sheet. Though expressed in professional phraseology—tactfully, often obliquely—it substantially confirmed the criticisms that had been, and continue to be, levelled against India's administrative system. There remains, however, the puzzling question: Given this damaging diagnosis of the system, why did the good Dean begin by eulogizing it in eye-catching capital letters? For the answer one should perhaps turn to a little-known episode that had preceded his mission.

One of the earliest, and ablest, U.S. experts to visit India after independence, on Prime Minister Nehru's personal invitation, was Dr. Solomon Trone. A man of high stature, with decades of experience piled up while serving as an industrial expert in many countries,[9] he was eminently qualified to assist India as she prepared to launch out boldly on a programme of economic development. And from the start he occupied the best conceivable vantage-point—as Industrial Consultant he reported direct to the Prime Minister.

Dr. Trone toured extensively in the country, visited numerous projects, old and new, held discussions with officials, drew his own conclusions, and submitted concrete recommendations in instalments. His analysis, always sympathetic and constructive, was incisive, forthright, often blunt. All these attributes climaxed in his final report, a scathingly critical document in which he ran down the civil service on several counts—its callous standoffishness, its narrow self-centred outlook, its authoritarian approach, its scintillating superficiality, its domination over scientists and technicians, its deadening grip over talent in general.

All through his stay in India Dr. Trone repeatedly deplored the utter failure of the government to mobilize and utilize the youth of the country—thousands of gifted men and women who had received enough education and had high potentials for growth, who were patriotic, anxious to work and serve, but were restlessly marking time mostly in jobless isolation, who had been left high and dry on the wayside of life. This tragic neglect of what was unquestionably India's greatest resource boded ill for her future. Dr. Trone foresaw it with prophetic vision, and was tormented by what he saw around him.

The Trone Report was a bombshell. It wounded the pride of the Civil Service, and dealt a blow to its prestige as nothing else, before or after. Some "corrective" action was urgently needed, and this, evidently, led to the Appleby mission for which the initiative, significantly enough, came from the Civil Service itself. The haste with which the Trone Report was shelved, and the care with which it has been locked up in the dark chamber ever since, *prima facie* lend credence to this hypothesis.[10]

It would be interesting if, after a lapse of two decades, this report were allowed to see the light of day to enable people to see things better even if only in hindsight, unless it has meanwhile been obliterated.

---

[9] Dr. Trone had, *inter alia*, served in both czarist and post-czarist Russia as representative of the General Electric Company. The writer, while working in the DVC, had occasion to come into close contact with him and to admire his deep convictions based on profound experience, and his uncompromising realism.

[10] Andrew Roth gave an excellent character sketch of this remarkable man whom he called "Mr. Point Four" (*Nation*, 27 Jan. 1951). Nehru urged him to stay, but Dr. Trone decided to pack up and leave when he saw no hope that his advice would be accepted because of hostility from "conservative bureaucrats and private interests." From India he went to Israel. By then Dr. Trone was over seventy and had already served in many countries—Russia, Germany, China, Japan, India among others.

## APPLEBY REPORT AND AFTER

Dean Appleby's mission was an exceptionally delicate one, and he was obviously at some pains to strike a balance between a conciliatory note and professional rectitude. He went out of his way to compliment, yet pinpointed with care the shortcomings he detected in the course of his survey. What he said was, in essence, strikingly similar to Dr. Trone's diagnosis. But, in contrast to the latter's stinging style, he was euphemistic and circumlocutory. His views were heavily sugarcoated, and readily ignored.

The mountain in labour did produce what, apparently, was more than a mouse. Following Appleby's recommendations O. and M. offices were established; but, in general, they have proved more ornamental than innovative, and they have added to the flow of paper rather than rationalizing it.

Perhaps a more important outcome of his mission was the establishment of an Institute of Public Administration in New Delhi. Since then it has, through its diversified courses, helped train many Indians in what had been a neglected field of study. However, the Institute has been more academic than action-minded in its orientation. And dominated by old-line civil servants, it has, once again, tended to perpetuate its own type.

In the all-important matter of personnel policy—that is, in recruitment, placement, and training—the progress, despite Appleby's urgings, has been close to nil.

Another recommendation of great significance related to finance, though this, too, went virtually unheeded. If it were true that India was already getting about all the tax revenue she could hope to get, "the outlook would be distressing." But Appleby refused to accept that this was in fact the case. For one thing, appraisals of land values were hopelessly out of date, and in most cases heavily in arrears. One revenue commissioner had told him that the land taxes for certain farms were much too low, "amounting to the value of one bundle of grain-straw per acre."

Appleby also stressed the need for an agricultural income tax, both as a source of revenue and as an "additional approach to the land tenure problem." Land speculation in areas where large irrigation works were in prospect, he urged, should be countered by a capital gains tax and other legislation "making for a proper spread of benefits."

Besides, India's fiscal policy was, in his view, "conventionally conservative, with too much emphasis on budget-balancing—and especially a balancing in single-year terms." He wanted "spending" to be properly defined and classified; for, after all, while spending money the government was often "performing functions of credit and capital formation."

In effect, he was pleading for a substantial dose of credit, or "deficit," financing for sound development projects.

This was a remarkably imaginative view to take, especially in India where treasury orthodoxy of the worst kind had consistently dashed the hopes of quicker economic development. Dean Appleby sounded quite optimistic about the future. He believed that the policy "as it was unfolding in India," would be "flexible and progressive." Presumably, what he had in mind was the large dose of deficit finance which India was contemplating at that time, with the full backing of the then Finance Minister, Mr. C. D. Deshmukh. How things have developed after this first ill-planned and ill-fated experiment in deficit financing in India has been discussed in the preceding chapter.

Dean Appleby, without doubt, brought with him a wealth of principles and concepts from his wide professional experience, to bear on the Indian situation. There is, however, little doubt that they were not adequately "adapted" to the complex conditions of India and its peculiar human environment, and this gave rise to some unfortunate consequences.

The Centre, as he had diagnosed, was all "staff" with no administrative "line." This was, and still is, largely true. Yet its real weakness lay not in an excess of the one or deficiency of the other, but in performing neither function well enough. The "staff" work it was vested with was done perfunctorily, and the "line" authority it enjoyed was not effectively used.

A vast country like India with 360 million people—this was about the size of its population at that time—and large regional differences—in physical conditions, languages, culture, and the level of development—can be governed only with a large delegation of responsibility to the member-states. This is the premise the Federal Constitution had been based upon. For a great many fields there could be only one rational guideline: *Centralized policy-making with decentralized operation.*

The policy-making functions could be carried out at the Centre, within the framework of the Constitution, even when the subjects fell outside its jurisdiction. In several instances it has indeed done so, and has passed "enabling legislations" for the states or has recommended model bills to them. The same techniques could, and should, have been adopted for a great many other fields to provide leadership to the states, to stimulate right actions on a nationwide basis, and to maintain a reasonable degree of uniformity in important matters. Lack of adequate Central initiative has often been a major handicap; but this was due not to a lack of administrative authority, but to a lack of proper leadership.

For tax collection, enforcement of law, maintenance of internal order, the "line" authority of the Centre has not been sufficiently used. For example, the country is riddled with income-tax evaders; the Centre could certainly employ its civil service arm to apprehend and punish them; yet that arm has not been used resolutely enough. Again, the reason is not lack of authority, but lack of will.

With a strong bias in favour of centralization Dean Appleby leaned heavily against the autonomy of the DVC.[11] And he wanted large river valley projects to be exclusively carried out by the Centre, without control being shared with the states. This verdict, to say the least, was hasty. It was given without even caring to know the reasons that had induced some of the best minds—of Britain, India, and the USA—to set up the DVC after discussions extending over many years. It showed little understanding of the importance of integrated resource development covering river basins, and of the grassroots operations without which such development would not be feasible.

And it played right into the hands of irrigation engineers who already had to their credit wanton mismanagement of India's water resources; who have built dams at high cost, and have allowed the reservoirs to be filled with sands brought down by monsoon waters gushing down from the eroded uplands; whose autonomous behaviour needed to be curbed, not further extended.

At this moment[12] a Minister-engineer of the same genre that had spear-headed the fight against the DVC is working hard for its dismember-ment. The Centre, having watered down its autonomy, now seems deter-mined to demolish all prospects of rational water management in this river valley. Centralization, as this example shows, can easily degenerate into a powerful tool to serve perverse objectives.

On Community Development Dean Appleby, in effect, lent his sup-port to the Civil Service view, which had frowned upon, even opposed, its lurch towards an independent role. He criticized it rather strongly on several grounds, and pleaded for "consolidating administrative re-sponsibility" for executing the Community Projects. The advice took no account of the reasons that had led, in the first place, to the creation of a separate, people-oriented programme. Nor was he able to spot the real weakness of the CDP—that without science and without scientists it would fritter away energy and resources, and would produce very little lasting benefits.

However, a year later, on his second mission, Dean Appleby retracted much of his earlier criticisms. "Most of what I said in my Report of a year ago about Community Projects," he said in a personal note to Minister S. K. Dey,[13] "is now wholly irrelevant." The essential diffi-

[11] "I do not believe that it should be any more autonomous than it is. (The T.V.A. in the United States goes too far in that direction.)" Ibid., p. 40.

[12] In September, 1972. Also see the comments made in Chapter 16 under "A Postscript."

[13] Quoted in Community Development—A Chronicle, 1954-61, by S. K. Dey, Minister of Community Development, etc., Government of India, New Delhi, 1962, pp. 14-15.

culties had been overcome, the general success of the programme "speaks for itself." It had expanded more rapidly than had been expected, and was much ahead of schedule "in course of translation into a national extension programme." Holding out the possibility of greatly extended efforts on the part of 80 per cent of India's people, it was "peculiarly hopeful and important," also "peculiarly exacting of the highest administrative abilities and arrangements," and should therefore receive "corresponding attention." Mr. Dey called this "a terrifying compliment," and gloated over it.

On a more fundamental level, Dean Appleby misjudged the needs of *development administration*—his emphasis was far too much on the second word, and far too little on the first. There can be no worthwhile development in the modern world unless modern science and technology are, to a very great extent, built into every development programme or project. To Dr. Trone this was an axiom; he burnt with fury to find it slighted at too many places on too many occasions. Dean Appleby missed the axiom without being aware of its implications.

And he missed something else too—the signs of the times. He failed to see how the civil service, without much qualms, preempted for itself the top positions in public-sector enterprises; how, instead of acting as a moderating influence, it fed the prejudices of the neophyte political leaders against private enterprise; and how, instead of counselling a go-slow policy, it encouraged them to bring the "commanding heights" of the economy within the public sector and then commandeered those heights for itself; how, in short, an overweening civil service was overreaching itself.

Thus, Dean Appleby pandered, however unwittingly, to the prevailing myth of India's omniscient Civil Service, and thereby hindered development. And, in the process, what could have grown into a movement towards administrative reform was halted, if not sidetracked.

A high-powered Administrative Reforms Commission was appointed in January 1966 to examine the public administration of the country and to make recommendations for reform and reorganization, where necessary. The Commission which laboured for several years, until 30 June 1970, made, among other things, a fresh diagnosis of the old malaise in familiar terms. But so far few fundamental changes have been noticeable in the ossified system.

Several institutes for training in public administration or management have been established in India—in New Delhi as mentioned before, at Hyderabad, Ahmedabad, Barrackpore near Calcutta, Pawai near Bombay, and very recently at Bangalore in Mysore. And they are turning out a large number of trained personnel every year, including young people of great promise. But the contribution they can actually make to better management of public affairs has been severely limited because they

59

have to serve within a system which, in its top echelons, continues to violate the first principles of scientific management.

In general, it seems the trainees of these institutes have done better in commercial firms which offer them wider scope and greater incentives to deploy their abilities, and more opportunities for quicker promotions. Obviously, their future will depend very largely on the future of the private sector itself.

How frustratingly slow has been India's journey towards administrative reform can be well illustrated with one simple fact. In 1969, the Fourth Plan recognized "the need to incorporate in our administration, including that of the public sector undertakings, the technician, the specialist and the expert in an appropriate manner." The structure of the older organization and its line of command had been "inevitably constructed round the generalist administrator." This had to be modified to enable the specialist, the technician, and the expert "to make their contribution in a responsible manner at all levels of administration."[14] The hardest thing in India, it seems, is to discover the most obvious. How soon this latest discovery will begin to yield practical results still remains moot.

## AGRICULTURAL ADMINISTRATION

It was inevitable that a system, flawed so seriously in its fundamentals, would badly hurt agriculture. The Second Evaluation Report on the IADP made some trenchant remarks on the subject which are well worth quoting:[15]

> The administrative system, based essentially on checks and balances, evolved in a different time and for a different purpose, has proved woefully inadequate for any operation, the aim of which is not to maintain the *status quo* but to change it. The IADP has thus been a square peg in a round hole. The main objective of the IADP is to accelerate the rate of growth by bringing about a basic change in the situation in which it operates. The main purpose of the administrative system that India has inherited is, on the other hand, to ensure security and hence allow only the minimum possible change. The IADP puts a premium on the technician who is the harbinger of change. The Indian administrative system gives primacy to the administrator whose main function is to lay down and administer the rules designed to ensure conformity. The basic idea of IADP is

[14] *Fourth Five Year Plan 1969-74*, p. 111.
[15] Second Evaluation Report on IADP, 1964; also quoted in the Fourth Evaluation Report on IADP (1960-68), p. 23.

that it should be a tailor-made programme to suit the needs of a particular area which can be adjusted by the local authorities promptly and effectively, as and when the situation changes. The main concern of the Indian administrative system has been to lay down general patterns of conformity to which the areas must adjust rather than otherwise and leave the least possible discretion to the authorities lower in the hierarchical structure.

The Fourth Evaluation Report repeated this extract which, it believed, still held good.

Another expert, focussing attention on the administrative drawbacks, made similar observations:[16] "While it is necessary and appropriate to have a leader trained in decision-making process and willing to make decisions, it is even more important in a developing agricultural economy for that administrator to have empathy and understanding of the processes necessary for this to happen and some understanding of the technology which is essential for development."

The most sensible policy, he argued, would be to give well-trained agricultural officers—at the block, district, and Central levels—opportunities for administrative leadership, and, for this purpose, to supplement their experience by an administrative training programme. Similarly, a civil service administrator "who has a genuine interest in agricultural development" could, by a special course or programme, be better equipped to serve on development posts. The first alternative, he might have added, would in general prove more practicable since it normally takes years of study and experience to acquire enough knoweldge and skill in applied agricultural sciences.

The Fourth Evaluation Report drew attention to a primary condition which had been laid down in the original Ten-Point Programme, namely, that "the full production potential can be realised only when all the essential elements are combined into an integrated programme." This meant, the Report reminded, that if any one component in the IADP was inadequate in quantity or quality, it would "retard the growth in general," and if any one major input or service was not available at all, "the entire programme would fail."

The administrative system, the Report held, was a major retarding factor for reasons of which it specifically mentioned the following: deficiencies in organization, at the Central and the State level, split levels of command at the district and block levels, lack of adequate delegation of powers to the lower levels, centralization of financial powers, too frequent transfers of key personnel, lack of adequate incentives and

[16] Marvin A. Anderson, Dean, University Extension, Iowa State University, USA. Quoted in the Fourth Evaluation Report, ibid., p. 24.

469 A RICHER HARVEST

facilities to the staff, and lack of effective coordination mechanism between various development departments and agencies.[17]

Modernization of agriculture clearly depends, among other things, on modernization of administration. The system evolved in the bullock-cart age must be redesigned to serve the dynamic needs of today. Many of the reforms needed are common to all sectors of public activities, such as unified instead of divided responsibility, greater delegation of authority including financial powers, an enlightened and merit-based personnel policy, and effective coordination of interrelated activities.

In addition, agriculture calls for several specific changes in the organization as it now obtains in India. In a broad sense, they all relate to a reallocation of functions so as to better serve the farmers with science and technology as well as with other essential inputs.

The high priests of the green revolution, it cannot be emphasized too often, are the scientists. This is now better understood than before; and, as a result, scientists have been given a bigger role to play. This new trend is most clearly reflected in the reorganization of agricultural research and education at the Centre. The ICAR is now headed by a scientist, instead of a civil service administrator, and he is given a great deal of financial and other powers and responsibilities, which would have been unthinkable only a few years ago.

However, this process has much further to go. At the state level, the post of the director of agriculture is, in many instances, filled by a scientist, which, no doubt, is a great improvement over the past. But its advantages are often largely lost because he is still placed under a civil servant secretary of the department. There is no reason, except the force of tradition, why this latter post should not be filled by a competent scientist-administrator. Alternatively, the director of agriculture should be allowed to function with much greater delegation of authority than is currently the case.

At the district level, the situation in general is even worse. The "line" authority is arbitrarily bifurcated; the district agricultural officer is virtually subordinated to the district collector, a civil servant who, following the old custom, is in charge of all activities, technical and non-technical, and therefore controls the extension arm of the agricultural service at the block and the village level. Yet, in most cases, he is too much of a "generalist" to do justice to the technical functions, including agriculture, for which he is made responsible; and he is invariably much too overloaded with non-technical work to devote enough attention to them.

This organizational anomaly, carried over from the past, must be ended urgently. The split command that now plagues the extension service must be replaced by a vigorous, unified command—with a line authority

[17] Ibid., p. 24.

running from headquarters through the district, the block, and the village down to the farm. In addition, the extension service must be "de-amateurized," and turned into a competent instrument staffed with trained scientists.[18]

There remains yet another obstinate question to be definitively resolved: What should be the location of agricultural research and extension? More specifically, should it be the state department of agriculture or the newly-established agricultural university?

The answer, most definitely, should be—the latter, and this for a number of reasons.[19] That agricultural education should be broadbased and located in a university is now readily accepted. What is not yet sufficiently recognized, however, is that it must not be divorced from research and extension; otherwise it will quickly degenerate into a purely academic enterprise, and will fail to serve its primary objective —to lead the farmer from primitive to scientific agriculture and to build up farm productivity.

Similarly, research centred on a government department is invariably slipshod and insufficiently production-oriented. A departmentally-run extension service is badly organized, lacks the needed flexibility, and cares perforce more for bureaucratic rules than for the farmer's interest. These shortcomings are writ large on past experience extending over half a century. There is no need to repeat them today.

If agriculture is to prosper, its three fundamentals—education, research, extension—must be treated as one single package. And that package can be best handled not in the rule-ridden, suffocating confines of a government department, but away from it on a university campus enjoying the freedom to initiate, to innovate, and to investigate with uninhibited minds.

## MANY THINGS TO DO

There is yet another reason no less overriding why such a division of functions is essential. Intensive agriculture on scientific lines brings in

[18,19] See Chapter 22.

its wake a great many more new tasks than is commonly realized. To drive this point home, a simple graphic was devised (reproduced above) some time ago at the Mysore University of Agricultural Sciences.

Even after research, teaching, and extension are transferred to a university, the residual functions would still be enormous and will tax to the hilt the capacity of a responsible government department. For the range they cover is extraordinarily wide and complex. They were spelled out as follows by the Government of India Committee, set up in 1962, to advise the state governments on the legislation for establishing agricultural universities in India:[20]

*Marketing* : Setting and enforcing grades and standards of agricultural commodities, labelling containers, storage facilities, transportation.

*Processing* : Grades and standards, plant sanitation, quality control, additives.

*Consumption* : Product standard and purity of food.

*Regulation* : Weights and measures, seed purity and varieties, fertilizer grades, formula labels, serums, vaccines, medicines, and drugs for livestock, insecticide standards, labels for using insecticides and fungicides, nursery stock standards.

*Quarantine* : Livestock diseases, plant diseases, insects, eradication work.

*Service* : Vaccination, livestock treatment, spraying for insect and disease control of farm crops and livestock, surveys to determine presence of dangerous population of insects, disease incidence or animal pests, collect and compile agricultural statistics.

*Supplies* : Since there is a limited supply of many necessary items of production, supply at the proper time and amount is vital. Assist farmer co-operatives and local agencies in obtaining supplies of seed, pesticides, fertilizer, containers, transportation, equipment, foundation livestock and poultry, nursery stock, seedlings, etc.

These functions are far from adequately discharged today. Moreover, as intensive agriculture spreads and deepens, they will grow correspondingly in magnitude. Yet there is no escape from them; they must be handled competently, on the requisite scale, and often to meet inexorable deadlines; this is a precondition for agricultural progress. And since they are regulatory in nature, often requiring specific legislation and enforcement mechanism, they can be best carried out only by a state government through its department of agriculture.

An agricultural university has an entirely different set of functions. The Cummings Committee defined its distinctive features in clear-cut terms. It is not just a seat of learning and scholarship; it recognizes a "responsibility and responsiveness to the needs of the cultivators," and

[20] The so-called "Cummings Committee," see Chapter 22.

works towards that end. Its staff engages not only in resident teaching for degree candidates, but in applied and fundamental research in agriculture; and such research must go "beyond the laboratory and into the fields and homes." Finally, it has "an extension limb," the medium through which the benefits of training and research actually flow to the cultivators. It must therefore be fully integrated with teaching and training. Only then can there be a smooth and effective flow of the results of research and training to the cultivators. And only then can there be a reverse flow of the cultivators' problems from the field to the research and training centres to be tackled promptly and effectively.

These, from their very nature, are not departmental functions. They preeminently belong to a properly conceived agricultural university.

These views were wholeheartedly endorsed by the University Education Commission of 1964-66. The Kothari Commission, as it was called, urged a separation of extension work proper from the supply services of the agriculture departments. Experience had shown that the officers concerned had "hardly any time" when both these functions were combined. The extension workers should be attached "not to officers, but to research centres and demonstration farms." This would enable them to carry on extension work "by example rather than by precept," and it would create "greater confidence and trust" in the farmer about "their competence to advise him." The Commission, therefore, welcomed the decision to separate "the supply services" from extension work; and as and when such separation took place, the extension work, it urged, should be transferred to the agricultural universities.

The logic behind these principles was clinching. The need to accept them was clear and gained in urgency. Yet they met with tardy recognition; the tussle with vested interests continued and delayed progress. Nevertheless, it was assumed that the battle of principles had been finally won, and that their unqualified acceptance was only a matter of time.

This optimistic assumption has been unexpectedly belied, and a rude setback, it seems, is now in the works. The National Commission on Agriculture, in an interim report,[21] has recommended that the agricultural universities should develop into "centres of excellence for fundamental and basic research," and it would like problem-oriented research on practical problems to be left with the state departments. Besides, it has sought to distinguish between "applied" and "adaptive" research, and would restrict the university to the former while keeping the latter within the departmental domain! In short, it would tear apart research which is the soul of agriculture, and revert to an old system which has long been discredited.

Clearly, the Commission has misjudged the role of agricultural univer-

[21] *Some Aspects of Agricultural Research, Extension, and Training*, Interim Report, National Commission on Agriculture, November 1971.

sities, overestimated the capacity of the state agriculture department, especially its competence to conduct purposeful research, and grossly underestimated the demanding character of modern agriculture in terms of regulatory, law-enforcing, and supply functions on the one hand, and of education, research, and extension on the other. What is most curious, and disturbing, is that it should have passed such *obiter dicta* almost in an *ad hoc* fashion without taking into account, apparently without even knowing, the conclusions other authoritative bodies had crystallized through long debates and discussions.

One cannot but suspect that the Commission has tried to make a political compromise in what is a strictly scientific field and where politics should have absolutely no role. In the medical field, it is taken for granted that education, research and clinical work, and an efficient health service can be best run within an overall policy framework laid down by the government, but in separate and autonomous institutions outside departmental control. Agriculture, too, needs the same pattern. For the problems of health, nutrition, and disease control are essentially the same in the plant and animal world as in the human world, and therefore they call for the same fundamental approach.

The Punjab Agricultural University, in its comments[22] on the Commission's recommendations on research, has underlined their grave implications. If accepted, it will be "a very damaging decision.... It will only put the clock back and gains made so far will be nullified."

It would indeed be most ironic if such a retrograde policy were advocated by the National Commission on Agriculture from which the nation has been eagerly expecting a vigorous and enlightened leadership to move India's agriculture forward at an accelerated pace. Is it too much to hope that the Commission will still muster enough wisdom to scrap its interim proposals on research and replace them by more responsible ones in its final report?

Its task has been greatly simplified in recent years. All it needs to do now is to take a good look at what has happened, say, at the PAU—how effectively it has organized research, how deftly it now wields research as a tool to raise farm productivity and farm incomes, how harmoniously it has been working with the agriculture department, and how progress has been stimulated in the rural sector by intimate cooperation based on a rational division of labour between the government and the university —and then to uphold the PAU as a model for other states, and to persuade them, with its full authority, to move rapidly in the same direction. This, indeed, is what the Commission must do if it is to measure up to high responsibilities.

[22] Made available to the writer during a visit to the PAU on 22 August, 1972.

## DANGER OF WRONG REFORM

Today, once again in India, administrative reform is in the air. There are talks of "commitment" on the part of the civil service. At this moment,[23] Parliament is debating a legislation that would clip all the special privileges of the ICS, even reduce its retirement age by two years to 58, the same level as for other public services. Some parties are ready with their own brands of reform.

While the reformist zeal is in the ascendancy, one must sound a note of warning. For there is a real danger today that the ills of administration may be diagnosed wrongly, leading up to wrong remedies.

That the ICS has been an asset of tremendous value to the nation no knowledgeable person will deny. Things went awry mainly because it was not used sufficiently for jobs it was best qualified to handle, and was used too much on jobs for which it was ill qualified. It was diverted too frequently from its three prime functions—internal order, law enforcement, revenue collection—and was saddled with technical, managerial, and diplomatic responsibilities. The blame for this non-use and misuse must be shared between the political leadership that allowed this to happen and the Service itself which failed to exercise enough self-restraint and wandered too far afield. The quest for reform must begin with a rectification of this double error.

The importance of the three primary functions must not be underestimated. Together, they constitute the very foundation of national life, and no orderly development is feasible where they are neglected. Moreover, since independence the three functions have enormously grown in dimension because of the mounting population, expanding state activities, and the flood of new legislation.

How internal disorder can jeopardize economic development was dramatically illustrated by West Bengal where the law-and-order situation had deteriorated to such an extent that many Indians were ready almost to write it off. And it has also dramatically illustrated how quickly even such a desperate situation can be redeemed when an able civil servant is entrusted with this responsibility.[24]

Another highly desirable reform would be the creation of one single Public Service comprising ICS, IAS and the various specialized services, all merged into one, with frequent inter-transfers, bearing in mind the specific professional qualifications needed for specific jobs. This was one of the major recommendations made by Dean Appleby in 1953. As he then correctly pointed out, such consolidation would reduce inter-service rivalry and jealousy.

[23] In September 1972.
[24] This challenging task was handled with remarkable ability by the Governor of West Bengal, Mr. A. L. Dias, a retired ICS officer.

India's administrative structure was defective in design in another respect, Dean Appleby implied. It was very wide and dense at the base, reached out to a high peak, but was too thin and narrow in between. He wanted more layers to be created in its middle stretch to give it a truly "pyramidal form." The suggestion is no less valid today. Despite the changes that have taken place in the intervening years, a well-shaped "pyramid" is yet to emerge.

That the old administration was much too paternalistic is well-known. This did not escape Appleby's notice, despite all the praise he had bestowed on it, which explains his plea for democracy within administration. In fact, it is the absence of this in a nation governed by a democratic constitution that has irked the public and hurt the civil service most. This deep-seated weakness is yet to be remedied.

In development administration, by far the most pressing requirement is to rescue it from amateurism and to build into it higher technical competence and greater managerial ability.

There is every reason to demand greater commitment from the civil servants. But, surely, the commitment can only be to a cause and a code —the cause of public welfare and the code of civil service behaviour, consonant with the latter and therefore nonpartisan and nonpolitical. There is an urgent need to de-paternalize the administration, to de-amateurize it for development projects, but also to resist the growing tendency to politicize it.

CHAPTER 29

# Road to Survival

## A FITFUL WAR

India's food problem must be tackled "on a war footing," the nation has been repeatedly told. There is only one trouble about the analogy: It is true.

The brave words have reflected panic, not determination. They have echoed and re-echoed in times of searing droughts and alarming food gaps. But once the crisis blew over, panic subsided, the battle cry faded, and the nation lapsed back into a relaxed mood.

Yet the war is already on, and India is mercilessly caught in it, whether she recognizes it or not. It is a war against the oldest enemies of mankind, hunger and poverty, a war in which the enemy ranks are constantly reinforced by a powerful ally—*Time*. For time is swelling the population at the frightening rate of a million a month. Time is thus accentuating hunger and poverty, and is jeopardizing the prospects of victory in this grim struggle.

It will take more than mere declaration of war, and spasmodic display of valour, to clinch victory. Like all wars, it needs the right strategy backed by adequate mobilization. Given the nature and magnitude of the struggle, and the formidable time-bind, the strategy must be foolproof to forestall wastage of time and motions; and it must be accompanied by an all-out effort on all fronts.

In addition, it will need something else—a ruthless reappraisal of past policies and actions to determine what went wrong and why, and to correct the mistakes once identified. There must be strategic retreats in some instances—from battlefields which were hastily opened and have led to long attrition and no advance. The greatest of all errors would be persistence in past errors. The quest for the right strategy must begin by scrapping what has already proved wrong.

The three fronts from which India must beat a quick retreat are community development, panchayati raj, and cooperation, not because the goals are not covetable, but because the roads chosen are wrong and will lead not *towards*, but *away* from them. The reasons have been fully explained elsewhere.[1] Briefly, they cannot trigger development in a poverty-stricken, elite-ridden rural economy; they were doomed to prove non-starters. The goals they aimed at will be realizable, and therefore truly relevant, only when development is already well under way; when, as a result, caste and class barriers begin to crumble down and the rural community is increasingly democratized.

There are other errors which must be rectified, errors of false premises and strange omissions which have bedevilled India's planning right from the start. Her five-year plans have sought to bring together Soviet-style planning with heavy emphasis on the public sector and heavy industries, Gandhian-style approach to village industries centering on the spinning wheel, Western-style theorizing along with macro-economic model-building, and colonial-style financing with a tight treasury grip on public expenditures. The Plan thus became a bizarre package of incongruous principles.

And to make matters worse, it has lacked some vitally important dimensions. Maimed and truncated, and lacking in inner cohesiveness, it could not grow into the powerful propelling force it was expected to be. India's planning must be rescued from its built-in limitations. Only then could she expect to formulate an aggressive, winning strategy.

### SOME GLITTERING FALLACIES

It would be wrong to put all the blame for faulty planning on India's planners. Erudite scholars from abroad have made solid contributions to it, whether directly or vicariously.

First of all, there is the contagion spread by the macro-economic model-builders. Recent history of the U.S.A. is replete with examples to show how often they make forecasts based on bold abstractions only to find them belied by the march of events, and how, unbaffled by such experience, they persist in this theortical exercise. Apparently, the mathematical perfection of the models they are able to build with modern computers has a charm which few of them are able to resist.

Harvard Professor Wassily W. Leontief has unreservedly lamented this trend. He blames the economics profession for vastly over-emphasizing the role of abstract theorists and model-builders at the expense of empiricists. They do too little work to develop relevant data; they

[1] In Chapters 8 and 9.

underestimate the value of observation in science; they rely on beautiful mathematical models for the solution of "dirty, complicated problems." And so Professor Leontief refuses to be impressed by their handiwork.[2]

Such nonconformists, alas, are much too rare. And they are seldom found where they are needed most—in the developing countries. For, these countries lack the countervailing forces available in the industrialized societies—bankers, industrialists, businessmen, even administrators—who hold them in leash and prevent them from running away with their computerized fallacies. No wonder that the model-builders, encountering strong opposition from such unregenerate groups in their homelands, often pop up in underdeveloped countries, dazzle their leaders with a display of econometric wizardry, and lure them into an economic wilderness.

Take, for example, a country like India. It lacks an integrated macro-economy and consists, as even the lay public knows, of thousands of mini-economies functioning mostly in rural isolation. How absurd it is, then, to mobilize the ultra-refined tools of macro-economic analysis to work out solutions of her still-primitive problems!

There is a cognate problem that further complicates matters—the paucity of reliable data in many vital fields. Here again, the modern statistician, armed with the latest techniques of random sampling, bravely rides over a rough terrain through masses of illiterate people, conjures up endless series of glittering figures practically on every subject, and with them easily impresses the simple-minded leaders. The random samples they operate with produce, at best, random truths; in most cases, they contain significant untruths, and since there is no independent means of verifying the data, they are, *faute de mieux*, relied upon by the planners.

The fact is that macro-economic analysis can be relevant only when there is a macro-economy which can emerge only when a country has already reached a fairly high degree of development. And even then it has to be used with great caution because it involves too many abstractions which never fully square with the facts of real life, and a vast amount of statistical data which can never be wholly accurate; because, in short, it is a precision instrument used to deal with complex and elusive facts of an imprecise world.

Add to this the currently fashionable savings-centred theory of capital formation, and the damage done to the cause of development can be well imagined. It has not only created a theoretical trap with false premises, but has propagated, almost boastfully, the cynical thesis that poor nations must remain poor because of their very low national incomes

[2] This is how Professor Leontief reiterated, in December 1970, his long-held views as retiring president of the American Economic Association.

which give them an exceedingly low rate of savings which can support only a dismally low rate of capital formation. As explained earlier,[3] it errs profoundly because it has misconceived the real problem in a developing country, which is: development and utilization of its idle resources.

And it has virtually ignored the amazing advances science has made in recent decades, the knowledge explosion which has changed the very character of development, the infinite variety of factor combinations it has made possible, which need not be capital-intensive, which can be labour-intensive, and can yet prove astonishingly productive provided they are also *science-intensive*.

The so-called "trickle down" theory of economic growth—that fiscal and monetary stimulus applied to business and industry will stimulate the economy and lead to full employment—does not hold good beyond a certain point even in a developed country because of the numerous frictional factors it inevitably runs up against. How much relevance can it, then, have to an underdeveloped economy which is still unintegrated and is only a congeries of a great many fragmented parts? Investments made in a few industrial pockets cannot in such a case trickle down any more than water through a clogged sieve.

These misconceptions have been accompanied by yet another no less unfortunate—about the role of agriculture in a developing economy. Albert Hirschman, for example, had no doubt about its "inferiority" to manufacturing. For agriculture, to quote his well-known words, "certainly stands convicted on the count of its lack of direct stimulus to the setting up of new activities through linkage effects: the superiority of manufacturing in this respect is crushing."[4]

This crushing judgment stands self-convicted by the questions it begs. Obviously it relates to primitive agriculture pursued in remote areas, "delinked" from the general economy. But, then, why should one compare it with modern manufacturing industries, and not with primitive cottage industries? It is this illogical comparison that produces a "crushing" contrast.

The contrast will certainly cease to be so—indeed, the scale may well turn the other way—when modern industries are compared with *modern* agriculture. Its linkage effects are enormous. There is, first of all, the physical or spatial linkage—all the farms all over the country must be linked, by roads and transport facilities, with market-towns and cities to produce one integrated system. In addition, modern agriculture needs a host of supporting industries, new services and other facilities to ensure smooth flow of inputs to the farms and outflow of farm produce to the markets; and, in turn, it supports a whole range of processing and other

[3] See Chapter 2, the section on "Capital Error"; also Chapter 27, pp. 444-48.
[4] Albert O. Hirschman, *The Strategy of Economic Development*, Yale University Press, New Haven, 1958, pp. 109-10.

industries. The "new activities" it sets up through "linkage effects" have been grossly underrated in Hirschman's sweeping thesis.

And why, finally, should one be so obsessed with "new activities" and "linkage effects?" After all, what matters is their profitability, or the output-input ratio; and, in this respect tropical agriculture, if adequately backed by modern science and technology, would outperform manufacturing industries, and in most cases by extraordinarily wide margins. Not only that; the quantum jump it can bring about in GNP would create the market for, and thereby stimulate, a great many manufacturing and service industries.

Hirschman's thesis has been echoed, in one form or another, by the "industry first" school all over the world, which also happens to be in line with a cardinal tenet of Marxian thought.[5] This widely-held view has been a major factor in holding back agriculture in the developing countries.

Oddly enough, the United Nations family, instead of counteracting these negative influences, has been instrumental in reinforcing them. The UNDP has made a fetish of pre-investment study. It applies the approach more or less mechanically to agriculture with land-and-water surveys, consumes much valuable time—each project requires some four to five years for completion without any guarantee of follow-up action, whereas a great deal of progress could be made, here and now, to boost production if the scientific knowledge and technology already available were systematically utilized. The backbone of today's agriculture consists of adaptive research, education, and extension. It is precisely here that the UNDP and FAO have been at their weakest.[6]

The net effect of erroneous thinking and faulted policies has been to divert national effort away from what could be by far the most powerful growth-boosting force in a developing economy, and thereby to derail development.

And as if even this was not enough—it has been sanctified by what may be called the fallacy of a predetermined growth rate. Walt Rostow's analysis of the stages of economic growth is an intriguing, and courageously simplified, version of the trends of the Western economies as they zigzagged through a century, often marked by stormy economic and social upheavals. Original, perspicacious, alluring, a masterpiece of speculative interpretation of history, it is wholly irrelevant to today's problems of development.

History may repeat itself, although this oft-repeated maxim needs to be heavily qualified. Its validity for economic history is much more dubious. The West, through its very development, virtually guarantees

---

[5] See Chapter 1, pp. 9-12.
[6] For further comments on this question, see Chapter 31, pp. 517-23.

that its nineteenth-century experience need not, and will not, be repeated in today's underdeveloped countries. It has changed the planet itself, accumulated vast amounts of investment capital, and piled up scientific discoveries and mechanical inventions on a staggering scale. All this can be drawn upon by a developing economy for its own growth. Its "take-off" can be faster and smoother if the runway is well-designed and well-paved.

How naive it is, then, to assume that the poor nations, because of some imaginary historical constraint, must be tied down to a growth rate around 4 per cent per annum! And how absurd it is to postulate further that a higher growth rate is contingent upon a correspondingly higher rate of savings, a condition the poor nations, because of their very poverty, are unable to satisfy! Yet these irrational ideas have, for some mysterious reasons, cast a magic spell on contemporary economic thinking.

Thus, an astonishing *non sequitur* based on Rostow's highly subjective analysis of economic growth has forged formidable fetters for development. Chorused by a redoubtable array of economic pundits, it has been raised to the status of an immutable truth and made the major premise of all economic planning. And so planners have obligingly kept their sights low, and have consistently fixed a rate of economic growth that can barely match the population growth. As a result, poor nations are nervously "backing" into a cheerless Rostovian future.

Clearly, this stands development economics right on its head. Economic growth, to repeat, is a function of science and technology applied to physical resources. The optimum growth rate can be derived only from a field analysis of the actual potential, and not dictated from an ivory tower. It follows that a development economist, to be worthy of his salt, must leave behind his mathematical models, however "beautiful," and undertake studies of the "dirty" and complicated problems of real life, however mundane and unappealing. And he must carry out a whole range of micro-economic analysis based on careful input-output calculations before he can have any reliable notion about the feasible growth rate.

To do this job well, he must bring to bear on his conventional analysis two special attributes: a keen resource-sense and a fairly good understanding of science and technology in many key areas, especially of their economic implications. This involvement in science is absolutely essential. Only then can he expect to work out what the developing countries most urgently need in most cases, namely, tailor-made factor combinations to extract optimum wealth from a given resource-base, especially land and water, with skilful use of scientific knowledge, high input of labour which they are most liberally endowed—or burdened—with, and minimum input of investment capital, particularly foreign exchange, which is their scarcest resource.

India's agricultural scientists, it has been seen earlier, could make very little contribution to her development until they redirected their efforts to face and solve practical problems for increasing production.[7] The economists, too, will have to do the same if they are to fulfil their primary function.

The path developing countries must travel runs not from savings to capital formation to higher growth to better living standards, but from science-based resource development to higher growth to higher incomes, rising living standards, and larger savings. This is the only way they can break the vicious circle of "poverty perpetuates poverty"; and it is also an infallible way. There is no need for them to remain trapped in poverty when they have easy access to this escape route.

## PLANNING FOR HIGH GROWTH

India's economic growth has been agonizingly slow—on an average barely one per cent net per capita per annum. Once again, the fault lies not in her stars, but primarily in her planning. It is not fate, but folly that must take the lion's share of the blame.

The foremost task today is, first, to free India's planning from the false dogmas and paralyzing fallacies discussed above; and, second, to build into the Plan several new dimensions which, though vital, it has, for one reason or another, missed all these years. Planning will turn into a vehicle of rapid progress only when the imperatives listed below are fully respected and acted upon:[8]

### 1. *Add a resource dimension.*

To mention only the most conspicuous examples, there are several million acres of potentially fertile land which can be reclaimed and put to work; vast tracts of wastelands which should be planted with forests; several million acres of irrigated lands which are deteriorating for lack of drainage and need to be rehabilitated; and large areas of eroded uplands which should be protected with conservation measures and put to more productive use. Such measures are essential also to prevent rapid silting-up of rivers and storage reservoirs.

There has long been a colossal waste of water, the life-blood of tropical agriculture; the waste must be stopped. The surface, subsurface, and ground water has to be harvested systematically and managed efficiently. In recent years some progress has been made in that direction, but a great deal remains to be done.[9]

[7] In Chapter 22, esp. pp. 334-42.

[8] Several items briefly touched upon in this section, viz. items 1, 2, 3, 4, 5 and 7, are discussed in *Reaping the Green Revolution—Food and Jobs for All.*

[9] See Chapter 16.

## 2. *Add a vastly expanded public works programme.*

India's planning has been particularly timid in this respect. Yet a bold public works programme will serve a dual purpose. It will provide employment to idle manpower, and will build a great many sorely-needed productive assets. It should embrace such items as land reclamation, drainage works, reforestation; minor irrigation, soil conservation with contour-building, gully-plugging, and headwaters control; remodelling of major irrigation projects with provision of field control facilities; roads, markets, godowns and warehouses, cold storage; power transmission lines with substations; schools and hospitals.

The needs are vast. The work must therefore be properly phased to cover the whole country in suitable stages. What is important is to launch out courageously on such a programme. Without these essential works there can be no real economic development.

## 3. *Add a bold dimension for job creation.*

The most grievous, also the most cruel and cynical, default of India has been in this field—the lack of a sensible employment policy. And in this respect her performance has not been noticeably better than that of the pre-independence regime. Such callousness, at a time when the population grows by leaps and bounds, can only lead to disaster. Neglect of manpower, coupled with the neglect of natural resources, especially land and water, has kept the Indian economy in its present deplorable state. And it has made a mockery of planning.

The plea here is not for a make-work, or fake-work, programme. That would be both reckless and unnecessary. To rush to doles or subsidies, whether to create jobs or to support people, would be foolish at this stage of India's development. For tens of millions of highly productive jobs can be created here and now to employ the jobless, to boost economic growth, and to promote welfare.

The greatest potential job-creater is agriculture, or the green revolution; it will directly absorb billions of idle man-days, and indirectly many times more, if it is spread rapidly and regulated properly. A public works programme, as outlined above, will make a vast contribution to the same end, apart from feeding and speeding the green revolution. Roads, market-towns, and transportation facilities leading to an effective rural-urban continuum will stimulate countless manufacturing and service industries. All this will create a demand for millions of trained professionals and skilled workers. Health and education, the backbone of modern development, are still grossly neglected. They have to be expanded and improved, and this will call for a vast army of professionally trained men and women.

These are obvious possibilities, and there are many others. They have been crying out for far greater national effort. The tragedy is that they continue to be largely ignored even today.

### 4. *Build land reform into the Plan as a concomitant of the green revolution.*

It must be land reform with teeth. This means abolition of absentee landlordism in whatever form, imposition of meaningful ceilings rigidly enforced, and family holdings for "owner-cultivation" strictly defined. Such reforms will provide the best guarantee against blind mechanization and consequent displacement of labour, a danger which has already become real in some areas. It will also ensure more intensive cultivation of land, greater productivity per acre, and therefore also more farm jobs. These are vital objectives for India; without them she cannot support her surging population.

Land-reform-with-teeth will, in addition, yield several precious byproducts. It will end the domination of the poor by the rural elite, which has perpetrated so much injustice and misery in rural India. It will "homogenize" the farming community and will thus create, for the first time in India's history, a favourable environment for real cooperation to grow and prosper from below.

It will end the fiscal bleeding to which the economy has been subjected by the affluent farmers who grow rich on subsidized services, refuse to pay taxes, and use political muscles to thwart all proposals to tax agricultural incomes. Farmers in a homogeneous community, it is safe to predict, will be ready to pay taxes when they see that the tax proceeds are going to be ploughed back for their own benefit—to build better facilities and services which, in turn, will build up their farm incomes.

Even the rural elite, as mentioned before, should in the end stand to gain. Once deprived of their easy life and of opportunities to make easy money by social exploitation, they will, with their considerable talent and resources, almost certainly turn to other activities. Today's exploiters may, and most probably will, become tomorrow's entrepreneurs to enrich themselves as well as the rural economy and the country as a whole.

What about compensation? Can the public exchequer stand what looks like a colossal burden? Compensation must be paid in accordance with the law, and on a fair and equitable basis as assessed by an impartial public body. But it can, and should, be paid only partly—say 20 per cent —in cash, and the rest in guaranteed long-term bonds bearing an attractive yield—say, 7 per cent per annum—and maturing in 15 to 20 years. The extra agricultural production the redistribution of land will stimulate should be enough to amortize all the bonds within a few years. In addition, it will wipe off the nation's food deficit, vastly speed up its economic growth, and yield other far-reaching benefits as indicated above.

Land reform, properly conceived, will not be burdensome; it is the status quo that is intolerably so, both financially and economically. For two decades India has elaborately fiddled with land reform and has timorously evaded the crux of the problem. Development planning will remain futile in what is the most vital sector of her economy until this omission is finally made good.[10]

## 5. Undertake space planning and development as an urgently needed component of the Plan.

India's war against poverty and hunger, her war of survival, must be fought in the rural areas, her most critical battlefields. And as in all wars, transportation and communication are all-important. Without them vital problems of logistics cannot be solved, and therefore no wars can be won.

The greatest problem of India's villages is their isolation. The markets are too few and, in most cases, too far from the farms; and all-weather link-roads are the exception, not the rule. There can be no future for her agriculture as long as this situation continues. It will remain spatially paralyzed.[11]

What she desperately needs today are market-towns—some 20,000 to 25,000 of them by 1980—with warehouses and other facilities, along with several million miles of metalled—not necessarily concrete—roads in different categories. It would be futile to talk of rural development until farms are market-linked, families are hospital-linked, children are school-linked, and the villages are town-linked.

Nucleus market-towns can often be built rapidly, also inexpensively, if warehouses, power substations, hospitals, schools and a host of other facilities already approved are clustered in carefully chosen centres. Once established, they will grow on the strength of their inner dynamism and, like magnets, will attract a great many other activities to support and enrich the rural economy. Such functional towns will not only pay their way; they will, in addition, act as powerful growth-boosters.

This is exactly what the macro-economic analysts should busy themselves with today—to link farms and villages to market-towns—to cities—to the great metropolitan centres in order to weld them together with an effective transport system, to create a smoothly functioning rural-urban continuum; in short, to build a true macro-economy. Only then will their analysis begin to acquire some semblance of validity.

## 6. Add a massive credit dimension to the Plan.

This omission, more than any other single factor, has kept India's

[10] Yet this evasive exercise was re-enacted as late as August 1972. The decisions about ceilings legislation have once again been riddled with so many loopholes as to make them virtually meaningless.

[11] See Chapter 2, p. 27, and Chapter 24, esp. pp. 376-88.

economic growth absurdly low.[12] The imperatives are perfectly clear: Turn the credit faucet fearlessly on, but make sure that the credit flows in the right direction—not towards the hungry capital cities devouring steel and concrete, or government offices to support an expanding bureaucracy and an army of clerical and other low-paid staff, nor to the money-losing management of public-sector undertakings, nor to the giant projects inspired by engineering megalomania, nor to the alluring election-eve projects conjured up by politicians anxious to placate their constituencies, but into the fields to produce more crops, and into numerous agri-related activities discussed earlier, especially to disseminate the green revolution far and wide.

In the past, India has liberally used the government printing press at Nasik and the credit-creating mechanism of the Reserve Bank in Bombay to finance wars and the current deficits in the Central and state budgets to meet unproductive expenditure, and has expressed great worries about inflation. It is high time to rein in the lavish use of deficit financing of budget deficits, but to use it boldly for high- and quick-yielding projects centering, above all, on agriculture. This is the only way she can combat the inflation fuelled by shortages of food and the multiplying number of mouths to feed.

## 7. Strengthen the family planning programme with a socio-economic dimension.

The population surge continues almost unabated. The family planning programme, after its initial successes, threatens to hit a plateau. This is inevitable; it is futile to expect that jobless, homeless, hopeless people will favourably respond to it. To them the very concept of family planning is a cruel irrelevancy.

The population problem calls for a two-pronged attack. Knowledge, devices, and chemicals, now relied upon by the programme, may suffice for the relatively small elite sections of the population. But to involve the vast masses of people a second front is absolutely essential—to provide jobs and incomes which constitute the foundation of family life, amenities like housing, power and water supply, and social services, particularly health and education.

The two packages complement each other. Rapid progress can be made only when this complementarity is recognized, and vigorous attempt is made simultaneously on both fronts. Otherwise the programme will never get very far and will only invite vast frustration.

To put it differently, economic development depends largely on a slowdown of population growth, a fact that is incessantly emphasized. What needs to be stressed with equal force and pursued with relentless

[12] Discussed at length in Chapter 27.

effort is the corollary truth, namely, a slowdown of population growth is contingent upon a speed-up of economic development.

## 8. *Revamp and restructure the administrative system for effective execution of the Plan.*

The reforms needed have been fully discussed in the previous chapter. The most urgent requirements are for greater reliance on scientists and experts in different fields, a vastly strengthened organization to cope with expanding Plan activities, and therefore a greater effort to mobilize and utilize the professional manpower, such as scientists, engineers, doctors, teachers, business managers.

## 9. *Add a Time dimension to the Plan.*

A chief-of-staff is aware of the crucial value of time in formulating war-time strategy. Delays, he knows, may entail defeat.

The analogy is no less valid for India's fight against poverty. The war is on, and it grows more desperate with time as her labour force swells by some half a million people per month. Yet India's planning breathes no sense of urgency. Growth rates are fixed, targets in various fields are laid down, pilot projects are recommended as if time does not matter when, in fact, it matters most.

Only in agriculture the scientists have, of late, begun to show a time-sense—they now talk of output per unit of land per unit of time, or *per acre per day*, so as to maximize production and income. This concept should be built into all other sectors, and into the Plan as a whole, to maximize growth.

India's planning will come to life only when these dimensions are fully incorporated into it. What will be the resultant rate of growth? No categorical answer is possible for lack of precedents—no developing country has yet tried out a resource-based, agri-centred strategy on a comprehensive scale as suggested here. Nevertheless, enough hard evidence is already available—from the numerous scientific breakthroughs solidly field-tested, the brief but startling performance of the green revolution in several countries, and the longer record of achievements in Mexico and Taiwan—to suggest that a 15 to 20 per cent annual growth can be achieved, and can be sustained for a good many years.[13] This is the kind of target India should aim at and work for to raise the masses of people well above the subsistence level, and to ensure her own survival as a healthy and dignified nation.

Some economists might swoon at the very suggestion of such a growth

---

[13] This will be the case if today's infant green revolution is followed by systematic efforts to gather a full harvest with multiple-cropping, livestock and fishery development, agri-business, agri-related industries, and other activities, as discussed in *Reaping the Green Revolution.*

rate, especially those who have been wedded to the concept of a near-4 per cent annual growth long enough to look upon it as an unchanging truth in a fast-changing age of rapid scientific advances; whose thinking has congealed into a slow-growth dogma. It may be some time before they are able to shake off the dogma and begin to reevaluate the realities. Development planning cannot, however, wait till then as a hostage to late-reacting theoreticians.

Meanwhile, the budding green revolution is changing the general outlook. The dwarfs have dealt a decisive blow to a great many resource-blind planners and administrators. Agriculture, they have suddenly begun to realize, is not the hopeless cripple as they had hitherto assumed, to be carried forever in a subsidy-built wheelchair; that, on the contrary, it is the best hope of a developing country, the prime source of its national wealth, a growth-booster and a pace-setter of its economy. What is needed today is to build fast on that foundation, to work out its full implications, and to formulate a new action programme embodying the dearly-learnt lessons.

## GROWTH FOR WELFARE

What about the quality of growth, distribution of income, social justice? Contrary to the view held by some, these issues are of vital significance not only in an industrialized society, but also in a developing economy. Development will be a mockery if it fails to alleviate mass poverty. Nor can there be any real prosperity unless it is widely shared; to be vigorous and durable, it needs the underpinnings of mass purchasing power. Add to this the fact that, in general, population explodes more uncontrollably among masses when steeped in stark poverty, and it becomes perfectly clear why social justice, based on equitable distribution of wealth, must be an essential component of a sound development programme.

However, it would be wrong, indeed fatal, to frown upon growth *per se*, as some are inclined to do today in their anxiety not to import into the developing countries the moral and environmental pollution suffered by the industrialized societies. What they are apt to overlook is the fact that poverty pollutes too, in addition to the aches and pains, and the agonies of no-growth bodies and minds with which it fills a country. Growthlessness is not a blessing; it is the worst affliction that may befall a developing nation.

Surely, the fight must be not *against* growth, but *for* the quality of growth. What a developing country needs is *growth for welfare*. There is no inherent conflict between the two; and it is the business of policy-makers to see that, as far as possible, no such conflict develops.

The design suggested above shows how a high growth rate can be coupled with a broad measure of social justice. An ironclad legislation for land reform, giving land to the tiller and clamping down fairly low ceilings, will purge rural India of its worst injustices; it will be a major safeguard against accumulation of too much wealth in too few hands. Besides, agri-centred development gives the topmost priority to food production, and since food is the foremost necessity of life, it also meets a crucial test for the quality of growth.

Furthermore, roads and market-towns with transportation facilities will bring modern amenities into the rural areas and will stimulate countrywide exchange of goods and services, which will benefit the entire nation. They will also help establish a new rural-urban balance with a greater decentralization of industries and a better spatial distribution of population, which will enrich rural life and spare the overcrowded cities much of the crushing onrush of rural in-migration.

Thus, the high growth rate, as proposed here, will not militate against other desirable objectives—quality of life, social justice, pollution control, protection of the cities. On the contrary, it will go a long way towards their realization. Fiscal measures and social services, if fashioned properly, can be relied upon to do the rest.

## GARIBI HATAO : A REALIZABLE DREAM

In March 1971, Prime Minister Indira Gandhi won a stunning electoral victory. Several factors contributed to it, but the most decisive of them were two words emblazoned on her campaign manifesto: *Garibi Hatao*, or liquidate poverty. These magic words touched the soul of a nation long hungering for escape from a poverty-crushed existence.

The masses have given her a massive mandate. And since the expectations she has aroused will clamour for fulfilment, the massive mandate also poses a massive challenge. Will Indira Gandhi meet it? And can she? Or, was *garibi hatao* only an empty slogan for electioneering, a mere vote-catching ploy?

The last thought, though whispered around, is too cynical to deserve credence. There is every reason to believe that Mrs. Gandhi would like to do her utmost to fulfil the tall mandate she had asked for from the people and has, perhaps to her own surprise, been overwhelmed with. There is also every indication that she is still groping around for a strategy that will really work, and will lead the nation rapidly towards the proclaimed goal, but that she is still unable to lay her hand confidently on any.

Nor has her task been simplified by the fact that there are too many cynics around who believe India's poverty is too vast to be liquidated, too many pundits who use their talent to confound the issues, too many prophets ready with their apocalyptic predictions.

Luckily, the cynics are wrong. Garibi hatao *is* a realizable dream. Mrs. Gandhi *can* fulfil her historic mandate. She *can*, if she adopts the *right strategy*, breach the maginot line of negative forces and stage a blitz to produce an economic miracle of her own.

The first task confronting her today is to rescue planning from the morass it has been landed into by outdated attitudes, sterile punditry, and ideological follies, both exotic and home-made, and to integrate into it all the missing but vital components outlined earlier. Her second task is to speed and spread the green revolution all over the country with measures which have already been fully discussed.

There is a third and related task—to use the green revolution as the spearhead to bring about an all-round economic and social development, which calls for an all-out mobilization of effort embracing all sectors of the national economy.

In working out this strategy, the planners have something valuable to learn from the plant-breeders. As seen earlier, the green revolution, in its genesis, is a gene-revolution—the dwarfs have been designed with genes collected from widely-scattered sources. Like the yield-packed dwarfs, a growth-packed strategy needs the same kind of discerning, eclectic approach; and like biological engineers, social-economic engineers, too, must collect the right "genes" from all over the world. To mention the most conspicuous ones needed in India today, they could best turn to —

*USA* : For agricultural sciences and their application through education, research and extension; soil conservation work, integrated resource development in river valleys as demonstrated by the TVA, especially in its first two decades; and management principles as applied to various fields.

*Soviet Russia* : For its jobs-for-all, food-for-all, education-for-all, medicare-for-all policies; emphasis on public work programmes and country-wide geological exploration, especially as carried out under its first five-year plan; and its bold approach to credit financing.

*Japan* : For science-intensive agriculture based on small farms and owner-cultivated with small equipment, giving, for some crops, the world's highest productivity per acre.

Also for something amorphous, but most precious and very rare in today's world: harmonious relationship among all the interests involved in production—government, businessmen, working-class, and farmers. This is one of the main secrets of the high growth rate Japan has been able to maintain for many years. "Japan Inc.," though pejoratively used, represents a valid ideal for other countries, and most definitely for India.

*China* : For man-power mobilization with a large people's army used extensively on nation-building projects—but as a means to promote not a "cultural," but an agricultural revolution.

*Britain* : For an able, nonpolitical civil service, and the institution of an autonomous, nonpolitical public corporation for expert management of public-sector undertakings.

*The West in general* : For freedom of individual initiative and private enterprise; and for the techniques of stimulating and regulating the private sector for overall national benefit.

These are the positive genes India needs today to "breed into" her plans and policies in order to produce a high-growth economy. At the same time, she must take extreme care not to "breed out" precious ones inherited from her own hoary past: compassion for the people which Gandhiji, Vinobaji, and the best souls of India have cultivated throughout the ages and have upheld as the highest ideal of national life; and an attitude that enables people to live modestly, yet happily, unencumbered by a consumption craze. For, true happiness is as much a function of the mind and the values it nurtures as of the goods and services it commands.

But, finally, one must remember that there are some negative, or "black," genes as well which can harbinger blights and diseases, which must not therefore be allowed to get into the system. India must be particularly vigilant about three of them:

*First*, large-scale farming with blind tractorization will be completely misplaced in India's socio-economic environment, as also its two more strident variants—collectivization and communization. For farm-size and the degree of mechanization, India must, as emphasized before, look towards neither the USA nor the USSR, nor even West Europe, but to Japan and Taiwan.

*Second*, Marxism may be ideologically numb about numbers, but India cannot. It would be suicidal for her to take the cue from this source whether directly or indirectly, and to neglect the population problem. She must go all out to control numbers by all feasible means.

India's private sector is an asset of inestimable value, a tremendous dynamic force which, given the right climate, can greatly accelerate the right kind of economic growth. It must not be sacrificed, for the sake of an illusory ideological gain, to an all-devouring public sector which can only smother progress like a bureaucratic albatross.

Garibi hatao, to repeat, is a realizable dream. With an aggressive, growth-cum-welfare oriented strategy as outlined here, India can stage a spectacular turnaround; and thanks to the progress already made in the last quarter century, she can do so surprisingly fast. In five years

India can set *garibi* definitely on its way out even if, by then, it is not fully exorcised.

Will there be enough vision, and enough courage, to embark on such a programme? And will there be the requisite leadership, at this late hour, to carry it through with unflinching determination? An impatient nation expectantly waits for the answer. The world watches. The sands of time are running out.

PART THREE

# NEW HORIZONS FOR
# DEVELOPING COUNTRIES

# CHAPTER 30

# Challenges and Opportunities

## A DE GAULLE HOMILY

"You can't eat what you don't produce," President de Gaulle used to say; and this served as a guideline of his domestic economic policy. It is easy to find fault with it when applied to an industrialized nation like France, more so in the context of a Common Market he was anxious to forge for Western Europe. Yet this de Gaulle mystique holds a vital truth for most developing countries. They do need a large dose of physiocracy.

In the 1960's a frightened world nervously debated if it could at all feed the bulging world population. Thoughtful souls agreed then that this was a global problem which had to be tackled on a global basis. Soon spirits were buoyed by such noble ventures as the Food for Peace Programme, the World Food Programme, and a Freedom From Hunger Campaign. The highly-developed nations stepped up their production of grain, dried milk and other products frantically, spurred by very generous price supports. Food flowed out, as grants and subsidies, to the needy nations to meet their growing shortages.

The hungry world, it was quickly assumed by many, would have to be fed increasingly from the Western granaries. The idealist blessed the thought in a Christian spirit; farmers smiled at the prospect of more production and more profits, and promptly declared their willingness to play their part; farm-politicians nodded approval of what miraculously conformed to their enlightened self-interest; some economists sharpened their analytical tools to justify the new trend.

All these humanistic ventures had one thing in common—they over-looked the longer range interests of the developing countries which were the object of so much concern. What would be the impact of massive food imports on their poor farmers, and of the negative multiplier effects they would induce—depressed farm production, farm jobs and incomes —on their fragile economies? How much charity could they survive, and for how long?

And what would happen to them if the donor nations suddenly began to feel that the burden of altruism was, after all, too burdensome even for them, and decided to shrug it off? These questions were not asked; perhaps they were too profane or too inconvenient to deserve serious thought. In any case, globalism easily carried the day, aided by an admixture of humanism, enlightened and not-so-enlightened self-interest.

## NOT FOOD AID, BUT FOOD PRODUCTION AID

As a specimen of the skewed thinking that prevailed at the time one may cite a paper that was presented by Dr. Kristensen of OECD at the International Conference of Agricultural Economists in 1967. In it he suggested, in all seriousness, that from a global angle it might be better to step up agricultural production in the highly-developed countries and to sell the surplus for export to the developing nations.

Dr. Colin Clark saw "a fatal defect" in the proposal. How would the poor nations pay for the food imports? Dr. Kristensen was silent on this point, though he implicitly assumed that they would do so by expanding their manufactures. But would their exports grow fast enough for the purpose? Dr. Clark saw no likelihood that they would, although, in effect, this is the solution he eventually fell back upon, adding to it a strong plea that the developed countries should be more generous to the poor nations and actively help them to expand their exports.[1]

As for the comparative advantages in food production, Dr. Clark cited a study apparently showing that it was "actually cheaper to produce sugar in East Anglia, paying British wages, than to produce cane sugar in Jamaica, paying the recognized wages there." In explanation of this phenomenon he made a perceptive comment: "One reason for this is that the whole disposition of agricultural research (not only in sugar) has been directed far more towards the improvement of temperate than of tropical products." He thus came, it seems almost inadvertently, to what was the heart of the problem; but instead of pursuing it further, he immediately shied away from it.

After this passing remark Dr. Clark slipped into his pet discourse as to how FAO had exaggerated the extent of world hunger, starting with Lord Boyd-Orr's famous declaration of 1950 that two-thirds of the

---

[1] "Too Much Food?" in *Llyods Bank Review*, January 1970. On several occasions, Dr. Clark expressed the view that there was over-production of food because the world's food needs were exaggerated by FAO.

world were living in permanent hunger;[2] how, despite subsequent amendments of his thesis, the Agency persisted, with a set of excessively high calorie standards, to prove that a large part of the world was living in hunger; and how the inflated estimate of world food deficit resulting from these miscalculations led to excessive price supports in Western countries to produce large surpluses "at great cost to their taxpayers and consumers."

Boyd-Orr's observation on hunger, one may readily concede, was not mathematically precise; nor was it, one may further presume, intended to be so. After all, it is common knowledge that, even in advanced industrial countries, hunger and malnutrition do not lend themselves to accurate measurement; and in most developing countries, they encounter almost insurmountable statistical problems. Yet who would deny that vast masses of their people were, and still are, in the throes of what Gandhiji called "the eternal involuntary fast"? It is this broad, incontestable fact that mattered to Boyd-Orr; and it was enough for him to serve as a basic policy guideline. To belabour it on the ground of its statistical imprecision seems futile and largely beside the point.

The same remark applies to the various studies and investigations FAO has subsequently carried out in this field. It has tried to do the best it could in tackling an inherently difficult statistical problem, and to provide at least some notional estimates of the magnitude of hunger in the world when none at all were available. And who could help fill this knowledge gap if not FAO?

For example, in a study published in 1962,[3] FAO estimated that 300 to 500 million people out of the world's 3,000 million were "underfed," and that "up to one half of the world population—perhaps even more—suffer from hunger or malnutrition." The conclusions it arrived at looked grim: at the then-prevailing rate of annual growth, the world population would exceed six billion by 2000 A.D.; world food production had barely kept pace with the population growth and, unless sharply stepped up, would increasingly fall behind; in short, mankind was steadily drifting towards a global food shortage of staggering dimensions.

The study projected that, by the year 2000, the world food supplies would have to rise "by some 110 per cent in cereals, 200 per cent in pulses and 190 per cent in animal products over and above the supplies available today."

FAO served out these basic data year after year, threw a steady spotlight on the losing food-population race and the looming world food

[2] Boyd-Orr, writing in the *Scientific American* in 1950, had observed that "a lifetime of malnutrition and actual hunger is the lot of at least two-thirds of mankind." Colin Clark contested, in 1960-62, that this was "the most incorrect statement of human history."

[3] *Six Billions to Feed*, FAO, Rome, 1962.

63

crisis, and went all out to rouse the conscience of mankind. This was an outstanding service, for which it is entitled to the gratitude of all concerned people.

In another respect, however, FAO booked an outstanding failure. Like other people preoccupied with the problem, the Agency, too, misread its true character and misjudged the solution it needed. Freedom from hunger cannot be achieved simply by matching global food production with global population. The battle against hunger must be fought and won *within each hungry nation*. To spoonfeed a poor nation with imported grain would be a poor strategy. It could, at best, be a short-term palliative, never a permanent cure; indeed, in the long run it could only aggravate the problem.

To eradicate hunger the first task is to discover its root cause, and then to tackle it within each country. It should not have been all that hard, especially for FAO with all its expertise, to identify the cause. In any case, the diagnosis of the problem should no longer be in doubt: People in the developing countries are starved of food because their farms are starved of science and technology; their per capita calorie intake is low because their per acre productivity is low. The remedy, it follows, lies not in importing grains to meet food deficits, but in importing and adapting improved varieties and technologies to step up their own production.

Food aid as charity, uncharitable as it may sound, has badly hurt many developing countries. The reasons should be easy to understand. These unfortunate lands could not participate in the modern industrial age; they were left on the wayside by the march of history. In many instances, their old handicrafts have been cornered, or squeezed out of existence, by imported manufactures. And so while their population has swollen, their economic base has shrunk, and all that they are left with as a source of livelihood is agriculture. If this, too, is disrupted by imported foodstuffs dumped on their domestic markets, depriving farmers of whatever incentive they might have to produce any marketable surplus, it could only drive them deeper into poverty and desperation.

To look at things from another angle, the Western world is keenly aware of the importance of jobs, and full or near-full employment is now a primary objective of its economic policy. Developing nations, overwhelmed as they are with unemployment—year-round or seasonal, visible or concealed—need jobs no less urgently. Domestic production of food would help meet their most important domestic need, directly create employment for millions of people and, through its multiplier effects, raise their GNP and employment to significantly higher levels. Food aid, on the other hand, would kill countless jobs and set in motion a negative spiral in their economies.

Can they produce industrial goods and export them to pay for imported food, as has sometimes been suggested? To choose such a route is as good as to chase a chimera. It is the most uphill, the most hazardous, also the most expensive route the developing countries could follow.

Historically, this was the royal road Britain travelled for two centuries as she rode to unprecedented prosperity. For a nation that pioneered the industrial revolution and had a sprawling Empire at its disposal, this was the most obvious policy to pursue. For a developing country to copy this British model would be absurd, although many of them—and their Western advisers—often find it hard to resist the magnetic pull of a blind historical analogy.

Significantly enough, other Western nations, even though early entrants to the modern industrial age, discovered that the British model was less relevant to their conditions, and, therefore, relied more heavily on home-grown food. And some of them, Holland and Denmark in particular, found it more expedient to make intensive agriculture and agri-processing industries the foundation of their prosperity even in an industrial age. To a large extent, this has proved to be the case also with the USA, Canada and Australia in the earlier phases of their development.

It should be easy to see why, in the developing countries, the industry-first school errs fatally. Given the investment capital, foreign exchange, and expertise available to them, how many industries can they develop, and run efficiently? Given the low per capita income and, for most products, very narrow domestic markets, what would happen to their economies of scale, and how many of them would escape infant mortality? Given the strong protectionist-nationalistic attitude of the industrialized nations, how many of them could, in fact, expect reasonably free access even for their lower-priced manufactures to the expanding markets of those nations? Moreover, given the fast-growing population, how will the developing countries meet the mounting demand for food if their slender resources are diverted away towards manufacturing industries? And, finally, given a widening food gap, what will be the fate of the industries they may establish at great sacrifice?

By contrast, the food-first school has a foolproof case. In a developing country, food accounts for the largest segment of its domestic market,[4] and spurred by population growth, it is expanding fast. The cry for more food is becoming increasingly louder, and it cannot go unheeded much longer. Technologies for growing more food are already available; they can be borrowed in good part, and adapted and utilized to produce quick results. Increased production of food need not involve large capital investment, at least initially; on the other hand, it can absorb a good

[4] The average American family spent 12.5% of after-tax income on food in 1972, against 16.1% a decade earlier. The corresponding figure for Britain is 22%, for France 23%, for Japan 28%, for USSR 45%. In the poor nations the proportion is of course much higher—maybe 60% or more.

deal of labour which is in abundant supply. It will yield an outstanding cost-benefit relationship—in both economic and human terms—which no other economic activity could remotely equal in most of the developing countries today.

The food-first approach in no way implies that development should not, or will not, go beyond production of food. It is, needless to say, only the first step, not the last. In fact, it will immediately provide a solid base on which one could—indeed, will have to—erect a great many viable, agri-related industries—for farm inputs, for processing farm products, for agri-support services. And in due course, agri-centred development will fan out to embrace a large sector of the economy, including a great many manufacturing industries as well.

What has been said above does not apply to all developing countries; there are exceptions, though rather few. The most conspicuous of them are the oil-rich desert lands which lack an agricultural base. Even here, however, one wonders if they should not start exploring the possibility of ploughing back some of their oil revenues to set up desalination plants so that, some day, they could make at least part of the deserts bloom with desalted water. Oil, after all, is an exhaustible resource; and as it is depleted, the resource-base of these areas will shrink and may some day prove inadequate to support their still-growing population. From oil via desalination of water to irrigated agriculture would, at least *prima facie*, make a lot of economic sense as it would help diversify the oil economies.

Some developing countries are now overwhelmingly dependent on a single commodity destined for the international market, as Ghana on cocoa. They, too, would be better off if they begin to diversify their agriculture with greater emphasis on production of food to meet their domestic needs. This will make them less vulnerable to the sharp price fluctuations on the international commodity markets, and also help improve the inequitable terms of trade more in their favour. And it will equip them, while there is still time, with the means to feed their growing population.

The industry-first school has usually spoken, and acted, with the weight of authority, and from a historical bias, but without enough knowledge of modern agriculture and its great potential in the tropics. It is time to dethrone it from the high pedestal it has so long occupied. That task should now be easy to accomplish. For, the green revolution, despite its piecemeal performance so far, has dispelled much of the ideological fog, and has blazed an unmistakable trail for the developing countries pointing to a brighter future. There should be no more reason for them today to lose their way in a jungle of tangled ideas.

What the poor nations really need is not food aid, but food *production* aid. Maximum autarky in food should, in most cases, be their foremost economic goal. They should remember de Gaulle's injunction: "You can't eat what you don't produce"; follow Voltaire's exhortation: *"Il faut cultiver notre jardin";* and cultivate their own farm-gardens—for their home markets.

## RESOURCE-BASED DEVELOPMENT

Can the developing countries really produce what they eat? Today the answer, most definitely, is—Yes, provided, however, they unflinchingly satisfy four basic conditions.

*First,* they must eschew false, growth-inhibiting concepts which have so long encumbered their path:[5] Macro-economic gimmicry that evades the real problems of development; "savings-centred" planning that wrongly equates national savings with investible resources; the pseudo-historical premise of an arbitrarily low rate of growth, routinely accepted by planners but wholly unsupported by contemporary facts; the fashionable undervaluation of agriculture without an understanding of its high intrinsic potential; the newfangled dogma of pre-investment that mostly diverts efforts and delays development; the will-o'-the-wisp that lures the developing countries away from their fertile home base into industrial misadventures. The litany of pitfalls is long. To make real progress in their uphill journey from the depth of poverty they must bypass them carefully.

*Second,* they must turn their attention, far more than has hitherto been the case, to their vast but unused and underused physical resources, and develop them with modern science and technology combined with their superabundant manpower. For them, as previously reiterated in this study, this is the only valid definition of *development.* It is erroneous to think that there can be any other.

"A fact of overriding importance," says the President's Report almost at the start of this voluminous study, "is that the cornerstone of economic progress is the development of *resources.* Most developing nations must look to the land and to agriculture for the resources with which to build self-sustaining, productive national economies."[6]

Though not spelled out here, it is easy to see why land and water, that is, agriculture should be given priority over other natural resources—forests and minerals. They are the commonest resources of the developing countries; much of them is already in use, though on a low level of productivity, and can be further developed with relatively small capital to yield quick results; and they will produce more food these countries agonizingly need today.

[5] See "Some Glittering Fallacies" in Chapter 29.

[6] President's Report on *The World Food Crisis,* The White House, Washington, D.C. May 1967, Vol. I, p. 8.

Mineral development, on the other hand, is much more capital-intensive; the foreign exchange and the expertise it needs must frequently come from abroad; once developed, most of the minerals have to be exported since the domestic market for them is small, if not nonexistent; and most of the profits, too, usually flows out of the country. In the end, the game may not prove worth the candle.

In essence, this is what happened in many countries during the colonial era, and this, more than anything else, gave rise to the charge of "exploitation." Few of them, it may be presumed, would like to repeat this experience. In any case, the point to be borne in mind is that the opportunity cost of mineral development in poor nations is very high. In this respect it is no match for agriculture.

*Third*, it follows from what has just been said that these countries must give the foremost priority to agriculture in their development planning and, within the limits of their capacity, back it up with necessary allocations.

"This hard, mundane, and unexciting fact," to quote again from the President's Report, has yet to be accepted as it "must be" by the political authorities in most of these countries. "Indeed, it is not well enough understood by the developed countries which offer foreign assistance."

In explanation of this failure the Report offers the following comments: "Agricultural development has never been a particularly appealing or inspiring national goal; it is politically unglamorous, unrecognized, and unrewarding. It does not raise visions of the 20th century, the age of technological revolution, in the minds of most people."[7]

All this is no doubt true, but it is not the whole truth. Agriculture, for a long time, has been mistakenly sold short on economic grounds, the prevalent view being that it could not pay its way. To compound the problem, there was no way to disprove this thesis as long as agriculture in the developing countries was starved of scientific research and was, perforce, carried out with low-yielding varieties and without any inputs only to give shockingly low yields. The dwarf wheat and rice have, at long last, shaken the deep-rooted bias against agriculture. They have already added some glamour to it. But the process has a long way to go.

And this leads up to what has been the greatest stumbling block so far: the failure to understand what it takes to develop agriculture, a failure that has been shared universally—by the policymakers and the educated elite in the developing countries, by their counterparts in the developed world, and by the aid-giving agencies, both bilateral and multilateral, though not always for the same reasons.

Instead of diagnosing the problems correctly, they have all shown a strong predilection to underrate the payoff from agriculture, to blame the farmers for their supposedly unprogressive outlook and lack of enter-

[7] Ibid., p. 8.

prise, to grapple with symptoms, to apply palliatives in a piecemeal fashion. Altogether, there has been too much beating about the bush from all sides.

Thus, it is not enough to give the topmost priority to land-and-water development and to agriculture. Many developing countries, India in particular, did attach great importance to agriculture in their planning and made liberal allocations, yet reaped mostly frustrations.[8] The priority, in such cases, was right. What went wrong was—to use an overworked but inescapable word—the strategy behind it.

Here, then, is the *fourth* condition the hungry nations must satisfy to grow more food from their domestic resources: They must understand, adopt, and apply the correct strategy to develop their agriculture.

## PACKAGE APPROACH—THE ONLY WAY

Urban planners know that it is easier to plan and build a new city than to renew an old one. A Brazilia or a Chandigarh poses less complex problems to them than rebuilding a war-shattered Warsaw or a quake-devastated Shopje crowded with countless inhabitants. But life does not always offer the choice of a clean-slate start. Quite often one must build on a given foundation, which, moreover, may be in a pretty bad shape, and this complicates matters.

Agriculture, to a large extent, poses a similar problem in the developing countries. It is the oldest art of mankind, and their farmers have cultivated it for centuries. How to write modernism on a slate cluttered with so much primitivity is a uniquely complex task. And it naturally evokes a host of ideas, often unrealistic and contradictory, ranging from the romantic to the ultra-modern, about the new blueprint.

Much of this study has been devoted to an in-depth analysis of these ideas, along with the policies and actions, as they have evolved in India over the past quarter century for tackling the problems of modernizing her agriculture. Though treated here as a case study, India, it must be admitted, is not a typical case. Her problems are vast and extraordinarily complex because of the vastness of the country, the size of her population, the pressure on land, a long history, rigid customs and dogmas, a caste-ridden society, appalling poverty. Yet all this simply means that if the problems of rebuilding agriculture can be solved in India, they can certainly be solved in other countries where they are, quite often, much less intractable.

Besides, the experience of India confirms that there are certain fundamentals which must be followed by *all* developing countries, large or small, if they want to bring their agriculture into the late-twentieth century. It is therefore most desirable, at this point, to bring to a sharper

[8] See Chapter 6, pp. 78-81.

focus the fundamentals which are painfully emerging out of the confused thinking and experimentation extending over two decades or more. They can be best conceived as several *groups of complementarities*, or package programmes, different in size and content, but intimately interlocked:[9]

*Group 1 : Education, research and extension.* This is what one could call the *core-package* of agriculture. Some of the basic research can be carried out elsewhere, but a good deal of it must be done locally.

Not long ago it used to be assumed that agriculture in the developing countries could be quickly improved; that all it needed was a massive transfer of the knowledge already available in the West. Today the world knows better. Since agriculture is a biological industry, much of its technology cannot be transferred across climatic barriers. In this respect it radically differs from industrial technology.

"Plant varieties, animal breeds, and farming practices must be developed for each environment," emphasizes the President's Report. Most developing nations have climates, soils, cropping systems, and harvesting, processing and marketing techniques "vastly different" from those of the United States and Europe. Technology cannot therefore be transferred "without extensive adaptive research. The misconceptions of 'know-how, show-how' must be erased."[10]

Dwarf Mexican wheats, for example, had an unusual breadth of adaptation; according to Dr. Borlaug, some 75 per cent of their original characteristics could be retained in India and Pakistan, but 25 per cent had to be changed through local research to suit local conditions. The IRRI rices needed adaptive research to an even greater extent to enhance their disease resistance and to improve their grain quality to suit local taste. And so it goes endlessly with plant-breeding.

Research in plant protection, farm economics, farm mechanization, to mention some of the more obvious categories, must be conducted locally.

A competent extension arm is needed to carry the research results—improved varieties and better agronomic practices—to the farms, and also to take the farmers' problems back to the research centres for solution.

Clearly, research and extension can be effectively organized only when a country has enough trained scientists at its disposal, whence the crucial importance of agricultural education.

There are still too many people at policymaking levels—in developed and developing countries, and in the UN agencies—who have yet to grasp the significance of this core-package. Yet all they need to do is to look at the medical field: no country can expect to improve the health

---

[9] The items listed in this and the next section have been discussed more fully either in the preceding chapters or in *Reaping the Green Revolution*. The latter also deals with the critical but oft-neglected role of forestry.

[10] Ibid., Vol. I., p. 95.

of its people without doctors, nurses, and para-medical personnel, without diagnostic facilities, hospitals and clinics, without medical education and training. Essentially, agriculture needs the same kind of services to improve the health and nutrition of plants and animals, and to protect them from pests and diseases. There is, however, one major difference—most of these services have to be provided on the farms or in farmers' homes. This underlines the need for a nationwide network of an extension service.

Most developing countries are not in a position to build these facilities and services. It is therefore right here that the aid-givers—UNDP, FAO, USAID and others—must heavily concentrate their attention.

*Group 2 : Farm production package.* This is what the IADP was concerned with in India. Its background, underlying principles, actual progress, and the results achieved have already been discussed, also the reasons why the complementarity principle embracing all inputs—irrigation water, improved seeds, fertilizers, pesticides, farm équipment, and production credit—represented the first big leap from primitive into scientific agriculture.[11]

The package of inputs had, as its complement, a package of services, tailored to meet the specific requirements of each improved or high-yielding variety. The integration of the two is essential to give the full benefit in terms of production. And it has to be backed by a policy of guaranteed minimum prices.[12]

Progress with India's IADP would have been much greater, especially after the introduction of the high-yielding varieties, but for its weaknesses on three critical fronts. Supply of credit was hopelessly inadequate; in addition, it was made needlessly dependent on badly organized cooperatives.[13]

The administrative organization was old-fashioned and weak; it hindered rather than helped the execution of the new programme.[14] Roads and markets are regarded as an indispensable component of agriculture all over the world; they received practically no attention from the IADP authorities.

These were serious omissions, enough to jeopardize the success of the package approach. Developing countries must take special care not to repeat them.

*Group 3 : A larger production package including land reform.* In general, owner-cultivation is essential for rapid adoption of the package

---

[11] In Chapters 11 through 14.
[12] See Chapter 23 on Price Support, also the comments made further below.
[13] See Chapter 27, also Chapter 12.
[14] See Chapter 28.

approach. An owner-farmer has the incentive to learn and apply better techniques since he knows that he would enjoy the fruits of his own labour. It is also easier for an owner-farmer to build up his good name to obtain farm credit. Absentee landlordism undermines the incentive to production; and only too often, the landlord is inclined to exploit not his land, but his tenant. To wean him from past practice is a difficult task which may succeed only in exceptional cases. Moreover, tenant-farmers and sharecroppers not only lack the incentive to change and improve; as non-owners they are mostly unable to obtain the necessary production credit.

When effective land reform—that is, a land-to-the-tiller programme—is coupled with the package programme, the result will invariably be a tremendous plus. In that sense there is a real complementarity between the two.

*Group 4 : Post-harvest package.* Increased production is only one aspect of agriculture. The other is marketing which must go hand in hand with it. Without it all efforts to produce more will be foredoomed to frustration.

To fulfil the marketing function, a developing country needs new markets or market-towns—in most cases a great many of them, located in densely populated rural areas, equipped with warehouses and other essential facilities, including cold storage where feasible, and in any case linked to farmlands with all-weather, functional roads.[15]

There is a vital complementarity between the farm production package and this post-harvest marketing package. Agriculture can really take off only when the two are firmly geared together.

*Group 5 : Poultry, cattle, other livestock and fishery development; also perishable but higher-valued crops, e.g. tubers, vegetables, fruits.* These will diversify farm activities, and will boost farm output and income, once the other four packages are brought into the picture, along with marketing facilities, including warehouses and cold storage.

Here, then, are the widening circles of complementarities. Together, the five groups constitute what may be called the *super-package programme* for agriculture, a programme that every developing nation must set out to design and implement in all its components and with all the essential inputs and services. This is the only way it can modernize its agriculture to unlock the vast wealth that lies buried in it.

## NATIONAL COMPLEMENTARITIES

The concept of complementarity, defined as joint application of all

[15] See Chapter 24 on "Marketing, Transportation, Storage."

elements—inputs and services—under optimum conditions so as to produce the best results through their mutual interaction, can be extended beyond the immediate confines of agriculture to other sectors of a national economy. Here again, one could, broadly speaking, identify five distinct but related areas to which the concept can be applied to maximize benefits:

*Group 1 : Farm and nonfarm sectors.* The two are interdependent in the economic sense. Farm products must be sold largely in the nonfarm sector, the growth of which will determine the size of the market for them. At the same time it constitutes the largest potential market for nonfarm, or industrial, goods. In fact, the fate of most manufacturing industries in a developing country will, for a long time to come, hinge directly on the growth of the farm sector which contains some four-fifths of the population and, therefore, most of their would-be customers.

From this it does not follow that the growth of the one will *automatically* benefit the other. New industries may, for example, create demand for more food; but unless appropriate measures are taken in time to step up food production, the result would be higher food prices, or a demand-push inflation, which has, in fact, been the case in many developing countries. Alternatively, farmers may be able to increase their production to meet the growing demand, yet unwilling to do so in the absence of a remunerative price system or for lack of necessary transportation facilities.

The mutuality of benefits between the two sectors can be best ensured when they are developed in lock-step. And the first and most logical step in that direction is to set up various agri-related industries, such as manufacture of farm inputs, processing of farm produce, their transportation, distribution, and numerous related services. Together, they will build up a large nonfarm, but farm-related sector, which will represent a giant step forward for both sectors and will benefit both.

*Group 2 : Villages, towns, cities, and metropolis.* They constitute what may be called the *spatial complementarities.* The linkages among them, with a great many more new market-towns established in rural areas as hubs of economic activities, must be rated as one of the foremost needs in all developing countries today. They alone can ensure a free flow of goods, services, and ideas throughout the length and breadth of a country, which is indispensable for building up a vigorous economy.

*Group 3 : A package programme to curb population growth.* Dissemination of knowledge, chemicals, and devices now relied upon by the family planning programmes can help only up to a certain point. The programmes will be vastly more effective when they are, in addition, backed by socio-economic measures to provide families with jobs and incomes, health and education services, and some essential amenities.

*Group 4 : Government, public sector, private sector, and cooperatives.* Cooperation based on a rational division of labour among these four principal partners of an economy will greatly help progress in agriculture, also quicken economic development in general. And, in that broad sense, they, too, call for the complementarity approach.

*Group 5 : National and international,* and *developed and underdeveloped.* This is a specially sensitive area if only because the forces of nationalism seldom conform to a rational pattern of behaviour. Nonetheless, a latent mutuality of interest does exist also here. And a wide-ranging give-and-take between the "have" and "have-not" nations will benefit both, and will help raise world prosperity to a higher level.

This global complementarity can, however, be best evoked only after today's "have-not" nations have travelled the "complementarity path" as charted here, far enough to acquire for themselves a good bit of the status of "have" nations. When the hungry nations cease to be plagued by hunger, and are able to produce genuine surpluses for the international market, they will be able to bargain from positions of greater strength. The exchange of goods will then be more meaningful, and the terms of trade, too, will be much less one-sided.

## ROAD TO ABUNDANCE

A few years ago, Orville L. Freeman, Secretary of Agriculture in Kennedy-Johnson Administrations, analyzed the underlying causes of the phenomenon he described as the emergence of North America "as the breadbasket of the world."[16] With a few simple figures he illustrated the dramatic shifts that had taken place in just three decades ending in the mid-sixties (see Table on the next page).

In the late 1930's, only one of the world's seven main regions—Western Europe—was deficit in grain. Its import requirements, totalling 24 million metric tons, were met with supplies drawn from three main sources—Latin America, North America, and Eastern Europe. Australia, too, made a small contribution—of 3 million tons. Asia and Africa were just about self-sufficient (with a very low per capita consumption, of course) and showed a nominal surplus.

Thirty years later, the total deficit soared to 70 million tons, of which Asia alone accounted for 30 million; Eastern Europe, including USSR, lost its surplus position by 1960, and, six years later, it was engulfed in a

[16] "Malthus, Marx and the North American Breadbasket," *Foreign Affairs,* July 1967, pp. 579-93.

## WORLD GRAIN TRADE BY MAJOR GEOGRAPHIC REGIONS

(In million metric tons)

| Region | 1934-38 | 1960 | Estimated 1966 |
|---|---|---|---|
| North America | + 5 | +39 | +60 |
| Latin America | + 9 | 0 | + 2 |
| Western Europe | −24 | −25 | −23 |
| Eastern Europe (inc. USSR) | + 5 | 0 | −14 |
| Africa | + 1 | − 2 | − 3 |
| Asia | + 2 | −16 | −30 |
| Oceania (Australia & N.Z.) | + 3 | + 6 | + 8 |

NOTE: plus = net exports; minus = net imports. Minor imbalances between world imports and exports in a given year may be due to rounding or variations in reporting methods used by various countries.

deficit of 14 million tons; West Europe's position hardly changed over the period.

Even more startling was the jump in the grain exports from North America, which rose from 5 million tons in the late 1930's, to 39 million in 1960 and 60 million in 1966. Australia's share, too, increased in absolute terms, but as a proportion of the total grain trade, it remained stable at around 12 per cent.

Of the total grain exports from North America, the USA alone supplied about three-fourths, half as wheat and half as feedgrains; while Canada accounted for the remaining one-fourth, mostly as wheat. Even more significant is the fact that the United States alone, as Mr. Freeman emphasized, "could export easily the entire sixty million tons yearly if it were to remove all remaining production constraints."

The contrasting trends between the communist, or "socialist," countries and North America in food production are one of the most remarkable phenomena of recent economic history. The reasons are worth noting as they have a special significance for the developing countries now looking around for guideposts to their own future.

The comments Mr. Freeman made on communist economies conform to the views nowadays accepted in knowledgeable quarters. They have one characteristic in common, he underlined: "a poorly performing farm sector. To name a communist country is to name a country having problems with agriculture."

This is no accident. Marxist ideology does not recognize the special problems of agriculture, which was supposed to be just another industry that could be organized on a large scale and run directly under state control. In practice, agriculture was given an inferior status, and was exploited ruthlessly in the interest of industrialization. It was denied the investments and inputs it badly needed for further growth. And it suffered from a chronic lack of incentives.[17]

The decision to organize agriculture "on a large-scale, authoritarian basis has cost the communist countries literally billions of dollars in inefficiently used resources and lost economic growth," concluded Mr. Freeman. This verdict is now well documented by history.

By contrast, productivity of agriculture in the USA has soared to astonishing levels. What are the reasons? Mr. Freeman attributes this to a combination of factors which is of special interest in the present context:

1. The USA has *an excellent piece of real estate.* "Its Midwest, or Corn Belt, is one of the largest areas of fertile, well-watered farmland in the world." Only three other areas could be remotely compared with it in both size and inherent fertility—Northwestern Europe, the pampas of Argentina, and the Gangetic plains of India.

2. The USA has done "an excellent job" of developing the good farmland it was fortunate enough to start with. It has made the inherently fertile soils even more fertile through *scientific soil and water management.*

3. Then there is the *family farm* which, according to Mr. Freeman, is perhaps "the most important single factor" contributing to the USA's unparalleled productivity. As a production unit it is "the most efficient yet devised." In the family farm, the social unit and the production unit are identical; as a result, there is "a stronger link between effort and reward," and this ensures continuous growth in both size and efficiency.

Even where the production units are large, running into several hundred acres with assets exceeding $100,000 in value, they are still family farms and operated mostly by family labour.

4. "Careful delineation" of the *government's role* has been another important factor. It has encouraged private settlement and production, for example, through the Homestead Act of 1862. But it has never been directly engaged in agricultural production. Nor has it involved itself in producing and distributing any of the numerous inputs used in modern agriculture. This has been treated as the domain of private industry.

5. On the other hand, the government did take the responsibility for agricultural *research and education.* Its involvement in research began even before the Civil War. The Land Grant Colleges, established under the Hatch Act of 1887, have been a powerful driving force in agricultural research.

The State Colleges of Agriculture, it may be noted, functioned as

[17] For further comments on this subject see Chapter I, pp. 9-12.

autonomous bodies. They are funded mainly by the state governments and partly by the Federal Government, supplemented—at times quite liberally—with private contributions from industries and foundations to finance individual projects.

6. The government sponsored research only as a tool for development. It therefore recognized the importance of extending new ideas and techniques from the laboratory and experimental plot to the farm, a task for which it assumed full responsibility. This led to the now-famous *Extension Service* of the USA.

The results of research, it should be noted, are made available to the public. For example, when new varieties are developed, they are immediately released, and *private industry* is encouraged to multiply and distribute them.

7. Finally, there is the question of *price support*. This came only in the late 1930's, after considerable struggle, and aided by the great depression. This triggered what is now termed "the modern agricultural revolution." With an assured price level guaranteed by the government, farmers found it safe to make more investments—as working capital in production inputs and as long-term capital in land improvements and other capital assets to build up productive capacity.

Why should price supports be all that important? As Mr. Freeman puts it, three million production units—producing dozens of commodities and scattered throughout the country—were no match for the nonfarm sector in bargaining power. Prices could not be left to the free play of the so-called market forces. For, in that case, the terms of trade would inevitably go against the farmers. Government had to step in on their side to keep an equitable balance in bargaining strength. Without government support and the guarantee of a fair price, farmers could not engage in modern agriculture with expensive inputs.

This rationale of guaranteed price has been widely accepted by other countries. In fact, it is now regarded as the indispensable foundation of modern, input-intensive agriculture. There is no country in the world today which can boast of a progressive, high-productivity agriculture and does not operate price-support programmes for its major crops.

The same remark applies, *mutatis mutandis*, also to the other characteristics of US agriculture as outlined above: family farm operated mainly by family labour; scientific soil and water management; deliberate involvement of government in agricultural education and research with a strong and competent extension service; but an equally deliberate non-involvement in actual farm operations, nor in the production and distribution of agricultural inputs or in processing and handling of farm products; and encouraging, instead, private industry to deal with these functions.

These are the hallmarks of agriculture in the non-communist Western countries today, which have sent their farm productivity soaring to unprecedented levels, and have thereby brought about what may be called the *rich nations' green revolution.*

How far is the above pattern relevant to developing countries? Its basic principles are unquestionably sound, and have a validity that transcends both geography and ideology. Within this framework, however, there will always be need for local adaptation.

The family farm concept, for example, has an overriding importance for developing countries in general. But the optimum farm size, and therefore the degree of mechanization, must vary from one country to another. And heavily-populated countries like India and Pakistan must look not to the USA, nor to West Europe, but to Japan for their model family farm.

A good case can also be made out for corporate or plantation-type farms in sparsely-populated areas of Africa and Latin America in the transitional stage, that is, until modern owner-operated family farm units are solidly established there.

As for agri-related industries, whether for manufacturing inputs or for processing farm produce, countries like India and Pakistan, which can count on an enterprising private sector, would be wise to harness it to the utmost possible extent in the service of agriculture, if only because the government will have its hands more than full with a multiplicity of other agri-related activities. However, not all developing countries may be in such a fortunate position, and some may altogether lack a private sector they could rely upon. In such instances, the government may well have to involve itself actively in input production and distribution, also in processing and marketing operations. A wise government will, however, decide to saddle itself with such activities not in the first, but only in the last resort.

The other elements cited by Mr. Freeman—scientific soil-and-water management aided by government where necessary, government-run education, research and extension, and officially guaranteed price-support programmes—are absolutely essential. Nowhere in the world has agriculture prospered, nor can it prosper, without them.

## BREAKING POVERTY-POPULATION SPIRAL

The real snag with the Freeman package lies somewhere else: it is not enough for developing countries because it does not stretch far enough to encompass the basic needs of their agriculture.

In an industrialized country, farmers have long been familiar with modern inputs; they have also been aware of the importance of using them in combination in order to achieve optimum results. Credit facilities are readily available to them, thanks to a highly-developed banking industry. A modern system of transportation and communication, built largely as a concomitant of industrial development, has brought marketing facilities practically to their doorsteps. The USA has never been plagued by a land reform problem,[18] while West European countries were able to resolve theirs on the eve of their industrial revolution.

In these and other respects, the developing countries have many more gaps to fill, often starting almost from scratch. These deficiencies must be met if they are to develop a modern agriculture. Luckily, they can be met today, but the only way to do so is through the complementarity approach, the super-package programme, as delineated above.

The foremost need of the poor nations today is to turn to resource-based development, with maximum concentration on science-based agriculture backed by credit-based financing, and nationwide physical linkages tying farms and villages to markets, towns, cities, and metropolis.

The green revolution, even in its nascent form, has already given an exhilarating glimpse of the future prospects. What is needed now is to strengthen it with the various components discussed above. This will produce a tremendous multiplier effect. With such a strategy the developing countries can move rapidly towards a high-growth economy, not only to produce enough food to support their expanding masses of people, but also to raise their living standards to more tolerable levels.

Not only that; the psychology of progress it will engender, and the tangible benefits of family-size limitation it will exemplify, should dampen the runaway rates of their population growth. And this should decisively break the grim poverty-population spiral that now threatens their very existence.

---

[18] Except for the limited problem posed by sharecroppers in the South and company farms in the Mid-West.

# CHAPTER 31

# International Aid to Agriculture

## "LATE IN ALL THINGS"

"If you are late in doing one thing in agriculture, you are late in all things," so said Cato in the second century B.C. Time has not detracted from the wisdom of this remark.

Indeed, in this age of explosive population growth, soaring demand for food, the fascinating new vistas opened up by science for agriculture, and the need to apply a good many inputs in well-measured and well-timed doses, the dictum has gained a new validity.

It is the aptest maxim the developing countries could follow today. In fact, one might very well add a corollary to it: "If you are on time in doing all the things needed in agriculture, you will be on time in all other things"—in food supply, industrial development, and economic growth leading to higher employment, incomes, and living standards.

Yet agriculture, in almost all developing countries, is riddled with delays, not in one thing but at all critical points, thereby delaying all else and plunging the masses of their peoples deeper into hunger and poverty.

And here is the crowning paradox: Both developed and developing countries have massively contributed to these delays, and are doing so on a grand scale even today. Aid-givers, aid-receivers, and the UN family as aid-administrators—all have been responsible, however inadvertently, for holding back agriculture in the underdeveloped world and, therefore, its economic development which they have been so anxious to promote.

## DISENCHANTMENT WITH AID

Foreign aid has become the greatest hit-or-miss affair of the century—with far fewer hits than misses.[1] Its apologists have been quick to argue that since this is a novel venture attempted on a global scale, an initial period of trial and error was unavoidable; that one had to learn from experience before one could confidently design a dependable blueprint for development.

This can be accepted as an extenuating factor, but only up to a certain point. For, it is taking an unconscionably long time to wake up to the realization that the wealth of the underdeveloped nations consists of their natural resources; that the food needed for their undernourished peoples must come from their own land—that is, from their agriculture; that there can be no future for their agriculture until modern science—genetics to improve varieties and chemicals to feed and protect plants—is applied to it systematically the same way it has been applied to temperate-zone agriculture.

The failure to grasp these truths appears all the more surprising in retrospect. That hunger is widely prevalent in the developing nations has long been perfectly clear. And it was highlighted by Boyd-Orr's famous statement of 1950 quoted in the previous chapter—that malnutrition and actual hunger was the lot of two-thirds of mankind.

What could, then, be more urgent for foreign aid programmes established to improve the economic conditions of the poor nations than to concentrate effort, first and foremost, to produce more food, the first need of every human being, and thereby to reduce the incidence of hunger. Instead, they debated priorities for years in a scholarly fashion —until the commonsense-dictated priorities were sufficiently obscured.

Then there was the community development programme which, for several years, was believed to be the panacea for rural ailments. Its champions solemnly propounded the thesis that the key to progress lay in discovering the "felt needs" of the people at a time when countless millions felt, day after day, the pangs of hunger, often before their very eyes, when food was most obviously their most acutely felt need.

Yet, ironically, the right ideas were already there, carefully worked out and sufficiently field-tested. By early 1950's, the experiment pioneered by the Rockefeller Foundation in Mexico had begun to make its impact. The pattern evolved there could, in its fundamentals, be copied and applied to other countries to produce similar results.[2]

The disenchantment about foreign aid is now widespread, though the

[1] Only some brief reflections are made here since the writer has analyzed the issues in: *United Nations in Economic Development—Need for a New Strategy,* op. cit.

[2] See Chapter 3, pp. 31-37, and Chapter 4, pp. 62-64.

reasons advanced vary widely. The major donors are critical mainly on political-budgetary grounds. It is hard for their leaders to be generous with aid when countries supposed to have been liberally aided appear to be inadequately friendly, or when the donor nations are themselves pruning essential social expenditures to balance their own budgets. Some argue that the aid dollars, as now administered, are not remotely producing the benefits they could in the receiving countries.

The believers in foreign aid see the situation differently. In their view what is really wrong with it today is the inadequacy of the quantum of aid. They fervently plead for larger aid to achieve speedier growth in the developing countries. Some of them have eloquently advocated a sizable transfer of wealth from the rich to the poor nations. What they forget is that altruism has to be tempered by realism; that, in the present mood of the major donors, their pleadings can fall only on deaf ears. Moreover, it is not simply a question of the quantum of aid. Quality matters too, and it matters a great deal more than is commonly realized.

Foreign aid proper, that is, official development assistance (ODA) has stagnated around $6.5 billion since the mid-sixties; in real terms, it has actually been declining. The International Development Strategy outlined for the Second UN Development Decade (i.e., the 1970's) wants "a major part" of the assistance flows to be provided as ODA, which is offered on concessional terms and directly aims at promoting economic and social development of the recipient countries. It has also laid down a target for ODA—each donor country should "progressively increase" it and "exert its best efforts to reach a minimum net amount of 0.7 cent cent of its GNP at market prices" by 1975.

Several donor countries, it should be added, declined to accept any quantitative target for the ODA or a definite deadline by which it should be reached. The total GNP of the 16 DAC Member countries has been on the increase, while ODA, expressed as a percentage of this total, has been steadily declining since the mid-sixties. In 1970, it worked out to 0.34 per cent, or about one-half of the target for the Second Development Decade. The position has not much changed since then. These facts have aroused considerable gloom among the friends of the poor nations.

Meanwhile, another school of critics has been taking a significantly different line. They have begun to question the achievements of foreign aid. Whatever growth it has been able to produce, they argue, has benefited only the elite sections of the population; the masses of people had little or no share in it; as a result, unemployment is rapidly rising among them, and with it poverty, despair, and the threat of social disturbances.

Few will challenge these facts today—they are writ large all over the underdeveloped world. Nonetheless, one must be careful not to draw hasty conclusions from them, as some have been prone to do. Nothing is wrong with aid or growth *per se*, though both can easily go wrong.

Foreign aid, it cannot be stressed too strongly, cuts both ways. If planned imaginatively, it can greatly stimulate progress in a developing country; but it can also produce the opposite effect, if dumped haphazardly. Aid can hurt; and, indeed, it has done so in too many cases.

Broadly speaking, foreign programmes have suffered from three major weaknesses. First, they were established with one sole object in view—to promote the development of the world's poor nations. But soon they perceptibly strayed away from their declared goal. For example, the US aid programme, though born of a humanitarian impulse, was encumbered with other motives—commercial, ideological, and military. It grew rapidly in size and ran into billions of dollars, but its aid content was overwhelmed by the non-aid components, until the very word aid became largely a misnomer. Foreign aid suffered because it was packaged with elements totally "foreign" to it to serve contradictory ends.

The UN programmes were distracted by their special brand of politics, namely, of the specialized agencies and their secretariats.

Second, all aid programmes were insufficiently oriented towards the physical resources of the poor nations, especially their land and agriculture. The importance of this was not understood well enough by the aid-givers and aid-administrators, as was underscored in the President's Report.[3]

And, finally, even the limited attention given to land and agriculture was faulted by a failure to understand their specific needs, and therefore of the measures required to produce concrete results.

These factors are enough to explain why the performance of the aid programmes has fallen woefully short of expectations, also of their true potential. Stagnation in foreign aid is not its worst feature. What really matters is not how much aid, but what kind of aid.

## UNDP : PREINVESTMENT FAD

History has placed a unique responsibility on the United Nations and its agencies to help the world's poor nations out of their economic backwardness. It also provided a great opportunity to the UN family—by effectively serving such a cause it could strengthen its own foundations and attain an unchallengeable position of prestige and influence in the world. That was not to be. To the misfortune of all, it has proved itself unequal to this task.

Its performance so far has been outstandingly poor, especially in terms of missed opportunities and lost growth. This, in the final analysis, has to

---

[3] See the quotations given in the preceding Chapter, pp. 501 and 502.

be attributed to two fundamental causes: the fragmented structure of the UN family, and its misguided approach to the tasks of development.

What the developing nations sorely needed from the UN was imaginative leadership—to enlighten them about their priorities, to explain to them how their limited resources could be best utilized to serve their most pressing needs, and to help them with technical assistance and essential supplies from its own programmes. The UN family, as a conglomerate of specialized agencies, has been unable to fulfil this function.

Instead of dealing exclusively with the interests of the developing countries, it has been largely concerned with the interests of the Agencies and how to ensure "distributive justice" among themselves. Instead of the needs and potentialities of these countries dictating the programme priorities, these have been frequently tailored to the special interests of the Specialized Agencies. Instead of providing a unified leadership to them, the UN has usually spoken to them in a babel of contradictory voices. And so instead of elucidating their priorities, it has further obfuscated them.

To quote the words the writer has used elsewhere to sum up this perplexing situation: "The UN family was expected to function as a catalytic agent in the developing countries; instead, it has managed to catalyze itself." This has been, and continues to be, its "worst predicament."[4]

The vision of development has been mystified by another factor—the grossly exaggerated role assigned to preinvestment study. Ironically, the United Nations stumbled into it as a purely political compromise after almost a decade-long debate. But having done so, it proceeded to extol it as if it represented the best answer to the needs of the developing countries! When the SUNFED school—that is, the countries which had pleaded year after year for the establishment of a Special United Nations Fund for Economic Development—was about to carry the day with majority support despite the persistent opposition of the main donor countries, it was agreed upon, as a compromise between the two viewpoints, to set up a Special Fund as a separate programme, but to restrict it solely to the pre-investment phase of development.

Once established, the Fund was placed in charge of an outstanding personality, whose missionary zeal, coupled with superb salesmanship, soon built it up to an impressive level. As a result, the underdeveloped world has been covered with some 1200 pre-investment projects. The result has been tragic, although those directly involved in this numbers game are apparently unable to understand its implications.

It is one thing to carry out geological prospecting to explore mineral deposits or to survey forests to make inventories of the stands, and to prepare feasibility studies for their utilization, although—even here—

[4] In his UN study, ibid., p. 305. The study discusses at length the points touched upon in this section.

one must be careful not to concentrate too much attention on these studies and too little on their actual execution. With land and water it is an entirely different matter. What is needed here is not the kind of surveys and studies undertaken by the Special Fund, barring some very special situations. The greatest need in this case is *actual development, or better utilization of these two vital resources, to build up a vastly more productive agriculture.*

A few years ago, Sir Robert Jackson, in his so-called Capacity Study,[5] gave a painstakingly elaborate analysis of the UNDP's organizational structure and methods of operations. The UNDP "Machine," as he then put it, had "a marked identity of its own," and it had acquired "great power"; nor did it lack intelligent and capable officials. But it was so organized that managerial direction was "impossible."

The machine as a whole, he concluded, had become "unmanageable in the strictest use of the word"; it was becoming "slower and more unwieldy, like some prehistoric monster." For many years he had looked for the "brain" which guided its policies and operations. His search had been "in vain."[6]

To remedy this deficiency Sir Robert made wide-ranging recommendations, mostly intended to centralize the decision-making responsibilities at the UNDP headquarters, to expand its establishment with the addition of several new divisions, to curtail the autonomy of the Agencies, to strengthen the position of the Resident Representatives, and to unify in their hands the responsibility for field operations.

The measures he proposed were generally in the right direction. But they were also open to some serious questions. The degree of centralization envisaged in the study at the expense of the Agencies did not, and could not, prove feasible. The so-called UNDP machine was anything but a machine; it consisted of a family of living organizations; the family members did not relish the prospect of being bypassed under the reorganization scheme. And, predictably enough, they asserted their rights.

Moreover, they had enough logic on their side. After all, they had been solemnly established as Specialized Agencies of the United Nations, with their separate charters and with clear-cut responsibilities which they could not ignore. Besides, over the years they had built up their organizations with high-grade experts to do their jobs. Not to make use of these experts and to duplicate them at UNDP headquarters would be both senseless and wasteful.

If the UNDP-Agency relationship proposed in the study left much to be desired, so also did the headquarters-field relations it contemplated. Here again, the study revealed a strong bias for over-centralization. It is

[5] *A Study of the Capacity of the United Nations Development System*, United Nations, Geneva, 1969.
[6] Ibid., Vol. 1, pp. (iii), 13, 17.

absolutely essential to build up the Resident Representatives, if the UNDP is to function effectively; no knowledgeable person will disagree on this point. But this buildup must be *vis-à-vis* not only the Agencies, but also the UNDP headquarters. The delegation of responsibilities from the UNDP to its field representatives still remains woefully inadequate.[7]

The Capacity Study was off the mark in an even more fundamental sense. It failed to see how the UNDP had been conceptually incapacitated. *Preinvestment is not development*; in most cases it does not therefore meet the most urgent needs of the developing nations.

The "dinosaur" did not change its innate characteristics. The attempt to transplant a brain on it created, for a while, a good deal of motion and commotion. The end-result, however, has been to add to it even more bulk, not brain.

## FAO : KEYS TO NON-SUCCESS

FAO, as a participating organization of the UNDP, had its full share of the preinvestment extravaganza. And to this it has added a few foibles of its own.

Should FAO engage in research? The answer has been consistently in the negative. The general view was that research was an academic affair, and therefore a matter for universities, not for an action agency like FAO.

Some even went the length of saying that the FAO constitution did not envisage research as a function of the agency. This is simply not true; the Constitution, in Article 2, enjoins that the Organization "shall promote," and, where appropriate, "shall recommend" national and international action with respect to "scientific, technological, social and economic research relating to nutrition, food and agriculture." The same Article also urges similar action for improvement of education and administration relating to nutrition, food, and agriculture; the conservation of natural resources and the adoption of improved methods of agricultural production; the processing, marketing and distribution of food and agricultural products; and the adoption of policies for providing adequate agricultural credit.

The terms of reference could hardly be more comprehensive. Yet in practice the agency has evinced an aversion to research, even though this is the soul of modern agriculture. On this point the President's Report is emphatic: "Major attention must be directed to a wide range of

[7] The writer has discussed the question of proper UNDP-Agency relations and the role of the Resident Representatives in Chapters 18 and 19 of his UN study, op. cit.

research on problems of crops and soils of the developing nations and highest priority needs to be given to this objective by both the developed nations helping with technical assistance and the recipient countries."[8]

Lack of emphasis on research in FAO's programmes is a major default, equivalent to *Hamlet* without the Prince. Of late, there has been a slight shift in its policy; it has begun to participate in regional agricultural research institutes with other organizations (see below). This is welcome, but not remotely enough if FAO is to fulfil its mission worthily in a hunger-ridden world.

Must FAO function in a purely advisory capacity? Strange as it may seem, a kind of active passivity has long been a dominant feature of the UN programmes.[9] This thesis: the government requests, the Agency complies if funds permit, smacks of a cheap alibi unbecoming of a great organization. Surely, it is FAO's business, as of other UN bodies, to explain, to enlighten, and to persuade the recipient governments to take urgently-needed steps to promote their development and general well-being.

On top of all this, the Agency suffers from another grave shortcoming —excessive "compartmentalism" within its own organization. If the UNDP is hamstrung because of the exaggerated autonomy of the Specialized Agencies, an Agency like FAO is hampered by the preoccupation of its various departments to grind their own specialties. Its implications are most unfortunate. A common failing of the developing countries is that they approach their agricultural problems in a piecemeal fashion; how to wean them from this practice and persuade them to adopt the package approach instead is a task of overriding importance. Yet FAO, as it is now structured, is unable to help them in this matter. On the contrary, with its own "unpackaged" approach, it has further reinforced their failing.

Given these facts, it is small wonder that FAO's impact so far should have been minimal. This is all the more regrettable because it certainly has assembled a large number of highly qualified experts, many of whom have been unwittingly turned into paper-processing bureaucrats.

As a source of basic data on world agriculture, FAO now occupies a position of unchallenged supremacy; indeed, it has grown into *the* international centre of information on all major aspects of agriculture, fisheries, forestry, and nutrition, and supplies statistics on production, trade, and consumption of hundreds of commodities, compiled on a worldwide basis. It also provides a valuable meeting ground for policymakers, planners, and scientists from all over the world. But as an action agency for

[8] President's Report, loc. cit., Vol. I, p. 26.
[9] This is typified in the story, which is now part of FAO folklore, of the non-performing bull because it had been assigned only an advisory role.

agricultural development it remains deplorably weak for reasons that are both conceptual and organizational.

Today, FAO accounts for the lion's share of the UNDP allocations, amounting to some 43 per cent. This fact is often cited as a measure of their concern for the world food problem and of their willingness to make the maximum contribution towards its solution. But the tragedy is that so much resources and good intentions should continue to yield so little tangible results, especially in terms of increased production.

Public relations men will no doubt seek to refute the suggestion with success stories, such as the sheep-and-wool project in India, poultry development in India and other countries, promotion of pond fish culture in Nepal, fishing in the swamps of Northern Nigeria, increased sea-fish catches in several instances, introduction of light Japanese ploughs, called "Takakita," at a small cost in Chile to help Mapuche Indians to improve their cultivation of potatoes and other crops. The surprising thing about such success stories is not that they do exist, but that they are so few and far beween. Even those eager to blow FAO's trumpet are constantly embarrassed by their paucity.

And worst of all, success stories are virtually nonexistent where they matter most—in the production of foodgrains which constitutes the foundation of a prosperous agriculture, including livestock development.

When Dr. Norman E. Borlaug was awarded the Nobel Peace Prize, in October 1970, the UNDP and FAO publicized, with evident pride, their association with the Nobel Laureate. Dwarf wheats evolved by him were being used in UNDP-assisted wheat improvement projects in Latin America and the Middle East; FAO-executed projects provided him with data on the performance of these varieties under different local conditions; the International Maize and Wheat Centre (CIMMYT) in Mexico, supported by the Rockefeller and Ford Foundations and USAID, was also helped by the UNDP and the Inter-American Development Bank; and many young scientists, in particular from the Middle East, had attended courses at the Centre on UNDP fellowships.

The comments reflect exemplary modesty; they are also painfully revealing. It did not strike FAO in all these years that what Dr. Borlaug and his colleagues had achieved in Mexico under the leadership of the Rockefeller Foundation could be repeated in other countries; that the model they had built here had, in its essentials, a validity for the entire underdeveloped world; that there could be no greater and more pressing task today than to transplant it in other developing countries; that the initiative for doing so could come most appropriately from FAO; and that, until it wakes up to these possibilities and grabs the leadership role to realize them, it will fail to measure up to its historic responsibilities in the struggle to win the food-population race.

The Indicative World Plan (IWP), drawn up by FAO in the late sixties,[10] is a product of imagination mingled with misconceptions. And, in that sense, it is, once again, indicative of its chronic deficiencies.

By 1985, the IWP estimates, food demand in the developing countries as a whole will be about 140 per cent above the level of 1962 (the base year); at least two-thirds will be due to population growth, and one-third to rising incomes. Without a faster increase in food production, developing countries will be faced with mounting outlays on food imports —by 1985, the amount will soar to $40 billion at constant prices, compared with $3 billion in 1962. A more rapid rise in food production within the developing countries for their own consumption was imperative to avoid such overwhelming dependence on high-income countries. The Plan tried to estimate, in considerable detail, the future requirements of food in different categories, also of the various inputs which would be needed for the additional production.

The emphasis, it will be noticed, is now laid on the need to produce, and retain, more food within the developing countries. This is a welcome departure from the earlier attempts simply to balance demand for food with its supply on a global basis.

The most worrisome question the IWP is likely to provoke is: What role does FAO assign to itself, and what strategy will it follow, to increase food production rapidly within the developing countries? The Plan sheds little light on this point.

Meanwhile, FAO has decided to concentrate its efforts primarily on five key areas: reduction of waste, closing the protein gap, promotion of high-yielding cereal varieties, earning and saving foreign exchange, and utilization of human resources. Curiously enough, it calls them "five keys to development,"[11] a label that clearly reflects a lack of understanding of the problems involved and of the kind of action needed to solve them.

For the fact is that FAO's five keys are not keys; they are more in the nature of symptoms, the offshoots of a scienceless, anaemic agriculture. The real key is what in the preceding chapter has been called the "core-package" comprising research, education, and extension. This is the key that unlocked the green revolution in Mexico. And this is the crucial key that FAO must set out to forge and multiply jointly with the developing countries if it wants to play its own part in realizing the IWP goals.

A MOMENTOUS STEP

What has been said above clearly shows how progress is still hampered by confused thinking. Nevertheless, there are solid reasons for hope as

---

[10] *Provisional Indicative World Plan for Agricultural Development*, 2 Vols, FAO, Rome, 1969.

[11] *Five Keys to Development*, FAO, Rome, 1970.

well. The most important of them is the fact that scientific research in tropical agriculture is now visibly gaining in momentum. What began in Mexico, some thirty years ago, with corn and wheat has widened to embrace other regions and virtually all major tropical crops.

The Rockefeller Foundation-Mexico Programme led to the establishment of the International Maize and Wheat Improvement Centre, or CIMMYT, as seen earlier.[12] This was followed by the International Rice Research Institute (IRRI), established at Los Boños, Philippines in 1961 to deal with the most important foodgrain of Asia.[13]

The green revolution, as seen in Chapters 3-4, is essentially an offspring of the research pioneered at these two institutes. The spectacular results they achieved led to the establishment of three other regional research centres in fairly quick succession: the International Institute of Tropical Agriculture, called CIAT from its Spanish title, at Cali, Colombia to deal with forage and livestock problems in the humid tropics; IITA at Ibadan, Nigeria to concentrate on cultivated crops of the humid tropics, especially cassava; and the International Potato Centre in Peru to deal with this important tuber crop.

To these has just been added a sixth regional institute—the International Crops Research Institute for the Semi-Arid Tropics, or ICRISAT to use its acronym. Established near Hyderabad, India in May 1972, it will serve as the world centre for improvement of sorghum (jowar), pearl millet (bajra), pigeon peas (arhar or red gram), and chick peas (chana, also called Bengal gram). A fair amount of work has already been done in India on the first two; the new Institute will not only continue this work, but will also deal with their problems much more comprehensively.[14] Its initial programme will, of course, be extended as and when deemed advisable.

The funding of these institutes has broadened over the years. The earlier initiatives came from the Rockefeller and Ford Foundations, and later they were joined by the USA through USAID. Canada, too, stepped in with support in some instances. Thus IITA was established at Ibadan, in April 1970, with backing from the two Foundations and the United States and Canadian Governments.

An even more significant move was the creation of an international Consultative Group on International Agricultural Research (ICGIAR), which was announced on 6 December, 1971. It was the culmination of an idea which was stimulated by the Ford and Rockefeller Foundations and was readily supported by the World Bank. The declared objective of

[12] In Chapter 3, pp. 31-37.

[13] See Chapter 3, pp. 37-40.

[14] To ensure quick progress in the immediate future, it is essential to make full use of the extensive knowledge already accumulated. Plant-breeders should therefore concentrate their effort largely on *adaptive* research to start with, as underscored in the President's Report (loc. cit., Vol. II, pp. 215-19).

this newly-created body is to promote research programmes designed to raise the quantity and quality of food production in the developing countries of Asia, Africa, and Latin America.

As for finance, it was decided to make about $15 million available for 1972. The funds were intended to support the five international research centres which were then in existence. It was also agreed to set up two major new programmes, in India and Africa respectively. Thereafter, it took just about six months to establish ICRISAT, the first to be born under the new international initiative sponsored by the World Bank.

The composition of the Consultative Group has some unusual features. It consists of 27 members: the Rockefeller, Ford and Kellogg Foundations, the pioneers of the movement for scientific research in tropical agriculture, and advocates of a more broadbased international initiative; three bodies of the UN system—FAO, the UNDP, and the World Bank—which co-sponsored the proposal; 12 donor governments;[15] three regional banks—for Africa, Asia, and Latin America respectively; International Development Research Centre, Canada; and representatives of five major developing regions on a rotational basis.

In addition, a Technical Advisory Committee consisting of 12 international experts has been set up to advise the Group on research programmes.

The historic importance of this new move cannot be overstressed. For, by far the most important single factor that has held back food production and agricultural development in the poor countries, and thereby also their economies, is the lack of scientific research to improve tropical crops, in terms of both yield-capability and quality. Dwarf wheat and rice have already demonstrated what research can do, also how much potential wealth can be lost if there is no research. The recent actions are so heartening because they will, at long last, fill the greatest, and also the most crucial, void in tropical agriculture.

The ICGIAR carries with it the best possible guarantee that, henceforward, research to improve tropical crops and to develop new high-yielding varieties will receive high priority; that the regional research institutes will be adequately funded; and that, in addition, they will be backed by high-level scientific experts. The string of six international research institutes now in existence should cover most of the major tropical crops, and new programmes will, no doubt, be added to them as and when deemed necessary.[16]

[15] They are the governments of Belgium, Canada, Denmark, France, the Federal Republic of Germany, Japan, the Netherlands, Norway, Sweden, Switzerland, the UK, and the USA.

[16] In fact, a horticultural research centre, with some international support but outside the ICGIAR programmes, has recently been established in Taiwan to breed improved varieties of vegetables. It is headed by Dr. Robert Chandler Jr., the first IIRI Director.

More high-yielding varieties of crops, it may now be assumed, will flow out of these research centres. How far will the developing countries be able to capitalize on them? Clearly, they will have to adapt the new varieties to local conditions; and, in addition, they will have to build up competent extension services. For this they will, at least initially, need the kind of leadership and teamwork that was provided to Mexico by the Rockefeller Foundation.

And beyond that, they will have to attend to a number of other complementarities, as spelled out in the preceding chapter. Only then can they expect to reap full benefits from the high-yielding varieties. This is a truly gigantic task to which all concerned must address themselves.

## IBRD AID TO AGRICULTURE

In the last few years, the World Bank, under the dynamic leadership of its President, Robert S. McNamara, has greatly expanded its activities—in terms of both money and functions. Education, population, and health have been brought within its ambit because of their direct bearing on economic development; agriculture, with genetic research for crop improvement as seen above, and rural development are receiving greater attention; loans for road construction and transportation in general have been substantially stepped up. These are all encouraging signs.

Yet there are several snags. In spite of its new dynamism, the Bank's programme still contains critical gaps, and it is these gaps which will retard future progress. They can be remedied only when the package concept discussed earlier is adopted and applied *in toto* to agriculture and agri-related activities.

Can the Bank, for example, take the leadership, maybe jointly with the UNDP-FAO, to help build up national extension services staffed with trained people? This will call for an enormous expansion of agricultural education. But there is no escape from it. Every developing country must be equipped sooner or later—and the sooner, the better—with its own extension service to cash in on the results of production-oriented crop research which the Bank has now decided to promote jointly with others through the newly-created International Group. If the task is inescapable, it will also be extraordinarily rewarding.[17]

Another area where the Bank's initiative, again with possible UNDP-FAO cooperation, could make a tremendous impact is development of market-towns in selected areas, each serving a cluster of villages and, therefore, linked to them with all-weather rural roads. Markets and village-to-market roads represent one of the foremost needs in every

[17] For the role agricultural extension service must play in developing countries, see Chapter 22.

developing country. Without them, its agriculture—and therefore its economy—will never get very far.[18]

In India, for example, the Bank has helped finance hundreds of miles of expensive highways. The most striking feature that hits one's eyes while driving through them is the paucity of traffic. Some are therefore inclined to view these investments as premature, if not uneconomic. Yet the fact is that the highways are starved of traffic because they are not supported by feeder roads. What is really needed is to link them with fine-mesh rural roads, especially in densely populated areas, to generate traffic which will boost the payoff from the investments made in highway construction.

The combination of these two packages—research-extension-education and roads-markets-transportation—will revolutionizee the countryside. And together they will do far more to stimulate healthy economic growth in the immediate future than any other strategy one could contemplate.

## US AID—AN ANGUISHED QUERY

The US aid programme has, for some time, turned its attention increasingly to agriculture. The valuable assistance it has rendered to India, especially to establish agricultural universities, has been described earlier (Chapter 22). After the arrival of dwarf wheat and rice, the Agency further increased its support to agriculture. Nevertheless, a great deal more remains to be done. A comparison of the aid programmes now in operation and of the concentric circles of complementarities described earlier will indicate what further actions are required, and where.

Agricultural development, it cannot be stressed too often nor too strongly, depends on a whole series of elements that are closely interlinked. It is a kind of seamless web; each action meshes into and reinforces the rest.

In an address delivered in New York, in October 1972, Mr. Pedro G. Beltran, former Prime Minister of Peru, made some pointed comments on this subject. How could the USA, he wondered, wage an endless war in a remote corner of Asia and ignore the problems of "the restless peoples right near you." Yet he did not plead for any grandiose schemes, not even for a revival of the Alliance for Progress. All he asked for was a systematic extension to other countries of Latin America of the methods for boosting food production which had proved spectacularly successful in Mexico.

What could be more sensible for foreign aid administrators than to heed this counsel? And what could be more exciting, and more reward-

---

[18] For the vital importance of rural roads and market-towns, see the relevant sections in Chapter 24.

ing, for them today than to spread the green revolution throughout the underdeveloped world? This does not call for a multi-billion dollar enterprise; even a slimmer programme, if well-directed, can make a vastly greater impact in terms of concrete results. The real problem of foreign aid is not one of funds. The problem, to put it bluntly, is now to depoliticize, and to rehumanize, it so as to serve the ideals for which it was established.

# CHAPTER 32

# Towards New Horizons

## THE MASTER-KEY : SELF-HELP

The situation in the developing countries today is highly paradoxical. It is both exciting and exasperating.

Dwarf wheat and rice have given them enough glimpses into a future brimming with abudance. By now, they know very well that before long more of them, and like them, will flow out of the scientists' laboratories. The hopes are running high.

Yet they are frustrated, at too many points, in their attempts to exploit the new opportunities; only a tiny section of their farmers has so far been able to benefit from them. The great majority are still marking time, unable to join the fortunate few for lack of inputs and physical facilities.

Can the developing countries overcome the obstacles that stand in the way, step up the adoption rate of the new varieties, accelerate their progress? This is the agonizing question they are wrestling with today. And to their misfortune, the light they receive from external sources, such as the UNDP, FAO, IBRD, and USAID, to guide them through their troubles is too dim and diffused, often distorted. The leadership they are themselves able to produce at home is no more clear-sighted, and suffers from its own brand of myopia.

This is the cruel dilemma in today's world. But it must be broken, and, as things now stand, it can be broken only by the developing nations themselves. After all, it is their future that is at stake; outside effort, even at its best, can modestly supplement their own—aid can only be an aid, and no more.

But there is a deeper reason why they must rely primarily on themselves, and treat self-help as the ultimate master-key to their destiny.

67

"Biological engineering," which evolved in the North and remained confined to it for a long time, imperceptibly crossed over to Mexico some thirty years ago. And from there it spread, especially since the early sixties, over other regions of the South, unleashing in its wake a revolution in tropical agriculture.

Now, the progenies of biological engineering must be suitably accommodated within each environment if they are to produce the wealth they have been designed for. Hence the need for extensive socio-economic engineering within each developing country.[1] This is a prodigious task, often intricate because it is laden with local political and sociological overtones, and so it can be effectively tackled only by each country acting individually on its own behalf. All that outsiders can do is to enunciate the basic principles, clarify views and ideas, pinpoint the specific requirements, and provide occasional support at key points.

An analogy may be useful. When the steam engine first arrived some two centuries ago, countries of West Europe got busy reshaping their physical and social environments to meet the needs of the new invention in order to exploit its full wealth-producing potential. And, as factories sprang up in different places, every country was provided with an increasingly dense network of rural-urban linkages to facilitate nation-wide exchange of goods and services.

Just as the mechanical inventions of the eighteenth century ushered in the industrial revolution in the West, today's biological inventions have set the stage for an agricultural revolution in the underdeveloped world. And just like the former, the miracle rice and wheat, too, require a radical redesign of the rural landscape. In fact, the need for such redesigning is, if anything, even greater in this case. For, the production units to cash in on their high yield-potential are the farms which, unlike factories, are scattered far and wide, and so they need a vaster network of countrywide transport linkages interspersed with strings of suitably located market-towns.

This is the most fundamental task facing the developing countries today. Will they be able to tackle it effectively? On the answer will depend their ability to harness the sturdy dwarfs to ride to prosperity.

## QUICKENING THE PACE

Some newly-independent nations have treated the West to strident denunciations of neo-colonialism. The truth is that, in a broad sense, we are all captives of the past, with much of our thinking still attuned to a world that has died in this scientific age; that we carry with us, often

---

[1] See Chapter 4, pp. 64-66, Chapters 16 and 20 through 24. Much of *Reaping the Green Revolution* has been devoted to the same theme.

subconsciously and in varying forms and degrees, some vestiges of the colonial era.

Perhaps the most telling evidence of this fact is currently provided by the superpower game plan that has brazenly revived in-camera diplomacy —nineteenth-century style—to pursue peace in our compact world in this nuclear age.

Nevertheless, the most persistent practitioners of neo-colonialism, strange as it may sound, are the developing nations themselves. They have liberated their countries, but not their minds. Their economic policies, in particular, are geared to assumptions that hark back to a bygone age and fly in the face of contemporary realities. To take the most conspicuous examples:

They have kept the old administrative system virtually intact with its emphasis not on development but on law and order, not on progress but on the status quo. They have conspicuously failed to utilize the available talent and to release the energies of the people.

They have kept feudalism very much alive with all its attendant ills. And even when they have vociferously talked of land reform, in practice they have hardly touched the fringe of an exploitative status quo.

They have clung to the old go-slow or do-little policy for social services. They have shown no burning concern for education and have readily tolerated mass illiteracy. They have cared little to provide their masses with minimum health care.

They neglect land and water almost as callously as was the case in the colonial days. They still fail to see that these resources constitute the very foundation of their economic life.

They still believe that the best economic growth can be achieved only by setting up industries. They are unable to see that, in today's changed conditions, the only sound strategy is to move from agriculture to industries, and not the other way round. "Even the highest towers begin from the ground," says a Chinese proverb. Even the strongest economies in today's underdeveloped world must begin from the farms.

They still cling to the old concept of treasury finance, and are unable to distinguish, in their budgets, between consumption expenditure and production credit. For example, a dollar invested in the cultivation of dwarf wheat and rice would give a gross return anywhere from five to ten dollars in about four months. Even then, they lack the courage to create credit for crop loans to reap a many times richer harvest!

They grudge a remunerative price to the farmers, and fail to see that no farmer, any more than a manufacturer, can work to earn a loss, that he must be assured of a good profit margin if he is to exert himself to maximize production. Instead, they show a chronic tendency to keep down farm prices in the interest of urban consumers. They are unable to see the elementary fact that depressed farm prices mean not only less food, but also depressed farm incomes and, therefore, truncated markets for consumer goods.

This leads up to what has been the worst feature of neo-colonialism in the ex-colonial countries. In each of them a small elite group inherited the political power after independence; the economic power automatically shifted to the few urban centres, mostly port-cities that had sprung up in the colonial days. And since these cities were also the normal habitats of the ruling elite, they were fully assured of the most-favoured economic treatment.

The point not to be missed is this: Independence changed little in the status of the rural areas; they became *de facto* colonies of the urban centres. And, as in the colonial days, the terms of trade were skewed, often cold-bloodedly, against the farmers; public policy, in general, was swayed primarily to subserve urban-cum-industrial interests.

All this could happen the more easily because rural areas continued to remain isolated, more or less as before, without the essential village-market-town-cities linkages.

Urban prosperity has no doubt benefited rural areas, but its extent should not be exaggerated. The trickle-down effect has been minimal; it did not, and could not, penetrate very far.

Of late, under the impact of the green revolution, things have begun to change in some countries. For example, in several instances price-support policies have been adopted, however hesitantly, and farm credit, too, is expanding, however slowly. This precisely leads to what is the heart of the matter: Should one wait for changes to occur only when they are compulsively brought about by the dynamics of the green revolution, which would mean delays, attrition, and tension? Or, should one, using forethought and foresight, bring about those changes which are imperative in order to spread the green revolution rapidly, yet in an orderly fashion? To put these questions is also to answer them.

The tasks, then, are clear for the developing countries. They must free themselves from the economic anachronisms that are dogging them in a radically changed world. They must update their thinking, revamp their leadership, and remould their policies in order to create systematically the conditions necessary to make a resounding success of the green revolution.

And once they have taken action on such lines, they will also know how to make the most out of international aid programmes. They must learn to dictate to them the kind of assistance their programmes should furnish, and to reject outright what does not fit in with their priority needs and would divert their attention away from them.

This may look like a topsy-turvy relationship between the aid-givers and the aid-receivers; for the aid programmes were supposed to help the developing countries help themselves. Yet in today's conditions this is the only rational line the recipient countries can take. Sometimes even the masters have to be taught. The restless farmers of India, having seen the performance of the dwarfs, are now forcing the hands of the planners and policymakers to give them the assistance they urgently need and can rightfully claim.

A veteran US expert, with a lifelong experience in agriculture, put the same thesis somewhat differently. "When the management of a bank is oblivious of the shareholders' interests," he said in effect, "there is only one way to set matters right—through a shareholders' revolt." For UNDP-FAO he saw no prospect of change in the right direction until some of their influential customers banded themselves together to impose a policy change.

The developing countries are politically free to mould their own destiny. Science has given them the tools to shape it to their liking. The skill to use these tools is no longer a secret. They now have the means to outpace—and to outwit—the demographic demon that threatens to overwhelm their future, and to banish poverty. Success is within their reach. Indeed, they have no more alibis not to succeed.

Over half a century ago, when the national upheaval was at its height in India, poet Tagore cried out (in "The Call of Truth"): "The obstacle to our forward movement lies at our back. We have been bewitched by our past." This was true of India then; it is also true today—of India, of the developing countries, and, in many ways, of mankind as a whole.

The horizon is bright with a new hope as never before in man's history. It beckons reassuringly even the world's poorest nations. The roadblocks they have to overcome are largely mental. Can they shed them to quicken their pace? This, more than anything else, will determine how soon they can arrive at the promised land of plenty.

# Appendices

## I. LIST OF STATISTICAL TABLES

1. Rice : area, yield and production—an international overview
2. Optimum doses of N (kg/ha) and *profits* from fertilization for different wheat varieties
3A. Area Under High-Yielding Varieties—by crop
3B. Output of five HYV foodgrains
4. Growth of population in India (1901-1971)
5. Area, population, density of population in India
6. Production of selected industries
7. Import of cereals
8A. Area under principal crops
8B. Production of principal crops
9. Average size of holdings
10. Area, production, and average yield per hectare of important crops, 1966-67
11. Production of nitrogenous fertilizers in India
12. Imports made for Central Fertilizer Pool
13. Consumption of nitrogenous fertilizers in India
14. Production, imports and consumption of phosphatic and potassic fertilizers—All-India

## TABLE 1. Rice: Area, Yield and Production—An International Overview

| Country | Area (1,000 ha) | Yield (kg/ha) | Production (1,000 met. ton) |
|---|---|---|---|
| Spain | 64 | 6,230 | 399 |
| Australia | 23 | 5,910 | 142 |
| United Arab Republic | 345 | 5,840 | 2,039 |
| Japan | 3,272 | 5,240 | 17,157 |
| Italy | 115 | 5,120 | 589 |
| U.S.A. | 717 | 4,440 | 3,187 |
| Taiwan | 749 | 3,500 | 2,623 |
| South Korea | 1,165 | 3,230 | 3,167 |
| Malaya | 380 | 2,290 | 869 |
| South Vietnam | 2,358 | 2,100 | 5,327 |
| Ceylon | 567 | 1,810 | 1,026 |
| Indonesia | 6,738 | 1,740 | 11,764 |
| Pakistan | 10,294 | 1,720 | 17,724 |
| Thailand | 6,387 | 1,590 | 10,168 |
| Burma | 4,789 | 1,560 | 7,457 |
| India | 35,474 | 1,540 | 54,734 |
| Philippines | 3,129 | 1,220 | 3,223 |

Source: *World Crop Statistics: Area, Production and Yield, 1948-64*, FAO, Rome, 1964.

## TABLE 2. Optimum doses of N (kg/ha) and *profits* from fertilization for different wheat varieties*

| Variety | Optimum dose of N (kg/ha) | Yield at optimum dose (kg/ha) | Response over no fertilizer (kg/ha) | Net profit (Rs./ha) | Net profit per Rupee spent on (Rs.) |
|---|---|---|---|---|---|
| Sharbati Sonora | 124.0 | 4,415 | 2,225 | 1,532 | 6.2 |
| S—277 | 95.2 | 3,949 | 1,571 | 1,066 | 5.6 |
| S—308 | 105.2 | 3,694 | 1,475 | 970 | 4.6 |
| PV—18 | 95.2 | 3,821 | 1,441 | 962 | 5.1 |
| Chhoti Lerma | 105.2 | 3,817 | 1,631 | 1,094 | 5.2 |
| Sonora 63 | 84.4 | 3,291 | 840 | 503 | 3.0 |
| Sonora 64 | 118.0 | 3,888 | 1,748 | 1,162 | 4.9 |
| Lerma Rojo | 92.0 | 3,596 | 1,221 | 793 | 4.3 |
| J—277 | 92.8 | 3,652 | 1,172 | 752 | 4.0 |
| Safed Lerma | 89.6 | 3,422 | 1,223 | 799 | 4.5 |
| C—306 | 69.6 | 3,154 | 785 | 489 | 3.5 |

* It has been assumed here that the cost of a kg. of Nitrogen is Rs. 2.00 and that of a kg. of wheat Rs. 0.80, corresponding to a price ratio of 2.5.

Source: *Five Years of Research on Dwarf Wheats*, New Delhi, Indian Agricultural Research Institute, 1968, p. 14.

### TABLE 3A. Area under High-yielding Varieties—by Crop

*In million acres*

|         | *1966-67* | *1967-68* | *1968-69* | *1969-70* |
|---------|-----------|-----------|-----------|-----------|
| Wheat   | 1.33      | 7.26      | 11.86     | 11.81     |
| Rice    | 2.20      | 4.42      | 6.42      | 10.21     |
| Maize   | 0.52      | 0.72      | 0.99      | 1.11      |
| Millet  | 0.15      | 1.04      | 1.73      | 2.94      |
| Sorgham | 0.47      | 1.48      | 1.73      | 1.28      |
| Total — 5 crops | 4.67 | 14.92 | 22.73 | 27.35 |

Source : Agricultural Division, Planning Commission, Government of India, mimeo. 1971.

### TABLE 3B. Output of Five HYV Foodgrains

*In million m. tons*

|         | *1964-65* | *1965-66* | *1966-67* | *1967-68* | *1968-69* | *1969-70* |
|---------|-----------|-----------|-----------|-----------|-----------|-----------|
| Wheat   | 12.26     | 10.42     | 11.39     | 16.54     | 18.65     | 20.09     |
| Rice    | 39.31     | 30.66     | 30.44     | 37.61     | 39.76     | 40.43     |
| Maize   | 4.46      | 4.76      | 4.89      | 6.27      | 5.70      | 5.67      |
| Millet  | 4.52      | 3.66      | 4.47      | 5.19      | 3.80      | 5.33      |
| Sorgham | 9.68      | 7.53      | 9.22      | 10.05     | 9.80      | 9.72      |
| Total — 5 crops | 70.23 | 57.02 | 60.42 | 75.66 | 77.72 | 81.25 |

Source : Same as above.

### TABLE 4. Growth of Population in India (1901-1971)

| *Year* | *Population* in millions | *Decennial Increase* in millions | as % |
|--------|--------------------------|----------------------------------|------|
| 1901 | 238.34 | — | — |
| 1911 | 252.01 | + 13.67 | + 5.73 |
| 1921 | 251.24 | − 0.77 | − 0.30 |
| 1931 | 278.87 | + 27.63 | +11.00 |
| 1941 | 318.54 | + 39.67 | +14.00 |
| 1951 | 360.95 | + 42.41 | +13.31 |
| 1961 | 439.07 | + 78.11 | +21.64 |
| 1971 | 547.37 | +108.30 | +24.66 |

## TABLE 5. Area, Population, Density of Population in India

| | | |
|---|---|---|
| Total geographical area | — 328 | million hectares |
| Population, 1971 census | — 547.37 million | |
| Density of population in 1971 | — 182 | per sq. km. |
| Arable land in 1967 | — 181.22 million ha. | |
| Cultivated land in 1967 | — 151.76 „ „ | |
| Arable land per capita | — 0.35 ha. (= 0.86 acre) | |
| Cultivated land per capita | — 0.30 ha. (= 0.74 acre) | |

## TABLE 6. Production of Selected Industries

| | 1950-51 | 1960-61 | 1968-69 |
|---|---|---|---|
| Coal (million tons) | 32.80 | 55.50 | 74.50 |
| Iron ore (million tons) | 3.00 | 11.00 | 21.20 |
| Iron ore (million tons) | | | |
| (incl. Goa, Daman and Diu) | 7.50 | 18.70 | 30.80 |
| Pig iron (million tons) | 1.69 | 4.31 | 7.73 |
| Steel ingots (million tons) | 1.47 | 3.42 | 6.50 |
| Aluminum (000 tons) | 4.00 | 18.30 | 125.30 |
| Electricity : | | | |
| Installed capacity (million kw) | 1.83 | 5.65 | 14.29 |
| Energy generated (billion kwh) | 5.30 | 17.00 | 44.90 |
| Nitrogenous fertilizers (000 tons of N) | 9.00 | 101.00 | 541.00 |
| Phosphatic fertilizers (000 tons of $P_2O_5$) | 9.00 | 43.00 | 210.00 |
| Sulphuric acid (000 tons) | 101.00 | 368.00 | 1,034.00 |
| Soda ash (000 tons) | 45.00 | 152.00 | 401.00 |
| Caustic soda (000 tons) | 12.00 | 101.00 | 314.00 |
| Cement (million tons) | 2.73 | 7.97 | 12.24 |
| Refractories (000 tons) | 237.00 | 567.00 | 630.00 |
| Petroleum, refined (million tons) | 0.20 | 5.80 | 15.40 |
| Paper and paper board (000 tons) | 116.00 | 350.00 | 659.00 |
| Locomotives (000 nos.) | 8.60 | 10.70 | 11.70 |
| Coaching vehicles (000 nos.) | 20.80 | 28.70 | 34.60 |
| Wagons (000 nos.) | 211.90 | 309.40 | 383.30 |
| Automobiles (000 nos.) | 16.50 | 55.00 | 78.00 |
| Motorcycles (000 nos.) & scooters | — | 19.40 | 70.80 |
| Power-driven pumps (000 nos.) | 35.00 | 109.00 | 322.00 |
| Diesel engines (000 nos.) | 5.50 | 44.70 | 119.50 |
| Bicycles (000 nos.) | 99.00 | 1,071.00 | 1,957.00 |
| Automobile tyres (million nos.) | 0.87 | 1.44 | 3.42 |
| Bicycle tyres (million nos.) | 3.33 | 11.15 | 24.78 |
| Sewing machines (000 nos.) | 33.00 | 303.00 | 429.00 |
| Jute textiles (000 tons) | 837.00 | 1,097.00 | 998.00 |
| Cotton cloth (million metres) | 4,215.00 | 6,738.00 | 7,905.00 |
| Art silk (million metres) | 287.00 | 544.00 | 1,002.00 |
| Index of industrial production* (1960 = 100) | 54.80 | 100.00 | 161.00 |

*For calendar years. Index for Jan-Sept. 1969 = 171.1.
Source : *INDIA 1970*

## TABLE 7. Import of Cereals

*In thousand m. tons*

| Year | Rice | Wheat and Wheat flour | Other Cereals | Total |
|------|------|------|------|------|
| 1956 | 330 | 1,113 | — | 1,443 |
| 1961 | 384 | 3,092 | 19 | 3,495 |
| 1962 | 390 | 3,250 | — | 3,640 |
| 1963 | 483 | 4,073 | — | 4,556 |
| 1964 | 645 | 5,621 | — | 6,266 |
| 1965 | 783 | 6,583 | 96 | 7,462 |
| 1966 | 787 | 7,833 | 1,738 | 10,358 |
| 1967 | 453 | 6,400 | 1,819 | 8,672 |
| 1968 | 466 | 4,766 | 482 | 5,654 |
| 1969 | 487 | 3,090 | 295 | 3,872 |
| 1970 app. | 200 | 3,400 | — | 3,630 |

Source : *INDIA 1971*
  *Indian Agriculture in Brief,* 11th ed., Ministry of Agriculture, New Delhi, 1971.

## TABLE 8A. Area under Principal Crops

*In million hectares*

| Crop | 1950-51 | 1955-56 | 1960-61 | 1965-66 | 1969-70 |
|------|---------|---------|---------|---------|---------|
| Rice | 30.8 | 31.5 | 34.1 | 35.2 | 37.7 |
| Jowar | 15.6 | 17.4 | 13.4 | 17.5 | 18.6 |
| Bajra | 9.0 | 11.3 | 11.5 | 11.6 | 12.5 |
| Maize | 3.2 | 3.7 | 4.4 | 4.8 | 5.9 |
| Ragi | 2.2 | 2.3 | 2.5 | 2.3 | 2.8 |
| Small millets | 4.6 | 5.3 | 5.0 | 4.4 | 4.7 |
| Wheat | 9.7 | 12.4 | 13.0 | 12.7 | 16.6 |
| Barley | 3.1 | 3.4 | 3.2 | 2.6 | 2.8 |
| Total Cereals | 78.2 | 87.3 | 92.0 | 91.1 | 101.5 |
| Gram | 7.6 | 9.8 | 9.3 | 8.0 | 7.8 |
| Tur | 2.2 | 2.3 | 2.4 | 2.5 | 2.7 |
| Other pulses | 9.3 | 11.2 | 11.9 | 11.6 | 11.6 |
| Total Foodgrains | 97.3 | 110.6 | 115.6 | 113.2 | 123.6 |
| Potatoes | 0.2 | 0.3 | 0.4 | 0.5 | 0.5 |
| Sugarcane | 1.7 | 1.8 | 2.4 | 2.8 | 2.7 |
| Groundnut | 4.5 | 5.1 | 6.5 | 7.4 | 7.2 |
| Sesamum | 2.2 | 2.3 | 2.2 | 2.5 | 2.3 |
| Linseed | 1.4 | 1.5 | 1.8 | 1.7 | 1.7 |
| Rapeseed and Mustard | 2.1 | 2.6 | 2.9 | 2.9 | 3.1 |
| Cotton | 5.9 | 8.1 | 7.6 | 7.9 | 7.7 |
| Jute | 0.6 | 0.7 | 0.6 | 0.8 | 0.8 |

Source : *INDIA 1971-72*

### TABLE 8B. Production of Principal Crops

*In million m. tons except cotton and jute*

| Crop | 1950-51 | 1955-56 | 1960-61 | 1965-66 | 1969-70 |
|---|---|---|---|---|---|
| Rice (cleaned) | 20.6 | 27.6 | 34.6 | 30.7 | 40.4 |
| Jowar | 5.5 | 6.7 | 9.8 | 7.5 | 9.7 |
| Bajra | 2.6 | 3.4 | 3.3 | 3.7 | 5.3 |
| Maize | 1.7 | 2.6 | 4.1 | 4.8 | 5.7 |
| Ragi | 1.4 | 1.8 | 1.8 | 1.2 | 2.1 |
| Small millets | 1.8 | 2.1 | 1.9 | 1.7 | 1.7 |
| Wheat | 6.5 | 8.8 | 11.0 | 10.4 | 20.1 |
| Barley | 2.4 | 2.8 | 2.8 | 2.4 | 2.7 |
| Total Cereals | 42.4 | 55.8 | 69.3 | 62.2 | 87.8 |
| Gram | 3.7 | 5.4 | 6.3 | 4.2 | 5.5 |
| Tur | 1.7 | 1.9 | 2.1 | 1.7 | 1.8 |
| Other pulses | 3.0 | 3.8 | 4.4 | 3.9 | 4.3 |
| Total Foodgrains | 50.8 | 66.9 | 82.0 | 72.0 | 99.5 |
| Potatoes | 1.7 | 1.9 | 2.7 | 4.1 | 4.1 |
| Sugarcane (cane) | 57.1 | 60.5 | 110.0 | 119.6 | 13.1 |
| Groundnut (nuts in shell) | 3.5 | 3.9 | 4.8 | 4.2 | 5.1 |
| Sesamum | 0.4 | 0.5 | 0.3 | 0.4 | 0.4 |
| Linseed | 0.4 | 0.4 | 0.4 | 0.3 | 0.4 |
| Rapeseed and Mustard | 0.8 | 0.9 | 1.3 | 1.3 | 1.5 |
| Cotton (million bales*) | 2.9 | 3.9 | 5.3 | 4.8 | 5.2 |
| Jute      ,,         ,, | 3.3 | 4.2 | 4.1 | 4.5 | 5.6 |

* Bale = 180 kg          Source : *INDIA 1971-72*

### TABLE 9. Average Size of Holdings

| Country | Year | Hectares |
|---|---|---|
| Belgium | 1951 | 6.6 |
| Denmark | 1959 | 15.8 |
| Germany (Federal Republic) | 1960 | 9.5 |
| India | 1961-62 | 2.6 |
| Japan | 1960 | 1.2 |
| New Zealand | 1959-60 | 231.6 |
| Norway | 1959 | 17.5 |
| Sweden | 1961 | 14.6 |
| U.K. | 1960-61 | 40.6 |
| U.S.A. | 1959 | 122.5 |
| Yugoslavia | 1950 | 4.7 |

Source : FAO Yearbook of Production

**TABLE 10. Area, Production and Average Yield per Hectare**
of Important Crops, 1966-67

| Country | Area<br>'000 hectares | Production<br>'000 m. tons | Yield per<br>hectare<br>'00 kgs. |
|---|---|---|---|
| **1. RICE (Paddy)** | | | |
| Brazil* | 4,005 | 5,802 | 14.5 |
| Burma | 4,516 | 6,636 | 14.7 |
| China (Mainland) | N.A. | 88,000(F) | N.A. |
| INDIA | 35,251 | 45,657 | 12.9 |
| Indonesia | 7,668 | 14,103 | 18.4 |
| Japan* | 3,254 | 16,552 | 50.9 |
| Pakistan* | 10,480 | 16,410 | 15.7 |
| Philippines | 3,081 | 4,165 | 13.5 |
| Thailand | 6,878 | 11,846 | 17.2 |
| Turkey | 65 | 250 | 38.5 |
| U.A.R.* | 486‡ | 2,000‡ | 41.2‡ |
| U.S.A. | 796 | 3,858 | 48.5 |
| U.S.S.R.* | 248 | 712 | 28.7 |
| **2. WHEAT** | | | |
| Argentina | 5,214 | 6,247 | 12.0 |
| Australia* | 8,205 | 12,570 | 15.3 |
| Canada | 12,016 | 22,516 | 18.7 |
| China (Mainland) | N.A. | 25,700(F) | N.A. |
| France | 3,992 | 11,297 | 28.3 |
| INDIA | 12,838 | 11,393 | 8.9 |
| Italy | 4,274 | 9,400 | 22.0 |
| Iraq | 1,737 | 826 | 4.8 |
| Pakistan* | 5,276 | 3,933 | 7.5 |
| Romania* | 3,034 | 5,065 | 16.7 |
| Spain @ | 4,190 | 4,812 | 11.5 |
| Syria | 858 | 559 | 6.5 |
| Turkey @ | 8,069 | 9,715 | 12.0 |
| U.A.R.* | 605‡ | 1,620‡ | 26.8‡ |
| U.K. | 906 | 3,475 | 38.4 |
| U.S.A. | 20,180 | 35,699 | 17.7 |
| U.S.S.R.* | 69,958 | 100,499 | 14.4 |
| **3. MAIZE** | | | |
| Argentina | 3,275 | 7,040 | 21.5 |
| France + | 964 | 4,336 | 45.0 |
| Hungary* | 1,237 | 3,907 | 31.6 |
| INDIA | 5,074 | 4,894 | 9.6 |
| Italy | 988 | 3,510 | 35.5 |
| Indonesia | 3,186 | 2,874 | 9.0 |
| Mexico | 7,460 | 8,454 | 11.3 |

*Contd.*

## TABLE 10. (Contd.)

| Country | Area | Production | Yield per hectare |
|---|---|---|---|
| | '000 hectares | '000 m. tons | '00 kgs. |

### 3. Maize

| | | | |
|---|---|---|---|
| Pakistan* | 557 | 590 | 10.6 |
| Philippines | 2,167 | 1,435 | 6.6 |
| Romania* | 3,288 | 8,022 | 24.4 |
| Turkey | 655 | 1,000 | 15.3 |
| U.A.R.* | 661 | 2,358 | 35.7 |
| U.S.A. | 23,040 | 104,585 | 45.4 |
| U.S.S.R. § | 3,229 | 8,416 | 26.1 |
| Yugoslavia §§ | 2,500 | 7,980 | 31.9 |

### 4. Sugarcane (in terms of cane)

| | | | |
|---|---|---|---|
| Australia** | 230 | 16,968 | 738 |
| Brazil ++ | 1,636 | 75,788 | 463 |
| China (Mainland) | 420(F) | 25,000(F) | 595(F) |
| Cuba** | 1,700(F) | 53,000(F) | 312(F) |
| INDIA | 2,301 | 92,826 | 403 |
| Indonesia | 100(F) | 7,500(F) | 750(F) |
| Pakistan ++ | 817 | 30,182 | 370 |
| Puerto Rico | 105(F) | 7,403 | 705(F) |
| U.S.A. @@ | 194 | 11,449 | 590 |

### 5. Cotton

| | | | |
|---|---|---|---|
| Argentina | 441 | 116 | 2.6 |
| Brazil | 3,898 | 622 | 1.6 |
| China (Mainland) | 4,553‡ | 1,301‡ | 2.9‡ |
| INDIA | 7,836 | 895 | 1.1 |
| Mexico | 787 | 619 | 7.9 |
| Pakistan | 1,635 | 466 | 2.8 |
| Sudan | 441 | 159 | 3.6 |
| Turkey | 712 | 382 | 5.4 |
| U.A.R. | 781 | 462 | 5.9 |
| U.S.A. | 3,866 | 2,085 | 5.4 |
| U.S.S.R. | 2,463 | 2,045 | 8.3 |

### 6. Jute

| | | | |
|---|---|---|---|
| Brazil | 34 | 44 | 13.2 |
| INDIA | 797 | 964 | 12.1 |
| Pakistan | 876 | 1,161 | 13.3 |

### 7. Groundnut

| | | | |
|---|---|---|---|
| Argentina | 333 | 411 | 12.3 |
| Burma | 499 | 278 | 6.2 |

*Contd.*

**TABLE 10.** (Contd.)

| Country | Area | Production | Yield per hectare. |
|---|---|---|---|
| | '000 hectares | '000 m. tons | '00 kgs. |

7. GROUNDNUT

| | | | |
|---|---|---|---|
| China (Mainland) | 1,980‡ | 2,360‡ | 11.9‡ |
| Congo (Democ. Rep. of) | 190(F) | 112‡ | 5.9(F) |
| INDIA | 7,299 | 4,411 | 6.0 |
| Japan | 65 | 139 | 21.4 |
| Senegal | 1,117 | 861 | 7.7 |
| Uganda | 250(F) | 163‡ | 6.5(F) |
| U.S.A. | 574 | 1,093 | 19.0 |

8. TOBACCO

| | | | |
|---|---|---|---|
| Brazil | 265 | 228.3 | 8.6 |
| Bulgaria | 117 | 132.2 | 11.3 |
| Canada | 50 | 106.1 | 21.1 |
| China (Mainland) | 375(F) | 450.0(F) | 12.0(F) |
| Greece | 123 | 92.0 | 7.5 |
| INDIA | 424 | 353.4 | 8.3 |
| Indonesia | 153 | 137.0 | 9.0 |
| Japan | 87 | 198.0 | 22.8 |
| Pakistan | 102 | 137.3 | 13.4 |
| Philippines | 86 | 58.1 | 6.8 |
| Southern Rhodesia | 84 | 113.1 | 13.5 |
| Turkey | 285 | 167.7 | 5.9 |
| U.S.A. | 395 | 856.6 | 21.7 |
| U.S.S.R. | 165‡ | 235.0‡ | 14.2‡ |

(*)     Area sown.
(@)    Includes Spelt.
(+)    Main, associated and catch crops.
(**)   Cane crushed for sugar.
(++) Planted area.
(@@) Excluding cane for seed.
(‡)     Unofficial estimate.
(§)     Crops harvested for dry grain only.
(§§)   Area refers to principal crop, production includes mixture.
(F)     FAO estimate.

Source : FAO Yearbook of Production, 1967

## TABLE 11. Production of Nitrogenous Fertilizers in India

*In 1,000 m. tons*

| Year | Sulphate of Ammonia 20.6% N | Urea 46% N | Ammonium Sulphate Nitrate 26% N | Calcium Ammonium Nitrate 20.5 % N | Ammonium Chloride 25% N | Ammonium Phosphate 16% N | Total in terms of Nitrogen |
|---|---|---|---|---|---|---|---|
| 1951 | 53.6 | | | | | | 11.0 |
| 1956 | 396.9 | | | | | | 81.8 |
| 1961-62 | 403.6 | 13.6 | 55.4 | 200.8 | 17.8 | 14.1 | 151.7 |
| 1962-63 | 422.8 | 18.7 | 62.2 | 314.8 | 19.6 | 9.2 | 182.8 |
| 1963-64 | 440.4 | 18.1 | 47.2 | 493.8 | 19.6 | 28.7 | 222.0 |
| 1964-65 | 435.0 | 17.9 | 47.8 | 558.0 | 19.3 | 49.2 | 237.4 |
| 1965-66 | 420.2 | 27.5 | 55.3 | 496.7 | 22.5 | 52.1 | 232.0 |
| 1966-67 | 437.5 | 131.9 | 60.0 | 538.7 | 22.6 | 77.7 | 307.9 |
| 1967-68 | 407.3 | 224.9 | 61.5 | 332.3 | 25.3 | 92.6 | 366.0 |
| 1968-69 | 585.3 | 409.6 | 49.1 | 180.0 | 26.7 | 93.2 | 545.2 |
| 1969-70 | 612.7 | 771.5 | 42.7 | 14.1 | 24.0 | 75.4 | 715.8 |
| 1970-71 | 630.5 | 1009.0 | 41.2 | — | 33.2 | 73.2 | 850.0 |

NOTE on fertilizer statistics given in Tables 11-14: The data have been extracted from *Indian Agriculture in Brief*, 11th ed., Ministry of Agriculture, New Delhi, 1971. Some minor details are ignored. The figures are for fiscal years (ending 31 March) except 1951 and 1956 in Tables 11 and 14 which stand for calendar years. Figures for 1970-71 are provisional.

## TABLE 12. Imports made for Central Fertilizer Pool

*In 1,000 m. tons*

| Year | Total in terms of N | $P_2O_5$ | $K_2O$ | Sulphate of Ammonia 20.6% N | Urea 45% to 46% N | Ammonium Sulphate Nitrate 26% N | Calcium Ammonium Nitrate 26% N | Nitro-Phosphate 20% N 20%$P_2O_5$ | Ammonium Phosphate 20% N 20%$P_2O_5$ |
|---|---|---|---|---|---|---|---|---|---|
| 1951-52 | 29.3 | | | 142.2 | | | | | |
| 1956-57 | 56.4 | | 0.1 | 233.7 | 10.1 | 14.5 | | | |
| 1957-58 | 141.6 | | | 294.0 | 129.7 | 29.1 | 61.8 | | |
| 1962-63 | 251.9 | 10.2 | | 670.9 | 219.3 | | | 20.2 | 30.6 |
| 1963-64 | 226.4 | 12.0 | | 440.1 | 261.1 | | | 17.2 | 48.8 |
| 1964-65 | 213.7 | 11.9 | | 317.1 | 294.0 | | | 30.5 | 39.9 |
| 1965-66 | 309.5 | 12.8 | | 852.8 | 251.9 | | | | 62.4 |
| 1966-67 | 601.7 | 150.4 | 2.4 | 1,209.3 | 482.0 | 41.7 | 93.9 | | 220.5 |
| 1967-68 | 866.5 | 348.5 | 55.3 | 1,052.2 | 918.4 | 16.1 | 125.1 | | 256.5 |
| 1968-69 | 841.9 | 137.5 | 213.0 | 1,255.3 | 1,028.5 | 10.5 | 90.4 | 27.4 | 50.2 |
| 1969-70 | 667.2 | 93.5 | 45.2 | 790.1 | 937.6 | — | 83.4 | 7.0 | — |
| 1970-71 | 480.0 | 32.0 | 111.0 | 66.0 | 761.0 | 25.0 | 335.0 | 17.0 | — |

## TABLE 13. Consumption of Nitrogenous Fertilizers in India

*In 1,000 m. tons*

| Year | Sulphate of Ammonia 26.6% N | Urea 45 to 46% N | Ammonium Sulphate Nitrate 26% N | Calcium Ammonium Nitrate 20.5% N | Nitro-Phosphate 20% N | Ammonium Phosphate 20% N | Total in terms of Nitrogen |
|---|---|---|---|---|---|---|---|
| 1956-57 | 601.2 | 7.4 | 9.2 | 0.8 | | | 130.6 |
| 1961-62 | 669.5 | 113.6 | 79.9 | 149.3 | | 4.1 | 242.4 |
| 1962-63 | 833.7 | 154.4 | 53.7 | 234.9 | 0.03 | 4.5 | 305.8 |
| 1963-64 | 984.3 | 214.2 | 51.9 | 408.7 | 1.3 | 3.0 | 399.4 |
| 1964-65 | 1,015.1 | 342.9 | 62.4 | 671.5 | 36.2 | 64.1 | 538.3 |
| 1965-66 | 1,183.0 | 312.1 | 46.5 | 592.3 | 84.6 | 6.3 | 540.8 |
| 1966-67 | 1,581.7 | 596.8 | 86.8 | 507.3 | 61.2 | 194.6 | 856.5 |
| 1967-68 | 1,330.1 | 1,016.5 | 86.2 | 202.5 | 35.4 | 220.6 | 1,070.8 |
| 1968-69 | 1,669.5 | 1,290.3 | 41.7 | 164.9 | | | 1,254.0 |
| 1969-70 | 969.1 | 1,308.3 | 41.1 | 448.1 | | | 1,040.2 |
| 1970-71 | 933.4 | 1,451.1 | 60.3 | 490.9 | | | 1,149.1 |

## TABLE 14. Production, Imports and Consumption of Phosphatic and Potassic Fertilizers—All-India

*In 1,000 m. tons*

| Year | Phosphatic fertilizers, all kinds,[1] in terms of Phosphorus $P_2O_5$ | | | Potassic fertilizers, all kinds, in terms of Potash $K_2O$ | | |
|---|---|---|---|---|---|---|
| | Production | Imports[2] | Consumption | Production | Imports | Consumption |
| 1951 | 16.3 | 0.4 | 13.5 | | 8.0 | 8.0 |
| 1956 | 18.5 | — | 22.0 | | — | .— |
| 1960-61 | 60.7 | 0.2 | 69.8 | See | 22.6 | 20.3 |
| 1961-62 | 72.5 | — | 66.4 | | 32.3 | 29.4 |
| 1962-63 | 87.5 | 10 2 | 88.8 | Footnote 3 | 39.9 | 36.4 |
| 1963-64 | 126.0 | 12.0 | 140.5 | | 64.1 | 50.6 |
| 1964-65 | 133.5 | 11.9 | 172.7 | below | 57.2 | 70.4 |
| 1965-66 | 123.0 | 12.5 | 156.5 | | 93.6 | 77.7 |
| 1966-67 | 150.8 | 150.4 | 272.6 | | 143.3 | 114.2 |
| 1967-68 | 200.0 | 349.0 | 363.5 | | 270.0 | 170.0 |
| 1968-69 | 210.0 | 138.0 | 382.0 | | 213.0 | 170.0 |
| 1969-70[4] | 220.0 | 93.5 | 434.7 | | 120.0 | 176.0 |
| 1970-71[5] | 230.0 | 32.0 | 562.0 | | 111.0 | 250.0 |

1. Includes bonemeal, estimated at 6,000 tonnes $P_2O_5$ for both production and consumption.
2. Imports made for Central Fertilizer Pool.
3. Only 1000 to 2000 m. tons of Muriate of Potash (about 60% $K_2O$) is produced annually in India.
4. Estimated.   5. Targeted.

69

## GRAPHS

1.  Wheat production in Mexico
2.  Maize production in Mexico
3.  Comparative performance of low-nitrogen-response and high-nitrogen-response varieties, IRRI, 1965
4.  Effect of plant type and season on the nitrogen response of indica rice, IRRI, 1966 dry season
5.  Wheat in West Pakistan : area, production and yield per acre, 1954-55 to 1968-69
6.  Rice in West Pakistan : area, production and yield per acre, 1954-55 to 1968-69
7.  Average annual rise in real GNP per capita, 1962-67
8.  Adjusted production of foodgrains in India, 1900-01 to 1967-68
9.  Production of foodgrains in India
10. Monsoon's effect on foodgrain production and estimated demand during 1946-47 to 1975-76
11. Average annual rainfall and rice yield in the IADP District of Raipur
12. Consumption of plant nutrients—per hectare and per capita—in 1965-66
13. Production, consumption, targets and unfulfilled targets of fertilizers in India
    A. Nitrogen (N)
    B. Phosphoric acid ($P_2O_5$)
    C. Potash ($K_2O$)
14. Production and imports of pesticides in India—technical equivalent

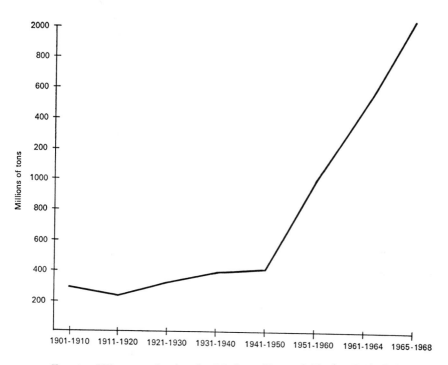

FIG. 1 : Wheat production in Mexico. (From Calderón, José Guevara, "Wheat and Maize in Mexico," in *Some Issues Emerging from Recent Breakthrough in Food Production*, Editor Kenneth L. Turk, Cornell University, Ithaca, New York, 1971.)

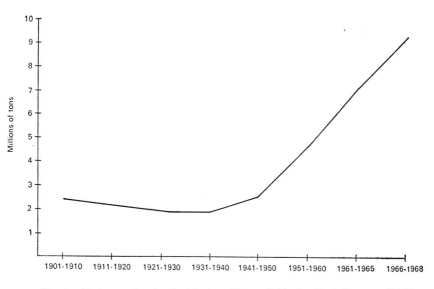

FIG. 2 : Maize production in Mexico. (From Calderón, José Guevara, ibid.)

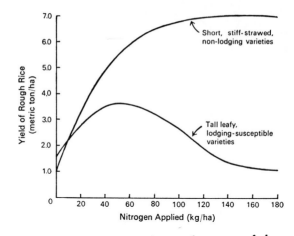

FIG. 3 : Comparative performance of low-nitrogen-response and high-nitrogen-response varieties, IRRI, 1965. (From *Rice Information Cooperative Effort*, **22**, p. 157.)

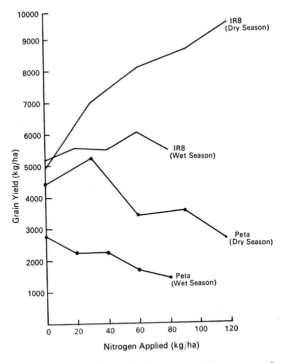

FIG. 4 : Effect of plant type and season on the nitrogen response of indica rice, IRRI, 1966, dry season. (From *Rice Information Cooperative Efforts*, 22, p. 158.)

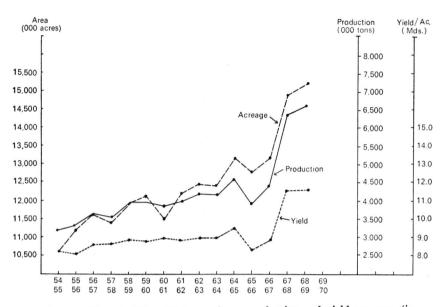

FIG. 5 : Wheat in West Pakistan : Area, production and yield per acre (in maunds per acre; 1 maund = 82.286 lbs. = 0.037324 metric ton, or 1¹/₃ bushels), 1954-55 to 1968-69. (From *Agricultural Statistics of Pakistan*, 1970.)

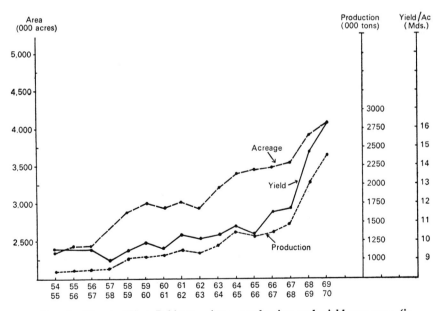

FIG. 6: Rice in West Pakistan : Area, production and yield per acre (in maunds per acre) 1954-55 to 1968-69. (From *Agricultural Statistics of Pakistan*, 1970.)

Fig. 7: How the nations rank in economic growth—average annual rise in real GNP per capita, 1962-67. The growth of real gross national product (GNP) per capita is a better measure of economic performance than dollar levels because, for one thing, conversion into dollars, using official exchange rates, inaccurately reflects internal prices. In dollar terms, the USA leads with a per capita GNP of $2,801; Canada, $2,686; Switzerland, $2,519; Denmark, $2,340. (From *CERES*, FAO, Rome, March-April 1969.)

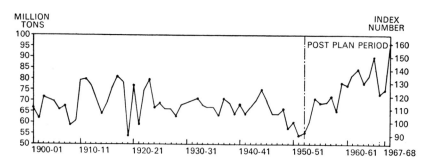

Fig. 8: Adjusted production of foodgrains in India 1900-01 to 1967-68.

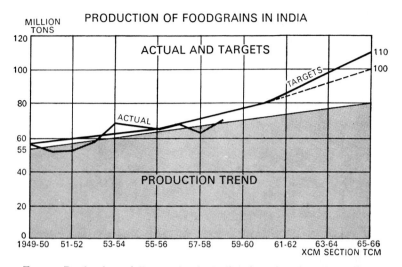

FIG. 9 : Production of Foodgrains in India—Actual and targets. (From *Report on India's Food Crisis and Steps to Meet It*, Agricultural Production Team, Ford Foundation, 1958.)

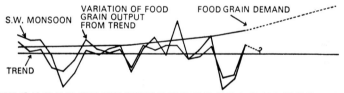

FIG. 10 : Monsoon's effect on foodgrain production and estimated demand during 1946-47 to 1975-76. (From A. A. Johnson, "Putting International Agronomy into Action—the Indian Experience," American Society of Agronomy, Inc., Special Publication No. 15, June 1969.)

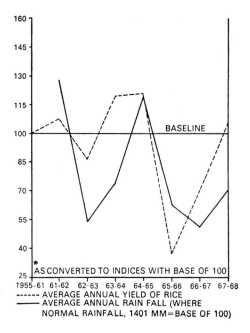

Fig. 11 : Average and annual rainfall and rice yield in the IADP District of Raipur. (From A. A. Johnson, ibid.)

BASELINE

* AS CONVERTED TO INDICES WITH BASE OF 100

1955-61  61-62  62-63  63-64  64-65  65-66  66-67  67-68
------ AVERAGE ANNUAL YIELD OF RICE
——— AVERAGE ANNUAL RAIN FALL (WHERE
NORMAL RAINFALL, 1401 MM=BASE OF 100)

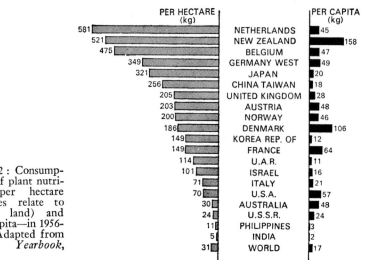

Fig. 12 : Consumption of plant nutrients—per hectare (figures relate to arable land) and per capita—in 1956-66. (Adapted from *FAO Yearbook*, 1968.)

| PER HECTARE (kg) | | PER CAPITA (kg) |
|---|---|---|
| 581 | NETHERLANDS | 45 |
| 521 | NEW ZEALAND | 158 |
| 475 | BELGIUM | 47 |
| 349 | GERMANY WEST | 49 |
| 321 | JAPAN | 20 |
| 256 | CHINA TAIWAN | 18 |
| 205 | UNITED KINGDOM | 28 |
| 203 | AUSTRIA | 48 |
| 200 | NORWAY | 46 |
| 186 | DENMARK | 106 |
| 149 | KOREA REP. OF | 12 |
| 149 | FRANCE | 64 |
| 114 | U.A.R. | 11 |
| 101 | ISRAEL | 16 |
| 71 | ITALY | 21 |
| 70 | U.S.A. | 57 |
| 30 | AUSTRALIA | 48 |
| 24 | U.S.S.R. | 24 |
| 11 | PHILIPPINES | 3 |
| 5 | INDIA | 2 |
| 31 | WORLD | 17 |

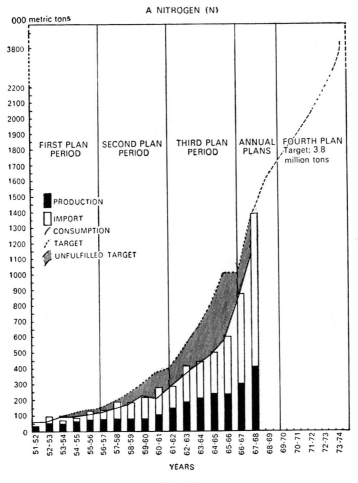

A NITROGEN (N)

FIG. 13A

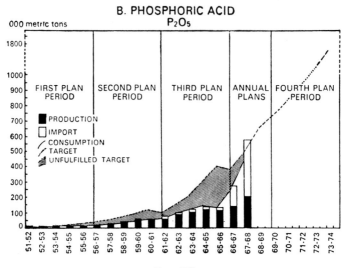

FIG. 13B

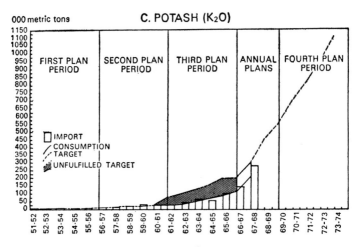

FIG. 13C

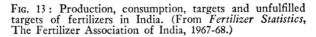

FIG. 13 : Production, consumption, targets and unfulfilled targets of fertilizers in India. (From *Fertilizer Statistics*, The Fertilizer Association of India, 1967-68.)

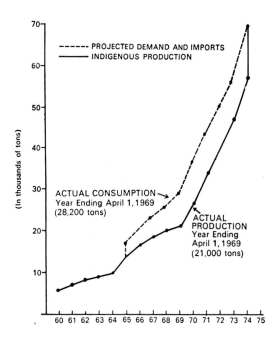

FIG. 14 : Production and imports of pesticides in India
—technical equivalent. (From *Pesticides Association of India—Special Number*, 1969.)

# CONVERSION FACTORS

## Area

| | | | |
|---|---|---|---|
| 1 | acre | = | 0.40469 hectare |
| 1 | hectare | = | 2.47109 acres |
| 1 | square mile | = | 2.5900 square kilometres |
| 1 | square kilometre | = | 0.38610 square mile |
| 1 | square mile | = | 640 acres = 259 hectares |
| 1 | square kilometre | = | 100 hectares |

## Weight

| | | | |
|---|---|---|---|
| 1 | ounce (oz.) | = | 28.3495 grams |
| 1 | gram | = | 0.0352740 ounce |
| 1 | pound | = | 0.43359 kilogram |
| 1 | kilogram | = | 2.20463 pounds |
| 1 | long ton | = | 1.01605 metric ton |
| 1 | metric ton | = | 0.098420 long ton |
| 1 | short ton | = | 0.90718 metric ton |
| 1 | long ton | = | 1.10231 short tons |
| | | = | 2,240 pounds |
| 1 | metric ton | = | 1,000 kilograms |
| 1 | short ton | = | 2,000 pounds |
| 1 | metric ton | = | 2204.63 pounds |
| 1 | maund (standard) | = | 82.2857 pounds |
| 1 | maund (standard) | = | 0.037324 metric ton |
| 1 | metric cent. | = | 26.792 maunds (standard) |

## Volume

| | | | |
|---|---|---|---|
| 1 | cubic foot | = | 0.02832 cubic metre |
| 1 | cubic metre | = | 35.31 cubic feet |

## Numbers

| | | | |
|---|---|---|---|
| 1 | lakh | = | 100,000 or 0.1 million |
| 1 | million | = | 10 lakhs |
| 1 | crore | = | 100 lakhs or 10 millions |
| 1 | million | = | 0.1 crore |

## Length

| | | | |
|---|---|---|---|
| 1 | inch | = | 2.54 cm. |
| 1 | cm. | = | 0.393701 inch |

## Rice-paddy

| | | |
|---|---|---|
| cleaned rice (not in the husk) | = | 2/3 of paddy (rice in the husk) |

## GLOSSARY OF SOME INDIAN WORDS

*Crop by season*

| | | |
|---|---|---|
| Kharif | — | monsoon or wet-season crop |
| Rabi | — | winter or dry season crop |
| Boro (rice), also called *Aus* | — | early rice |

*Some cereals*

| | | |
|---|---|---|
| Jowar | — | sorghum |
| Bajra | — | pearl millet |
| Ragi | — | finger millet |

*Main pulses*

| | | |
|---|---|---|
| Arhar (red gram) | — | pigeon peas |
| Channa (Bengal gram) | — | chick peas |
| Matar | — | peas |
| Masur | — | lentil |
| Moong | — | green gram |
| Urad | — | black gram |
| Charkha | — | spinning wheel |
| Khadi, also khaddar | — | hand-woven fabric made from hand-spun yarn |

# Select Bibliography

The literature on tropical agriculture, or the green revolution, is already vast and is growing rapidly. To keep pace with it is wellnigh impossible. Nor is this necessary for the present purpose since most of it is of a descriptive character.

This bibliography is limited to the material, both printed and mimeographed, which has been actually used or consulted in order to clarify or exemplify, or to develop or substantiate, points of major importance.

*A Note on Impact of Agricultural Programmes on Small Farmers*, mimeo., New Delhi, Planning Commission (PEO), 1969.

Appleby, Paul H., *Public Administration in India—Report of a Survey*, New Delhi, Government of India, 1953.

Balis, John S., *Farm Machinery Input in Agricultural Development*, mimeo., New Delhi, USAID, Sept. 1969. Also other papers on farm mechanization.

Borlaug, Norman E., "Wheat, Rust and People," in *Phytopathology*, USA, vol. 55, No. 10, October 1965.

——"National Production Campaigns," *Strategy for the Conquest of Hunger, Proceedings of a Symposium, 1968*, New York, The Rockefeller Foundation.

——*Mankind and Civilization at Another Crossroad*, McDougal Memorial Lecture, mimeo., FAO, Rome, 1971.

Cabanilla, Nathaniel B., *Technological Innovation in the Philippines—Highyielding Rice Varieties*, mimeo. thesis, Manila, University of the Philippines, 1969.

Chandler Jr., Robert F., "The Case for Research," in *Strategy for the Conquest of Hunger*, see above.

——*Keynote Address* delivered at a meeting of West Africa Rice Development Association, held 22-26 March 1971, mimeo., FAO, Rome.

Clark, Colin, "Too Much Food," *Lloyds Bank Review*, London, January 1970.

Currie, Lauchlin, *Accelerating Development*, New York, McGraw-Hill Book Company, 1966.

De, Rajat, *The Spread of New Wheat Varieties in India*, mimeo., New Delhi, IARI, 1968.

Dey, S. K., *Community Development—A Chronicle 1954-61*, New Delhi, Ministry of Community Development, etc., Govt. of India, 1962.

——*Community Development—A Bird's-eye View*, Bombay, Asia Publishing House, 1964.

Ensminger, Douglas, *An Evolving Strategy for India's Agricultural Development* (an Address), New Delhi, The Ford Foundation, June 1968.

——*India and the 1970's—An Overview*, do, July 1970.

Fertiliser Association of India, *Annual Report* (Fertilizer Statistics), 1969.

Food and Agriculture Organization (FAO), Rome:
  —*The State of Food and Agriculture* in 1970, 1971, 1972.
  —*Production Yearbook*, 1969, 1970.
  —*Fertilizers—An Annual Review*, 1969, 1970.
  —*Agricultural Commodity Projections 1970-1980*, 2 vols.
  —*Six Billions to Feed*, 1962.
  —*Possibilities of Increasing World Food Production*, Basic Study No. 23, 1970.
  —*Agricultural Development: A Review of FAO's Field Activities*, Basic Study No. 23, 1970.
  —*Provisional Indicative World Plan of Agricultural Development*, 1969, 2 vols.
  —*A Strategy for Plenty*, 1970.
  —*Report of the Second World Food Congress*, June 1970.
  —*Five Keys to Development*, 1970.

Ford Foundation, *Accelerating Development in West Godavari District*, mimeo., New Delhi, May 1969.
  N.B. Other Ford Foundation publications have been listed under the respective authors' names.

Freeman, Orville L., "Malthus, Marx and the North American Bread Basket," *Foreign Affairs*, New York, July 1967.

Freeman, Wayne H., "Seed Problem and Seed Production of New Rice Varieties," *Seed Specialists' Seminar Proceedings*, April 1969, mimeo., New Delhi.

Gill, K. S., *Wheat Market Behaviour, Post-Harvest Period*, 1968-69, Ludhiana, Punjab Agricultural University, 1969.

Galbraith, John Kenneth, *Ambassador's Journal*, Boston, Houghton Mifflin Company, 1969.

Hansen, A. H., *The Process of Planning—A Study of India's Five-Year Plans, 1950-64*, Oxford University Press, 1966.

Hill, F. F. and Hardin, Lowell S., "Crop Production Successes and Emerging Problems in Developing Countries," in *Some Issues Emerging*, etc., see under Turk, Kenneth L., ed.

Hirschman, Albert O., *The Strategy of Economic Development*, New Haven, Yale University Press, 1958.

Hopper, David, and Freeman, Wayne H., "From Unsteady Infancy to Vigorous Adolescence—Rice Development," *Economic and Political Weekly* (Special Issue on India's Agriculture), Bombay, 29 March 1969.

*INDIA* (Yearbook), 1969, 1970 and 1971-72, Publications Division, Govt. of India.

Indian Agricultural Research Institute (IARI), New Delhi:
  —*Diamond Jubilee Souvenir, 1905-1965*.
  —*Five Years of Research on Dwarf Wheats*, 1968.
  —*National Demonstrations*, 1969.
  N.B. Other IARI documents are listed under the respective authors' names.

*Indian Agriculture in Brief*, 11th edition, Ministry of Food and Agriculture, Govt. of India, New Delhi, 1971.

Intensive Agricultural District Programme (IADP), Reports of the Expert Committee on Evaluation and Assessment: First Report 1961-63; Second Report 1960-65; Third Report 1965-66 and 1966-67; and Fourth Report for 1960-68, titled *Modernizing India's Agriculture*, 2 vols., Ministry of Food and Agriculture, New Delhi.

Indian Council of Agricultural Research (ICAR), *Agricultural Research in India—Achievements and Outlook*, New Delhi, Ministry of Agriculture, 1972.

Indian Council of Applied Economic Research, *Market Towns and Spatial Development*, New Delhi, 1965.

*Indian Farming*, Central Rice Research Institute Jubilee Number, October 1971.

*Indian Farming*, Maximizing Production and Income from Water Resources, May 1972.

International Rice Research Commission Newsletter, IRRI, XII. No. 4, 1963.

Jackson, Sir Robert, *A Study of the Capacity of the United Nations Development System*, Geneva, mimeo., 1969, 2 vols.

Johnson, A. A., "Putting International Agronomy into Action—the Indian Experiment," American Society of Agronomy, Special Pub. No. 15, June 1969.

——"Present Position and Future Prospects for Rapid Increases in Rice Yields," *ORYZA*, Vol. 6, No. 1:4-22 (1969).

——*Indian Agriculture in the 1970's*, New Delhi, The Ford Foundation, 1970.

Johnston, Sherman E., *The IADP Path to Intensive Agricultural Development*, New Delhi, The Ford Foundation, Expanding Horizons Series, Dec. 1968.

Johnston, Bruce F., and Kilby, Peter, *Agricultural Strategy and Industrial Growth, Report on Visits to Taiwan, India and West Pakistan*, mimeo., 1969.

Kellogg, Charles E., "Interactions in Agricultural Development," paper presented at UN Conference on the Application of Science and Technology to Development, Oct. 1962, and World Food Congress, Washington, D.C., 4-8 June 1963.

Lewis, John P., *Quiet Crisis in India*, Washington, D.C., Brookings Institution, 1962.

Malone, Carl C., *Background of India's Agriculture and India's Intensive Agricultural District Program*, mimeo., New Delhi, The Ford Foundation, 1969.

Mavi, Harpal Singh, *Roads in the Rural Punjab*, Ludhiana, Punjab Agricultural University, 1970.

Mayer, Albert, *Pilot Project, India, The Story of Rural Development at Etawah, Uttar Pradesh*, University of California Press, 1958.

Miles, Harold A., *The Outlook for Farm Credit in India*, New Delhi, The Ford Foundation, Expanding Horizons Series, June 1969.

Mosher, A. T., *Getting Agriculture Moving, Essentials of Development and Modernization*, New York, Frederick A. Praeger, 1965.

Naik, K. C., *A History of Agricultural Universities—Education, Research and Extension Concepts for Indian Agriculture*, New Delhi, USAID, 1968.

National Commission on Agriculture, *Some Aspects of Agricultural Research, Extension and Training*, Interim Report, New Delhi, Nov. 1971.

Nurkse, Ragnar, *Problems of Capital Formation in Underdeveloped Countries*, Oxford University Press, 1953.

Ogura, Takekazu, ed., *Agricultural Development in Modern Japan*, Tokyo, Japan FAO Association, 1963.

Paddock, W. and P., *Famine 1975? America's Decision : Who Will Survive?* Boston, Little Brown, Mass., 1967. Also *Hungry Nations*, do, 1964.

*Partners in Development, Report of the Commission on International Development*, New York, Praeger Publishers, 1969.

Patrick, Niel A., *India's "Package Programme" for Intensive Agricultural Development*, mimeo., New Delhi, The Ford Foundation, Sept. 1972.

Pesticides Association of India, *Annual Report*, 1969.

Planning Commission, Government of India, New Delhi:
—*Five Year Plans : First Plan 1951-56; Second Plan 1956-61*;
  *Third Plan 1961-66*;
—*Towards a Self-reliant Economy—India's Third Plan*, December 1961;
—*Third Five Year Plan Progress Report*, March 1963;
—*Fourth Plan—A Draft Outline*, 1966;
—*Fourth Five Year Plan 1969-74*;
—*Study of Wastelands including Saline, Alkali and Waterlogged Lands and their Reclamation Measures*, Committee on Natural Resources, 1963.

Planning Commission's Programme Evaluation Organization (PEO), Reports on the Working of the Community Development Programme, First through Seventh Report, issued during 1955-60.

——*The High-Yielding Varieties Programme in India—*Part I, Draft, mimeo., jointly with the Australian National University, 1971.

Randhava, M. S., *Green Revolution in Punjab*, Ludhiana, Punjab Agricultural University, Jan. 1972.

Rath, Nilakanth, and Patvardhan, V. S., *Impact of Assistance under P. L. 480*, Bombay, Asia Publishing House, 1967.

Revelle, Roger, "Education for Agriculture in India," in *The World Food Problem*, President's Report, Washington, D.C., 1968, Vol. III, Ch. 5.

*Report of the Administrative Reforms Commission* : Economic Administration, July 1968; Delegation of Financial and Administrative Powers, June 1969.

Report of the *Jha Committee on Food Grain Prices* for 1964-65, and of the *Agricultural Prices Commission* on Price Policy for Kharif Cereals for 1966-67 Season, Department of Agriculture, Govt. of India, New Delhi.

*Report of the Working Group* for Formulation of Fourth Five Year Plan Proposals on: *Minor Irrigation and Rural Electrification*;
Ditto : *Plant Protection*; mimeo., Dept. of Agriculture, New Delhi, 1965.

*Report on India's Food Crisis and Steps to Meet It*, by the Agricultural Production Team sponsored by the Ford Foundation, issued by the Ministry of Food and Agriculture, etc., Govt. of India, April 1959.

Reserve Bank of India, Bombay:
—*Report of the All-India Rural Credit Survey Committee*, 1953, 2 vols.
—*Report of the All-India Rural Credit Review Committee*, 1970.
—*Financing of Agriculture by Commercial Banks*, 1968.
—*Report on Currency and Finance*, 1970-71.

71

Rockefeller Foundation, *Strategy for the Conquest of Hunger*, Proceedings of a Symposium, 1 and 2 April, 1968.

——*Agricultural Development*, Proceedings of a Conference, 23-25 April, 1969.

——*Proceedings of the Third Wheat Seminar* held in Ankara, Turkey, 29 April–13 May 1970, mimeo., issued by FAO, Rome.

Roth, Andrew, "Mr. Point Four" (Dr. Solomon Trone), *Nation*, New York, 27 January 1951.

Schultz, Theodore W., *Transforming Traditional Agriculture*, New Haven, Yale University Press, 1964.

*Seed Specialists' Seminar Proceedings*, 8-11 April, 1969, mimeo., India International Centre, New Delhi.

Sen, S. R., "Indian Agriculture: Retrospect & Prospect," *Round Table*, London, July 1969.

Sen, Sudhir, *United Nations in Economic Development—Need for a New Strategy*, New York, Oceana Publications, 1969.

——Other publications as cited in the text.

Shastry, S. V. S., "New High-yielding Varieties of Rice—Jaya and Padma," *Indian Farming*, New Delhi, Feb. 1969.

——"New Dwarf Rice Varieties for India in the Seventies," *Indian Farming*, CRRI Jubilee Number, Oct. 1971.

Sisler, Daniel G., "The Role of Transportation in the Process of Economic Development," in *Some Issues Emerging*, etc., see under Turk, Kenneth L., ed.

Stakman, E. C., and others, *Campaigns Against Hunger*, Cambridge, Mass., The Belknap Press of Harvard University Press, 1967.

Streeten, Paul, and Lipton, Michael, *The Crisis in Indian Planning—Economic Policy in the 1960's*, Oxford University Press, 1968.

Streeter, Carroll P., *A Partnership to Improve Food Production in India*, A Report from the Rockefeller Foundation, New York, 1969.

Swaminathan, M. S., *Recent Research at the IARI*, mimeo., New Delhi, 1968.

——Address at IARI Convocation, mimeo., March 1969.

——*Agriculture Cannot Wait*, mimeo. address, 1972.

——*Can We Face Widespread Drought Again Without Food Imports?* Dr. Rajendra Prasad Memorial Lecture, New Delhi, 26 March, 1972.

——Other papers, mostly mimeo.

*The Green Revolution*, Symposium on Science and Foreign Policy, Committee on Foreign Affairs, House of Representatives, Washington, D.C., US Printing Press, 1970.

*The World Food Problem*, A Report of the President's Science Advisory Committee, Washington, D.C., May 1967, 3 vols.

*Towards Self-reliance in Agriculture*, New Delhi, Indian Agricultural Research Institute, 1972.

United Nations, *Report of the Community Development Evaluation Mission on India*, mimeo., New York, 1959.

Vohra, B. B., *Balanced Development of Surface Water Resources* (1970); *Current Trends and Prospects in Irrigation Development* (1970), *Groundwater Comes of Age* (1972), and other papers, Ministry of Food and Agriculture, etc., New Delhi.

Warriner, Doreen, *Land Reform in Principle and Practice*, Oxford, Clarendon Press, 1969.

Wortman, Sterling, "The Technological Basis for Intensive Agriculture" in *Agricultural Development—Proceedings of a Conference*, The Rockefeller Foundation, New York, 1970.

# Index

Ackley, Gardner, 446
Adoption, of HYV's, Ch. 4, 44-64
Adoption breakthrough, 193-4
Adaptation of HYV's, 51-5, 55-8, 336-9
Adaptive research, 46-8, 49-59, 504, 524
Administrative reform, Ch. 28, 452-74;

historical background, 452-4;
Indian Civil Service (ICS), 454-8, 472-4;
Appleby on, 459-60, 462-6, 471-2;
Trone on, 460-1, 465;
——in agriculture, 466-72;
Danger of wrong reform, 472-4

Administrative Reforms Commission, 465
Agricultural administration, 466-72
Agricultural aviation, 278-80
Agricultural credit, Chs. 25-26, pp. 398-431; also 230, 316-7, 350-1, 397, 434-8, 449-51, 484-5;

Background, 398-9;
"Credit Agricole" of Egypt, 399-402;
Integrated Rural Credit Scheme, 127-8; the Scheme in retrospect, 402-7;
Multi-agency credit, 407-10; Agencies involved, 414-8; its inadequacies, 412-4, 416-8;
Nationalization of banks, 410-1;
Urgency of a unified system, 422-31; its imperatives, 422-3; a new all-India agency, proposal for, 423-31;
Also see Cooperation, Credit shackles, and Deficit financing

Agricultural credit corporations, 415
Agricultural education, see Education
Agricultural Prices Commission (APC), 366-7, 370-1

Agricultural Refinance Corporation (ARC), 390, 415
Agricultural universities, 323-9
Agro-industries corporations, 415
All-India Agricultural Credit Corporation, proposal for, 423-9
All-India Agricultural Modernization Programme (IAMP), 202-7;

Case for, 199-203, its urgency, 204-7;
Multi-tier approach, 203-4

All-India Coordinated Maize Breeding Scheme (AICMBS), 331
All-India Coordinated Rice Improvement Project (AICRIP), 49, 56, 339
All-India Coordinated Wheat Trials Programme, 45, 336
All-India Rural Credit Review Committee (AIRCRC), 128, 402-7, 408, 409
All-India Rural Credit Survey Committee (AIRCSC), 126-30, 162, 388, 402
Anderson, Marvin A., 467
Anderson, R. G., 53, 61
Andhra Pradesh Agriculture University (APAU), 56-7, 328, 340
Appleby, Paul H., 459-60, 462-6, 473
Ashby, A. W., 27, 383
Athwal, D. S., 340
Attlee, Clement (Prime Minister), 453
Axioms, of development, Ch. 2, 22-9; 137-8
Ayacut development, see Irrigation

Bajwa, M. A., 55
Balis, John S., 290
Beltran, Pedro G., 527
Bengal famine, 399

Biological engineering, 40-2, 132, 530
Biological industry, agriculture as, 28
Borlaug, Norman E., 31, 34-7, 41, 44-5, 47, 48, 49, 55, 61, 206, 266, 336-7, 433, 504, 522
Boyd-Orr, Lord, 496-7, 515
Bradfield, Richard, 31
Brezhnev, Leonid I., 12
Bright, John, 13
Brown, Dorris D., 369
Brown, Lester R., 298

Cabanilla, M. B., 60
Calcutta, problems of, 90-1, 135-6
Calcutta Metropolitan Planning Organization (CMPO), 194
"Capital Error", 23, 444-5
Casey, Sir Robert G., 399
Cato, Marcus Porcius, 514
Central Rice Research Institute (CRRI), 178, 338
Central Roadbuilding Corporation, proposal for, 395
Central Tractor Training Centre, 300
Central Warehousing Corporation (CWC), 389-93, 395
Chalam, G. V., 50
Chandler Jr., Robert P., 31, 37-40, 41, 57, 206, 339, 525
China, 11, 200, 490
Charka (spinning wheel),
   Gandhiji on, 94-8;
   versus machine, 96-9

Chemical fertilizers, see Fertilizers
Clark, Colin, 496-7
Classical economics and agriculture, 7-9
Cobden, Richard, 13
Coldwell, M. J., 116
Colanial era, agriculture in, 15-6
Community Development Programme (CDP), Ch. 8, 107-18;
   Etawah pilot project, 107-12, and after, 112-7;
   also 205, 324, 345, 378, 386, 387, 464, 476, 515

Complementarity principle, 154-6, 393;
   groups of complementarities, 504-8
Compost-making, 251, 256
Cooperation, 125-9, 389, 476, 508, 418-21;
   Wrong roads to, 126-9;

Cooperative credit, 126-7, 414;
Cooperative monopoly, 127-9, 158, 163;
   underlying misconceptions, 129-31
Overemphasis on credit, 126-7, 426;
Cooperative marketing of fertilizers, 258;
Cooperative warehousing, 392-3;
Building true cooperatives, 426-7
also see Agricultural credit, Credit shackles, and Deficit financing

Credit shackles, 432-9, 484-5;
   HYV's as collateral, 432-4;
   High-payoff activities, 434-8;
   Green Revolution credits, case for, 449-51

"Crisis Report", see Ford Foundation
Crop improvement, 32-3, 34-42, 46-8, 55-9, 329-34, 335-44, 504, 523-7
Crop loans, 162-3, 434
Cummings, Ralph W., 206, 327, 329
Cummings Committee, 327, 470-1
Currie, Lauchlin, 23

Damodar Valley Corporation (DVC), 85-91, 108, 109, 118, 134-7, 153, 234, 308-10, 455, 464
   origin, 85-6; years of struggle, 88-9; success mutilated, 89-91, 134-7

Darling, Malcolm, 126
DDT controversy, 275-6
Deficit financing, 442-51;
   past abuse of, 442-4; current fallacies, 444-9;
   Green revolution credits, need for, 449-51;
   also see Agricultural credit, and Credit shackles

de Gaulle, Charles, 496, 501
Deshmukh, C. D., 463
Dey, S. K., 112, 115, 116, 119, 153, 464-5
Dias, A. L., 473
Droughts (of 1965-66), 147-8
Dumont, René, 116
Dunkerley, Harold, 369
Dutt, A. K., 153
Dwarf wheat:
   genesis, 31-7;
   adaptation to India, 45-8; to Pakistan,

48; to both, 504;
further breeding, 136-7; spread of 44-9, 184, also 76

Economic growth, 479-81, 486-7;

Prerequisites of high growth, 481-7; Growth for welfare, 487-8

Education, 320-9;

A mindless system, 320-3; Agricultural universities, 323-9

Economic Planning in India:

A bizarre package, 476; bedevilled by fallacies, 476-8;
Need for new dimensions, 481-8, see Planning Commission

Elmhirst, Leonard K., 21, 108, 399
Ensminger, Douglas, 206
Etawah Pilot Project, 107-12
Exploratory Tubewells Organization (ETO), 211, 218-21
Extension service, agricultural, 344-9, also 28, 188, 191-2, 350, 437, 504-5;

Rebuilding the service, 347-9

Family planning, 485-6, 507-8, 523
Farm and nonfarm sectors, interaction, 201, 507
Farm Mechanization, Ch. 20, 284-301; also 54, 182, 344, 437;

problems of selection, 284-5;
need for better implements, 285-8;
special needs for heavy machines, 288-90;
machinery for green revolution, 290-3;
dangers of blind mechanization, 293-9;
tasks ahead, 299-301

Farm planning, 159-62, 189
Farmer, Indian, reflections on, 19, 20-2, 131-2, 153, 162, 449-50
Fauzi, Mahmud, 401
Fertilizers, chemical, Ch. 18, 248-64; also 16, 133, 136-7, 153, 180, 190

Delayed start, causes, 248-52; production, imports, consumption, 252-3, Tables 11-14, Charts 12-13; future targets, 253-6;
Prices, 256-8; excise duty on, 257-8;

Distribution problem, 258-9; fertilizer credits, 435-6;
Fertilizer Committee (1964), 249, 259;
Fertilizer Promotion Council (FPC), 259-61

Fertilizer responsiveness of traditional varieties, 41, 133, 153
Food aid, 147, 360-3, 495-6, see Public Law 480
Food aid versus food production aid, 496-501
Food and Agriculture Organization (FAO), 48, 60, 276, 339, 479, 496-8, 505, 520-3, 525-6, 529, 533

Five keys, 521; Indicative World Plan (IWP), 322-3

Food Corporation of India (FCI), 366-8, 370, 389
Food Crisis, Ch. 10, 139-50; background of, 140-43; the droughts, 147-8; and their effects, 148-50
Foodgrains Enquiry Committee (1957), 362
Foodgrains Policy Committee (1966), 369-70
Ford Foundation:

Crisis Report, 143-6, 151-8, 206;
on chemical fertilizers, 249; farm implements, 285, 288;
irrigation, 152, 209, 213, 225; pesticide use, 274; plant breeding, 190-1, 339; seed multiplication, 237-8, 339
F.F. and Package Programme, for details see Intensive Agricultural District Programme (IADP), Chs. 12-14;
F.F. support to Calcutta Metropolitan Planning Organization (CMPO), 193-4; to water management in India, 225; to international crop research centres, 37, 324-5; general, 352

Foreign Aid, disenchantment with, 515-7
Fredrickson, C. J., 276
Freeman, Wayne H., 49, 52, 244

Galbraith, John Kenneth, 117-8, 155, 205, 448
Gandhi, Mrs. Indira, 488-9
Gandhi, Mahatma (Gandhiji), Ch. 7,

93-106; 114, 117, 136, 287, 308, 490, 497;

economics of, 94-104; cult of khadi, 95-8; *charka* versus machine, 96-9; on population, the cow, diet, medicine, prohibition, education, class struggle, land reform, and back-to-the village, 100-4; Legacy of Gandhiji, 104-6

*Garibi hatao*, 488-91
Gill, K. S., 379
Gill, N. S., 236, 247
Gorwala, A. D., 459
Grain Golas, 236
Grant, U. J., 330-1
Green manuring, 251, 256
Gregg, B. R., 241
Griliches, Zvi, 64, 351
"Growth points", 180, 395

Hanna, H. W., 325
Hanson, A. H., 124
Hardin, Lowell S., 59
Haringhata Scheme for Livestock Improvement, 108, 400
Harrar, George, 31, 34-5, 206, 271-2
Haryana Agricultural University (HAU), 327
Heller Walter W., 446
High-yielding economics, Preface
High-Yielding Varieties (HYV's), 133, 177, 183, 190, 243-7, 250, 292-3, 310, 342; also *see* Dwarf wheat *and* Miracle rice
High-Yielding Varieties Programme (HYVP), 177, 196, 254, 277, 318, 408
Hill, F. F., 59, 206
Hindi, Kamel, 401
Hirschman, Albert O., 478-9
Hixon, Ephriam, 327
Hoffman, Paul G., 113
Hoffman, Walter, 210
Hopper, W. David, 18-9, 52
Howard, Sir Albert, 335, 336

Imperial preference, in tariff, 14
Indian Administrative Service (IAS), 454, *see* Administrative reform
Indian Agricultural Research Institute (IARI), 45-6, 178, 183, 225, 327, 328, 329, 330-1, 423;

crop improvement work, early days, 335-6; recent achievements, 45-7, 336-7, 341-2;
A post-graduate university, 327-8;
Soil analysis, 261-2

Indian Civil Service (ICS), 452-8, *see* Administrative reform
Indian Council of Agricultural Research (ICAR), 45, 250, 250, 326, 330-1, 334-5, 337, 423, 468;

background, 326, 334;
slow progress, 335-6, 337-8;
reorganization, 334-9;
accelerated research, 339-40;
all-India coordinated projects, 335;
new tasks, 342-4

Indian farmer, 20-2, 129-32, 162, 177, 449-50
Indo-US aid programme, 113, 155, also *see* USAID
Indica rice varieties, 38
Indicative World Plan (IWP), FAO, 522-3
Industry versus agriculture, 81-5, 478-9, 498-9;

"agriculture-firstism", 91, 499-500;
India's steel industry, 82-4, and industrial policy, 84

Innovative districts, IADP, 185
Institute of Agricultural Research Statistics, (IARS), 183
Institute of public administration, 465
Integrated Rural Credit Scheme, 126-8
Intensive Agricultural Area Programme (IAAP), 179, 184, 187, 204, 408, 422
Intensive Agricultural District Programme (IADP), Chs. 11-14, 151-94;

origin, 146, 151-6; 10-point programme, 156-8;
Package programme at work, Ch. 12, 159-75;
significance of guidelines, 159-65;
selection of districts, 163-70; imperfect selection, 165-8;
inter-district variables, 168-70;
Financial arrangements, 170-1; slow start, 171-5; inhibiting factors, 173-5;
First decade of IADP, results achieved, Ch. 13, 176-85; retarding factors, 184-5;

criticisms and appraisal, Ch. 14, 186-94;

an adoption break-through, 193-4;

other references: 109, 112, 132, 133, 181, 185, 196, 197, 202-4, 205, 244, 248, 252, 251-3, 288, 299, 365, 367, 369, 407, 408, 429, 434, 466-7, 505

Intensive Agricultural Modernization Programme (IAMP), 202-4, 207

Inter-Asian Programme for Corn Improvement, 333

International Bank for Reconstruction and Development (IBRD), 83, 88, 309, 524-5, 526-7, 529

International Consultative Group for International Agricultural Research (ICGIAR), 524-5

International Crop Research Institute for Semi-Arid Tropics (ICRISAT), 341, 343, 524-5

International Institute of Tropical Agriculture (CIAT), 524

International Institute of Tropical Agriculture (IITA), 524

International Maize and Wheat Improvement Centre (CIMMYT), 34-7, 524

International Potato Centre (IPC), 524

International Rice Research Institute (IRRI), 37-40, 50, 51, 57-9, 338, 340, 524

Irrigation, Ch. 16, 208-34; 15, 80, 85-8, 89-90, 166-7, 168, 180, 454;

agricultural credit for, 217-8, 230;

command area, or ayacut, development, 229, 233;

drainage, neglect of, 214, 227-8, 232;

Fourth Plan target, 218;

groundwater development, 211, 218-21, 227;

high dam and canal irrigation, 85-92, 213-4, 232-3;

Irrigation Commission, 225-6, 231-4;

low return on investments in, 213;

new policy (conjunctive approach), 217-8;

north-south irrigation grid, 230-1;

poor quality of, 212-5, 226-7;

potential and present status, 210-2;

small irrigation projects, 215-7; energized pumpsets, 216, 228;

Tasks ahead, 226-30

Jackson, Sir Robert, and "Capacity Study", 519-20

Japan, 4, 36-7, 38-9, 98, 154, 196, 253, 255, 261, 268, 297-8, 300-1, 344, 489, 490, 499

Japonica, rice, 38

Johnson, A. A., 239, 243, 331

Johnson, Sherman E., 176, 188, 190

Joint Indo-US Team, of 1954, 325; of 1959, 326, 334

Jones, Paul H., 220

Johnston, Bruce F., 297, 298

Kamel El Far, Mustafa, 401

Kellogg, Charles E., 154

Keynes, John Maynard, 74-5, 446; neo-Keynesian approach, 74-6

Khosla, A. N., 210, 231

Khrushchev, Nikita, 12

Khusro, A. M., 439

Kilby, Peter, 297, 298

Kothari, D. S., 323

Krishnaswamy, S. Y., 407

Kristensen, 496

Land development banks, 414

Land Grant Colleges, 191, 324, 325-8, 510

Land reform, 16, 91, 301, 344, 427-8, 483-4, 505-6

Leeuwrick, Dick, 133

Lenin, Vladimir Ilyich, 317

Leontief, Wassily W., 448, 476-7

Lewis, John P., 74-6, 91, 206

List, Friedrich, 13

Lipton, Michael, 19

Macro-economic planning, weakness of, 445-6, 447-8, 476-8, 501

Malone, Carl C., 368

Malthus, Thomas Robert, 7, 9

Mangelsdorf, Paul C., 31

Marketing, Ch. 24, 376-97

Importance of, 376-7;

Regulated markets, 380-2;

Scarcity of markets, 377-80; need for market-towns, 378-80, 381-2;

Transportation, importance of, 382-8; rural roads, critical lack, 384-8;

Warehouses, 388-93; present deficiencies, 391-3;

How to speed progress, 393-7

Marshall, Alfred, 7
Marx, Karl, 9-12, 508
Marxism and agriculture, 9-12, 509-10
Mavi, Harpal Singh, 394
Mayer, Albert, 108-12, 115
McNamara, Robert S., 526
Mead, Margaret, 116
Mehta, V. L., 399
Mexico, 31-7, 44-5, 62-4, 148, 332, 351, 427, 486, 504, 524, 527, 530
Miles, Harold A., 423, 429
Mill, J. S., 7
Minor irrigation, *see* under Irrigation
Miracle rice, 37-40, 76, 504;

Adoption and adaptation, 51-5, 504; Jaya, Padma, etc., 55-9; Lagging progress, 49-51

Monsoon, influence of, 142, 147-8; Ch. 16, esp. 208-12 and 221-4
Morgan, A. E., 323
Montagu-Chelmsford reform, 104
Mosher, A. T., 27, 29, 192, 298
Myers, Will M., 239, 331
Myrdal, Gunnar, 452

Naik, K. C., 322, 327, 329
National Commission on Agriculture, 350, 471-2
National Council of Applied Economic Research (NCAER), 377-80, 390-3
National Demonstrations programme, 348-9
National Extension Service (NES), 113-6, 348-9
National Planning Committee (NPC), 81, 96, 99, 162, 388, 398-9
National Seeds Corporation (NSC), 51, 57, 238-40, 242, 246, 337
Nehru, Jawaharlal, 76, 81, 96, 98-9, 106, 108-9, 398-9, 458, 461, 462
Neo-colonialism, 357, 530-2
New agricultural strategy, Ch. 15, 196-207;

Not so new, 195-6; only a beginning, 196-8
"Food enough" policy inadequate, 198-9; need for new dimensions, 199-202;
Towards all-round modernization, 202-4; and its urgency, 204-7

Nicholson, Fredrick, 125
Nightsoil, utilization of, 136, 255-6
Nixon, President R. M., 446-7
Nurkse, Ragner, 23

Occam, William of, 131

"Occam's law", "Occam's razor", 131

Official Development Assistance (ODA), 516
Ogura, Takekazu, 263
Okun, Arthur, 446
Organic manure, 255-6
Osaye, Roberto, 63
Ottawa agreement, 14

Package approach, 154-8, 159-70, 501-8, 512-3
Package Programme, *see* Intensive Agricultural District Programme (IADP)
Paddock, W. and P. (Paddock Brothers), 30
Pakistan, 48, 60
Pal, B. P., 335
Panchayati raj, 118-24, 476
Pant, Govind Ballabh, 110
Pantulu, Ramdas, 399
Parker, Frank W., 206, 325, 329
Parker Committee, 334
Parker, Marion W., 206, 334
Patrick, Niel A., 171
Patvardhan, V. S., 361
Pearson Commission, report, 4-5, 71
Permanent Settlement, 16
Pesticides Association of India, 436
Pesticides, Ch. 19, 272-83, 436

Chemical control, 272-3;
Why pesticides, 273-6; Thacker Committee on, 274-5; DDT controversy, 275-6; WHO-FAO on, 276;
Use of pesticides in India, 276-80; aerial spraying, 278-80;
Weed control, 280-3;
Need for realism, 283;
also *see* Plant protection

Philippines, 37-40, 60, 148
Physiocrats, 358-9
Pigou, A. C., 7

Planning Commission, Govt. of India:
priority for agriculture, Ch. 6, 78-92,
149; allocations to agriculture, 79-80;
on agricultural prices, 365-6;
on cooperation, 127, 417-20;
on community development programme, 113, 118;
on deficit financing, 442-4, 448;
on farm equipment, 287, 299-300;
on panchayati raj, 119-20;
on rural electrification, 318-9;
Targets for:
fertilizer production, 251-3;
foodgrains production, 142, 199;
HYV programme, 254-5;
irrigated areas, 212, 216, 218;
electrified villages, 311-2, 318;
energized pumpsets, 303, 318;
power production, 306-8, 314-5;
Missing dimensions of planning, 481-7;
Other references, 149, 210, 219, 270,
305-6, 385-6, 389, 466, 476

Plant breeding, general, 65-6, 196, 224,
496, 504-5;

In Mexico, 31-7, 62-3, 351; at IRRI,
Philippines, 37-40; at other international centres, 523-6;
In India, 129-42; wheat, 45-7, 335-7;
rice, 49-51, 55-9, 337-9; maize, 330-4;
sorghum, 340-1; millets, 340-1; pulses,
341; other crops, 341-2; plant breeding and IADP, 191-2

Plant protection, Ch. 19, 265-83, 181;

food for men or pests, 265-6;
biological control, through breeding,
266-7; through parasitic agents, 269-
70;
protection through cultural practices,
267-70;
control through quarantines, 270-2;
Destructive Insects and Plants Act
(1914), 271;
chemical control, pros and cons, 272-5;
need for realism, 283;
also see Pesticides

Poor nations, definition of, 4, also referred as "backward", "low-income",
"underdeveloped" and "developing"
Population growth, 6, 7, 11, 72, 507-8,
512;

Gandhiji on, 100; Ford Foundation
projections (1958), 144; later projections, 149; 1971 census results, 198;
also see 'Family planning'

Post harvest complementarities, 376-7, 506
Power, electric, Ch. 21, 302-9; growth of,
306-7; Fourth Plan target, 307-8; power
famine, 302-3; and load-shedding, 319;
power for green revolution, 303-6; also
see Rural electrification
Prerequisites of agricultural development,
26-9;

Technical prerequisites, Chs. 16-22;
Other prerequisites: price support, Ch.
23; marketing, transportation, warehouses, Ch. 24; credit, Chs. 25-7;
administrative reform, Ch. 28

President's Report (The World Food
Crisis), 41, 267, 269, 273, 282, 285, 292,
329, 332, 357, 383-4, 395, 501-2, 504,
520-1, 524
Price Support, Ch. 23, 355-75, also 28,
196-7, 505, 511;

critical importance of, 355-7; "bon
prix" or "bon marché", 357-9;
Consumer-oriented prices, 359-63; their
effects, 363-4; P.L. 480 imports, 360-3,
and IADP, 365-6;
shift to incentive prices, 363-8; its
effect on fertilizer use, 368-9; implementing the new policy, 369-73;
danger of policy reversal, 373-5

Priority, for agriculture, 78-88, 90-1; agriculture versus industry, 81-5
Private sector, 13, 84, 242, 261, 277-8,
279-80, 396, 490, 508
Prohibition, Gandhiji, 101-2
Public Law 480, 360-1; imports under,
361-3;

P.L. 480 funds, 317, 425, 439-42

Public works programme, need for, 192,
438, 482
Punjab Agricultural University (PAU),
328, 340, 379, 394, 472
"Pusa bin", 391

Radhakrishnan, S., 321
Rainfed areas, 201, 221-4; multipronged

approach, 223-4; and changes in agronomy, 224

Ramiah, K., 338

Rath, Nilakanth, 361

Regulated markets, 380-2, 437

Research, agricultural, 28, 190-1, 196, 224, 329-44, 350-1, 504, 510, 520-1, 523-6; also *see* Plant-breeding

Research, agr. (in India), 329-44; 15, 28, 190-1, 194, 437, 504;

    reorganization of, 329-35;

Rockefeller Foundation—India programme, 329-34;

    ICAR restructured, 334-5;

    crop research, then and now, 335-9;

    accelerated tempo of, 339-42;

    some new tasks, 342-4

Resource-based development, 22-9, 481, 501-3, 518-9

Revelle, Roger, 329

Ricardo, David, 9

Rice, traditional varieties, 38, 41; *see* Miracle rice

River valley projects, 213; TVA era, 85-8; travesty of TVA, 88-91; silting up of reservoirs, 232-3; also *see* Damodar Valley Corporation (DVC)

Roads, importance of, 27, 377, 382-4;

    roads in India, 384-8; village-to-market roads, 377, 383, 386-8, 437

Rockefeller Foundation, 46, 48, 191, 194, 237, 238, 322, 326, 346, 352, 435;

    R. F.'s Mexico programme, 31-7, 62-3, 515, 524, 526;

    R. F.'s India programme, 329-34;

    as partner in other international efforts: IRRI, 37, other centres, 524

Rostow, Walt W., 479-80

Roth, Andrew, 461

Roy, B. C., 98

Royal Commission on Agriculture, 126, 136, 322, 380-1, 388, 396

Rural electrification, Ch. 21, 302-19, 437;

    slow progress of, 302-3; power-starved villages, 305-6; villages electrified, 311-2;

    loaded question, 308-10; vast potential demand, 301-6;

    energy resources, 314; installed capacity, 306-7, 314; poor capacity utilization, 314-5;

    Fourth Plan target, 306-8;

    power for green revolution, 303-6; energized pumpsets, progress of, 303-4;

    power famine and load-shedding, 303, 319;

    power tariff, 309-10

    financial constraints, 316-9;

    tasks ahead, 312-6; lever of rural progress, 317-8

Rural Electrification Corporation (REC), 303, 312, 317, 441

Rural Institutes, 324

Rural Universities, 333-4

Russel, Sir John, 36

Sahai, L., 327

Salmon, S. C., 36

Samuelson, Paul, 446

Santiniketan, 20, 108

Saraya, R. G., 399

Schultz, Theodore W., 9, 17-8, 22, 351

Seed, multiplication and distribution, Ch. 17, 235-47;

    Lagging seed-consciousness, 235-7;

    Recent progress, 237-42; breeder seed, 239; certified seed, 240; foundation seed, 239-40; marketing and distribution, 242; modern seed farms, 240; National Seeds Corporation, 238-9; Seed Law, 240-1; seed processing, 241; seed storage, 241; seed-testing laboratories, 241; variety release procedures, 238, 243

    Tasks ahead, 243-47; purity of seeds, 235-6, 246, 247; seed programmes, credits for, 435

Seed, export potential, 245

Seed treatment, 268

Self-sufficiency in food, 141-3, 198-9, 200

Shafie, Abdella, 401

Shastry, S.V.S., 49, 55, 56, 337-9

Singh, D. P., 115

Sisler, Daniel G., 386-7

Sivaraman, B., 249

Small farmers, 179-80

Socio-economic engineering, 64-6, 485-6, 530

Soil chemistry, 249-50, 261-4; soil-testing laboratories, 181, 261-3
Spatial development, for agriculture, 27, 377-80, 391-3, 484, 507
Sprague, E. W., 331
Sriniketan, 20-1, 108
Stakman, E. C., 31, 206
Stampe, Sir William, 209
Storage, and warehousing, 388-93; metal bin, 391
Streeten, Paul, 19
Streeter, Carroll P., 59, 62, 329, 333
Subramanian, C., 50, 132-3, 177, 196
Swaminathan, M. S., 46, 348-9

Taccave loans, 406, 414, 415, 425
Tagore, Rabindranath, 20, 106, 108, 533
Taiwan, 39, 51, 253, 298, 301, 344, 427, 486, 490
Tax, Sol, 17-8
Technical Cooperation Mission (TCM), 113, 325, 330; also see, USAID
Ten-Point Programme, 156-8, see IADP
Tennessee Valley Authority (TVA), 85-8, 464;

  travesty of TVA, 88-91
  also see River valley projects

Time, India's race against, 72-7, 476, 486, 491; on time-dimension in planning, 486-7
Trace elements, 263
Traditional agriculture, 17-23, 26-9, 132-7; see Indian farmer
Transportation, 27, 376-7, 382-8
Tropics, subtropics (defined), 6
Trone, Solomon, 460-1, 465
TVA approach in India, 85-9;

United Nations Development Programme (UNDP), 221, 479, 505, 518-20, 521-2, 525-6, 529, 533
University Education Commission (of 1949), 321-3 (of 1964, Kothari Commission), 323, 328, 471
US Agency for International Development (USAID), 505, 522, 527-8, 529;
Aid to India: agriculture, 191, 215-6, 225, 241, 276, 279, 290-1, 352-3;

  community development, 113, 117-8;

agricultural education, 325-8
USA: agriculture in, 150, 281-2, 273, 275, 285, 330, 332, 341, 481, 490, 499, 510-3;

  Indo-US cooperation, 117-8, 327-8; 352-4;
  Food aid, see Public Law 480
  also see US Agency for International Development (USAID), Tennessee Valley Authority (TVA), and other relevant entries

USSR, agriculture in, 9-12, 455-6, 489, 490, 499, 509-11
Uttar Pradesh Agricultural University (UPAU), 178, 323, 345

Varghuese, George, 46
Variety release, procedures, 238, 339
Vinoba Bhave, 490
Virdi, S. S., 241
Vogel, Orville A., 36
Vohra, B. B., 224
Voltaire, 501
Warriner, Doreen, 117
Water management, see Irrigation
Warehousing, 437

  Central Warehousing Corporation (CWC), 388-91
  growth of, in India, 389-90
  critical gaps, 391-3

Weed control, 280-3

  special problems of tropics, 280
  weedicides and herbicides, 281-2; versus manual labour, 282-3

Wellhauser, E. J., 330
Wilcocks, Sir William, 134
Woods, George D., 82
World Bank, see International Bank for Reconstruction and Development (IBRD)
World grain trade, trends, 509
World Health Organization (WHO), 276
Wortman, Sterling, 31, 351
Wright, B. C., 53

Yokoi, Tokikata, 268

Zila Parishad, 121